# THE AMAZING BO JACKSON

## BY RANDI HACKER

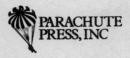

PARACHUTE
PRESS, INC

Parachute Press, Inc.
156 Fifth Avenue
New York, NY 10010

ISBN: 0-938753-34-7

First printing: March 1990

Printed in the USA

Design by Bob Feldgus

Typography by Mel Kaplan

Cover photos by Jeffrey E. Blackman

# TABLE OF CONTENTS

# CHAPTER I

# BO MANIA!

"My motto is like the commercial:
'Never let them see you sweat.'"
Bo Jackson

Once in a lifetime—and if you're lucky, it's your lifetime—an athlete comes along who breaks all the records and redefines the words "living legend." Vincent Edward "Bo" Jackson is such an athlete.

Unless you've been traveling to the edges of the universe on Voyager VII, you know Bo! He's the Kansas City Royals' outfielder who plays professional football with the L.A. Raiders as a hobby. Since 1986 when he started playing

1

baseball with the American League and football with the National Football League, Bo has been blasting records into the stratosphere. Not only does he break records set by other baseball and football players, he keeps on setting and breaking his own records.

And records aren't all he breaks. Bo is the only player in baseball history who has broken a baseball bat over his knee to show how mad he was at striking out!

Bo Mania! It's everywhere! It's at the Kansas City Royals' Stadium when Bo cracks a 400-foot homer! It's on the line of scrimmage when Bo rushes 91 yards for a touchdown for the Los Angeles Raiders!

Bo Jackson is an athlete who keeps on astounding his fans. It's no wonder they shout "Bo! Bo! Bo!" as soon as he steps out of the on-deck circle and takes his place behind home plate. Bo can hit a 400-foot homer left-handed even though he's a righty. Bo can scoop a line hit off the stadium wall and fire it into home plate from 300 feet away. Bo can outrun a ball when he steals a base.

And then there's Bo the football phenomenon, too. As a running back for the Raiders, he set a team record the first year he played, then broke his own record two years later!

2

Bo Mania is even in *your* living room during the now-famous Nike commercial where Bo plays not one, not two, but *eight* sports! He plays baseball. He plays football. He plays hockey, tennis, and basketball. He also runs, bikes, and lifts weights.

Bo isn't the only famous athlete in the ad. A top name from each sport appears with Bo in each super segment. Los Angeles Dodger Kirk Gibson says "Bo knows baseball." Ram quarterback Jim Everett says "Bo knows football." Michael "Air" Jordan says "Bo knows basketball." Tennis pro John McEnroe says "Bo knows tennis?" and marathon gold medalist Joan Benoit says "Bo knows running."

Only Wayne "The Great" Gretzky has some doubts about Bo's hockey skills. "No" he says after Bo knocks into hockey team members one after another. The ad goes on to say how Bo knows cycling and weight lifting, too. Then Bo tries the guitar and makes a terrible, ear splitting noise. In the first version of the ad rock 'n' roll legend Bo Diddley comes in and says "Bo, you don't know diddley!" But a newer version adds a segment that shows that Bo even learns to play the guitar!

It isn't very far from reality. Anyone who's followed Bo's career knows the 225-pound, 6-foot

2-inch powerhouse can pretty much do every sport in the commercial.

Bo Jackson has already been called the greatest athlete of our time.

"There's always the feeling that you're going to see something you never seen before and we don't want to miss it," says Seattle Mariners' catcher Scott Bradley.

"A mistake to a normal player isn't a mistake to Bo," says John Wathan, the manager of the Kansas City Royals, the baseball team Bo plays left field for. "He can outrun and outthrow mistakes."

"Bo is the only baseball player you sense can do whatever he wants," says Willie Wilson, the Royals' center fielder. "And you can't wait to see him do it."

Bo's awesome athletic skills are not the only thing his teammates and fans admire about him. There's a kind heart in his strong body. Ever since he was in high school, Bo's been helping others whenever he can. If he sees an accident on the road, he stops to be sure no one is hurt. If he thinks an award has been given unjustly, he speaks up in favor of the person he believes deserves it. And he wants kids to stay drug-free. That's why he's made two anti-drug videos. One for his college, Auburn. And one for the

Methodist Hospital Systems in Memphis, Tennessee.

This book will tell you all about Bo. Where he grew up. How many sports he played in school. When he hit his first home run. Who gave him the nickname "Bo." What he does to stay in shape. Why he likes to help other people. It will also tell you how you can get into shape like Bo.

And when you're finished reading, we hope you'll know Bo!

# CHAPTER II

# BO'S BOYHOOD

**"All my life I was determined
not to be a loser."
Bo Jackson**

Close your eyes and send yourself back, back, back in time. Nineteen years before MTV changed the way we listened to music! Seven years before "Sesame Street!" changed the way we learned to count! Twenty-six years before Teenage Mutant Ninja Turtles changed the way we look at sewers! Where are you now? 1962 in the good ol' U.S.A.

John F. Kennedy was in the White House. The Cold War with the Soviet Union was at its peak—

we didn't trust them, they didn't trust us, and both countries were building nuclear weapons at a frenzied pace. "The Donna Reed Show," "The Beverly Hillbillies," and "My Three Sons" were top TV shows. And outer space was the place to be.

On February 20, 1962, Lieutenant Colonel John Glenn hurtled into the stratosphere in Friendship 7 space capsule and became the first American to orbit Earth. The marine pilot circled our planet three times before splashing down in the Atlantic Ocean.

On November 30, 1962, ten months after the United States entered the Space Age, Vincent Edward "Bo" Jackson was born in Bessemer, Alabama.

His mom Florence worked as a maid at a Ramada Inn near Bessemer. She never married Bo's father. Baby Bo came home to a small, three-room house where he shared one of the two bedrooms with some of his nine brothers and sisters.

Vincent Edward became "Bo" when he was six years old. His eldest brother gave him the nickname. Bo is short for "boar hog" and that's one tough animal. Boar hogs are big and strong and built for running. They have vicious curving tusks that grow up from their lower jaws.

Except for the tusks, this is a good description of Bo Jackson today. He's big, strong, and built for running. Even then, the nickname fit.

"I was tough like a wild boar," Bo says about himself when he was a kid.

Young Bo liked to show everyone just how tough he was. He often challenged his brothers and cousins to punch him in the stomach. They would wind up and let loose their hardest blow, and young Bo would laugh and say he didn't feel a thing.

Bo showed signs of the strength and power he has today when he was just a third grader. That was the year Bo discovered sprinting. It was love at first dash. Soon Bo was cutting classes to run with the school track team.

At the time, the Raimond Elementary track team was off limits to everyone except the fourth, fifth and sixth graders. Then came Bo. Because he was such a super-speedster, the principal made an exception and let him compete with the older team.

Outside of racing, Bo was a bully. Trouble was his middle name. He broke windows, beat kids up, stole bikes, and threw rocks. When he was a third-grade track star at Raimond Elementary school, he bullied the sixth graders. He took lunch money away from other kids—then loaned it back to them with interest!

To try to teach him a lesson, his mother used to wake him up before dawn and make him take out the garbage or mow the lawn! But nothing worked. Bo kept right on acting wild.

Then, when he was 14, something happened that made Bo think about and change his behavior.

It was a hot summer day and Bo and his friends were on their way to a local swimming hole to cool off. Along the way they passed a hog pen that belonged to a Baptist minister in town. Bo and his friends picked up some rocks and threw them at the pigs. They kept on throwing rocks at the trapped animals until all the pigs in the pen were dead.

Bo's mother was at the end of her rope.

"If you want to send him to reform school, go ahead," she told the minister. "I just can't do a thing with him."

When Bo heard that, he knew it was time to straighten up. He and his friends went to work and earned enough money to pay the minister for the pigs they had killed. Then they all took up track, baseball, and football. All the athletics made Bo too tired to get into any more trouble!

Bo continued to build his reputation as a super athlete while he was a student at McAdory High in McCalla, Alabama. It was here his awesome athletic powers really paid off. He became a star player in three sports.

Let's start with track. As a member of the McAdory track team, Bo set state records in the 60- and 100-yard dashes, the 60- and 120-yard high hurdles, the long jump, and the high jump. He racked up enough points to win the state decathlon two years in a row even though he only completed nine of the ten events. He never competed in the final mile run. Why? He didn't like running such a long distance!

Sometimes it seemed that nothing could stop Bo—not even an injury.

In the high school state championships, Bo was competing in the triple jump. He won the state title with his 48-foot 8¼-inch leap but he twisted his ankle on the effort. That didn't stop Bo! Later that day he returned to the field with his ankle taped and set a new state record of 9.54 in the 100-yard dash!

Meanwhile, on the baseball diamond . . .

Bo's batting average was a whopping .493 in his senior year of high school! He also set a school record of 20 home runs. Though he mostly played center field and shortstop, Bo sometimes spent some time on the mound. At 18, Bo's fastball was clocked at 92 mph and he threw two no-hitters during his final season. And he didn't even play in every game! He missed seven games because he was competing in track meets at the time!

And then there's football. As a defensive player for the McAdory Yellow Jackets, Bo rushed for 1,173 yards on 108 carries with 17 touchdowns.

Bo was even good at sports he hated—like basketball.

One day, Bo was sitting in the gym studying. Basketball practice had just ended and though the team had gone, some balls were still on the gym floor.

Bo looked around to make sure no one was around. He didn't know that his baseball coach was watching him. Bo closed his books, walked over, and picked up a basketball. He took a couple of steps and executed a perfect reverse slam dunk. Then he simply picked up his schoolbooks and went home. Two points, Bo!

Sports really turned Bo around. Instead of being afraid of him, the other kids looked up to him. The new improved Bo started to show people what a good heart he has.

During his senior year, the McAdory Yellow Jackets football team had a proud 9–0 record.

The school decided to hold a pep rally. There were cheers. There were speeches. Then the Who's Who award, the school's top honor in athletics, was announced. Bo Jackson wasn't the winner. The award was given to another multi-sport athlete who just happened to be white.

The pep rally turned ugly. The white kids took over one side of the gym. The black kids took over the other and refused to stand or clap for the white athlete. The teachers rushed the football players out of the gym and the seniors were taken into the library for a meeting.

After the team had been sitting in the locker room for a while, Bo made his move. He said he wanted to talk with the students and teachers who had put the pep rally together.

"I wish you wouldn't," said Coach Atchison.

"I'd like to get things settled," said Bo.

So Bo went over to the library, opened the door, and walked in. Everyone stopped talking. The room fell silent. Then Bo spoke up.

"I didn't come to school here to get all the glory and win trophies," he told them. "I came here for my education. Y'all better get your act together."

As soon as Bo finished speaking, everyone started hugging each other and kissing each other and crying. Bo saved the day.

Naturally, Bo's stunning sports record in high school got him some attention from the pros. In his senior year, Bo was drafted by the New York Yankees. Even though the Yankees offered him a $250,000 contract to play ball with them when he graduated, he turned them down. He didn't want to go pro in one sport right away. He wanted to keep on being a multi-sport athlete. So he decided to go to college where he could run track, play baseball, and play football for four more years.

# CHAPTER III

# BO AND THE TIGERS

"When the time comes for me to make big money, if it's time, I'll make it. I'm in no rush. The money's not going no place. I'm not going no place."
**Bo Jackson**

Colleges all over America wanted Bo to come play for them. The University of Southern California Trojans called. The Tennessee Volunteers made him an offer. The Florida State Seminoles were after the big Bo. The University of Hawaii Rainbow Warriors even invited Bo down to look around the campus—all expenses paid.

But Bo didn't go. He felt that Florida and Hawaii had reputations as party schools. He didn't want to flunk out in his first year. Besides, he wanted to stay in his home state. The University of Alabama and Auburn University were his two top choices.

In 1982, any football player would have been proud to wear the University of Alabama's crimson and white uniform. 'Bama's Crimson Tide was *the* team to beat in the Southeastern Conference. They'd had 24 straight winning seasons and played in 25 consecutive Bowl games.

Bo loved 'Bama. He had learned the famous "Roll Tide!" cheer when he was a little boy and he had his mind set on hearing that cheer for him! 'Bama was interested in Bo, too. In fact, the coach told Bo he belonged at Alabama.

"There's no place else for a player like you to go," the coach told Bo. "'Bama really wants you."

Of course Bo loved what he was hearing. He'd waited all his life to hear those words! Then the coach told Bo that he probably wouldn't see any gridiron action until his second or third year on the team. Bo didn't like that at all. He didn't want to wait two years to play in the games. Especially when Auburn University needed running backs and would let freshmen play. So

Bo said "No" to 'Bama and accepted Auburn's football scholarship. He planned to study family and child development and play all the sports he loved.

Bo's decision made his mother happy, too. Some Alabama players had been in the news because of drugs and other unlawful behavior. Bo's mother was glad to have him as far away from that scene as possible.

Bo started school in 1982. By the time he left in 1986, he had become the first man in ten years in the Southeastern Conference to letter in three sports—baseball, football, and track.

As a center fielder for the baseball team, Bo played 89 collegiate games and had a career .335 batting average with 28 home runs and 78 RBIs.

In track, Bo ran the 60-yard dash in 6.18 seconds and was a member of the 4 X 100 relay team. His all-time best 100-yard time was 10.39. Fast, but not fast enough to qualify for the 1984 Olympics. Because he couldn't qualify, Bo quit track and began to concentrate on football.

Auburn always had a decent football team. But it had been ten years since the team had beaten the powerhouse team from 'Bama. With Bo's help, the Auburn Tigers turned the Tide.

The Auburn-Alabama game is always played the first Saturday after Thanksgiving. The first

Saturday after Thanksgiving 1982 was a cloudy, slightly rainy day. The stands at Jordan-Hare Stadium on the Auburn campus were jammed with excited fans from both schools.

The game started out badly for Auburn and stayed that way for the first three quarters. By the fourth quarter, 'Bama was ahead 22–16. Then the Tigers got going.

The Tigers faced a fourth-and-goal on the Tide's one-yard line. Over the noise of the screaming Auburn fans, the quarterback called for Play 43 in the huddle. That meant a hand-off to freshman Bo Jackson.

When Bo got his hands on the ball, he found himself facing a wall of red shirts. But that didn't stop him. Bo wriggled and pushed and finally dived over the top of the Tide to score the winning touchdown! With the 23–22 victory, the Auburn Tigers beat 'Bama for the first time since 1972!

Bo continued to lead the Tigers to victory—even when he was sick! In a 1983 game against Florida State, Bo had a pretty bad virus. But he still managed to score twice, once running 55 yards to a touchdown and again running 80 yards. Auburn won 28–21.

One summer between college terms, Bo took a job as a teller at the Colonial Bank in Birmingham, Alabama. As he was driving to work one morning, he accidentally clipped the rear of another car. The woman who was driving jumped out of the car and started yelling at Bo and demanding he tell her his name.

"Bo Jackson," he told her.

"The Bo Jackson who plays for Auburn?" she asked, very surprised and not as angry as she had been. "Oh, are you all right?"

After everything about the cars was settled, Bo and the woman drove off on their separate ways.

A few months later, just before the Auburn-Texas game, a Mailgram arrived for Bo.

"SMASH TEXAS LIKE YOU SMASHED MY CAR!" it said. It was from the woman he had clipped in his car!

Bo often spoke up if he thought something wasn't fair. In 1984, Bo was on the Auburn team when they beat University of Michigan 9 to 7 in the Sugar Bowl. Bo was elected Most Valuable Player that year. When it came time to accept his award, he turned it down. He felt it belonged to his teammate and running mate Lionel James.

The next year was a big year for Bo. He helped Auburn beat 'Bama again. He became a first draft choice for the Tampa Bay Buccaneers. And he was nominated for the Heisman Trophy.

The Heisman Trophy is the highest honor a college football player can win. It's given each year to the outstanding college player. A lot of famous pros won the Heisman Trophy when they were college athletes. OJ Simpson won in 1968 and went on to play with the Buffalo Bills. He held the rushing record in 1972, 1973, 1975, and 1976 with a total of 6,574 yards. Hershel Walker was a Heisman winner and became a Dallas Cowboy. He was the NFL's 1987 individual leader in rushing and scoring. One other Auburn Tiger had also won a Heisman. That was quarterback Pat Sullivan back in 1971. Would 1985 be Bo's turn?

Bo was not impressed by his nomination. It wasn't that he didn't care. It was just that he loved playing football and he wanted to do his best whether he won the trophy or not.

Still he continued to rack up the stats. In 1985, he became the leading rusher, scorer, and all-purpose runner in the Southeastern Conference. He rushed an average of 162.4 yards per game, scored an average of 9.3 points per game, and ran an average of 169 yards per game. In 1985, Bo also set a school record by rushing over 100 yards in eight games. And in four games, he ran over 200 yards!

In addition to his hectic football schedule, Bo also traveled around and talked to schoolchildren near Auburn. He told them about how bad he had been as a boy and advised them to stay out of trouble. He also asked them to steer clear of drugs and alcohol.

Because of his outstanding performances in football and the good work he was doing in the community, Bo Jackson won the 51st Heisman Trophy on December 7, 1985.

That same year, the Tampa Bay Buccaneers offered Bo a contract. Though he practiced with them one summer, he decided not to go pro right away and stayed at Auburn for another year.

All through college people had been asking him whether he planned to go pro in football or baseball. Bo never gave a straight answer.

"I may play professional football," he said, "or I may play professional baseball. Or I may chuck 'em both and go fishin'."

Many people thought the Heisman Trophy would help Bo make up his mind. Every Heisman winner since 1958 had gone on to play professional football. But Bo took the sports world by surprise. In 1986, Bo became the first Heisman winner in almost 30 years to leave college and play professional baseball!

# CHAPTER IV

# BO GOES PRO

**"It's just like this two-sport thing. This is just the way I want to spend my time. It has nothing to do with trying to be the world's greatest athlete. It's just me."**
**Bo Jackson**

When Bo signed a contract with the Kansas City Royals in 1986, he became the first college football superstar in over 25 years not to play pro football. The last trophy winner to do it was Army running back Pete Dawkins who went to Oxford on a Rhodes Scholarship and competed in crew, European football, and cricket.

"My first love is baseball," said Bo. "I went with what's in my heart."

Bo didn't get any special treatment from the Royals. That June, they sent him and the rest of their handpicked 1986 draftees down to the minor leagues to start learning the way the pros play the game.

The minor leagues are made up of farm clubs. These farm clubs are divided into different levels from the lowest rookies to the top AAA clubs. Most major league players are chosen from the AAA teams. Each pro team has four or five farm clubs to choose players from. And each pro team places its rookies in a farm club that best suits his abilities.

Bo played with the Memphis Chicks, a team in the Southern League that develops ball players for the Kansas City Royals. Chicks is short for "Chickasaws," a tribe of Native Americans that lived in that area. The Chicks are a Class AA team from whose ranks have also come the Royals' Gary Thurman and Kevin Seitzer.

Bo's life in the minor leagues wasn't as glamorous as it might have been if he had decided to play pro football. Instead of riding in limousines and eating expensive food, he found himself riding for 15 hours in a bus and eating greasy hamburgers. But Bo didn't mind. He was playing the sport he liked best.

Bo played his first professional baseball game on June 30, 1986. More than 150 reporters from all over America were at Chicks Stadium to cover it. During batting practice Bo cracked one hit after another. One crashed into an inflatable beer can on the left-field roof. Another slammed into the back of the bleachers.

Then the game began. As designated hitter, Bo came to bat with two men on base and two outs. After swinging and missing on two good pitches, Bo crouched and faced the mound for his third and final chance.

The pitcher went into his windup and threw the ball. Bo swung. Though it wasn't one of his rocket balls, his hit was good enough to bring in one of the men on base. An RBI on his first try!

Two weeks later, on July 13, Bo hit his first home run playing against the Knights from Charlotte, North Carolina. Soon after that he was named the Southern League Player of the Week (July 15–July 21) with an 11 for 25 effort that included a double, three triples, two homers, eight RBIs and five walks. He hit safely in an incredible 40 out of 48 games with the Chicks.

The Royals decided Bo was ready for the majors on September 1, 1986. You might say they let him skip a grade by bypassing the Class AAA club. This promotion made Bo the first player in Royals' history to go straight from the college campus to a major league ball club in his first year as a pro.

Bo didn't have to wait long to play in his first major league game. The Royals put him in the lineup against the Chicago White Sox the very next day! He hit a single in the bottom of the second inning.

Later that month, Bo hit his first major league homer in a game against the Seattle Mariners. The ball flew three quarters of the way up the outfield embankment at Royals' Stadium and was speeding so fast that when it hit the grass, it got stuck in the ground!

Bo quickly became the sixth Royals' rookie—and the first since Willie Wilson in 1977—to have a four-hit game. Because he racked up the hits by the time he had played his fifth big league game, Bo also became the first rookie to do it in such a short time.

Bo's record-setting continued in 1987. On April 10, Bo had a four-hit night in a game against the Yankees. Then, just four nights later, he had *another* four-hit night against Detroit. Two of those four hits were home runs including a sixth inning grand slam. He also drove in a Royals' team record-tying seven runs in the same game!

Just to balance out all the good stuff that happened, Bo also led the club in strikeouts in 1987 with a colossal 158!

As it turned out, 1987 was not only a year of highs and lows, it was also a year of surprises. In July, Bo decided to take up a "hobby"— professional football. The Los Angeles Raiders were delighted to sign Bo, even as a part-time player. At first the Royals' fans were angry. They felt betrayed. Some of his teammates even turned their backs on him. Still, Bo knew what he wanted, and he wanted to play football, too.

In his first year with the Raiders, it was clear that Bo had not lost any of his football style. Though he missed the first five games of the season because of baseball, Bo was still second on the team in rushing with 554 yards and a league-leading 6.8 yards per carry average. He also set an all-time Raider record in a game against the Seattle Seahawks when he ran 91 yards for a touchdown. The Raiders beat the Seahawks 37–14.

1988 was just as awesome a year for Bo. When he wasn't sidelined because of a recurring hamstring injury, Bo continued to push the outside of the sports envelope in both his sports. In no time, fans of both the Royals *and* the

Raiders had a major case of Bo fever.

And the amazing Bo didn't disappoint them. He became the first 25/25 player in Royals' history: batting 25 home runs and stealing 27 bases. He was elected the Royals' Player of the Month in May when he hit safely in 21 of 27 games. He belted five home runs and drove in 19.

When the Royals' season ended in October, Bo joined the Raiders' action in progress. He had the Raiders' longest touchdown in 1988 with a 22-yard score against Kansas City. He averaged 4.3 yards per carry and rushed a total of 580 yards on 136 carries.

In 1989, his fabulous feats continued. On March 5, 1989, Bo blasted a 515-foot shot that cleared the 71-foot scoreboard. It was the longest home run ever hit at Baseball City, the Royals' spring training camp in Florida.

On May 23, 1989, Bo was placed fourth in the batting lineup for the very first time. In baseball, the fourth man at bat is in the important cleanup position. The thinking is that if the first three batters can nail a single, the fourth man can start bringing in the runs. If he hits a single, the man on third will score. If he hits a double, two men will score. And if, by some chance, he hits a homer, four runs will cross the plate. That's called a Grand Slam homer.

Far from being nervous about batting clean-up, Bo was cool. He cracked the ball 461 feet, making it the longest measured home run ever hit in the history of Texas' Arlington Stadium.

What's even more astounding, it was the first hit Bo ever got off the legendary Nolan Ryan. He had faced the Rangers' pitcher six times before and struck out six times.

In a game against the Seattle Mariners, Bo showed that the strength of his throwing could equal the power of his batting.

It was June 5, 1989. The Royals were playing the Seattle Mariners. The score was 3 to 3. The Mariners were at bat. Steve Farr was pitching for the Royals. He threw the ball. Mariner Harold Reynolds had left first base on the pitch and was on his way around the bases when Scott Bradley connected and drove a line drive deep into the corner of left field. Reynolds was past third when Bo Jackson caught the ball as it rebounded off the Kingdome wall, 300 feet from the plate.

Jackson turned and fired the ball toward home. He didn't even have time to take any steps toward the plate. That ball shot past Reynolds and landed in catcher Bob Boone's mitt before Reynolds could slide into home. Not only did Bo throw the ball 300 feet for an out, he also threw a perfect strike!

In the 1989 All-Star Game Bo led the American League to a 5–3 victory over the National League. He started off with a 448-foot home run, then drove in two runs, stole a base, played flawless left field, and was named Most Valuable Player.

And in 1989 Bo Jackson broke his own Raiders' record. He ran 92 yards against Cincinnati for a touchdown.

For now, Bo just wants to divide his time between his two pro sports. He trains with the Royals down in Florida and plays with them for the entire baseball season. While he's working for the Royals, he lives in a five-bedroom house in Leawood, Kansas, with his wife, Linda, and their two sons, four-year-old Garrett and two-year-old Nicholas.

When the last pitch of the season's been thrown and the last homer has been hit, Bo moves into his apartment in California and starts the football season.

But what about the future? What if he ever retires? "I may take up golf," says Bo. Watch out, Jack Nicklaus!

**Auburn running back Bo Jackson
awarded the Heisman Trophy.**

**The Royals' newest addition gets a hug from Mom.**

**Bo at Bat.**

**Bo Royal.**

**Bo coming home**

O say can you see . . .
Bo and his team on the  sidelines before a game.

**A rare moment at rest.**

**Bo breaks loose for a major gain.**

**Will he make it?**

Jeffrey E. Blackman

**Not this time!**

**Ready for action.**

**Jackson to Jackson**
Michael fakes a pass to Bo at Michael's recording studio.

Jeffrey E. Blackman

A teammate helps Bo limber up before a game.

Jeffrey E. Blackman

**New meaning to the word Giant trouble.**

Just a regular guy

Bo returns to college to finish his degree.

# CHAPTER V

# TAKE A BOW, BO!

**"Even if it was my worst enemy,
I'd stop and help."
Bo Jackson**

You know Bo can hit a homer. But did you know that for every home run he hits, he donates $25 to the Marillac Foundation to help children with learning disabilities?

That's typical behavior for Bo. He's a guy with a good heart. Bo likes to help people and so he's always spent a lot of time doing just that. If someone is in trouble and Bo is around, you can count on him to come to the rescue and do what he can to make things better.

There are a lot of stories about Bo's good deeds. These are a few of them.

## NO SHOES? NO PROBLEM!

A player on the basketball team at a junior college in Missouri was a guy with big feet. He wore a size 21 and he just couldn't find any basketball shoes to fit him. This was putting a cramp in his hoop-shooting style.

While Bo was watching TV one day, he heard a report about this player's plight. He felt sorry for a guy who couldn't play his best game because his shoes fit badly. So Bo put in a call to Nike. Have some shoes made to fit this guy's size 21 feet, he told them, and send them to this athlete.

The shoes were made and delivered. Because Bo didn't want a lot of attention for what he'd done, he never revealed the name of the college or the player.

## THAT'S WHAT FRIENDS ARE FOR

One day, Willie Wilson, the center fielder for the Royals, was leaving Milwaukee County Stadium. With him was his fiancée Catherine. As they walked, some people started shouting racial insults at him. An argument broke out and it looked like things were going to get violent.

Wilson went over to the Royals' bus to see if anyone would help him out. Danny Tartabull, Thad Bosley, Frank White, and Bo all stepped down to see what they could do.

The gang of hecklers took one look at Bo rolling his sleeves up over his bulging arm muscles and ran right out of there!

## BO ON THE ROAD PART I

One day, not long before spring training began, Bo went out to buy a pair of shoes. He was driving down the highway when he came to the scene of an auto accident. Eight or nine cars slowed down and stared but no one stopped to help.

Except Bo. He pulled over, called for an ambulance, and then stayed with the couple from Nashville, Tennessee, until help arrived. Then, when he saw that everything was under control, he left before anyone had a chance to thank him.

Later, when a policeman told the couple that Bo Jackson had been the one who helped them out, they couldn't believe it.

"I thought he was just a nice guy," said the man from Nashville. "He was a real gentleman."

# BO ON THE RUN

It was two days before A-Day, Auburn's annual spring game in which the football squad is divided into two teams—blue and white—and pitted against themselves. David Housel, the director of Sports Information at Auburn, was sitting in his office when Bo Jackson came to see him. Bo missed spring training because of track and wasn't playing in the big game.

"I got an idea for A-Day," said Bo.

He wanted to invite a bunch of kids to come up to the game. Before the game begins, he said, he'd race them all from goal line to goal line. Bo promised to buy supper for any kid who could beat him. Housel set it up.

On the day of the game, hundreds of kids showed up at the stadium ready to race against Big Bo Jackson. Bo gave them all a 15-yard head start. The race began. Bo caught them, passed them, and vaulted the fence at the end of the field into the end zone seats. He spent the next few hours signing autographs for his fellow racers.

# GOOD CITIZEN BO

While he was in college, Bo loved to play video games in an arcade on College Street in Auburn. One of his favorites was Galaga, a space shooting game. Troops of evil aliens march down from the top of the screen while you shoot at them from your triangular-shaped spaceship at the bottom. Bo liked it because he was "dodging bullets all the time."

On this particular day, Bo parked in front of the arcade and went inside.

When he came out a while later, he found a parking ticket on his windshield. Bo jumped in his car and drove right over to the police department to pay the 50¢ fine then and there.

"If you don't pay within 24 hours," said Bo, "it goes up to a dollar."

## BO ON THE ROAD PART II

One summer Bo was driving on his way to a summer job. Suddenly, a car near him lost control, hit the guardrail, and came to a stop with smoke pouring out from under the hood.

Even though Bo knew that a smoking car is a ticking time bomb that could explode into a gasoline fireball at any time, he stopped his car, got out, and quickly pulled the driver out. He made sure she was safe, then he jumped back in his car and went on to work.

On the day it happened, Bo didn't tell anyone what he'd done. Not even his wife, Linda.

"I was just doing what was right," said Bo.

# CHAPTER VI

# BO-LIEVE IT OR NOT!

**"I just want to be looked at as a baseball player. Not a phenom. Not a legend in the making. Just a baseball player."**
**Bo Jackson**

The fact is that Bo is a phenomenon! He is a legend in the making. But Bo is not the first super athlete to come along. There have been plenty of other record breakers through the years. Here are some quick facts about the Bo Man and four other ultra-athletes: Jesse Owens, Babe Didrikson, Bob Mathias, and Jim Thorpe. It's up to you, sports fans, to decide who—if anyone—is tops.

# BO JACKSON

Some people think Bo Jackson is the best athlete ever. He plays two pro sports. He switch hits. He steals bases. He broke his own rushing record a year after he set it!

● **Switch Hit:** Bo blasted a 450-foot homer that was only 30 feet short of being the longest ball ever whacked in the Minneapolis Metrodome. And he hit left-handed.

● **Speed Demon:** Bo can run from home to first base in 3.82 seconds!

● **Quick Step:** During a game against the Baltimore Orioles, Bo stepped out of the batter's box to ask for a time out. Jeff Ballard, the pitcher, didn't notice and went into his windup. Bo quickly jumped back into the box as the ball whizzed toward home plate and hit a homer over the center-field fence!

● **Right This Way:** Bo is the first right-handed batter ever to hit a ball into the right-field upper deck of a stadium. He did it in Minneapolis at a game against the Twins off a pitch by Francisco Oliveras.

● **I Break for Bats:** Once, after striking out, Bo broke a baseball bat over his knee. The fans loved it! Even when he strikes out, Bo makes the sports page!

- **First:** In 1989, Bo became the first 25/25 player in Royals' history. He hit 25 home runs and stole 27 bases.

- **Hit and Run:** Bo is only the second player in baseball history to hit a homer and steal second base in the same game. The first player to do it was the legendary Willie Mays who did it in 1960.

- **Double Header:** Bo is the only man in the last 20 years who has a chance to play in the Super Bowl and the World Series in the same year.

- **Perfect Strike:** In a game against the Seattle Mariners, with the score tied 3–all in the tenth inning, Bo threw a 300-foot sizzler to stop Harold Reynolds, the Seattle Mariners' fastest runner, from scoring the winning run. The amazing Bo was standing flat-footed in the outfield when he made his astonishing toss, and what's more, his throw was a perfect strike, right in the zone!

- **Number 8 With a Bullet:** In the 1980's, 1,083 stories were written about Bo Jackson— enough to make him #8 on the Top 10 Baseball Story list.

- **It's My Record and I'll Break It If I Want To:** In 1987, Bo set a Raider rushing record by running 91 yards for a touchdown. In

1989, Bo broke his own record by running 92 yards to a touchdown.

● **Royal Rise:** Bo is the first player in Royals' history to go straight from college to the big leagues in the same year.

## BABE DIDRICKSON

Babe Didrickson was a multi-sport superstar back when women didn't do much competing at all. Babe won championships in running, javelin throwing, swimming, diving, high jumping, hurdling, baseball, boxing, rifle shooting, horseback riding, and billiards.

● **Don't Call Her Mildred!** Babe's real name was Mildred Ella. She earned the name Babe after she hit three home runs in a sandlot game. The kids gave her the nickname that stuck because her homers reminded them of baseball's Sultan of Swat, Babe Ruth.

● **Wonder Woman:** In high school, the Babe played forward on the boys' basketball team. She was so good, she won All-City and All-State honors.

● **Team Babe:** When Babe was 18, she *was* the Cyclones of Dallas track team. There were no other athletes on the team. Babe single-handedly won an Amateur Athletic Union track meet against other girls' teams with 15 and 20 athletes who specialized in different races and events. Babe came in first in five of the eight events, tied for first in the sixth, placed second in the seventh. Her total score for the day was 30 points—almost twice the number of points the team in second place collected. They scored 16 and they had 22 members!

● **Golden Oldie:** Babe competed in three events in the 1932 Olympics. She got the gold and set world records in two of them: the 80-meter high hurdles and the javelin throw. The only reason she didn't win the third event—high jump—was that the judges didn't like her unusual style.

● **Tee Time:** After her Olympic triumphs, the Babe decided it was time to play golf. The fact that she'd never played before didn't stop her. She sometimes practiced 15 or 16 hours a day and hit as many as 1,500 practice balls. In no time at all, Babe was winning every tournament in sight! In the 1940's, she set a record by winning 17 major golf tournaments in a row. Babe was even the first American woman to win the British Women's Amateur Golf Tournament.

● **Woman of the Year:** Babe was the only

woman ever voted "Woman Athlete of the Year" six times!

# BOB MATHIAS

Bob Mathias was a high school track star. When Bob's coach first mentioned decathlon to him, Bob said, "What's a decathlon?" Then he went on to win the Olympic decathlon two times in a row. The decathlon is a track event that's made up of ten individual track and field events. Decathletes have to be able to throw the javelin, shot put and discus, complete the broad jump, high jump, pole vault, hurdles, and run two long-distance races and a sprint. Athletes win by racking up points in each event. Whoever has the most points at the end of two days of competition wins.

• **Point by Point:** Bob got 7,094 points in the first decathlon he ever competed in at the 1948 Pasadena Games. And he had never done five of the ten events before!

• **Hold That Gold Part I:** In the 1952 Olympics, Bob came from behind and racked up 8,042 points—a score that broke a 14-year record! He got the gold!

• **Hold That Gold Part II:** He got the gold again in 1956, shattering the records he had set in 1952 and scoring an impressive 7,887 under new rules.

● **Twice and Only:** Bob Mathias is the only man to win the Olympic decathlon twice! He's also the first athlete to appear on a box of Wheaties!

## JIM THORPE

Jim Thorpe was a Native American athlete. He played college and pro football, semi-pro baseball, and competed in the pentathlon and decathlon at the 1912 Olympics. The pentathlon is half the decathlon—there are five events: broad jump, discus, 100-meter and 200-meter dash, and the javelin.

● **A Point a Minute:** As a running back for Carlisle College, Jim Thorpe scored 17 points in 17 minutes in a game against Dickinson College.

● **Rocky Mount High:** He pitched for the Rocky Mount baseball team while still in college and helped them win 23 games.

● **Getting the Gold:** Jim Thorpe became the first man in history to win the Olympic gold medal in both the pentathlon—where he came in first in four of the five events—and the decathlon.

● **Losing the Gold:** The Amateur Athletic

Union stripped Jim Thorpe of his gold medals when they discovered he'd played baseball for money during college. Even though Jim hadn't known he was doing anything wrong, the AAU made him send his Olympic medals back and they erased his name from the record books.

● **Pro and Pro:** Jim played professional baseball for the New York Giants. A few years later he played professional football for the Canton (Ohio) Bulldogs.

● **Mr. President:** In 1920, Jim Thorpe became the first president of the American Professional Football Association, which later became the National Football League.

● **Getting the Gold Back:** Jim Thorpe died in 1952. But Jim's family never stopped the fight to get his medals and titles back and have his good name restored. In 1973, the AAU decided they were right. Not much later, the U.S. Olympic Committee also came around. Finally, in 1983, the International Olympic Committee restored Jim Thorpe's gold medals and reinstated his name in the record books!

## JESSE OWENS

Setting and breaking track records was no problem for Jesse Owens. He was one of the greatest track stars in the history of sports. And he brought home the gold from the 1936 Olympics, the year Adolf Hitler told the world that the Germans were superior beings. Hitler even said that black people like Jesse Owens were inferior. Jesse showed Hitler and the world a thing or two!

● **Leading the Fast Breaks:** Jesse made the track team when he was in fifth grade. But he had an after-school job so he couldn't make it to practice. The coach thought Jesse was good enough for special treatment. He met young Jesse every morning before school began. Those sessions paid off! Jesse broke his own school record six months after he set it!

● **Not Bad for a Day's Work! Part I:** While still in college, Jesse broke three world records and tied a fourth in under an hour. During a Big 10 track meet at the University of Michigan, Jesse got down to business. At 3:15, he tied the world record by running the 100-yard dash in 9.4 seconds. At 3:25, he broke the world record by jumping 26 feet 8½ inches in the long jump. At 3:45, he set a 14-year world record by running the 220-yard dash in 20.3 seconds. At 4:00 he shattered the 220-yard low hurdles record by completing the course in 22.6 seconds. And he did it all with a bad back!

● **Not Bad for a Day's Work! Part II:** At

the 1936 Olympics, Jesse set three records and tied a fourth to win four gold medals in track. He equaled his own record when he ran a 10.3-second 100-meter dash. He set a new Olympic record of 26 feet 5/16 inch in the long jump. He ran the fastest 200 meters ever, blazing to victory in an amazing 20.7 seconds. And he helped set another record as the lead runner in the 400-meter relay.

# CHAPTER VII

# BO—
# UP CLOSE
# AND PERSONAL

**"I leave everything related to sports at the park. And when I hit the driveway, I become a husband and father."**
**Bo Jackson**

It's no secret that Bo likes to keep a low profile. As far as Bo is concerned, his private life is private, period. And who can blame him? Just think for a minute about what it's like to be a celebrity in America today.

Your picture would appear on the cover of *People* and *Sports Illustrated*. Reporters would be in your face all the time and follow you everywhere asking you questions about everything from how your hamstring feels today to what you like to read in the bathroom. You'd receive tons of mail and not all of it would be friendly. Hundreds of chattering fans would push you and crowd around you after every game asking for your autograph. Magazines would want photos of you in the kitchen, photos of you in the bedroom, photos of you taking a nap on the couch. Some people might even start bothering your family if they couldn't get through to you.

This much attention might seem like fun at first, but pretty soon no privacy at all would be no fun at all.

Bo knows that too much of the celebrity life can interfere with an athlete's concentration and wreck his or her performance. Bo has his own way of handling this kind of situation. When reporters get too pushy, Bo simply stops talking to them.

"I've talked enough to you guys," he has said. "I can't concentrate if I keep talking to you guys. I gotta play ball."

Bo has always kept to himself. Even when he was in high school, he never hung out with the other kids. He went to class, practiced whatever sport he was competing in that season, and went home.

Today Bo is no different. He's happy to hear

61

the roar of 50,000 to 80,000 fans screaming "Bo!" when he hits the breaking pitch or rushes 92 yards for a touchdown. But when he takes off his uniform, and leaves the stadium, he expects to leave his fans there, too. Off the playing field, Bo is very much a family man.

Bo's wife's name is Linda. He met her while they were both students at Auburn University. They didn't marry right away. They waited until Bo had left school and joined the Kansas City Royals before they tied the knot.

On July 13, 1986, Bo and Linda had their first child, a boy, and they named him Garrett. A younger brother for Garrett, named Nicholas, was born two years later on August 2, 1988. Bo takes being a dad very seriously.

"My sons are my best investment," he says.

While Bo is working for the Royals, he lives with Linda, Garrett, and Nicholas in a five-bedroom house he just bought near Kansas City.

Linda is still in school. She's studying psychology. Bo recently went back to school, too, to finish his degree in child and family development. Someday Bo and Linda hope to open a clinic for kids and families in trouble.

Bo's so private about his private life that not even his best friends know everything about him.

Many of them don't even know that he's deeply religious. He believes that his strength, speed, and stamina are gifts from God.

"I'm blessed," says Bo. "The athletic ability and skill I have is not because Bo Jackson was born with them but because the Lord gave them to me."

For all the time he spends on the field, Bo Jackson loves his hobbies! He likes to spend quiet time outdoors in nature. Hunting and fishing are two of his favorite pastimes. He also likes to take long walks in the woods with Linda. In other words, Bo's just a regular guy.

"Once people get to know me, they say, 'Wow! I didn't think you hung around with normal people,' says Bo. "But I'm not going to try to change what people think of me. I'm just going to be myself."

# CHAPTER VIII
## BE LIKE BO!

*"For me, the athletic part of both sports comes easily. If I can handle it in my mind, everything else comes easily."*
**Bo Jackson**

Bo is in tip-top condition. And it's no accident. He knows he has to take care of his body if he wants it to perform like the super sports machine it is. That means he pays attention to what he eats, he doesn't strain himself, and he doesn't smoke or drink.

Because Bo actively plays aerobic sports professionally all year long, he doesn't really have a strict training schedule. That is, he doesn't go to a gym or jog five miles a day or swim. He stays in shape because it's his job.

Bo thinks everyone should be and can be in shape. That's why he's a spokesman for the President's Council on Physical Fitness and Sports. He even did a video for them called "On Your Mark" that's all about the Presidential fitness award program and how kids can get in shape and win one.

The President's Council on Physical Fitness gives out two awards to kids only: The Presidential Physical Fitness Award and the New National Physical Fitness Award. The first one is for kids who achieve an outstanding level of fitness. The second is for kids who achieve a basic fitness level.

On the following pages is a Fitness Challenge based on the President's test. Bo can do everything. Can you?

## THE FITNESS CHALLENGE

**1. Curl-Ups:** Lie on the floor with your knees bent. Ask a friend to hold your ankles down. Cross your arms over your chest so your hands are on your opposite shoulders. Curl up so your elbows touch your thigh, then lower yourself slowly to the floor. See how many you do.

**2. Shuttle Run:** Put markers about 30 feet apart. Put two building blocks down behind one of the markers. Stand behind the other marker. Ask a friend to hold the stopwatch and say "Go!" Then run to the other marker, pick up a block, and run back. Put the block down behind the first marker—don't throw it. Then run back and pick up the other block and bring it back.

**3. One-Mile Walk:** Your parents will have to help you with this one. Ask your mom or dad to measure a mile course that starts and ends at your house. Then walk it with some friends. Don't forget to time yourself.

**4. Pull-Ups:** Only try this in a properly supervised gym class with mats and other safety equipment. Make sure you have a spotter watching you. Hang from a bar using an over-hand grip—that means your palms are facing away from your body. Now pull yourself up until your chin is higher than the bar. Then lower yourself slowly until your arms are extended. See how many you can do.

**5. V-Sit Reach:** Sit on the floor with your legs spread about a foot apart. Lock your thumbs together and place your hands on the floor in between your legs. Now creep your fingers forward. Keep leaning forward with your legs straight until you can't bend anymore. First try to reach your thighs, then your knees, then your shins, ankles, and finally your toes.

If you want to enter the President's Challenge officially and qualify for an award, ask your school to write to the Council and ask for the Fitness Program Order Form. Here's the address:

The President's Challenge
Poplars Research Center
400 E. 7th Street
Bloomington, IN 47405

# CHAPTER IX
# GET YOUR BO QUESTIONS ANSWERED HERE

**"Bo Jackson is about dreams . . ."**
**Al Davis**

There's never been a pro like Bo. He does things his way. And he does them better than anyone else.

Here are the answers to some questions you might have about Bo.

**Q:** Did Bo really get on the ice with Wayne Gretzky in his Nike commercial?
**A:** No. The Royals and the Raiders and Bo's agents were afraid he might hurt his ankles if he were to ice skate. So Bo's sliding around in

socks, not hockey skates. And he's not sliding on ice, either. He's sliding on a gym floor. By the way, Bo didn't play eight sports in the European version of the ad. He played ten. Bo added cricket and soccer to make it a total advertising decathlon!

**Q:** Is there any sport Bo isn't good at?
**A:** Bo might have a hard time getting on the Pro Bowlers' circuit! In a promotional bowling match set up at the Royals Stadium, Bo hit only 22 pins in ten frames! He finished last behind third baseman Kevin Seitzer who hit 34 pins and pitcher Bret Saberhagen who hit 27 pins.

**Q:** Does Bo ever make mistakes?
**A:** Sure. Bo led the league in strikeouts in 1987 with 158 strikes out of 396 at bats.

**Q:** Did Bo ever finish college?
**A:** Bo didn't graduate with his class from Auburn University in 1986. But he's back at Auburn now. He's still studying family and child development. Someday he hopes to open a clinic for kids and families in trouble with his wife, Linda, who is studying psychology.

**Q:** Since baseball season lasts so long, how does Bo get to California in time for the first football game of the season?

**A:** He doesn't. He finishes up his season with the Royals and *then* goes over to play with the Raiders. He usually joins them about five games into the season.

**Q:** Does Bo have a speech impediment?
**A:** Bo used to stammer. He would trip over letters and have a hard time saying what he wanted to say. He had a particularly hard time with the word "I." That's why he referred to himself as "Bo Jackson" so often. But Bo decided he wanted to change. He worked as hard on his speech as he does on his sprinting and pretty soon he beat the stammer.

**Q:** Does Bo lift weights? What does he do to stay in shape?
**A:** He doesn't. He says that if he lifts, his muscles get too big and he can't move as fast as he has to. He only does weight training to strengthen his wrists.

As far as other training goes, Bo doesn't have any formal stay-in-shape routines. He trains with the Kansas City Royals at their spring training camp and then plays baseball. The rest of the year, he plays football. That's a schedule that's physical enough. He doesn't have to jog or swim or walk to stay in shape.

**Q:** What other sports does Bo play?

**A:** Bo likes to hunt, fish, and shoot a bow and arrow. Some days he even shows up at the stadium with his archery equipment. He sets up a target in the batting area underneath the stands and then shoots one bull's-eye after another.

"Bo loves archery," says John Wathan, the Kansas City Royals' manager, "so he does it—better than anyone else."

**Q:** How come Bo doesn't get a swelled head from all the attention he gets?
**A:** Bo is very religious. He believes that his super sports skills are a gift from God. That keeps him humble.

**Q:** Would Bo be better at baseball if he gave up football? Would he be better at football if he gave up baseball?
**A:** There are three schools of thought on the Great Bo Debate.

School of Thought #1—Some people think he should give up football and concentrate on baseball. They think he'd play more consistently and improve his low batting average if he weren't distracted in mid-season by football. John Wathan, the manager of the Kansas City Royals, thinks that when football season begins, Bo starts thinking of rushing and touchdowns instead of batting and stealing bases.

"I think there's a little tendency for him to start thinking about football once the NFL training camps begin," says Wathan. "In '88 . . . he was not running as well the second half."

School of Thought #2—Some people think Bo should give up baseball so he can train with the football players as well as play with them. They say anyone can play three or four good games but not everyone can play that brilliantly for a whole season. They want him to decide where his dedication lies—football or baseball.

School of Thought #3—Some people think Bo should just keep right on doing what he's doing: playing two sports and breaking records in both of them!

And for now, that's exactly what Bo plans to do.

# CHAPTER IX

# BO AT A GLANCE

"I won't let anyone outdo me."
Bo Jackson

Here they are!
All the stats from Bo the statbuster!

**Personal Stats**
Name: Vincent Edward "Bo" Jackson
Height: 6'2"
Weight: 225 pounds
Birthday: November 30, 1962
Favorite Book: *The Old Man and the Sea*
Brothers and Sisters: 9
Marital Status: Married to Linda;
  2 sons, Garrett, 4 and Nicholas, 2
Car: Ferrari Testarossa
Football Team: Los Angeles Raiders
Football Position: Running Back
Baseball Team: Kansas City Royals
Baseball Position: Left field
Throws: Right handed
Bats: Right handed—but he can wallop
  them lefty, too!

# BASEBALL CAREER STATS

| YEAR CLUB | AVG. | G | AB | R | H | 2B | 3B | HR | RBI | BB | SO | SB |
|---|---|---|---|---|---|---|---|---|---|---|---|---|
| 1986 Memphis | .277 | 53 | 184 | 30 | 51 | 9 | 3 | 7 | 25 | 22 | 81 | 3 |
| KANSAS CITY | .207 | 25 | 82 | 9 | 17 | 2 | 1 | 2 | 9 | 7 | 34 | 3 |
| 1987 KANSAS CITY | .235 | 116 | 396 | 46 | 93 | 17 | 2 | 22 | 53 | 30 | 158 | 10 |
| 1988 KANSAS CITY | .246 | 124 | 439 | 63 | 108 | 16 | 4 | 25 | 68 | 25 | 146 | 27 |
| 1989 KANSAS CITY | .256 | 135 | 515 | 86 | 132 | 15 | 6 | 32 | 105 | 39 | *172 | 26 |
| M.L. Totals | .244 | 400 | 1432 | 204 | 350 | 50 | 13 | 81 | 235 | 101 | 510 | 66 |

*Led League

1986 Selected by Royals in 4th round of June Free Agent Draft, scouted by Ken Gonzales and signed by Royals front office.

# JACKSON'S BESTS

**Season**

| | |
|---|---|
| AVG. | .256—1989 |
| H | 132—1989 |
| HR | 32—1989 |
| RBI | 105—1989 |
| SB | 27—1988 |
| Hit Strk | 11—1988 |

**Game**

| | |
|---|---|
| H | 4—5 times, latest vs. Bos., 5-10-88 |
| HR | 2—5 times, latest at Oak., 7-4-89 |
| RBI | 7—vs. Det., 4-14-87 |
| SB | 3—3 times, latest at Oak., 7-5-89 |

# PLAYERS WHO HAVE HOMERED IN THEIR FIRST ALL-STAR AT BAT

| PLAYER | YEAR |
|---|---|
| MAX WEST | 1940 |
| HOOT EVERS | 1948 |
| JIM GILLIAM | 1959 |
| GEORGE ALTMAN | 1961 |
| JOHNNY BENCH | 1969 |
| DICK DIETZ | 1970 |
| LEE MAZZILLI | 1979 |
| TERRY STEINBACH | 1988 |
| **BO JACKSON** | **1989** |

# PLAYERS WHO HAVE HOMERED LEADING OFF AN ALL-STAR GAME

| PLAYER | YEAR |
|---|---|
| FRANKIE FRISCH | 1934 |
| LOU BOUDREAU | 1942 |
| WILLIE MAYS | 1965 |
| JOE MORGAN | 1977 |
| **BO JACKSON** | **1989** |

# FOOTBALL STATS

## FOOTBALL WITH THE RAIDERS

| Year | Gm | Rushing | | | | Receiving | | | |
| | | No. | Yds. | Avg. | TD | No. | Yds. | Avg. | TD |
|---|---|---|---|---|---|---|---|---|---|
| **1987** | 7 | 81 | 554 | 6.8 | 4 | 16 | 136 | 8.5 | 2 |
| **1988** | 10 | 136 | 580 | 4.3 | 3 | 9 | 79 | 8.8 | 0 |
| **1989** | 11 | 173 | 950 | 5.5 | 4 | 9 | 69 | 7.7 | 0 |
| Total | 28 | 390 | 2084 | 5.5 | 11 | 34 | 284 | 8.3 | 2 |

## VERBAL AND VISUAL INTERACTIONS    339

## STRUCTURE IN THE MODERN FILM    355

## APPENDIX    377

## INDEX    397

# Introduction:
## Toward a Film
### Idea

The central idea of a narrative—the recounting or imitation of an action—traditionally originates in the mind of a storyteller, who then proceeds to develop a structure suitable for the communication of his basic concept. The structure in its broadest sense, however, does not follow the conception but appears at the very moment the idea itself begins to take shape. This idea often incorporates a complexity of notions about personal feelings, human relationships, and intellectual and social problems, but presumably an artist does not conceive and elaborate his idea first and then decide whether he will turn it into a poem, a novel, an opera, or a ballet. Regardless of the process of creation, we find that a meaningful narrative succeeds only when its informing idea—which tends toward abstraction because of its potentially wide application—coheres with the particular characteristics of an art form.

As numerous as abstract narrative ideas may seem, audiences have always had a knack of simplifying them into sentences or even phrases ("the evil of man's inhumanity to man," "the suffering of unrequited

love," etc.). Any narrative form can communicate such ideas as these, yet obviously these abstractions do not themselves contribute quality to an individual work of art; they are too easy to establish, too commonplace to demand constant attention, too frequently found in trivial contexts. On the other hand, without such ideas, narratives lack that universal application that makes art a serious human endeavor in the first place. Therefore, what ultimately matters is the assimilation of these ideas within the framework of an esthetically appropriate form. For the film artist, the fulfilling of his creative impulse can be achieved only by shaping a narrative idea within the specific expressive mode of the film medium. The process of turning a general narrative idea into a specific film idea includes both the formulation of the idea and the actual development of it into a finished work of art.

Every authentic art form communicates through its unique expressive mode. Sophocles, Tolstoy, Gilbert and Sullivan, and Fellini all employ dialogue in the presentation of their narrative ideas. Obviously, however, both the style of effective dialogue and the degree of information it imparts change significantly from the dramatic mode to the fictional mode, to the operatic mode, and to the cinematic mode. Dialogue belongs properly to several narrative forms, but its potential value for any one art form depends very much upon its capacity for expressiveness within the medium.

Thus, the full sense of any narrative idea cannot be comprehended unless one has a total awareness of the nature of the particular art form under consideration. Assuredly, no one attempts to analyze *The Pirates of Penzance* according to the esthetic criteria Aristotle evolved for *Oedipus Rex*, nor does anyone insist that *War and Peace* meet the standards of greatness by which Sophocles' play is judged. The expressive modes of these three art forms are generally familiar and never seriously confused. The cinematic medium, however, originating with no esthetic principles of its own, borrowed its narrative ideas from drama, fiction, and (oddly enough) poetry, and took with the ideas some of the techniques found in the original sources. As a result, filmmakers around the turn of the century could provide merely the *imitation* of an imitation of an action. Their products lacked a direct approach to the reality of the events recorded by the camera, and this limitation meant that the best the new medium could hope to accom-

plish was a literal transcription of the process of an event. It could not communicate any abstraction, any intellectual process, any feeling other than what was immediately observable on its surface.

But filmmakers soon learned from the early films of D. W. Griffith the technique of conveying the sense of a complete action without actually depicting it in its entirety. Griffith demonstrated the method by which the arrangement of selected visual images of an action could effectively convey a complete story with the clarity and coherence of any comparable literary version of the same narrative materials. The discovery that in controlled circumstances the visual imagery could suggest meanings beyond its immediate physical reality made possible a distinctly cinematic form capable of narrative art of a very high order. In fact, by the end of the second decade of this century, filmmakers, by intuition and by trial and error, had worked out a truly cinematic mode of communication. The purpose of this book is to examine the nature of the film medium, its possibilities for expressiveness, and the ways it is utilized by filmmakers in the process of shaping a film idea.

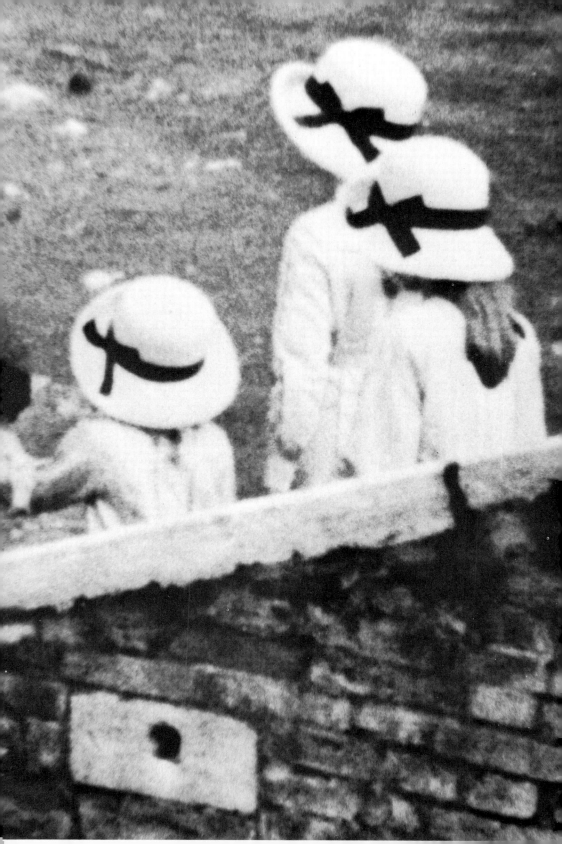

# Part One
# The Nature of the
# Narrative Film

Part One examines the foundations of cinematic meaning. In shaping a film idea, the filmmaker proceeds to develop the basic elements of the medium in regard to both their inherent properties and their capacity to be structured and designed to yield new possibilities of expressiveness. His technical proficiency is directly related to his knowledge of how these elements tend to function in any general context, how suitable they may be for the special presentation of his ideas, and how to employ them so as to extend their implications beyond the limitations of the mechanical nature of the medium.

All artists manipulate their material and thereby, to an extent, their audiences—not to mislead them, but to emphasize areas of importance. But audiences have a responsibility to themselves of intellectual awareness, a need to evaluate not only the effects of the art experience but the procedures and techniques that the artist uses to achieve his purposes. The film audience, in particular, constantly faces two difficulties in evaluating the cinematic experience: the uninterrupted progress of the narrative while that experience is occurring (which allows for very little reflection at the time) and the complexity of the medium's expressive mode (a combination of dramatic, literary, musical, and photographic modes).

Basically, the narrative film is made up of numerous selected views of reality, arranged so as to suggest events, activities, thoughts, and feelings. The origin and design of these parts, the development of the film idea, often involves the joint effort of several people as well as the unifying sensibility of a controlling artist. To understand the art of the cinema we must evaluate not only its elements but also the nature of the contributions made by the artists and craftsmen responsible for creating and executing the film idea.

5

# 1

# Film as Motion and Fixity

## The Material Nature of Film

The circus cars roll out of town, raising clouds of dust and leaving in their wake the solitary figure of Charlie the Tramp. He had loved a girl and just witnessed her marriage to another; and once again alone, his brief moment of glory as a circus performer passed forever, he prepares to walk along the backroads of respectable society confronting the hazards of his ever-precarious destiny. Then suddenly Charlie's step turns into a little skip and a kick of his heels. And with that gesture and his jaunty cane, he figuratively shrugs off his misfortune, dispelling the mood of sadness by determining to affirm the possibilities of his existence. Charlie refuses to be bound by his outward condition, for he lives an extraordinarily rich emotional life, and he tells us by his movement that his experiences justify his pain. Growing smaller and smaller as he strolls down the distant road, this final image of Charlie from *The Circus* extends itself into a symbol of spiritual triumph.

By its nature the film medium has the capacity to present images of tremendous suggestive power that at the same time retain an immediate link to the ordinary physical world. The characters in a filmed story are always tied to an environment that we find either identifiable or false but that we never ignore. A tramp walking down a road is not a particularly remarkable aspect of reality, but when an artist like Charles Chaplin works

with great awareness of the possibilities of the medium he can, through the camera's emphasis, transform the ordinary into the extraordinary. In Chaplin we move from the literal image of the physically small man to the symbol of the spiritually great man; this movement takes us from a precise detail of the physical environment to an abstract idea, a larger truth than the environment seemed at first to contain.

Yet in one sense even the greatest film artist cannot transcend the nature of his medium. The communication of ideas in any art form supposes difficulties, but the problems are magnified in film because of the fact that the raw materials must be shaped in terms of the various mechanical apparatus that record, arrange, and project the images that make up the cinematic experience. After all, when audiences see the tramp walking into the distance at the end of *The Circus* they are witnessing something slightly different from the dramatization of an image that occurred to Charles Chaplin, the writer-director of *The Circus*. The image on the screen was recorded by a cameraman and processed by a laboratory before Chaplin himself could actually see the strip of film projected. But this does not mean that somewhere along the line the film artist must lose control of his original idea or compromise his intentions. Rather, it means that he must anticipate all the steps from the conception through the production of the work. He must conceive his ideas in a specifically cinematic sense that takes into account the mechanical reality of the nature of film.

When we examine the essential nature of the motion picture we discover that it resembles several other art forms in its esthetic implications, incorporating many modes of expression within the scope of its own. Film communicates by music, speech, picture, and motion as well as silence, darkness, and stillness; by detail and by abstraction; by erratic design and by patterned narrative. But multiple modes of communication derive from the nature of film, not the other way around.

Fundamentally and inherently, film is deceptive. It presents us with the *optical illusion* of motion (based on the working of the eye, whereby the brain retains an image a fraction of a second after the image has disappeared), yet its mechanical nature reveals a series of fixed pictures. Although this much is common knowledge, few have concerned themselves with the implications suggested by the film's double nature, the appearance of motion as opposed to the reality of static images. What may be the most exciting moments in a film—for example, the acrobatic feats of a Douglas Fairbanks escaping from an army of pursuers— consist actually of a number of separate photographic images (called *frames*) on a transparent celluloid strip. The chase in fact was never completely recorded, for the camera that filmed it simply took a number of still pictures of a continuous action at a predetermined rate of 16–24 frames per second. If the entire action took one minute and was photographed at, say, 24 frames per second, then the complete action is suggested by 1440 still pictures. But why should we be satisfied with merely 1440 glimpses of this action within a

minute? Obviously a greater number of pictures would come much closer to a truthful description of the human form in movement. The answer, of course, is that the eye is not sophisticated enough to notice the difference between 1440 pictures flashed per minute and as many as 14,400,000, for the smaller number does the trick, and to all viewers the illusion of continuous action is absolutely convincing. For similar reasons, audiences cannot tell that the screen is without a picture 1440 times during that same minute. Each picture stops for a fraction of a second for the eye to record it; then the screen must be darkened so that in the replacement of one picture by another, the image is not blurred.

Let us consider first what the optical illusion of motion suggests. Most obviously, it implies that the material recorded by the camera ought to move. If not, the film projected on the screen will tend to duplicate the esthetic nature of a filmstrip, and there is no reason to use a moving picture camera to perform a function that is performed quite well by a still picture camera. While some parts of the modern motion picture are not depictions of motion, clearly movement in one form or another, suggested or shown, is a distinguishing aspect of film. Movement, of course, may be highly subtle: the study of the slightest change in facial expression, virtually unobservable on stage, might be extremely emphatic and of ultimate significance in a film. However, a full-length film cannot be composed entirely of raised eyebrows; much overt movement is needed, and that movement, as we will see later, must be related to the meaning of the film. In any case, the illusion of depicted movement must occur frequently for a film to be expressive in terms of its unique nature.

By the very fact that the film has to do with motion, we know that it is related to other art forms that reveal their meaning primarily in a linear or chronological progression, for example, drama, certain types of dance, and the novel. Motion not only allows for narrative, it suggests that narrative is fundamental to the mode of expression of a particular art form. The film, then, except in its experimental short forms, exists as a narrative art, though not always concerned with fictional narrative. (For instance, film is also a suitable form of narrating process: how mail is delivered by Great Britain's postal system, how Eskimos exist, how battles are fought.)

On the other hand, the mechanical nature of film—that it consists of fixed pictures on a celluloid strip—suggests a relationship between film and motionless arts such as still photography. A majority of ordinary filmmakers seem to ignore this relationship, but it remains a continual challenge to the film artist. In effect, it demands that filmmakers pay attention to the esthetic requirements of such art forms as painting and photography that do not reveal their meaning in a linearly progressive way. Like the graphic arts, film requires a permanent arrangement of parts by a creative artist—in spite of the fact that these parts are recordings of motion. This instability in his basic material, as compared to the basic material of a painter, precludes the likelihood of absolute control over the smallest particulars, but it does

not free the film artist from the necessity of establishing a fixed arrangement for the presentation of the moving elements.

Thus, although cinematography clearly differs from photography, the filmmaker—if he wishes to take advantage of all the possibilities of his art form in order to achieve maximum expressiveness—must strive to attain many of the goals that the artistic photographer achieves, for instance, control of light values and harmonious arrangements of planes and volumes. Control is essential, for a film is not a "happening," not an improvisation. It is quite unlike the mechanical process most closely identified with it, the video tape recording, which is designed primarily to record an event and which captures, but does not arrange, the facts of a reality (a state funeral, a trip to the moon, a late-night variety show, a television play) as that reality is in progress. In contrast, a film presents what *has happened* after the process is finished. Even when the actors have partially improvised the script (as is quite common), the film, by virtue of its mechanical nature, is ultimately an arranged or controlled set of photographs. A film cannot simply be developed and projected; if it is to express the meaning of the recorded event, the context of the event must be established.* (This is achieved through editing, as we will see later.) Thus, the peculiar nature of film— that it involves both motion and fixity, and by implication both real action and conscious arrangement—determines the possibilities and limitations of the medium for the expression of meaning.

## Motion: The Impressions Recorded

If we agree that the recording of motion is a primary function of the film medium, we must still distinguish the kind of motion most useful for film art. When the camera captures living things, some degree of motion always appears. If we watch long enough, the crocodile will move. But surely there are some types of movement so subtle or ordinary or boring that they do not repay the effort of observation. For the fisherman in his boat the slightest stir beneath the surface may be of absorbing interest; but to the casual spectator on shore even the much more evident movement of a swaying boat and a peering fisherman is too tedious to look at for more than a few seconds at a time.

On the other hand, we must not expect the film to deal exclusively with very broad movement such as we associate with violence or sports. It is sometimes necessary for men to sit and talk as well as to wrestle. To

---

* Some arrangement must be evident even in the extreme instance of the news film that is rushed through development and projected exactly as filmed on the television news broadcast the same day. The news commentator usually uses the film merely as a vivid illustration of the story he has already related, thus verbally supplying a context for the film.

demand that film emphasize the physically exciting moment is to limit its possibilities for the depiction of human emotion.

The sense of movement required by the nature of film may be achieved through a progression of images that convey the *idea* of human activity without showing actual motion. For instance, at the beginning of one Fritz Lang film we are presented with a series of separate images that include a man sitting at a desk, a close-up of a revolver, and a view of a woman standing on a stairway. While we are looking at the woman we hear a gunshot. Since the woman remains standing, it becomes almost immediately clear that the man at the desk has committed suicide. With an economy of visual material, Lang has depicted a physically violent and emotionally powerful act.

The sense of movement may sometimes be conveyed by a moving camera when the subject is stationary, but camera movement alone cannot sustain an audience's visual interest for very long. Yet many films made in the last several years use camera movement to enhance the motions of human subjects. For example, in Akira Kurosawa's *Rashomon,* the camera rushes along with a woodsman as he hurries through a forest, involving us in the character's perceptions of his environment, intensifying the tempo of his movements even as he slows down or stops, and carrying us to the emotional peak of the sequence, the sudden discovery of a corpse.

Another type of movement particularly suited to the medium is human gesture. But mere gesticulation, appearing in scenes where such movement is dubious, may convey a sense of stagnation rather than motion. Many silent films of the first two decades of the twentieth century, in a futile attempt to achieve grand art in the manner of the stage play, utilized famous stage stars who tried to compensate for their inability to use their voice by means of elaborate arm gestures. Actresses such as Sarah Bernhardt as Queen Elizabeth and Mary Garden as Thaïs appeared in utterly ridiculous poses, waving their hands up and down, while the audience waited for frequently inserted titles to explain in a flash what these actresses were so long in doing. In contrast to the use of broad, inappropriate gesturing of this sort is the truly meaningful moment in D. W. Griffith's *Intolerance* when the close-up of a woman's hands is used to express her tremendous anxiety while awaiting a jury's decision regarding her husband. Considered outside the emotional context the nervous movement of Mae Marsh's fingers would be insignificant, but within the framework established by Griffith the movement arrests our visual interest.

We see, then, that the movement in a film ought to have specific cinematic significance; it must not be mere kinetic activity. Neither should it be incidental or gratuitous to the narrative, but ought rather to be linked with the general progression of images on the screen. Whenever visual points of origin and destination can be shown for the movement depicted, and these locations justified by some reasonably clear motivation for the

**1** A typical example of Muybridge's many studies of animals in motion.

movement, chances are that the material is truly cinematic, as is almost always true with chase sequences.

According to one anecdote, which may not be true, the immediate impulse that led to the invention of the motion picture camera was the desire to record the motion of a racing horse. In 1872, Governor Stanford of California staked a large bet on the question of whether a trotter's four legs leave the ground simultaneously. There had been no accurate way of knowing this at the time, though the fact could be established nowadays by a still picture camera with a high shutter speed. The cameraman hired by Stanford, Eadweard Muybridge, devised a battery of cameras that produced a series of pictures at regular intervals (fig. 1).

But the desire to record movement in order to study its nature was only part of the instinct behind the invention of the motion picture. If a still picture of a horse with four legs off the ground had been sufficient, there would have been no need to refine the camera or to develop a projector. Cinematography by no means improves upon the earlier art form of

**12** | Film as Motion and Fixity

photography; it is something else entirely. Glancing at a display of separate images taken from successive frames recorded by a motion picture camera, we see only photographs (*stills*). We can see them either simultaneously or in sequence, but our eyes can do nothing with a series of photographs to simulate in any way the effect of a motion picture.

In other words, the recording of movement is only half the process; the other half is projecting that movement in time. The brain's response to the projection of images on a screen has been described by Sergei Eisenstein in *Film Form:*

> We know that the phenomenon of movement in film resides in the fact that two motionless images of a moving body, following one another, blend into an appearance of motion by showing them sequentially at a required speed.
>
> This popularized description of what happens as a *blending* has its share of responsibility for the popular miscomprehension of the nature of montage [editing]. . . .
>
> . . . Placed next to each other, two photographed immobile images result in the appearance of movement. Is this accurate? Pictorially—and phraseologically, yes.
>
> But mechanically, it is not. For, in fact, each sequential element is perceived not *next* to the other but on *top* of the other. For the idea (or sensation) of movement arises from the process of superimposing on the retained impression of the object's first position, a newly visible further position of the object.*

The important implication of Eisenstein's point is that movement in film requires not only a record of spatial progression but also a suggestion of temporal progression.

## Movement and Time

The relationship between time and movement in film has never been studied in detail, but certain basic premises are generally understood by most spectators. For one thing, film time (the time it takes to depict an incident on screen) is almost always greatly abbreviated in comparison to real time (the time it would actually take for the identical incident to occur in reality).†

* Sergei Eisenstein, *Film Form,* ed. and trans. by Jay Leyda (New York, Harcourt Brace Jovanovich, 1949), p. 49.

† Occasionally films have attempted to duplicate real time for long segments; for example, in Agnès Varda's *Cleo from Five to Seven* and Hitchcock's *The Rope,* an hour of screen time supposedly equals about sixty minutes in the lives of the characters. These experiments, however, were notably unsuccessful. Of course, film time can also exceed real time; although such lengthening is quite rare, a single great instance, the "Odessa Steps" sequence from Eisenstein's *Potemkin* (discussed at length in Chapter 15), proves that extending real time is a thoroughly valid cinematic technique.

Because almost everyone is acquainted with the precedents of literature and drama, the fact that a hundred-minute film usually contains events spread over many days causes no difficulty in comprehension. But our particular concern here is not with the relationship of film time to the story but with movement and time.

Even in the depiction of physical movement film tends to distort real time. This distortion has nothing to do with trick photography or variation in camera speed to produce the effect of "slow motion." It is simply a matter of visual economy. We do not always need to see a gesture or an ordinary procedure in its entirety to grasp the idea of the whole action. It takes a man five minutes to shave, but no film can spare five full minutes for such an incident. Without literally reproducing the activity, a filmmaker in a matter of seconds can easily convey the idea of shaving.

A film that portrays every movement in a time span of exactly the same length as it really took to complete the movement is likely to be visually dull. The sort of descriptive camera method that fastens on every aspect of motion runs counter to a basic premise of art in general: that art is selective. All narrative arts are necessarily selective in the elements of the story they choose to emphasize. (The limits of human patience and attention are factors here.) But film has an additional problem inasmuch as the projected images themselves are to a degree selective. The very dimensions of the visual area, set by the darkened sides of a rectangular plane in a movie theater, inform the viewer that he sees only a portion of the event observed by the camera crew.

The nature and degree of any selectivity beyond that implied by the spatial limitations of the camera lens depend on several factors, many of which are not primarily concerned with time. For instance, the film artist must consider the composition of the picture flashed on the screen at any given moment. How many irrelevant elements appear within the frame, distracting our attention from the most important visual aspect of the picture? How far are we from the object filmed? Is the recording of the activity worthwhile in the first place? Such questions merely begin to indicate the difficulty of selecting the proper way to film any sort of movement.

The problem of selectivity with respect to time presents the filmmaker with two alternatives for portraying any human activity. He can record the entire incident, movement, or gesture, or only suggest it by describing selected fragments of the whole. Most filmmakers use both techniques many times within the same film. For instance, if John Wayne is supposed to ride a horse from one town to another, no filmmaker could spend five hours depicting the ride (unless the entire film concerned that ride), especially if nothing particularly eventful occurs on the way. The five-hour ride will probably be suggested by a shot of Wayne mounting a horse and riding off, followed perhaps by four of five glimpses of him along the way, and

finally a view of him arriving at his destination. Five hours need not take more than a minute of screen time.

But what about the filming of Wayne mounting a horse? The camera can describe this complete action either in whole or in part. Yet since the act of mounting requires only a few seconds, it would be difficult to justify the effort involved in dividing the motion into separate images. In fact, such a division of imagery would create an emotional distortion, for the audience's attention would be focused for no apparent reason on an activity of no apparent importance. Furthermore, the division of an action that would take only a few seconds to depict in its entirety would likely produce a wasteful expansion of film time.

On certain occasions a director might choose to dissect a brief action even though this will extend film time beyond its equivalent time in reality. In *Marnie,* Alfred Hitchcock decided to film the fall of a woman and her horse from different angles, repeating a fragment of the incident on screen immediately after its first appearance. But this is a major incident, not a casual gesture. The audience is shocked into a second view of a horrifying accident; we know, suddenly, what the precise nature of such an event is, and the disruption of the narrative visually is justified by the point Hitchcock is making.

The division of movement into fragments, then, can either lengthen or shorten real time. As mentioned earlier, lengthened time is rare and not a significant aspect of the film style of any one director, including Eisenstein. On the other hand, the shortening of real time is part of the essential nature of film style. The film could never have developed its narrative potential without the discovery of elliptical use of time through editing of film sequences; for this the narrative tradition is indebted to D. W. Griffith, who, though not the originator of the method, was the first man to see the significance of the relationship of movement and time.

## Movement and Space in Some Primitive Films

Students viewing several of the outstanding one-reel Griffith films of 1912 are often confused by what appears at first to be a less advanced manner of filming movement than that in some earlier films. In many of these films Griffith does not employ a single moving camera shot! The explanation is that Griffith was working out a more sophisticated approach to movement in the cinema than earlier filmmakers ever achieved. But to appreciate what Griffith was doing, we ought to look at the most primitive examples of movement in the film.

One of the very first motion pictures was the Edison Company's 1894 filming of Fred Ott, an employee of the company, in the act of sneezing. This film (a sound film, by the way) consists of nothing more pictorially

interesting than the sneeze and suggests no conflict on a pictorial or thematic level; it simply presents an action, rather pointless without a context, but of great curiosity because of the newness of the mechanical recording devices. Surely the sound portion would dominate one's attention, as in many ordinary films today. The visual depiction of the action makes no great contribution to our knowledge of the act of sneezing and leads to no deeper understanding of the visual world around us. Yet the film had value at the time because it portrayed in detail something about the ordinary world.

The technique of visually emphasizing a movement was further developed in *The Kiss* (1896), the earliest extant film that still interests us, even aside from its historical position as the first film known to raise the cry of censorship. No one, we assume, intended *The Kiss* to be a daring movie. It simply reenacted a kissing scene from a popular play, *The Widow Jones,* and in a certain sense the Edison Company was performing a public service by showing for a penny a scene from a play that few could afford to see in person. But Mrs. Grundy saw more in it and complained.

What she saw was John Rice and May Irwin from the chest up against a dark background (fig. 2). The two performers are not particularly young or charming, nor in fact do they seem involved in any serious relationship.

**2**  *The Kiss*

Rice goes through the act of kissing in a very overstated manner that might indicate his own imminent laughter. Then the film ends, as abruptly as it began. The offensiveness of the film to some spectators cannot be dismissed as merely an example of late-Victorian prudery. The scene actually is sexually daring inasmuch as it discovers a basic means of depicting the erotic on screen: the camera has isolated two people presumably alone in a room. (As a matter of fact they are virtually outdoors; all films at that time relied on sunlight for sufficient exposure, and the roof of the Edison studio slid back to admit sunlight from any direction.) The couple is presented for no other purpose than to be revealed in the act of kissing—an intimate gesture that fills most of the screen in front of an indefinite background. The anonymous cameraman, working on no apparent conscious esthetic principle, has given overwhelming pictorial emphasis to a single motion. He has produced the first significant example of the basic principle of cinematic art: the isolation of a segment of reality in a single shot.

*The Kiss* does not show us anything that the normal view of a standing observer would fail to catch. In this sense, it is typical of the films shown around that time, for no one had yet come upon the idea that the camera ought to show something distinctively different from the eye's view of reality. Nevertheless, the film achieves an important, though unconscious, advance: it creates a visual emphasis on an ordinary gesture that could never be equaled on stage or in real life. For a moment, the entire world excluded, each viewer becomes absorbed in an intimate scene. Mrs. Grundy was alerted, and she was not to enjoy much peace of mind in the years ahead.

Shortly after *The Kiss*, purposeful human movement began to be used to convey the meaning of the narrative of a film. At this time films were necessarily short for technical reasons, often lasting less than a minute, and therefore the possibilities for storytelling were indeed limited. A primitive example of this sort of film is the Edison Company's *Streetcar Chivalry* (1901), in which several actors crowd into a studio set that supposedly resembles the interior of a streetcar. The painted background, patently false, might have been entirely effective on stage, but at this point in film history, it was not yet clear that artificial settings are obtrusive in films that rely basically on pictorial realism.

Although the action is anecdotal, as we would expect from the brevity of the film, it does relate movement to idea without difficulty. The plot concerns a group of men sitting in the crowded streetcar who are willing to give up their seats to an attractive lady; however, when a fat lady arrives, the men pretend to ignore her until, as a result of a sudden movement or stopping of the streetcar, she falls upon them, thus innocently punishing them for their bad manners. The entire action is shown in one shot and lasts about a minute. Since the artificial setting is immobile, the "motion" of the streetcar depends completely on the miming of the actors. This expedient does not work in any serious sense—nor does it have to, since the film is

intended to serve as the most superficial type of comedy; nonetheless, it is an interesting example of the way in which an idea, and a social one at that, can be conveyed swiftly and understandably without the slightest need for verbal clarification.

*Streetcar Chivalry* has charm rather than artistry, and a certain historical attraction that all primitive films now hold for us, yet it is not a completely cinematic experience. The movement of the film is arbitrarily limited (because of the undeveloped techniques of the industry) by its location, which clearly is not real; thus, the cameraman's decision to simply film what he saw indicated that he saw only a casual relationship between the event and its expression. Had the event been presented the same way on stage, the effect would have been better, for a theater audience would have appreciated the simulation of motion as acting, whereas the film audience could only consider it an unsuccessful attempt at verisimilitude.

The next significant steps in the development of the narrative film were a turning away from the filming of vaudeville bits and anecdotes, which are essentially of the theater, not of the cinema, and an extension of movement spatially beyond the confines of the set. These advances were accomplished in two ways: first, while sets were retained, an impression of spatial movement beyond that of the theater was suggested by taking each scene in a different place, thus switching locations at a greater speed than even the revolving theater stage could do. A second method, more cinematic than this, was to use real locations (that is, exteriors) to take the narrative visually beyond the confined space of the theater. This method not only introduced a new sense of reality into the narrative film, but quickly dissociated the film from its theatrical tendencies.

A primitive example (but not the first) of the spatial extension of a narrative by cinematic means is seen in Edwin Porter's *Romance of the Rails* (1902). The story is simple and uninteresting: a couple sitting on the rear, outdoor platform of a train go through the process of courtship and are married on board. All the while the continuous motion of the train is followed by a camera mounted in front of the couple. Told in several shots, the story for all its contrivances seems real, for the setting is real, and the setting—the moving world observed by the camera—is more interesting than the characters because it had not yet become familiar. We are outdoors exploring a delightfully rustic but solid world; no painted backdrop could achieve this effect. Apparently the romantic background inspires the lovers and perhaps even determines the marriage. The psychology need not be perfectly clear. Here the smooth train ride and the passing scenery are made to count for everything.

It is no accident that the train became the major symbol of movement in cinema. The engine itself represents the complexity of an industrial society and the functional beauty that can develop with it. A moving train provides a variety of natural scenic images, and if a camera is placed near

it, the motion picture screen will reveal interesting linear patterns of motion. Even today, thousands of Americans collect plotless movies of trains. *Romance of the Rails* is a title with applications to both the filmmaker and the audience.

By about 1905 Porter had completed his contribution to the film. He had made important experiments in both realistic and nonrealistic cinema, and his perception of what kind of material is truly cinematic was essentially correct. One of his greatest contributions was his development of the relationship between space and movement. By considered use of a background —of necessity it was often outdoors, to take advantage of natural lighting— Porter was able to construct patterns of movement that emphasized the figure or object traversing an identifiable area. He took the film out of abstract space and located it *someplace*. Thus, movement in space became meaningful: a character or an object—for instance, a bandit in *The Great Train Robbery* or a fire truck in *The Life of an American Fireman*—had somewhere to go as well as a point of origin. In addition, Porter expanded the field of view (primarily along a horizontal plane) by occasionally moving the camera and gradually revealing an area beyond the immediate environment. The art of the film widened as the possibilities for utilizing spatial relationships became enormous.

# 2

# Film as an External Medium

## Film and Eye

Because much of a film is taken up with images of everyday reality, the motion picture camera necessarily competes with the human eye, for in order to justify any visual art, we must be able to say that it makes us see something more clearly or more penetratingly than we have seen for ourselves. In construction, the human eye is more sophisticated than any camera. It is more flexible in terms of focus and distance than anything man will likely invent for quite some time. But it is equally true, though hardly ever remarked, that a great many cameras collectively can be even more sophisticated perceivers of reality than any one pair of eyes. The modern motion picture takes advantage of that premise: it may actually use only one camera, but that camera can be in five different places in one room—not at the same time, of course, but for all practical purposes, the results of filming from five different camera positions can be reconstructed (edited) to present the equivalent of five alternating views of one thing.

The eye shifts its focus too, quite naturally, even when a person simply sits in a chair gazing across the room at a bowl of fruit. Incapable of focusing attention for very long on an object that is not doing anything interesting, the mind directs the eye to look at something else, probably another object in the vicinity of the bowl of fruit. In other words, the eye can expand the area around the fruit or constrict it. Instead of concentrating on the bowl alone, it might concentrate on the bowl as an object on a table; it might

next see the bowl and the table against the background of the wall; it might then go back to one of the earlier perceptions and return again to another. Whatever the pattern, and very likely it is a random one, the eye may well have absorbed a dozen distinct impressions in a few seconds. The mind may never be aware of this accumulation of impressions. Other thoughts may occur spontaneously and simultaneously. The eye continues to send visual impressions to the brain, but they do not always register consciously.

Considered from another point of view, the eye always perceives the vastest possible area before it, its angle of vision much wider than that of a normal camera lens, but less than that of some specialty lenses (called *fish-eye* lenses). Yet as the eye takes in the total area as far as it can see, the brain almost always excludes from consciousness the larger part of what the eye perceives. It has learned to do this by experience. A baby in its earliest days was once thought to be incapable of seeing anything; we now know that a baby does see at a very early age but has a problem focusing on specific objects. A white wall ten feet away, a mother five feet away, and a rattle hanging one foot away are equally interesting to a mind that has observed nothing previously. But the adult eye, trained by billions of visual experiences, has learned to distinguish depth more readily than a camera can ever do, except in stereoscopy; more importantly, it has learned to shift areas of concentration instantly.

The eye then does instinctively what a filmmaker does by art: it selects images to focus on, always excluding the extraneous or the uneventful. When we look at the Grand Canyon, the eye surveys everything. But when we talk to a friend, the eye notices only the friend, or rather the brain excludes most other visual information. Thus, the eye can choose to see only a tie, then a face, then an entire body, all without any movement of the head. The variation of visual images is natural, instinctive, and continuous while we are awake.

## Camera Shots: Basic Considerations

The early development of the motion picture narrative is described most clearly in terms of the development of a variety of shots from cameras that sought new possibilities for capturing movement. The very first films were done in a single camera shot—that is, from one point of view at one set distance. D. W. Griffith changed this basic approach forever by popularizing (but not inventing) the procedure in which the camera interpreted the action of each episode by filming it in a variety of ways. In the earlier films the camera served mainly to record action; with Griffith it began to define it.

An examination of some terminology will be useful at this point. The basic vocabulary of film is so much a part of the general vocabulary that one has to be reminded that he has rarely heard the words defined with any

attempt at precision. Even within the industry, the paucity of terms is a hindrance to clear descriptions of the art. The essential term, *shot,* is known in some sense to practically everyone. It can be defined as any length of continuously projected film in which the image *seems* to have been captured continuously by a motion picture camera. *Seems* is used because in the very first films made, stop-motion photography was used for trick effects. For example, a man could be photographed holding a package, the camera stopped and the package removed while the man remained exactly as he was, and then the camera started again. This would literally mean two shots were taken of the man, but when the film is projected only one shot is visible: it *seems* as if the package mysteriously and instantaneously disappears from the man's hand. This definition of a shot allows for the effects of trick photography but does not require the spectator to figure out when or how often the camera actually stopped. As long as the projected film gives the appearance of continuous filming, we can call the result a single shot.

The shot, then, may be considered the basic unit of film meaning. A shot may be composed of any number of frames * and may be of any duration. However, the modern filmmaker, seemingly obsessed with the fear of boring his audience, will only rarely allow a shot to exceed a minute in length; and most shots are much shorter. The original one-shot motion pictures were quite short, but as technology developed, some films were extended to five or more minutes and still contained only one shot.

At the other extreme, a shot may consist of only one frame. Since 1927, the projection speed has been standardized for sound films at 24 frames per second. Thus, a one-frame shot would have a duration of about one half of one twenty-fourth of a second (allowing for the amount of time when the image moves into place behind the lens of the projector). At this speed many people in the audience would not even see the shot, though it is not true that no one could see it. For others, the shot might register subliminally.† Shots of very short duration—five or six frames (one quarter of a second)—are not unusual, but because they are almost impossible to comprehend in any complexity, the context of the brief shot must be carefully established for the audience. Sometimes the very brief shot or series of shots within the duration of a few seconds is used to suggest fleeting or haunting memories. In Hitchcock's *Marnie,* such shots appear several times;

---

* In Chapter 1, the word *frame* was used to mean a separate, fixed picture on the celluloid strip of film. The term may also refer to the entire rectangular pictorial area of the image as projected on a screen or other surface.

† In the 1950's some advertising men thought of a supposedly clever scheme to sell products. They assumed that if the picture or slogan of a commercial product was flashed on the screen for a frame or two right in the middle of a film, the name of the product would register in the minds of the viewers, though they would never know they had seen anything. The experiment failed, however, for many people did see that bottle of Coke in the middle of the love scene, and at the end of the film they did not flock to the Coke machines in gratitude for the imposition.

although their precise meaning remains unclear, the audience understands that they represent memories of a harrowing sexual experience. The rapid pace of several consecutive brief shots within a single context frequently produces considerable tension. Physical violence of various sorts—for instance, an automobile crash or a fistfight—is sometimes depicted in such a series of shots, and the audience, unable to evaluate rationally the objects and movements flashing so quickly on the screen, becomes emotionally involved in the action.

Perhaps the clearest way of approaching the shot as a basic film unit is to divide the subject into two categories: the moving camera shot and the stationary camera shot. The latter category is further subdivided according to the *distance* between the camera and the subject (essentially, long, medium, and close shots) and the *angle* at which the camera photographs the subject (*i.e.*, high angle, low angle, or eye level). With moving camera shots, though the angle and distance are important of course, the usual description refers to the kind of movement (*i.e.*, up, down, sideways). Because these few terms represent the essential vocabulary of the medium, they should be considered in detail.

## Moving Camera Shots

When used to describe a shot, the word *moving* refers only to the camera, not to the subject being photographed, which may be moving or still. Subjects that move a great distance rather quickly (*e.g.*, airplanes, running animals, football players) are usually photographed with a moving camera. The reason for this is that an object moving, say, from right to left, would continually pass outside the visual range of a stationary camera, necessitating multiple stationary camera setups to show the whole movement. Another chief function of the moving camera is to keep characters in approximately the center of the frame when they move in certain ways. For example, if a character sits down, the moving camera can keep him in the center of the screen and avoid the awkwardness of having the major subject appear in a lower corner. A third traditional use of the moving camera, to reveal vast scenery, is especially important in the modern wide-screen color film. Great areas need to be filled up, and for the uninventive director the moving camera shot often becomes a saving grace.

There are five basic types of moving camera shots, plus the shot using the zoom lens, in which the camera merely appears to move:

(1) For up-and-down movement, the camera can be tilted by placing it on a device that enables its angle of vision to be shifted vertically. The *tilt shot* is often used to suggest the viewpoint of a character looking down from a great height or looking up at signs or pictures high on a wall.

(2) The camera can be attached to a device commonly called a crane or mounted on an elevator of some sort and moved up or down without changing its angle of vision. The *crane shot* can give a level view of a man racing up or down a flight of stairs.

(3) In a *pan shot* (the sideways equivalent of the tilt shot) the camera, though mounted on a nonmoving device such as a tripod, is itself turned on its vertical axis, for example, to follow a car moving from left to right.

(4) If the same movement of a car is followed by a fixed camera mounted on a moving vehicle, the procedure is called tracking (or trucking, in England). A distinction is made at times (though not in this book) between a *tracking shot,* in which the camera moves at the same speed as the subject, and a *traveling shot,* in which the camera moves at an independent speed.

(5) For interior sequences or shots in which the camera is to make various kinds of movements while covering a relatively small area, the camera is placed on a dolly. A *dolly shot* allows for extreme flexibility, as the camera can move in many directions; it is particularly useful for moving toward or away from an object unobtrusively.

(6) A fixed camera fitted with a zoom lens (a lens with a variable focal length) can make distant objects seem to draw continuously nearer or close objects seem continuously to recede. Difficult to use artistically because of its readily apparent artificiality, the *zoom shot* frequently diverts one's attention from the thing being photographed to the photographer himself. Nevertheless, it is commonly used, though rarely with skill in the fiction film; in the documentary film and in amateur cinematography, the zoom lens may help greatly in filming distant objects that the photographer cannot get close to.

The five basic camera movements may be used in virtually any combination. For instance, a camera mounted on a rising platform may be tilted upward at the same time as it pans the scene, thereby combining three separate movements.

It is sometimes difficult to draw a line between a moving shot and a stationary one. For example, a continuously running camera may move for a while and then take a stationary position, or vice versa. In such an instance, if the shot is long enough, it might be useful to consider it as two separate shots, especially if the filmmaker is trying to tell us something by the change from movement to nonmovement or from nonmovement to movement.*

* Most such shots, however, are made simply to save money (two shots cost more than one and take longer to set up) or, even more commonly, because someone suspects that the shot is visually boring.

## Stationary Camera Shots

A stationary camera shot is simply one in which the camera does not move. The subject of course can be moving or still, as is the case with a moving camera shot. If the stationary camera is placed higher than the subject, the result is a *high-angle shot;* if lower, a *low-angle shot.* Most shots fall in between and are roughly *eye-level shots.* However, the terms are somewhat less than precise, for after all, what is eye level to a seven-foot basketball center is high angle to his baby daughter. The great Japanese director Yasujiro Ozu saw the world from the point of view of the typical Japanese at home; but to an American audience, Ozu seemed to be filming on his knees. The earliest films were shot almost exclusively from some approximation of eye level, for this was considered the normative view, as it is today in the cinema of the western world. In German films of the 1920's, a great deal of attention was paid to weird angles, which seemed in themselves artistic. Not only high and low angles but oblique ones became fashionable. Unusual angles are still not normative and therefore call attention to themselves, so if they are used, they are chosen self-consciously and often for a good reason.*

Stationary camera shots are also described in terms of the distance of the camera from the subject. Again, the terms are relative, and although within the Hollywood industry the terms are more rigidly confined to specific measurements, even shooting scripts for Hollywood films use the terms loosely. The first shot to consider is the *long shot,* or *distance shot,* which depicts an area large enough for several human figures to move in. The long shot can cover an enormous area, but increasing distance reduces our perception of details, resulting in an abstraction of the image and a decrease in audience comprehension. However, most long shots cover a decidedly narrower area than the human eye would observe if it were in the same position as the camera. After all, with even the largest theater screens a shot of enormous distance can disclose very little, and an aerial view of the world cannot sustain audience interest for more than a few glimpses.

The term *full shot* is frequently used to mean a shot in which standing human figures more or less fill the screen. Obviously, this is a variation of the long shot, but the distinction has some pragmatic value inasmuch as it tends to define the long shot as any shot filmed at a greater distance than a full shot. Thus, it is worthwhile to use one term or the other to distinguish between long shots of many characters (*e.g.,* fig. 25) and somewhat closer shots in which one or two characters fill the frame vertically (*e.g.,* fig. 5).

Long and full shots are frequently used to "establish" an area, that is, to inform the viewer of the location of the action. When they introduce a sequence, they are often referred to as *establishing shots.* In practice they

---

* For a discussion of the question of whether angle conveys meaning see Chapter 13.

do much more than point out the nature of the environment, for they continually relate the characters to their background.

The *medium shot* (also called a *mid-shot* or *three-quarters shot*) is even more difficult than the long shot to define precisely. For the purposes of this book, the term will refer to a shot that covers an area of which the vertical dimension is approximately equal to the height of a seated adult or an adult from the waist up (see fig. 44). American technicians who are bothered by the vagueness of the term further define such shots as *medium full, medium close,* and so forth. The medium shot is important because it serves to exclude much of the unnecessary environment in scenes where the relationship between a few people is more important than the background or the relationship of any one person to the background.

The *close shot* and the *close-up* are difficult to distinguish from each other but easily distinguished from the other shots. Usually, a shot in which a human head fills the screen is described as a close-up, but some contemporary filmmakers habitually bring their cameras closer than that, and they would call a close-up only a shot that fills the entire screen with an actor's eyes. (In the 1940's, such a shot was sometimes referred to as a big close-up.) With the advent of the wide screen, some of the definitions have shifted slightly, but for the purposes of this book, a close-up will be any shot in which a person's head or a small object just about fills the screen. Shots falling between the close-up and the medium shot will be referred to as close shots (see fig. 39).

The relativity inherent in these definitions may prove disturbing in a technologically oriented age, but we require some terminology to describe films, and perhaps if the terms were made scientifically precise they would be limiting. A visual medium is not enhanced by precise verbal definition, anyway. Understanding the relative nature of the terms referring to camera distances and angles, we may make good use of them in analyzing films.

Some shots cannot easily be classified by their distance from the object because the focus is shared or divided. In *Strangers on a Train,* Hitchcock uses a shot in which the insane Bruno, in a close shot, tries to arrange over the telephone for his father's murder. Normally the conflict would be confined to the telephone call itself and to the expression on Bruno's face as he tries to convince another man to commit the murder. But just prior to this shot Hitchcock has for a few seconds introduced the father, about whom we know nothing except that his son hates him. Now in the shot where Bruno speaks on the telephone relatively close to the camera, Hitchcock also shows the parents talking to one another in long shot. The two conversations proceed simultaneously, dividing our aural attention just as the division of the visual image causes us to look at Bruno on one side of the screen and his parents on the other (fig. 3). Usually when a character is close to the camera, the visual emphasis falls entirely on him, not on people who are far beyond him. But in this peculiar shot, the audience is just as

interested in finding out about the father as about Bruno's telephone call; furthermore, the visual conflict actually concerns Bruno's indifference to his parents' presence and his dislike of them. Thus, the foreground and the background require equal visual attention, although there is no physical interaction between them. It would be impossible to describe this shot as either a close shot or a long shot.

## Selecting the Appropriate Shot

Almost every object or person can be filmed from an infinite number of camera angles at an infinite range of distances from the camera. Naturally, not all angles or distances are equally effective for any one shot. One of the prime responsibilities of the filmmaker (usually with the assistance of the cameraman) is to choose the most appropriate angle and distance for each shot. But he often makes this sort of decision on intuition, sensing that the camera ought to frame just this part of a scene rather than another. Film-makers with a very highly developed pictorial sense—such as Jean Renoir, Fritz Lang, and Sergei Eisenstein—tend to do it right almost all the time, which means nothing more than that a spectator cannot quarrel with their

choices. With other filmmakers, even with some very good ones, it often seems that one angle would serve as well as another. And with inferior filmmakers, the choices frequently seem awkward or contrived.

The appropriateness of such choices may be evaluated in terms of style and content regardless of the subjectivity of the creative process involved. Unlike nonnarrative filming, which for its special purposes may emphasize either attractive visual representations or information, the feature-length narrative film aspires to combine style and content in each shot of an esthetically unified work of art. We have no rules for assuring such a successful balance—instinct is important here—but the alternative imbalance is often easily observed in the finished product.

When style is the overriding interest of a filmmaker, the result is usually camerawork unsuitable to the subject matter. In such cases a strong visual sense, characteristic of several avant-garde filmmakers, obtrudes upon the narrative, continually calling attention to the presence of the camera. The technical innovation or the charm of this kind of film may temporarily obscure its narrative deficiencies. Most of us are eager enough to be entertained by something new and thereby to overlook a degree of emptiness in appreciation for it—but only the first time around. In a film that endures for more than its season, technical virtuosity and fine photography are not ends in themselves but means to an end. The stylistically overemphatic shot —say, with a self-consciously odd angle (lovers seen through the fire in a fireplace) or with excessive motion (a child photographed from a helicopter's view)—calls attention to the cameraman and distracts us from the underlying film idea.

The other kind of imbalance—of content over style—is even more common, since there are more filmmakers convinced that they have something important to tell us than those who claim technical skills at cinematography. The former sometimes try to convey a story without much of a preference for one shot or another, and in these instances the cameraman really determines the effectiveness of presentation, the filmmaker serving largely the role of scenarist or stage director. Yet even the greatest cameramen cannot be expected to impose a stylistic unity on the material. When content is virtually the sole concern of the filmmaker, he may occasionally interest or surprise us, depending on both his intelligence and his subject matter, but he must always be limited by a lack of discernment regarding the functions of his shots. No longer can a significant anti-war statement be made merely by accumulating close shots of corpses, though the point about war's horror and wastefulness is reinforced by each shot. In other words, even the most powerful content demands carefully selected images for effective expression.

Clearly, some shots are more effective than others in communicating the subject matter. A close-up will not tell anything about the general environment, and a long shot will lose the minute detail of a setting or

entirely miss a subtle gesture. Furthermore, the problems of choosing the camera's vantage point and of electing to use a moving or a stationary camera are even more complicated than the problem of determining the best distance from which to shoot. Decisions based on technical ingenuity or social commitment rather than artistic appropriateness always ignore the full expressive possibilities of the shot.

In discussing the criteria for selecting shots, we must not underestimate the general assumption of film studios that any shot held for too long a duration becomes visually boring. Actually, there are two kinds of tedium in films, visual and verbal. Evidently, many directors feel they can compensate for the former by improving acting performances and dialogue; in so doing, however, they ignore the visual nature of the problem and fail to meet the standards implicit in the nature of the film medium. Similarly, the attempt to combat verbal boredom by changing the shot is also essentially futile; it can work only with spectators who have seen so few films that the process of filming itself still holds a good deal of fascination for them. There is no need to belabor the point: a dull film is a dull film. But when one is caught in a movie theater watching such a film, it is sometimes worth the price of admission for the sake of education to look for the strained camera setups and unnecessary movements contrived by the hard-pressed director in order to keep the show going.

## Special-Effects Shots

In addition to moving shots and stationary shots, the movie industry has developed an enormous number of special-effects shots, about which a great deal has been written in older film books. That these shots are used neither consistently nor frequently by the great filmmakers indicates that they have not functioned as particularly important aids to the filmmaker. However, that they were ever used at all is enough to justify mentioning them.

*Slow motion* and *fast motion* (*speeded-up motion*) are produced by projecting the film at a different number of frames per second from the rate at which the camera recorded the action. Slow motion is achieved when the rate of projection is less than the rate at which the film was shot. Fast motion occurs when the projection rate exceeds the rate of shooting. Since the projection rate of sound films is now standardized, the usual method of producing slow or fast motion is by varying the rate of shooting. However, some projectors are equipped with a variable-speed motor, so it is possible also to vary the rate at which the action is shown.

Both slow and fast motion are essentially comic, but not funny enough to produce laughter automatically because they have been seen too often.

They did enjoy some successful uses in the early days of slapstick comedy, and speeded-up motion was found frequently in those weekly serials when the heroine seemed doomed to some tragic fate, tied to the tracks as a speeding train approached. (The train, of course, was not speeding.) Speeded-up filming helps certain biological studies that otherwise defy human patience; for example, the laying and hatching of an egg can be projected in one minute when filmed by stop-motion photography over many hours of time. Slow motion, more commonly and possibly more sensibly used, is an essentially cinematic device of great usefulness in non-narrative films, for it can show the process of motion in a way that the human eye could not otherwise perceive. In the narrative film, slow motion is sometimes used to record particularly graceful movements of men or animals. In recent years, it has evolved a connotation of the grotesque, as in the portrayal of the violent deaths at the conclusion of Arthur Penn's *Bonnie and Clyde.* Contrary to the apparent belief of many directors, slow motion contains nothing inherently poetic or dreamlike (do *you* dream in slow motion?), but its use for such moods in many second-rate films has made slow motion a kind of film cliché for the symbolic representation of innocence and beauty. In Sidney Lumet's *The Pawnbroker,* some flashback sequences are done in slow motion to suggest memory or a man's groping with fleeting images of his past. The effectiveness of such filming is likely to be evaluated on the basis of one's subjective responses.

*Superimpositions* are optical effects in which one or more images can be seen on top of the main image. This was once a weird effect and could be used in films that dealt with the supernatural. Nowadays, ordinary television shooting of nonvisual performers (primarily singers) commonly employs one type of superimposition, the *double exposure,* and viewers hardly make a mental note of the effect. A once popular usage—to begin a flashback—has virtually disappeared.

*Split-screen filming,* which allows a director to portray simultaneously, by means of multiple images, actions that may or may not be simultaneous, was briefly popular in the late 1960's. The device has been exploited mainly by television, where its creative possibilities are necessarily limited by the small size of the screen. (Five or six tiny pictures would be difficult to see, let alone to comprehend in regard to stylistic patterns or sophisticated relationships.) Its recent film use may be an instance of the influence of television on cinema, though it is not clear which medium popularized the style first. Certainly split-screen filming has been used on rare occasions for a great many years, and variations of it can be found in Georges Méliès' films at the turn of the century. But it has functioned as a consistent aspect of style in surprisingly few films. It was used masterfully in John Frankenheimer's *Grand Prix:* in one sequence, several individually framed images of the cars engaged in a particular race are shown within the larger frame. In another, more striking sequence, several images reveal the same

car from different points of view. In *The Thomas Crown Affair,* Norman Jewison employs the multiple-image device to show us various activities of the main character in relation to his planning of a theft; these incidents are simple in themselves and do not require visual concentration, so that our eyes need not roam all over the screen to pick out the proper frame to watch.

The trouble with projecting different images in separate sections of the screen is the resultant loss of focal attention; therefore, the actions portrayed in multiple images cannot be especially subtle. On the other hand, so much may be gained from clever visual arrangements of simultaneous or closely related activities that one wishes to see the technique used more often so that its potential may be fully realized.

In the short development of the film from silent to sound, one of the most useful of all shots went out of fashion and is very rarely seen today. This is the *iris shot,* in which the frame is completely dark except for an area—usually circular—that is clearly illuminated. The technique of "irising in" used an iris shot at the beginning of a segment of film, followed by a gradual widening of the circle of light until the entire frame was illuminated. The iris shot, employed very often by D. W. Griffith, thrived throughout the silent age, notably in many classic films such as *The Cabinet of Dr. Caligari.* Perhaps it lost its popularity because it seemed too contrived; perhaps it was overdone. In any case, few these days lament its loss because its great value has been forgotten. The iris shot really functions as an alternative to the close-up; it focuses attention on a part and can have an even more powerful effect than a close-up because the entire environment is not ignored but merely hidden for a moment. And as the iris expands, with each frame it reveals something new about the relationship between the object or person emphasized and the general background. No shot has replaced the iris for its special effectiveness, but it seems unlikely that it will return to popularity in the near future. Most filmmakers have never really considered the possibilities of the partially darkened screen, which Eisenstein once proposed in the form of an expanding or contracting picture.

# Editing
# the Film
# Idea

## Connections of Shots

The two basic procedures of filmmaking are shooting the film and assembling the shots. We have considered some of the problems of choosing what shots to take and will now consider some aspects of editing.

Shots are connected to each other in a limited number of ways. The basic connection is the *cut,* which is a joining of two shots with no intervening frames. In any modern film at least ninety percent of the shots are connected by simple cuts; sometimes no other joining device is needed. Occasionally modifying terms may be attached to the word, but they do not often connote much that is different from just the plain cut. For instance, the *jump cut* supposedly refers to a joining of two shots in which the content of each indicates a lapse in time; however, the distinction is seldom more than academic, since the very nature of film suggests a jump in time between many shots, possibly even most shots. Perhaps the term could be made meaningful if it were restricted to extended leaps in time or elliptical connections of shots where the camera position remained identical.

The other devices for joining shots—for example, irising in—now have limited value, though at one time they were used extensively. The *fade-in* is still found occasionally: the darkness following one shot yields

gradually to increasing light, which in a few seconds (or even just one second) reveals the next shot. It is sometimes used in connection with a *fade-out,* a shot that gradually becomes immersed in darkness (the process may take a second or two). An interesting variation is the *dissolve,* or *mix,* in which the laboratory technician superimposes the fade-in and fade-out. Shots are sometimes joined by frames completely overexposed or colored so as to suggest intense light (for instance, sunlight); the effect is the antithesis of the fade, but it accomplishes a similar purpose.

Finally, an unlimited number of tricks or special optical effects can be used to join shots. In the 1930's Hollywood went in for the craze of *wipes* and by the 1940's had exhausted their artistic possibilities. In a wipe, the new image is brought onto the screen, simultaneously "wiping off" the old image. The most common wipe was a simple replacement from right to left or left to right of one shot with another. But Hollywood really had a lot of fun with the wipe—it is an early example of American camp—and an enormous variety of wipes was invented, including zigzags, saw-teeth, and all sorts of geometric patterns. They were, while still new, visually entertaining on their own level, especially if the film was mediocre and audiences did not really care too much what the next image was to be. But wipes have almost completely disappeared in the last ten years—that is, from the movie screen; television relies on them extensively and apparently has invented some variations that even Hollywood in 1935 would have envied.

The choice of one technique or another in joining shots can be of considerable importance. The cut is standard; we now expect to see a conversation presented to us by cutting from one speaker to another. While the camera is focused on one speaker, we do not wonder where the other is. We are never disoriented by cutting, never disturbed by it unless the filmmaker blunders or wishes us to be confused. In recent years, audiences have been *temporarily* confused by cuts to flashbacks because they have not seen the device often enough. Younger people have less difficulty with this technique, since they have been brought up with it, and may not even realize that earlier filmmakers usually went into some elaborate verbal and visual preparation for flashbacks, sometimes using double exposures or coating the lens with vaseline to produce distorted pictures. As the cut to a flashback becomes standard, audiences will learn to accept it naturally and immediately.

Choosing a technique other than the cut to join shots results in a longer duration between shots; therefore, our attention is called to the linking device, though rarely with justification. But frequently a director wishes to isolate a shot and will fade or dissolve from it so that its import is not wasted. Such a joining method most often occurs at the end of some particularly dramatic segment of a film. Many such fades (if especially lengthy, they are sometimes called slow fades) can be found in Chaplin's films, where they are usually used to achieve an extension of pathos.

Optical tricks, superimpositions, and changes from soft to sharp focus are of less use, though perhaps entertaining in themselves and thus self-justifying.

## Editing and the Communication of Ideas

It is necessary at this point to consider the relationship between the individual shot and the material photographed only in a general sense. How does an externalized medium convey either an abstraction or an understanding of inner reality? Some people might challenge the premise behind the question and ask, "Why should the film deal with abstraction or with inner reality?" This attitude, that film is primarily a pictorial art devoted to the depiction of the beautiful and the interesting details of the world, is not shared by the general public. Even the moviegoer most committed to using the film as a means of escape apprehends that film deals with more than the visual aspects of life; he himself may prefer the fluff, but only because he has been made uncomfortable often enough by wandering into a movie theater where a serious film was being presented. Actually, one can hardly ignore the possibilities of film for exploring the nature of man. And such a task is not reserved for only the more artistic filmmakers, the Bergmans and Antonionis and Fellinis; even the ordinary film, for all its limitations as art, frequently attempts to say something meaningful.

So we come back to the problem of how film, tied as it is to surface reality and specific detail, can convey universal meaning. A glance at any film shows that a single shot by itself indeed cannot often convey much more than the specific details of the reality it is illustrating. Sometimes it can, only because the counterpoint of sound is suggesting something additional to the information given by the image. Yet a reliance on sound seldom contributes to successful filming—on the contrary, it often reflects rather second-rate competence, as in the usual photographed adaptation of a stage play. Still, there are some intriguing examples of the film shot in which an idea, as well as surface imagery, is conveyed visually; these occur especially in the works of great actor-directors such as Chaplin and Buster Keaton. For instance, Charlie will suddenly give a peculiar look at an object, and the look will tell everything. The shot described at the beginning of Chapter 1 is another example.

But there were never enough Chaplins to make common the type of filming in which the idea emerges immediately from the image. Those shots in which an actor's expression conveys meaning without reference to the preceding shots occur rarely because they almost always require a very close understanding between the actor and the filmmaker. Basically, the artistic merit of the film is the responsibility of the filmmaker, and no filmmaker relies entirely on the ability of even a fine actor. The film must

keep communicating ideas all along on a visual level; it cannot wait for close-ups of the same actor to express every key idea.

The real method for conveying inner reality, or universal truth, or any abstraction necessary for a meaningful analysis of the human condition, consists of assembling shots in such combinations that the individual specific details (of limited value by themselves) jell into an organization that makes us intuitively see beyond the particular, beyond the surface reality. The *sequence*—the collection of several shots that depicts each segment of the action of a film—is the basic unit for expressing ideas in the medium, just as the shot is the basic unit for expressing specific information.

Films are put together in terms of sequences, which are roughly equivalent to scenes in a play, though they tend to be shorter. A sequence can be composed of any number of shots. In the Edwin Porter film *The Great Train Robbery,* there was generally only one shot to a sequence. In the six-minute "Odessa Steps" sequence from *Potemkin,* Eisenstein required about 150 shots. For the average film of today, both examples are extremes. Nevertheless, any five-minute sequence in most modern films will likely have far more than a dozen shots.

As standard practice, directors film a great deal more than can be used in one motion picture, leaving much opportunity after all the shooting is finished to choose the arrangement of shots in a sequence. The process of putting together a sequence is primarily the work of editing. Theoretically, the director supervises the process of editing with the technical assistance of the film editor. However, a filmmaker frequently conceives much of the editing before the film has been shot, often explicitly indicating the sequence of shots in the shooting script—though in modern-day filming some of the leading directors claim to improvise shots in the studio or on location. But in major-industry productions, anything not preplanned tends to involve large sums, and sometimes a technician may attempt to decide what shots to film in the first place. Moreover, in the major-studio situation, the process of editing is not always under the control of the director, and often the picture is edited without the director's approval, or with so much interference by the producer or other interested, but not necessarily artistically knowledgeable, parties that the film is truly weakened. Perhaps it will be meddled with to the extent that it loses all value as an artistic creation, becoming merely a commercial product. For if the creative mind that initially shapes any long film does not have continuous control over the material, the final product must be of questionable artistic merit.

Generally, major-industry films cost a great deal. They are produced by huge corporations that have a primary responsibility not to the world of art but to the stockholders, who evaluate the film product only in terms of its commercial viability. Thus, any huge production system considers artistic concerns somewhat irrelevant, and in a situation where an artist's view of

the final editing of a film directly counters the studio's intuitive sense of what will make money, the artist's film is often taken from him and given over to technicians who seem to have a superior commercial sense. Sometimes directors of great talent have been unable to work within such a system because of studio interference (Erich von Stroheim is the classic example). Obviously, commercial pressures must always be a dominant factor in the manufacture of motion pictures by the major industries.

Less obvious but of much more interest is the fact that the movie business has always been run as something more than a commercial enterprise; manufacturers have always been influenced by the demands and opinions of critics, intellectuals, and artists. We are often surprised to realize the large number of major films, even great films, that have come out of the compromise between commercial and artistic standards. Great artists have frequently been able to function within a mass-production system. Eisenstein could not, but Hitchcock has,* though many of his films have been to some extent adversely affected by the studio situation (as when he was required to cast a performer who he felt was wrong for the part— *e.g.,* Farley Granger in *Strangers on a Train*).

Whereas in all major film industries, even in recent times, few directors are known to the general public, in many of the smaller-scale industries the situation differs, and sometimes the filmmaker's reputation accounts for part of the financing. If the reputation of a particular director has sold the picture to its backers, it might very well sell the picture to the public; consequently, in independent productions the great filmmakers almost completely control their product—though even there some allowance must be made for the usual compromises that any great artist must make to work in a popular medium in the first place. But Ingmar Bergman does not, presumably, have to fear that his films will be distorted in the editing room by a technically competent editor who has no real understanding of the meaning of individual sequences. The final print approximates as closely as humanly possible Bergman's artistic vision.

## Editing the Sequence

Editing must never be looked upon merely as the finishing touch put on a film. Sometimes in films of no special quality, the editing is actually regarded as a way of doctoring the original blunders of the production. A sequence that seems to drag will be compressed so that the shots are

* Of course, Hitchcock's peculiar genius enabled him to pre-edit a film mentally. Not trusting his employers, he shot less footage than other directors, leaving less for the studio to tamper with when the shooting was completed. In turn, the studio respected Hitchcock, not only because many of his films brought in big profits but because by shooting less, he saved them enormous sums of money.

shorter than had been planned and the tempo is accelerated; or dialogue will be dubbed in at places where nothing much was happening. (No rule says that something extraneous can't be added that was never shot as part of the film.) Of course, in all editing situations, editors discard thousands of feet of extra film. Of the usable footage, the editor and director must choose, first, the best shot of all the variants of any particular shot—and there might be twenty "takes" of a particular shot, depending on the director's drive for perfection, the actors' competence, and considerations of a mechanical nature such as lighting and sound. Second, the director and editor must decide upon the number of shots for any particular sequence.

One of the guiding principles of editing is surely the economy of shots. If a point can be clarified in three shots, what justification exists for using fifteen? As a visual medium, film continually conveys a great deal of explicit material, images that explain themselves clearly and immediately. When the point is simple, the editing ought not to complicate matters by dividing the information into innumerable shots—unless of course the filmmaker has some specific reason for analyzing the point in great detail. A sailor smashes a plate in *Potemkin* and Eisenstein shoots at least six different views of the action, for he wants to show the essence of the sailor's frustration by photographing the gesture piecemeal. But just imagine the results if every director ordered his cameraman to spend the entire day filming a small action, such as the lighting of a cigarette. Great art takes for granted the standard of brevity in showing anything, as long as the portrayal is clear and coherent and forceful.

Unfortunately, in too many films—especially those in which the editor has as much say in the editing as the director—sequences get cut mainly on the principle that the audience becomes bored with material in which one camera position is held for a long time. This is only partially true, for as we have said, visual boredom is not a result of a shot of lengthy duration but of inaction filmed in any detail by the camera—and inaction is, of course, more noticeable when the angle of filming remains the same. Thus, in many films, different shots appear in a sequence not because they tell us something that the previous shot did not say as well but because the editor wants *variety*. The desire for variety results in that constant switching back and forth from speaker to speaker so characteristic of dull, talky films.

The choice of how to edit a sequence is virtually unlimited. Let us say that after preliminaries have been considered for a scene in which three people sit in a room and talk for two minutes, the director has decided to use six different shots. There are 720 mathematically possible arrangements of six shots, which poses a problem to start with. Next, of course, is the length: if the shots can be cut so as to take (for this example) from one second to one minute and fifty-five seconds, the director can choose for any one shot a length of between 24 and 2760 frames. One may then multiply that number of possibilities by 720 and come up with some idea of the

total number of possibilities for arranging the sequence. Of course, the total number of possible choices is not really a key factor—shots are chosen for reasons, not at random. Still, regardless of the principle on which a film-maker chooses a series of shots—pictorial sense, intellectual content, artistic intuition, or whatever—the alternative possibilities are numerous.

With the overwhelming number of mathematical possibilities, the director must take into account the more serious matters of thematic emphasis. In a six-shot sequence portraying the conversation of three people, the director must evaluate all the dramatic properties of the situation, the tensions and conflicts built into the dialogue and manifest in the personal relationship of each character to the others. When one character speaks, who appears on screen? Sometimes the reaction of the listeners is more important than the speech or the speaker. If the speaker and one listener are of about equal importance (in regard to just one particular shot), they might be shown together in a medium shot—but from what angle? What about the view of the third person, or a neutral view, or a view from behind the speaker focusing on the more important listener, or from behind the listener focusing on the speaker? Surely it matters what view is presented. If any one of the six shots is out of keeping with the tone and style of the other five, the entire sequence will probably fall short of its narrative possibilities: some idea will be blurred, some gesture ignored, some piece of dialogue overemphasized.

Obviously, editing is every bit as important as the shooting of the film itself, though conceivably a film can tell a story without editing (especially on an amateur level), or with a minimal amount of editing, as in those pre-Griffith films in which shots were strung together in some simple narrative order. The purpose of editing, however, is not merely to make a narrative cohesive by structuring bits of film in comprehensible order, but primarily to make the film expressive cinematically.

## Intellectual Associations Between Shots

Before considering some particular examples of editing, we should examine the major premise behind any style of editing: that any two successive shots suggest a chronological or a spatial relationship, or both. The implications of this premise are far reaching. A viewer will assume some connection between virtually any two images in succession, whether they have any real relationship or not. Of course, a reasoned analysis of two completely disparate shots might prove to a spectator's satisfaction that indeed the shots are not connected; but during projection, images succeed each other at such a rapid pace that the mind usually cannot objectively analyze the parts and dispute the connection.

In regard to the relationships that the human mind infers between

shots, the great Russian director Vsevolod Pudovkin cited an experiment by his teacher Lev Kuleshov, also an important director:

> Kuleshov and I made an interesting experiment. We took from some film or other several close-ups of the well-known Russian actor Mosjukhin. We chose close-ups which were static and which did not express any feeling at all—quiet close-ups. We joined these close-ups, which were all similar, with other bits of film in three different combinations. In the first combination the close-up of Mosjukhin was immediately followed by a shot of a plate of soup standing on a table.
>
> It was obvious and certain that Mosjukhin was looking at this soup. In the second combination the face of Mosjukhin was joined to shots showing a coffin in which lay a dead woman. In the third the close-up was followed by a shot of a little girl playing with a funny toy bear. When we showed the three combinations to an audience which had not been let into the secret the result was terrific. The public raved about the acting of the artist. They pointed out the heavy pensiveness of his mood over the forgotten soup, were touched and moved by the deep sorrow with which he looked on the dead woman, and admired the light, happy smile with which he surveyed the girl at play. But we knew that in all three cases the face was exactly the same. *

Equal success with similar experiments can easily be anticipated. Perhaps an audience would not react very strongly to set-up scenes of this sort, where only the actor's presence seems to imply a spatial relationship between shots that are completely unrelated. More likely, we would think that the relationships existed, but that the actors and director had done a rather mediocre job in bringing the situation to life. In any case, our possible reservations will not negate the principle that audiences in general seek out chronological and spatial relationships between shots.

In fact, it requires some thought and effort on the part of the filmmaker to dissociate images in order to point out disconnections. He might, for instance, show a simple flash of color in a black and white film, and if no apparent connection is noted, the audience—because of the color more than the content of the shots—might not assume an association. Also, if a film is composed largely of unrelated images, eventually the audience will realize that the experiences depicted are disconnected. (A film of the sixties in which this type of seemingly random imagery prevailed was *You Are What You Eat*.)

But the exceptions are far too rare to disprove the general rule that any two consecutive images will suggest a physical or temporal relationship.

* V. L. Pudovkin, *Film Technique and Film Acting,* trans. by Ivor Montagu (New York, Crown, 1949), p. 140.

The rule stands because the human mind insists on attempting to perceive order even in chaos. The truth of this statement is borne out even in the case of those avant-garde films where unexpected imagery is the whole point. Luis Buñuel's *Un Chien Andalou* (1928) is composed of extraordinary images; but even with shots in which unusual objects—such as the head of a slaughtered mule—appear in a room, the viewer is constantly making mental associations in time and space. For instance, in one image, a man in a room is shot with a revolver and begins to fall. Buñuel cuts from the room to an exterior scene in a field, so that the motion is completed in an entirely different environment. There is no visual problem here at all. Although audiences do not generally understand Buñuel's symbols in the film and the narrative is quite difficult to piece together, the visual pattern is clearly impressed on our brain. The spatial association of two distinct environments is made so brilliantly by the image of the man falling that the mind reasons that *some* connection must exist, however obscure to our rational process. No doubt exists in our mind that the man who falls to the ground in the field does so because a second or two before he had been shot with a revolver in a room. The motion of the latter shot has been caused by the action in the former, regardless of the shift in place; in this example, the association of time is more convincing than the seeming dissociation of place.

Ordinarily, of course, a filmmaker wants the audience to perceive a connection between every successive shot: this is the way visual relationships develop the ideas of the film. If the spectator perceived every shot as a random one, he could not begin to see beyond the surface level of the reality being filmed.

## Ideas Through Editing: A Sequence from Niblo's *Blood and Sand*

With this tremendous advantage over the narrative arts that rely on verbal progression (which requires logical connections of sentences), the filmmaker can be certain that some connection will always be made. However, he cannot be sure that the ideas will be communicated clearly or interestingly by weak visual relationships. To a significant degree, the process of editing involves the selection of those aspects of a film idea which will prove intellectually cohesive and emotionally powerful when attached in a specific order. The sequence disassembled into its constituent shots may lack both cohesiveness and power—that is, the given shots could theoretically be assembled in a different fashion and relate approximately the same sense of incident, but the peculiar impact of a good sequence cannot be duplicated by any other arrangement.

Sometimes the filmmaker's arrangement of shots can create virtually the entire emotional and intellectual impact of a sequence. In Fred Niblo's *Blood and Sand* (1922), a silent picture presumably designed mainly as

a vehicle for Rudolf Valentino, one of the key sequences sustains our involvement through superb editing, in spite of undistinguished acting. In the sequence in which Valentino, the married bullfighter, is to be seduced by the "vamp," Nita Naldi, Niblo conveys with tremendous emphasis the inner torment of a man recognizing the conflict between his physical passion and his moral code (*i.e.,* his commitment to another woman). This is achieved with a minimum of titles (the few titles inserted are not particularly important, anyway), and, as was necessary, with a minimal reliance on facial expressiveness.

Valentino apparently had only one expression, that of painful indecisiveness, which in itself could not be counted on to reveal anything profound about the bullfighter's nature. But Niblo is quite adroit at depicting internal states on the basis of external evidence. First he shows Nita Naldi in full shot playing a huge harp, as a prelude to her seduction of Valentino. She has her back to the hero, who walks into the frame and gazes at her. Then follows an exceptionally clever choice of shot: a close shot of the woman's back—she wears a dress with a very low-cut back—as she leans toward her instrument. We are thereby informed swiftly and with a directness that could not be obtained by words alone of the specific nature of Valentino's desire and of the woman's awareness of her charms.

This shot is followed by a medium shot in which Valentino, affected by the woman's beauty, begins to bend down to kiss her bare shoulder (fig. 4); but as he bends, the rose he is wearing in his lapel falls to the floor. They both notice this. For a moment he is distracted and reminded of his

**4**  *Blood and Sand*

commitment to another woman. Caught in his usual mood of hesitancy, he vacillates between giving vent to his passions and retaining his fidelity to another. The spell is broken, however, and he finally determines to leave (he shakes her hand!) and walks past her to the door. Niblo then cuts in a close-up of Nita Naldi's foot crushing the rose. The shot immediately suggests her state of mind: she would like to destroy Valentino's will. A full shot shows her alone for a second while Valentino presumably heads for the door. Then her face shows a quick decision, which we understand from the context must have something to do with her desire to stop him.

The conclusion is swift and effective: in full shot she walks past Valentino and goes over to a vase; a close-up of the vase shows her hand plucking a flower; a mid-shot shows her putting the flower in Valentino's lapel. He does nothing to resist her as she stands next to him, replacing his fallen rose with her own, and we are now certain that he has been defeated by her. She holds him, and though he turns away his painfully indecisive single-expression face, we know that he can do nothing. Yet we sympathize with him in his weakness, for he has simply been outplayed by the vamp, though aware all the time of the danger. He represents, we see with absolute clarity, the good but weak man led astray against his better nature.

Niblo accomplishes a dramatically effective confrontation of complex psychological motivations by means of a variety of shots that express a condition or a reaction to a condition. The shots of a foot stepping on a rose and a woman playing a harp are purely informational. Their emotional force derives from Niblo's editing of the basic situation of Valentino alone with an attractive woman so as to focus our attention on those external signs suggestive of states of minds. The two performers do relatively little to communicate the subtlety of the sequence. The meaning is grasped through Niblo's careful association of carefully selected shots.

## Editing the Whole Film: Chaplin's *The Vagabond*

Narrative in film develops in terms of individual sequences, in the works of Griffith as well as in those of Fellini and Truffaut. Like a chapter in a book or a scene in a drama, a sequence is a natural unit of organization for plot materials and a natural step for progressing from one stage to another in the development of the basic intellectual ideas of the work. Yet certainly only one or two aspects of the entire thematic meaning of the work can be developed in one scene of a play, one chapter of a novel, or one sequence of a film. What relates one segment of the work to the others is the creative artist's sense of style. For a significant film style, we expect more of a director than a set of unassimilated attitudes toward the nature of his profession; style refers to the ways in which he conceives the film idea and goes about putting together his sequences in order to express that idea.

Editing involves not only the joining of shots but the structuring of

the sequences to produce a total work. Since a work of art always exceeds the sum of its parts, it is worth looking at the structure of a sample film in terms of its sequences. Chaplin's *The Vagabond* (1916) affords a good opportunity to examine the parts in terms of the whole because of its quality and its brevity (under thirty minutes). At the time of the film, as ever since, Chaplin was universally recognized as one of the great performing artists of all time. On the other hand, as the writer-director of his own films, Chaplin's position of supremacy can be disputed. Certainly, he is a great filmmaker (if that is distinguishable from his related greatness as a performer); but with respect to his technique, Chaplin is usually regarded as extremely simple: his camera angles are obvious, his filming never surprising or extraordinary, and his editing an almost naïve stringing together of a few shots that feature his great comic ability. However, Chaplin is essentially a classical artist, and his achievement should be assessed in terms of those goals generally prized by the classicist: simplicity, grace, profundity, harmony, and correctness. These classical ideals, which are of no value to many contemporary filmmakers, are nonetheless the essential premises behind Chaplin's technique. (Of course, we are not speaking here of his humanity or his emotional power, but—more narrowly—of the way he, as controlling artist, conceives an idea and portrays it through his editing.)

*The Vagabond* is in most respects a typical Chaplin film. Its story concerns an itinerant street violinist who comes upon a mistreated gypsy girl, rescues her from her cruel gypsy oppressors, sets up housekeeping with her in a little wagon, and prepares to live an idyllic, innocent, and somewhat paternal existence. A painter appears and inspires an attraction in the gypsy girl, who forgets her benefactor or else does not understand that Charlie has fallen in love with her. In any case, the triangle is not developed because the painter's portrait of the girl is seen by a wealthy woman, who discovers through a birthmark that the gypsy girl is her long-lost daughter. Charlie nobly rises to the occasion and parts with her. Reunited with her mother and driving off in a limousine, the girl suddenly decides that she must have Charlie and comes back for him, thus turning a sad ending into a happy one. Chaplin had originally planned an unhappy ending: the girl drives off and the fiddler commits suicide. But on further consideration, Chaplin must have seen that the sense of the story, regardless of whether the fiddler won the girl, predicates triumph, not defeat. The happy ending is closer to what the controlling idea suggests than the discarded suicide.

Structurally, the film contains ten sequences,* nine of which emphasize Charlie; the one sequence in which he does not appear, a very brief sequence

* The division into ten sequences is somewhat arbitrary. A sequence is sometimes considered to be all the action that occurs in one place; by this definition, the film contains only six sequences. However, in this book the term is used for any significant episode or series of shots that develops a clearly distinguishable and separate segment of action.

of four shots and an insert title, reveals a good deal about Chaplin's film-making technique. This sequence, which follows the much longer slapstick opening sequence, is necessary to get the plot started. It presents no comedy and serves a primarily functional purpose. But it is interesting because it is perfectly filmed and edited, without a wasted gesture or an excessive nuance, and not a second of time could be removed without affecting its tone.

A relatively rare (that is, rare for Chaplin at this early stage in his career) panning camera shot establishes a richly furnished interior, gradually revealing the central figure, who the insert title tells us is "The Mother." This minor character comes to us completely realized in only two dimensions: wealth and motherhood. Were she a main character we would have to know more, but in classical art, every bit of information must function in terms of the whole. To tell more would have been easy enough, but such detailing would have lent greater importance to the character, and Chaplin conceived of her as merely one of the external factors that intrude on Charlie's world.

A medium shot follows, serving to reveal the woman against a background of splendor. The first shot had been from a greater distance with a moving camera and emphasized the environment; the mid-shot now emphasizes the woman and links her naturally with this environment. In this same shot she leans over to get an object, a picture, from her sewing box; the action dislodges our eyes from the surrounding environment and prepares us for a sudden increase in emotional intensity. Next, a close-up of the picture she is examining, that of a young girl. No words, no insert title. We know from the previous insert title (the significance of which was purely intellectual when it was flashed before us) that the woman is to be regarded in a particular way; she is not mainly a woman who is wealthy but a woman who is a mother. The three shots so far make sense—that is, they are coherent—but they contain no film idea. No point has been made yet; the filmmaker has merely prepared us for something. Then, in the fourth and final shot of the sequence, it all jells. Another medium shot discloses the mother grown pensive. Obviously, yet profoundly, a point is communicated: a lost daughter (dead or missing, we do not yet know), a quiet, enduringly grieving mother. The shot slowly fades into the next sequence.

The third sequence immediately answers the question left by the last shot. It begins with the title "A Gypsy Drudge," followed by an iris shot of Edna Purviance's face. By immediately focusing on the small, dirty, but feminine face emerging from the blackness of the screen, Chaplin overwhelmingly reinforces the psychological association between the daughter and the gypsy (though the photograph was of a much younger girl), ingeniously letting us know that the girl is not dead but drudging away as a gypsy slave.

The segment from the beginning of the second sequence to this shot has taken only a few moments and has had the sole purpose of introducing

the plot. Yet it is the sort of classic filming that only a creative mind of the highest order could accomplish so conscientiously and successfully. How much time can a filmmaker spend on a scene that merely bridges sequences? A great director, however, will care enough to pay close attention to such a minor aspect of the film, because it *does* matter that the details of art provide authenticity for the intellectual meaning.

The third, fourth, and fifth sequences feature the confrontation of Charlie and the gypsies, led by that excellent, huge character actor of the Chaplin troupe, Eric Campbell, here the personification of idealized rage. The mere appearance of Campbell made up as a caricature of a devil or a man whose habitual anger has distorted his face is enough to establish him as the antagonist, though Charlie has not even appeared in the same location. When Charlie wanders on the scene with his characteristic lackadaisical stroll, his gentle innocence contrasts instantly with the cruelty of the gypsy. When he begins to play his violin for the equally innocent girl, their mutual attraction is depicted through Chaplin's miming of a concert violinist and Edna's rapt attention (fig. 5). There is a large tub of water near the girl. Charlie is aware of it and avoids it, but we feel that with Chaplin as filmmaker, some use must be made of this prop. As Charlie begins to play more

**5** *The Vagabond*

and more furiously, the danger increases; finally, carried away with himself, he falls in. He is not only playing the violin but also playing a role—he is pretending to be a great musician by imitating the gestures of a concert violinist. This is particularly true at the end of his performance when he dashes behind the gypsy wagon a couple of times, as if it were the wings of a concert stage, to emerge only for the applause of Edna. But his pride distracts him; he forgets about the barrel and in the middle of a majestic bow he falls in once again.

Although Chaplin's visual style was conservative throughout his career, his art was not limited in any way. In the fifth sequence, Charlie's escape with the girl and the pursuit of the frantic gypsies require a good deal of camera movement, but the movement is hardly perceptible, since Chaplin never calls attention to camera technique. A nontypical low-angle shot, with an unusual depth-of-field range, shows us the futile anger of the gypsies in the background as Charlie, on a wagon in the foreground, drives beyond their grasp. In a long shot of the rear of the escaping wagon, the camera remains stationary while the wagon becomes smaller and smaller as it recedes; the pursuers trail along the road behind the wagon. Behind the pursuers, a wicked old hag of a gypsy who obviously has no chance of catching the wagon, races furiously on; her joining the chase seems just another instance of her gratuitous evil. Her grotesque impotence in the chase is epitomized by a stumble and a ridiculous fall, which set her further back; but her rage makes her continue, though the wagon is almost out of sight. Through all this the camera has not moved, so that as the gypsy characters speed away, their images continuously diminish in size, in a perfect visual representation of their completely disintegrating personalities.

Sequences six, seven, and eight contain a number of Chaplin's great mime inventions (such as turning an old shirt into a tablecloth and napkins), but the sequences serve mainly to introduce the plot complication. Charlie and the girl have a chance to find life together in an idyllic country setting, seemingly isolated from the troublesome world. Then a painter enters; Chaplin employs a great deal of cross-cutting to show the girl and the painter meeting, while Charlie, happily unaware of his rival, prepares breakfast near the wagon. The audience, through the cutting, recognizes an irony that none of the three essentially innocent characters are aware of.

When the three come together to eat Charlie's simple meal, they are framed in medium shot, which requires us to concentrate on the developing relationships. The painter and the girl are almost oblivious of Charlie, but he is troubled by them as he begins to understand their growing fondness toward each other. Then Charlie goes to prepare more food on the side of the wagon; the camera shows him alone, presumably looking toward them and certainly thinking about them, as we can guess from his absentmindedness in sitting on a hot stove. A medium shot shows the girl and the painter alone, and when Charlie finally reappears and the three are together in full

shot, the painter stands in the middle. The editing here has effectively suggested Charlie's state of mind as he discerns his growing separation from the girl.

The last shot of the sequence, one of the best in all of Chaplin and one not easily translated into verbal language, shows Charlie and the girl in mid-shot looking toward the left as the painter leaves. The girl's expression remains fixed—she seems in love with the departed painter; therefore the visual interest resides in Charlie, who looks first in the direction of the painter and then again at the girl. Consider an alternative possibility: a close-up of Charlie's remarkably communicative expression as he evaluates the degree of the girl's feeling for the painter and ponders his own position. Such a shot would be less effective here, though most directors probably would have tried it. The idea that the filmmaker wants to convey in this shot requires the girl's presence in the frame, for the meaning relates not to Charlie's face alone but to his face as a reflection of what he surmises about her. The tension in the relationship, which is the basic visual information of the shot, is precisely portrayed in the mid-shot Chaplin uses.

In the ninth sequence the mother comes upon her daughter's portrait, recently done by the painter, and recognizes the birthmark of her child. In the last sequence the mother and her party, which includes the painter, come to reclaim the long-lost daughter. The sentiment appears so strongly here that it might distract us from an appreciation of Chaplin's technique. In one full shot we see the lovesick girl sitting on the wagon steps while a large car drives up. The chauffeur opens the door and four very formally dressed people emerge, led by the painter in a top hat (so dressed because they have all hurried there from the exhibition). The girl is overwhelmed by joy at being reunited with her painter and at discovering her real mother (the two other figures are unidentified friends or relatives). The second shot of the sequence shows Charlie receiving some eggs from a dairymaid, which explains his absence in the previous shot. The third shot is a continuation of the first. The master's touch is seen in the grouping: the four people around the girl are all tall, particularly the mother, and the men are wearing top hats. They stand in front of the wagon; only on the left is there any space between the characters. In that narrow white space between the wagon and the car Charlie appears, moving straight toward the camera, his natural shortness emphasized tremendously by his approaching from the distance between two rows of tall people. This arrangement of human figures according to size establishes the emotional point needed for the sequence to work: Charlie appears poor and insignificant in this grouping and yet dominates the group spiritually. He walks through the group, standing out because he is smaller than the others and because he is in motion—and also because when he learns of the great change in the girl's fortunes he drops his eggs on the painter's foot in surprise.

An almost imperceptible cut to a fourth camera shot, showing Charlie

in mid-shot between the much taller mother and painter, manages to elevate Charlie's stature, as he refuses the offer of money condescendingly held out to him by the mother. With a slight hand gesture he dismisses the offer, and the mother steps back, leaving Charlie in the forefront. He embraces the girl, kisses her good-bye, gallantly congratulates the painter, and watches in long shot as they all drive off. It is only when he is alone that he gives vent to his grief at the loss of the girl, leaning his head against the wagon in a compelling gesture of sadness.

At this point Chaplin supposedly had originally shown the fiddler jumping into a river to commit suicide. This act would have falsified the characterization presented earlier. In the very first sequence, one of some length, no plot material is presented; therefore, the purpose of sequence one must be to clarify Charlie's character. There, outside a barroom, Charlie sets up as violinist innocently competing with a band. Although his music is drowned out, he goes into the bar and collects in his hat the money that the customers think they are contributing to the band outside. In an incident typical of his life pattern, Charlie is victimized by circumstances beyond his control; yet in the ensuing battle, he does not yield to the odds but fights back and outsmarts the angered musicians, who cannot catch up with him. The same pattern is repeated with the gypsies. Pushed into a tub of water by the gypsy bully, Charlie figures out a way to defeat all the gypsies and escape with the girl. In this last episode, circumstances have defeated him in his plans to win the girl's love, but with his self-sacrificing nature, Charlie puts on his best face and sends her off in joy. As usual, he rises to the occasion. The loss of his beloved could not mean the end of Charlie. He is hurt, but even here we note a degree of spiritual triumph. The man accustomed to dealing with adversity is spiritually a conquerer, not a loser.

Thus, the switch at the end—when the girl, in the car, suddenly and instinctively begins to cry for Charlie—may be romance, but it fulfills the mandate of artistic consistency more than the alternative ending, whose cancellation most critics seem to regret. The whole tone of the film is romantic, for the plot is not really as important as the character revelations derived from individual incidents. The long-lost daughter, the gypsies, the birthmark, and the turnabout at the end are mutually compatible aspects within the film, though they are quite incompatible with the realistic tone of other Chaplin films. The girl's return to Charlie and his entering the car are a very tangible reward for his bravery and kindness throughout the film. In reality, good men are not frequently rewarded with princesses and gold, but the story is completely credible in the tradition of narrative art.

Working within the limitations of the two-reel film, Chaplin brought to the cinematic form the sensibility of classical art (classical in technique, though romantic in content—at least in *The Vagabond*). A high degree of technical sophistication was required to produce the effect of rustic simplicity. To make a point with great depth of feeling, yet to avoid bathos;

to move swiftly and yet to avoid the frantic pace of contemporary comedies (*e.g.,* Mack Sennett's); to assemble a clear, intellectual framework relying primarily on visual components—these were some of the problems successfully solved by Chaplin through editing. He undoubtedly edited much of *The Vagabond* in his mind before he even shot it, but this is not significant in considering the finished product—a perfect realization of a film idea.

# The Projected Film: Physical Properties

## The Movie as a Sense Experience

From their beginnings the movie theaters have assaulted the customer's senses in a deliberate attempt to produce a psychological and sensual state removed from ordinary experience. Early movie theaters surrounded the customer with lush appointments and plush carpets and swept him into a comfortable sloping seat in a darkened hall, forcing him to confront the only area of light, the screen, while soothing him with the constant music of an orchestra, piano, or Mighty Wurlitzer (fig. 6). Even today, long after the disappearance of live music, hardly a theater in the country will allow the spectator a moment for reflective silence, for as soon as a film ends and one group files out while another enters, recorded music is piped in to extend or introduce a euphoristic mood.

But we are concerned here with the psychological implications of the projected film itself rather than with the external trappings cleverly worked out by enterprising movie theater managers such as S. L. Rothapfel, who managed the Roxy Theatre in New York, the epitome of the motion picture "dream palace." The physical properties of the projected film include dimension (height and width), the illusion of depth, color, and sound. All

**6** The Roxy Theatre (opened in 1927)

these properties appeal to our senses simultaneously to convey the total esthetic experience. However, for the purpose of analysis, this chapter isolates the first three so as to consider their implications for the visual communication of the film idea. (Sound will be discussed later, in Chapter 10.)

## Dimension

One of the most basic considerations for a theory of film is the implication of the screen's height and width. There are two aspects to dimension, actual screen size and proportionate screen size. Actual size is obviously important psychologically but less so now than in the past. Undoubtedly, the huge size of ordinary objects, and particularly of faces, was one of the primitive attractions of the films of the first two decades of the century. It is well

known that the film industry's concern with large screens was a result of the decrease in attendance in the post–World War II era; the competition from television was fought with various quantitative methods. In any case, one of the significant properties of the art form lies in its ability to project a larger-than-life image of reality.

Some other minor concerns of actual dimension can be noted briefly. The large size of the image requires a large theater, which in turn hopefully implies a large audience. But the film did not start out as a medium of mass communication, and very likely its "public" role is not an absolutely necessary aspect of film. In other words, the form could conceivably have developed in the same way if the projector had not been invented. Many professionals and scholars do a good deal of their viewing on editing machines (*e.g.,* moviolas) that are simply refinements of the old penny-arcade peep-show machines or Edison Kinetoscopes. Of course, if the one-cent price of single viewings had continued as standard, the ten-million-dollar spectacle would never have been possible. But again, the question of whether the spectacle is itself essential to film art is debatable.

Yet the fact remains that for most people the actual dimension of the screen has made the movies the public art of the age. (It is the closest equivalent we have to the democratic theater of ancient Greece—one interesting difference lying in the fact that in Greece the theater was not simply an entertainment vehicle, but had official importance, and the state took care to see that most people attended.) For us, the esthetic experience of observing a film differs from, say, that of reading a poem; the latter remains a private experience intended by the author for an audience that might be vast but is reached personally and privately. Even at a play, an opera, a ballet, or a concert, although people may indeed talk, they try to do so discreetly; everyone considers it an offense to good manners to make noise at such an occasion. On the other hand, the movie house, to some extent in the past and to a much greater extent since television, accepts a wide range of sounds: whispers, coughs, giggles, popcorn, clapping, hooting, running commentary, and so on.

Although the film does not require a movie theater, it must be experienced in some projected form. Much less gets lost if one views a film on a small screen in his living room than if one reads the text of a play, though as Aristotle pointed out, reading a play is a valid dramatic experience. The small screen is, in fact, familiar to thousands of home-moviemakers, who are used to (but not comfortable with) two-inch by three-inch pictures on editing machines much smaller than their television sets. Nevertheless, we cannot ignore the fact that the large size of movie screens influences the content of shots. For example, the Western film represents one of the great breakthroughs in the development of the film idea. James Cruze's *The Covered Wagon* (1923), among the first Westerns filmed on location, stressed the grandeur of the open country. The Western film as a

genre is itself a case in point: its meaning very often is conveyed visually by the portrayal of the hero in conflict with the ruggedness of the terrain, the lone man challenged to prove himself against an uncompromising environment.

The other aspect of dimension is proportion, and its esthetic considerations are subtle but significant. The screen has generally been in the shape of a rectangular frame. For most of the silent screen days (from about 1906) and right up through the fifties, the frame size had been standardized in the proportion of four to three, slightly larger in the horizontal than in the vertical. The shape of the frame was apparently borrowed from a classical concept of painting called the Golden Section and was presumed to approximate the way in which the eyes normally take in a specific area (though the truth of this justification seems dubious). Many filmmakers would not have chosen the Golden Section proportions, but once they became the international standard everyone adhered to them as a necessary commercial consideration—unless every movie theater were to be re-equipped with projectors and all movie studios with new cameras. (Actually, the change to a wider screen can be accomplished by equipping the projector with a masking device or special lens.) Nowadays, since almost all new 16mm projectors are designed for the Golden Section in spite of the fact that almost all films are made for the wide screen, film distributors have solved the problem in a peculiar way: wide-screen pictures are sometimes reproduced so as to project on a normal Golden Section screen filling the horizontal portion of the screen, but sharply reduced from top to bottom. Thus, common new proportions—such as 2:1 or 2.2:1—can be maintained, but a large segment of the old Golden Section screen is blackened.

The four-to-three proportion had inherent limitations. For example, in showing a crowd or a football game or a horse race—any shot, in fact, where horizontal movement was predominant—the camera had to get farther away from the action than was always desirable. With the advent of the wide screen, it became possible to show a great deal more of an area or an action at a closer distance than previously. However, the change to a wide screen, presumably accompanied by a change to screens of greater total area, was motivated entirely by commercial considerations, not in the least by artistic ones.

The result was a sort of minor cultural disaster for the art form, for the changeover occurred internationally at a time when many filmmakers had not yet fully understood the nature of the proportions in use for fifty years. Now, with a little more than a decade of experience with wide-screen filming, the industry has even less of an idea of the implications of the new frame size.

With or without understanding, films continued to be made, and every director had to come to terms immediately with the wide screen. The first and primary problem is still what to do with the wide screen when there

is no particular movement in a horizontal direction. The old screen dimensions were much better suited to the mid-shot of two people talking than is the new size of the frame. In wide-screen filming, a mid-shot of two people leaves a great deal of space to be filled. What happens in that space? If the area is consistently dull, spectators will have to devote their attention to the center of interest, but then the artistic composition of the frame must of necessity be second-rate.

And what can be done with close-ups? A close-up of a full face, from the chin to the top of the head, is impossible in the wide screen. The frame will leave as much total space on both sides of the face as is covered by the face itself. Never again can we experience the effect—once possible for every ordinary film—of absolute emphasis on a complete face. Our eyes, from now on, will wander to the right and to the left in a close-up, trying to make out the background and losing the impact of the visual focus.

This sobering fact was, of course, immediately recognized by directors all over, who devised an alternative: to move the camera so close that the face virtually fills the wide screen, even though the chin and hair of the actor are omitted from the frame. The sacrifice is significant, for such a close-up creates an extravagant emphasis on the nose, mouth, and eyes. The camera automatically isolates the features of the face, but isolation usually implies something purposeful, and today, the choice of this overemphatic close-up is usually not artistic but necessary. What else can be done, the harassed director wonders, if the alternative is the weaker close-up of a face with distracting visual areas on the side?

Another technical solution to this problem makes use of soft focus, which involves blurring the background, thereby limiting the viewer's visual interest to the object or face (in sharp focus) emphasized by the close-up. A modern equivalent of the old masking shots (such as the iris shot), the soft-focus shot is perhaps less effective, for soft-focus images have a certain degree of interest for us, and sometimes the eye will actually concentrate on the background area in an effort to discern the objects out of focus, thus defeating the purpose of the shot. Probably popularized (though not invented) by Michelangelo Antonioni in *The Red Desert* (1964), the soft-focus technique impressed many directors, who saw the device used so effectively in this film that they did not have to experiment with it to discover its possibilities.

Still another way of coping with the problems of the wide-screen close-up is to skillfully arrange the visual components within the frame so that interest is fixed on the face in spite of whatever else is in the frame and might otherwise be distracting. An excellent example of this solution occurs at the very beginning of *Topaz* where Hitchcock, applying one of his remarkable crane shots, moves the camera in a swooping manner from a distance shot to a close-up of the reflection of a man's face on a glass surface. Our eyes are fixed on the face because of the circumstances of the shot, its movement, and the tension built up by the apparent conflict of

characters in the early part of the shot; yet even the ultimate close-up fills only a third of the screen.

Unfortunately, the wide screen has created problems that go beyond even the important matter of the use of the close-up. Eventually these problems will be solved—and in fact they already have been by a few directors such as Stanley Kubrick in *2001: A Space Odyssey* (plate I).* Primarily troublesome is the problem of locating a character in an environment that does not give him anything in particular to do. The whole problem of filming nonmovement (see Chapter 14) is emphasized by the greater width of the frame. Can the actor just sit down? If he does so, where will his chair be in relation to the rest of the room? In a normal size room, a seated actor shown in a full shot will be placed against almost the entire rear wall; in other words, every article of furniture will be vying for our attention, and in a color film where a designer has spent much time deploying an attractive color pattern, the actor will very likely be lost in that room. In fact, most directors seem to fear interior shots nowadays. Shooting on location, a frequently interesting contemporary innovation in production styles, is often necessitated by a director's overwhelming desire to get his characters outdoors so he can film them against natural scenery or real streets and take advantage of the horizontal emphasis of the camera. Living-room conversations are now being replaced by conversations in which the characters are strolling in the park (as in *The Owl and the Pussycat,* 1970) or sitting in a scenic area such as a beach (*e.g.,* in *Alex in Wonderland,* 1970). But while filming dialogue in motion takes advantage of the properties of the wider dimensions of the new screen, we sometimes get the feeling that we are seeing nervous activity, not truly cinematic motion.

## Depth

The development of perspective in painting took place over a period of centuries because the illusion of depth was, for a long time, not an immediate interest of the medieval painters. Besides, the illusion of depth in painting is not an inherent aspect of the medium. In contrast, the narrative film automatically suggests a degree of depth simply by photographing people or identifiable objects against a recognizable background. Nevertheless, depth perception is ordinarily limited even in the film unless an effort is made by the director and the cameraman to utilize the space between the foreground and background.

In the early silent films the primary concern of cameramen was to capture lateral motion. The preoccupation with movement across the horizontal plane was due in part to the influence of the stage, where characters enter and exit mainly from the sides, and in part to the limitations of the old lenses. Today, a greater area can be kept in sharp focus than

* All color plates following page 212.

was possible around 1925. Still, the industry itself has always felt that perspective was a problem in film, and various expedients have been devised to deal with it, for instance, the huge, curving screen (*e.g.,* Cinerama) and three-dimensional films requiring special viewing glasses. Stereoscopic pictures, still popular in slide viewers for children, hold a fascination for the industry. Undoubtedly, if some technical system can be perfected that is economically feasible in terms of investment in new equipment, we are bound to see greater attempts in the future to develop three-dimensional films.

There exists in this area a confusion between what is artistically necessary and appropriate to the cinematic process and what is technically desirable with respect to the achievement of a closer approximation of depth as perceived by the human eye. The three-dimensional movies failed quickly because the glasses proved unpopular with viewers. But had the glasses been accepted, it still remains doubtful that the film industry would have gone over completely to three-dimensional filming. After all, the illusion of a tiger leaping toward a viewer will cause the viewer to duck only so often. In due time he will catch on to the illusion, and it will cease to threaten him; long before that, it will cease to amuse him. The first film viewers sometimes even ducked when the speeding train seemed headed right for them; this illusion is impossible for modern viewers because we are too familiar with the properties of the present-day screen. In all the three-dimensional movies, objects or people suddenly appeared to spring from the screen, producing a mild sensation, a thrill perhaps, but acceptable only because the films were uniformly boring and audiences had come particularly for the visual experience of seeing an object dart toward them.

The real problems with depth and perspective in films have to do with occupying the area between foreground and background. This is not an absolutely essential part of filming because even without full utilization of movement in depth, it is possible to achieve a high degree of art. Nevertheless, extension of depth figured in the development of the narrative film inasmuch as it led to the abandonment of the old, stage-oriented style of filming. As long ago as 1903, when in *The Great Train Robbery* the train moved into the distance or the robbers, chased by the posse, rode into the foreground, we had a real sense of cinematic movement. The cinematic world was no longer limited to horizontal relationships. The so-called fourth wall of the stage—the perspective of the audience at a realistically staged play—no longer applied to the film. The camera was liberated when it was set up to express points of view beyond the artificial scope of the stage.

The sense of depth is achieved in a film by several means, the most common being simply the composition of items within the frame. If a cameraman photographs all volumes from the old eye-level stage view, he risks flattening out the perspective; the sense of depth is also diminished when he uses a telephoto lens. However, the human eye watching a projected

shot of a flattened perspective naturally tends to make some mental adjustments, as long as the scenery looks real. Nevertheless, if a good deal of money has gone into the production of sets, filmmakers will want to gain more than just a hint of volume—they will want to emphasize it and will take advantage of the solidity of the sets by varying the camera angle, using moving shots, or carefully arranging different, contrasting shapes and volumes. A technique popularized by Orson Welles in *Citizen Kane* (1941) was to present distant objects in sharp focus while closer objects were blurred; Antonioni often achieves the same effect using the opposite technique, blurring everything behind a character in a close shot.

The sense of movement forwards or backwards within the frame is aided by the spectator's mental adjustment of relative dimensions. Images recorded on a strip of film and by the retina of the eye are proportional to distance in the same way: in both cases, the image of an object at ten feet is four times as large as the image of that object at twenty feet, although—also in both cases—our automatic mental compensation makes the closer object seem only twice as large. Thus, we are able to judge relative depths in the film as well as in real life. For example, if a human figure appears in the frame, even without knowing whether the person is 6'4" or 5'8", we have a pretty good basis for judging the relative distances of less familiar objects in the frame.

Different locations, of course, affect our sense of depth. Standing on a mountain top, a character may be photographed against a background that suggests infinite space. Indoors, the depth is always limited by the back wall; spectators will feel uncomfortable if the camera continually photographs interior scenes from a high angle without showing walls. The element of fantasy can be achieved by blacking out the walls—that is, by not lighting them—or by photographing downwards so as to avoid them. This technique is used in Arthur Penn's remarkable experiment in allegory, *Mickey One* (1965): interiors are sometimes made to suggest infinite space, and in the final shot the walls actually disappear, leaving the character in an infinite space that proved too disturbing a visual concept for general audiences.

Finally, the lighting can be a decisive factor in suggesting depth. As Renaissance painters used light and shadow to create the sense of depth, so can filmmakers, though the subject is technically rather complex and usually under the control of technicians rather than the director. There is more variety in the intensity of light in black-and-white films than in color, not only because many black-and-white films require less light to produce an image but also because the industry believes that color, not lighting, is always the key factor in a color film arrangement. In any case, the movement of a figure from a light to a dark area or vice versa is one of the most obvious ways to show depth. Evenly lighted interiors are less popular today than in the past (the influence of poorly lit but dramatically powerful European films), and in general lighting has became increasingly sophis-

ticated not only in the depiction of depth but in regard to the creation of all sorts of moods and emotions.

## Color

Color is everywhere today in the film, and one can readily anticipate a time when no full-length commercial film in any Western country will be done in black and white. The reasons for the conversion to color in recent years probably have nothing to do with any innate superiority of color to black-and-white cinematography. Basically, the industry needs, first of all, to compete with color television, and secondly—almost contradictorily—to manufacture a commodity salable to television. For people of this generation, color is a pleasant addition to a film, regardless of the way it affects the content of the film, because we are not yet so used to color that we can be entirely complacent about it. Perhaps the next generation will be indifferent to color (when all television sets are color sets), and black and white will then have a peculiar, perhaps nostalgic, effect on viewers.

The earliest films were often in color—of a sort that might have been quite exciting, for they were handpainted. Around the turn of the century, the French filmmaker Georges Méliès employed a production-line technique: each woman would color certain parts of a few frames of a film and then pass the film down the line to the next woman, who would supply color for other parts of the frames. Obviously, this process was costly and not easily adapted to mass industry needs, for each copy of a film would have to be done the same way.

For the full-length silent film, a different type of color was commonly used: the tinted film stock. The effects of a colored stock were quite different from those in a full-color film, as we know from some of the striking results achieved in the surviving tinted prints of some Griffith films. In tinted films, the entire frame was one basic color, but the many intensities from dark to light would permit human figures to stand out against the background. Sometimes the charm of a scene could be rendered in ways unobtainable now that "true" color is standard and all sorts of garish exploitation of color schemes are preferred. But in the early days of film, the tinted stock had some significant values of its own, as Ivor Montagu has pointed out:

> The colours most favoured were amber, red, blue, and lavender. In the hand, this kind of film stock could be seen clearly to be coloured. Its colour was marked and apparent. When the image was projected onto a distant screen, the enlargement diluted it. The public for the most part was unaware when the first or fourth of these colours were being used. Red, used for scenes of fires, and

blue, for scenes of night, were highly apparent and suddenly dramatic; the change to them was not only appreciable but surprisingly acceptable and undisturbing as a convention. There was also an abominable refinement, a two-colour effect of blue and pink for sunrises and sunsets.*

The advent of color as we know it today came in the 1930's with the development of film stocks that would reproduce colors approximating the color values of nature. They did not then, and still do not, really duplicate "true" colors but tend to simplify the total range of shades and tones that occur in nature. This is not a defect, for the esthetic appeal of color films is probably related to the fact that colors appear brighter in films than they do in real life.

At first color films appealed to the eye in a completely sensuous way; the quality of the film counted for nothing in comparison with the simple fact that it *was in color.* Of course, as color became more popular and less extravagant as a cost factor in relationship to the generally mounting costs of moviemaking, audiences reacted in a less naïve manner. Color will never again insure the success of any film; yet audiences to this day are not entirely sophisticated about it—and the level of responsiveness to sensitive use of color is not being developed by television.

Surprisingly little critical thinking seems to have been done on the subject, though most critics now realize that the distinction between color and black and white is more than the effect of prettiness. In fact, all major industries devote a good deal of money to costuming for the color film, and the arrangements of color in the clothes of stars has always been a consideration. However, most movies go no further in accommodating the medium to the color process. The question of how color affects the internal structure of a film is hardly ever asked. Usually, a film is simply made in color just as if it were in black and white—the only difference being that the studio makes occasional attempts to display some attractive colors in the background (*e.g.,* in draperies) as well as in the costumes.

In considering the possible artistic uses of color, one of the greatest of all filmmakers, Carl Theodore Dreyer, remarked: "In the film in black and white, one works light against shade and line against line. In the film in color, one works mass against mass, form against form, and color against color." † Dreyer seems to be suggesting that in color films we see shapes or volumes of color; therefore, what is prominent in black-and-white films is not necessarily so in color films and vice versa. If our eye is constantly diverted by changing shapes or moving volumes of color, then certainly the effect of the typical color image differs *in kind* from that of the ordinary

* Ivor Montagu, *Film World* (Baltimore, Penguin Books, 1965), p. 72.

† Carl Theodore Dreyer, "Le film en couleurs et le film colorié," *Cahiers du Cinéma,* No. 148 (Oct., 1963), p. 2. [Trans. by S. J. S.]

black-and-white image. Such seems to be generally true of good color photography as compared to good black-and-white photography. The same picture taken in color and in black and white will not have the same esthetic effect, and good photographers seem to distinguish the proper subject matter for color from that for black-and-white photography.

In film, however, the predominant imagery tends to deal with human beings in their environmental relationships or interacting with each other. Therefore, films in color and films in black and white will necessarily have a similarity in subject matter. But should that similarity dictate a similarity in imagery? In conceiving of cinematic images, even talented directors may lack a highly artistic sensitivity to colors. A director is not a painter, not even a photographer. Dreyer suggested that painters be hired as technical advisers for all directors undertaking color films, but this hardly can achieve the desired effect. Ideally, the filmmaker's conception of his work ought to be in color in the first place.

This problem really defies solution for the time being. There have already been several fine color films—but there have been even more fine films that simply *happened to be in color,* rather than having been conceived especially for a color medium. The implications of color are largely ignored even by the good filmmakers with this qualification: great directors like Hitchcock are sensitive enough to know that there is a major difference between color and black and white, so they include several shots, even a few sequences, that make excellent use of color; and of course they see to it that colors are never garishly displayed simply for their own sake. A director should always reveal good taste, even when he has no particular aptitude or training in color cinematography.

Color, then, can be used tastefully if not brilliantly. Nowadays it is still an extraordinary occurrence when color is part of the basic film idea itself. That it could really be part of the structural concept of a film was made clear to critics only with the appearance of Antonioni's *The Red Desert.* In this film, Antonioni achieved a significant breakthrough by frequently using color to suggest the state of mind of the neurotic heroine. In other words, color was manipulated as another cinematic tool for the purpose of conveying meaning; it was not used merely to reflect pretty surfaces or colored spaces. It is almost as if Antonioni had followed Dreyer's suggestion (made in the previously cited article): "We have so often seen green grass and blue sky that we wish just for once to see blue grass and green sky." Antonioni actually did do some rearranging of nature: a marsh was supposedly sprayed with gray paint to suggest the mental outlook of one of the characters. In fact, Antonioni has said, "It is necessary to intervene in a color film, to take away the usual reality and replace it with the reality of the moment." He has also managed to suggest by the use of color the abstract concept that the new industrial world has a kind of functional beauty that we ordinarily overlook. In *The Red Desert,* the most colorfully

attractive areas are connected with the industrial age: the factory, with its neat, modern design, its vitality, contrasts with the more sterile elements of society. The stagnant landscape, itself a victim (presumably) of industrial pollution, contains somber gray and brown tones, and frequently the area is covered with an oppressive fog. The factory exudes a poisonous yellow gas—beautiful in itself but deadly for the environment—which symbolizes the shift in the balance of power between the natural world of the past and the industrial world of the present; the triumph of the mechanized world over the natural is brilliantly demonstrated by the volumes of gas filling the atmosphere around the factory.

Since that film, the artistic use of color has been less rare. Among the most successful works have been Federico Fellini's *Juliet of the Spirits* (1965), Buñuel's *Belle de Jour* (1967), Antonioni's *Blow-Up* (1966), and Visconti's *Death in Venice* (1970). Filmmakers are now self-conscious about colors, even when they do not feel particularly qualified to handle them, and in some cases this self-consciousness leads to wariness; colors are sometimes muted and less flashy than they would have been in the ordinary films of several years ago. Particularly noticeable is the improvement in films set in the West; nowadays when the chase is conducted against a background of natural splendor, the color tones may reinforce the somberness of the events rather than suggesting, as they used to, the conflict between natural beauty and somber incidents. In Abraham Polonsky's *Tell Them Willie Boy Was Here* (1969), the sheriff's chase of the socially victimized and generally sympathetic Indian, Willie Boy, is conducted along the barren crags of the mountains of the Northwest. The predominant colors are brown and white, and the relentless, pitiless chase is emphasized by the absence of vivid colors. In one particular sequence, the opening shot of the pursuers is presented in extremely bright sunlight that washes out all colors and makes it difficult to perceive the men against the absolutely white background; this shot follows immediately upon a sequence whose final shot shows Willie Boy and his girlfriend embracing in almost pitch blackness. The cut to bright daylight is disturbing to the eyes, almost duplicating the effect of walking out of a movie theater on a sunny afternoon, but it is deliberately achieved and serves well the purpose of depicting the clash between pursued and pursuers, characterizing the personalities without bringing them together in the same frame, or even the same general area.

## Meaning Through Color: Visconti's *The Damned*

One of the most effective uses of color in recent years occurs in Luchino Visconti's *The Damned* (1969), in which color evokes a cinematic sense that organizes the visual material into a stylistic unity. The material of this film seems at first primarily literary and sociological: the plot concerns a

wealthy German industrial family at the beginning of the Hitler regime (the burning of the Reichstag is reported during the first sequence), and the events deal with the struggle for power within the family and the collaborations of the various family members with the Nazis. Filled with complex intellectual attitudes and generalized insights into the workings of perverted minds, the film proceeds to elaborate the psychological conditions of hatred and envy through dialogue and dramatic confrontations. Visconti is well known in Europe for his staging of plays and operas, and this film has certain similarities with the other artistic media Visconti works in.

Yet *The Damned* is a truly cinematic work in its conception because the literary dimension of the film and its psychological depth are communicated visually at least as much as verbally. Even the verbal aspect acquires depth from its physical setting. Visconti accomplishes this blending of the cinematic and the literary by establishing two prominent levels to the story line. On one level we are introduced to a family torn by bitter feelings caused by aggression, ambition, pride, and sexual perversion; working out their inevitable destiny of destruction, the family is depicted collectively as possibly the most dislikable group of people ever encountered in a film. On this level the narrative thematically resembles certain works of fiction and drama (especially drama—a whole tradition related to this film can be seen from the *Oresteia* of ancient Greece to *The Little Foxes* of modern America). The plot of *The Damned,* however, is also conceived as an allegory, as one may readily assume from the title. The German subtitle, *Götterdämmerung,* is also allegorically suggestive.

In terms of its allegory, the film depicts people already in hell, damned by their passions, their very nature, and involved in working out their private and mutual torments. As there is no longer—and has not been for 500 years—a large segment of the public readily susceptible to allegorical presentation, a creative artist has a difficult task in communicating this concept. Visconti succeeds as well as anyone else ever has in visualizing the world of hell on film. There have been other depictions of hell—for instance, Jean Cocteau's version of it in *Orpheus*—but such treatments have been either figurative or highly imaginative, making no attempt to depict reality. Visconti's achievement is of another order; he conceives his hell completely within the realistic framework of the story. The allegorical implications develop simultaneously with the activities occurring on the strictly literal level of the narrative; that is, the allegory does not create the structure of the film but instead grows out of it.

To create this unity, Visconti relies on a basic color pattern, a color rhythm, so to speak, that emphasizes reds, orange-reds, yellow-reds, reds of all intensities. The colors of the film are carefully designed to keep the audience always aware of location. Even if we do not actually comprehend the setting as a type of hell in an intellectual sense, we certainly understand the attitude maintained toward the characters and the location. Visconti's

control of our responses to the environment and events is achieved most effectively by his careful color arrangements. We might say that the color here implies the film idea.

Bright, glowing orange-red-yellow colors evoke the concept of fire, and thus, of hell and of destruction. It is also the background color of the Nazi swastika and flag, which are increasingly displayed as the film progresses and the Nazi mentality encompasses Germany. The film's title shots are set against the fiery steel furnaces within the huge ironworks of the Von Essenbeck family. These shots establish from the start the association of the color pattern with great heat (the fires of hell presumably find a modern equivalent in the blast furnace). Although the steel foundry does not figure much in the film as a visible presence, it is always in the background of the conversations, eventually becoming the focal point of the family's internal struggle. And one shot of tremendous effectiveness shows the molten iron being poured into huge vats as a group of uniformed Nazis walk across a platform in the foreground. The bright blaze of the molten iron makes the shot seem very much like an illustration for Dante's *Inferno:* the Nazis are suggestively depicted as devils or inhabitants of hell against an environment of eternal fire.

More shots, however, are located inside the Von Essenbeck mansion, where most of the drama is played out. The conversations usually occur in rooms where the predominant lighting appears to come not from the electric bulbs but from the fireplaces, giving a reddish tinge to the area photographed. The extreme warmth is made manifest by the frequent perspiring of the characters. It is impossible to dissociate the characters from the theme; for even when the environment shifts, the color tone remains essentially the same. In one sequence the Storm Troopers entertain themselves at their retreat, where the dissipations, innocuous enough considering the more sophisticated perversions of the Von Essenbecks, take place in a kind of beer hall also apparently lighted by fires. In both locales, the reddish tinge flickers slightly, giving the impression of firelight, which on a literal level *is* the lighting. But the fireplace only symbolizes the greater fire, the hell-fire illuminating the souls of all the characters. In one part, the fire assumes an explicit identity as a destructive force, an identity only implicit in other parts: in this sequence a professor reads a list of proscribed books, which are then tossed into a huge bonfire by the students. The act of book-burning for the twentieth-century viewer stands for the supreme horrors of totalitarianism, although it is literally a somewhat lesser horror in itself.

We all associate the color red with blood as well as fire, and *The Damned* is expectedly filled with its share of that. The major episode of violence involves the internecine warfare within the Nazi party: in the midst of their drunken orgies, the Storm Troopers are methodically slaughtered by the Gestapo; the bloody scene is filmed with complete dispassion (a technique made famous by Eisenstein). The struggle for power among the

Nazis parallels the violence within the family that begins with the murder of the grandfather, the head of the Von Essenbeck dynasty, on the night of his birthday celebration—an assassination instigated by his daughter-in-law and her cousin and carried out by the man Von Essenbeck has just promoted to the vice-presidency of the steel company.

Of course, red is also commonly associated with passion; however, as the common color of lipstick, red might seem all too familiar to have much symbolic value in ordinary color films. But when the lipstick is worn by men—as female impersonators—it becomes suggestive of the perversion of passion, which is much in evidence throughout the film. At the beginning the sexually disturbed grandson, dressed as a woman, entertains the guests at the birthday party with a kind of Marlene Dietrich impersonation. His later sexual aberrations (which include child molesting and incest with his mother) are directly suggested by his painted face and leering glances during his tasteless impersonation. The motif of female impersonation reappears as the Storm Troopers are shown cavorting in feminine clothes during their debauchery, which is largely homosexual (plate VI).

*The Damned,* though certainly not a pretty film, creates its own kind of pictorial fascination. Its superb color does not reveal beauty but instead implies internal ugliness. Red becomes the color of evil, and Visconti understands that it is not a pleasant color to look at for a long period of time. He deliberately puts us at a distance from the spectacle, creating what Bertolt Brecht would call an alienation effect, so that we cannot sympathize with the various characters. Of course our eyes must be constantly relieved from the red color scheme, which if used in every shot would be physically uncomfortable regardless of the activity in the frame; thus, a great deal of movement from the basic color pattern to other colors (primarily dark blues and browns) is necessary (plate VII). But with each return to the basic color arrangement new associations are suggested, culminating in the final marriage-suicide sequence, in which the rich interiors of the Von Essenbeck home are hung with black Nazi insignia against massive volumes of red draperies.

The possibilities for the use of color are still being explored, and doubtless many interesting techniques will be developed every year, since color has now become standard. With color readily available, all the important filmmakers are adjusting their film conceptions so as to gain expressive value from color cinematography. Today, however, the key aim—to make color part of the meaning—is still only rarely accomplished, and *The Damned* remains a remarkable exception to the general level of color filming.

# 5

# Film as Production: The Craftsmen and the Artist

## The Director and the Specialists

Who is the filmmaker? The question is not rhetorical, for the answer is by no means obvious, nor can it be consistently applied to the predominant conditions in the major industries. This book has so far assumed that the filmmaker is the director, but the implications of the question have yet to be considered.

The traditional response of the major-studio executive suggests that the question is even unanswerable. In fact, in the tailor-made commercial vehicle there really does not seem to be any filmmaker. Certainly films get made, and title credits will always show a cast of performers, a producer, a director, a composer, a cameraman, an editor, a writer, a wardrobe mistress, and a host of technicians. The impression given, the impression intended by the Academy of Motion Picture Arts in their annual award ceremony, and the impression received by an audience that stops reading as soon as the cast of performers is replaced by the list of specialists suggest that every film is a joint production of dozens, perhaps hundreds of people. No one is entirely responsible for what happens on the screen; or, everyone concerned is partly to blame, but the responsibility is spread so widely that it is impossible to indict or commend any single person.

A film, if it aims to be a work of art, must have an artist designing it, and artistic sensibility creating it. We allow for helpers. When watching a

play by Shakespeare, for instance, we must always bear in mind that the play is made for performance, not for the printed page. Shakespeare demanded help from directors, designers, and performers for the total artistic expression of his works. Nonetheless, everyone who has seen *Hamlet* or *King Lear* goes away feeling that he has seen "Shakespeare" produced. The same feeling ought to be common to the movie audience, but it is not. The performers are always remembered afterwards, but frequently the creative artist is never even noted.

In the 1950's a movement among French critics established a method of evaluating artistic filmmaking in terms of the director.* Since that time, violent controversies have ensued, but the case for equating the director with the filmmaker has finally prevailed among critics, though less so in America than Europe. This theory has value because in most films of merit (but not all), the contribution of the director is basic, while that of the performers, writers, producers, cameramen, *et al.,* is secondary. Although we can never precisely discern each person's contribution, we can attempt to establish two different kinds of contributions: the interpretive and the creative. When the director is given some control over the script—when he is asked to supervise it or write it or change it, when he is given some control over the actors, and finally, when he controls the editing of the film, then only he can claim to influence the total sense of the film. These are the conditions that existed in the major films of Chaplin, Kurosawa, Mizoguchi, Renoir, Griffith, Bergman, Antonioni, and Fellini—and one could add the names of twenty major filmmakers. For the American industry, such total control until recently had been quite rare, but a degree of control was common, as we can tell from consistent results by various talented directors such as Arthur Penn, John Frankenheimer, Howard Hawks, John Ford, Frank Capra, and Preston Sturges. We can assume that the director is the primary creative force if there is a similarity in concept or style or theme among his films.

The problem of fully evaluating the director's role is complicated by the theatrical derivation of the term. In the theater the director is the unifying *intepretative* artist of the work of a *creative* artist, the playwright. In film the director has the same interpretive function, but it is merely part of his total job—and under ideal conditions it is not even the major part of his job. His primary function ought to be conceptual. For the purposes of this book, when we speak of the filmmaker we mean that kind of director who takes full charge of the film.

However, the peculiar nature of film requires a joint effort of specialist talents. For instance, consider the contribution of the composer, arranger, and musicians. From the earliest days, films were scored, even before the

---

* See Chapter 12 for a discussion of "auteur" criticism.

score was added to the film celluloid itself. The importance of music was so strongly felt that with some silent films musicians were hired to play while the actors performed. In the finished product, a musical score is often more than an accompaniment of the action. It frequently helps to establish mood and characterization and to anticipate action. From time to time, Hollywood studios hired the best available composers to score films and traditionally gave composers more freedom than directors. The score usually requires an orchestra and a conductor, who is sometimes the composer. It then requires a host of technicians to record it and to match it to both the visual portion of the film and the dialogue track. The technician who edits the sound track is obviously in a position to make significant decisions about relative sound levels and tones. Although Chaplin could compose music for his own films, composition of the musical score will almost always lie beyond the competence of the greatest directors, and so musical specialists will be required to contribute meaningfully to the production of a film.

To elevate the director as the key artist of a film is not to denigrate any of the other artists or technicians who work on the film. It means, however, that the specialists' contributions must be placed in their proper perspective. Denying the controlling influence of a creative mind in the film suggests a product without art. Nevertheless, the major industries have generally been slow to understand the concept that a film must be shaped by a central intelligence; it cannot be parceled out. Behind the studio attitude is a basic misunderstanding of the medium: the director is still regarded as a theater director, whose main job is to interpret a script and to guide the actors through their paces. The famous stars have always been more important in the American system than the best directors, but in turn the directors are always more important than the writers. This is because the industry feels, essentially, that the writers are the true creative artists behind the film, but that creativity is less important commercially than interpretation. Those considered interpreters (actors, directors, and top cameramen) are better paid, presumably because they come closer to the public and are therefore more essential to an entertainment medium than the originators of the ideas. The public wants performance, not illumination—or so the theory goes.

Although it has developed a production system of specialists—writers, actors, cameramen, technicians, editors, *et al.*—the industry has still failed to create a democratic art. If its ideal has been consciously to create art by committee, the studios have succeeded only in the limited sense that their product has wide appeal: parts of it appeal to almost everyone, but all of it appeals to no one. No production overseer with universal taste has been discovered, and each new film remains a commercial gamble prior to its release. Commercial uncertainties and financial pressures in the industry system in turn affect the degree of freedom given the filmmaker. Every

product of the industry system represents a substantial investment; therefore, artistic idiosyncrasies or unusual working habits are suspect—and often an extra expense.

Given the evident failings of the system, we must still recognize its occasional successes. If it has frequently harassed great filmmakers, it has also employed them. Furthermore, the fact that filmmakers must satisfy a broad-based public, necessitating some artistic compromises, is not an entirely negative aspect of the system. It has undoubtedly forced filmmakers to clarify personal insights and vague symbols that might otherwise have remained undeveloped or obscure.

In addition, the American industry in particular, with its specialist emphasis, has a record of interesting achievements in films that were directed by men of no known particular talent. To look at the situation another way, some extremely hard-working directors have made two or three good films in a career that is remarkable only for its mediocrity. Sometimes we are forced to account for this by the nature of the industry: the talents of some directors have been hidden by excessive studio interference with these directors' assignments. But perhaps a more reasonable way of accounting for the few good films in a career filled with bad ones is to assume that the good films were the result of a major contribution by someone other than the director.

## The Screenwriter as Filmmaker: Abraham Polonsky and *Body and Soul*

One might expect that the other most likely contributor to the creative idea of a film is the writer. However, normally the writer serves primarily as the source for raw material, the meaning of which the director then interprets. Occasionally the writer does a good deal more: he works with the director in articulating the film concept prior to shooting the film, and in this sense he supplies a script that verbally suggests the surface level of the film (to disclose its depth is still essentially the work of the director).

Sometimes even when a film is done well, when the director has placed his camera correctly and edited his shots so as to keep the pace swift and the tension as taut as one could hope for, the credit for the film idea has to be shared. The type of motion picture in which the director cannot be the sole creative artistic force behind the work is one in which the basis is primarily literary. This does not mean that films with literary antecedents cannot be truly cinematic works. But if a decision is made to remain faithful to the "spirit" of a producer's or studio's view of a literary "classic," a successful play, or a popular novel, the director is limited to someone else's basic concept, and whether it is Shakespeare's or Samuel Goldwyn's does not matter. His work is unlikely to yield truly cinematic substance.

**7** *Body and Soul*

Sometimes the literary quality of the screenplay dominates the film, as in Robert Rossen's *Body and Soul* (1947). This film is extremely well directed in terms of camera arrangements and pacing, but the concept of the film lies very solidly in Abraham Polonsky's screenplay, which embodies the theme clearly in the dialogue. It could conceivably have been transformed into a play, and certainly into a novel, with very little difference. Furthermore, the acting of John Garfield as the corrupted prizefighter contributes significantly to the meaning of the film. Polonsky is the creator, and both Garfield and Rossen are interpreters. The film is a successful one, and in its own way, a unified work; but it does not have the driving force of a work of genius. Its conception is quite good, as is its execution, but it is not the conception and execution of one man, one filmmaker.

*Body and Soul* relates through a long flashback the boxing career of Charlie Davis (Garfield) from his start as an amateur of local renown to his attaining of the championship. The story concerns an immature, uneducated pugilist who grows to achieve a tremendous depth of feeling, acquiring both sense and sensibility to the extent that he develops into a tragic

hero capable of spiritual redemption. As he rises to the position of fame and wealth he had always aspired to, he finds that he is gradually selling himself out, till at last he is owned "body and soul" by the criminal elements of the fight game and required by them to lose his precious championship in order to cash in on the betting (fig. 7).

Not only is the idea conceived in literary terms, but so is the method of presentation. It starts with melodramatic tension the night before the final fight: we first see Charlie completely distraught because "Ben" has died (and we don't know who *he* was); then Charlie visits his mother, whose cold antagonism toward him tells us that everything is wrong (though we have no information about causes). Finally, just before the fight, he lies down on the training table at the arena; what he thinks or dreams forms the main body of the film and proceeds chronologically from many years earlier right up to the present. Only toward the end of the film do we work our way back to the present. The final fight begins at the moment when Charlie's reflections have led him to the point of tragic revelation. He grasps the falseness of his values and the fact of his complicity in his tragic predicament, which leaves him the choice of betraying not only those who love him but himself, or risking the vengeance of the gangsters who control him. During the fight, he determines to accept the risks and to win, though he has bet all his money on his opponent. His victory is then a spiritual triumph as much as a physical vindication of his right to be champion; he has, in effect, reclaimed himself from the evil surrounding him.

Even this simplified summary of the film clearly indicates the kind of material that makes for excellent drama—but equally excellent on the stage or in the novel as on film. Without question the whole film could have been ruined through misdirecting or clumsy acting, and Rossen and Garfield do excellent—not just adequate—jobs. But would the film have been essentially different if it had been directed by John Huston and had starred Humphrey Bogart? Surely all the nuances would have been different—but the essential concept is located in the text of the film. In fact, the screenplay could have been published, for it would certainly be good reading with no changes at all.

Consider specifically a clever sequence in which the young Charlie Davis, who is little more than a crude, egotistical street fighter, meets a much more sophisticated girl, played by Lilli Palmer. She gets him to leave her apartment, but he lingers in the doorway, while she considers how to regard him. Physically attractive, but somewhat animal-like, Charlie can be manipulated by her. She recites Blake's poem, "The Tyger," which concludes, "What immortal hand or eye / Dare frame thy fearful symmetry?" Puzzled, Charlie says, "What's symmetry?" She answers, "Well built," and immediately kisses him goodnight. The visual counterpart of this sequence is adequate, but it does not match the verbal wit. If we closed our eyes, we could

still get most of the meaning from the sequence. Similarly, when the chief gangster brushes off all moral qualms concerning the role of money in moral life with the philosophical observation that "everything is addition or sub-traction—the rest is conversation," we know that perhaps the best a director can do with dialogue that so skillfully characterizes both speaker and listener is to avoid getting in the way.

Thus, *Body and Soul* inevitably seems the creation of Abraham Polon-sky more than of Robert Rossen. Following *Body and Soul,* Polonsky di-rected his first film, *Force of Evil,* which also starred Garfield. Similar in theme and tone to the earlier work, this film, while still literary to some extent, is more cohesive and powerful because the same mind interpreted and conceived it. Of course, few writers of screenplays have the capacity to direct films. What is really needed is a director who, without necessarily being a writer, can shape a screenplay into cinematic form. Oddly enough, most of the major directors seem to have literary backgrounds. Some of them were even writers, whether for the screen or for publication, before they were directors, (*e.g.,* Fellini, Truffaut, and Bergman). Many who went from performing to directing had obvious literary leanings (Griffith and Chaplin). And even the ordinary film director is likely to have some feeling for the narrative form, for the art of the story-teller.


## The Star System

The European movie industry has never been quite as commercial in its orientation as the American industry, perhaps because the European film-maker from virtually the earliest days had more status than his American counterpart. In America, the star system became standardized almost as soon as the movies became big business. The public first got to know the actors and actresses, and to a great extent even today the typical moviegoer does not consider the names of the leading directors in choosing the films he will see.

The star system was unavoidable in the United States because even before 1920 the industry had produced a number of great filmmaker-performers, people who were not only among the most talented actors in the entire history of the motion picture, but were also the creative force behind their films. No equivalent array of talent existed that early in any other Western country. Before completing his first year in the industry (1914), Charles Chaplin had become a tremendous box-office attraction. But even before Chaplin, audiences had learned to identify their favorites, although the industry, anticipating the possibility that popular personalities might demand more money, had tried at first to keep the performers' names secret. In 1908, Biograph Films paid actors a mere five dollars a day. Yet

when audience attendance indicated a popular preference for the anonymous "Biograph Girl" (Florence Lawrence), for example, it eventually became clear that her next employer would do well to publicize pictures by proclaiming her role in them, even though it must inevitably mean a raise in her salary. Nevertheless, in 1915, when Chaplin was able to demand the first of the fantastic salaries, the industry began to worry about the profitability of the star system.

They need not have worried, for it was indeed profitable and the high salaries were justified by the high box office returns. But as soon as the films were advertised in terms of the stars, the role of the filmmaker was de-emphasized in the mind of the public. Only two filmmakers remained truly important in a commercial sense at that time, D. W. Griffith (whose popularity was to decline steadily in the 1920's) and Mack Sennett. Stars very quickly became more popular than the studios themselves, though in the earliest days each studio sought to establish a public identity with a certain kind of product. Biograph succeeded in the period of 1910–12, for instance, in establishing itself as the industry leader in high-quality dramatic one-reel films, as the audience intuitively recognized the superiority of D. W. Griffith's work, even though for the most part his name too was not announced by Biograph.

The early comedy stars deserved their popularity, for almost invariably they created their own comic personalities in films that were nothing more than vehicles to exhibit their talents. In other words, even when they were not directors, these stars were primarily the "filmmakers," the creative forces behind the films they appeared in. Such is unquestionably the case in the films starring Harold Lloyd or Harry Langdon, though both great comedians did require competent directors to keep their films consistently paced. On the other hand, Chaplin and Keaton, generally conceded to be the two greatest comedians, were by and large their own directors and the creators of their own ideas. Keaton usually worked with the director, co-directing his films; Chaplin of course did everything from writing the script to composing the musical score for some of his feature films.

The silent screen demanded high-quality visual acting or style to convey a personality. Much of the acting required mobility, if not agility. Stunt men who had some ability to act could develop into significant performers in days when the stand-in or "double" was not common. Keaton was a professional acrobat before becoming an actor. Douglas Fairbanks was one of the most remarkable screen performers because he managed—it is difficult to verbalize how—to communicate a personality through his acrobatic exploits. The epitome of the romantic adventurer who rescued those in distress and escaped to torment the oppressors, he played at the same time the role of a self-conscious comic ironist; and all these roles derived essentially from his physical nature.

On the other hand, silent screen acting was often subtle. In general, the pace of silent films exceeded that of sound films, for one almost always grasps the visual image more swiftly than the verbal. Thus, the acting had sometimes to be remarkably resourceful in terms not only of facial expression but of the mobility and gracefulness of the entire body in contributing to the emotional effect of a scene. Of course we note a disproportionate amount of very broad hand waving in the silent films, but that was not typical of the best films. In the performances of Lillian Gish directed by Griffith, the technique of film acting is refined to a high art. One of the most

**8** *Broken Blossoms*

memorable scenes in film history occurs in Griffith's *Broken Blossoms* (fig. 8) when Lillian Gish is locked in a closet-sized room, terrified as her violent and half insane stepfather pounds on the door in an attempt to break in and beat her. Miss Gish runs frantically in tiny circles, absolutely desperate and unable to prevent the man from eventually reaching her. In this sequence, the actress never is seen as simply the trapped animal she has almost been reduced to; her ability to convey her humanity in this situation remains one of the highlights of a career filled with great roles in many films.

The tendency toward the star system received new impetus from the beginnings of the sound film. By its very nature, sound encouraged a reliance on the more traditional techniques of acting. In addition, there was now felt to be less need for significant physical movement, and the industry went back to its earliest conception of narrative film as similar to the stage play. All in all, sound seemed to promise new opportunities for the theater performer; a good stage actor, it could be assumed (and this dubious premise is still often accepted), should have no basic difficulty in mastering the sound film medium. After all, the ability to express meaning and emotion verbally—plus the natural requisite of being "photogenic"—was supposed to mean everything in the sound film.

After a relatively short period of director dominance in the industry, during the 1920's, the term *director* once more began to refer to a person who supervised performers in the interpretation of a script. Since inevitably many actors received better salaries than directors and represented more important commercial assets to the production, naturally the star system exerted influence on the director's interpretation in many significant ways. This has nothing to do with the well-known tantrums and idiosyncrasies of famous screen performers. Given the most placid nature, a star was likely to inhibit or mold many segments of the film whether or not he desired to make his presence felt on the set. For instance, the very fact that Greta Garbo was starring in a film meant, obviously, that in all sequences she dominated the scene. More tellingly, in the matter of close-ups, whether necessary or gratuitous, every pretty face was sure to be shown over and over again in a film. Films featuring a sex-symbol actress such as Jean Harlow, Jane Russell, or Marilyn Monroe displayed her anatomy sometimes as the only object of note. A whole series of Betty Grable movies seemed to consist of little more than sequences set up for the actress to show off her famous legs; in fact, these films seemed to be *conceived* in terms of Betty Grable's legs! The film idea had indeed become purely visual at last.

When stars dominate the film, the editing must of necessity try to utilize the best shots of the performers, regardless of whether they are the shots that best express the film's concept. Thus, producers began to

supervise cutting with a great deal of practical justification: if the audience comes to see its favorite performers, the studio must respond by supplying plenty of vehicles in which those stars employ their personalities in exactly the same way as they did in their last commercially successful film.

## The Performer as an Influence on the Film Idea

The success of a star is sometimes determined by his ability to communicate an interesting personality regardless of the quality of the film he appears in. Cary Grant has always radiated a warmth that suggested moral superiority, urbanity, intelligence, and the capacity to do things successfully, though with some versatility he can also play a parody of that aspect of his screen personality which has made him constantly successful (as in *I Was a Male War Bride*). In some roles his presence causes an ambiguity simply because he carries over from film to film an identification with previous roles. In *Charade,* the filmmaker Stanley Donen was able to capitalize on Grant's personality from previous films. Here Grant is always seen from the point of view of the heroine (Audrey Hepburn)—we never see him from his own view. He seems to her a potentially criminal mind, and she does not know if he is a ruthless murderer or a friend. Grant's characteristic charm is much in evidence in *Charade,* and we remember that in dozens of earlier films he always played the hero. (Some spectators might also remember that Hitchcock has already used Grant in exactly the same way in *Suspicion,* where in the eyes of the heroine the clues all pointed to his being a murderer until his vindication at the end.) Donen realizes that the audience has such great admiration for Grant that in spite of the accumulated evidence it will remain highly skeptical of his guilt. A tremendous degree of suspense can build up because we infer rationally that Grant must be guilty. If the role had been played by an unknown actor, the ambiguity would not have been felt: we would simply be sure that the man was guilty. At the end of *Charade,* Grant turns out to be a government official who had sought the criminals. An unknown actor in this role would have made the ending a surprise, but the role throughout the film would have been less effective.

Hitchcock's use of Grant serves as an interesting case of the great director in conflict with the commercial concerns of the studio system. Grant is a superb film actor, and his best performances have probably been in the films of Hitchcock. If films had been left to the control of great directors, the star system might have been beneficial to actor and film, but Hitchcock himself is controlled by the commercial demands of the industry. Using Grant as an actor whose charm unites with certain unsavory implications of his character, Hitchcock could turn out some remarkable studies of the ambiguity of personality: the guilty-innocent or good-bad man of

**9**  *Suspicion*

*North by Northwest* and *Notorious.* In *To Catch a Thief,* Grant is again cast as the suspected man who is really innocent, though this time he has been guilty in the past.

Hitchcock was always aware of the limitations imposed on him by his use of popular performers. When he made *Suspicion,* the gist of the film lay in the underlying evil of a charming man, Grant. The wife, Joan Fontaine, grows to suspect him to the point where she believes him capable of poisoning her (fig. 9). Hitchcock's original film idea was contrary to the version he finally had to make because he had cast Grant as the villain. Hitchcock has commented on this matter:

> The correct ending of *Suspicion*—which was never shot but which
> I wanted to do—was that Fontaine writes a letter to her mother,

saying that she is in love with her husband, but she feels he is a murderer. She doesn't want to live anymore and she's willing to die by his hand. But she thinks society should be protected from him. He comes up with the fatal glass of milk, gives it to her. Before she drinks, she says, "Will you mail this letter to mother for me?" And she drinks the milk and dies. Fade out. Fade in on one short shot: a cheerful, whistling Cary Grant coming to the mail box and popping the letter in. Finish. But, you see, Cary Grant couldn't be a murderer.*

In this case we cannot simply say that Hitchcock was wrong to cast Grant in the role, knowing the restrictions that are imposed by studios, agents, public relations men, and so on. Obviously, Hitchcock wanted to manipulate the personality Grant had created in the public mind prior to this film. As Donen was to do years later, Hitchcock made good use of Grant even though it meant a compromise with the underlying sense of the film. Grant's final image as the good man in *Suspicion* negates to some extent our impressions of essential selfishness and moral indifference that made the characterization so interesting throughout.

The contribution of a performer to a film production is difficult to assess. There have been notable examples of fine acting done by amateurs —or seemingly done by them; in such cases as Vittorio De Sica's *Bicycle Thief,* the amateur performers conveyed a sense of pathos unexcelled in cinema history, but the great depth of feeling communicated was really attributable to the filmmaker for establishing an emotional context so powerful that mere glances from the actors proved sufficient to represent the deepest sense of humanity. Eisenstein and Pudovkin sometimes employed inexperienced actors effectively, since they both believed that the filmmaker was the creator of meaning through the process of editing.

In special situations the filmmaker can entirely create the actor's role. Films have long demonstrated the more-than-adequate acting job of such otherwise limited performers as Rin Tin Tin, Lassie, Trigger, King Kong, and Flipper. The natural ability of not a few Hollywood starlets was no more in evidence than that of the rankest amateur, but cast as self-parodies of starlets they could perform adequately. In Stanley Kubrick's *2001: A Space Odyssey,* the computer was the most praised performer in the film.

Hitchcock has been criticized in recent years for sometimes using barely competent performers—very likely a deliberate choice of his, perhaps to avoid the kind of compromise he has always made in his craft because of studio restrictions on casting as well as the limitations placed on the star once he is cast. In films with a great deal of dialogue, too much is at stake to risk the use of amateurs; the actor must be able to suggest an idea through

---

* Quoted by Peter Bogdanovich in *The Cinema of Alfred Hitchcock* (New York, Museum of Modern Art, 1963), p. 23.

speech or facial expression. In general, acting creates a dimension of meaning that most filmmakers rely on.

## The Performer as Filmmaker: Fred Astaire

The star system has afforded some performers the opportunity—whether desired or not—to determine the style of the films they act in. However, almost all these films are second-rate, for usually either the work is intended as a vehicle for the star or else, once the star is cast, the concept of the film revolves around his screen personality. The success of Edward G. Robinson in *Little Caesar* and James Cagney in *Public Enemy* typed both of these fine actors as gangsters for much of their careers. Peter Lorre's brilliant job in Fritz Lang's *M* made him in the eyes of the American industry a character actor suitable for almost nothing but roles as a murderous yet pathetic psychotic. How many films require such a role? Obviously, the role was carved out of many films just for his presence. Other performers became cult heroes, and the individual films in which they appeared are forgotten except for their roles in them—for example, Boris Karloff horror films, John Wayne Westerns (though many of Wayne's films were directed by talented directors such as John Ford and have merit beyond the characterization of the hero).

Quality films that were styled by the personality of the star are comparatively rare. Humphrey Bogart does indeed seem to bear much of the credit for the conception of the hero in all of his John Huston films, such as *Key Largo, The Treasure of Sierra Madre,* and *Beat the Devil;* on the other hand, Huston very likely conceived of the film idea for such works in terms of Bogart's playing the main role. Bogart's performances implied so much about the depth of his reality in any role that no director could ignore his personality when considering the design of the film. A tremendous list could be drawn up of American performers who undoubtedly helped make their films meaningful as cinema (*i.e.,* not just as vehicles for themselves), including Gary Cooper, Bette Davis, Paul Newman, Marlon Brando, James Stewart, Katherine Hepburn, Gregory Peck—and each major national industry could boast of its own line of stars (Marcello Mastroianni, Sophia Loren, Vittorio De Sica, Vittorio Gassman, for example, in the Italian film industry).

There have in fact been a few stars who with complete justification could be deemed the basic, even overwhelming, force behind their films. As noted before, this was usually true of the great comics of the silent screen and frequently (but less frequently) true of the sound film comedy. W. C. Fields, however, would have to be included among the best comic filmmakers in the early sound films because he helped write the scripts and deter-

mined his own screen characterization. Similarly, no one would dispute the fact that the Marx Brothers and Laurel and Hardy kept a consistent tone to their peculiar artistry from film to film, regardless of the director—though they worked with greater and lesser directors. In fact, Mae West, the Marx Brothers, and Laurel and Hardy all starred in films directed by Leo Mc-Carey, a very good Hollywood director; however, their films done under McCarey, while good, were not necessarily better than the films they did with mediocre directors. Obviously, the determining factor in the films of these performers lay in their performances more than in some director's conception of a work of art.

Of all the stars other than comedians who influenced the style of their films, none was more effective than Fred Astaire. The unpretentious Astaire musicals of the thirties, such as *Top Hat, Swing Time,* and *Shall We Dance* (all made with Ginger Rogers), and even a few of the bigger-budgeted ones that appeared in later years, such as *The Bandwagon,* now deservedly rate among the gems of the American cinema, though the earlier ones, at least, were undoubtedly intended to be trivial, passing entertainment, not film classics. Their success depends on the character portrayed by Astaire, who —so the studio thought—was just a skillful dancer. With no immense budget at stake in these films, with no pretense of a meaningful plot, much less an idea, the studios seemed to allow Astaire to plan the filming of his dance numbers. No one in the thirties seemed cognizant of the fact that Astaire was one of the cinematic geniuses of the age—or else no one cared. After all, the musical comedy was the lightest of entertainment, something aimed at the lowest common denominator of American taste. The only major musical comedy artist before Astaire was that baroque self-parodist, Busby Berkeley, but most of his best work consisted of choreographic effects in other men's films. The time between production numbers in a Berkeley film is unrelieved tedium.

It is worth noting here the original evaluation of Astaire based on his screen test: "Can't act, is bald, can dance a little." Of course in the classical sense, the remark may have been true: Astaire playing Prometheus or King Lear on stage might have fallen short. But Astaire knew from the start what he could do as an actor on screen (and for one thing, he wore a hair piece). Of course he could dance, but what kind of screen character could or should dance? The various characters Astaire created on screen were exactly in line with the personalities revealed while he was dancing. When he was not dancing, he was frequently walking or moving about with the same sense of stylization that characterized his dances. His acting gestures were broad in that they involved more hand and arm movement than most actors employ —but these gestures served to unify the character of the dancer when not dancing, for Astaire's hands, his whole body in fact, are tremendously expressive of his personality.

The real unity is achieved by connecting the dance to the usual daily activities of the character. Astaire often plays a dancer in his films, but so did most other dancers in their films. The difference lies in the musical sense generated throughout an Astaire film. The dances, for instance, are not isolated from the plot. Equally important, the songs are frequently connected to the narrative line. Astaire begins his songs often to advance the film concept; seldom does a song interrupt the narrative.

Because Astaire's acting style connected his dancing performances with his nondancing scenes, he was able to structure a visual rhythm in relation to his movements throughout his films. It is for this reason that Astaire is undoubtedly among the great film *singers*. Although critics concede that he was the screen's greatest dancer, at least in this category others might be mentioned—most notably Gene Kelly, whose 1940's and 1950's musicals, especially the ones directed by Stanley Donen, are among the best ever done in this genre. Singing for the film differs as much from singing in a night club or a recording studio as screen acting does from stage acting. Some impressive voices have produced dull singing sequences (*e.g.,* Mario Lanza's voice could not compensate for a lack of film style). Of all the singing stars who succeeded in conveying songs effectively on the screen, perhaps Al Jolson was the best, but even Jolson has far fewer memorable songs to his credit in film than Fred Astaire. That Astaire's voice was often fragile and sometimes shrill is not really to the point. We are not comparing voices or even personalities, but the ability to convey film meaning during a song number. Frank Sinatra, for example, was unquestionably an inferior singer earlier in his career than later on, but he probably performed more credibly on screen in the silly, innocent roles he played as Gene Kelly's cohort than in roles as a singer in the later musicals.

In his films, Astaire courted his women by singing or dancing. It was his way of expressing himself within the framework of the character he played. In *Swing Time* (1936), directed by George Stevens, he tries to overcome a very bad first impression he has made on a dancing school instructor (Ginger Rogers). She won't talk to him, but in front of her employer he forces himself upon her as a novice dancer. He grabs her and with inept clumsiness keeps stumbling and falls down. When she has had enough of his supposed incompetence and refuses to continue, thus placing her job in immediate jeopardy, Astaire sings to her, playfully pointing out the need for forgiveness of all the stumblers of the world: even the greatest men had to fall in order to rise, "so pick yourself up, dust yourself off, and start all over again." He then proceeds to demonstrate to her angered employer that she is an excellent dance instructor, that in one lesson she has taught him to dance. Grabbing her again, he dances around the floor with her, this time superbly, and thereby saves her job (fig. 10). Some of Astaire's dance numbers were "spontaneous" in the sense that they took

**10** *Swing Time*

place in natural surroundings as part of the story line; others were performed "on stage" or in a nightclub, as part of his occupation in the films in which he portrays a dancer. The spontaneous numbers are always an external reflection of an inner emotional state, frequently of joy. Dancing with Ginger Rogers is his way of telling her that they belong together. His singing expresses his affinity to the person sung to; his dancing is equivalent to a ritual ceremony performed by a primitive man to show his desire and worthiness to win the hand of his beloved.

Astaire's character carries over from film to film. He seems always to play a man whose fantastic dancing ability has given him sufficient self-confidence to be his own man; yet as his own man, he is really an outsider. He wins the girl because his nature is essentially good, and he manages to inform her of this in unusual ways—for as an outsider, he seems radical on the surface. He *has* to dance, as the poet has to write, in order to make his inner life clear to the people watching. Since dancing is an entirely

visual art, the precise method of his accomplishment defies description. But, for example, in the sequence from *Swing Time* mentioned above, the dance that Astaire does with Ginger Rogers inspires two middle-aged on-lookers who cannot dance to get out on the floor and jump around with the extravagance of the two who inspired them. They have picked up the spirit of Astaire's joyful announcement of his good feeling for Ginger Rogers (who has also sensed this from his performance), and their dance, though a parody, also pays tribute to the inner life of the character portrayed by Astaire.

Even when dancing in public and joined by many other dancers, Astaire is capable of making the entire production number a reflection of the mood he establishes. In *The Gay Divorcee* (1934), directed by Mark Sandrich, Astaire and Ginger Rogers escape from the watchful eyes of the hired correspondent who is supposed to spend the night with her in order to provide grounds for a divorce from her husband. To effect the escape Astaire cuts out paper dolls and attaches them to a turntable so as to cast a shadow against the wall; to the correspondent in the next room it seems to be the couple dancing. Jubilant at the success of their trick, they rush off, not to seek some private spot but to join the ballroom dancers. Surrounded by other dancers, Astaire and Rogers communicate privately to each other "the rhythm in their heart and soul"—while dancing "The Continental."

Although most memorable were his dances with female partners, especially Ginger Rogers, Astaire used the dance to convey a variety of moods with no women present at all: moods of abandonment, sorrow, frustration, and many others (such as the sense of loneliness conveyed in singing "I'll go my way by myself" in Vincent Minnelli's *The Band Wagon*). At the very beginning of *Top Hat* (1935), directed by Mark Sandrich, in an extremely brief dance routine, he succeeds in establishing his major personality traits. The film opens in a very exclusive men's club; all the members are old, stiffly formal, and absolutely silent. No noise is permitted, and all the members are terribly disturbed by the sounds of a man reading a newspaper. The man turns out to be Astaire, who is immediately made to feel the outsider he is. But before leaving the club he does a short tap dance, practically driving the members frantic. The dance here expresses Astaire's unconventionality and style of humor. The sense of this number parallels that of the "Top Hat" routine later in the film. In that musical number Astaire dances in front of an all-male chorus, everyone dressed in top hat and tails. At one point in the routine, Astaire turns on the chorus and using his cane as a machine gun annihilates the entire line in what becomes a strange, but comic, fantasy production number. Again, as the outsider he undermines the stiff conformity of the rest of the world.

Astaire conceived of the method of filming his dances so as to produce a sensation of complete fluidity of camera: while he moved with spectacular

grace and technique, the camera followed him so unobtrusively that the audience could never reflect on the presence of a camera between them and the performer. Busby Berkeley, his contemporary, framed his routines in a camera that always took precedence over individual dancers, and he succeeded in making the audience take note of the clever camera angles. In contrast, Astaire aimed at an esthetic appreciation of the dance itself.

The ability to create a cinematic personality in terms of one's entire body occurs infrequently outside the silent comedy. Mae West had the ability too, creating a mythological personification of sex, which she nevertheless viewed with comic detachment. Many a screen beauty has for obvious reasons projected a personality in terms of her body, but almost always that personality was a good deal more formless than the body. Astaire's external manifestation of his internal life is the mark of a filmmaker as much as that of a star.

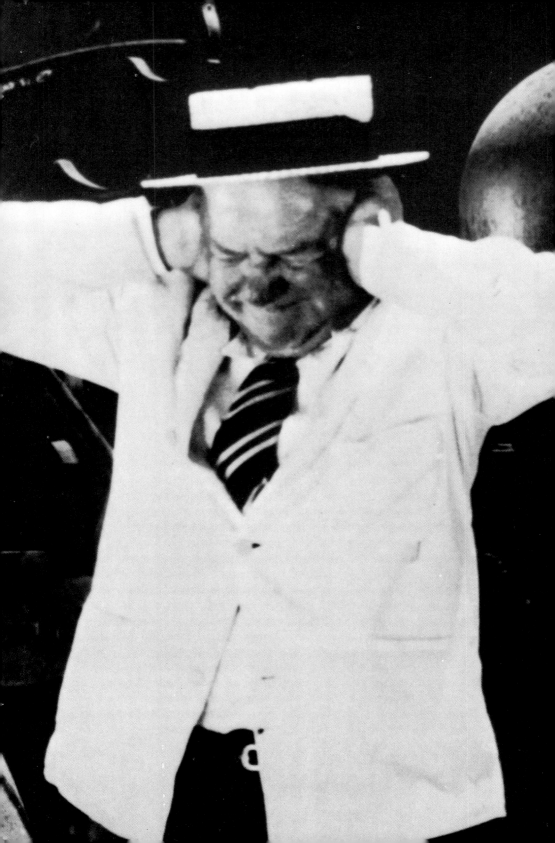

# Part Two
# The Development
# of Film Form

Part Two analyzes the development of the film idea in regard to the most significant innovations in narrative cinematic form. Particular importance attaches to D. W. Griffith's transformation of the primitive film into a sophisticated form capable of expressing the most complicated ideas. However, the pre-Griffith film warrants attention not merely as a historical curiosity but also because its limited powers of expressiveness help us to understand the ways in which film communicates. Although it is widely believed that sound was the esthetic completion of the motion picture medium, the silent film had developed means of visual communication that allowed great filmmakers to express quite fully the film ideas that interested them. The coming of sound really meant a total rethinking of the kinds of material suitable for the new medium. In dealing with the films of the last decade, we will be concerned with some of the far-reaching developments and recent trends in the nature and communication of the film ideas we encounter today.

# The Primitive
# Film up to
# Porter

## The Origins

Motion pictures originated as a mechanical device for recording moving images of reality, not as a narrative medium. Since its inception, the cinema has developed in many directions: it functions today as an art form, an educational tool, a means of dispersing information and news of current events, an entertainment medium, and, as it was originally designed, a process for recording reality—this last aspect still its most popular use for thousands of home movie enthusiasts throughout the world. As diverse as the modern uses of the movie camera might seem, they have mainly developed from the same fundamental approaches to film that were worked out in the first twenty-five years of motion picture history. The techniques used by an amateur with his Super 8 movie camera in recording the images of his baby daughter eating lunch (which, by the way, was the subject of one of the first films made in France by the Lumière brothers, in 1895) were discovered by cameramen like Edwin Porter and Georges Méliès at the turn of the century, developed by D. W. Griffith from 1908 to 1912, and are basic to the art employed by Ingmar Bergman and Federico Fellini in the 1970's.

These basic techniques for making good motion pictures—whether for purposes of art, education, business, sport, or any other use—had to be

worked out by studio experimentation rather than by *a priori* esthetic judgments, for none of the earlier devices for recording human experience, such as books, photographic plates, and phonograph discs, was similar to motion picture film passing through a projector. The first films, made in the 1890's in America, France, and England, were regarded as novelties of very limited potential. The few people seriously interested in the development of film technique were inventors, mechanics, and photographers rather than artists or estheticians, and no one handed out financial grants to encourage the study of what most people considered a toy. Thus, the first decade of motion picture history is characterized by experiments with the mechanics of the camera and the projector; people concerned with motion pictures directed their talents to matters of operation, while problems of film content and film form were of secondary interest.

Today, the beginner at taking home movies starts at a point esthetically far ahead of a typical film of 1895. Any contemporary home movie guidebook will contain such information as the following:

> A good story starts by setting the scene, so you could first shoot an over-all view of your back yard and house, preferably with some member of your family . . . getting ready for the cookout. This immediately establishes where the action is going to take place and need consume only about 6 to 10 seconds. You might then move in for a closer shot to show exactly what kind of work the person is doing, whether it be setting the table or dumping charcoal into the grill.*

As elementary as these suggestions might seem, had such a film been shot in 1899 it would have become a historical classic. Around 1900, G. A. Smith, an English inventor, had used some close-ups in his anecdotal films such as *Grandma's Reading Glass;* before this no one had thought the really close shot worth shooting. Filmmakers devoted themselves to opening a window on the world—they were not yet concerned with seeking out the fragment of reality that becomes expressive of the wider world when established in a context. Also, to intercut a shot of six to ten seconds' duration into a sequence would have seemed an unnecessary chore before dollies or overhead cranes or flexible tripods made it feasible to move the ponderous equipment needed for taking motion pictures in 1899.

In examining the primitive films of the 1890's, one should bear in mind the circumstances surrounding their manufacture and distribution. They look primitive not merely because modern technical improvements (such as fast lenses and indoor lighting) were lacking or because they fulfill nonartistic goals, but because producers were making films for

---

* Editors of the Eastman Kodak Company, *How to Make Good Home Movies* (Rochester, N.Y., Eastman Kodak Co., 1963), p. 19.

audiences with no experience in following any sort of narrative conveyed purely by visual images. The mere wonder of seeing these moving images disconcerted the earliest audiences, preventing them from evaluating any sophisticated artistry on the part of the filmmaker. The producers, as soon as they realized the commercial possibilities of their products (and they did not realize them for some years), began to turn out great quantities to meet the demand—and the demand was not for new expressions of cinematic art but for a repetition of formats that had already proven successful. The early growth of the cinema in the direction of art was severely hindered by the discovery of its vast commercial possibilities. With businessmen rather than filmmakers in control, the industry developed mainly as a commercial enterprise. What truly surprises us is the number of great artists like Griffith and Chaplin able to perfect their art within the restrictive framework of this materialistic industry.

## The Inventions

Some thorough historians of motion pictures are tempted to begin at the beginning. The prehistoric painter at Altamira, Spain, depicted a boar with many legs, in an evident attempt to capture the essence of motion by drawing. The basic principle of the cinema, that the mind retains a visual impression for a fraction of a second after the object has been perceived by the eye and removed from view, may have been known by Ptolemy in the second century, though formulated as the theory of the persistence of vision only in 1824 by Roget. And as for projection devices, Athanasius Kirchener demonstrated his *Magia Catoptrica* (magic lantern) in Rome in 1640. The date usually assigned to the origin of photography is 1839, when Louis Daguerre in France and William Talbot in England developed systems for exposing photographs on chemically coated plates.

In the late 1880's numerous inventors were discovering methods of photographing objects in motion and projecting the developed pictures so that they could be viewed by several people at one time. Not until Thomas Edison began to give some attention to the problem was the basic system invented that is used today. But Edison, however shrewd a businessman he was, completely underestimated the importance of this device and assigned to an assistant, William Kennedy Dickson, the task of inventing a visual counterpart of the Edison phonograph.* Thus, at its very earliest stage the motion picture was associated in a significant way with sound. The first films that Dickson made actually were synchronized sound films, though

---

* The latest scholarship attributes to Dickson the actual invention and credits Edison with assimilating the machines and ideas of earlier inventors, particularly Eadweard Muybridge.

the sound was not placed on the film celluloid as it is now; the date (which is controversial because Edison and Dickson came to an unfriendly parting of ways) was probably 1889. In that same year, George Eastman's company invented a more durable film stock than Dickson's, and it was soon put to use in the Edison camera, which was called the kinetograph. The machine through which one viewed the film, the kinetoscope, contained earphones for the sound. It did not project images on a screen; instead, the viewer looked through the window of the kinetoscope and turned a crank in order to see the motion pictures, which ran for about one minute.

When Edison finally got around to applying for patents on the kinetoscope and kinetograph, apparently two years after Dickson developed them, he thought so little of the financial value of the machines that he would not pay the extra $150 for the European copyrights, a blunder that probably lost him a fortune. An English manufacturer of scientific instruments, Robert W. Paul, learned of the absence of an English patent and began producing an improved version of the machine called the bioscope. The same thing happened with Louis and Auguste Lumière in France; they called their much-improved version of Edison's kinetoscope the Cinematographe. The early years produced a great many variants, with such descriptive names as Vitascope, Phantoscope, Mouvementograph, and Animatographe.*

## The Earliest Film Products

In 1893 Edison contracted with a manufacturer to market his kinetoscope. The first commercial exhibitor opened a kinetoscope parlor in New York City containing ten machines, each with a fifty-foot film (running about one minute) supplied by the Edison Company's new movie studio. This studio, the world's first, was a specially designed building measuring thirty feet by twenty-five feet; it was painted black and had a movable section of ceiling to admit light at any desired angle, since no indoor lighting in those days was bright enough for filming. The one- and two-minute films made there were written, designed, photographed, directed, processed, and produced by the cameraman, who was often Dickson.

Up to about 1899 only a very few such director-cameramen worked in the United States, perhaps as few as six.† In spite of the anonymity of the profession, two of them eventually achieved fame: Edwin Porter and Billy Bitzer (who became D. W. Griffith's chief cameraman years later). They mastered their techniques before the owners of motion picture com-

* See the long and amusing list compiled by Ivor Montagu, *op. cit.*, p. 25.

† *Cf.* Lewis Jacobs, *The Rise of the American Film* (New York, Harcourt Brace Jovanovich, 1939), Chap. 1.

panies cared enough about content to interfere. The early films consisted of reproductions of reality or short skits by entertainers. In Edison's studio, nicknamed the Black Maria, many films were made of celebrities such as Buffalo Bill, Sandow the Strong Man, and Annie Oakley. Parades, speeding trains, and natural scenery were indiscriminately considered suitable material for the public. No individuality of technique was displayed in the early films, most of which now seem impersonal glimpses of figures and events of the period.

Early nonnarrative filming did not develop into an art form; in fact the nonnarrative film as such did not develop at all, though the techniques of filming were constantly improving. Technique, however, will not supply theory, and until the Russian director Dziga Vertov began thinking about nonnarrative filming around 1915–20, very little was accomplished. Granting the validity of filming the contemporary world just to record impressions that may be of temporary interest, we regard these old films of celebrities, curios now, as ultimately uninspiring and imitative.

The nonnarrative, however, soon began to evolve into the story film. Porter's *The Life of an American Fireman* (1902) tells of a particular fire put out by firemen and shows a daring rescue from a burning building. It comes close to being either a documentary or a fiction film, but it is not quite either. The story is purely surface material, straightforwardly presented only for the visual interest of the movement. Yet it lacks a true documentary sense in spite of its detailing the day of a fireman, for it presents images of the fireman's day on a purely descriptive level (though it was partly staged, partly taken from stock). It seems authentic, but it is not interpretive. Not until years later did the documentary, in the hands of John Grierson and Robert Flaherty, go far beyond the recording of the events in the day of a fisherman or an Eskimo, the literal subjects of such films by them. The documentary in their sense bears no relationship to the dreary travelogue that still dominates the short feature presentation in American movie houses. The documentary explores the meaning of the surface reality it records; it is not, after all, totally different from the narrative fiction film. But in the primitive stage of the industry, the public was treated only to short external views of what cameramen believed would interest a wide, not well-informed, impressionable public.


## The Development of Technique and Content in the Early Films

The earliest film technique was borrowed from the art of photography and consisted mainly in choosing the best stationary vantage point from which to photograph the moving subject; the standard view, a long shot, framed the subject in the center of the picture. This most obvious approach to cinematography reflected the audience's absorption in the subject and

neglect of the art of the cameraman. The illusion of reality was always the main aim of the first films.* The static camera photographed films one to ten minutes in length, usually without changing locations or indicating time lapses, especially in the shorter films, and almost always without establishing a psychological or an esthetic relationship between the camera and the subject photographed.

Conscious cinematic technique first appeared when the single long shot from a static camera ceased to be the rule for all films—that is, when director-cameramen began making conscious choices. Film manufacturers believed for a long time that audiences would naturally prefer the stage view, in which all subjects are visible from head to toe and in which the audience, presumably sitting in the center of the orchestra, selects the area to concentrate on. (It should be noted that with modern stage lighting the area of focus is no longer left to the selection of the spectator even at stage plays.) They felt that audiences demanded the chance to see everything that was going on. The medium shot had been used by the Lumière brothers as early as 1895, but it was not often seen in films produced before 1900.

A typical early film, *The Execution of Mary Queen of Scots,* produced by the Edison Company for its kinetoscope in 1893 and later for its vitascope, exhibits both the virtues and the flaws of the early cinema. Running under a minute, this film reproduces the illusion of reality (the beheading of Mary) in a manner that immediately revealed to the public the superiority of a cinematic simulation of this sort of action over a theatrical representation in a stage play of the period. The film, however, is little more than a scene from a play; the static camera gives no particular emphasis to anyone present on the set. In a true narrative, real drama lies not in the fact of an execution but in the events leading up to it. At this point in the primitive film, narrative could attain only a pictorial effect.

Films such as *The Execution of Mary Queen of Scots* make it clear that the cinema had not yet found means of expression in truly cinematic terms. In 1893 cinema was hardly more than a cross between photography and stage representation, for the movie camera was merely a passive spectator at an unusual event. Yet even at this point in the development of the motion picture medium, as this film reveals, one cinematic technique had evidently been carefully considered by the director, William Heiss: he had grasped the possibilities of stop-motion photography. In filming the execution, he stopped the camera while a dummy was substituted for the actress portraying Mary; the result is one of the earliest examples of trick

* When the Lumière brothers exhibited the film of the train speeding toward the camera, some in the audience shrieked and dashed for the exits in hysterical fear. Sixty years later, three-dimensional movies created the same effect as far as the shrieking went, but audiences were forewarned and did not actually leave their seats.

photography in the movies, for the original audiences must have been completely bewildered by the head rolling off what they assumed was an actress. Of itself the trick is unimportant, but we take interest in an early example of a director exercising full control over his subject matter and making some imaginative use of the properties of the cinema.

Very shortly after its origins, the film began to develop a narrative focus. *Washday Troubles,* a brief comic episode filmed in 1895, represents a typical advance many films made over *The Execution of Mary Queen of Scots,* not in technique but in content. The same static camera is set up in front of the scene to record what happens, but what happens here is truly of cinematic interest: the central event, the upsetting of the wash, represents the intrusion of the ridiculous upon the detailed, commonplace environment, linking action and location in just the sort of slapstick incident that the motion pictures were to express so well in the Mack Sennett years ahead. Although not developed in *Washday Troubles,* a classic film idea, the chase, appears in one of its earliest forms. Arising from the spilling of the wash, this particular chase is largely unconnected with the rest of the film, but in general the chase came to mean visual movement in time and space; it could provide a film with an entire sequence readily comprehensible without the use of dialogue, and therefore in its innumerable forms the chase became the motivation for many of the first narrative films.

In films that followed, directors like D. W. Griffith employed greater and greater variety in their selection of camera techniques. Films of contemporary interest that featured a chase (*e.g.,* James Williamson's *Stop, Thief!,* 1901) or a combat scene (*e.g.,* Charles Urban's *Possibilities of War in the Air,* 1906) reveal much refinement in the handling of action by the cameraman. In Cecil Hepworth's film *Rescued by Rover* (made in Britain in 1905) we perceive some evidence of an acknowledged relationship between camera and subject matter. Hepworth uses some low angle photography in filming the scenes of the dog running. Thus, the audience is made to share Rover's view of the world.

The artistic claims of the primitive films are indeed modest. To appreciate most of these works requires an effort of imagination. Aside from their sociological and historical interest, such films can only be tolerated or apologized for. Yet the films of two men deserve to be separated from the rest because of their inherent quality. These men were the first conscious artists of what was to become the great art form of our age: Georges Méliès and Edwin Porter.

## Georges Méliès

The contribution of the French filmmaker Georges Méliès to the development of the narrative film remains difficult to assess, though he is now uni-

versally recognized as the first truly important creative artist working in the primitive cinema. He produced a great quantity of short films—estimates range from 500 to 2000 or more—between 1896 and 1913, when he ran his own company (Star Films), and all those that are still available (in this country only a small number can be seen) retain a degree of charm beyond mere historical curiosity. Yet regardless of the quality of his films, he was not the founder of a major cinematic narrative tradition; in fact, very little that we see in film today has descended from Méliès. A few talented followers such as Emile Cohl and Ferdinand Zecca remained within a limited tradition. Griffith supposedly said of Méliès, "I owe him everything," but the context of the remark is unclear. As far as we can see, Griffith's style owes nothing to Méliès, and this in itself is remarkable, for with the exception of Porter no other filmmaker emerges from the early days with any recognizable style. Therefore, the apparent lack of direct influence of Méliès on Griffith must remain a mystery.

Méliès worked outside the major film trend of his own day, which was, as it is today, toward realism, though sometimes he staged realistic works such as *The Dreyfus Affair* and *The Coronation of Edward VII*. However, what he will always be remembered for, what brought him his international popularity, were his innumerable fairy-tale and fantasy films such as *The Voyage Across the Impossible, The Bewitched Inn, Jupiter's Thunderbolts,* and *The Mermaid*. In films like these Méliès developed his famous camera techniques, so far advanced for his day that imitators around the turn of the century had to steal his prints or copy them to achieve his effects—they could not duplicate the effects in their own studios until the whole subject of trick photography became commonplace before the end of the first decade of the century. The following camera techniques were popularized—and some perhaps invented by Méliès: double exposure, stop motion, fast motion, slow motion, animation, fades, and dissolves. These innovations appealed to the imagination of filmmakers the world over, but although all these devices became standard in the cinematography of the narrative film, they are not of crucial importance to the development of narrative cinematic expressiveness. Méliès' real accomplishment was to bring imagination to bear on the story line. Even though he and his followers eventually glutted the market with more fantasy than the world cared to have, we must remember that he started to produce works in a period that was almost entirely without imaginative concepts for the medium. Ignoring the subject matter of his contemporaries, Méliès specialized in what he called artificially arranged scenes. These scenes were projections of the imaginative mind, not only his own mind but the minds of the other literary men whose fairy tales and science fiction stories he adapted to the screen.

In spite of his fertile and energetic concepts, Méliès now seems ultraconservative in his attitude toward the expressive qualities of the camera as

an interpreter of material brought before it. With Méliès, as with his least talented contemporaries, the camera still functions primarily as a recorder, though the images recorded by Méliès have a distinctive quality. Keeping the essential setup of a theater, he placed the camera at one end of a long room; at the opposite end was a stage or acting area. His shorter films consist of a single shot of a single stage setting; his longer films are made of twenty or thirty such shots, all roughly of the same duration, and all from exactly the same distance and angle.

In other words, Méliès conceived of a motion picture as a recording on celluloid of amusing incidents carefully staged before a camera. His success, therefore, must be attributed to the number of amusing things he created for the camera to record. In the history of film, only Méliès was able to rely exclusively on his own inventiveness and performance to produce artistically successful works time and again. Much greater artists like Chaplin, Keaton, Griffith, and Eisenstein could not do this—that is, they did not conceive of their art in so simple and basic a way as Méliès did. Méliès succeeded because of his intuitive feeling for a very limited cinematic experience. He had no major statement to make about human nature. He wanted to depict the surfaces of a fantasy world, and he did so brilliantly, in a manner that might be compared to the best work of current avant-garde or experimental filmmakers, who use his techniques. He knew what was funny, at least visually, and he contrived a hundred variations of all the little things that make for a comic idea.

His most famous film, *A Trip to the Moon* (1902), represents the high point of his artistry. Made in thirty scenes, the film was about three times the length of the average film of the day (fig. 11). Méliès based his material on a Jules Verne story but turned all the science fiction into parody. His ridiculous scientists from the Astronomic Club set off to the moon with great fanfare and consciousness of their own importance. They land their "projectile" in the eye of the moon (the landing is shown in animation, and the moon has a face), emerge to do battle with moon creatures, and return to earth to be decorated as heroes and to become the object of public rejoicings. As usual, everyone in a Méliès film is satirized, but the satire is intended to be neither bitter nor significant, for the characters have no human dimensions; they are all stereotypes or grotesques.

Prior to Méliès it had been assumed that the subject matter, not the filmmaker, determined the quality of a film. Méliès was the first filmmaker with a style recognizable from one film to another, and with this film, audiences could finally discern a creative mind in the cinema. However, our first critical reaction to *A Trip to the Moon* is that here, again, is the same old camera view of a stage setting; of course we are not too concerned about camera angle and technique in a Méliès film because the emphasis so clearly falls on the visual design of the area being photographed (for instance, the costuming and painted sets, everything designed by Méliès).

11  Scenes from *A Trip to the Moon*

All his films announce that their whole point is visual amusement through comic inventiveness. Surprise and humor mean everything. The stars in the sky twinkle with pretty actresses' faces; we watch a Méliès film for just that kind of design, and since we demand to be entertained in this way, we can only agree that Méliès succeeds in surprising us. It does not bother us that the film is a completely artificial contrivance, that the numerous trick shots and narrative twists are often gratuitous in regard to the main action. Méliès' effectiveness depends upon the rapport he establishes with the audience and its acceptance of the charm of the filmmaker. We understand that in such a work as *A Trip to the Moon* the filmmaker is creating a series of surprise episodes, really little jokes both in their cinematic form and in their content. This type of entertainment relates at least as much to improvised theater as to the dramatic stage.

Although the camera does nothing to aid in conveying a sense of movement in a Méliès film, the action itself is never static. *A Trip to the Moon* progresses in chronological order using a peculiar form that Méliès seems to have developed himself for the cinema: carefully staged "tableaux," each representing a step forward in time. Each tableau or sequence tends to contain its separate elements of humor. No intercutting is used.

Méliès' limitations have been perceptively noted by John Howard Lawson:

> Méliès was a screen poet; his technique points the way to Chaplin's unique vision. But the human emotion that underlies every movement of Chaplin's films lay beyond the purview of Méliès' art. His tableaux could not achieve emotional life. The difficulty did not lie primarily in his love of fantasy, for his imaginative use of transformations and illusions was the first suggestion that film *sees* physical and psychological relationships that we do not see with our eyes. Méliès could not free his imagination from the stage picture. He conceived of the camera as an eye watching the scene from a fixed position in the center of the audience. Technically, this meant that the action could not flow around the camera as it must for genuine cinematic movement. The technical limitation affected the portrayal of people. Without close-ups or intimate views of objects or persons, it was impossible to achieve human feeling or to give emotional substance to the tableaux. . . . [the characters] are not humanly funny, because neither they nor the audience are really participating in the experience. It is not an experience at all in an emotional sense. It is a self-conscious joke.*

This evaluation, for the most part just, does not take account of Méliès' cine-

---

* John Howard Lawson, *Film: The Creative Process* (New York, Hill and Wang, 1967), pp. 10–11.

**12** *The Magic Lantern*

matic intuition. In spite of his limitations, and in spite of the fact that no one else was able to use his approach to make truly cinematic substance out of staged scenes, Méliès did achieve entertaining cinema within the goals he set for himself.

The nature of this achievement can readily be seen by examining in detail one of his typical short works, *The Magic Lantern* (1903). There is no plot in the usual sense, just a series of incidents that seem to be occurring in a child's nursery. The entire film, which takes less than five minutes, is presented in a single shot and employs only one visual area. The two presiding characters seem to be toy clowns that have come alive in the nursery; during the course of the film a group of soldiers, toys presumably, appears, as does a group of girls (borrowed from the nearby Folies Bergère); and later more of the same dressed as ballet dancers (fig. 12). All the characters, though they are not supposed to be real, are played by real people in costume. The action of the film consists of the two clowns coming out and constructing a magic lantern (that is, a motion picture projector) large enough to hold several people. They show movies seemingly against a wall. Later the projector is used just as a large box from which the bevy of chorus girls emerges as if by magic (through stop-motion photography); and when the clowns start fighting with each other, a group of soldiers marches on as if to take them as prisoners. Finally, an India rubber man expands from

midget size to giant size and the soldiers flee. In the interim we see some lively dancing by the chorus and one particular dancer of some talent. None of the incidents seems determined by cause and effect. The major motivation seems to be only a desire to keep in motion.

As a general principle, prolonged reliance on the single shot taken at some distance in order to cover an acting area is not feasible. The long shot, though entirely cinematic, diminishes the human in relation to the environment, and therefore cannot be the sole shot in a cameraman's repertory. Yet in *The Magic Lantern* and virtually every other Méliès film such use of the long shot is justifiable because the subject matter is truly the acting area itself. A division into mid-shots and close-ups would damage the film idea that really lies behind his work: Méliès, though uninterested in human beings as psychological entities, wishes to concentrate on them as physical shapes, and by exaggerating various gestures and positions, to fill the area with motion. He might just as well—and he does just as often—use monsters or supernatural bodies (gods, stars, mermaids, animated forms, anything and everything). When humans appear they tend to move in comical ways: in *The Magic Lantern* the two clowns are continually doing jigs; the rubber man expands and contracts; the main dancer does some notable gymnastic feats, but her somersaults are essentially comic. The film idea of a Méliès work concerns the pictorial problem of filling an area with shapes in motion so as to present a burlesque of reality. Méliès had been a magician once, and magic is closely allied with his peculiar film art—not so much, as is always remarked, because Méliès was an illusionist, but because he was a creator of burlesque who specialized in pictorial deviations from the norm of reality.

His tableaux explode with unexpected movement in any direction. Everything is ridiculous, not only the incidents but the characters themselves. Yet sheer movement continuously recorded in long shot is potentially confusing. Méliès, however, knows how to create emphasis within the frame. When the magic lantern projects a circular image on the screen, the result is equivalent to an iris shot; even though the entire screen is visible, our attention is naturally directed toward the visual point that holds the interest of the characters on screen. When the dancers arrive, they separate into two rows for the performance of their "prima ballerina," who is costumed in a much darker shade, reinforcing visual emphasis.

The long shot in Méliès is further justified by the nature of his visual gags, which are scaled to the proportion of the entire human form, not just a part of it. When he creates an illusion of appearance or disappearance, it usually has to do with the human form. From within the magic lantern, which had seemed just a machine, a crowd of people surprisingly emerge, the idea behind the gag having to do with how many people can appear in an instant (via stop motion) from a large box. When the rubber man expands or contracts, the comedy has to do with his proportions relative to the realistic norm. Everything is measured implicitly against reality, but

reality itself is not depicted; nevertheless, the comedy suggests reality by parodying it, and there would be no humor without this suggestion.

Completely cinematic within carefully self-prescribed limitations, Méliès' art deals only with external perception; such restriction is never true of great narrative, nor even of great visual art that employs human figures. Yet Méliès' simplicity is surely legitimate; he is one of the first to alert us to the way the camera sees as distinct from the way the eye does. And if nothing derived directly from him, we may account him the spiritual parent of the Marx Brothers and Eugene Ionesco and the whole Theater of the Absurd.

## Edwin S. Porter and *The Great Train Robbery*

Porter, while not quite qualifying as a "great" filmmaker, is one of the most important figures in the history of the cinema. He deserves this position as the man who evolved the principle of editing, the concept of making a film by selecting and putting together separate shots. In Méliès' films, a single shot in most cases served to present the entire sequence, often the entire film. Porter's films, starting with *The Life of an American Fireman* (1902), were built up from many sequences. Still rather primitive, Porter relied almost exclusively on the single-shot sequence, as did Méliès, but he made his sequences connect logically with each other as necessary links in a developing plot, whereas Méliès remained satisfied with sequences that in themselves contained completed episodes.

A mechanic originally, with no feeling for art when he joined the Edison Company, Porter more or less instinctively worked out many basic types of editing techniques, such as parallel plot construction and cross-cutting. He remained the most important filmmaker until 1908, when an actor introduced in one of his films of that year, *Rescued from an Eagle's Nest,* began to direct his own films: D. W. Griffith.* It is from Porter rather than from Méliès that Griffith's work and the major tradition of filmmaking develop. Porter used techniques like the moving camera and the close-up five or six years before Griffith made his debut, though it must be said that Griffith was the first to understand the implications of Porter's contributions. Furthermore, Porter helped develop a new sense of cinematic space and clarified the relationship of the camera to subjects moving in depth.

The first sensational box-office smash was *The Great Train Robbery* (1903), and it is *the* landmark in American films. It was the first American film to tell a story in a manner unlike that of a photographed play. Méliès' narrative films had been simply a stringing together of chronological scenes

---

* The date of the film is always listed as 1907, except in the most authoritative recent source, Robert M. Henderson's *D. W. Griffith: The Years at Biograph* (New York, Farrar, Straus & Giroux, 1970), p. 29.

**13**   *The Great Train Robbery* (Shot #1)

performed before a camera, each complete in itself. *The Great Train Robbery* presents a unified action divided into shots that draw their emotional power from the suggestion of what might follow. These shots build with a tension never before witnessed in the movies.

*The Great Train Robbery* is composed of thirteen segments of film telling the story of a train robbery and the recovery of the stolen money, plus a fourteenth segment, consisting of a close shot of a bandit firing a gun point blank at the audience; this shot was sometimes shown at the beginning and sometimes at the end of the film. It has no narrative value, but it provoked sensations of fear and surprise in the audience (which considered it a very rare close-up, though for us it is almost a medium shot).

The thirteen segments detail the act of the robbery, emphasizing the event itself, with little regard for characterization or theme. Each segment of the film corresponds to a distinct stage in the entire event, and each is done in a single shot. In the eighth segment, a stationary camera setup tilts and pans with the robbers as they flee, and it is possible to consider this segment as a two-shot arrangement; however, Porter undoubtedly thought of it as a single shot capturing the action.

This remarkable film deserves an extended analysis because of its historic influence. In shot one, the interior of a railway station telegraph office is occupied by two robbers who tie up the operator after forcing him to signal the train to stop (fig. 13). Through the window we see the train coming to a halt. A moving background had previously been used by Méliès, but with this significant difference: in Méliès this trick effect was intended to make the audience appreciate the artifice—that is, to wonder about the

technique; in Porter's film, the technique is used for the exact opposite reason—to establish verisimilitude.

In shot two the train comes to a full stop to receive water for its boiler, allowing the robbers time to board it without being noticed. This is an extraordinary shot pictorially. The frame is dominated by the vertical planks that support the water tank: they are the basic stable pictorial elements, along with a ladder. In conflict, the mobile elements are horizontal: the train moves into the picture from the right to the center, and the robbers move from the left to the right. The directional crossing of the mobile elements parallels and balances a huge X shape formed by crossbeams. The shot contains action in regard to the plot and tension in regard to the composition of the frame. And, although some historians believe that in shot eight we have the first example of a panning camera in an American fiction film, it should be pointed out that the camera moves from left to right in this second shot, significantly but so subtly that no attention is usually given to it.

Shot three survives today in some prints in a green tint, reminding us that films were generally tinted in the silent days; in addition some prints show some remarkable hand coloring of the explosion of a strongbox. The robbers, having entered a car of the train, kill a loyal railroad employee who had locked the strongbox and thrown away the key before he shot it out with the robbers. A stick of dynamite is used to open the box; for about two seconds a beautiful puff of orange-red smoke rises against the pale green tint, the contrast being so remarkably sharp that we are surprisingly given a new awareness of the nature of an explosion.

Shot four shows two robbers climbing over the tender, one holding up the engineer and the other engaged in a fight with the fireman. This shot evokes laughter from modern audiences because a dummy is substituted for the fireman (through stop motion) and tossed overboard. So obvious and distracting is the substitution to modern viewers that it sometimes hinders an appreciation of the interesting camera angle: the camera on top of the third car follows the action while the train moves along at a good speed. It is one of the first exciting tracking shots to make use of natural surroundings.

Segments five through eight show the robbery. In the sixth shot, with the passengers lined up outside the train, one man decides to make a dash for it and is gunned down. This shot is evidence of a general filming problem (which Griffith would solve within a few years). Prior to his attempt to escape, the camera fails to single out from the crowd the man who dies; even on a second viewing, audiences can hardly make out the beginning of his movement (fig. 14). Nowadays, he would be distinguished by a separate shot. In shot eight, the camera makes a significant pan and tilt to follow the fleeing robbers down an embankment. Shot nine is, to quote the Edison Catalogue of 1904, "a beautiful scene in a valley" in which the camera

**14** *The Great Train Robbery* (Shot #6)

continues to move as the robbers take to their horses—with much less grace than in the modern-day western.

Segment ten is, to the historian, the most notable achievement of the film. We return to the telegraph office and see the operator, bound and gagged, struggling with his ropes. This must have occurred within seconds of the end of shot two; in other words, it seems to have occurred at about the time that shots two through nine took place. Whatever the case, it must be happening no later than the time of shot nine and is thus the first known instance of the portrayal of simultaneous time in the cinema.

Segment eleven is definitely simultaneous with segment ten. Here Porter has completely abandoned mere chronological time. In this hand-colored sequence of the dancehall, a dude (an easterner) showing off some dance steps is ridiculed by his more sophisticated western observers, who start firing pistols at him to frighten him. Then the telegraph operator bursts in through the door—another filming mistake, for we can hardly notice his entrance amidst the dancers—and a posse is formed. (Some viewers are so baffled by this sequence, probably because they miss the entrance of the operator, that they think that the dancehall crowd includes the robbers.)

Segments twelve and thirteen, both long shots, concern the chase and the gunning down of all the robbers (fig. 15). Many of the gunshots are painted to give the same effect as the exploding strongbox in shot three.

**15** *The Great Train Robbery* (Shot #13)

In these sequences Porter's excellent sense of camera placement is evident; it really allows us an emotionally powerful vantage point, the robbers and the posse riding from the background to the foreground, firing their guns in the general direction of the camera. Of course in modern filming the action would be broken up into many shots instead of one long shot for the chase and one for the closing in on the robbers.

One innovation in *The Great Train Robbery* was the technique of crosscutting, a technique suitable to the form of the cinema but unnatural to the form of nineteenth-century stage drama, which was at that time a significant influence on the new medium. When the bandits escape with the loot from the train, the camera leaves them fleeing into the wilderness (of New Jersey!) and returns to the telegraph operator whom they had bound and gagged (fig. 16). Without using any insert titles (and none were needed even though this technique had never been seen before), Porter informed the audience that two events were happening simultaneously. This is the first visual "Meanwhile . . ." we know of in the cinema. The following shot of the dancehall is another simultaneous action, and so there are three distinct actions occurring at one time; by means of crosscutting, Porter was able to convey the idea of simultaneity, as opposed to the concept of progression in time, much more usual in narrative dramatic art. Within a few years, Griffith realized the significance of this procedure and used it in his own work. But until Porter produced *The Great Train Robbery* for the Edison

Company, the cinema had no real mode of expression to distinguish it as a legitimate art form capable of presenting an experience in unique terms.

Later improvements in film technique based on the principle of editing extended beyond Porter's practice. Against the inclination of their conservative studio chiefs, directors began to use medium and close shots as well as long shots. When an actor fired point blank at the audience, ending *The Great Train Robbery*, it caused a sensation that could not have been achieved if filmed as a long shot. Thus, it was not primarily the content of the shot but the way it was filmed that accounted for its shock value. Nevertheless, the potential effectiveness of close filming was not appreciated until nearly a decade later.

Concerning the weaknesses of the film, Lewis Jacobs writes:

> The limitations of *The Great Train Robbery* were those of youth. The action of every scene was told in one long shot instead of a number of shots. Every shot, moreover, was a long shot, its action being confined to the proscenium-limited stage area. With the exception of the scenes in which the passengers are lined up outside the train, the robbery of the mail car, the hold-up of the engineer, and the battle between the posse and the bandits, the action was played in profile before the camera. Foreground and middle ground were equally ignored, the background alone serving as the acting area. The camera never moved from eye level. Tension and excitement were achieved by a quickening of the players' movements rather than by variation of the lengths of the shots. Within the simple framework, however, the kinetic possibilities of the new technique were convincingly demonstrated.*

Porter regarded the single shot as the equivalent of a building block. By placing a number of these blocks together he structured the edifice of the film. Although Porter was perhaps the first filmmaker to conceive a film idea in this way, the attitude is still primitive in comparison to Griffith's development of the film idea. Porter was limited to a degree by his sense of linkage: he conceived each section of the narrative in terms of a complete activity photographed in one shot and attached to the previous shot. Thus, Porter standardized for the cinema the essentially chronological method of fictional and dramatic narrative; the method is still standard. But Porter went beyond this basic linkage to invent simultaneous, or parallel, action in *The Great Train Robbery*.

The importance of parallel action has been rather exaggerated by historians of the cinema. Griffith and Mack Sennett were to make great use of it, but the device is not essential to film narrative. To show a train robbery in progress in one shot and a few shots later to suggest that during the rob-

---

* Jacobs, *op. cit.*, p. 46.

**16** *The Great Train Robbery* (Shots #9 and #10)

bery the stationmaster has been attempting to extricate himself from the ropes tied around him seems hardly astounding now. Parallel action in two entirely separate locations shown sequentially but intended to be understood as simultaneous is an interesting achievement for the primitive screen, and while the technique of crosscutting is exclusively cinematic, the result is not. The novel can achieve similar effects, which indicates that Porter's contribution in this line owed more to the general nature of narrative than to the particular nature of film.

But simultaneous action does have other important implications. It tended to show that real time and film time need not coincide. Film narrative really began to develop after the appearance of *The Great Train Robbery,* for Porter freed the camera from the restraints of real time and thereby opened the way for artistic development in the medium. Perhaps equally important, the use of parallel action dissociated locations from a spatial continuum. The first nine shots of the film portrayed areas adjacent or close to one another; the camera progressing from place to place clearly traversed consecutive points in the landscape of the robbery. But when in the tenth shot Porter cut back to the stationmaster, his camera skipped all the intermediate points touched in the previous shots and arrived again at the film's initial location. The camera simply went to a new place, or so it seemed to the audience, and the audience immediately grasped the spatial leap, as intuitively as it must have grasped the shift backwards in time.

The two principles upon which Porter worked out the basis of film editing were the selectivity of time and the selectivity of space. By interrupting the time continuum and by moving his camera from one location to another without showing the characters in the process of going from place to place, Porter created the possibility of distinctively cinematic narrative in which the visualized portions of an event perceived one after another could clearly represent an entire story, though in fact a great deal of the total action was not shown on screen. Yet Porter did not actually turn that possibility into a consistently employed aspect of style. His interests led him to try several kinds of subjects, and he made films of social protest (*The Ex-Convict,* 1904), realistic documentation (*The Life of an American Policeman,* 1905), satire (*European Rest Cure,* 1905), and magical fantasy (*The Dream of a Rarebit Fiend,* 1906). Throughout his career he remained committed to the standard narrative structure consisting of progressive stages of more or less continuous action. It cannot truly be said that he gave the film a unique form, for his narrative related a simple story in a straightforward way; other filmmakers would be doing the same thing for years to come, and some had already done it before Porter. Yet no one before had gone beyond merely thinking about the possibilities of camera technique to the achievement of a truly cinematic concept. Porter directed the focus of the cinema away from making film versions of literary ideas and brought it to the point of a film idea.

# 7

# D. W. Griffith and the Development of the Narrative Film Idea

## The Historic and Esthetic Contributions

The greatest contribution to the development of film narrative was made by David Wark Griffith, a man whose unquestioned historical importance has for a long time obscured the fact that he was the first great artist working in the film medium. A great artist is one who produces great art; he is not necessarily historically important, if by historical importance we mean having "influence." However, Griffith's influence was no less than the standardizing of all future filmmakers' approaches to their art. Therefore, most of the analyses of Griffith tend to emphasize, naturally enough, a historical perspective when dealing with his contributions. Yet the truly remarkable aspect of the man's career is that his works are in themselves great films.

Strangely enough, Griffith is today an underrated artist. Critics accept implicitly the attitude that his major innovations have become standard practice, and therefore when one sees his films they do not seem particularly impressive. Although the conclusion is either false or obtuse, the premise of such reasoning is true: a man can contribute significantly to an art form with a limited talent. Edwin Porter is also historically important, but his films do not hold a perpetual claim to our interest purely on their merit. With Griffith, the reverse is true; if he had not been an innovator, he would probably be rated more highly today for his artistic merit.

By himself, Griffith practically invented the film idea, in that he devised the method for making a concept both visual and dramatic. When he first began to make films, he proceeded like Porter and the other contemporary filmmakers to think in terms of transforming a literary story into a visually interesting film. But working constantly with the typical narrative procedures of his contemporaries and producing an incredible number of films, he gradually began to think in terms of stories conceptually and fundamentally cinematic. Although he never abandoned the literary story, he always reduced it to its basic narrative material and then reconstructed it into an entirely cinematic experience.

Griffith's major cinematic advance was the development of the sequence. Before him, others had divided their films into what we call sequences, but with both Porter and Méliès, the sequence consisted essentially of a single shot, and each shot functioned as another step in the development of the narrative. Griffith designed his films, even the one-reel films, in terms of several sequences, of which each usually had several shots. The meaning of a film became the total meaning of the sequences. No longer was the sequence used only to get the action from one step to another. In Griffith's hands the sequence became the basic unit of film meaning.

Griffith thus invented the modern idea of editing. To someone like Porter, editing meant choosing the best shot to keep the story moving swiftly and coherently. To Griffith, the sequence itself functioned as a visual concept. Shots within the sequence were not chosen mainly for the purpose of making the next shot clear; instead each shot was chosen for what it would contribute to the whole of the sequence. Griffith's style of editing was practically the last word in the visual development of film narrative. In the next decade or two the great editing directors such as Vsevolod Pudovkin and Sergei Eisenstein devised theories but did not significantly change the implicit theories of Griffith (who left no formalized analysis of his methods).

Griffith perfected a number of other technical and stylistic methods that have tremendous historical importance, even when earlier examples can be found of the same methods. For instance, he seems to be the first to use close-ups effectively, though they had been in use for a decade. The photography of his films—often under the technical control of Billy Bitzer, the first truly great cameraman in the industry—was remarkable; the pictorial quality of many of Griffith's images has never been surpassed. He also seems to have been largely responsible for introducing realism into the films: his actors and actresses eventually abandon the theatrical mannerisms so annoying in the work of his contemporaries. In addition, his pictorial realism, readily duplicated today, is evident in the use of sets and props that look authentic; painted backdrops largely disappear in his work. These important contributions shaped film style for every subsequent director; yet they might very well have become the norm for filming even

without Griffith. What might never have come about without an instinctive cinematic genius, however, is the development of the film idea.

To perceive that film idea, we sometimes have to plow our way through a morass of minor surface obstacles. Griffith larded over his cinematic sense with second-rate literary ideas. We know something about his frustrated ambitions to be a writer, and we can tell from his scenarios why he could never have been particularly successful as an author (further evidence can be found in his insert titles). Still, he picked up a good deal of the narrative sense, as Eisenstein pointed out, by his affinity with Dickens. One of Griffith's literary strains can be seen in his use of melodrama. His narrative concepts usually involved a moment of physical jeopardy leading to a frantic chase, the melodramatic aspects of which he heightened by various technical means; and, to extend the cinematic thrill, Griffith developed a penchant for using last-minute rescues.

Melodrama has a greater justification in cinema than in other narrative arts, for the melodramatic incident naturally emphasizes surface action more than the motives that provoke it, and film normally relies on surfaces more than other narrative media. Nevertheless, we have learned from our literary and dramatic experience that pure melodrama is not the highest form of art. As he developed, Griffith handled melodrama with more and more refinement. The hectic pace of a film became relevant to the inner life of the main characters. Griffith's achievement, certainly, should be measured on the basis of his successes, not on his early experiments or occasional failures. When he finally learned his craft—in the remarkably short space of a year or two—his films became notable for the way in which surface action, the motion of a film, paralleled theme and characterization.

## Griffith's Early Period: *The Lonely Villa*

Griffith practiced his craft within the rigid framework of the short film until the standard one-reel length became too confining for his ambitious ideas. Yet we can now feel grateful that he was forced to start with the short film; it gave him the opportunity to produce more films and develop more film ideas than any young director could do nowadays. He may have made as many as 141 films in 1909 alone (the equivalent of about twenty full-length films)!

Many critics categorize the beginning years of Griffith's career, from his first film, *The Adventures of Dolly,* in 1908, to his last Biograph film, made in 1913, *Judith of Bethulia* (released in 1914), as the period of apprenticeship. The category neatly divides the short films from the long ones and marks the division with his first film of any substantial length, the four-reel *Judith of Bethulia.* Actually, Griffith served his technical apprenticeship in the first two or three years with Biograph. Many of the extant films of

1911 to 1913 are the work of a master filmmaker. This is not to suggest that any short film of, say, 1912, rivals the full-length films of later years such as *Broken Blossoms* or *Way Down East*. That the long film served Griffith better than the short one should not lead us to ignore the amazing achievement of his one-reel films. Griffith so perfected serious narrative drama within the one-reel film that by 1913 he left virtually nothing more to be said in that form. (The comic one-reeler, however, had yet to be developed, and when it was it had a longer life and is still potentially viable today.)

He had in fact liberated the narrative form from the restrictions that Porter, himself an earlier liberator, had imposed by perfecting a narrative method that was not completely cinematic. An interesting connection between the first and second important names in American cinema occurs in *Rescued from an Eagle's Nest*, which was directed by Porter in 1908 and marked the film acting debut of Lawrence Griffith. (Apparently ashamed of any association with movies, Griffith hid his real name for several years.) The film relates the rescue of a baby by the father (Griffith), after he learns that an eagle has snatched the child. The highlight of the film is the animation a la Méliès of the eagle making off with the baby in its cradle. In Porter's usual style, the father is notified of the event, perhaps while the bird is flying off with the child, and with a good deal of action he saves the child after what appears to be a furious fight with the eagle, some of it outside the frame. The kind of melodramatic action Porter popularized was quite in keeping with Griffith's own sensibilities, and Griffith was undoubtedly encouraged by Porter's examples to continue in this vein when he began directing in the following year.

Griffith's earliest known film of real interest is *The Lonely Villa* (1909). The film has historical importance since it may be the first extant example of Griffith's prolonged crosscutting climax, sometimes known as the last-minute rescue. It thus reveals narrative interest, truly cinematic manipulation of visual excitement, and a much more sophisticated handling of parallel action than was ever shown by Porter, who popularized the technique. Although made within his first year as a director, *The Lonely Villa* plainly bears the mark of a developing craftsman with considerable experience and demonstrates that Griffith had already made some key improvements over the films of his contemporaries, for example, Siegmund "Pop" Lubin and Wallace "Old Man" McCutcheon. First of all, his camera is generally somewhat closer to the action (taking what we would call full shots), allowing us to see characters' faces more clearly than was then customary. Also, his scenery is much more convincing than Porter's flimsily constructed sets (even a film as late as *Rescued from an Eagle's Nest* uses blatantly unreal scenery). The few instances of cutting within a sequence tell us that film has come a long way in a very few years.

For all its improvements, *The Lonely Villa* interests us more as a

primitive film than as a work of quality. It is not a completely realized narrative idea, for only the action is plausible; the characterization is almost nonexistent, and therefore the single element of cinematic interest—the desperate predicament of a helpless woman and her three children faced with an intrusion of criminals in her isolated villa—is simply a situation occurring in a general way. It is not individualized but abstracted; the entire film revolves around a race against time, and for the ending Griffith needs only to present the situation and then cut back and forth between the trapped family and the rescuers. Griffith had figured out that shorter and shorter durations for particular shots would, in a chase sequence, result in increased tension. The ending has its dramatic effect, or rather melodramatic effect, as the husband and police arrive just as the criminals have knocked down the last barricade and seized the family.

Although Griffith was working now with materials that could not be effectively duplicated on stage, *The Lonely Villa* is really not totally cinematic. Griffith's understanding of spatial relationships is still limited; to get a person from one point to another, Griffith shows him moving there in stages. For example, a hallway separates the front door from an inner room in which the family sits and later secures itself from the burglars. To gain entry the thieves must knock down first the front door and then the inner door to this room. Hardly any significant use can be made of that hallway, though Griffith needs some spatial area between the front door and the inner room to prolong the suspense. Still, the hallway works adversely for most of the film because Griffith feels he has to move his characters from the door to the room and from the room to the door. The one time he omits the hallway is when the rescuers arrive. No needless extension of motion in this case is permitted. We had previously seen the rescuers rushing along in their horse-drawn wagon; now they appear in the very room with the criminals and the family. Finally Griffith seems to have realized that even the dullest viewer would instinctively know that the rescuers arrived by passing through that hallway.

The acting in *The Lonely Villa* is typical for the day, characterized by exaggerated gestures and a constant implication that the audience is sitting just where the camera is. Iris Barry says that this was the first film in which Griffith was allowed to reshoot scenes that were unsatisfactory to him.* If so, he did not seem to pay much attention to the acting here. In the middle of the film, the husband calls his wife on the telephone, and they engage in a long conversation (fig. 17) that seems almost a parody of the later Keystone comedy scenes, for the burglars are at that moment breaking down the door. The husband goes outside the building he has called from, remembers that he left a revolver in the villa, telephones his wife again,

---

* Iris Barry, *D. W. Griffith: American Film Master* (New York, Museum of Modern Art, 1965), p. 14.

**17**  *The Lonely Villa*

and talks at some length until—to the audience's relief—a burglar cuts the wires. The miming of the conversation, grotesque considering the imminent danger, indicates a mistake in editing, from our point of view; it takes too long to start the rescue.

*The Lonely Villa* then is apprentice Griffith. Its idea is limited in conception to achieving an emotional reaction on the part of a spectator; all the creative energy goes into the method of attaining the desired excitement. But Griffith learned quickly that a meaningful narrative must be embedded in a total film idea. Otherwise, when the surface movement *is* the whole film idea, the camera functions simply as a recording device, and most of its expressive possibilities are relegated to either unimportance or mere technique.

## Developing the Cinematic Sequence: *The Battle*

Without ever really abandoning his melodramatic tastes, Griffith began to formulate ideas in which the action is conceptually presented rather than recorded. That is, he learned how to suggest the narrative of a story with-

out actually *showing* it step by step, in the fashion of Porter and the other primitive filmmakers. Griffith did this first, apparently, by simply cutting within the sequence, a technique that was thought at the time to be both economically unfeasible and esthetically disorienting. Nowadays, scholars and critics are unmercifully scornful of the early company executives who demanded the single-shot "stage view" for each sequence, but it is only fair to remember that a real esthetic principle was involved: the belief that a shot establishes a frame of reference that allows the actors to interpret their roles within a carefully delimited area. The principle threw inordinate emphasis on the performer's ability to suggest meaning through gesture and motion, but it was at that time sincerely believed to be a sensible way of achieving art.

Griffith's early experiences with a few close-ups and a few sequences with more than a single shot convinced him that he could convey meaning more emphatically than anyone who relied on a one-shot sequence. The relatively little intercutting in *The Lonely Villa* prior to the concluding sequence was typical of the use Griffith conceived for the edited sequence: it was, evidently, just a device for increasing suspense. In other words, the practice of cutting within a sequence (as distinct from crosscutting—the switching from one location to another) seems to have developed merely as a way of emphasizing certain aspects of a film; in the case of *The Lonely Villa* that aspect was suspense.

*The Battle,* made in 1911, exemplifies Griffith's successful treatment of cinematic ideas. Griffith conceived of this film, presumably, in terms of the activity of warfare, as the title suggests, but he also managed to structure the battle scenes within the design of a significant dramatic action. The story seems to have Crane's novel *The Red Badge of Courage* as its source, with some major variations. It concerns a young man who loses his nerve in a Civil War battle and flees to his girlfriend's house, where he is not welcomed by her. Returning to the battle, his desertion unnoticed, he receives an assignment to bring ammunition to the troops. Accomplishing heroically his perilous journey with the powder wagon and saving the day for his side, he justly redeems himself in his girlfriend's eyes.

*The Battle* differs from the primitive cinema of the period, including Griffith's own early works such as *The Lonely Villa,* in that the action exists not just as the essence of the film but also as a suggestion of an intellectual framework, an idea that is not exactly the same as the literal portrayal of the plot. To portray the *idea* of battle, or the *idea* of the way in which war affects a soldier, Griffith chose certain precise images. Each major image consists of separate shots which, when put into an orderly sequence, take on a meaning that the individual shots do not have by themselves. The amassing of visual images leads to the presentation of the theme; however, the theme is not easily paraphrased, but stands as the total impression left by the images.

The first battle images occur in a sequence in which three stationary long shots establish the environment of warfare. These shots, taken from the usual advantageous viewpoint so typical of Griffith (as it was to a slightly lesser extent of Porter), convey the information of two armies firing at one another. The swiftness and effectiveness of Griffith's method can be readily understood by comparison with the more common method used in hundreds of battle films that followed up to the present day. The ordinary filmmaker's mind works more directly with the *subject* to be recorded rather than, as Griffith's did, with the *idea* to be communicated. In the former method we frequently see what the camera has recorded from, say, a hill or an airplane, as it pans the field to photograph the opposing sides. Both sides in the conflict are thus seen at a glance, and their proximity denoted exactly, as they are often revealed within the same frame. The limitations of such literalness in filming can be felt in its lack of both suggestiveness and emphasis; with everything presented on a grand scale, the environment containing the battle has no special point of emphasis except numerous individual confrontations observed remotely as mere spectacle. The recording of a large area with many performers engaged in warfare requires the camera to spend considerable time traversing the landscape, which naturally cannot be filled at every moment with objects or events of equal interest. Thus, the literal depiction of conflict is often surprisingly dull. In contrast, Griffith shows us three distinct shots of the two armies separately firing at the enemy from behind their lines. His camera remains close to the action, but no attempt is made to show us the entire field of battle. Griffith builds up to the *idea* of battle by the juxtaposition of *separate elements* of a conflict.

For Griffith, a film is composed of selected shots of his own total visual impression of the world he wishes to create. Working primarily in the realistic tradition, Griffith, like all major directors to follow, was tremendously concerned with detail. Yet he seldom records on film every detail that may be relevant. Much is omitted; what remains will readily suffice to represent the whole—it will even suggest many details that constitute the unfilmed parts—when arranged in the final sequence. All of the visual area is not seen at a glance, as in a typical modern-day panning shot, but constructed carefully in short segments so as to plan the total impression in the viewer's mind. Perhaps the truth is that the total impression is never presented on screen; it may exist in its fullest form only in the viewer's imagination. In any case, Griffith's way is a more demanding approach to filmmaking than is usually found today. In fact, this particularly "classical" approach to film art—the constructionist approach—reached its peak with Eisenstein in the 1920's and has more or less declined in popularity among filmmakers ever since.

## The Relationship of Technique to Idea: *Man's Genesis*

The long shot is actually more important in Griffith's short films than the close shot, which is much less common because Griffith always reserved it for particularly important times (although today the frequent use of the close-up is often a matter of course). Moreover, it must be accounted one of Griffith's major contributions to technique that he developed the purposeful long shot. Although long shots were standard when he began to film, Griffith soon made the full shot more useful for portraying the basic relationship of character to environment, particularly indoors. (Compare, *e.g.,* Porter's interior to Griffith's in figures 16 and 17.) Thus, once it was no longer the normative shot, the extreme long shot became a choice deliberately made by the director. (At about the same time, Griffith made the close-up a significant part of filming; thus, every shot became a matter of choice. It is, in fact, the use of close shots that makes long shots effective.) In other words, Griffith made the long shot a device for interpretation, not merely, as it had been, a standard technique of recording action.

*Man's Genesis* (1912) uses the long shot for purposes entirely different from those of *The Battle* because here Griffith's emphasis is on theme. This rather remarkable film dramatizes man's discovery that brains can defeat brawn. So abstract an idea can be shaped into a narrative only by inventing a specific story, which Griffith does in line with his understanding of Darwinian theory. The plot tells of Weakhands, a physically weak caveman whose woman is stolen away by Bruteforce, a bully. Angered but impotent, Weakhands mopes about his cave and comes up with an invention: the stone club (shown in the film's only close-up). With this weapon Weakhands engages stupid Bruteforce in combat and beats him, then flourishes his club overhead to frighten away other would-be attackers. In the end, Weakhands has clearly emerged as the man to be reckoned with in physical combat within his circle. The whole of the story is contained within a modern framework: in an opening shot an old man admonishes a boy about the use of force, telling him the story related above. The first shot fades into the main story of Weakhands and Bruteforce, and at the very end we return to the old man and the boy, who throws away his stick and renounces force (though the fable he has just heard ought to have convinced him that force is quite suitable, particularly if it is gained by the use of a weapon).

The long shot has probably never been better or more consistently used to communicate an abstract concept: the survival of the fittest—the fittest being the man with more brains than his neighbor. The film has three key roles, with only a handful of very minor characters to suggest the community of cavemen. The scenery is primarily barren and filled with craggy rocks seen from a considerable distance. All the actors stand in a manner that suggests a standing ape, but Weakhands is more stooped than

anyone else. Bruteforce moves through his environment with much greater confidence than Weakhands, for he is the master of this rough terrain, whereas Weakhands is dominated by it.

By using the long shot, Griffith achieves multiple cinematic values, all relevant to the abstract idea he is developing. First, he establishes the environment, giving us a sense of the reality of the place. The nature of this primitive world is thoroughly explained by the setting. Secondly, the long shot serves to bring within a single area the forces of conflict (but recall that Griffith determined to avoid this particular use of the long shot in *The Battle*). We see from a distance the actual pursuit and fight of the two men.

Finally, the long shot serves to define character in terms of the background environment. That environment, consisting exclusively of caves and rocks, looms there entirely physical and uncomfortable. Weakhands moves about in fear of attack from other men; he cannot function for long in this area. Thus, the theme is brought into focus early, dramatized in the form of Weakhands' struggle to continue his existence with some shred of dignity after his woman is taken from him. Necessity forces Weakhands to become a thinking man, a military strategist. The visual quality of the long shot conveys this idea to us immediately: constantly demeaned in an alien world, Weakhands cowers timidly before the impregnable stone surfaces rising in challenge to him. Undoubtedly these rocks will outlast the human figures that walk on them; if man is not to fall victim to his natural sur-

**18**  *Man's Genesis*

roundings, he must make this inert material serve him. The climax is Weakhands' discovery that by putting together a wooden club and a stone he can overcome Bruteforce (who has already been portrayed in his physical size and manner as akin to the stone environment, the personification of natural forces). The conquest of Bruteforce is followed by a brief moment when Weakhands reclaims his woman (fig. 18). He stands next to her in long shot, outlined against the environment, perfectly at ease and completely upright, no longer challenged by the stony peaks.

## Characterization Through Technique:
## *The Musketeers of Pig Alley*

Griffith's mastery of the short film is evident in such diverse works as *The Lonedale Operator, The New York Hat,* and *Enoch Arden* (a rare two-reeler). But even if he had done nothing else prior to 1912, *The Musketeers of Pig Alley* would have made him the best of all filmmakers up to that time.

The story line of this film is rather involved for a short work. The setting, the New York East Side, is really any urban ghetto. The Little Lady (Lillian Gish) and her husband, a musician, live there in a tenement with her mother.* While the musician is away earning money, a local gangster (musketeer) named Snapper Kid becomes attracted to the woman, but she refuses his advances and slaps his face. The gangster, a James Cagney type (played superbly by Elmer Booth), appreciates the independence of the Little Lady and does not resent her anger. Later, the somewhat stupid musician returns with a good deal of money, but he carelessly talks about it in the street and is overheard by the gangster, who attacks him in the hall-way of his tenement and takes his wallet. The musician goes out determined to recover his stolen money. Later, the mother dies; a good deal of time passes, but the action is so rapid that we have the feeling that everything occurs in the same day. In any case, a girlfriend of dubious virtue tries to entertain the Little Lady by taking her to a dancehall where the neighbor-hood gangsters hang out. Here she encounters a gang leader who attempts to slip a drug into her drink, but the other gangster, Snapper Kid, prevents her from drinking it, whereupon she gives both men the brush-off. The two gangsters confront one another and determine to settle the matter outside.

A large part of the film is then devoted to the preparations for the gang

* The Little Lady and the musician might be sister and brother or they might be engaged. Griffith is not clear on what ordinarily would have been a significant point: Robert Henderson, *op. cit.,* says Miss Gish plays the wife; Miss Gish has said she plays the sister. Some minor matters are clearer with one sort of relationship understood, other matters clearer with another alternative. However, the main elements are not affected by this confusion.

war, which is finally staged in an alley and interrupted by the police after much shooting. In the midst of the battle, the silly musician, more concerned to retrieve his money than to guard his life, sees Snapper Kid and grabs back his money while Snapper Kid flees from the police. At the end of the film, Snapper Kid takes refuge in the apartment of the musician and the Little Lady and unhappily learns of their relationship. After a wonderfully comic double-take to show his surprise at her connection with a character like that, he gallantly withdraws and is immediately arrested by a police-man. However, as the insert title says, one good turn deserves another: the musician and the Little Lady save Snapper Kid by supplying him with an alibi in return for his saving the Little Lady from the snares of the other gangster.

All this in fifteen minutes! Yet Griffith does not seem rushed. Every shot helps to create a visual impression about the nature of the various characters; nothing is wasted, nothing excessive. Even the costuming is revealing: every character wears a different kind of hat, except for the Little Lady, who wears a shawl. Snapper Kid's jaunty hat shows the characterization he has created for himself, the role he has determined to play as leader of his gang. His rival's straw hat is an attempt at sophistication, at playing the ladies' man. The slouched hat of the musician relates to his carelessness and essentially foolish nature. The broad-brimmed hat of the Little Lady's friend makes us suspicious of her moral character. These are, of course, merely surface clues, but they provide visual information quickly and are consistent with other evidence.

Snapper Kid is one of the first thoroughly sympathetic bad guys, en-tirely engaging in spite of his obvious criminal activity. Above all, he con-stantly acts tougher than he is underneath, and he has a sense of humor about his role-playing. A revealing shot shows him with his gang preparing for the gun battle. Suddenly a laundryman walks by and brushes up against him; he jumps wildly, thinking he has been attacked by his rival, but in-stantly he sees the source of his confusion and laughs at his own nervous-ness. Elsewhere, this nervousness is portrayed subtly in the mere gesture of his opening a bar door and glancing behind it. Were he to act timid about entering a supposedly safe place, he could lose the respect of his gang; yet he is aware that carelessness could cost him his life, and so he slyly manages to look behind a door without letting his gang see what he has done. Sim-ilarly, although he must lead his men through the alleys to the rendezvous with the rival gang, he is really too intelligent to be absolutely brave. In one beautifully filmed shot, a gate to an alley is opened by a hand extending horizontally across the frame; when no guns are fired, Snapper Kid "cas-ually" emerges. He is always attentive to his entrances. At the gangsters' dance, he enters a room only after we see a puff of cigarette smoke coming through the curtained doorway. His appearance is then properly underlined by his sophisticated toughness, calculated for its effect on his rival.

Griffith's use of significant realistic detail is especially impressive. For instance, early in the film, as the musician leaves his apartment to find work, we see a woman leading her daughter off screen. These two appear for a second and are gone forever; they could never appear in a play—not only because of the prohibitive cost of paying two actresses for one second's work every night, but mainly the art of stage writing requires a narrowing of dramatic focus, a cutting away of irrelevancies to the major dramatic action. A naturalistic film, in contrast, uses such a shot (here, a fraction of a shot) as one of the details needed to build up an environment. On stage, realistic details of setting and costuming are revealed in their entirety at a glance. In film, realism of setting and costuming is achieved gradually, by progressive revelation of details, shot by shot.

The more interesting kind of detail in *The Musketeers of Pig Alley* is found in the exterior shots of streets and alleys. The ghetto is teeming with life. In one shot we see several people pushing their way through the crowd from right to left. Then, rather quickly, the Little Lady manages her way through, moving by herself in the opposite direction (fig. 19). By establishing the movement within the frame in one direction, and then reversing it for a solitary figure, Griffith makes the woman seem almost heroic, cer-

**19**  *The Musketeers of Pig Alley*

tainly singular. Dressed in worn clothes, she maintains a tremendous dignity in a complex image of fortitude and courage. The background environment is not simply passive but almost antagonistic, in the sense that it isolates her. The shot seems extraneous to the narrative until we place it in the context of the next sequence, in which the woman discovers that the mother has died while she was out, and she weeps. Without the short, one-shot sequence of her moving through the street to serve as a bridge, the images we would retain of her personality would jar; conflicting images of hardness (slapping Snapper Kid) would be juxtaposed against her softer traits. She is more than just a poor suffering woman, and Griffith shows us her total personality by a series of situations which place her in relationship to the background.

Griffith somewhat prolongs the activities leading to the gang fight, creating narrative tension. The movement of the two gangs is handled by crosscutting, as we would expect; their movements are almost symmetrically parallel. The action in the alley is fraught with danger for both sides, but Griffith forces us to see it mainly from Snapper Kid's point of view because he is the most sensitive of the gangsters. The camera gets considerably closer to him as the film progresses. As he moves toward the showdown, we see him in a medium shot close against a wall; we watch as he turns a corner, knowing as he does that at any moment he may be shot down. His cronies follow in single file. In an artful close-up, his head fills the right-hand portion of the frame; the left-hand portion is just a brick wall. In this moment of extreme tension, the environment has defined him in terms of his essentials: a lonely figure in a desperate situation, frightened, yet forced to risk his life to retain his honor among his followers. And above all, the bricks indicate sheer blankness, the emptiness behind the impending confrontation.

Stylistically, the film's depiction of motion seems dominated by actors moving toward the camera and then past it. Such shots had appeared earlier (even in *The Great Train Robbery*), but prior to Griffith (who introduced the technique as early as 1909), close-ups of moving subjects were not dramatically integrated into the film idea. That is, in the shot referred to above, Snapper Kid moves into close-up from a medium shot; the members of his gang then follow one by one in the same manner. We have never before witnessed so intimately as this a group of men caught in a moment of absolute concentration on a single activity. Here and elsewhere in the film, the actors continue to move up to and past the camera. The effect, rarely seen again until recent times, is to separate a man from his environment for a moment and then to relate him again to the flow of activity as he moves on. In the reverse process, which is only slightly less effective, a gangster near the camera moves into a full shot. In either case, the effective use of depth in crowded or confined environments produces a greater sense of realistic dimension than we had seen before in films.

Nowhere else in the extant early Griffith works has movement been used as well to make us appreciate inner character. The film is full of actors in motion, and the individual movements reveal individual traits. The frantic rushing of the musician externalizes the chaotic or haphazard mind of an impetuous man. The slow, cautious movement of Snapper Kid through the alley tells us that the grin he wore earlier was only a facade for his truly human side, his fear of the consequences of his life style. The Little Lady's standing aloof at the dance while the dancers cavort in rather amusing short, quick steps clarifies her character in terms of theirs: her sense of self-respect, despite her poverty, makes her superior to everyone present.

It is notable that the film style can vary so greatly in two of Griffith's films made only a few months apart, *Man's Genesis* and *The Musketeers of Pig Alley*. In the former, the long shots isolate a character against an un-populated, dehumanized background. In the latter, closer shots are used to depict man against an environment crowded with a number of alienating aspects. Clearly, Griffith was among the first filmmakers to choose a de-liberate method of approach for each film. His style, recognizable from film to film, is yet different in each.

## The Narrative Structure of the Film Idea: *Intolerance*

*Intolerance* (1916) is one of the few indisputable masterpieces of the cinema, and yet in some ways it is not a successful film. Griffith aimed at a mass audience, but he grossly overestimated the film's popular appeal. Its subsequent commercial failure and its fantastic cost, for its day, make it the most notable "flop" of the twentieth century. In addition, there has never been a film as obviously ambitious as *Intolerance*. With elaborate care and new confidence after the commercial success of his first film epic, *The Birth of a Nation* (1915),* Griffith put together an enormously long film (it might have run four hours in its first few showings), invested great sums of money, and staked his artistic reputation on it. No doubt the sheer pre-

* *The Birth of a Nation* had been the first widely acknowledged great work of art in the cinema, but at the same time critics, intellectuals, and a large part of the public were dismayed by the racial bigotry they found in the treatment of stereotypes of black Americans freed from slavery and the glorification of the founding of the Ku Klux Klan. To the embarrassment of the American cinema up to the present day, this film really does rely on racial falsehoods that are not so distant from our contemporary world that we can divorce ourselves from the controversy for the sake of the art. Griffith was amazed at the antagonism that the film aroused, for he did not truly grasp the prejudices built into the film and did not consider the film biased against a minority. In fact, Griffith felt victimized, even martyred, by the controversies and attacks precipitated by the film. *Intolerance* is, in part, Griffith's answer to his critics: he is accusing them of exercising intolerance in regard to him, a preposterous self-justification that, fortunately, does not succeed in obtruding upon this film. That the same man could turn out both films shows a kind of colossal intellectual blindness or insensitivity, and yet both films are landmarks in the cinema.

tentiousness of such a project deterred a large segment of the public. In any case, *Intolerance* remains today, unfortunately, a film for the archives, considered by some only as a responsibility for every serious student of film to sit through once, but not *the* Griffith film for students or scholars to ponder.

Yet *Intolerance* is, after all, not a museum piece but a masterpiece. It may be long and difficult to take in during a single performance, but this is not an ultimate test of art. *Intolerance* runs longer than the endurance of most viewers, yet seen in segments, perhaps over a two-day period, it yields all the rewards one could desire of a great film—from emotional involvement to intellectual awareness. Its one basic flaw is its towering stature: it presents a tremendously wide view of human life, with so many instances of interesting film imagery that it cannot be absorbed until it has been seen several times, and modern life does not ordinarily provide the time for repeated viewing of a film that even in its shortened extant form runs longer than three hours.

Although *Intolerance* is unique even among Griffith's films, it does typify the filmmaker's ambitious manner of conceiving a gigantic film idea that leads to certain generalizations about human nature and human destiny, and the way he carries out that idea in magnificent detail in many parts of the film. At first the ideas behind any of the mammoth Griffith films may seem too amorphous ever to be shaped into a comprehensible cinematic idea. For example, *Intolerance* is structured around the conflict between the forces of intolerance and individuals who represent a love of life; the conflict is depicted in four separate stories, thematically related but far apart in time and plot development. The idea of the conflict is basic enough, yet in what sense can one make a convincing generalization about the history of mankind's conflicts based merely on any four stories? Griffith was continually drawn to great abstractions and believed that the generalizations were meaningful and relevant to ordinary lives. In other words, the manner in which intolerance attempts to thwart man's essentially innocent instincts (love is a reflection of the innocent heart), Griffith feels, is not just an idea but a fact of life, and a fact that man can do something about if he realizes its existence. To some extent, this attitude makes Griffith didactic, but despite the derogatory esthetic connotation of that word, the didactic impulse gives his films a depth of meaning and a seriousness of purpose that generate an internal unity within the most gigantic of projects.

Griffith conveys his ideas with amazing coherence in *Intolerance*. Since the film is composed of four stories, two of which were later released as separate films in an attempt to recoup the financial losses of the great work, critics and audiences sometimes felt that the problem with *Intolerance* was a lack of unity, for the stories could evidently be separated. However, the film idea is in its very essence a vast panorama of episodes that are meaningful because they are typical human experiences, not isolated examples

of bad human behavior. The film demonstrates that what Griffith called intolerance is a condition common to all societies at all times, a human condition related to certain failings of all men, but controllable by means of self-awareness. Griffith's concept spans the ages, from Babylon to Calvary to sixteenth-century France to modern America: the symbolic implications for all mankind cannot be missed.

A good summary of the weaknesses of the film has been made by Iris Barry:

> Audiences find it bewildering, exhausting. There is so much in it; there is too much of it; the pace increases so relentlessly; its intense hail of images—many of them only five frames long—cruelly hammers the sensibility; its climax is near hysteria. . . . The desire to instruct and to reform obtrudes awkwardly at times. . . . The Biblical sequence is weak, though useful dramatically to point up the modern sequence. The French episode seems to get lost, then reappears surprisingly.*

Miss Barry concludes, nevertheless, that in a film of monumental proportions shortcomings are to be expected and that the flaws in *Intolerance,* including some dramatic absurdities, do not lessen the total impact of its greatness.

The title of the film is confusing inasmuch as the stories seem to illustrate a number of ideas, not all of which can be categorized as types of intolerance. Perhaps "repression" or "tyranny" would be more accurate. Essentially, the stories illustrate ways in which the characters, who have some power over other human beings, act from extremely personal or selfish motives; their motivations have at least something to do with intolerant attitudes. The simplicity of the unifying concept works out in extremely complex terms within each story, as Griffith is always much better at developing his themes cinematically than at theorizing. The turns of the plot are so involved that audiences cannot possibly remember all the details, even as the film is in progress. In the modern story, the action begins with a group of "Uplifters," puritanical women who fervently wish to control social conduct so as to elevate the moral life of the lower classes. Griffith repeatedly scorns these women through pointed insert titles that seem excessive for so innocuous a group. (The trouble with Griffith's titles is that the author has seen the film, knows what is coming, and incorporates his ultimate evaluations into descriptions that are not borne out by the immediate images. Indeed, later on these women cause great trouble. To appreciate a Griffith film—if one is sensitive about his passages of purple prose that miss the mark—one must distinguish between what is presented in visual terms and what Griffith believes he has presented; they are not al-

* Barry, *op. cit.,* p. 26.

ways the same.) In any case, these silly women succeed in doing only one significant thing: they enlist the aid of a wealthy old maid, Mary T. Jenkins, in their cause—only after she realizes that her youth has passed her by. Griffith's point is that the innocent pleasure of the young is subject to repression by the old, who are frustrated by their inability to share this youthful joy. The psychology is only partially convincing, but it serves to start the plot.

Griffith's development of this story and of the others might seem unnecessarily complicated, but his concept apparently proceeds from the premise that any instance of intolerance (or repression) is likely to begin a chain reaction. In this situation, Mary T. Jenkins' avid espousal of the Uplifters' cause, which seems to be only securing legislation against public dancing and perhaps liquor, leads her to require more and more money from her "dividends" from her brother's company. Pressured by his sister, and puritanical too, Jenkins comes up with a startling idea for siphoning more money into the hands of his sister: he orders a ten-percent cut in the wages of his employees. Even in 1916 this was an outrageous labor practice. As a result, the men call a strike, the owner calls in a militia, some workers are killed, strike-breakers are hired, and the former workers are forced to look elsewhere for work.

All these events take place in a relatively short period of film time; meanwhile other things are happening. For instance, the main characters in the plot, a young worker (Robert Harron) and the daughter (Mae Marsh) of an old worker have left the town to find work in another city. Their lives are used as examples of the problems caused by Jenkins' sister's original decision to pursue her relationship with the suppressive Uplifters' movement. Harron, unable to find work in the city, resorts to a life of petty crime. Mae Marsh and her father, who had led an idyllic existence prior to the strike, have to leave their little house for unpleasant work in the city, where her father soon dies, abandoning his daughter to the evil environment.

This elaborate plot summary includes less than half the actual plot of just the modern story in *Intolerance*. All four stories are complicated, though the situation of Jesus in Judea is easily followed because its outline is familiar (though if one did not know the story he might get lost in the details here too). Nevertheless, despite our difficulty with the details, Griffith was fully conscious of the structural techniques needed to make the broad outlines of his materials intelligible. His preconceived design can be seen in his remark that the "stories will begin like four currents looked at from a hilltop. At first the four currents will flow apart, slowly and quietly. But as they flow, they grow nearer and nearer together, and faster and faster, until in the end, in the last act, they mingle in one mighty river of expressed emotion." *

* Quoted in Jacobs, *op. cit.*, p. 189.

Still, a film is not an abstraction, not a theme, but a vivid recreation of the surfaces of reality as they involve human beings in specific situations, and no other film captures for us so many memorable scenes of reality.* More important than the elaborate Babylonian scenery is the authenticity of the situations as perceived by the characters. The reality of the environment is established not by the scenery but by the manner in which Griffith handles his characters within his sets, the way he makes a huge area abound with life and turns a studio set into a city, not of spectacular edifices but of real people. (Griffith claimed to have employed as many as 15,000 extras for some of his scenes, but whatever the actual numbers, the filming gives the impression of many thousands more.) The spectacle is an added feature. After more than half a century, *Intolerance* remains the screen's greatest spectacle—though this achievement is somewhat less remarkable when we consider the execrable extravaganzas that approach it in terms of spectacle alone. Even *Intolerance* suffers from the magnitude of the settings, for some of the nuances are impossible to catch at first against the extravagant backgrounds of the film. Yet what is finally memorable about this film's gigantism is the way in which characters rush through their environments with all the vitality of real life.

The greatness of Griffith's achievement can be seen in virtually any sequence. Everything is motivated by the force of the general film idea, which permeates the smallest segment and thus relates each shot to the total sequence, each sequence to the individual story, and the four stories back to their source in the film idea. The bridge Griffith uses to unite the parts, one of the weakest elements in the film, consists of a shot of a mother rocking a cradle (Lillian Gish in her most nondescript role) and is often accompanied by an insert title from Walt Whitman, "Out of the cradle, endlessly rocking . . ." The image is endlessly repeated as a link between stories, but we are spared the link often enough so that each time it recurs it is a fresh annoyance.

The general plea for the tolerance due any person merely because he is a human being takes either of two basic forms. Sometimes it appears as an indictment of those concerned in some great historical tragedy: the Crucifixion, the massacre of the Huguenots, the betrayal of the Babylonian Empire by self-serving priests. Elsewhere, less spectacular instances of intolerance show us real-life situations, often with quite telling images. It is the nature of the mammoth film to drown our sensibility in the larger

---

* Apparently Griffith was desperate to inculcate a sense of reality in his audience through a series of footnotes appended to the insert titles; he wanted them to know that his grandiose scenery was based on historical reconstructions and scholarship. For example, he claims that the Babylonian hall he copied measured a mile in length. The footnotes are indeed trivia, more likely to produce laughter nowadays than the gasps of awe the director must have anticipated.

**20** *Intolerance* (Modern story)

images and make us miss the subtlety of the smaller ones, but that is the price Griffith pays for specializing in long films. However, we might note some of the literally innumerable small instances of the underlying film idea.

A persistent difficulty in many of Griffith's films should first be remarked: his delight in generic names. Perhaps Griffith hoped to achieve a leap from the specific to the general by labeling some characters with names such as Brown Eyes, the Friendless One, and the Mountain Girl (other characters in the same stories have real names). It was a mistake he repeated throughout his career, for to the extent that he artificially moves us from a particular awareness of an individual into a conceptual appreciation of a type, he denigrates the marvelous individualizing touches that make him a great director of performers. These names are oversimplifications that do not at all sum up the essence of the particular characters.

In contrast to the simplistic names, the visual images of the characters in action are highly suggestive. In one section of the modern story, the Boy

**21** *Intolerance* (The Massacre of the Huguenots)

(Robert Harron) decides to quit his gang to go straight and marry the Girl (Mae Marsh).* The gang leader (called a "Musketeer of the slums") objects, and a fight ensues between the two men. At this point a woman enters, presumably from the bedroom, and stands in the back of the room watching as Harron knocks down the gangster and leaves (fig. 20). It is a long shot, but somehow focused intently on the woman in the rear, clearly the mistress of the gangster. We remember that this woman (played by Miriam Cooper) was introduced much earlier as the Friendless One, a victim of the workers' strike who was forced to move to the city and was unable to find work. At the time that Harron first turned to crime to survive, this pretty girl, similarly motivated, became the mistress of the Musketeer. Her role was a small one—though she is extremely important later on—and seemed to be simply another example of the lives wrecked by the labor troubles. Yet Griffith here expands on the image of the morally isolated and

---

* Silent-film audiences by and large could read lips. They would notice that these two characters call each other "Bobby" and "Mae," though the names do not appear in the titles.

frightened young woman. She watches as her contemporary breaks his bond with the gangster, but realizes that she has neither the courage nor the resources to follow this example and is thus committed to remaining. Her pathetic condition is caught for a few seconds by Griffith with all his understanding of feminine fragility and hopelessness. That she should later murder her oppressor is made plausible by the implications of this shot. By itself, the sequence evokes complicated responses on the part of the audience, but it merely suggests that we need to understand the woman who has abandoned her morality against her better inclinations in an evil world that she did not create.

Griffith's greatest success in this film occurs with his images of overwhelming pathos. Our feelings for the dire predicaments of his characters are stimulated by our sense of the universality of human suffering, a theme that *Intolerance* drives home with great force. In the massacre-of-the-Huguenots story (fig. 21), a fleeing child throws herself down before a doorway where a Catholic priest stands, close to the turmoil in which the Catholic soldiers are methodically killing the Protestant population. He looks down at the child begging to be saved and then he looks around to see if anyone is watching him. Our sense of the impending destruction of the child and the priest's fear of detection are balanced in a moment of hesitancy. The timing is as impressive as the visual image: we know that another moment's hesitation will be fatal to the child, as we have already witnessed the soldiers' propensity to slaughter every last Huguenot. Finally the priest takes her, hiding her in his robes. Later in the story, the heroine's family is marked for annihilation, and their house invaded by the soldiers, led by a mercenary, who wishes to force the heroine, Brown Eyes, to yield herself to him. As the soldiers break in, the girl is sleeping with her sister. In the hallway the father fires a rifle at the soldiers, a final impotent attempt to defend his family; he, the mother, and a baby are killed. Then the mercenary approaches Brown Eyes and locks her in a room with him. The camera reveals her absolute terror in close-up as the man advances toward her and begins to untie her clothes. The intercut shots of her lover Prosper's attempts to get through the city to save her only increase our realization of the complete hopelessness of her condition. We see that he cannot possibly rescue her, and she is finally killed by her tormentor before the lover arrives.

The last two reels (of the total of thirteen in the extant circulating versions) are among the most exciting sequences in all cinema. As the four stories head toward their conclusions, Griffith begins to cut back and forth much more quickly than he did earlier--mainly without the interference of the image of the rocking cradle. He starts one chase and then cuts to another, delaying the outcome of each story and building up a tremendous amount of suspense. The earlier reels usually developed a story idea that left us with a sense of completeness in each episode; the change to an

editing procedure using incomplete episodes is of course noticeable, and the cinematic value of the procedure—judged purely on the basis of the excitement it generates—is obvious.

On the other hand, suspense melodrama results from technique, not theme, and in a film of this sort we would expect Griffith to maintain a steady hold on the film idea, which is ultimately more important than the thrill of a great chase. Indeed, Griffith never does lose sight of the motivating concept that intolerance leads to a complicated set of disasters. The fabric of the film has from the beginning been based on the unpredictable ways in which intolerance becomes socially destructive. The initial intolerant actions at first do not seem capable of yielding so large a destructive force. The plotting of the Pharisees against Jesus, the joining of the Uplifters' society by Mary T. Jenkins, and the High Priest of Bel's hatred of a rival religious order are almost random instances of intolerant attitudes that reveal evil potentiality within human beings, but they do not in themselves suggest the particular kinds of personal disasters that will follow. They are not meant to. The forging of the chain of intolerance is circumstantial. Thus, the increased pace of the four stories at the end is an additional representation of the organic unity that the theme imposes on the materials. Events are out of hand: the original decisions, bad in themselves, create conditions that cause universal tragedy. The swift movement suggests that humans cannot control the outcome of the evil they loose upon the world.

The three stories that conclude with chases move in the direction of tragedy. Regardless of their ultimate conclusions, they jointly counterpoint the fourth story, the Crucifixion of Jesus, which establishes a tone for the others in the sense that its outcome is known, and thus inevitable. The Crucifixion story is a grand example for Griffith of what his theme is all about; although relatively little time is devoted to this story, its final shot is one of the most effective in the film. The Crucifixion, shown from a great distance, takes place on a stormy night, and what our eye probably catches first is the large crowd in a somber mood; it takes a few seconds to make out the three wooden crosses in the background, and as a result the emphasis is thrown onto the significance of the event to the watching crowd.

The Crucifixion story and the massacre-of-the-Huguenots story are finished before the Babylonian and modern plots. Thus, Griffith can concentrate on the two more spectacular chases, at the same time prompting us to measure them against the outcome of the other two stories. The massacre of the Huguenots ends with a symbolic sequence summarizing the senselessness of the slaughter. Prosper, arriving too late to save Brown Eyes, carries her body to the door and berates the soldiers in front of the house. A group of soldiers simultaneously shoots him, though he wears an official badge of safe conduct and is carrying a dead body.

The end of the modern story, the one hopeful event in the film, epit-

omizes the sort of last-minute rescue Griffith introduced in *The Lonely Villa*. Harron, sentenced to die for the murder of the Musketeer, for which he was falsely convicted, is shown being prepared for execution by a priest. Meanwhile his wife and a policeman have gotten the real murderer (the Musketeer's mistress) to confess. These three have to reach the governor to get him to sign a pardon, and the final chase consists of a racing car trying to catch up with a train, which unfortunately is somewhat reminiscent of chases by the Keystone Kops. Harron, on the gallows with the noose already around his neck, is finally saved. The most effective parts of the sequence are the close-ups suggestive of the tension inherent in the situation —for example, the shot of a foot on the gas pedal of the racing car. At the end, three executioners stand ready to cut three cords, one being the real string that releases the platform on which Harron stands. Griffith indicates that the execution is interrupted literally at the last second by a close-up of the poised hands hovering over the cords.

Because of the enormity of its settings, the Babylonian story is probably the most memorable of the film. It has a more complicated moral outlook than the other segments because in this case the victims, the Baby-

**22** *Intolerance* (The Gates of Babylon)

**23**  *Intolerance* (Belshazzar's Feast)

lonians, are guilty of leading an excessively luxurious life. (After all, the
city has for us the connotation of an evil place.) The overthrow of the
kingdom occurs during a victory celebration when Prince Belshazzar and his
Princess Beloved are at the height of their glory as a result of the Babylonian's defeat of the Persian army of Cyrus. They believe their position
unassailable, and judging from the glorious battle scenes we have previously
witnessed, we assume that the gates of the city could not be successfully
stormed by the enemy (fig. 22). But Belshazzar and his people do not
realize the possibility of human perfidy; sure of themselves, they relax their
guard and are victimized by the treachery of the priests. The gates are
opened by traitors and the city overthrown almost before the Babylonians
are aware of what is happening. This treachery takes place while the camera
moves about at great distances in amazing crane shots of the feasting and
dancing in the city.

In spite of the moral character of the city, we sympathize with the
people of a civilization about to be overthrown by internal subversion.
Griffith induces us to align our sympathies with the Babylonians by relating
the fate of an individual to the general fate of the society in chaos around
him. Much as he did in the story of the slaughter of the Huguenots, Griffith

focuses on the plight of a woman caught up in historic events over which she can exercise no control. Through the role of the Mountain Girl (Constance Talmadge), he shows the best traits of the Babylonians—loyalty, in contrast to the treachery of the priests, and courage. The Mountain Girl does not come from the city and so lacks the Babylonian propensity for luxuriousness; instead, she is somewhat unsophisticated, wild, but entirely feminine in spite of her Amazonian skill with the bow and arrow. Although the Babylonian segment of the film is on a consistently large scale, Griffith establishes a balance between spectacle and personal story by cutting within the sequence from shots of the background, revealing the sprawling, crowded city, to shots of the girl, following her as she moves from one place to another in the crowded environment. Treated kindly by Belshazzar when she is forced by the judicial system to appear on the marriage market (and humiliated when no one bids for her), she falls in love with her prince, though she can only observe him from a distance. Later, the Mountain Girl learns of the conspiracy between Cyrus and the priests. As the Persian army prepares for its second attempt at Babylon, she rushes to the city in a chariot to warn Belshazzar of the impending attack. We see the hopelessness of her race against time, for the whole city is preoccupied with feasting and dancing and evidently is entirely incapable of defending itself (fig. 23). Moreover, though she arrives a few minutes before the invading army, Belshazzar cannot believe her immediately; finally he can muster only a dozen soldiers to defend the palace. The Mountain Girl herself joins the combat and is killed, as Belshazzar and the Princess Beloved commit suicide.

The four stories demonstrate the cause-and-effect relationship between individual acts and broadly based calamitous events. This narrative superstructure required Griffith to depict widely representative acts of personal or political self-interest that develop consequences of great scope to the communities involved. The concept of filmmaking that Griffith evolved in the one-reel film carried over into all the twelve- and thirteen-reel films he created during his prolific career. That concept held that in the peculiarly suggestive medium of film, visual information ought to consist of fragments which, when carefully chosen and sensitively edited, would produce the idea of a completed action. It was not necessary, Griffith discovered, to link each movement or stage of an action to convey the totality of that step within the framework of a plot, as Porter had done. And when Griffith applied his usual procedures for suggesting the totality of an action to *Intolerance,* a film of enormous scope, four distinct civilizations were made concretely visualized realities, each with an overwhelming number of details. Furthermore, because the film idea functioned so clearly within each story, Griffith could relate the parts thematically without muddling our capacity to perceive the specific development of each.

The financial failure of *Intolerance* kept Griffith from attempting other films of similar structural complexity. It did not stop him from turning out

some lengthy masterworks that were in some respects more successful (though less monumental) than *Intolerance* because they were simpler to absorb, even though they were of about the same length: *Hearts of the World* (1918), *Way Down East* (1920), *Orphans of the Storm* (1921), and *Isn't Life Wonderful?* (1924). In the middle of the 1920's, Griffith began to lose his popularity at the box office, and by 1931, at the age of fifty-six, he was finished as a director; embittered, he was to live another seventeen years largely forgotten by the industry that he, more than anyone else, had created. The new master of the spectacle became Cecil DeMille, a talented but far inferior filmmaker. Griffith, it should be noted, did not need spectacle to produce major films; *Broken Blossoms* and *True Heart Susie* (both 1919) are simply personal dramas about the difficulties encountered by lovers. To the public he remains a historical figure awaiting reevaluation on artistic, not historical, grounds, for his artistry lies outside the limited concerns of the film historians who only enumerate his technical contributions. As Andrew Sarris has said, "Griffith invented this 'mere' technique, but he also transcended it." * He was the first man to have an artistic conception of the film, the first to conceive of the film idea. The scope and depth of his many fine works attest to a cinematic sense attained by only a handful of filmmakers in this century.

---

\* Andrew Sarris, *The American Cinema* (New York, E. P. Dutton, 1968), p. 52.

# Narrative Comedy
# in the Silent
# Film

## Mack Sennett and the Keystone Style

The kind of slapstick comedy Mack Sennett made famous did not originate with him; indeed such antics seem to exist at the very start of the narrative film. In 1895, the Lumière brothers produced *L'Arroseur Arrosé* (Watering the Gardener), a film in which, through a boy's prank, a gardener turns a watering hose on himself; the evident success of the film is attested to by immediate plagiarisms and duplications, which showed that slapstick was thoroughly adaptable to the primitive film. Mack Sennett may have originated nothing more than the custard pie and the funny cops; his genius lay in the perfection of cinematic properties inherent in the comedy of his day. A student of Griffith, he learned from his master the techniques of editing, and moving on to the Keystone Film Company in 1912, he turned out an enormous number of well-made one- and two-reel films through 1916. His career lasted far into the sound era, though he is best remembered for his early work. Sennett was a masterful supervisor of films, running a studio with many directors and supervising many productions simultaneously. Even when he did not direct the films, his style pervaded the works of the men under him. Sennett's was the first recognizable American comic style, and the Keystone and later Triangle comedies show definite stylistic similarities. Working with performers who had genius of their own,

Sennett let some of them, like Mabel Normand and Fatty Arbuckle, direct their own films. Nevertheless, for all the vast differences among the styles of the performers, the comedies all look like Sennett's. His ideas of visual humor dominated the influence of any individual performer, retaining an amazing consistency for five or six years of extraordinary output.

Practically everyone knows what the Sennett films look like. For his audiences, to see almost any one of them was to experience something of the visual awakening that spectators must have had at the early Méliès films. Like Méliès, Sennett emphasized the absurd, though with less geniality, for his world was the identifiable, everyday world of reality. Of course, Sennett dislodged the reality from that world, but Méliès never intended to approach the real world in the first place. Both men delighted in camera technique, though Méliès really wanted to call attention not to the camera but to the effect produced. Sennett's audience was more familiar with the possibilities of camera manipulation, and few would have thought his speeded-up motion or slow motion an exact-time recording of the movement performed on the set. Lewis Jacobs' apt distinction is that whereas Méliès aimed at magic, Sennett aimed at nonsense. Sennett was also more cinematically complex than Méliès, for American comedy took advantage of the innovations of Griffith. In fact, Sennett's are probably the best-edited American films of the age, after Griffith's own.

The Keystone world exuded violence and vulgarity, but its incessant energy was always appealing. Perhaps the films progressed too quickly to develop the serious moral sense that was shortly to characterize those greater filmmakers, Chaplin and Keaton. Much of the comedy was satiric, and some of it had a moral implication. However, the satiric premise was really overwhelmingly broad, and maybe too broad to sustain serious moral implications. In Sennett's view *everybody* reveals a degree of ego or self-interest, and that self-interest ought to be exploited for comic purposes. The mayhem that follows touches everyone in the films. The comic actors were fortunately capable of the rough-and-tumble antics they had to go through, for not all the feats could be simulated by the camera. In spite of the ever-present violence, the smashing of cars and heads, in general no one seems to get permanently injured in the Keystone world. Watching the incredible collisions detaches us sufficiently from the real world so that we can laugh at a car accident.

Within the framework of a Sennett film, the individual idiosyncrasies of the comedians were never buried, since the loose plots favored by the Keystone Film Company frequently consisted of little more than a premise for the characters to become involved in a chase, to call in the Keystone Kops, or to provoke a marital squabble. The sense of formula is usually apparent, but it is never mere stereotyping. The real art of Sennett was to ring an infinite number of changes on the same story material, and perhaps we should evaluate a Sennett film according to the ancient Greek esthetic

principle that originality lies in making familiar materials vivid and entertaining. The films swarm with basic human traits, stripped of civilizing restraints: greed, lust, vanity, miserliness, envy—in fact, all the sins that medieval religious writers allegorized, often with a good deal of slapstick humor themselves. Because Sennett's plots and characterizations were rudimentary, the films seemed improvised; but truly fundamental to his film idea were the ingenious comic bits, the incongruous associations, the total disintegration of sanity resulting from the intrusion of the comic nightmare of absurdity. Kalton C. Lahue describes the nature of Sennett's comic world:

> Except for Mabel Normand and Chaplin, every member of his motley stable of comics was absurd in some respect: Roscoe "Fatty" Arbuckle, cross-eyed Ben Turpin, leering Mack Swain, impish Chester Conklin, pathetic Harry Langdon, and so on down the list. Even Chaplin's screen character, as it developed in his Keystone films, contained absurd elements which were later reduced to more human terms as he polished his portrayals.
>
> Sennett realized that if one policeman was humorous, a group of them would be riotous. . . . Pretty girls were also essential in Sennett's brand of comedy. A dozen luscious girls fawning over Ben Turpin was a guarantee that the house would come down in an uproar. Custard pies flew all over the place, cops fell headlong into mud and water, cars careened crazily along the edge of cliffs and plowed through houses, motorcycles mowed down pedestrians, and buildings exploded with regularity as Sennett went about his business.*

Sennett edited his films seemingly on the premise that slapstick comedy has to present dramatic situations quickly. No slow spots survived his cutting; and he had the unusual reputation (for an early filmmaker) of omitting about 90 percent of his original footage from the final negative. The statistic probably highly exaggerates the facts, but it does suggest that Sennett's conception of editing was like Griffith's in that the final film was an assemblage of carefully selected elements of a film idea. Aside from Griffith and Sennett, the only American filmmaker of note at this time was Thomas Ince, and not even his early films are as thoroughly intercut as Sennett's. Sennett specialized in crosscutting to build up the chase sequence, and his final rescues (*e.g.,* of Mabel Normand tied to the railroad tracks in *Barney Oldfield's Race for a Life*) were almost parodies of Griffith's rescues (*e.g.,* in *The Lonely Villa*), but oddly enough they were still used straightforwardly by other directors in the serial craze that had already begun in Hollywood.

* Kalton C. Lahue, *The World of Laughter* (Norman, University of Oklahoma Press, 1966), p. 73.

A typical Sennett chase would include at least two elements. For instance, in *Love, Speed and Thrills* (1915)—the title of which is a perfect general description of about half of all Sennett's works—Chester Conklin flees with Mack Swain's wife. The intercutting consists not only of Conklin's flight and Swain's rescue efforts but of the pursuing cops; finally, all elements come together in some proximity, and a series of disasters follows such as someone's riding a motorcycle off a bridge. The separate shots within such a sequence permitted individual responses (*i.e.,* comic bits by individual performers). The method employed by Griffith, shorter and shorter lengths of film for successive shots, was essentially duplicated by Sennett to build up the frantic pace, and of course the camera was frequently speeding up the action in addition.

Even when not employing a chase, Sennett would crosscut a good deal between parallel actions. One of his favorite subjects was the marital arrangement; husbands were particularly fond of other men's wives—which meant that the other men might be attracted to their wives. This naturally allowed for two plot threads of similar action, inevitably linked in the denouement. In *Fatty's Chance Acquaintance* (1915), Fatty Arbuckle and his ugly wife, who holds the money, are in the park, when the penniless Fatty espies a prettier woman. Meanwhile her male companion is out to steal the pocketbook from Fatty's wife. Sennett cuts back and forth to emphasize attitudes about money as Fatty buys his new girlfriend food he won't be able to pay for. The complexity of the plot is added to by Fatty's fear of being seen in this compromising situation by his nearby wife, which inevitably happens (fig. 24). All the characters are misbehaving and are punished for it, but in this madcap world all men are guilty just for being alive, police as well as pocketbook thieves.

The Keystone performers, as wild as they seemed, were essentially self-effacing, for they worked as a team, and many a smaller role was filled by a performer who would become a feature star in later years. Perhaps this is why talented performers eventually left Sennett; the films, by bearing the stamp of his style, may have impinged upon what the performers felt was the true development of their own styles. Chaplin certainly needed to move away from the Sennett mold. Harold Lloyd never developed a great style under Sennett. And the big names of Keystone, like Fatty Arbuckle and Mabel Normand, felt they could do better elsewhere—financially of course, but probably also artistically.

Nevertheless, Sennett's influence permeates the independent work of all the silent comics, including the four most individualized, Chaplin, Keaton, Lloyd, and Langdon. Even the comedy teams show his influence. Laurel and Hardy develop directly from that tradition, as witnessed in the peculiar absurdity of their situations. To the list of these six distinguished performers, one could add virtually every major name that followed. Earlier comics and those who developed at about the same time that Keystone was achiev-

**24**  *Fatty's Chance Acquaintance*

ing its comic heights may have been immune to Sennett's influence, but they are not in the major tradition of American film comedy, which is Sennett's. The six comedians mentioned above produced works greater than any of Sennett's, but in terms of the development of national attitudes toward comedy, not even Chaplin's influence was so widespread.

## Buster Keaton and the Short Comedy: *Cops*

Buster Keaton has risen in reputation over the last decade to the point where he now rivals Chaplin and has been decidedly elevated over Lloyd and Langdon in critical esteem. Undoubtedly Keaton deserves his present status, for no other film mind except Chaplin's was so successful in finding visual equivalents for internal emotional conditions. In some ways, his task was more difficult than Chaplin's, for Chaplin often relied on one of the most expressive faces any performer ever had. The face is the external passage to the soul, and so Chaplin had an immediate advantage over everyone else who cared to turn comedy into a reflection of the inner man. Not everyone cared to: Harold Lloyd performed brilliantly in the guise of an extremely superficial character. Sennett's films were almost allegorical in their dimension: they were certaintly not attempts to portray an individual's psyche.

Keaton, however, attempted to do what Chaplin did, but by other means. As his technique evolved, he turned his face into a mask (he became known as the Great Stoneface). Unusual for the age he worked in, the mask of course has an honorable tradition for actors. In the Greek theater, masked performers appeared with countenances that represented a single state of mind. This is not exactly true of Keaton, for even without wide variation in facial expression, very much could be read in his face. Yet the real effectiveness of his face has to do with the context. The comedy lies in the obvious emotional turbulence beneath the exterior mask. To express that inner nature Keaton had to rely on various external equivalents.

Keaton excelled in the two-reel as well as the full-length film; his two-reelers, like Chaplin's, sometimes show remarkable comic inventiveness that is occasionally equaled but not surpassed even in his more intellectually significant features that followed such as *The General* and *Steamboat Bill Jr.* One of Keaton's best short films, *Cops* (1922), is also one of the classics of the silent screen. And like many of Chaplin's fine short films, it is not entirely integrated, though in *Cops,* everything leads up to the chase (which takes up most of the second reel), in which the whole police force tries to capture the hero, played by Keaton. The plot concerns the hero's attempt to succeed at business so as to marry his wealthy but snobbish girlfriend; however, this aspect of the plot disappears once the chase begins.

In spite of the film's episodic structure, Keaton's attitude toward the comic film idea remains consistent from the opening sequences. The gags are conceived in terms of surprise, the surprise itself deepening our understanding of the tragic irony that surrounds the hero. An expanding iris shot opens on what seems to be an imprisoned Keaton sadly conversing with his girlfriend; they shake hands and she leaves. The second shot, however, reveals to us that the girl is within the gates of her estate—the bars symbolizing Buster's exclusion from the social company of a girl who won't marry him until he becomes a successful businessman. The nature of this exclusion is emotionally conveyed to us because our intellectual anticipation of a jail scene is met with a shot of a free man, but one who is surely imprisoned spiritually by the circumstances. The comedy is tempered by our immediate awareness that the illusionary imprisonment symbolizes an internal state.

Keaton's comedy continually calls into question the justice of the universe. His role in *Cops* is that of an innocent man confronted with accidents and wicked designs of others. But although he suffers through his involvement with people and situations beyond his control, we do not feel that he is simply a victim. Faced with a series of surprising cruelties dictated by not an indifferent, but an antagonistic, fate, Keaton's hero, like Chaplin's, refuses to remain passive.

Buster passes a huge, angry man (who is later revealed to be a detective) calling a cab. He returns the man's dropped wallet; ungratefully, the man pushes him away. Getting into his cab, he falls and is helped up by

Buster, who is once again treated with disdain. The falling reinforces the impression that the man is a caricature of Ingratitude, and the hero's generosity is set off by the man's rough pride. Thus, when Buster picks up the dropped wallet a second time, we feel that he ought to keep it. The man, however, grabs it away from the bewildered hero's hand. Then, driving away in his cab, the man discovers the wallet is empty. He goes back for Buster and gets out of his cab, but then we see Buster driving away in the same cab, innocently holding the money. The several surprises of this sequence produce comedy and direct our sympathies to the hero. Nevertheless, Keaton's universe is metaphysically more complex than one that doles out punishments and rewards according to merit, though in this instance the passive, good man has gotten away with the bad man's money.

In Keaton's pessimistic and unusual world view, the innocent man frequently imposes on others. *Cops* contains a number of incidents that attest to the filmmaker's firm control over the rather grim cinematic idea behind the amusing visual gags. At one point, the hero thinks he is buying a horse, but mistakenly pays a bystander, not the owner—nor, for that matter, is the horse really for sale. The man who receives the money is just as confused as Buster. The humor of the situation momentarily blinds us to the tragedy of the world we inhabit: a horse is actually being stolen, and a second innocent man is brought into the perpetration of this act. In a separate incident, Buster is swindled out of his money (the money he had accidentally taken from the angry detective) when a con man talks him into helping an imaginary poverty-stricken family by purchasing a load of furniture that happens to be piled in the street (awaiting a moving van). Buster thinks he is setting himself up in business as a seller of second-hand furniture; he then rides off with the furniture, which in fact belongs to a policeman's family who are in the process, they think, of moving to a new residence. Thus, the hero has involved himself with the law twice and committed serious violations without the slightest intent to harm anyone. What, in fact, increases our perception of the tragedy on thinking over the incidents is that the hero has actually been too good in his intentions, first, in helping the angry detective to get back his wallet, and second, in trying to help a family who were being dispossessed, or so he thought.

The idea is firmly established even in minor incidents. Buster, riding along on his furniture wagon, decides to be the responsible citizen who gives traffic signals. He arranges a hand-operated signal by using a boxing glove on an expanding clothes rack; but instead of obeying the law, he unwittingly knocks down a policeman with his signal. Clearly, the film idea postulates a certain number of offenses perpetrated by the hero, not for the reason of justifying the impending disaster, but for elaborating on the film's inherent logic. As unjust as the demonstrable universe is, it still runs on a peculiar legalistic system, and Buster is going to be punished for his infractions.

The climactic incident, which sets off the pursuit by the police, is

**25** *Cops*

typical. Buster's wagon gets mixed up in an annual policeman's parade (fig. 25), and as he marches along with the entire force, an anarchist tosses a bomb that lands on his wagon just as he is lighting a cigarette. (He needs that cigarette to retain his composure now that he is involved in a parade and can't get off the street because he is passing the reviewing stand— on which sits the mayor's daughter, Buster's girl, who will witness the key event.) Almost without looking, he lights his cigarette with the bomb and tosses it away as one would a match. It explodes, and every policeman in the city runs after Buster, who is assumed to be the anarchist.

This prolonged chase, stylistically arranged largely in terms of visual surprises in repeated patterns, is one of the greatest sequences in film comedy. In one pattern, for example, the hero is chased by a large number of cops but runs toward a single officer waiting to grab him; once he runs around the officer, another time he slides under him. We watch for the variations on the same situation, for this is Keaton's true genius, even more so than the acrobatic feats he performs under duress (here, balancing a ladder like a seesaw on a high fence while his pursuers stand at either

end waiting for him to come down). The chase is characterized by the enormous number of cops in pursuit of one man. Of course the photography is partly responsible for suggesting the thousands of cops, as the same actors are filmed over and over again; the audience is not supposed to be deceived by the method, but rather amused by it.

Keaton's characterization emphasizes the courage, fortitude, and ingenuity of the hero while he resists being conquered by superior numbers. He outwits the cops time after time, finally convincing us that intelligence can triumph over sheer might. Up to the end it looks as if the chase is really a tribute to the greatness of the hero's character under pressure. Yet the film idea is complicated by the filmmaker's philosophic attitude, as pronounced in *Cops* as in any so-called serious film. Just as he brings the hero to the verge of a magnificent victory, the pessimistic filmmaker channels the action into a new direction—not really reversing his attitudes, but joining certain ideas developed prior to the chase. The hero is not going to escape punishment just because his superior abilities under fire have gained him a victory against his human opponents. The fates are eternally cruel to him. The final image is astounding in its implicit bitterness. Buster has seemingly been cornered at last by thousands of cops in the station house, and just after they pour inside to vent their rage upon him, he suddenly emerges (another complete visual surprise) disguised in a police uniform and locks the doors on his tormentors, at last freeing himself from the chase. Most viewers would have been content for the film to end there, happily enough, with this human triumph against impossible odds. But Keaton cannot neglect the theme he has so carefully planted in the first half of the film. Buster's girlfriend appears, takes one look at him, and snubs him again. In despair, realizing the uselessness of trying to win her over, he unlocks the station house and enters. The final shot, shocking in tone for this film, shows a tombstone with the hero's hat on it so it cannot be mistaken for anyone else's. In comedy, people just do not die at the end. Death introduces an ambiguity that causes us to reevaluate the tone of the comedy we have witnessed. Ultimately, Keaton's mixture of the tragic and the comic works because it is implicit in the total concept of the film.

If we have any doubts about Keaton's ability to portray an inner state of mind, the pathos elicited by the man's final gesture of despair, the opening of the station house door, surely indicates a very high level of cinematic originality, whatever we think about the unhappy ending. Yet because of the extravagant physical activity, Keaton has to rely on the impact of each sequence in order to establish the audience's sympathetic relationship with the main character. Other talented performers, particularly Harry Langdon, immediately elicit a degree of sympathy merely from their appearance or their gestures. Keaton's art, then, consists of supplying a context within which his overtly physical comic performance becomes emo-

tionally meaningful. One of his major visual means for structuring our response to his characterization is through numerous images of isolation. In *Cops* the hero always appears racing away from an enormous crowd. The image of the isolated man is sometimes established more subtly by simply moving everyone else away from him, as when he hides in a trash can and the police pass him by. Whatever the particular technique involved, the result transforms that outer physical condition into a symbol of a man's spiritual state. Thus, even though the cinema of Keaton is pre-eminently one of surface movement, the filmmaker consistently achieves a correlation of the circumstances of that movement with the essential mental processes of a hero highly responsive to the continual challenges of his environment.

## Harold Lloyd and the Feature Comedy:
## *Safety Last* and *The Freshman*

Of the four leading silent comedy stars, Chaplin, Keaton, Lloyd, and Langdon, the first two were filmmakers in the truest sense: their comic ideas and style controlled the production of their films. For this reason, and of course because of their genius, Chaplin and Keaton are among the greatest filmmakers, without regard to classification. Lloyd and Langdon did not exercise the same degree of control over their productions; they were performers more than filmmakers, but their genius was clearly great enough to shape most of the comic vision of their major films. Langdon, because his comic role frequently employed a good deal of the same pathos, suffers somewhat by implicit comparisons we tend to make with Chaplin. Although it is not fair to Langdon to think of him as an imitator of Chaplin, it is true that for the present age his screen personality is less sharply defined for us than Harold Lloyd's.

On the other hand, Lloyd's full-length silent films are not in regular distribution at this time, with the exception of *The Freshman,* and even this film is rarely exhibited. Until the six or seven major Lloyd films from *Grandma's Boy* (1922) to *Speedy* (1928) are made more generally available, final evaluation of Lloyd's position is not feasible, but on the strength of *The Freshman* alone, Lloyd must be judged one of the great comic artists in the film.

After a long apprenticeship in one- and two-reel comedies, Lloyd evolved a distinctive screen personality that would operate in a set way with carefully established comic materials. This consciously imposed limitation was not at all an artistic limitation but a successful attempt to derive a comic style as comprehensive in its intellectual implications as any, short of Chaplin's and Keaton's. He created a character who was completely involved in following some of the American ideals now fallen into dis-

repute, though presumably never fully accepted because of their overt falseness. Instead of questioning the values of the society he moves in or wishes to move in, the Lloyd character (frequently called Harold, even Harold Lloyd), accepts them implicitly. The comedy is not satiric, for it does not attack the values even through implication. On the contrary, Lloyd's comedy results from the increasing difficulties encountered in living with these values and gaining acceptance by the money-oriented society the hero is interested in. Having money and exhibiting the outward trappings of those who "have arrived" are only part of the system. What the Lloyd hero is always vainly seeking is status; he wants to be liked or loved, he wants to get ahead, he wants to win a particular girl who seems to have these values also.

Furthermore, Lloyd is a *successful* comic hero in the most obvious way. Chaplin triumphs too, of course, as all comedy usually moves toward a favorable resolution of the main character's problems. But Lloyd triumphs as he goes along because he has the resourcefulness to turn life's little tragedies into small successes. When Chaplin gains a point during a film, it is commonly because of a trait in his personality manifestly superior to that of the other people concerned. Lloyd succeeds because of his quick wit. He thinks his way out of jams and embarrassing situations. His cleverness is not really intellectual but almost a matter of reflex: continually placed in situations of great pressure, he needs to come up with something or he is finished. When, in some of his films, he finds himself in a situation of precarious physical peril, he is always forced to meet the challenge. He does not go out and deliberately get mixed up in events that seem headed for disaster, but these things continually happen to him from the pressures generated by the society he feels compelled to join. In *Safety Last* (1923, directed by Fred Newmeyer), Harold's friend, a "human fly," is being chased by a cop, and Harold must take his place and climb up the side of a building—only to the second floor. But when he gets to that floor, his friend informs him that he'll have to continue to the third floor while the friend again tries to get rid of the cop. At each floor, Harold is instructed to continue, and naturally the imminent perils increase in intensity, culminating in the classic acrobatic feats involving the hero's hanging from the building's clock (fig. 26). The point, however, is that he succeeds; he does an extraordinary job and nearly gets killed several times, but he does reach the roof, and there the girl awaits him. Typically, he ends up with the girl—and a thousand dollars for the feat.

Since the comic action of the films relates to the resourceful ways Lloyd gets himself out of tight situations, the comic idea is essentially a development of those conditions of desperation which will require the hero to act. Lloyd's genius in part consists of his ability to involve us in his hero's sense of panic. This is especially difficult because the character of the hero has very little of the endearment that the Chaplin, Keaton, or

**26** *Safety Last*

Langdon characterizations conveyed. We ordinarily will not feel a great deal of sympathy or empathy for a man as aggressive and yet as simple as the character Harold. But the psychology of situation overrides the psychology of character, as Lloyd constructs his film idea. He makes the situation so threatening that we feel every moment that we ourselves are in danger of defeat or failure.

An interesting example is the department store sequence from *Safety Last*. Harold has told his girlfriend, who lives far away, that he has a responsible job in the store, though he actually is only a clerk. We know enough of the girl to see that she would never care for him if she thought he was not a success. Now looked at objectively, this is the quite ordinary situation of a man trying to impress his girl by exaggerating his importance, by lying, in fact. The girl hardly gets our sympathy either, for our evaluation of her must be based mainly on the estimate she makes of Harold's worldly position. When she suddenly arrives at the store, the situation immediately takes on an air of panic, for we know that Harold, far from having any status at the department store, is in danger of losing his fifteen-dollar-a-week job.

The Keaton or Chaplin characters, in such a situation, would not pull it off; they would at last be found out, and if they later won the girl

back it would require recouping their reputations after the embarrassment of discovery. Lloyd, in contrast, does get away with his pretense to status by a series of ingenious incidents which demonstrate to the girl that he really is important—that in fact he is the general manager of the whole store. While these incidents reveal one thing to the girl, they tell us something else: we watch in perpetual amazement the variety of things Harold can do to cover his story, to save himself from seemingly inevitable rejection. We do not start out by particularly liking him, and we may consciously dislike the pretense he has made of his position, but we end up rooting for him because we very quickly become involved, for two reasons. First, he makes himself so vulnerable that any slip will destroy him in the eyes of the girl. Second, he does not rely on luck to get himself out of a difficulty (in fact, his luck is all bad, but he overcomes bad luck too). He seizes any small opportunity to support his role in front of the girl, and we can't help admiring the way he improvises his strategy to get clear just as he seems trapped.

Every small incident is filled with danger. A fellow clerk shows him a cartoon of the floor manager, and Harold signs it officiously, as if he had been given a paper that needed his okay. It puzzles the clerk, but it impresses the girl. When she sees him selling behind the counter and is just about to be disillusioned, he pretends to be demonstrating sales techniques to fellow clerks. She insists that he show her his office, and so when the general manager walks out of *his* office, Harold takes her in. The surprise return of the manager, which would seem the impending peril, is turned into a triumph by Harold's pretending that the girl was a customer who had fainted; he even gets the manager to rush out for a glass of water, and his girl assumes that the manager is Harold's subordinate. When he accidentally presses all the buttons on the manager's desk and several employees rush in to see what is required, Harold simply fades into the background, pretending that he too was one of the employees summoned mysteriously, and so everyone leaves assuming it was some mistake made by no one in particular. The effect is that whatever happens, the audience expects it to be the end of the game for Harold. Although he anticipates nothing, he is ready for everything. Of course he does not welcome the challenge, for he is clearly suffering in every episode; the pressure almost destroys him—as it would anyone else. Yet his ability to react brilliantly always saves the day: the girl never notices the extraordinary means he employs to pursue his role.

Lloyd's character in his films represents an aspect of the American dream of success. As the social effects of ambition and aggressiveness are not portrayed in their negative aspect, the comedy succeeds in accumulating images of an essentially innocent man struggling with adversity and overcoming it. The crass materialism that such a portrayal might be associated with in real life is not the subject of the films. What finally emerges is a

sympathetic hero who personifies American determination to succeed, to climb out of a lowly class, to gain general acceptance. Lloyd's masterpiece, *The Freshman* (1925), is a major statement of this part of the American character, and as film art it remains one of the three or four great silent comedies.

Like the best of Keaton's and Chaplin's feature films, but unlike Lloyd's typical work, *The Freshman* moves on the periphery of the tragic. Indeed, Harold's brash ambitiousness for once runs into the realities of life and leads him to a short-lived but profound discovery of his failure. It is also unusual for him in that it relies for background humor on a degree of satire (of the life and times of the "Roaring Twenties" undergraduate), and the comedy proceeds without the acrobatic element so prominent in *High and Dizzy* and *Safety Last.* Yet the film is undeniably typical in the essence of its comic drive and in the characterization of the hero, Harold Lamb.

The environment of *The Freshman* is the fantasy-type academe of Tate College, where not a single classroom, teacher, or book is ever in evidence—or to describe it in the words of an insert title, the institution is a large football stadium with a college attached. To this world comes Harold, a freshman motivated by the sole desire to succeed in the only area that counts to him, the social life of the college. Amazingly enough, apparently nothing else counts to the other students either, for even football is but one category of the fun-and-games atmosphere that is Tate. The academic hierarchy is personified in but two authority figures, the Dean and the football coach, and for all we see they may constitute the entire administration and faculty of this hilarious school. Even in the Marx Brothers' academic world of *Horse Feathers,* at least the cap-and-gown brigade seems to be represented. At Tate, Harold Lamb can concentrate all his tremendous energies on gaining popularity and trying to make the football team, unimpeded by the irrelevancies of the outside world or a program of studies.

The premise of college life as an absolutely trivial existence has just enough contact with the reality of 1925 to make it satiric rather than fanciful. The satire is directed as much at the students trying to make the hero look foolish as it is at Harold. Since everyone accepts the idea of college as a social enterprise, then obviously Harold's goal to become number one in student popularity merits an effort. The general respect afforded such a position guarantees that Harold's struggle will not be ignored by his contemporaries. In fact, he is quickly singled out as a student who is desperately aiming to be popular, and because he is so earnest in his endeavors and so unsophisticated, he is immediately made the laughing-stock of the college. That we know this and Harold does not creates an increasing sympathy for him and, more importantly, a developing awareness of the potential tragedy in the situation.

Surely, since much of the film consists of the students' encouraging Harold to reveal his socially gauche sensibility, we anticipate a time of reckoning, a time when he will discover that he is the college sap, not the popular character he imagines himself to be. For this reason, we tend to like Harold though the truth shines as clearly here as in any Lloyd film that the values the young man represents are false and deserve to be deflated. It is an evident indication of Lloyd's genius that he can manipulate our attitude toward the hero in spite of our despising what the hero stands for.

The motif of the pathetic and the ludicrous that runs through *The Freshman* is summed up by a recurring visual and verbal image. At the beginning of the film, we see Harold preparing to leave for Tate College, practicing weird sounds from a pamphlet entitled "College Yells." Wearing a beanie and a sweatshirt with a big T on it, Harold has been perfecting a routine he saw in a movie about a college hero, a little dance step or jig followed by the self-introductory remark: "I'm just a regular fellow—step right up and call me Speedy!" He tries it first on his father, and we realize immediately that Harold is doomed to abysmal failure. His father tells his mother that the jig will lead the boy to heartbreak, but Harold is so enthusiastic about his little formula for winning friends that no one ever tells him it is ridiculous. Off he goes to Tate convinced that he has only to do the jig and repeat that idiotic refrain and everyone will like him.

The jig and the refrain, we know, will not work, and we would not want to see them work, for at this point in the film the error is all Harold's. At his age he should not be so insensitive to human nature as to think that he can win friends merely by repeating a magic formula. He deserves the failure he is bound to meet, but at the same time we feel sorry for someone who tries so desperately to achieve something that seems hopelessly beyond him. Lloyd's development of this motif strategically overcomes our initial reluctance to be wholly sympathetic toward Harold, for what happens is that the boy is not rejected outright by his fellow students when he performs his jig; instead, they play along with him, having sized him up as a naïve freshman who can provide them with a semester's entertainment. This obvious cruelty takes advantage of a human simplicity that is not by itself socially harmful. Their mass joke at one person's expense naturally aligns us emotionally with Harold the victim (thus, his surname, Lamb), who we understand will be spiritually distraught if he learns his true standing in this community

Throughout the film, then, the image of Harold dancing and repeating "I'm just a regular fellow—step right up and call me Speedy" underscores the development of the plot inasmuch as it characterizes the fall and rise of Harold's reputation. However, since the cinema of Harold Lloyd is one of triumph, not tragedy, this key image is later used to symbolize the eventual triumph of the hero. Persistence does it again in this film, the pure drive to succeed against overwhelming odds. Harold, who becomes known as

Speedy among the mocking students posing as his friends, must go through a series of humiliations before he finally triumphs, but in the world view of this film (and his others), that triumph is deserved because the human spirit is capable of rising to the challenge. In reality, the reward for the good-natured man sometimes does not arrive in his lifetime, but in Lloyd's films Harold's reward comes after he avoids defeat at the last moment; he wins because he tries harder.

His main tormentor, who pretends to be his friend, is named the College Cad (in an insert title). He tells Harold, early in the film, that each new student is supposed to address the student body in the auditorium (filled by students waiting for the Dean's speech). On the stage, Harold faces an amused, eventually hysterically laughing, audience. He can't think of anything sensible to say, and so he finally blurts out his "call me Speedy" routine. The whole college cheers and joins in on the campus joke. When Harold offers to buy a few "friends" ice cream, the Cad invites dozens of students, gaining Harold the ironic nickname of Speedy the Spender, a social climber on his way to the top. Harold finds his only friend in the kind, charming girl, Peggy, who falls in love with him for his simplicity. She knows the truth about the way the others treat him, but she does not tell him, in order to spare his feelings.

The film builds up to a public humiliation, but not all Harold's encounters are total failures. The Cad insists that to be really popular, he must try out for the football team (fig. 27). In one of his greatest sequences, Harold shows up for practice, accidentally trips and knocks down the coach, and then does his jig in front of him. After he knocks the hard-boiled coach off his feet a second time, the coach bans him from the field, but reconsiders because he needs a tackling dummy. We witness Harold manhandled as a human prop, thrown to the ground over and over again by the team and the coach, who seems unaware that Harold is even around. Finally, beaten and totally exhausted, Harold gains the attention of the coach, who, admiring his spirit, does not want to tell him that he can't make the team. At the suggestion of a player, the coach makes Harold the water boy, but pretends that he's on the varsity. Thus, in this sequence we have an example of what ultimately will win for Harold: his stamina in putting up with anything to gain his end will eventually wear down resistance to him. Peggy learns that he is only the water boy, but even she refuses to tell Harold the truth.

The sequence that leads to the climax, the Fall Frolic, is the most effective representation of the film idea, an entirely typical sequence in that its momentum builds up tremendous tension from a series of incidents related to a basic prop, in this case the prop being the tuxedo worn by the hero. Harold, who hosts the affair, arranges to get a suit made by Adam the tailor, but because of the tailor's dizzy spells, the suit is not quite finished by the time the party begins. Adam goes along with Harold to the party

**27** *The Freshman*

just in case the basted suit tears at the seams. Of course the suit does tear, piece by piece (finally leaving poor Harold in his shorts), which is the ideal Lloyd comedy procedure. The humor is associated with our perception of Harold's dread of being found deficient: he does not want to be ridiculed as a man whose suit comes apart. He wants above all else to be treated as an equal, and his fear of scorn over the suit reinforces our awareness that he is always the school clown in everyone else's eyes.

The comic virtuosity of the Fall Frolic sequence is impressive: the remarkable number of variations on the gag of a suit that falls apart shows the same type of ingenuity we find in Keaton and Chaplin and marks the super comic star. The first part to go is the sleeve, which attaches itself to a girl's dress, necessitating Harold's chasing her around the floor to retrieve it without her knowledge. He not only gets it back but has Adam sew it on while under the obligation to shake hands with guests; he even uses the tailor's arm as his own, as the tailor stands behind drapery sewing the sleeve while Harold sticks his own arm behind him. Another time his suspenders snap off, forcing him to dance holding up his trousers. A girl sees the suspenders on the floor and assumes that her own undergarments have fallen off. This fabulous comic idea, though unique, is yet altogether typical of Lloyd's style: the pressure is on Harold, but he avoids being

found out—and meanwhile someone else has the problem transferred to her. Even his worst moment is partially redeemed by a success. A tablecloth getting mixed up with his shirt, Harold pulls everything off a table; the waiter arriving to clean up the mess pulls the tablecloth—and Harold's pants are swept away with it. In complete humiliation before all his peers, Harold runs from the party. In his flight he sees Peggy, who is the hat-check girl, struggling against the Cad, who is trying to kiss her. Harold admirably stops running to rescue the girl by knocking down the Cad.

This heroic gesture of his leads to the moment of disclosure. The Cad, enraged by Harold's hitting him, reveals the truth, telling Harold that the college considers him the school boob. This knowledge almost completely destroys Harold, who nevertheless tries to pretend to Peggy that it doesn't matter. First he laughs, but then, in the most pathetic moment of the film, he cries in Peggy's lap. At this point, Peggy, an entirely sympathetic character, makes an appeal to Harold that is astounding considering the fact that Harold's social ideal of popularity has been exploded and shown to be false: "Get out and make them like you for what you really are and what you can do!" Since the rest of the film implicitly supports the inherent value of her declaration, it turns out that what we thought had been a showing up of an ideal has only been a revelation of a bad example of attaining this ideal. However, the moral nature of Lloyd's comedy does not bear scrutiny, and indeed we do not feel the facile morality a flaw while the film is in progress. Lloyd's comedy turns on the hero's will to succeed within a given social and moral culture; it is not an examination of the mores of that culture (which is often the case with Keaton's and Chaplin's comedy).

His goal of achieving popularity reaffirmed by Peggy's inspiration, Harold vows to show them what he can do on the football field, not realizing that he is only the water boy (though he has never gotten into a game). In the final comic sequence, the big football game with Union State, we have the culmination of Harold's determination and the visual affirmation of the American ideals of initiative and hard work. In the fourth quarter, Harold watches as one by one all the Tate substitutes are used up as injuries reduce the squad. Trailing 3–0, Tate finally runs out of men, and Harold asks the coach to send him in. The coach has to confess that he can't use him because Harold is only the water boy. This might have been made into another tragic scene, as it duplicates the sort of information the Cad passed on to Harold in that previous moment of realization. But this is a new Harold—or rather the epitome of the Harold roles in all the films: he becomes completely aggressive, taking a verbal stand that proves he is no longer to be victimized by others. He tells the coach: "You listen, now! I wasn't kidding! I've been working—and fighting—just for this chance— and you've got to give it to me!" The coach finally agrees to let him in, but only when the referee threatens forfeiture.

Once he is in the game, Harold's personality begins to take command

of the situation. He has neither athletic skill nor even much knowledge of the rules of the game, but he has fantastic drive. His pep talk inspires a beaten and mauled team. On the first play he is knocked unconscious and carried off on a stretcher, but he recovers and though dazed gets back into the lineup before the next play. He even manages to catch a pass in a semi-conscious state. This football sequence became the classic model for comic football scenes down to the present day. When, in 1927, Keaton made the full-length *College,* he had sense enough not to use any football sequences though his film was almost entirely concerned with college sports; this is itself high praise of Lloyd's earlier film, for it indicates that not even Keaton felt he could top the comic variations Lloyd invented in this sequence. The sequence contains such classic maneuvers as Harold's running for a touchdown with a hat he has mistaken for the ball, his waiting to catch a punt and losing sight of the ball as he gets it mixed up with some balloons (the 1925 football was much rounder than the current one), and his refusal to give up the ball to the referee after the whistle has blown.

Lacking in athletic ability, Lloyd has to rely on his enthusiasm, drive, and brains. In one shot he unties the lacing of the ball, puts the ball next to him on the ground, and when his opponents dive for it, he pulls the ball back by the lacing and walks away with it behind his back, looking nonchalant. But he commits an almost fatal blunder: mistaking a steam whistle for the referee's whistle, he stops a foot short of the touchdown, puts the ball on the ground, with no one near him, and the opposition grabs it. The coach and team are infuriated at this error, and with only a few seconds left, Harold has to rise to the occasion once more. He blocks a kick by Union State, but the ball unluckily bounces into the hands of a State player, who rushes off toward the goal line. Harold prevents a touchdown by jumping on the back of the runner, causing him to fumble the ball. Then Harold picks it up and races the length of the field; just as the game concludes, the valiant Harold, resisting the efforts of the State tacklers by sheer will power, scores the winning touchdown.

The ultimate symbol of Harold's success comes at the very end, in the dressing room, when a teammate calls him over and shows him what is going on outside the window. There Harold's tormentor, the Cad, is imitating the famous "call me Speedy" jig. However, there is no ridicule in the imitation, for next we see the coach doing the same jig. In fact, everyone is doing it—it has become a craze, a way of emulating the newest hero. In the world of Harold Lloyd's films, determination by itself has led to competence, and competence to success. In its own way, *The Freshman* is a celebration of human effort and therefore highly optimistic. Its peculiar genius does not, of course, lie in the theme, but in the way the film idea informs a great variety of extraordinary comic incidents. Lloyd's work is not a collection of visual gags but a representation of a structured comic vision, the incidents illustrating aspects of a fully conceived comic personality.

# The Comedy of Situation:
## Douglas Fairbanks and *The Mark of Zorro*

American silent screen comedy developed in two basic ways. The first type of comedy, the comedy of incident, originated as an artistic form with the Mack Sennett Keystone films. From this style most of the great comic actors perfected their individual personalities, many actually working under the auspices of Sennett. The comedy of incident sometimes featured a strong plot, but the humor was characterized by its immediate appeal from sequence to sequence. It was highly visual and sometimes quite broad; in the tradition of Sennett, it was frequently physical, sometimes violent. This was the tradition within which Keaton and Lloyd always worked. The comics were all funny in themselves, even in small roles. The comedy of incident relied on the performer as filmmaker, since much of it was either improvised or entirely related to the actor's special style. The great directors of this comic form were, aside from Sennett, great performers (and even Sennett appeared in many comedies). Emphasis was placed upon each actor's developing a recognizable characterization, and sometimes a great artist took years to develop a sufficiently original approach, as in the case of Harry Langdon and Ben Turpin. Up through the early twenties, the world of this type of comedy was visibly removed a step from reality. Even in the great Mutual Films of Chaplin (1916–17), the world is populated by people who are frequently grotesques (*e.g.,* Eric Campbell's characterizations). Of course, the connection between comedy and reality is never totally lost even in the madness of the Sennett films, but by and large, comedy of incident deviates from the realistic tradition, perhaps in order to comment on it.

The second type of comedy, that of situation, developed later, probably because the comedy of incident fit so well into the pattern of the pre-Porter films, made before it was possible to sustain a complicated narrative idea. In any case, the 1920's saw the real blooming of this kind of comedy in the work of directors such as Ernst Lubitsch and, later, Frank Capra, Frank Borzage, and Leo McCarey (all these directors eventually distinguishing themselves in the sound film). The comedy of situation is often romantic in tone but usually realistic in presentation. In general, it contrasts with the rougher comedy of incident, which, though not realistic in presentation, was so in tone. When the sound film appeared, many of the greatest silent comedians had trouble adjusting their techniques to it; on the other hand, the comedy of situation—since it was primarily a director's work rather than a performer's—was much more easily assimilated into the mainstream of the sound film. Obviously, the comedy of situation is by nature closer to the verbal comedy of manners; in fact, the two are indistinguishable in the sound film. (In the silent film, manners were certainly the subject of many comedies, but the absence of sound required films to

be highly visual and connected them more closely to the comedy of incident than they were later to be.)

Before 1920, one actor had developed great talent in the comedy of situation, Douglas Fairbanks, and his style had a great affinity with the comedy of incident. Fairbanks had the same sort of agility and physical prowess that characterized so many of the Sennett troupe as well as Buster Keaton. However, Fairbanks starred in a series of films that were definitely developed around a plot that in itself suggested the comedy: *The Lamb* (1915, written and perhaps supervised by Griffith), *Wild and Woolly* and *Reaching for the Moon* (both 1917 and directed by John Emerson), *The Mollycoddle* (1920, directed by Victor Fleming), *The Three Musketeers* (1921, directed by Fred Niblo), *Robin Hood* (1922, directed by Allan Dwan), and *The Thief of Bagdad* (1924, directed by Raoul Walsh). The association of a leading actor and a talented director is typical of the comedy of situation.

Because Fairbanks was a comedy star in somewhat the same way as his great contemporaries Chaplin, Keaton, Lloyd, and Langdon, it is not surprising that he is often considered the creative force behind his films. That Fairbanks deserves to be thought of as a filmmaker is unquestionable, but one should not overlook the fact that most of his directors are not simply anonymous figures who merely called the actors together for the shooting schedules. It is more proper to suggest that Fairbanks is the co-creator of his films along with directors such as Niblo, Dwan, and Walsh.

Fairbanks reached his comic height with *The Mark of Zorro* (1920, directed by Fred Niblo), a film that altered the nature of his career, though it actually resembled the sort of thing he had been doing all along. However, the film's popularity owed more to Fairbanks' acrobatics and the heroic character he portrayed than to the essentially comic conception of the film. He had almost accidentally hit upon a great cinematic genre, the costume adventure film, the life of which seems perennial. (Since in the remakes of *The Mark of Zorro* the comedy is removed and the swashbuckling swordsmanship emphasized, audiences come to the original version predisposed to watch it as a straightforward adventure film.) After *Zorro,* Fairbanks himself felt bound to continue in the heroic mold, and his subsequent pictures are only partially comic in conception. However, it must be noted that the character presented in all the films has to a certain degree a self-consciously comic attitude.

In his silent films (and even in his sound films), Fairbanks projects some consistent personality traits. In this respect—as well as in the physical nature of his performance and most importantly, in the relationship between the character and his actions—the performer of the sound period Fairbanks most resembles is Fred Astaire. Both men achieve the admirable feat of creating a character who extends his personality in terms of an amazing physical talent; that is, part of Fairbanks' expression of his inner character

comes from swinging through the air. In their roles, both Astaire and Fairbanks, when not exhibiting their special skills, pretend to be quite ordinary —or at least they never allude to their spectacular talents. And the roles of both dominate the film idea, requiring it to accommodate acting styles that reflect the character's awareness of what he can do when he assumes his special identity as dancer or adventurer. The best term for this role—the underlying characteristic of Fairbanks' characterizations—is the Greek concept of the *eiron* (from which we derive *irony*), the man whose characteristic behavior is understatement.

Fairbanks is the *eiron,* or ironist, par excellence in *The Mark of Zorro.* He plays two roles, one of them the masked avenger of the wrongs meted out to innocent victims by the representatives of tyranny; the other, that of the quiet, unimpressive, ordinary man, waiting for the proper moment to reveal his true identity, his more romantic, idealized life. But the rather effete caballero played by Fairbanks in his day-to-day humdrum existence (characterized by his own frequent yawns) is also a reflection of his real character; this is the *eiron* in disguise, the man who appreciates his own jest at the expense of the entire world. As an unassuming, weak young man, Don Diego laughs at the world's misconception of his capacity. But it is a joke that harms no one, for at the final moment he can merge his two personalities. No other characters are offended at his joke, since they do not know at the time that he is laughing at their opinion of him (they think him spineless). Of course, once he reveals himself, the film must come to an end because the character no longer exists as he was conceived; he is no longer an *eiron* when everyone knows that the effete man is the famous Zorro. And Zorro no longer exists when the mystery about him disappears and he is established not as the almost divine source of retribution he was thought to be but as a member of the community.

The film opens ominously with insert titles that announce the theme of the punishment of oppressors. There is no hint of comedy in the first shot: a close-up of the face of a man whose cheek bears the scar left by Zorro's sword, a Z. The scene is then revealed as a tavern, and we learn that the scarred man was punished by Zorro for beating a peasant. Almost immediately intercut into this long tavern sequence (about twenty percent of the entire film) is a shot of the chief source of the oppression: the Mexican governor of the province of California in the early nineteenth century. Immediately Zorro is spoken of as a menace to the authority of the governor, who has committed himself to finding and destroying the masked swordsman. Thus, a mood absolutely in line with romantic adventure is established from the outset. Although later treatment of such material, probably based on a tradition that this very film began, always features the romantic rather than the realistic, this film attempts to strike some balance, with much of the comedy undermining the romance.

Under the direction of Fred Niblo, the carefully structured first se-

quence cuts from the tyrannical governor not immediately back to the tavern again but to the hut of a poor native who is telling some others that Zorro is their only friend. Then once more Niblo extends the dramatization of the theme by cutting to a fourth locale, the home of the wealthy Don Carlos, who reads a piece of paper to his wife and daughter, informing them that a new decree of the governor will ruin them. Thus, the poor and the wealthy alike suffer from misrule. Now when Niblo cuts back to the tavern—and we realize that we are still in the first sequence, not the fifth (as we have seen three additional locales after the tavern)—we begin to put a good deal of expository information into place. But this is not stage exposition; the drama has been going on all the time, simultaneous with the exposition. The situation becomes suddenly intriguing when the tavern door is thrown open and a man stalks in with his head down. Is this the ghostlike Zorro? (The reference has been made to him as ghostlike earlier.) It turns out to be Sergeant Gonzales, who comes in kicking chairs and people, visually establishing his character as *miles gloriosus,* the braggart soldier. He is, however, decidedly more villainous than comic at this time. Gonzales starts to brag about what he would do if he ever came across Zorro, but in the midst of his drawing a sword to demonstrate, again the door swings open. In the blackness of the rainy night, nothing is seen, till slowly an umbrella comes through the doorway pointed at Gonzales, who is frozen on the spot, terror-stricken with the thought that this might be Zorro. Instead, it is the exceedingly mild-mannered Don Diego Vega.

The sergeant's fear not only undercuts his character; more importantly, it turns the mood of the sequence into comedy. If Zorro had entered at this point, we would have been unprepared for the kind of man he is. We know that he is the hero, certainly, but we might expect him to be severe or cruel in confronting his military opponents. His subtle play-acting and his sense of humor would be difficult to perceive if he entered in a moment of great tension. Niblo immediately establishes that Gonzales will be no match for Zorro by demonstrating in this shot that the bully can sustain his power only through his military rank. Knowing this, of course we look forward to seeing him upstaged. Yet had Zorro appeared, the comedy would not easily have begun; the audience might have been misled into expecting a violent encounter at the start of the film, which might effectively preclude any likelihood of later comic sequences. Zorro, in fact, consistently avoids violence and never kills anyone, for he is a thoroughly good-natured super-man, but we could not appreciate this yet.

Ironically, the man who has entered is indeed Zorro, in his everyday role, as most spectators must have assumed, since Fairbanks was already a star before this film. Even if we were not suspicious of the dual role, we would be amused by him as Don Diego Vega, emerging from under the umbrella, dressed as a Spanish dandy, and ordering a pot of honey for himself while treating everyone else to wine. In front of him, Gonzales can

resume his act and pretend he is sorry that it was not Zorro who entered. Don Diego seems gentle, harmless, friendly to all. But the effeteness of his characterization is modified by his constant grin. This smile radiates overwhelming self-confidence; it is the only jarring note in his appearance, yet no one but the audience notices. The *eiron* signals to those who must ultimately evaluate him (the gods or the audience) that he knows what he is doing.

The sequence continues with Gonzales demonstrating how he intends to cut up Zorro at swords, while Don Diego grimaces and winces at the imaginary slaughter, which concludes with Gonzales's characteristic kick. When Don Diego leaves, he tells Gonzales that although he detests bloodshed, ridding the country of a menace is a noble deed; these words are meant to appear as approval for Gonzales's claims about getting rid of Zorro, but an audience, even if it does not know that Diego is Zorro, knows that the menace is Gonzales and the government he stands for. Thus, Diego remains on friendly terms with Gonzales and yet avoids losing our esteem through an endorsement of the tyranny.

The sergeant continues to bluster and kick servants, but as the talk gets back to Zorro's seemingly supernatural power of showing up anywhere, Gonzales's real cowardice appears in his face. A loud sound alarms everyone, but it is a false alarm. Then, a close-up of a hand pounding on the outside of the door increases the tension. All inside are sure that it must now be Zorro, but once again it is not: a man enters and posts notice of a ten-thousand-peso reward for Zorro. Each false alarm increases Gonzales's self-confidence. Finally, he is told that if he really wants Zorro to materialize, all he has to do is pick on a priest or a peasant. Accordingly, Gonzales goes over and knocks down a peasant near the fireplace.

In a long shot, all the onlookers are shown intently gazing in front of them, while behind their backs a caped figure enters, silently lights a cigarette, and nonchalantly blows smoke toward the group. He is then noticed by the men, several of them soldiers, who are not sure of his identity, but do nothing as he, unconcerned about them, goes about shutting windows and bolting the door. Finally he turns on them defiantly and his mask reveals he is Zorro. All of the men attack him at once, eager for the reward, of which he has reminded them by ripping off the poster. But he draws a pistol on them and herds them into a corner, where they sit as a gallery while he proceeds to humiliate Gonzales in a duel.

Gonzales's clumsiness is set off by the grace and agility of Zorro, who characterizes himself by his sense of comedy. To Gonzales, the struggle is one of life and death; to Zorro, it is a game, in which, between great gymnastic leaps, he invents means to humble his opponent (he manages to soak Gonzales with water and to throw a berry in his eye). For a time, Zorro duels while sitting on a table. The shots are intercut with the gleeful response of the spectators, who are supposed to be rooting for Gonzales.

Yet one of the motifs of the film idea is that graceful physical activity can win the admiration of men. Here, the men are clearly glad to see the feats of Zorro; perhaps, too, they are glad to see Gonzales defeated—though no hint of their dislike for him has appeared. Zorro gives his opponent an unusual variation of the mark: he carves a Z in Gonzales's trousers and later backs him into the fireplace to the laughter of his supporters. Finally soldiers arrive at the tavern, and in the commotion Zorro slips away, ending the sequence. It is notable that he retains his nonchalance even when he seems —to us—to be in immediate peril.

The next sequences show Don Diego's character, very much in the light of what we have already seen in the tavern. Now, however, it is perfectly clear that Diego is perpetuating a disguise; inwardly, he is not at all the same man. He makes his gestures deliberately effeminate to amuse himself, for no one else could possibly conceive of the elements of his disguise as what they are—the props of an actor. He constantly clutches a flowing handkerchief, for instance, and uses it to wipe his face. He dangles his sombrero by its string so that when he hands it to someone who puts it on a table, he comically pulls it back without anyone observing it. This and his amateur magic tricks relate Fairbanks' performance to the style of the comedy of incident. The difference is that Fairbanks' mannerisms are meant to show us the actor in the process of creating a character. The finished character wears the face he presents to the world as Don Diego, but the humor appreciated by the movie audience stems from the total context of the Diego-Zorro world.

At the same time, the characterization of Zorro also provides self-conscious parody. Just as Diego is meant to be a self-parody of the over-privileged young man, the idle rich boy, so Zorro stands for the "cool" hero, the undaunted individualist without the slightest fear for his safety. No one in the film regards either Diego or Zorro as parodies; both are accepted for the real thing. The only one who knows they are parodies is the character himself, whose true existence lies somewhere in between the two extremes. Yet Diego-Zorro knows he has no world to live in under the present conditions. He is an ironist who has lost his identity except for his own mental image of himself. When he straightens out his world, he can reveal himself and become the integrated character that could exist only in his mind prior to the end of the film.

The hero enjoys both his roles equally. As Don Diego he has to be more comically inventive, perhaps, than as Zorro, for Diego, a passive man, responds to situations created by others rather than by his own design. For instance, his father, who scorns his son's effeminate nature, insists that he court Don Carlos's daughter, Lolita. Diego, of course, cannot marry and maintain his dual disguise. To discourage a potential marital relationship becomes his main goal. Niblo films the first courtship meeting of the would-be couple with a good deal of understatement. The girl sits across a

**28** *The Mark of Zorro*

table from Diego; they are filmed together or singled out in medium-close shots, intercut with several insert titles. Diego first of all convinces her that he is there at his father's bidding; by himself he lacks all the energy of a young man courting. He does everything deliberately calculated to make her conclude, as she does, that he is a "fish," not a man. He tells her that he will send his servant to play the guitar under her window; she counters by saying that she will send her maid to listen. Then he shows her a silly trick with his ever-present handkerchief (fig. 28), yawns, and leaves.

The contrast between his two roles is vividly emphasized when Zorro enters ten minutes after Diego leaves. Sneaking up to Lolita in the garden, Zorro kisses her hand. She resists, slapping his face, but his persistence and romantic verse capture her affections in spite of her inclinations (Zorro is, as far as she knows, only an outlaw). Their next encounter occurs when Zorro saves her from the film's chief villain, Captain Ramon, the local leader of the government's repressive troops. Ramon manages to gain entrance to the house while Lolita is alone and attempts to force himself upon her (he had previously asked for her hand), but he is now more repulsive to her than ever, for she has Zorro to think about. Of course at the moment of greatest peril, Zorro emerges, crosses swords with Ramon, and forces him to make a humiliating apology to the girl.

The next contrast is just as telling: Diego, as the official suitor, hears from Don Carlos of Ramon's insult to Lolita. The father insists that Diego take blood revenge, but all Diego says is that since so many unpleasant things occur these days, "it is most fatiguing." Later he promises Lolita that he will ride over to see Ramon and "rebuke him"—after Diego finishes his siesta! Diego's characterization of the fop is completed by his taking snuff

at a crucial point where Don Carlos, his wife, and their daughter turn their backs to him to mull over their misfortunes in regard to the dishonor given them by Ramon's conduct. Diego sneezes, and they all turn around suddenly, realizing his hopelessness as an avenger of the family's honor.

The pervading ironic tone of *The Mark of Zorro* is of an unusual kind, since the irony springs from the manipulations of a character. The hero misleads everyone, but because of his peculiar moral drive his irony does not alienate us. The Zorro role must be kept up until enough support can be gained from the aristocracy to destroy the tyranny of the governor. And the Diego role must be kept up to enable the hero to move within society without being forced to take a public stand against the governor. He aims at nothing less than a social revolution, which he cannot accomplish as an ordinary man, nor even as an extraordinary one. However, he can achieve his end in the guise of a supernatural scourge of evil who appears from nowhere and disappears without a trace. Yet the actual results of even the fantastic Zorro's accomplishments would not alone be sufficient to achieve his goal. He wounds relatively few, and all he can do physically is disrupt the forces of oppression in the ordinary course of their activities.

The real distinction of Zorro lies in his ability to present himself as a symbol that means a great deal more than the sum of his known encounters with the soldiers. The symbol he establishes for himself is that of a man with the power to do as he pleases in the face of his opponents; and more than that, to accomplish with grace and style the humiliation of his enemies. Thus, there is a real need for the hero to act in such a manner that he radiates total self-assurance despite considerable peril. For him to show fear would be to admit a human characteristic; for him to wreak havoc and disappear would be to turn into a mere terrorist. Instead, the hero chooses a role that eschews prudence and makes his valor even greater since he is always risking his life; yet he knows that he must do these things to create a certain impression in the minds of the enemy. They must grow to believe him not merely invincible but beautiful—that is, not merely the better man but the man who stands for the truth. In that way, the final irony of *The Mark of Zorro* consists in the salvation of the opposition. They observe, and they discover the error of their ways. The turnabout is, naturally, comic and romantic, but it is in keeping with the comic irony throughout. Never before had a film idea structured and integrated a full-length work through a pervasive tone, and very rarely since then has the ironic tone of a film been conceived in terms of the hero's manipulation of the world around him.

Although the plot or basic situation is comically ironic, the hero's own predicament is almost tragic in its conception. He has no public identity that he desires to claim until the end. In other words, he lives in a twilight world between two roles, neither of which he really feels is natural. Certainly, he is the antithesis of Don Diego, but he could not wish for a life as a masked avenger. In fact, he never ignores his goal—to destroy the

tyranny—though he realizes that it will make the Zorro figure unnecessary in his world. He has, on the contrary, stated a couple of times as Diego that he abhors bloodshed; as Zorro he assiduously avoids killing his opponents. Clearly, he has no innate desire to harm people, even villains. His purpose is mainly moral, though he has a secondary delight in life: he really enjoys climbing and swinging and all forms of dangerous physical activity.

The underlying tragic aspect of the hero's predicament is not emphasized, but it appears in certain moments of confrontation with his father, a nobleman who concludes that his son lacks manliness. In one sequence, Don Diego leaves a gathering of caballeros at his father's table because he claims to be fatigued. His father tells him that he is more ashamed of his son than ever before. Diego seems to hesitate for a moment, but his moral mission wins out over his relationship with his father; the hero must leave so that he can put in an appearance as Zorro before the caballeros and rouse them to his side. He finally makes his speech and it works, but at the cost of alienating his father.

Nevertheless, *The Mark of Zorro* maintains its comic tone in almost every part, despite some notes of solemnity, particularly when the nature of the tyranny is depicted (as in the whipping of a priest and the jailing of innocents). The comedy is kept afloat by the hero's dedicated portrayal of the two roles. Zorro is always trying to structure his encounters so that the underlying ridiculousness of the opposition is revealed. Don Diego, in his own way, tries to portray the inherent selfishness of the privileged class by his detachment from all the serious events around him. His faked indifference to evil presents a satiric indictment of his contemporary society.

The last quarter of the film shows Zorro achieving his goal of unifying the opposition to the tyranny and leading that side to victory. To effect a triumph conducive to the comic tone so carefully established, Zorro must bring about a reconciliation of sorts rather than an Armageddon; that is, the military forces must be converted, not destroyed. Niblo accomplishes this by means of a magnificent chase sequence in which Zorro taunts the soldiers and at length proves beyond doubt that they are no match for him.

The sequence begins with Zorro posting a notice on a tree that unarmed he will be eating lunch in the village; it is a challenge to the troops pursuing him, led by Gonzales. (Unknown to Zorro at the time, the much wickeder villain Ramon has abducted Lolita.) As the soldiers chase Zorro throughout the town, a pattern emerges: Zorro's graceful leaps surpass the physical abilities of his pursuers, who, on horse, rush in the wrong direction (see fig. 29), or on foot, following in Zorro's path, cover the same ground with clumsy enthusiasm. Zorro jumps over all obstacles, but the soldiers are barely able to climb over them. As for leaping into windows, Zorro can't even be badly imitated; the soldiers have to go in by the doors, thus giving him enough time to come back out through these same windows. For some reason they never suspect that Zorro will leave the same way he

**29**  *The Mark of Zorro*

entered; his psychological superiority parallels the physical advantage he has over them.

The sequence gathers its comic effect not only from the blatant contrast of grace and awkwardness but from our renewed understanding of Zorro's underlying good-humored attitude toward his opponents and himself. He succeeds in convincing them of his capacity to elude them forever, but he has no wish to harm them. He aims to make them look funny, even in their own eyes, as he had done earlier. Not surprisingly, we note that he finds physical challenge stimulating regardless of his audience, for even when his opponents are not present he sometimes swings into windows. This is the power of the disguise operating on a man who is by nature the complete outsider. As he has no one to discuss his adventure with (the only one who knows his identity is a mute servant), he must please himself by the activity. Thus, he never does anything to indicate that even in solitude he would let his guard down or his style lapse—as long as he wears the disguise.*

Immediately after this most spectacular of the chases in the film, Zorro rescues Lolita and lures the troops led by Ramon and the governor to his father's house for the final sequences. He takes off his Zorro disguise and resumes his role as Don Diego as the troops search the house for Zorro.

---

* In Chapter 14, a further detailed analysis of this sequence examines Niblo's method of portraying Fairbanks' exploits.

Diego appears in a robe as if he were still half asleep; his yawns contrast strikingly with the bustle of the soldiers. When he protests, he is shoved disdainfully by Ramon, who then insults him in front of Lolita by saying that Diego was not man enough to win Lolita and that the house has become a rendezvous for Lolita and her lover.

Diego's reaction is his first gesture out of character. He punches Ramon in the face, knocking him down. This completely atypical action takes everyone by surprise, and of course it signals the fact that the hero is giving up his effeminate characterization. His next gesture is to reveal the Z he has previously cut on Ramon's neck, indicating that now he has also given up the mystery of the Zorro role. Ramon, however, does not know that Diego is Zorro until they duel, and when his opponent gives him his second Z—this time on his forehead—he realizes that Diego is Zorro unmasked. By this time, Diego's father and all the noblemen have assembled for the showdown. Everyone is properly shocked to discover that the meekest of men is also the most terrifying. The two most interesting reactions are the governor's and Gonzales's. The hero announces that all the noblemen are on his side and that the tyranny is finished. The governor rather humbly asks what he can do. The answer is to abdicate, leave the country, and take Ramon with him. The governor hesitates for a moment, then bows and acquiesces. Gonzales, however, runs over, slaps Zorro on the back, and instantly but sincerely converts to the side of his old antagonist, swearing to keep his soldiers with him. His conversion, comic as it is on the surface, is thematically right to the point of the film. The Zorro role had been created to demoralize the opposition into an awareness that Zorro could not be suppressed. The final chase sequence proved the point visually, and the conversion of the "bad" soldiers proved it thematically.

The last shots of the film show the hero and Lolita embracing. Lest we assume that Diego has now allowed his personality to be submerged by Zorro, the hero turns to the crowd watching him and says, "Have you seen this one?" He then proceeds to do his final handkerchief trick (an unsuccessful attempt to cover up their kissing). Of course, it would be just as impossible for the hero to revert back to the effeminate Diego as it would be for him to don a mask and swing from balconies. The truth is that he was never really Diego or Zorro; whatever he was, he can now live with that real identity. He may in the future practice his gymnastics, but he really does like those handkerchief tricks too. As with most comedy, the sense of social reconciliation is dominant at the close. The evil has been exiled and the natural order of good men concerned with justice for all has been restored.

# 9

# Narrative Drama in the Silent Film

## Narrative Drama Contemporary with Griffith's Films

The film has never developed a tragic genre that approximates the genre of tragedy on the stage. Quite likely, this has something to do with the decline of the tragic narrative sense in the twentieth century, as evidenced in today's theater. Although tragic films have occasionally been made, most films, like most modern plays, present a narrative that can be characterized by the popular term drama, if by drama we mean simply all narrative works that do not fit into the category of comedy.

In the silent film, comedy achieved a degree of artistic dominance (judged from our point of view today) because of the surprising amount of great comic talent that developed in the American industry, which emerged at the beginning of the sound era as the major film industry in the world. Cinema had very quickly achieved artistic supremacy in regard to a kind of hilarious comedy unmatched on the stage or in the novel, but this sort of art—as exemplified by Mack Sennett's films—was never considered the sort of material that would give the film significant status in the intellectual community (though many intellectuals, then as now, admired the Sennett films).

Comedy succeeded artistically before drama in the film perhaps be-

cause comedy is inherently much more adaptable to the one- and two-reel form than is drama. Although Griffith accomplished a great deal in making drama artistically feasible in one reel, he himself felt confined by the one-reel form. The first attempts at longer, artistic dramatic films were the Italian spectacles, the most famous being *Quo Vadis?* (1912), and the products of the French Film d'Art movement, which turned out *Queen Elizabeth* (1912) with Sarah Bernhardt. The Film d'Art is of interest in that its pretentious name signified one of the earliest attempts to elevate film by turning it into a form of literature. This attempt was misdirected, despite its good intentions, for by relying on famous theater performers and famous literary sources (such as Ibsen and Shakespeare), it did little to improve the development of a true cinematic style. In an equivalent American film production of a French play, *Cleopatra* (1912), the stage star Helen Gardner labored mightily for very meager effects. Film versions of famous novels and plays were as common in the silent era as they are now. These literary properties could not be transferred to a nonverbal medium with any real fidelity to the original, but to change them drastically would be to defeat the purpose of bringing high art to the cinema. Thus, the completely static film with Helen Gardner is a ludicrous version of a play, with Cleopatra denied

her voice and forced to rely on extravagant hand gestures to distinguish herself from the surrounding characters when she speaks and to convey any idea (fig. 30). Of course, since the ideas were almost entirely verbal, the gestures are ambiguous without the insert titles. On the other hand, the numerous insert titles explain everything, and the visual images become disruptions of the continuity of plot developing from title to title.

In fact, the only really bright spots in the early narrative films outside of Griffith's and those of filmmakers he immediately influenced in America were Scandinavian films by Victor Seastrom (Sjöström) (*The Outlaw and His Wife*, 1918; *The Phantom Coach*, 1920) and Maurice Stiller (*The Song of the Red Flower*, 1918; *Sir Arne's Treasure*, 1919).* In retrospect it seems amazing that the dramatic film would suddenly flourish at the beginning of the second decade and reach artistic fulfillment within the six or seven years remaining to it before the sound film would significantly alter the nature of cinematic art.

With the production of *The Birth of a Nation* and *Intolerance*, Griffith, it could be said without overstatement, had worked out the essential premises of narrative drama. If the film had made no other technical advance after 1916, it would have remained a formidable art form for the rest of the century. Significant developments followed Griffith's innovations, of course, but Griffith had established the viability of film form for the expression of a great variety of narrative ideas. The filmmakers who came later modified the techniques and introduced new styles. As a matter of fact, the epic structure in which Griffith excelled in his 1915–16 masterpieces was very quickly modified to fit the much less ambitious drama that was to become the standard film fare of the century. In the forefront of those who remolded the epic structure to fit the domestic or realistic materials of the films for the last decade of the silent era was the master himself. Griffith turned out some truly beautiful films such as *Broken Blossoms* (1919) and *Way Down East* (1920) as he led the way toward the development of a cinema of personal narrative, as distinct from the broad epic that told the story of a great many people.

What remained to be done, then, after *Intolerance*, was to perfect the presentation of psychology and of realism. In its struggle for artistic status, the film competed with the two other major narrative forms of the early twentieth century, the novel and the play. Both verbal arts had already developed a realistic mode and a method for conveying psychological depth. Easily enough, the film soon rivaled or surpassed literature in the depiction of surface realism, but found inner reality more difficult to portray.

There are two basic ways for the film to depict visually the conditions

* The films of these men are not easily accessible. The best known, Stiller's *The Story of Gösta Berling* (1923), is available in a two-hour version from the Museum of Modern Art; the film originally ran four hours. The positions of these filmmakers in the history of film are undisputed, but their work has not been truly evaluated yet.

within man. The first way requires symbolic references that stand for the workings of the mind. Because narrative films are so insistently realistic in terms of the images presented, filmmakers cannot often derive a consistent pattern of symbols that is neither too literal nor too obscure. Thus, a second, and more fruitful, possibility is to *imply* an inner condition by creating an environment that clearly exemplifies the attitudes of a particular character; this method, of course, uses the camera and the techniques of editing to turn the objective recording of reality into what is ostensibly a single individual's view of the world. Both methods are examined in this chapter, the first as observed in *The Cabinet of Dr. Caligari,* and the second as seen in *The Last Laugh.* Both films are important beyond their considerable artistic achievement because as popular and critical successes they awakened the public to the possibilities of psychological cinema and therefore greatly expanded the range of the dramatic film idea.

## The Symbolic Representation of Inner Reality: Wiene's *The Cabinet of Dr. Caligari*

Once Griffith revealed the capabilities of narrative drama, filmmakers of considerable talent began appearing in several different countries. In the 1920's the first European country to achieve a consistently high level of narrative drama was Germany, which led the way in psychological studies. Although Hollywood was able eventually to lure most of them away and revitalize its own industry in the twenties and thirties, the following major filmmakers worked in Germany: G. W. Pabst, E. A. Dupont, Fritz Lang, Ernst Lubitsch, Josef von Sternberg, and F. W. Murnau.

The first German film of international importance was Robert Wiene's *The Cabinet of Dr. Caligari* (1919), with the scenario by Hans Janowitz and Carl Mayer. The film caught the public's imagination perhaps because it represented a break with the developing tradition of realistic settings for the feature film and yet retained real characters engaged in unusual but not implausible activities. Besides, it is a fully conceived murder mystery with elements of eeriness, if not of the supernatural. Much influenced by German expressionistic drama, then at its height, it was the first (and virtually the last) film to employ an unreal environment throughout a serious narrative.

Perhaps the most remarkable aspect of *The Cabinet of Dr. Caligari* is its mastery of a personal or subjective point of view. This notable achievement is, even today, not at all characteristic of film narrative. However, it is commonplace in prose fiction, where the first-person point of view, in which a narrator tells what he has observed or what he has participated in, is easy to achieve; in fact, this method is older than the novel itself (Defoe uses it in *Robinson Crusoe,* for instance). In film, the personal point of view is usually established by shots of a person followed by shots of the things

that he was either looking at or thinking about.* But a first-person approach to a whole narrative film is ordinarily not feasible, because even if the narrator appears in every sequence (as, for example, in Orson Welles's *The Lady from Shanghai*), details such as shots of other faces not readily observed by the narrator ruin attempts at absolute consistency.

In *The Cabinet of Dr. Caligari,* everything appears structured so as to be a story within a story. The film begins with one man announcing to another that he has something strange to tell. From this point until the very end, when we return to the narrator, the story is consistently related from the narrator's viewpoint. What makes *Caligari* so unusual is that the narrative is revealed at the end to have been untrue, a fabrication of an insane mind. On first seeing the film, the audience could not anticipate the conclusion, which Wiene intended as a surprise. In 1919, at least, there was no audience of sleuths who came predisposed to question the materials of the mystery designed by the filmmaker. They might note some lapses— that is, the story is supposed to tell the events as they appeared to the narrator, but several parts give details that the narrator presumably could not know but only guess at. Naturally, too, the audience is struck by the unrealistic sets, but soon accepts the decor as essential to the mood. It is only at the end that the significance of the environment is clarified and the audience informed that the sets represent the narrator's distorted perception. Thus, these questionable parts turn out to be entirely consistent with the rest of the narrative.

The story told by the narrator, Francis, seems plausible enough; at least no hint appears of any motive for Francis's not telling us or his listener the truth. He relates an account of a traveling carnival entertainer, Caligari, and a somnambulist, Cesare, who sleeps in a cabinet. The community in which this act is being shown is victimized by some inexplicable murders, one of them of Francis's friend. Francis becomes suspicious of the sinister figure of Caligari, but the investigation of the authorities cannot prove anything about Francis's theory that Cesare commits murders at the command of Caligari (see fig. 31). Toward the end of the film the persistent Francis tracks down Caligari, who flees into an insane asylum, followed by Francis, who makes the shocking discovery that Caligari heads the institution. In the original screenplay, according to Siegfried Kracauer's well-known analysis of the film in *From Caligari to Hitler,* Francis overcomes

* In a dialogue sequence, two characters' personal points of view may be shown just as simply: by filming the listener, we have the speaker's personal view; by filming the speaker, we have the listener's viewpoint. This method has never caused the audience any difficulty in comprehension, probably because we are used to looking at speakers this way in real-life situations. But prose fiction can never present the viewpoints of two characters simultaneously. A prose writer can at best print dialogue without indicating "he said," "she said," etc. Thus, written dialogue is presented always from an objective point of view. In film, shifting the point of view is entirely natural.

**31** *The Cabinet of Dr. Caligari*

his adversary and unmasks him for the murderer that he is; however, Wiene changed the ending by devising the structure of a story within a story. In the film version, when the narrator concludes his story, we return to the first scene of the film, where it becomes clear that the narrator is himself an inmate of Dr. Caligari's asylum. Caligari appears at the very end as the kindly doctor who diagnoses Francis's madness and announces his hopes of curing the patient. This ending ties everything together neatly without leaving us with the feeling that we have been cheated, as is almost always the case with modern variants on this structure in which a man wakes up at the end and the whole narrative turns out to have been a dream.

Wiene's film attempts to relate its environment to its tone more immediately than other films had done. Quite apart from any interest the viewers might find in the expressionist scenic pattern, the settings in *Caligari* are intended to provoke a sense of mystery and psychological disorientation (fig. 32). The visual design was sharply angular, emphasizing props and backgrounds and even streets that were patently out of proportion to the real world they represented. They were clearly patterns borrowed from the popular expressionistic theater. Audiences generally assumed that

**32** *The Cabinet of Dr. Caligari*

such stage settings suggested the way people actually dreamed and also the way people with various psychoses looked at the world; as such, they stand as the equivalent of our generation's psychedelic designs, which supposedly serve the same functions. Despite its great success, *The Cabinet of Dr. Caligari* did not exert a tremendous influence on the settings of films that followed. Expressionism was sometimes used in small doses within realistic films to suggest a disoriented view of the world, as well as in stylized horror films like *Frankenstein* and science-fiction works like Lang's *Metropolis*. Even in the tradition of experimental filming, where *Caligari* stands out prominently as a source of inspiration, the best films to come did not make use of a primarily realistic narrative with real enough people in contradistinction to a deliberately contrived, artifical background.

Because the discovery of Francis's insanity is intended to be, and is, a surprise ending, the film's expressionistic images should be evaluated for their cinematic effectiveness while the film is in progress, not after it has ended. The scenery transforms reality into two-dimensional sets and designs, throwing the human figure into rather sharp relief: flattened out backgrounds detach themselves from the characters, who must, because of their

three-dimensional bodies, appear in a different light. The camera then has the main responsibility for emphasizing either the falseness of the human in a world of unreality or the falseness of the settings in a world of reality. The latter tends to get the emphasis in *Caligari,* for as we become accustomed to the background we concentrate more and more on the murder mystery that structures the narrative.

In the film, the camera simply presents the setting objectively, doing little if anything to stress the unreality of the narrator's concept of the world—it merely shows that world in its distorted design. Whatever weird effects the film attains are achieved by set design, not by editing or cinematography. The use of numerous iris shots—which for modern viewers tends to heighten the effect of mystery—was a commonplace stylistic technique even in the Mack Sennett films. In the experimental films that followed, and in those made today, special effects are achieved by the editing or the camera itself—that is, real objects are made unreal, distorted, or pulled out of context, or else the entire film is made surrealistic, as in animation.

The effect of the camera's objectivity in *Caligari* is that the narrative is unimpeded by the background. The background affects the tone and establishes the context for the reversal of our premises in the end, but the story itself could have been filmed in perfectly realistic city streets. When a modern film adopts the surprise ending, it basically foregoes the unreal setting: when a character awakes from a dream, what the spectator had assumed was reality is revealed to have been false, but while in the process of depicting the dream, the photography did not physically distort the environment. In *Caligari,* the environment is overtly unreal; the characters relate to it only casually, until the ending reveals a much deeper connection, and we find that what we have assumed to be a fantastic setting is actually reality, completely intelligible as the reality of a sick mind.

The camera in this film remains rather static and conventional. It does not function to interpret but to report, and in that sense reminds us of the primitive films. This surely does not mean that no creative mind is apparent in the conception; it is definitely a new cinematic experience shaped by Wiene in close collaboration with Janowitz, Mayer, and the cameraman. The peculiar subject matter almost requires a degree of detachment during filming, in order to portray without the bias of reason the personal ravings of a madman: an objective camera lets us see what the madman saw or at least thought he saw.

## Subjective Reality by Implication: Murnau's *The Last Laugh*

F. W. Murnau's *The Last Laugh* (1924) is one of those films that exert tremendous influence in their day and therefore take on a historic importance that may restrict appreciation of the artistic value in the work

itself. The film remains significant in its own right, but what originally made it a landmark in the cinema now may obscure its artistry. For instance, the American print lacked insert titles except for a note from the filmmaker introducing the epilogue (though some scholarship today suggests that in fact the German version did have titles); in any case, the feat is not truly important. Conceivably, if it were worth the effort, feature films could have been made earlier without titles, as they were sometimes done after Murnau's film became popular. The absence of titles does suggest that the visual images carry the whole meaning, but it may also suggest excessive simplicity or overextended visual demonstrations that could be better handled with a few inserted titles. Some directors used titles well, Eisenstein superbly. Furthermore, Murnau's film contains a number of written words— signs, a letter shown in close-up, and a newspaper story, for example.

More impressive and more important was the use of the moving camera in this film. Murnau moved the camera more than other leading filmmakers had done, sometimes with telling effects. However, viewing *The Last Laugh* today we would have to say that the emphasis placed on the moving camera by film historians is simply out of proportion to its actual use in the film. Hardly any film made today, for instance, would employ so *few* moving camera shots. Murnau was an innovator, but his instinct was primarily classical. Camera movement made the film a landmark in the development of technique, but to think of the film in terms of only one technique is misleading. The forcefulness of his moving camera is due perhaps to the restraint with which it is used—at least in comparison with the number of stationary setups and the emphasis on editing to convey the film idea. One film historian writes, "Throughout the film his camera was constantly on the prowl, roaming freely through the city streets, crowded flats and long hotel corridors." * In fact, it may be that Murnau did discover the secret of moving the camera effectively by choosing to move it from time to time rather than "roaming freely" as often as he could.

*The Last Laugh* is notable for the carefully defined area of its plot. It is a truly cinematic narrative rather than a literary one. Murnau's script was written by Carl Mayer, who had shown in *Caligari* skill at the kind of narrative that would be truly expressive in a visual medium. The story of *The Last Laugh* is simplicity itself: an aging hotel doorman is given an inferior position as washroom attendant because he is no longer physically able to meet the requirements of his more exalted position. Because of his pride in his old job and the status it gave him in his community, he feels that his demotion robs him of all dignity; this turns out to be true, for later, in a nightmarish sequence, his neighbors join in mocking him. In terms of the plot, the single most important event of the film is his pathetic robbery of his former doorman's uniform, which he needs so as to deceive

* Arthur Knight, *The Liveliest Art* (New York, Mentor, 1957), p. 61.

his neighbors about his condition (though he is found out by them at last). At a certain point, when Murnau has gone as far as possible in depicting the misery of the ex-doorman, the filmmaker suddenly switches direction. He inserts a message to the effect that in real life the main character would simply deteriorate, but that the director has decided to add an unrealistic epilogue. This lengthy epilogue takes up more than fifteen percent of the film and completely reverses the story: a millionaire dies and leaves his fortune to the washroom attendant. Although this material seems a perversion of the truth contained in the larger part of the film, no decline in the quality of filming is evinced in the epilogue.

In its conception the main part of the narrative is both realistic and psychological. That is, the doorman is placed in a convincingly real environment (though the film was shot in a studio), surrounded by real people; yet the interest lies not so much in the character's relationship with his environment as in—if we can separate the two—his reaction, mental and spiritual, to the loss of his position in the world. The drama of *The Last Laugh* is conceived in purely cinematic terms. Visual imagery predominates, and the exploitation of commonplace images, unsuitable to the theater or the novel, transforms the everyday reality into an ever-deepening revelation of the human soul. Thus, the picture need not be turned into a literary statement for us to grasp its human meaning.

No subplots and no extended characterizations of minor figures distract us from Murnau's insistent portrayal of the doorman. The role was handled with tremendous feeling by Emil Jannings, only twenty-nine at the time, but made up to look sixty. Aiding Murnau and Jannings, Karl Freund, the cameraman, beautifully conveyed the relationship of form and content. In *Caligari,* the characters moved through a maze of disjointed scenery, though in truth the characters paid no attention to the unreality of setting. In *The Last Laugh,* the environment is perfectly ordinary and familiar, but Freund's camera captures Jannings' constant awareness of place. The result is to bring us ever closer in our emotional involvement with the doorman in his plight. Jannings' situation makes the environment seem almost alive and certainly antagonistic; in turn, the environment gives greater dimension to the character. Photographed constantly as an isolated figure, the doorman both in prosperity and in sorrow takes on a stature as a human being that he could not have achieved had he continually shared the picture frame with the various minor characters set off around him.

Oddly enough, Murnau intercuts a good deal during certain sequences, though no minor plot is developed. When he incorporates in a sequence occurring in one location a shot of activity occurring somewhere else, he enlarges the audience's perspective of the particular dramatic incident within the sequence. For instance, when the doorman, while in the manager's office, discovers he has been removed from his job, some shots of his successor performing the duties of that position are intercut into the se-

quence to suggest to the audience Jannings' understanding of the impact of the event on his life. Later, working as a washroom attendant, Jannings slowly eats some food from a bowl while sitting in the rear of the washroom (fig. 33); this shot is paralleled by one of hotel guests dining luxuriously upstairs. Actual crosscutting is used sparingly, but effectively, in the sequence where Jannings' neighbors have learned of his demotion and prepare to greet him with derisive laughter; shots of the poor man in the washroom and on the way home increase poignancy because of our knowledge of what awaits him when he arrives.

The predominant stationary camera setups are apparently chosen for their expressiveness, but whenever possible the camera is placed in an unusual position. However, Freund's skillful stationary camerawork avoids calling attention to itself—even though he is filming from unfamiliar vantage points. This is a tribute to Murnau's visual conception of the film. The first shot, indeed, does emphasize the camera inasmuch as its cleverness caused immediate interest: the camera comes down on an elevator in the Atlantic Hotel and continues to move through the lobby. But from this camera movement Murnau goes on to establish the hotel environment mainly by means of stationary setups.

We first glimpse Jannings' face from behind a car window. While the

**33**  *The Last Laugh*

camera photographs the front of the hotel from across the street, a taxi stops between the hotel and the camera. We look through the window at the doorman on the other side of the taxi as he hurries to assist the emerging woman, sheltering her from the pouring rain with an umbrella. Then the camera switches to the opposite vantage point, looking from the hotel toward the street. A fairly close low-angle shot emphasizes a trunk on top of the taxi. Then a high-angle shot from atop the taxi shows the doorman struggling under the weight of the trunk. Once it dawns on us that the doorman is the main character, we have already been predisposed to sympathize with him (because he works in the rain and has to lift heavy weights). This sympathy has been engendered "objectively" inasmuch as the camera is not recording it from any particular person's point of view.

After the rain has stopped, the doorman, in the process of removing his raincoat and putting on his gloves, reveals a new dimension of his character: a degree of pride in his magnificent uniform and his occupation, as indicated by the care with which he puts on his gloves. We see him in long shot moving with a full sense of his prominence against a background of cars and people that pale into insignificance behind him. He stands more than erect, almost as if his chest were inflated. Murnau humorously fastens onto his small vanity by showing him looking into a mirror and checking the grooming of his moustache. The doorman enjoys his work, whistling for cabs, saluting guests, escorting ladies to their taxis, and just generally presiding over the passing world. In this last aspect, he turns his back to the camera to gaze at the people walking in front of him—but as they are further from the camera than he is, they seemed dwarfed by his large body.

In the next sequence, the doorman is placed in the environment of his neighborhood, a lower-class section filled with the life of the city—mothers getting their children to go into their apartments, husbands doing the same to their wives. But the appearance of the doorman in his uniform immediately uplifts the general tone. Greeted with respect by the neighbors, he tips his hat in return. Obviously no wealthier than the rest, he is nevertheless the most dignified member of the community. Here some more appealing traits of character are shown in his tender relationship with a young woman (his daughter or perhaps his niece) who is to be married that day and in his befriending a little girl in the street who has been mistreated by her playmates—he picks her up, gives her candy, and wraps her cloak around her (fig. 34).

When the doorman returns to work, he discovers another, younger man occupying his position. Some of the same camera setups from the beginning of the film are used, but now the meaning of the shots is quite different, for Jannings shares the frame with the new doorman, who is even larger than he is. Also, for the first time, Jannings stoops a bit, just enough to contrast with the new doorman; more importantly, it is clear that Jannings really is an older man, for now that he is emotionally stung and

**34**   *The Last Laugh*

thinking of something else, he forgets to pose himself in his former proud fashion.

The sequence in which the manager informs Jannings of his demotion exhibits Murnau at his best. Up to this point the cutting has been fairly rapid. Now, however, as Jannings goes to the manager's office for an explanation, we watch him from behind glass doors receiving a letter from the hands of the manager. The manager sits at his desk at the left of the frame, facing the camera. Jannings stands half turned away from the camera with the letter in his hand, his back more stooped than we have noticed before. This one stationary shot is held for an almost unbearable duration while Jannings, barely moving, fumbles for his glasses. Finally the camera moves in through the glass door and frames Jannings in a close shot. The letter tells him he is no longer of an age to carry on his duties and therefore is being assigned another job. We see a mixture of sadness and disbelief in a series of close shots and close-ups of Jannings' face, intercut with some medium shots of the manager, his back to the doorman.

Then Jannings notices a trunk in the corner of the room. A close-up

of the trunk suggests immediately what is happening in his mind: he has the idea of proving himself. Now the speed of the cutting increases with the tension. Jannings rushes across the room; the camera in mid-shot focuses on the trunk, and Jannings, coming from behind the camera, moves past the camera and reaches for the trunk. A close shot indicates Jannings straining to hold it over his head. A close shot of the trunk falling to the ground and opening is followed by a close shot of Jannings collapsing from the effort. The manager hesitates over whether to assist the fallen man. Finally he comes over to Jannings, and not knowing what to do and obviously annoyed at being put into the situation, he bends toward the doorman, who is in a sort of stupor. The manager resolves his quandary by clapping for an employee, who comes and helps Jannings.

Because few incidents divert us from the main narrative development, Murnau felt free to examine his material from varying perspectives. *The Last Laugh* is unusual in its smoothness in changing from objective to personal presentation, switching frequently from one point of view to the other throughout. No equivalent in traditional literature can be found for this technique, and its full esthetic implications for the cinema have not yet been worked out by theoreticians. In any case, no question arises of its effectiveness here.

Most of the film presents an objective study of the degradation of a human being by external forces. For instance, in the sequence that begins the doorman's humiliation, after he realizes that he has lost his job, we see him on his feet but propped up and in fact virtually unconscious. A bellhop struggles to take off his uniform-coat, while in another shot the manager goes over to a sink and washes his hands. Murnau's visual statement about the manager's reaction to the event and the stupefied reaction of the doorman represents no character's view of the situation; the idea is structured in the mind of the audience by the editing.

Other sequences, equally effective, clearly attempt to bring our perspective in line with the doorman's personal view. There are basically two ways of achieving this. The first is Murnau's habitual use of the camera to describe the appearance of the world to the mind of the doorman. For instance, after the man has stolen his uniform and fled the hotel so that he can return home in dignity by pretending he is still the doorman, Murnau shows us the immediate reaction of a guilty conscience. The buildings seem to swarm over the cringing doorman as he looks up from apparent safety in a street across from the hotel. He will not, certainly, be pursued (indeed, the theft is never discovered), but for a moment it seems to his distraught perception that the city itself has taken note of his robbery. An even more famous example of the use of this first method of subjectivism is in the drinking sequence. When the doorman returns home he joins a wedding party and eventually becomes intoxicated. Murnau shows this by having the camera duplicate the movements of a drunken man. Freund may have

strapped the camera to his chest and whirled around to produce the effect, one of the most famous in the film.

As a tour de force of cinematography, such subjective filming is of interest. The first example intended to simulate the doorman's anxiety, the second to describe his momentary escape in drunkenness. We may have some reservations, however, about the artifice employed to achieve such an effect. It requires bringing the camera into the film as a character—that is, it calls attention to the presence of the mechanical device.

But Murnau uses a second, much more effective method of conveying subjectivity, and it remains one of the major achievements of *The Last Laugh*. Murnau was among the first to prove that a subjective view of reality can be clearly presented without camera distortions or chaotic camera angles *and* even with the presumed subjective perceiver himself in the picture frame. He achieves the subjective effect by leading us into a position where we have a complete understanding of a character's emotional predicament through a total comprehension of the entire visual area that the character is himself absorbed in. If the character is to appear within the frame during a shot that supposedly represents his point of view, then we must be able to assume that he is keenly aware of his being in that particular position at that particular time.

Some examples will clarify this method. In one shot, Jannings climbs the stairs to his apartment, depressed and guilty for wearing a uniform no longer rightfully his; he has just stolen the uniform and put it on, and now he is immensely weary from the events of his day. But this is the day of his daughter's (or niece's?) wedding. He is about to join the celebration going on inside. When the door opens, he confronts family and friends, and with a tremendous effort, he forces himself to receive congratulations and to take part in the joyous occasion. We see the responses of others as he sees them, and we see him turning his weariness and sorrow into a broad smile. This is surely a subjective shot even though the camera's point of view technically is objective because Jannings, the perceiver, is also perceived in the frame. But the entire emotional force of the incident lies in our awareness of Jannings' knowledge that he must act a certain way in front of these people.

The tragic moment of the film is also primarily done from the point of view of the main character. A relative (usually called the daughter's aunt) has unexpectedly gone to the hotel to bring him something to eat. Shocked by seeing a new doorman, she asks for Jannings, and a messenger is sent down to him in the washroom while she waits at the head of the steps. Jannings is on his knees cleaning the floor. The situation is remarkably tense, for the audience is aware that the impending discovery of his condition will be the ultimate humiliation of his life. But it becomes immediately clear that Jannings fears this too, though he probably does not know who has sent to see him.

As he slowly picks himself up and moves toward the door, the camera photographs the washroom from the outside. It is primarily an objective shot, and no one is in the frame. Then the door swings open slowly, and Jannings' face appears in close-up. The subjective element here is not Jannings' physical presence, but the fear of exposure, the destruction of the psychological being whose ability to survive hinges on his retaining the illusion of status. The shot is followed immediately by an overtly subjective shot, as Jannings sees the woman's horrified expression (her world too is collapsing) as the camera moves from close to very close (the effect comparable to a zoom shot today). Then Murnau cuts back to a close-up of the horror in Jannings' face; then a full shot of the woman fleeing, followed by a mid-shot of Jannings virtually folding up, withdrawing into the washroom, and a close shot of him leaning in total despair against the washroom door. The portrayal of the internal turmoil of the man is unsurpassed in the cinema. No words could bring us any closer to what is going on inside him. The subjective camera here goes far beyond that earlier depiction of what a man sees when he is drunk; here we have what a man feels at the climactic moment of his life.

For sheer virtuosity in filming, what follows the climactic sequence is as good as anything Murnau ever achieved. Yet the continuation occurs with such natural smoothness that we are not even aware of the transition into the next sequence. The old man leans against the door, his pride destroyed, his life ruined, when suddenly a completely indifferent hotel guest appears, demanding service. Murnau immediately switches to an objective presentation. Objectivity derives from Murnau's directing our attention away from the old man's view of his misery to a dramatic confrontation between the guest and Jannings. We still retain a sense of what the main character is feeling; however, the emphasis in this sequence falls not on his subjective view of the world, but on the way he appears physically in the conflict that develops because each man is preoccupied with his personal thoughts. The guest wants his towel, he wants his jacket brushed. Jannings' mind is completely taken up with the tragic awareness of his decline. He has no interest in the guest, who in turn has no interest in him. But the guest insists that Jannings perform his duties, and Jannings has no will to resist.

Here Murnau creates two amazing shots. One of them is a close-up of Jannings' hand holding a rag over the guest's shoe. He is supposed to polish that shoe—the guest demands it—but somehow Jannings cannot bring himself to be concerned. Thus, Murnau's close-up of a hand conveys a mental attitude as effectively as the more famous shot of Mae Marsh's hands in *Intolerance*. Jannings' seeming absentmindedness sends the irate guest into a fury: it is the final straw; he has suffered from bad service too long and storms out to complain to the manager. At this point, Murnau holds the camera in a long shot outside the glass washroom door. The camera seems fixed to the spot as the man runs out the door, up the stairs,

past the camera, and through the glass doors above. Some seconds elapse with no one in the frame, but the camera remains fastened on the washroom. The angry guest and the manager appear from behind the camera, walk down the steps and enter the washroom; their figures are observed through the washroom door as dark, somewhat ominous shapes. Again some seconds pass with no one in the frame. Finally, the manager and the guest emerge, walk up the stairs, and continue past the camera and out of sight.

This long shot—that is, long in distance—is held for a surprising length of time, considering the fact that Murnau generally prefers relatively short durations for individual shots. In any case, this shot and the preceding sequence of shots, from the moment the guest enters the washroom, are all filmed from a basically objective point of view simply because the characters are really unconscious of each other. Murnau thus shows us how even in a moment of tragic revelation human beings are thrown together casually into forced social situations. Both men, wrapped up in their own thoughts, cannnot comprehend the whole significance of the scene, as the viewer does from the vantage point of the objective camera.

At the conclusion of the dramatic action of the film, the subjective and objective points of view seem to have merged. Our last images of Jannings show him sitting hunched over a chair in the washroom late at night, incapable of being comforted by a humble watchman who has befriended him. Here both the watchman and Jannings are involved with Jannings' mental state—which is complete despair. Yet this subjective feeling has been enlarged into an image of human despair in general. Murnau achieves this symbolic abstraction partially through a curious effect: he has the watchman continually frame Jannings in the darkness with a flashlight beam; the result is the pictorial equivalent of an iris shot. The overwhelming emphasis lies, of course, on Jannings' state, not on the perception of the watchman. But the watchman stays there to objectify the situation. As an outsider, he is introduced to represent the audience's basic reaction of sympathy toward intense human suffering.

The epilogue of *The Last Laugh* is comic in style and represents a considerable let-down in tone from the dramatic portion of the film. Critics tend to ignore the ending because it seems so gratuitous that it invites just such a critical response. On the other hand, Murnau's happy ending is neither brief nor carelessly thrown together. It affords us an alternative view of a man's life again manipulated by an irrational fate beyond the individual's control. This time the last laugh is Jannings' in his newly found wealth. The epilogue reverses the image of the pathetic figure seated on a small chair in the washroom at the end of the dramatic portion of the film.

Some critics interpret the device of inherited wealth as used in the epilogue as a parody on happy endings, but more likely, it functions as a quick way of presenting a reversal of fortune without developing this re-

versal in terms of realistic plot manipulation. Murnau might have assumed that to establish verisimilitude for a reversal once he has brought Jannings to a seemingly hopeless position would require a chain of incidents as long as the film itself had been up to that point. And even if such a series of events could be made realistically convincing, it would seriously change the nature of the entire work. For a long film half devoted to Jannings' fall and half to his subsequent rise would result in saga, not tragedy. Murnau apparently was quite willing to sacrifice realism to preserve the tragic nature of his film idea.

Nevertheless, it remains unclear why Murnau attached an ending that seems detachable. Why did he feel a happy ending of any sort was necessary to his cinematic concept? A tentative answer might be found by considering the cinematic content of the epilogue rather than simply the story of it. That is, perhaps what Murnau intended to achieve in the ending was not simply a reversal of the plot but a contrast in characterization that would enable us to see the personal tragedy in another light. By describing two contrasting alternatives to a man's life, Murnau might be suggesting an inherent opposition in all men between inner reality and external circumstances.

To substantiate this, we must first question the accepted sense in which *The Last Laugh* ends happily. At the dramatic conclusion to the story, Jannings, a humble figure of man's despair, has been stripped of his status in the world and is without hope of regaining it. An insert title informs us that the "author took pity" on Jannings and "has provided a quite improbable epilogue," since in real life the old man "would have little to look forward to but death." The epilogue fades in with a series of fourteen shots of guests and employees laughing hysterically over the newspaper story of the eccentric millionaire who left his money to a washroom attendant in whose arms the millionaire happened to die. This is followed by one of the best moving shots in the entire film: the camera dollies backwards through the hotel dining room, passing from table to table where people are presumably reading or talking about the same newspaper story. It finally comes to rest on a table surrounded by waiters, and as they move away they reveal a serving dish heaped with a fantastic variety of exotic foods; when the dish is removed, we discover Jannings behind it, tasting the food and various wines. The camera, through a long, winding process, has moved us in on the object of everybody's mirth, the old man made suddenly wealthy, now no longer a subject of pathos.

Except for overindulging in luxurious food, Jannings is the same man we saw earlier in adversity, but now, with all adversity gone, he shows the better aspects of his character—he is charitable toward his replacement in the washroom and has become the lavish patron of the watchman who befriended him at the close of the dramatic portion of the film. He gives tips to the small army of hotel employees who serve him. And when his

former antagonist, the manager, walks by, Jannings shows that no ill will has been harbored by graciously acknowledging him.

Yet with all these good traits displayed, the poor man turned rich is somehow a lesser person than he had been while suffering. Murnau has portrayed him in the epilogue in such a way that we must feel his human stature undermined by his changed fortunes. Without status, without a respectable job, the old man was pitiable, but in that condition he rose to gigantic proportions as a human being. He had been reduced by his circumstances to nothing more than a man, "A poor, infirm, weak, and despised old man," as King Lear says of himself on the heath. Stripped of everything, Jannings becomes pure humanity, identifiable with everyone in his universal condition. Once his position is reversed, he becomes a *type* of man, typical in his foibles of others of that type: wealthy but naïve and simple, he squanders money because he does not understand it. He is kind to the poor not primarily because he was once poor or because he is naturally kind (though both aspects are operative in his conduct) but because the role of the truly wealthy man as he idealizes it is one of noblesse oblige. No longer wearing his innate dignity as a human being, he dons another uniform (*i.e.,* expensive clothes) and acts out his new role in life.

In this final role, he is not being satirized; the ending is essentially genial, and the old man is too simple and benevolent to deserve satire. Murnau just reminds us that the trappings of status make us lose touch with the man underneath the costume. The comedy stems from his not fully comprehending the role he plays; his tips and his gestures (such as kissing the attendant in the lavatory) are extravagant, and he does not recognize that people are extremely amused by him. The final images of Jannings are highly comic. He takes a beggar into his carriage, but there is no room, and the beggar slides to the floor. Undaunted, Jannings rides off waving like a prince to the crowd of employees he has just tipped.

The ending, then, may have been intended to draw the emphasis away from the narrative idea that structured the dramatic portion of the film, namely, the declining fortunes of the doorman. What Murnau wanted to achieve in the total film was a portrait of a man particularized by his condition and environment but generalized into a universal or prototype figure. Plot movement is necessary, as Aristotle knew, for convincing character development in a narrative work. However, by undercutting the logic of the story line, Murnau may have been hoping to limit the implicit importance of the plot. It is, of course, open to question whether he succeeded in the epilogue, or even whether he ought to have attempted to do so.

Regardless of our attitude toward the ending, *The Last Laugh* represents one of the ultimate refinements in the art of the narrative film. *The Cabinet of Dr. Caligari* stands as an excellent demonstration of the manner in which an essentially literary idea can be translated into a truly cinematic experience. But that film remains limited by the nature of its original

concept. With *The Last Laugh,* the film form derives totally from a film idea. The difference is especially interesting, since both *Caligari* and *The Last Laugh* were written by Carl Mayer. With *Caligari* Robert Wiene adapted the scenario to a film structure, but the creative force behind *Caligari* is as much Mayer as Wiene. F. W. Murnau, however, is unquestionably the shaping force behind *The Last Laugh,* for his version transforms whatever amorphous substance lay in the scenario into cinematic meaning. Murnau's achievement in this sense compares with, for instance, Sophocles' or Chaucer's; both writers always adapted other people's stories for their plots, but were of course among the most original artists who ever lived.

*The Last Laugh* brought the art of the film great distinction in the eyes of an international public. Its real importance lay in its being a profound psychological delineation. Its thematic material was completely embedded in its images. No words were needed, and no literary antecedents sought. It was one of the first films to convince a large public that a film idea was capable of total development in a purely cinematic manner.

# The Sound Film

## The Advent of Dialogue in the Film

The sound film is neither better nor worse than the silent film, but something different. To the masses of filmgoers in the late 1920's, dialogue represented the fulfillment of the esthetic experience of film; while to some few theorists who believed that the esthetic experience had already been fulfilled in the works of Eisenstein, Griffith, Lang, Pudovkin, Chaplin, and others, the addition of a synchronized sound track meant the imminent deterioration of an art form. Although the general quality of ordinary films did decline temporarily, the effectiveness of the first artistic sound films immediately made clear that new possibilities for art were available in this new form. Regrettably, the sound film put an end to the feature-length silent film, but it is inconceivable that both sound and silent narratives could thrive side by side.

A new cinematic tradition developed with the coming of dialogue. It was not of course completely outside of the older tradition, but the change was significant and cannot be overlooked. Therefore, to complain, as several did, that the sound film of 1930 could not duplicate the artistry of the best silent films was to ignore the modifications in film form created by the sound track. No longer was sustained purely visual expressiveness a

necessarily desirable goal. The problem immediately recognized by the best filmmakers was how to use sound to open a new dimension of expression in the film. Some of the relatively early experiments with sound proved so remarkably successful that within a decade of *The Jazz Singer* (1927)— the first popularly successful sound film—filmmakers had developed virtually all the opportunities for artistic use of sound that still prevail today.

The major consideration is that the sound film remains primarily a visual medium and that possibilities for conveying essentially cinematic materials on the sound track are limited.* Film sound can be categorized under the headings *synchronous* and *asynchronous:* that is, either the sound can be known to originate within the pictured visual area (or its suggested immediate environment), or it can be unconnected to the visuals inasmuch as its origin is uncertain. A third possibility occasionally utilized effectively is total silence within a predominant sound environment. Silence in a sound film is frequently found in suspense situations, but naturally it is impossible to sustain silence for a very long time without switching the presentation to the mode of a silent film. Similarly, a sound track composed only of music does not properly constitute a sound film. Virtually all commercial silent films were intended for musical accompaniment. In fact, the initial audience response to the sound film was, at times, negative because spectators were annoyed at the prospect of losing the magnificent live orchestral accompaniment supplied at many large movie theaters and in turn being given the low-quality reproductions then available on discs or attached to the film celluloid itself!

Of course what made the sound film viable was not music or background sounds but dialogue. In the later period of the silent film, the German industry had succeeded in equating the absence of most insert titles with artistic achievement of a very high order, and most American films of more than ordinary ambition avoided excessive titling by the late 1920's. But the attempt to cut down on titles in the silent film was not generally a satisfactory solution to the artistic problem raised by the difficulty in depicting complex ideas in a visual medium. Thus, looked at from one point of view, the sound film solved a major problem of the medium: it provided a shorthand method of conveying the difficult verbal ideas that filmmakers were concerned with. Yet if the problem is considered in a special sense, the solution of sound was not entirely successful, for it clouded the larger issue, which was never, in fact, clearly articulated. That issue certainly was a matter of choosing the proper ideas for a visual medium. Now, after *The Jazz Singer,* the assumption was that any idea that was literary or dramatic was also cinematic.

The result was a temporary eclipse of the characteristic film idea and a great number of very poor films right through the early thirties. Recorded

* For a theoretical analysis of the problem, see Chapter 17.

dialogue, perhaps because of its novelty, for a number of years clearly out-weighed the visual element. It also restricted the visual part of the film because of the control exercised by the technician in charge of the sound, in an age when the rather crude equipment required performers to keep close to the hidden microphones. As anticipated, many of the leading per-formers of the silent screen were forced to compromise their particular skills and to adopt the methods of the stage actor—an ironic reversal of the conditions prevalent thirty years before, when great stage actors were enticed to the new film medium.

## Esthetic Problems in the Sound Film

With dialogue, the industry reached a new level of confidence. The belief was that now film could do what drama and fiction had always done: tell complicated stories about people who could verbalize their problems. After the coming of sound it seemed that now movies could not only rival the other narrative arts but surpass them. Suddenly the movies found them-selves right back where they were at the turn of the century. The talking films were little more than stage dramas with close-ups—or as Alfred Hitchcock calls them, "photographs of people talking"—which is really another way of saying they were something less than stage dramas, for the film in comparison to the live stage can hardly compete as a primarily verbal medium.

The point cannot be stressed sufficiently. The verbal idea on film comes to us wrapped in a visual form. The visual portion is now basically discontinuous—a series of shots, partial glimpses of the total environment; the verbal portion is essentially continuous—a series of sentences pursuing a consecutive train of thought. We hear within shots, and when, as is usual, the dialogue is carried beyond one shot, we still hear in terms of several shots in succession. The visual portion of a shot conveys information about the external shape, size, and proportion of things. Whatever information we see in a shot, the verbal portion of the film must either relate to it or distract from it. Hearing is, for most people, a less impressionable way of receiving information than seeing. The simplest, most ordinary sights are received by our minds more emphatically than their accompanying sounds. Thus, it becomes a touchy esthetic problem to handle the most common-place event in a sound film—for instance, a plane taking off. If we see it, the sound portion only repeats to our brain the same piece of information. If, in fact, we only hear the sound, we know immediately what it means and do not need the picture. Usually, we get both the picture and the sound of a plane taking off, but what is gained by the duplication of informa-tion? A three-year-old child could absorb the same information through either the sound or the picture alone. On the other hand, a sound track that

attempts to do something different for the visual image of a plane taking off (say, a lion's roar) is likely to call too much attention to itself; it either distracts or overwhelms. For the narrative film, the numerous images that require no sound, or sounds that require no image, create a difficult problem, only partially solved to this day.

There was, surely, an advantage to having a visual art without dialogue, inasmuch as filmmakers in the silent days could concentrate on communicating primarily through the visuals. The insert title in itself had certain advantages over sound, though they were not at all appreciated when such titles were considered an unfortunate expedient. For example, the insert title could save a great deal of time by omitting unneeded visual material: "Two weeks later, after securing the money, John returns to Mary." A simple title of this sort merely serves to put into the equivalent of a program note a good deal of expository information that now requires depiction one way or another. Every shot used merely to bridge a time gap is likely to be harmful to the total design of a film—not necessarily destructive, but still wasteful. And if John's getting money and returning to Mary is simply a matter-of-course process, the filming of it is also largely irrelevant to the narrative's development. Thus, sound, which was theoretically viewed as a means of moving along more quickly and concisely, is often an artifice that slows the pace of a film.

On the stage, dialogue is usually presented against a static background by actors speaking from essentially arranged positions that vary in visual patterns easily assimilated by the eye—easily because the spectator views the continuous movements of all characters. Film, on the other hand, communicates dialogue in terms of ever-changing backgrounds, or sometimes no discernible background at all (as in close shots). The visual patterns shift more readily than the verbal patterns in film. The difficulty for a film writer lies in establishing the kind of dialogue that will relate to the environment in some way. On the stage, the dialogue creates the entire context, and the background and sets must fit the dialogue. In staging Shakespeare, any kind of background might work—abstract, realistic, bare, baroque; as long as the designer makes the set functional and attractive, it doesn't matter too much what stylization is worked out.

The problem for the sound film, then, revolves around the relationship of dialogue to the special way in which the visual portion of the film creates a place and a sense of incident. The film atomizes its reality; the bits, the shots, communicate visually at the same time that the sound track, more or less continuously, gives us additional information. Since the picture is constantly shifting, and we are shown one character, then another, then both together, normally we end up with a number of different views of a single conversation. In most films, the frequent mutual reinforcement of sound and image makes the visual aspect trite or subservient to dialogue because the images are usually designed so as to correspond with the

dialogue shift from one character to another. Even without cutting back and forth among speakers, the camera must often wait upon the conclusion of a discussion in an environment of no particular visual interest before moving to a different location. Where such visual interest exists, and the physical environment of the conversation changes markedly with each shot, we may have difficulty absorbing the meaning of the dialogue.

## Sound and Comedy: W. C. Fields and the Marx Brothers

The kind of comedy that employed sound best in the thirties featured performers who reacted to an environment that was tangible and patently open to absurdity: Mae West, Laurel and Hardy, W. C. Fields, and a few more. Other comedians relied on verbal material that may have been funny in itself but bore little relation to cinematic substance. In the early days of sound, audiences were willing to accept dialogue just for the fun of enjoying the synchronized visual-sound medium, but eventually even popular taste began to sift out the truly cinematic from the merely verbal.

One of the best comedians of the sound era, W. C. Fields, made a few excellent short films by turning his peculiar stylized wit into a commentary on the environment. The sound track frequently amuses us in these films even when Fields is silent (for instance, the sounds of the storm in *The Fatal Glass of Beer,* the noise of the steam engine in *The Barbershop* (fig. 35), and the best of all, the horrifying scraping sound of a razor as Fields shaves a customer, also in *The Barbershop*). In *The Barbershop* (1933), Fields' caustic remarks are motivated by the visual images of his world. We see him first sitting in front of his small-town barbershop greeting people and talking to a man who never puts down his newspaper. The people are inane and boring. Fields may be a braggart and a liar, but at least he is alive, and we can't help feeling that he is what he is because he is surrounded by nincompoops. Next we see him with his wife and son. His son delights in riddles, but lacks charm; he will grow up as a small-town joker. His obnoxious wife scorns both him and his son. The only one who treats him with particular respect is the simple manicurist in his shop, who is infatuated with him, for no observable reason.

For his own part, Fields abuses his customers, and in turn they threaten him. A huge man shrunk into a small, emaciated man by Fields' steamroom angrily leaves, threatening revenge. One man burned by hot towels almost strikes Fields, but here the customer gets what he deserves, since he returned after his scars from the previous week's encounter with the same barber had just healed.

As a man who reverses the usual sentimental attitudes inculcated by films (*e.g.,* he dislikes children), Fields stands as a realist; but to make his realism meaningful his films must establish a context to support his

**35** *The Barbershop*

observations. The reason for his success is that his comments were aimed specifically at matters suggested in the visual portion of the film. Other comedians tended to deliver verbal gags that floated in the air without touching anything that we could see. Understanding the nature of performer-audience relationships in the theater, they attempted to link their personalities to certain conceivable characteristics likely to elicit audience approval. But the film medium relies on specific surfaces constantly presented to our eyes. If an actor detaches himself or his humor from the visible world, his verbal jokes alone will fail to communicate very much to us.

The Marx Brothers might seem at first an exception to this generalization. Actually, however, they succeed because in their best films all their movements counterpoint a remarkably familiar world. They themselves might be introducing an element of absurdity into this world, but they are by no means comic maniacs. In fact, the demolition created by the Marx Brothers seems almost divine in its inspiration, given the contexts in which they function. What's wrong with bringing down the opera house in *A Night at the Opera?* Certainly, the action is anti-establishment, but the stodginess of the establishment, in its refusal to come to terms with reality, makes it deserving of the kind of undercutting the Marx Brothers give it. When the orchestra is tricked into playing "Take Me Out to the Ballgame" in the middle of the opera score, the humor has to do with the inflexible attitudes presented within the context, the excessive seriousness of the establishment faced with blatantly comic incongruity.

The solution to the problem of verbal wit and visual relevance is the key to the Marx Brothers' films. For example, Groucho's scenes with the marvelous character actress Margaret Dumont, who always plays straight roles (as a dowager) might seem noncinematic, since all the comedy is contained in the remarks and the puzzled reactions they provoke. Yet this type of sequence is more than mere radio or vaudeville filmed. The success of the comedy here hinges on Groucho's ability to create a context that stresses deflation of a pompous or pretentious personality. The environment is itself commonplace, consisting of overly humorless people excessively concerned with decorum. The people Groucho assaults, the establishment set, do not understand their own absurdity until Groucho insults them.

Groucho's conversations are, of course, irrelevant to the plot, but then again the plot is irrelevant to the film. For instance, in *Duck Soup* (1932, directed by Leo McCarey), Groucho is head of state of Freedonia. To avert an imminent war, Margaret Dumont comes to tell him how to deal with the representative of the rival small nation. The subject is hardly broached before Groucho says to her, "Would you mind giving me a lock of your hair?" Since she has been attracted to him throughout, her answer expresses hope that finally their feelings are mutual: "A lock of my hair? I didn't realize. . . ." To which Groucho replies, "I'm letting you off easy— I was going to ask for the whole wig." The remark satirizes her momentary exaltation and her general attitude of self-satisfaction; very indirectly it also accuses her of meddling in affairs of state by implying that a ridiculous woman should not be suggesting ways to avert a war. On the other hand, it also hints that Groucho really does have some feeling for her—at least he needs her as a "straight man." In any case, the scene works because a mood is built up and destroyed, but the destruction is not nihilistic; it reveals the emptiness beneath the pretensions implied in appearances. Later, during the battle, Groucho rallies his followers by pointing to Margaret Dumont and saying, "Remember, you're fighting for this woman's honor, which is probably more than she ever did." The deflations are immediate and devastating, but also deserved.

Sometimes, the mere appearance of the Brothers suffices to deflate the scene. Groucho often plays roles within the establishment, and no serious explanation accounts for his getting to be where he is: for example, the president of a college, dressed in academic cap and gown at the beginning of *Horse Feathers* (fig. 36). Harpo, of course, has only to appear in any scene to turn logic to shambles and to confuse even Groucho (only Chico can consistently interpret Harpo). Whatever their antics, the background situation is always serious enough. Generally people are scheming to get what they don't deserve, and often all sorts of criminal activities and con games go on in the stodgy world until impeded by the interruptions of the Marx Brothers.

**36** *Horse Feathers*

The ideal arrangement for Groucho's verbal deflation is naturally a sequence in which the visual pomposity of a person or group has clearly been impressed upon us prior to and simultaneous with the comic remarks. *Duck Soup* abounds in such possibilities because of the situation: the head of a government comes into contact with just the sort of people most in need of being disturbed. The first sequence in which Groucho appears in *Duck Soup* includes a classic setup. At a formal ball attended by government dignitaries, everyone awaits the newly installed head of state, Rufus T. Firefly. Dozens of uniformed attendants form two rows for Groucho to walk through, after a group of flower girls take their positions in front of the attendants. Everyone is singing, "Hail, hail Freedonia, land of the brave and the free." A pause, but no one appears, and so the refrain is sung again. The first shot of Groucho shows him waking up in bed, removing his night-shirt—under which is his tuxedo—and then sliding down a firepole to appear in the grand ballroom—but behind the attendants. Everyone looks in the other direction. Finally, he is recognized by Margaret Dumont, who comes up to him and on behalf of the country officially greets him. His first words are, "Never mind that. Choose a card!" And he proceeds to offer to do a card trick. Thus, the apparent irrelevancy of Groucho's re-marks explode the whole mood of this solemn ritual. His lack of concern hits at the ridiculousness of everybody else's submitting to the social artifice

of greeting him as if he were a great man. His position alone imposes upon them and elevates him, not, certainly, the quality of the man. Yet somehow, his quality seems supreme, for he alone realizes the pretentiousness of the situation.

Later we see him presiding at a cabinet meeting in which the opening shot shows him and everyone else at a long table, but whereas everyone seated somberly awaits the beginning of the meeting, Firefly is playing jacks. During the course of the meeting, a minister rises and requests, "How about taking up the tax?" Groucho replies, "How about taking up the carpet?" The minister is humorless and urges again: "I still insist we take up the tax." To which Groucho answers, "He's right. We have to take up the tacks before we take up the carpet." After this, the minister resigns. The humor of the situation does not really have anything to do with the quality of Groucho's pun, which is at best dubious. Rather, it concerns his poise, the lack of it in others, and the need for comedy to humanize situations that have been turned into rituals devoid of human thought or feeling. Groucho does not blast the environment in a moment of tension. He explodes the stagnant atmosphere that results from people's insistence on maintaining, and operating in, formalized patterns to avoid having to think.

*Duck Soup* ends amidst the chaos of war, not a serious war, but one for which the only apparent cause is Groucho's slapping the ambassador of Sylvania for calling him an upstart (he does not mind being called a worm). For some reason Freedonia wins, though we have only seen them suffering defeats during the few minutes that the war seems to last. Margaret Dumont brings the word of victory to the Marx Brothers, who are throwing vegetables at the trapped Sylvanian ambassador. Victory is ours, she says proudly, and begins to sing in her best operatic style, "Hail, hail, Freedonia," when the Brothers turn and start pelting her with the vegetables as the film ends. The shooting, the shouting, and the singing are reduced to nonsense; patriotism has been exposed as humbug, for previously humbug had been raised to patriotism. Life is a game, and the Brothers are the best players. The sound of the Marx Brothers is incessant noise, but it is finally a noise that makes more sense than the logical progression of the trivial, but somber, dialogue of everyone else.

## Sound and Drama: Lang's *M*

Although some comic actors made the change from silent to sound films with considerable success, much of the great visual comedy was not easily adapted to the sound medium because an interesting verbal equivalent or counterpoint could not often be developed. The dramatic film, however, afforded directors certain obvious opportunities for expressiveness, which they were quick to develop. Silent film directors like Hitchcock, Ford,

Renoir, and von Sternberg seemed to adjust immediately to the dialogue film, and today they are thought of as directors of sound films, few people realizing that part of their technical achievement results from their training in a cinema of visual expressiveness that required them to develop narrative art in terms of moving images.

One of the great directors of the silent screen, Fritz Lang, created a sound film masterpiece in his first effort in 1931: *M*. The film does not contain any astounding special sound effects—though undoubtedly the sheer technical achievement of relating speech and image was thoroughly novel for its time and established methods of editing the sound track that were either new or generally unknown in 1931. Also, Lang's creative use of sound goes beyond the employment of dialogue; human and nonhuman sounds (footsteps, breathing, whistles, etc.) are incorporated into the texture of the film to develop character and theme as well as mood.

The basic film idea is itself an amazing achievement, as it includes a sociological analysis of considerable understanding of the most gruesome subject ever dealt with in film—the child-murderer. Working with materials based on the Dusseldorf child-murderer, a contemporary criminal case that would have been known by a large part of his audience, Lang moves from the victim's mother's point of view to society's and finally to the killer's. Since he has first portrayed the awesome horror and grief that results from just one of the murderer's adventures, the technical achievement in creating sympathy for the murderer is all the more notable because of Lang's typically objective mode of presentation. Lang, more than any other director, tends to convey a sense of linear rigidity in each of his shots; that is, he frames each shot so carefully that it communicates a fixed geometric pattern, which seems to lock characters into narrowly circumscribed areas within the established environment and limit the range of their mobility so as to maintain the pictorial balance of the frame. And this is the case even in the many graceful moving shots typical of any Lang film. We get the feeling that Lang is studying the destiny of his characters as a scientist does microbes under a microscope. Even within this pervasive stylistic pattern, with its characteristically beautiful photography, Lang manages to move us into the point of view of various characters. And although we remain aware that an artistic mind is always in control of the movement of the characters, the effect is not alienating in *M*.

Toward the unifying tone of horror and terror, the sound track contributes not merely reinforcement of the visual element but its own psychological associations that deepen the total impact of the film. The first shot establishes the grimness of the tone in a way that could hardly be duplicated, even by Lang, in a silent film. The camera looks down (a characteristic angle in this film) on a group of little children playing a game. The complete innocence of the children's play is ominously contrasted by the song they are singing (not translated in the subtitled version circu-

lating in America): "Just you wait a little while, / The evil man in black will come. / With his little chopper, / He will chop you up." * The song bothers a neighbor troubled by the fact that a real child-murderer is at large, and once we know this we too are alarmed for the safety of the children.

Lang's skill at developing a sense of horror with great economy is revealed in a nondialogue sequence that follows (the sounds are the natural ones of the environment for each shot). After showing us Mrs. Beckmann cleaning her apartment, the camera gives us a close-up of a cuckoo clock at midday, and instead of merely duplicating the picture with cuckoo sounds, Lang brings in the tolling of bells as well, thus creating an emphasis on the time that is not intellectually understood at the moment but that registers with great emotional force. The scene switches to the street entrance to a school, where the tolling bells link the image to the previous shot, and we understand that the Beckmann child is the little girl who goes off with her friends. Lang cuts back to the mother in the kitchen laying the table, and back again to the girl, who runs along a street. Our previous information about the murderer and our awareness that Lang has some purpose for developing the sequence through crosscutting prepare us for the horror we dread seeing. While the girl proceeds along streets filled with people or is crossed by a policeman, we feel a degree of safety. When she bounces her ball against a pillar, the camera moves in as the ball rebounds from a poster, and we read of a reward offered for the murderer. The impending horror quickly encompasses the frame in the form of the shadow of a man that falls across the billboard. Our immediate psychological response associates that shadow with the murderer. At this point, the first dialogue of the sequence is heard, and it is absolutely chilling because of its indirectness. The unseen man says, "What a pretty ball," and we observe his shadow bending down. We know, of course, that he is not interested in the ball, and therefore we can guess that he is about to lure the girl to her doom. Lang now cuts between the girl, as she proceeds along with the murderer, and the mother, who becomes increasingly worried about her daughter's absence. The murderer buys the girl a balloon, and for the first time we hear a refrain from Grieg's *Peer Gynt* whistled inaccurately by the murderer (a sign of his nervousness and a recurring sound motif).

The sequence concludes with a remarkable series of shots, increasing the idea of terror and culminating in profound pathos, perhaps never surpassed in the cinema. Lang uses sound to drive home the particular human predicament of the mother's developing terror, while creating visual metaphors of pathos to substitute for what might have been an intolerable display of violence and sadism. However, the images shown together with the sound track comprise an impression that is far more powerful than even a

* *M* (New York, Simon and Schuster, 1968), p. 15.

gruesome murder scene. The mother calls, "Elsie," and we see the cuckoo clock again as it strikes once. Then the mother calls a second time, "Elsie, Elsie," from the window. Now the camera shows us (for the second time) the stark geometric pattern of the staircase, from above; its emptiness is an image of hopelessness. The third cry, with the mother off screen, is accompanied by a shot of building lofts, deserted, except for some hanging laundry. The fourth time the mother cries, we have a shot of the girl's empty chair at the table, neatly set for her. The mother cries again. Now Lang's image becomes the perfect symbol for a murder of the innocent. Outdoors, we see on a patch of ground Elsie's ball rolling from the bushes. Then the doll-shaped balloon that the killer bought her floats up and catches on telegraph wires, until it is finally blown free and carried away. Then for the last time we hear the mother's voice off screen calling the girl. The scene fades out, and the next shot, a long shot tilted down toward a city street, is followed by the cry of newspaper sellers proclaiming an extra edition about the latest murder.

A good portion of the film deals with the tracking down of the killer prompted by the public outrage over the murders of several children. Using sound, Lang captures the sense of the public response with his usual econ-

omy. We have voices of a crowd attempting to read the "wanted" poster, then a radio announcer's voice takes over from theirs, and in turn the voice of a man reading from a newspaper blends with, and then takes over from, the announcer's. The linking of voices indicates that everyone is preoccupied with the same subject. Public opinion is aroused.

Lang frequently links visual ideas by means of the sound track. For instance, a policeman remarks that anyone in the street could be the guilty man, and while he speaks, the camera cuts from him to an unrelated city street where we see an old man innocently speaking to a child and being accosted by a mob as if he were a legitimate suspect. The sound link immediately transforms the general to the specific image, making both mutually effective because they reinforce the same basic idea, but not the same precise information.

There are times, however, when the use of sound to link visual ideas may seem questionable, though clearly Lang thought it was effective at the time the film was made, for these links are part of the film's style. In one sequence, for instance, the chief of police is first seen speaking on the telephone, obviously to a superior, attempting to justify the police's handling of the case. His voice is then heard over a variety of images: when he says that his men are getting very little sleep, the picture shows us weary policemen; when he remarks that they are checking candy stores, a shot shows us a detective at a candy store. This continues for about sixteen brief illustrations, the dialogue always being duplicated almost exactly by the picture, which makes the sequence informationally repetitious. It does give the film a documentary feeling; we are shown police routine for one of the first times on screen, and the processes are permanently interesting. However, the duplication of sound and visual sense deviates from the typical moments of Lang's art.

In the course of its narrative, *M* shows us two different procedures for tracking down the criminal. The first is the slow and methodical process of police investigation. The second is the more flamboyant approach of the underworld, united in an effort to find the murderer in order to take the pressure off themselves. The police have been cracking down with a good deal of Germanic authoritarianism on all the criminal elements in their search for the killer, since the public demands action. In their roundups of criminals, naturally, the police uncover a number of illegal activities and make numerous arrests. Thus, the persecuted villains form a league to track down the murderer and presumably punish him. Lang handles the meeting of a small committee of criminals as if it were a board meeting of a corporation, with considerable verbal humor as the criminals complain to each other of the unbearable conduct of the police in wrecking their "business" activities.

With a good deal of visual wit, Lang draws a parallel between the organization of the underworld and the organization of the establishment,

as represented by the police. He cuts between the criminal meeting and a similar meeting of high-ranking police, who are sitting around a long table. Schranker, an arch criminal, conducts the underworld meeting, and at a particular point, he says, "I am appealing to you for advice." In the middle of Schranker's sentence, Lang for the first time cuts to the police meeting, where the chief is in the middle of the same sentence, and in fact finishes Schranker's. The parallel is immediately established on both the visual and the verbal levels. In terms of their techniques, the criminals and police of course differ: the police continue to work scientifically from clues and to spend a great deal of time checking out the records of mental patients; the criminals, on the other hand, enlist the organization of beggars to watch every street in Berlin. They hope that the next attempt by the murderer will lead to his detection, and in fact this actually happens. Ironically, the police method also works, though they are just slightly behind the criminals in locating the man, Hans Beckert. However, the long sequence in which the dual search for the murderer organizes along parallel lines helps create the concept of coalition. Beckert, we know, is now bound to be destroyed because the whole world, in two separate movements, is converging upon him. Though the criminals and the police do not actually cooperate, the abstract idea of their alliance against a common enemy has been clarified by the oral-visual cutting in parallel terms.

Thus, relatively early in the film Lang begins to redirect audience sympathy, though of course we do not at this point sympathize with the murderer as a human being. All we see is the combination of great forces moving against a man who is clearly deranged. Beckert is played by Peter Lorre, in his greatest performance. His timid appearance, after the first time we see him as a shadow against the "wanted" poster, mitigates the threat of his behavior. During the sequence with Elsie, we do not see his face, and the first time we do see it, he is grimacing into a mirror. As a small, frightened-looking man, clearly a psychotic personality, he looks much less dangerous than the criminals who set out to track him down. In a classic shot, Beckert stands munching an apple and gazing into a cutlery window; the knives in the window are reflected in a pattern encircling the murderer's head, a striking simile for the state of Beckert's mind.

In another shot, out of the corner of his eye, Beckert spies a young girl's reflection in a window; his face reveals tremendous excitement as he wipes his mouth, his eyes bulge, and he seems to have a slight fit. We see the reflection of the girl moving away, and then Beckert sets off to follow her, whistling the now ominous refrain from Grieg. He begins to appear as a man obsessed by an uncontrollable urge to kill. The awkward whistling certainly serves him as a release for the tension he feels in his pursuit. Suddenly the girl greets a woman and goes off with her, and instantly the whistling stops. By unexpectedly shutting off a sound, Lang uses the sound track to indicate a sudden turn in the narrative. The Grieg refrain symbol-

izes the killer's resolve to perform another murder, for when we hear him stop as the potential victim goes off with the woman, he seems distraught, completely shaken by the interruption in his plans. Only after he buys a couple of drinks can he resume whistling; thus, we realize he is about to stalk another victim.

This time, however, the tune is recognized by a blind beggar, part of the organization prepared to seek out the murderer. As this beggar remembers having sold a balloon to a man whistling the same tune on the day of the previous murder, he signals to another beggar to follow Beckert. Now the sequence becomes ironic, for Beckert is luring another girl and does not know that he is himself pursued (fig. 37). The second beggar manages to bump into Beckert and chalk an M on the killer's coat as a sign for others who will continue to follow the man. The bumping causes Beckert to drop his knife, with which he was peeling an orange. His face shows sheer terror at the beggar's bumping into him and then bawling him out, but the scene becomes almost pathetic when the girl retrieves Beckert's knife and hands it to him, calling him "Uncle."

Once the actual chase of the murderer begins, the sound track is cleverly employed to aid the visual design in building up an external representation of an internal condition; even without dialogue the sound track helps us to understand the fear in Beckert's terrified mind. When he discovers the M chalked on his back, he knows immediately that he is being followed. He hears the whistling of a beggar and correctly assumes that it is a signal to pursue him. Beckert runs away and more whistles are heard. From a high angle we look down on a deserted street in which beggars appear from different sides, creating a pattern of converging movements in their attempt to corner the killer. The scene resembles a hunt, with Beckert the animal pursued by the hounds. The ordinary sound of a man running is made frightening not only because he is being chased by many men who appear from different directions, but also because of Lang's framing Beckert against geometric shapes, buildings and street corners, that clearly suggest rectangular boxes of severely limited area. Beckert is defined by the amount of room he seems to have between himself and his pursuers, for all we see of him is animal-like. We do not sympathize with him for any redeeming traits of personality, for we know of none, but we do understand the claustrophobic sense of converging lines. The sounds are minimal—those of a man running down empty streets—but they are ominous sounds, and the weariness and heavy breathing indicate a man reduced to an inhuman state because of the pressures of survival.

Taking refuge in an office building just as the employees leave for the day, the murderer hides in various places to avoid the watchmen. However, the underworld organization, informed of his whereabouts by the beggar, arrives at night to search the building. At this point, Lang relies on a predominant silence to reinforce the tension involved in the killer's situation.

The criminals make considerable noise when they take over the building and tie up the guards. In contrast we are given several shots of Beckert cringing in his hiding place, the only audible sound being his heavy breathing, which is much louder than it could conceivably be in reality. It is not merely the recording level of the sound but the isolation of it on the screen that produces a successful image of fear.

The murderer tries to pick the lock of a door in a storage attic where he is hiding, using some mild expletives as his pocket knife fails to open the lock. Finally, his one weapon, his knife, breaks and his entrapment becomes more and more obvious to us, though he does not know that the building is being searched for him. The numerous criminals meanwhile conduct a thorough search of the premises, and their dedication and numbers make us realize that in a matter of time Beckert will be found. By this time we feel considerable sympathy for the helpless plight of this fearful, lonely man, and the thoroughness and professional procedures of the criminals have begun to turn the conflict into an abstract struggle in which the dehumanized, machinelike world crushes the human being, turning him in his fear into something less than human.

Finally, the lock-picking of the murderer is heard by the criminals, who assemble on the other side of the door to surprise him if he manages to get out. The sound of the murderer hammering the nail into a skeleton key accompanies a shot of the outside of the door; the result is considerable irony, for our eyes tell us what the result of Beckert's activity will be. But when Lang cuts to the view on the other side of the door, we see Beckert's satisfaction (at having made a key) change to horror as he notices the handle of the door revolve slightly. Beckert turns and flees back into the recess of the attic. Knowing his own freedom will be gone in a matter of seconds, he cringes pitiably in a compartment, listening to the sound of doors being broken down (fig. 38). A scene of great commotion ensues because the criminals' watchman has given the alarm. The criminals get Beckert inside a bag and run off with him.

The police, when they arrive, catch a criminal who was left behind in the scramble to evacuate the building, but since he does not talk they are puzzled as to the motive for the massive breaking and entering that has occurred. One of the most effective uses of the sound track occurs in a sequence that employs crosscutting. Back in the police station, Inspector Lohmann glances through the police report of the criminal activity of the evening and expresses his bewilderment, while the visuals graphically examine the details of the building where Beckert was caught. This sequence is a kind of "comic relief" from the severe emotional strain produced by the capture of Beckert. We listen to Lohmann's commenting on the report, while through a series of dissolves, we observe a commentary on his comments. For instance, the inspector remarks that the breaking and entering happened in a very quiet neighborhood, and the picture before us shows an

unconscious watchman lying on the floor of the office. Lohmann wonders what they were hoping to steal and if they intended to empty the whole place; the picture shows us the forced door to the coal bin. His verbal comments such as "It's incredible!" express his amazement that the criminals could bother to take apart the entire building, while the images (which are apparently described in the written report) show us the attic and the doors to the various compartments broken in. When Lohmann says, "Ah, now it makes sense. They were after the safe," the image is a close-up of a safe obviously untouched, as are two others. We are amused by the innocence of the police indicated by the disparity between what they know (as seen in the images of the interiors of the abandoned building) and what we have previously witnessed.

In the next sequence, the criminals carry Beckert to an abandoned distillery to face a "kangaroo court." Being Germanic, the criminals insist on an orderly procedure, which is itself a parody of traditional judicial procedure and therefore does not uphold established modes of dealing with any type of murderer. Beckert is first identified by the beggar who sold a balloon to him on the day that Elsie was killed. When a similar balloon is

produced, Beckert's own defense—that there must be some mistake—quickly crumbles, as he turns in terror, gasping the name of his victim.

The court sequence is arranged in such a way that the criminals, assembled in a huge crowd—including a sizable contingent of prostitutes—are both judges and accusers. Schranker conducts the prosecution, but everyone is already convinced of the murderer's guilt and their right to punish him. The cutting builds up the panic and fear of the killer and the criminals' vindictiveness and outrage. The dialogue depicts the psychological bullying of the accused, which parallels the physical brutality of the sequence. Schranker shows Beckert pictures of the victimized girls, and the murderer crouches, with those marvelous bulging eyes that became Peter Lorre's trademark, exhibiting horror at the accusations and uttering feeble denials. When Beckert insists that they have no right to hold him, he infuriates the mob, of course, who chant, "Kill him!" Schranker, who has a theatrical instinct, has no intention of presiding over a lynching—at least not until he has finished his role as prosecutor, obviously a role he has studied first-hand during the various times he has been prosecuted.

The criminal assigned to him as a lawyer informs Beckert that he is on trial for his life, provoking Beckert to wonder aloud, "But, but . . . do you want to kill me, then?" The derisive laughter of the mass jury when Beckert insists that killing him will be "cold-blooded murder" further separates him from the inhumanity of the mob. Lorre's innocent appearance is not just an irony of casting, for Lang conceived of the murderer as a psychotic personality who does not consciously control his violent actions. The murderer is truly childlike, and therefore the sense of the trial scene, as the "defense lawyer" sees it, is that a man like Beckert needs to be committed, not executed, and evidently the movie audience is supposed to arrive at a similar conclusion. The jury, however, does not. Schranker suggests that Beckert might eventually escape from an institution or be set free and murder again.

Beckert's humble plea eloquently expresses his own defense. He claims he can't help himself: "I haven't any control over this evil thing that's inside me—the fire, the voices, the torment!" * In his compulsive state, he follows his private demon. "I have to obey it. I have to run . . . run . . . endless streets. I want to escape." † After he commits the murders, which he learns about only later on, when he reads the posters, he cannot remember anything. On his knees, he puts his hands over his ears to shut out the sounds of his oppressors. The defense lawyer pleads that lack of responsibility on Beckert's part means that he cannot be killed by them or even by the state, but instead must be committed. The crowd of criminals does not accept this view, the prostitutes in particular affirming the need to get rid of the murderer for the sake of the mothers. As the roars and whistles of the crowd

* *Ibid.,* p. 103.    † *Ibid.,* p. 104.

reach a peak and the mob is about to seize Beckert, everyone freezes in sudden silence. We hear off screen the voice of the police and see all the criminals raise their hands. A policeman's hand is placed firmly on Beckert's shoulder, indicating that he is to be put into protective custody—that is, committed.

Lang's *M* is one of a number of films of the early thirties that experimented with the synchronized sound track and worked out many of the possibilities for using sound and dialogue in the shaping of the film idea. In *M,* Lang both complements the visuals and counterpoints them. His sound track is frequently meaningful in itself, but always subordinated to the gist of the idea behind a particular sequence. He was among the first to perfect the use of asynchronous dialogue (a voice talking while a shot of something other than the speaker is seen). He also realized the dramatic effectiveness of "dead spots" on the sound track—silent moments when the sudden stopping of dialogue can have a jolting effect. In *M,* the sound track continually shares with the visuals in the presentation of Lang's ideas, for as striking as both sound and image are, their true effectiveness is understood only inasmuch as they relate to each other.

# 11

# Film
# Genres

## Film Genres and Narrative Art

When we speak of genre in the motion picture industry, we apply the term vaguely to suggest any kind of category. Different countries have different popular genres: in Japan, the term "samurai film" connotes a large number of works with a related historical environment and a good deal of physical action; in America, the category of the Western similarly suggests a time and a place on the one hand and a style on the other. The major industries in the various countries usually try very hard to work within genres. If a certain film has received approval, the industry hopes to turn that successful film into a genre quickly enough to maintain public interest. Yet once the industry commits itself to a genre, it often works the genre to death by glutting the market with imitative films. In America in the 1960's the spy film became tremendously successful for a while, particularly with the production of a series based on the fictional exploits of James Bond. But even as the Bond films were appearing, an anti-spy-film genre caught on and a slew of parodies was made. In fact, undoubtedly the best of the Bond films, *Goldfinger* (directed by Guy Hamilton), was itself a parody of the genre. It did not matter, for during the three years or so of its popularity, the spy film and its parody anti-spy film continued to thrive together,

in spite of the execrable quality of most of the films cranked out to take advantage of popular taste.

Although the use of genres is closely associated with commercial considerations, examining their use can be a helpful way of approaching the development of narrative art. This is more true of a genre that is based on style (*e.g.,* the private-eye film) or location (*e.g.,* the courtroom drama) than of one based on similarities in theme or subject matter (*e.g.,* race relations or juvenile delinquency). The former generic types are conceptually relevant to a visual medium; the latter are essentially literary. Most often the concept of a genre suggests the utilization of pre-existing patterns —of style, place, setting, plot, or characterization. However, a series of films conceived primarily in terms of a theme or a vague subject currently popular with moviegoers will most likely establish patterns that are cinematically irrelevant. When a work originates with a studio executive's judgment that what the world wants now is, say, a film about a young man's first encounter with the adult world, the second step must be the locating of a literary property to supply the requisites. Thematic emphasis, therefore, is unlikely to lead to a truly cinematic genre film.

In evaluating the contribution of genres to the development of film narrative, we must recognize the fact that although some genres are especially cinematic, all genres are without intrinsic artistic quality; that is, we cannot tell anything about the merit of a film simply from the category it belongs to. Although no one has ever claimed artistic merit for a film just because it was a musical or an adult Western, frequently a film is condemned simply because it is part of a genre that has no status. Producing a film in one of the less reputable genres is a sure way to alienate critics; however, minor genres have occasionally yielded very good films. In Europe, Alfred Hitchcock has long been known as one of the great filmmakers in the history of the cinema, but in America he was, right up to the 1960's, considered only the best suspense director. The suspense film and the closely related mystery genre have always been popular entertainment, but in this country they simply lacked status. Therefore, while Hitchcock was appreciated for being what his French admirer Truffaut called "the least dull of all directors," he had here a very limited appeal for exactly those movie sophisticates who ought to have been studying his films.

Some genres have even less status than the suspense film. The horror film, for instance, has been a significant source of ideas for the experimental cinema, but to the literary mentality that dominates our film criticism this genre is only a source of scorn. Yet within the horror genre, the Dracula subgenre has itself been an attraction to two of the world's greatest filmmakers, Carl Dreyer (*Vampyr,* 1931) and F. W. Murnau (*Nosferatu,* 1922); in America, Tod Browning's *Dracula* (1931) is an interesting example of expressionism and in tone reminds us somewhat of the film that might be said to have first made the genre of horror popular, *The Cabinet of*

**39**  *Dracula* (The pattern of a genre,)

**40**  *Stagecoach*

*Dr. Caligari* (fig. 39). In fact, expressionism often blended into the American horror film of the thirties—the most notable examples being the very fine mixing of comedy and pathos in James Whale's, *The Bride of Frankenstein* (1935) and the original *Frankenstein* (1931).

By choosing to work within the patterns of a well-defined genre, a director risks losing a degree of critical esteem that his film might otherwise be entitled to, for often the surface similarities of a meaningful work of art and many ordinary films are so evident that audiences may respond casually to the pattern, overlooking its artistic use in the particular film. While few major filmmakers have worked consistently within one genre, those that have are frequently defined by the type rather than the quality of film they have produced. John Ford is the most notable example of a major artist returning frequently to the genre film, in his case the Western (fig. 40). Since the landscape of one Ford Western looks like that of the others, critics are inclined to assume that the genre limits the artist. Actually, the genre offers a director like Ford the possibility of developing a consistent world view over a number of works, as did Shakespeare in regard to English history in his chronicle plays and Faulkner with the Southern heritage in his novels.

Yet the advantages of working within a genre can be significant even to the director who approaches the genre only once, if he is intent on using a new perspective that is set into relief by the usual properties of the type. In other words, genre means that a given film comes equipped with a place or a setting or a group of characters familiar from a dozen or a hundred other films. To the ordinary director on a routine assignment, those familiar materials are placed into a recognizable pattern to elicit the same old responses on the part of the audience. In contrast, the best directors may choose these materials because they provide an easily identifiable background for new film ideas. The familiar properties of the genre set into relief a filmmaker's reinterpretation of human motivation in particular situations of crisis. For this reason the Greek tragic drama dealt repeatedly with the same legends and the Elizabethan playwrights were fond of so-called revenge tragedy.

## The Cinematic Nature of Genres

While it is obvious enough that we ought not condemn a particular film because it represents a genre made up largely of second-rate films, it is somewhat less clear that we ought to recognize, if not appreciate, certain values that belong to the genre and are shared in fact by many an ordinary film. In the first place, any genre that survives a number of years very likely exhibits inherent cinematic qualities. The distinction between implicit cinematic values and the artistic utilization of these values is obvious—in ordi-

nary films we need consider only the inherent qualities, not the applications of them. Secondly, the establishment of a pattern is frequently invaluable for the finest of films within a given genre.

Every genre that has flourished seems to contain truly cinematic qualities. The gangster film of the early sound period is an interesting case in point because a number of effective films appeared, including Mervyn Le Roy's *Little Caesar* (1930), George Hill's *The Big House* (1930), and Howard Hawks's *Scarface* (1932). Even some of the great silent screen directors had tried the genre: Griffith in *The Musketeers of Pig Alley* (1912), Fritz Lang in *Doktor Mabuse, der Spieler* (1922) and elsewhere, and Josef von Sternberg in *Underworld* (1927). After a period of great popularity in the early thirties, this genre was temporarily brought to an end through the pressures of censorship, though of course it could not be permanently ignored, since it reflected a contemporary aspect of American life that is still with us. Undoubtedly, many of these early gangster films were designed for their sociological relevance, but as more of them appeared, it became apparent that their true effectiveness lay in their entertainment value rather than in their attempts to document the life of the criminal personality. Possibly only William Wellman's *The Public Enemy* (1931) retains any significance as a documentary study of the rise and fall of the gangster. As the genre developed, it seemed to the public that films began to glamorize the villain, who was becoming heroic.* Certainly, the later film biographies of criminals like Roger Touhy, John Dillinger, and Al Capone turned their subjects into a type of folk hero.

Regardless of its relevance or irrelevance to reality, the gangster film contributed to the development of cinema, particularly to the sound film, where the short, tough colloquialisms of these films provided an equivalent for the visual realism being depicted. The language of these films is stilted now because the slang has changed substantially, but perhaps in the larger perspective of history, this sort of dialogue will be recognized for its effective cinematic quality. The inarticulate criminal could express himself perfectly with grunts and sneers and language that touched directly on the idea at hand. Of course, actors like Edward G. Robinson, James Cagney, and later Humphrey Bogart could always convey a great deal through their clipped dialogue; when playing criminals, they were extremely verbal in spite of their limited vocabulary. The gangster was, however, a man of action more than words.

It is as films of action, of course, that the gangster genre proved most interesting. For some it had too much action, too little thought, and for everyone it was melodrama—a word that is always at least slightly pejorative in American English. Yet melodrama is in general not an apt descrip-

* See Robert Warshaw's famous article "The Gangster as Tragic Hero," reprinted in his book *The Immediate Experience* (Garden City, N.Y., Doubleday, 1962).

tion of film, as it is of a certain kind of dramatic literature, for the truth seems to be that the structure of film is quite different from that of the idealized dramatic form. The form of the gangster film always took note of the content of the imagery: a world of violence, machine guns, speeding cars, and gangland vengeance (fig. 41). Since the gangster world predicated sudden violence as the norm, the form of the film narrative suggested to audiences that violent death was virtually unavoidable and just a matter of time. Thus, the inevitable "melodramatic" conclusion was actually rather well prepared for: Cagney or Robinson or George Raft was going to get his due, and when he was finally "mowed down," the film would end. In fact, the real plot of each gangster film concerned the establishment of this premise, and the suspense consisted in the amount of time remaining to the "hero" before the anticipated destruction was achieved.

Gangster films illustrate the principle that a genre may be inherently cinematic, even though the subject matter may not seem particularly elevating. This genre is concerned with the way in which criminals function, and they function in terms of specific extravagant actions. They commit crimes and run and shoot each other, all naturally graphic materials for the medium. "Gangsterism" represents a type of activity that we ought to know about but not observe (hopefully) in our everyday lives. Thus, it takes us

**41**  Edward G. Robinson in *Little Caesar* (The imagery of a genre)

back to the original intention of the motion picture: to bring to the masses those views of the world most people could not directly experience.

Though the gangster genre can in this sense justify itself despite the frequent assumption that it (like the horror genre) remains intrinsically low-brow, we should also note that this genre—as is true of every genre—creates a pattern of human activity that is extremely important for those films considered the better or exceptional examples of the type. In other words, several minor films taken collectively and absorbed into the mainstream of our popular culture produce a pattern that supports the more artistic films—films like Penn's *Bonnie and Clyde,* Kubrick's *2001: A Space Odyssey,* and Hill's *Butch Cassidy and the Sundance Kid,* which most people assume could stand on their own without the existence of their genre, but which gain in innumerable ways from their associations with earlier examples of the same type.

In their establishment of patterned activity, film genres, because of their wide appeal, serve the purpose of creating modern mythic structures. Among the most enduring in its appeal is the private-eye genre (which might also include those films about police detectives who operate independently). In this genre, representatives of the dark world of hypocrisy and greed impinge upon the moral order until the hero is alerted and single-handedly sets about restoring the proper moral balance. The transformation of this originally literary genre to the screen resulted in strangely formidable visualizations of the vague shadow world of evil common to the private-eye novel. In the private-eye novel, people continually steal and kill but they are not real; the reality of everyone except the hero is played down in order to emphasize the method of solving the mystery. On screen, however—and many of the private-eye films are taken rather directly from novels—the background becomes more vivid, more menacing. The somewhat disembodied villains of a novel take on the same physical reality that the hero has; they share his world and threaten him. Thus, the generic pattern of confrontation between the good man, the intellectual mind sorting out the evidence of extremely complicated corruption, and the bad man (or frequently bad woman) and his criminal cohorts underlies the plot and implants a certain degree of moral depth in the film's structure.

## The Private-Eye Genre: Huston's *The Maltese Falcon*

The first film John Huston directed, *The Maltese Falcon* (1941), which starred Humphrey Bogart, remains the best, or close to the best, of the private-eye genre. It surpasses in quality not only the other films of the genre but most films of its day that were made with more serious claims on the public's attention. It was presented, after all, as just an adaptation of a well-known Dashiell Hammett novel, without pretensions to saying anything

relevant to life outside the romantic world of its conception. And it must be noted immediately that it *is* really a genre picture; it goes beyond the limitations of genre (that is, of stereotyping), but it never moves outside the recognizable world we associate with such films. It contains a proper number of murders and a complicated story line that few could recount after seeing the film for the first time. The hero has the usual virtues of masculinity, the typical resourcefulness, and the inevitable success. Private detectives are invariably calm and collected in the face of danger, relying primarily on their brains to keep alive, though in moments of crisis they have the necessary capacity to outfight their opponents.

These and other stereotyped aspects of the world of *The Maltese Falcon* are not really shortcomings of the film that need our apology. In fact, the generic devices used provide a source of the film's strength. Knowing in advance something about the qualifications of the hero and the duplicity of his antagonists prepares us for a pattern of action that we can analyze more easily for its surface, more deeply for its meaning, than we could a less familiar pattern. In other words, we know in general what it is all about; what we want to see is the significance of this film's particular variations on the theme.

As in the best sound films of the 1930's, dialogue is used to establish much of the background, a world of evil within which the hero moves while attempting to derive the truth. Little is made of location—it is not important that the story takes place in San Francisco; it really takes place in rooms that could be anywhere. The kind of people that move in and out of these rooms define the environment, and the people in turn are defined in terms of their words. Truly cinematic dialogue reinforces the darkening tone of the film, continuously calling our attention to the corruption of the characters. The dialogue constructs the central image of this corruption: the Maltese falcon, a priceless *objet d'art*. At the end of the film, the verbally constructed image materializes visually: the bird is delivered wrapped in torn newspapers by a man who dies on the spot. When the Maltese falcon is finally uncovered from its dirty wrappings, it proves to be a fake, a copy. It was referred to all along as a mysterious object more valuable than anything the evil characters could imagine—certainly more valuable than the human lives taken for it. Ultimately, then, the object is exposed as a fraud, but the real exposure concerns the values and life styles of the three people most eager to acquire the Maltese falcon. Evil is first revealed as a moral nullity, and then its human manifestations are destroyed by the hero. Indeed, the whole film has been a demonstration by the hero of the worthlessness of that evil.

Huston handles this demonstration subtly; in fact, the hero's veneer of moral indifference—an element common to the genre—is cracked decisively only in the peculiar ending of *The Maltese Falcon*. The most skillful part of the presentation lies in the hero's insights into the psychology

of all the other characters in his environment and his subtle responses to their words and actions. The complexities of the Bogart characterization in this film resemble those revealed in other Bogart performances directed by John Huston such as those in *The Treasure of Sierra Madre, The African Queen,* and *Beat the Devil.* Undoubtedly, the Huston-Bogart film is a kind of collaboration of filmmakers, since the actor exerts a significant influence on the way in which the film idea is conceived. Much of the film's success comes from the hero's ability to convey a level of awareness about the apparent disorder around him, and this level cannot, of course, be verbalized directly without alerting his would-be antagonists in the surrounding environment.

Playing the tough-minded, wisecracking Sam Spade on the outside, Bogart remains something else inside. He has never—or at least not often—come to terms with this other self. His outer being establishes a kind of facade; however, it would be untrue to assert that he is not really the tough-minded, wisecracking detective. He *is* that, but he is something more too, something he seems to hide from himself because in a way it is his better self and therefore an implicit criticism of his life. That external life contains many crude elements, which he might be ashamed about, though he has convinced himself that it is a necessary guise for his professional activities.

The narrative begins with a woman, Brigid O'Shaughnessy, played by Mary Astor (the casting, as Andrew Sarris has observed, is one of the best in the history of American film), requesting that the Spade-Archer detective agency find her sister and her sister's lover. In this first sequence we learn as much about Archer as about Spade; we see Archer, an apparent ladies' man, eyeing the attractive woman, while Spade is more aloof. Later in the film we learn that Spade became suspicious of the woman immediately because he didn't believe her story and the retainer she left was too high. The first sequence visually emphasizes the name of the partnership both on the door and on the window; at first the reason for the emphasis is not clear, though its significance is obvious on a second viewing. The interesting personality of Archer is never explored, for before long we see him being shot to death on his assignment. The information we soon receive tends to put Spade's character in a bad light. We see a close shot of a telephone on a table standing near a window with its curtain blowing; it rings, and a hand takes it from the table out of the frame. While the camera fastens on the window, Spade's voice, from off screen, retains its surface calm in spite of his obvious surprise at learning from the police that his partner has just been murdered. The sense of detachment evoked by our hearing a telephone conversation in which Spade demonstrates no emotion is reinforced by the shot's pictorial omission of the human element from the frame. Later, at the scene of the murder, he briefly but cleverly reconstructs the incident and hurries away, refusing the police offer to show him the body.

I   *2001: A Space Odyssey*                                    II   *Death in Venice*

**III**   *The Touch*

**IV**   *Fellini Satyricon*

**V** *Fellini Satyricon*

**VI–VII**  *The Damned*

Again, no emotion at all is evidenced by Spade, and this is peculiar, for the situation would seem to call for some of the usual remarks one makes about the sudden demise of a long-time associate.

We know, of course, that Spade's mind is working on the crime, though we never know till the end that he suspects Brigid on the basis of his brief analysis of the scene; however, we do realize that she might be involved, since Archer was going to meet her. Shortly after this, we have the encounter between Archer's widow and Spade in his office, when she comes in not as the bereaved widow but as Spade's lover. They kiss, but without any passion on his part. (His secretary asks him later if he plans to marry Mrs. Archer, and he answers, "Don't be silly.") Many pieces here begin to fit together. The lack of emotion Spade showed at the news of Archer's death indicated indifference or dislike for his partner; this opinion is now confirmed by our knowledge that he was deceiving Archer. Neither Mrs. Archer nor Spade seems happy at the death of Archer, but neither pretends to be emotionally touched by his absence. Later Spade hints that he might suspect Mrs. Archer. Actually, however, Spade's suspicions of her implication in the murder probably are aroused more by Mrs. Archer's double-dealing with him than by any serious notion of her as a murderess.

The environment continually tempts him to become involved in hypocrisy, though if we condemn Spade for anything at this point it is not his conduct toward his late partner's wife as much as his excessively placid reaction to the event of murder. Yet his attitude reflects the essential personality of the generic private eye: the man who keeps cool under conditions of strain, whose mind must operate effectively and unemotionally in all kinds of precarious situations. Sam Spade has by extensive experience learned to perform well while appearing hardened and corruptible. From the outside he is indiscernible from the villains he meets in the film. The police, who like him for his toughness, think him capable of either of two murders. Criminals take it for granted from their observations of his hardness that he is as corruptible as they are. They try to deal with him rather than kill him, for their instinct tells them that he is one of their kind.

His secret is that he is not one of them. He has earned their confidence by deliberately misleading them, and eventually he intends to destroy them. The point of interest here lies in the psychological transformation always potential in role playing. Has Sam Spade to some degree become the character he has invented for himself somewhere in the past? This seems likely in the early part of the film. But his coldness, his reserve, has made even Spade himself uneasy. The whole film, in fact, may be seen as a gradual unfolding of his role, a divesting of his emotional reserves up to the last sequence where he removes his disguise and tries to verbalize the conditions he works under. Only then is he free to speak of his abiding ethical code.

The disparity between his inner nature and the role he assumes begins to implicate him in the evil all around him. His relationship with Mrs. Archer

seems dispassionate, but it undermines his moral stature from the beginning. Not only do the police at different times have some justifiable suspicion about his involvement, but Mrs. Archer too thinks he might very well have killed her husband. All along he finds himself increasingly attracted to his client, Brigid, though he knows she is mixed up in various illegal activities relating to the Maltese falcon. The two others interested in the falcon, Kasper Gutman and Joel Cairo, at different times try to hire Spade to get it for them. At the end they consider him a partner in their enterprise; even when the recovered falcon proves to be an imitation, Spade claims a thousand-dollar fee, and Gutman pays it. Finally, Brigid O'Shaughnessy, revealed as the killer of Archer, assumes that Spade will cover up for her. These are not casual events but part of the hero's continual dilemma regarding his association with evil people. Ultimately, he manages to have all of them arrested and the complicated crimes solved, but the accomplishment costs him a great deal along the way.

The key to the Bogart characterization is integrity. Integrity is consciously important to Spade, though because of the nature of his role-playing career he has already sacrificed some of it at the beginning of the film. We realize how much when we discover the relationship of the hero and his partner's wife. Still, the man has a great deal of integrity as yet uncompromised, and he fights to save that much and to regain that which seems lost at the beginning. To make *The Maltese Falcon,* then, a narrative of moral redemption, Huston applies the generic form of the private-eye film (which does not inherently contain any such theme) to the particular characterization of the hero (which does contain the material for this theme).

What Huston borrows from the genre is what we would expect to find in the Hammett novel: plenty of nefarious activities, evil characters, and a brilliant detective mind, not to mention a perplexing mystery plot. The filmmaker's job was then to combine these elements through some cinematic style that would allow for the usual fast action of a detective thriller but would not obscure the hero's quest to regain his moral identity. The film's scenario, which Huston wrote, conveys ideas in an extremely concise way; it had to, because the villains are played by actors so talented—Sidney Greenstreet is Gutman, Peter Lorre is Cairo, and Elisha Cook, Jr., is the gunman Wilmer—that they create their own visual interest each time they appear and thus tend to develop their own characters and their own mannerisms that range suggestively beyond the narrative's immediate scope.

The villains are the alternatives to Spade, people who have no integrity at all. They roam freely throughout Spade's environment, and the last time we see them—and Brigid—is in Spade's own apartment; it is almost as if the evil spirits had moved in and Spade had to exorcise them, which he does. He never lets anyone forget that these men, who appear comical, actually do kill people. Several times Spade deliberately gets them to talk about criminal activities, but his disapproval emerges in understatement, and they do not see through his irony.

Huston relies on the generic qualities of the private-eye narrative not only in establishing swiftly and recognizably the background of evil, but in defining the normal function of the hero. In the genre, the hero's major job is fitting together the clues and solving the crime. In *The Maltese Falcon,* Huston makes this literal search for the solution to the crime the external dramatization of the hero's search for moral redemption. Spade has a way of asking questions that not only are aimed at eliciting facts but at probing for what he himself calls "the truth." He tells Brigid a few times that she is not merely lying but—a subtle distinction—not telling the truth. To lie is to change the facts; to fail to tell the truth may be not only to lie but to ignore the issue—to act hypocritically, and by implication, to obscure the possibility of reaching moral certainty. The truth that Spade seeks concerns not just the mystery of the Maltese falcon but the real moral identity of Brigid O'Shaughnessy, the girl he is falling in love with.

Mary Astor interprets the role of Brigid as practically Spade's image reversed. He senses this from the start, and the ambiguity surrounding her fascinates him. She seems a beautiful and innocent woman; yet essentially she is as evil as the villainous grotesques we encounter in the film. The role she plays in front of Spade evolves from the prototype of the feminine creature imposed on by hardened, greedy men who will stop at nothing to achieve their goal (securing the falcon), while her own concern is only self-protection. She never claims that she wants the falcon, merely admitting to having accompanied one of the murdered men who was also after it. Spade's external toughness is matched by her inner cruelty. Her role-playing is more dangerous than his, for she pretends to be better than she is, he just the opposite.

Except for his involvement with Brigid, Spade does not show any natural admiration for evil in the film. He despises and openly scorns Wilmer, the young hood, and makes a point of humiliating this innocuous-looking man each time they meet. Of course, Wilmer is not really innocuous, for he has murdered at least two men. Indeed, at the end, Spade warns the police that Wilmer is extremely dangerous. Spade also taunts Gutman and Cairo. Only Brigid attracts him, and probably it is because of her own evident skill at role-playing that he falls in love with her. Then it becomes a matter of his finding out her true identity, in the course of which he has to confront his own dual nature. She seems to see through him to some extent—at least she knows how to appeal to him, how to get him to help her in spite of his voiced suspicions about her. She relies on her femininity, asking him to "be generous." He responds always with skepticism or anger over the fact that she never tells him the truth. Spade tries unsuccessfully to intimidate her by his anger: once he takes almost all of her money, and at other times threatens to abandon her. Yet her dishonesty is essential to her self-preservation, for if she revealed the extent of her depravity, Spade, she assumes correctly, could not continue any relationship with her.

The predominant pictorial view is odd: much of the time the camera

films from an angle slightly below eye level—that is, tilted up toward the actors. The events are presented only partially from Sam Spade's point of view. Most of the time Spade himself appears in the frame, and frequently, Spade's back is caught in the frame as we focus on other characters. This is not the sort of film that benefits from a close audience identification with the hero, and the low-angle camerawork tends to put us off slightly from personal involvement with Spade, the only decent man in the film and the one with whom we would naturally sympathize. Remaining at a distance from him is perhaps the only way we can discern the difference between his outer role and his inner life. The oblique camera angle might indeed suggest Huston's own view toward the irregular moral world under examination, a world off-center, askew. The particular values gained from such shots are of some importance: for instance, Gutman, the voluptuous symbol of indulgence, is filmed from a very low angle, his huge stomach and hanging jowls caricaturing the sensitive refinement he pretends to have at the basis of his characterization.

Looking at this world is Sam Spade, ironically disguised as the callous man of this world, but actually, an observer studying the degree of corruption about him (fig. 42). Often he is photographed apart from the two or three others grouped together in a room. Sometimes he provokes quarrels among his opponents and laughs at the dissension he creates among those he calls "a fine lot of thieves."

The film always retains the typical movement we associate with the genre: the detective methodically plows through the chaotic mass of details toward a successful conclusion. Since Spade's search for the answer to the puzzle really postulates a search for the truth about the woman and himself, the generic structure of the film leads him into a series of exciting encounters that serve to dramatize his interior condition. Huston's method is established primarily through contrasts in characterization. In one sequence, Joel Cairo draws a gun in Spade's office and announces he will search the place. Spade proceeds to disarm him—using only one hand, as clear evidence of his disdain for his antagonist. What Cairo actually wants is to hire Spade to retrieve the falcon, which Spade agrees to do (though his true interest lies only in discovering the murderers). Spade innocently returns the gun to his new client, who immediately points it at him again, indicating he will search the office anyway. The image fades out on Spade's laughter at himself for being gullible enough to hand over the gun, but it reveals the disparity in the codes of the two men. Spade, as cynical as he is, would never have drawn a gun on a man who had struck a bargain with him. The contrast illuminates the somewhat precarious balance Spade has attained between his moral being and his disguise as the tough, amoral private eye. The truth is that Cairo would be foolish to trust him, though Spade has trusted Cairo. Thus, ironically, Cairo, with no inner nature at all, acts consistently; it is only Spade who constantly jeopardizes his integrity.

42  *The Maltese Falcon*

43  *The Maltese Falcon*

In fact, throughout the film he repeats the pattern of making pacts with the criminals, and at least once he suffers humiliation for it. In that instance he seemed to have reached agreement with Gutman in the latter's hotel room, but suddenly he passes out, drugged by Gutman, and is then kicked by the henchman, Wilmer (fig. 43). Although hired by Gutman, he has also been hired at different times by Brigid and Cairo, each supposedly the enemy of the others. In fact, however, the three of them, Cairo, Gutman, and Brigid, can try to kill each other at one moment and form alliances at the next. (At the end Cairo and Gutman comically start off together to Asia to continue their tracking down of the falcon.) Their betrayals are without passion; their murders are casual and indifferent. When Spade, at the end, wishes to demonstrate conclusively the ultimate moral perversion of these people, he insists that they set up a "fall guy" for the police to pin the murders on, and he turns to Wilmer, Gutman's loyal retainer (who ironically did commit two of the murders). Gutman professes great love for the "boy," who he claims to consider as his son, but as Spade continues to talk, the expendability of Wilmer is made attractive to his master. Gutman agrees, saying that if he loses a son he can get another, "but there's only one Maltese falcon." In the ensuing confusion over the discovery that the bird is fake, the terrified Wilmer slips out before he can be turned over to the police.

By this time, Spade's cynical humor has been satisfied, even glutted. He has solved the mystery of the murders (though he has not yet told Brigid that he knows she killed Archer), demonstrated the evil of the falcon's devotees, and had his laughs. But he remains in the grim process of withdrawal. His last joke of sorts seems almost pointless, but he sets it up at his own expense for his own purposes. He insists that Gutman pay him a thousand dollars even though the search has proved futile. When Gutman and Cairo leave, he phones the police and tells them where they can arrest the men for murder. Then, as if to complete his demonstration that the pursuit of money is totally futile within this particularly materialistic environment, he sardonically gives the police the thousand dollars as "material evidence," though it signifies a considerable sum of money to him. Why does he return it? It seems that this final gesture is a way of washing his hands after the case has been closed and perhaps of proving he was not corrupted. Yet it clearly means more than that: it is a token of moral affirmation. Presumably his keeping that sum would not be dishonest or deceptive. Yet his gesture provides his own comment on the external role he plays; it is his way of showing that, after all, it is just a role. Spade refuses to be motivated by the materialistic goals that pervert the sensibilities of the others. He will not yield to every easy temptation. It seems likely that the gesture of returning the money is a demonstration of the claim of honesty he made for himself to Brigid. There he very specifically informed her that the corruptible exterior he presented to the world was a lie only to enable

him to carry out his ordinary business. And that business, the last two sequences prove, is the destruction of social evils.

The beginning of *The Maltese Falcon* found Spade in the early stages of corruption. It was difficult to see the moral fervor beneath the placid exterior of the hardened, worldly detective. Only his angered verbal attacks on Brigid for not telling him the truth exhibit his inner commitment to some moral code that will continuously protect his nature from the environment he works in. Still, for the dramatic sense of the film to be convincing cinematically, some major specific action must testify to the development of character with respect to the search for redemption or the affirmation of moral values.

The need for such a demonstration must have been evident at some early stage in the conception of the film idea. Peculiarly, Huston placed it at the end, requiring viewers to reexamine the film in the light of the last major sequence, an unusual request for a filmmaker working in this genre. Thus, Huston had to plant a good number of indications throughout, while working within the usual generic structure of movement toward the solution to a specific crime. In any case, the final key sequence illuminates the conflict within Spade and shows as clearly as any film has ever done a man making a moral choice against his emotional inclination.

On the road to redemption, Spade has been given the opportunity of reclaiming that inner self he was close to losing early in the film. His redemption required of him some sacrifice; it required of John Huston a striking scene in which the sacrifice would gather tremendous emotional force in order for us to witness Spade's achievement of his quest. The sequence in which Spade confronts Brigid with his knowledge of her murder and turns down her plea for mercy is in many ways brutal. She has never appeared to the audience as a murderer, but as a frightened, defensive woman, lying to save herself, of course—but we did not know it was to save herself from being arrested for murder. For the sequence to work, Huston has to make it clear that Spade still loves her, and the hero claims he does. Having no moral nature of her own, she expects that Spade will let her go, even go off with her. She is completely puzzled by what seems to be a gratuitous moral action.

Spade tells her his chief reason: "When a man's partner is killed, you're supposed to do something about it." The simplicity of the phrasing of this idea baffles her. He says that he can't let her go because it would be "bad all around, bad for detectives everywhere." His creed admits of nothing more specific, and it abstracts the whole issue for her. Then he tries to come up with some other reasons, such as the possibility that she might kill him if he let her go; but the reason sounds false, even while he speaks it, and he himself dismisses it. The truth persists that his main reason is profoundly real to him, but he cannot articulate it clearly to a woman who lacks a moral nature that could ever comprehend the abstraction of responsibility and

obligation. The affirmation of his code requires the sacrifice of personal ambition, that is, his love for a woman. Were he to put aside his code at this particular moment of great temptation and choose her, he would really be abandoning his integrity and choosing to accept the external life he has been leading, thus becoming as corrupt as the villains, which Brigid herself believed him to be.

He tries to make her grasp the horror of her particularly vicious murder, but all she perceives is the horror of a long prison term, and his promising to wait twenty years provides no comfort. He says, "I'll be waiting for you. If they hang you, I'll always remember you." Delivered straightforwardly to a desperate woman, the remark is strikingly blunt; it takes a moment to absorb because we are not certain about the direction of either the bitterness or the irony. Primarily, Spade is trying to cut through the personal relationship by bringing in an objective consideration; in turn this consideration will illuminate something about his personal feelings that cannot be communicated as long as Brigid insists on dealing with him in terms of her private responses to the situation. First of all, Spade lets her know that the problem involves an objective criterion: the legal system that will not condone her activities because of her personal designs. He is saying that she has committed a terrible crime, that in this case the opinion of the world permits no extenuating circumstances, and that she will be punished for it. Secondly, the tone of his statement very strongly suggests that he agrees with the assessment of the external world—that Brigid indeed deserves the stern punishment awaiting her. Thirdly, at the same time, he very clearly states that although he will not do anything to help her avoid the punishment, he personally regrets that it has to happen because in spite of her guilt he does love her. He places his personal feelings for her against the reality of the future and demands that she see that reality. Fourthly, the implication of all this reinforces the motive for his bitterness because her crime means that he has to lose her; she has betrayed and deceived him, and as a result he too is stuck with the fact of her impending punishment. She deserves blame for what she did to him because he had done nothing to her that should have made him liable for any suffering at all. By stating that he will always remember her, he puts before her in the most rational (i.e., the least emotional) way the pertinent truth: his own life will not come to an end, but he will always be affected by the memory of her dishonest treatment of him.

Spade is certainly sensitive enough to realize the implicit cruelty of his remarks: he wants to force Brigid into an awareness that there are objective considerations beyond her continual subjective analysis of the world—and he relates this point to her moral indifference by asserting that the outer world will judge her so harshly that she can no longer avoid making her own objective assessment of the life she has led. Since he fails to enlighten her as to his justification for turning her in to the police, he tries to tell her

something about himself and his integrity, but this too cannot move her. As he explains moral philosophy, she attempts sexual allurement, and clearly enough neither one communicates to the other.

The genre creates a familiar pattern of private-eye action, arousing certain audience expectations. Spade's verbalized moral analysis disrupts the familiar pattern, alerting us to the disparities between what we normally anticipate and what in fact occurs. We see Spade surrounded by evil he despises; we see him ironically participating in conspiracies with men he evidently intends to destroy once he solves the riddles of their cross-involvement. He manipulates them as he carefully arranges for the denouement. Never do we have the feeling that he seriously intends to join them; we know he is just acting—because the genre is premised on the basic honesty of the private eye. We are challenged to examine the surface to find clues to support the premise. The use of a genre pattern affords us a new perspective on the conventional moral predicament of the good man in a bad moral environment.

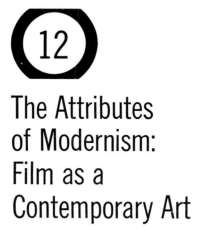

# The Attributes
# of Modernism:
# Film as a
# Contemporary Art

## The Responsiveness of the Medium

In Part Two we have so far emphasized certain key developments that have
shaped the narrative film into the art form of today. We now need to examine
some of the internal and external influences on the film industry that have
shaped our image of the contemporary film's most interesting characteristics.
When we examine the attributes of modernism in film, we find—as we would
expect—innumerable changes in both the form and the substance of
cinematic art in those works which best represent the spirit of our times
compared to the major artistic films of other eras. Since some of the
developments in film form, particularly the general structure of the modern
film, raise issues relevant to the larger questions of film theory studied in
Part Three, the major discussion of these aspects of the current cinema
will occur in Chapter 18.

  Our concern here is with the kinds of influence that have affected the
substance of the contemporary film—that is, with the way in which filmmakers have responded to the cinematic environment in which they work
creatively. So responsive is film to every sociological and historical change
in our era that it would be futile to attempt even a summary of the main
ideas and values of this society that have affected the subject matter of the

cinema. But it seems both feasible and profitable to examine instead certain general attitudes that have significantly influenced the actual presentational mode of film narrative, contributing to the manner in which audiences and filmmakers alike conceive of the special traits of cinematic modernism.

In any case, the characteristics of a contemporary art form will usually have more to do with the artist's approach to his material than the particular subject he deals with. It is quite common for a modern filmmaker to treat familiar subjects, but we need only compare any ambitious contemporary retelling of conventional cinematic materials with any 1940's treatment of that subject—for instance, Penn's *Little Big Man* (1970), a depiction of General Custer's last stand at the Battle of Little Bighorn—to realize the nature of the change. It is not just Penn's deflation of Custer's usual heroic stature, which presumably could have been accomplished by any historically-minded filmmaker of the past, but the modern director's feeling for narrative form, the anthropological emphasis on the depiction of Indian life, the mixture of serious and comic events, and the central focus on the main character's growth of consciousness that mark the contemporary approach.

Since every filmmaker's approach to his craft is influenced (though not absolutely determined) by the interests of his era and the attitudes of his audience, to understand the nature of the contemporary film requires an evaluation of some of the major forces affecting our present cinematic sensibility. For an audience to perceive film as an art form (a relatively recent attitude) means that filmmakers, in turn, will become responsive to producing works that strive to reflect a deepening level of human awareness. At the same time, segments of the mass audience may raise counter-claims that film has nothing in particular to do with art: witness, for example, the evident interests of some producers in the exploitation of violent or sexual imagery. The narrative film has always been susceptible to the vagaries of fashion, but just as surely, key filmmakers and significant stylistic trends are responsible for many of the essential attributes that define the modern film.

## Public Recognition

Probably the most important development since the introduction of sound was the rapid acceptance by a significant portion of the public of the opinion that film was a major—perhaps *the* major—art form of the age. Public acceptance of what now seems an astoundingly simple fact occurred in the late 1950's and was no longer seriously challenged by the early 1960's. Thus, the 1970's find the bastions of culture, the institutions of higher learning, teaching film as part of the general curriculum, a situation that seemed unlikely as late as 1965 and was undreamed of in 1955. Film has invaded the cultural scene of America and Europe (where it always had more status as a serious art form than it had here) and virtually conquered

that segment of the younger generation with any pretensions to artistic interests.

This signifies an important development for the film historian because it helps to explain the shift of this mass medium from a certain kind of narrative to a variety of newer, more experimental forms. Up to the time that the public began to accept the film as an art form the industry saw its function primarily as a provider of mass entertainment. When the industry finally decided to come to terms with the fact that the arrival of television had demolished the old patterns of weekly and biweekly moviegoing, it began to recognize the claims of that portion of the new public that did go frequently—but selectively—to the cinema. It seems strange to us now that for a long time to the general public the idea of going to see a film meant going to see whatever was there. Bad films were not necessarily successful under the old system, since some degree of selectivity was always apparent (even when most of the selecting was done by the distributors in choosing what films to show where), but many mediocre vehicles for star performers became sufficiently popular to encourage numerous productions of what Hollywood itself called the Grade B film.

Selectivity means quality appraisal, and though the audience of today indicating its preference exerts no very obviously higher degree of taste, it patronizes a wider variety of films than the equivalent public had in the past. The audience of college students, for example, wants to get the feeling that it has witnessed not only something entertaining but something that might qualify as an artistic experience. Almost all the movie theaters built in the last twenty years (aside from those in shopping centers) have relatively small seating capacities and are implicitly built for a limited portion of the public that might have particular standards for motion pictures. Nowadays, with movie theater attendance finally rising again, the industry has recognized that people will not always accept the superficial product that was the staple of the past. The industry itself has become as pretentious as its early critics would have wished: it now advertises its products in terms of artistic quality, profundity, reflection of contemporary values, and the like.

More important, however, the filmmaker as artist has been allowed to work regularly and exhibit his feature films, and also to make a very good return on them. In the past, many major film artists were inactive for a period of years, though they had considerable reputations among their contemporary critics: Carl Dreyer turned out no feature narrative films between 1931 (*Vampyr*) and 1943 (*Day of Wrath*); Luis Buñuel, so remarkably admired today, directed no films between 1932 and 1947; Erich von Stroheim directed no films for the last twenty-five years of his life. But today, the film artist (unlike the poet) is supported in grandiose style, and the result is that filmmakers like Antonioni and Bergman can work regularly at the kind of film they think important.

## "Auteur" Criticism

In considering the evolution of the public's attitude toward the contemporary film as an art form—as well as the renewed sensibility of artistic goals on the part of filmmakers themselves—we must take into account the contribution of a loosely associated school of criticism that originated in France in the middle of the 1950's and spread significantly in England and America. These critics' approach to film, their basic starting point, is the "auteur theory," which holds that film is the expression of a filmmaker, more than a collective art, and that what is of primary interest consists in the self-expression of the creative artist from film to film. Thus, the filmmaker, like an author, creates his vision of life within a body of works. In other words, these critics emphasized first the filmmaker (who is almost always the director) and then the body of films he produced.

The impact of this theory has been extensive even though few people read serious film journals. These critics supplied an approach to film that only a small part of the public was intuitively arriving at without any formal theory. Nowadays, to devoted followers of the art, a new work by Antonioni or Visconti would be a significant event of the film season regardless of the critical reviews of the particular film. The individual film no longer rested purely on its apparent merits but required discussion as a reflection of the filmmaker's world view as seen in the total context of all his films. To speak knowledgeably of a film by a major director, one analyzed that particular film in regard to those distinguishing characteristics peculiar to the film artist.

A necessary corollary to this approach was the ranking of directors.* Some were considered great—which in itself was an offensive idea to many scoffers who did not really believe that the cinema was capable of producing more than very rare films of high quality. The auteur critics, led in America by Andrew Sarris, seemed to be deliberately trying to arouse critical controversies by their innumerable lists of major and near-major and even minor directors. There was much disagreement among the English, French, and American critics, particularly noticeable in divisions made along nationalistic lines. Although from the general consensus much indisputable praise was heaped on artists like Jean Renoir, Charles Chaplin, and Carl Dreyer, the controversial nature of the selections can be seen in the promulgation of claims for the filmmakers these critics felt were the nearly great men.

Some extremely interesting quarrels arose among critics supporting the auteur theory and those who felt the theory was unimportant and the appli-

---

* The most extensive ranking occurs in Andrew Sarris's *The American Cinema,* an extremely useful source of information even when the opinions are highly controversial.

cation of it outrageous. In their attempt to establish reputations, the auteur critics were consistently guided by the principle that the filmmaker's personality is as clearly visible in his films as an author's is in his novels (thus the coinage of the term, established by François Truffaut's challenging slogan, *Politique des auteurs*). This premise stirs up less controversy than the one that follows it: a consistent personality observable in film after film is *the* decisive proof of a filmmaker's quality. Opponents dismiss this premise out of hand, claiming that it equally justified the practices of a terribly bad filmmaker whose stupidity might also carry over from film to film. Presumably, the auteur critics would answer that a second-rate filmmaker could not conceivably shape his views consistently time after time; his bad films would not express the same kind of badness over and over.

With most directors, one of two attitudes became apparent on the part of opponent critics. For instance, with Hitchcock, American writers who were never accustomed to thinking of him as an important artist were slowly convinced of his importance. With directors like Sam Fuller (*I Shot Jesse James, Underworld U.S.A.*), Robert Aldrich (*What Ever Happened to Baby Jane?, The Dirty Dozen*), and "the Orson Welles of Z films," Roger Corman (*The Masque of the Red Death, The St. Valentine's Day Massacre*), opponents have refused to go along with the evaluations of the auteur critics. But the case of Howard Hawks became the testing ground for the theory and continues to be a problem because Hawks has always been recognized as at least a moderately talented filmmaker. In America, his reputation is probably lower than John Huston's; yet Huston, unpopular with auteur critics, is rated by them far below Hawks. Huston's *The Treasure of Sierra Madre,* to many a film classic, is scorned by auteur critics, who pay serious attention to Hawks's African hunting film, *Hatari!,* or his parody of a fisherman in *Man's Favorite Sport?* To opponents, it is an absolutely trivial point that the comedy in, say, *Man's Favorite Sport?* can be related to a much earlier and more popular Hawks film, *Bringing Up Baby.* In the first place, *Bringing Up Baby* is not a classic, and secondly, even if it were, its similarities with a second-rate later film cannot save that other film. An exact estimate of Hawks still poses a difficulty for anyone not engaged in the controversy.

In the almost total absence of a theoretical attitude toward the art form, the auteur theory has been a valuable stimulus to thought, or a provocation to argument, depending on one's point of view. Regardless of our feeling about this school of criticism, we can recognize its significant historical contributions toward the general recognition of the cultural standing of the medium. Auteur critics can also be singled out for establishing an aura of respectability in the examination of certain types of films that have significant cinematic value. The French auteur critics, in fact, have raised the esteem of the American films of the 1930's and 1940's (films considered of no value by the industry that made them).

Consequently, the auteur critics are in part responsible for making the public aware, first, that a vast body of cinematic works of high merit is available and, second, that many of these films deserve study, not simply casual viewing. The lists of great films and great directors continually drawn up by these critics may be arbitrary and personal, but they reflect serious interest in film study. They also serve to throw some historical perspective on the study of film, for many of their favorites are silent films pretty much forgotten by most moviegoers and in need of a rehabilitation of reputation. On the other hand, certain directors have never been very popular with the auteur critics—among them many filmmakers whom one might consider intellectual, including creative artists as truly great as Akira Kurosawa and Ingmar Bergman—in spite of the fact that they qualify as having the most noticeable "directorial personalities" in their films. The choices of the auteur critics are, of course, somewhat arbitrary, for these critics exercise a highly subjective critical faculty in determining quality; in practice this subjective attitude toward evaluation has disturbed non-auteur critics.

Ultimately, however, it is not so much the understandable arbitrariness of decisions that makes the practice of these critics suspect. More dubious is their tendency to impose literary criteria on the cinema. This is surprising, since the critics have decidedly firm commitments to cinema as an art form (several followed Truffaut's lead and became directors themselves). They entirely lack the snobbishness of literary critics in evaluating genres, for instance, and one of their major contributions has been to awaken interest in such subliterary cinematic categories as the crime film (*e.g.,* ex-critic Jean-Luc Godard's love for the fast pace of American gangster films is obvious in several of his films), the horror film, and the Western. Still, they tend to apply literary analysis and have never derived a consistent cinematic approach to criticism. Their criticism persistently aligns film with literature inasmuch as the emphasis falls on the general themes and motifs of a director's works as evidenced by a particular film. Yet unlike literary critics, they seldom evaluate the quality of the ideas, merely the implementation of them in the films under analysis. For this reason, directors like Hawks will outrank men like Bergman. Hawks's ideas are indeed limited, but the application of his notions is clearly established and can be traced easily from film to film. Although Bergman's style is so remarkably personal that it cannot be mistaken for anyone else's, his ideas tend to be concerned with abstract psychological, moral, and theological matters and change significantly over the course of his career.

Certain notable directors, therefore, receive limited attention from auteur critics because they do not fit readily into the desired patterns of motifs and themes. Similarly, the industry director who, working steadily, turns out a large number of mediocre films and one or two fine ones cannot profit from auteur-theory analysis. (Occasionally, these critics will admit to liking such films, but these exceptions, such as Michael Curtiz's *Casa-*

*blanca,* are rare.) New directors find a more receptive audience among auteur critics, but the problem arises that a first film can only show "promise," not fulfillment. (*Citizen Kane,* one supposes, might be an exception to the usual evaluations of first films as merely promising.)

Whatever their shortcomings, the auteur critics appeared at a moment in film history when some formalized approach to film criticism was required, especially in America, where random evaluations by critics who had never thought twice about a film theory were the rule. The auteur critics have rescued some reputations and established others. They have not succeeded in convincing many people that Roger Corman's films are worth serious consideration, but their rating of Max Ophüls (*Lola Montès, La Ronde, Caught*) among the great directors called attention to a fine filmmaker whose reputation had never been made with the general public. They have also managed to rescue the reputations of films that the public at first disapproved of (*e.g.,* Hitchcock's *The Birds*), but which taken in the light of later films became more intelligible and more effective. In general, these critics have done more good than harm as an influence on standards for evaluating the contemporary film, for establishing the primacy of the director as artist, and for creating a greater audience awareness of the artistic development of the medium.

## Ingmar Bergman and the New Intellectualism

The filmmaker most responsible for the public's increased recognition of the film as a major art form was Ingmar Bergman. Of course, he was not the first great filmmaker to catch the public's attention; Griffith, Eisenstein, and others in the silent screen era were generally well known, and certainly Chaplin was a household word. But the film artist in the past succeeded because he qualified in the mind of the public, as an entertainer first and an artist second. When Griffith started to make films that were less and less commercially successful, his reputation did nothing for him. Sergei Eisenstein, on the strength of his reputation, was invited to make a film in Hollywood, but his fame did not serve him well once here; the studio deemed his projects unsuitable for the mass audience, and he never completed a film outside of his own national industry. Chaplin's artistry was popularly considered only that of the performer—the interpreter's, not the creator's.

Bergman's reputation in America was made rather suddenly on the basis of *The Seventh Seal* (1957). Before Bergman became well known here, the only filmmakers whose names meant anything to the public as an inducement to go and see a new film were Alfred Hitchcock and Cecil DeMille. (A few others, like Frank Capra and John Ford, had followings but were unknown to many.) Bergman's films had some limited distribution in this country before *The Seventh Seal,* but for the most part he was so far

removed from anything resembling an artistic reputation that such films as *Monika* and *The Naked Night* were booked by sex-exploitation movie houses.

Working with a superb group of performers in what was virtually a repertory company, Bergman wrote and directed a series of major films in which he had control over his product to a greater extent than most contemporary filmmakers. His output was much larger than that of any serious director of his generation, and thus he was afforded many opportunities to try different approaches to his craft. Bergman worked in both comic and tragic genres, and his films often reveal a mixture of modes, but the films that gained him his following were serious dramas that were marked by a highly literate dialogue spoken by intelligent characters who were played by brilliant performers like Max von Sydow, Gunnar Björnstrand, Ingrid Thulin, Harriet Andersson, and Bibi Andersson. The photography of Gunnar Fischer and Sven Nykvist received unanimous critical approval, though sometimes it was the stark beauty of the Swedish landscape that got the credit for the effects of the cameraman.

Bergman's appeal for many intellectual filmgoers had much to do with his willingness to create films around broad philosophical ideas. This has rarely been attempted in the cinema because the particularizing surface of the medium seldom suggests conditions favorable to the articulation of such ideas. Yet Bergman's famous works are not discussions nor theatrical plays photographed but true films in which the visual surface absorbs our interest and justifies the quality of the thought verbalized or suggested by the characters. Aside from Akira Kurosawa, who does the same thing, no filmmaker known in the West consistently creates films that present a viable intellectual microcosm. Certainly there are such films—Dreyer's *Ordet,* Renoir's *Rules of the Game,* Chaplin's *Monsieur Verdoux,* and, since Bergman, a number of films including those by Fellini, Buñuel, and Antonioni—but they do not seem to be plentiful. Of course, artistic greatness does not rely on the level of the intellectual themes discussed in a film: the characters in De Sica's *Bicycle Thief* cannot express verbally the ideas of this classic film, whereas the pseudo-religious Biblical spectacles cranked out by large studios are filled with babbling about great issues, but are decidedly not great films. Bergman was the first popular artist to conceive of films repeatedly in terms of an intellectual environment.

And much more important for artistic purposes, Bergman's environments were fully cinematic in the sense that, interacting with the characters on his landscape, they made every aspect seem truly credible. Conceived in regard to situations that created plausible conditions for the raising of philosophic problems, the major Bergman films of the 1950's present characters in confrontation with great issues. *The Seventh Seal* made perhaps the greatest impact on the public of any film of its decade and typifies the filmmaker's approach. First of all, in this film (as in *The Virgin Spring* and

*The Magician*), Bergman evolves a vivid sense of an earlier period in a situation of crisis, thus making feasible some of the theological considerations of the characters. Certain supernatural devices are used in *The Seventh Seal,* the main one being the personification of Death. Still, the visual level carefully sustains the sense of realism despite Death's literal presence and despite the unfamiliar landscape of the medieval world. In other words, Bergman's films, regardless of their tendency to remove the idea from the particular situation to the level of either allegory or general human conditions, remain very close to the surface iconography recorded by the camera; real objects are continually given symbolic values, but the objects are indeed real all the same.

In *The Seventh Seal,* for instance, a medieval knight disillusioned from many years in the Crusades returns to Sweden in the midst of a plague that has ravished the country and reduced much of the population to a state of paranoia; antisocial acts such as rape and thievery are becoming common as men turn cynical. We have numerous graphic examples of the conditions of the times, and set against this morbid backdrop is the knight whose increasing disillusionment requires him to commence a spiritual journey in search of a certitude that is theologically tenuous. Death himself, the personification of a force that everyone believes in, tells the knight that even he does not know if God exists. The film makes it increasingly clear to the knight that faith precludes certainty. In a world where man can neither be totally knowledgeable nor totally indifferent, the knight must recognize that faith supposes a degree of doubt. A man who sees God can have no need of faith.

Given this premise, the film really makes visual the problem of how to respond to a world of evil in an age of uncertainty. The characters act in different ways, representing common alternatives. Some, through fear and cowardice, abandon all moral principles; others renew their religious affirmations. The squire, who unlike his lord has completely lost his faith during the Crusades, verbally insists on denial, but his integrity requires him to rise to heroic heights to defend the humanistic principle he operates on (*e.g.,* he saves a girl from rape or murder and might even have attacked a group of soldiers to prevent a witch-burning). The knight, whose search for spiritual certainty is at the center of the narrative, learns (from Death) that his time on earth has run out. Playing a prolonged game of chess with Death at intervals in the film, the knight manages to stall for time, not because he fears dying or because he desires knowledge of God, but because he feels his life has been insignificant and wishes for the opportunity to do one significant act (he does not know precisely what kind) before he dies (fig. 44). At the climax of the drama, he seizes an opportunity to save the life of an innocent young couple, distracting Death by upsetting the chessboard. It is so unobtrusive a gesture in comparison to the many striking images of this photographically beautiful film that some critics never discern that

this act is the structural climax of the narrative of *The Seventh Seal*. In any case, once the action is performed, the knight has to his own satisfaction at least partially redeemed the emptiness of his past years.

Throughout *The Seventh Seal,* the characteristic questioning and spiritual searching always seem plausible within the context. Plausibility tends to make the film an emotional as well as intellectual experience, for we believe in the problems of the knight and the squire and the subsequent reactions they have in critical moments. But it was not necessary for Bergman, even in the 1950's, to use a distant time to involve us emotionally in the spiritual problems of his characters, for *Wild Strawberries* is contemporary in its setting and rivals *The Seventh Seal* for honors in the Bergman canon. In that film, less technical virtuosity is apparent, but perhaps even more is present, for Bergman enables a man to evaluate his entire past during a long car ride. However, Bergman had some difficulty in establishing a philosophical problem in visually effective terms in most of his films with contemporary settings. In *Winter Light,* a character's remarking to his minister that he suffers from fears of a great calamity (the explosion of a nuclear

bomb) reflects not so much a general spiritual burden of modern man as a particular neurosis of an unstable individual. *Winter Light,* itself a remarkable intellectual film, falls short of being a major accomplishment because the issues are too broad for the environment and situation depicted. However, in *Shame,* Bergman found a magnificent contemporary setting for a spiritual allegory of the crisis of modern man—the conditions of war in the modern world dehumanizing the civilians; the allegory is about war in general, but it is particularly relevant to the Vietnam war.

At a certain point in his career, Bergman turned from the philosophical-theological issues that had helped shape the film ideas in his major works toward a more personally derived view of experience that emphasized his psychological interests. He had always shown considerable evidence of an interest in probing the psyche, but with *Through a Glass Darkly* (1961) he first moved into the realm of psychoanalytical drama. In style, most of the later films up to *The Passion of Anna* (1970) emphasize the isolation and somewhat inarticulate agony of various characters, mainly women (both these films take place on sparsely populated islands, making possible intense concentration on the distressed psychological conditions of the heroines). This style led Bergman to an increasing reliance on actors to convey through facial expressions and dialogue their interior mental states. *Through a Glass Darkly* was judged a particularly difficult film, though fascinating in many ways, especially since its spider imagery (visualized by a young woman during her breakdown) is communicated with theological overtones that tenuously link the film with his earlier efforts. The film, in its interpretive challenge to viewers and critics, marked what for many seemed a decline in Bergman's ability to communicate visually. The films that followed were provocative but increasingly difficult to interpret: *Winter Light, The Silence, Persona,* and *Night of the Wolf.* The director had begun to lose a good part of his audience in America, and not even the more comprehensible *Shame,* which followed the others, was given its deserved consideration, though it was well received by reviewers.

The difficulty with the later Bergman films reflects one of the unresolved problems of the contemporary cinema: the increasing use of intellectually complex ideas frequently corresponds with the encroachment of a literary mode of expressiveness upon the cinematic mode. The continual challenge to embody an equivalent to the logic of spoken or written language in the imagery of the cinema is particularly notable in the works of such fine filmmakers as Antonioni, Kubrick, Frankenheimer, and Pier Pasolini. Rejecting the literary impulse to explore ideas primarily in dialogue, today's major filmmakers, with a propensity to intellectualize, on occasion seem to lack suitable visual symbols to convey the film idea. In one of the most remarkable film experiments of recent years, *Death in Venice* (1970), Visconti confronts the problem in the most direct way, borrowing the distinguished and profound literary text of Thomas Mann

and turning it into virtually a silent film (a minimum of dialogue is used) in which photography, the musical score, setting, and background sounds substitute largely for Mann's authorial insight and his descriptions of the hero's consciousness. Obviously, Visconti could not have intended a duplication of the literary mode in Mann's story, for the logical verbal processes of literature can never find a precise equivalent in either literal or symbolic visual images of motion. But what Visconti tries to achieve here is an emotional response to the total impact of the narrative that in some way resembles what readers derive from the Mann text. Whereas Mann analyzed the interior world of the hero, Visconti depicts the external; for some, the results of the film are entirely different from those of the literary work. Regardless of whether Visconti's experiment will eventually be considered a success, it is clear that one of the attributes of modernity— most apparent in the works of Visconti, as in those of Bergman—is the determined effort to develop new cinematic resources, not exclusively verbal, to deal with the demands of a new intellectual cinema.

Bergman has always evinced a strong literary background, but in the past it had been an advantage, for it added depth to the texture of his films. In his later work, the literary background vied for attention with the visual presentation. He had failed to find a narrative, cinematic myth to convey the mental anguish of his characters. Overt narrative action was minimized, and the dialogue too became more suggestive than it had been, but less concrete. There is a sequence in *Persona* in which two women look at each other while one speaks; immediately after the conclusion of the sequence, the same dialogue is repeated, with the camera taking the view of the other woman's face. It is a clever feat, the relating of two views of the same situation, but it is all technique; clearly it could occur only in a film where the narrative interest is so slight that an interruption of the surface order is welcomed by an audience that lacks interest in what is literally happening on screen and is impatient to delve behind the visual imagery.

Exploring the process and effects of psychological alienation in his color films of the 1970's, *The Passion of Anna* and *The Touch,* Bergman moved away from the internalized landscapes of his typical films of the 1960's, which dealt with similar subjects but were characterized by rather stark black-and-white photography. Because color has the capacity to endow the images of ordinary objects with an objective reality—that is, they occupy clearly depicted spatial volumes in the environment, easily distinguishable by their color from adjacent volumes of at least different intensities or hues—these recent Bergman films situate the characters' psychological problems in an identifiable landscape.

Yet if color resolves some of the difficulties of abstraction notable in his films of the 1960's, it also creates some new problems for the intellectual cinema of the 1970's. In *The Touch* (1971), for instance, the three main characters relate quite naturally to their surroundings, so well in fact that

when the woman casually but very quickly enters into a relationship with a highly unstable archeologist who lives in a dreary apartment, painted an unpleasant dark green, we are unclear as to her motivations for abandoning her commitment to her family and her attractive home, decorated and furnished in a variety of bright colors, with white prominent (plate III). We understand that the woman is drawn to the weaknesses of the archeologist while she is in the process, largely subconscious, of rejecting the security and comfort of her role as a doctor's wife (although she does not verbalize any complaints about household routines); her dissatisfaction has to do with her fear of aging, but the fear is not reflected in the immediate environment shown on the screen. Because the contrast in the settings is so vividly detailed, the environment so persistently present to affect our awareness of what the woman can gain or lose, the film probably needs a more explicit demonstration of her motivation or a more precise articulation of the problem than Bergman characteristically employs.

In the intellectual cinema, it is frequently necessary to create visual symbols to compensate for the absence of an extended literary or psychological discussion of the internal predicament. In *The Touch* the symbol is a medieval wooden Madonna that the archeologist has discovered sealed in a church alcove; the Madonna is slowly being destroyed internally by insects that had been dormant in the statue for hundreds of years, and it cannot be saved. The futility of the lovers' relationship, their personal instability, and the conflict between the beauty of the Madonna and her inner decay may be read into the symbol, but proportionately much less time is spent on the sculpture than on the ordinary surroundings of the main characters. Occasionally, the literary tendencies of the intellectual cinema require us to read visual symbols as we read literary symbols in drama or poetry, but such moments cannot be totally effective in a film like *The Touch,* in which the physical reality of the settings is continually meaningful and interesting on its own level.

Bergman, an incessant experimenter, will certainly go through other forms of cinematic expression as long as he keeps making films. His screenplays retain a literary quality beyond that of virtually every contemporary, even in those few instances where the idea bogged down on a cinematic level. When his screenplays were at their best they were characterized by a strong sense of the reality of the imagery. Sometimes, as in *The Virgin Spring* (1960), the simplicity of the imagery and the solidity of the narrative combined to provide the ideal framework for the communication of ideas. The advantage of maintaining a surface clarity in a conceptually complex film is that viewers can relate the image to the idea as the film is unfolding. *The Virgin Spring* affords us numerous examples of Bergman's ability to impress upon us a striking visual equivalent for an emotional or intellectual state, so that regardless of our grasp of the intricacies of the philosophic argument underlying a film, we know very

deeply what the sequence proposes. This film abounds in images of violence, of crime and punishment, and of man's revulsion in the face of physical terror. The sequence in which three brothers, one only a boy, participate in the rape and ultimate murder of Karin, stands as one of the most brutal scenes in Western cinema. The lust and fear of the brothers at the time of their involvement and their inability to extricate themselves with any shred of decency before they murder the girl prepare us for their passionless execution at the hands of Karin's father later in the film. The father performs a pagan ritual of cleansing, purging himself of pity and fear prior to slaughtering his daughter's murderers. The father, himself a devout Christian, does not really take revenge for his daughter, nor does he allow himself to become emotionally involved in what he is doing. Instead, he is presumably carrying out a civic responsibility, as lord of a medieval manor, to eradicate a force of evil. His responsibility requires him to destroy the murderers, and by bathing and scourging himself and delaying the impending event for a few hours he succeeds in quenching that passionate hatred that came over him when he discovered that his guests had killed his only child.

The unpitying coldness of his subsequent execution of the obvious penalty in a semi-darkened room just around dawn is itself formalized and terrifying. Having finished what he felt was necessary, the father, with his

**45** *The Virgin Spring*

remarkably clear moral conscience, accepts a degree of guilt as a Christian for his actions (fig. 45). What one remembers about the film longer than the theological concept is the visual manifestation of that concept as it appears in the lives of the characters. The film idea, as in *The Seventh Seal,* has to do with man's questioning of a silent God and seemingly gratuitous evil as revealed in the imagery of the simple setting, so palpably open to the intrusion of violence. Bergman infuses the narrative and the setting with the sense of universal concerns underlying the particulars of place and time. Thus, the miraculous occurrence of a spring beneath the body of the daughter at the film's conclusion serves as a sign of the restoration of spiritual balance in a world that seemed to be running dry. It presents the characters with a chance to reaffirm their faith; however, the father had witnessed the appearance of the spring after his insistence that he would reaffirm his faith despite the indifference of God, who, he feels, allowed the evil to transpire without providing a meaningful context for evaluation. That spring can be interpreted as a sign that such a context does exist, regardless of whether he comprehends it. In any case, the miracle is not tacked on to the tragedy but appears as a plausible component of the realistic environment.

Typically, the vitality of Bergman's best images derives from their being conceived in a world where the characters provide or seek to provide a commentary and interpretation for what occurs. Moreover, events do not just happen, but happen in a way that requires some simultaneous analysis from each spectator as well. Bergman succeeds in depicting the event and the process of its analysis within a consistently realistic framework. As long as that narrative framework is itself clear, the analysis is practicable; but at times in the later films, audiences are urged to devote their energy to deciphering the surface imagery, and the result is a blurred impression of the film idea.

## Stylistic Movements

Film is an enthusiast's medium. A sizable portion of each year's crop of films is greeted by some segment of the public as "masterpieces" or "great works," and reviewers constantly tell us we "can't afford to miss this one." Perhaps because of its brief cultural history or because of the lack of sophistication among reviewers in general, the contemporary cinema always seems creatively fertile. Indeed, the medium teems with experimentation, though no more so than many of the other arts, but what has distinguished the reception of film experimentation from that of experimentation in most other arts is the willingness of the public to assume an equation between quality and novelty. Film experimentalists from Griffith on have

frequently found quick acceptance, and since the 1950's, when film as an art form began to find a large public, filmmakers who represented departures from the traditional narrative structure—like Antonioni, Fellini, Godard, Resnais, and Truffaut—found either public support or a large amount of critical acclaim.

If nowadays we hail everything new as interesting, and much of that as "truly important," it becomes difficult to sort out that which seems to have lasting impact or value from that which is merely of contemporary cultural significance. The intent of this section is to take note of some of the major film influences of the last decade on the cinema of the 1970's rather than to evaluate the quality of the contributions.

To speak in terms of broad trends, we can say that the film of today reveals pretensions to an awareness of social and intellectual interests, at least in contrast with the ordinary films of the 1930's and 1940's. This is a result in part of the decline in the production of films aimed at being second features (B films) or aimed at theaters that changed their program twice a week. This was an economy measure for the industry more than an artistic commitment to better films, though it was accompanied by a campaign to indoctrinate the public with the slogan "Movies are better than ever."

In this era, even the most ordinary film is designed to show some superficial relevance to modern problems or issues of the day: the generation gap (with the younger generation coming off better than the parents), the civil rights movement (with the black man, at long last, reversing the old stereotypes and appearing as heroic and superior), the "sexual revolution," reappear as motifs in many films and are occasionally main themes. Intellectual pretentiousness may sometimes encourage worthwhile developments, but it has had a narrowing effect on the kind of product that could be the ordinary fare of the major studios. One problem is that introducing "big issues" into films that aren't equipped to deal with them weighs down potentially successful entertainment vehicles with messages that can rarely be implanted in the visuals. The emphasis is redirected to a dialogue that is not referable to any pictorial meaning, and the extraneous message is too readily discerned as an artistic irrelevance.

In terms of style, the contemporary cinema has moved in several directions. As the American industry began to lose its dominant position in the European markets, it became more susceptible to foreign influence than in the thirties and forties. As a result, what might have remained avant-garde filming has become stylistically familiar to the mass audience everywhere. Antonioni, an unusual case, is himself part of the avant garde and, since *Blow-Up,* also a part of the industry establishment. Even without the American *Zabriskie Point,* Antonioni's influence was felt subtly in the creation of ambiguous tones in many films. Equally obvious is the effect the

French New Wave had on the industry at large without really exerting major economic pressure on American studios. Naturally, American producers and directors themselves attend movies and pick up ideas and techniques that they would like to try out within their industry. Our country has always prided itself on a technical competence that has proved adaptable to changing conditions, and it is not difficult for studio men to emulate the practices of other, foreign productions.

The French New Wave directors were first noticed in the late 1950's. Since several of them wrote film criticism, they managed to popularize their own work by analyzing their friends' films. That they ever formed a stylistic school is hard to prove, but their impact was felt as a group challenging the traditional well-made films, the glossy but sometimes superficial products of the French industry or the popular American films widely available in France. The movement included filmmakers as diverse as François Truffaut, Jean-Luc Godard, Alain Resnais, Agnès Varda, and Claude Chabrol, plus a few who were felt to have some spiritual affinity (that is, men like Jean Renoir and Robert Bresson who had stature and were not New Wave, but whose work was appreciated by the New Wave critics).

The early films of Truffaut (*e.g., The 400 Blows, Shoot the Piano Player, Jules and Jim*) and Godard (*e.g., Breathless, My Life to Live*) seem almost casual in construction. The action does not build toward an elaborate climax but sometimes starts immediately, before we know the characters, before they have been carefully established for us in terms of place, time, and social context. Even when finally introduced to them, we do not fully understand the motivation for their decisions. Sometimes we are made to believe that the characters themselves lack insight into the reality of their lives, so that they could not articulate the reasons for their responses to life. The world depicted by the New Wave filmmakers, Godard in particular, is intelligible and true insomuch as the story is externally plausible and without regard to the characters' personal interpretation of events.

In *Breathless* (1959), Godard's main character, Michel, steals a car at the beginning of the film and, pursued by a policeman, kills the man almost casually. We do not get the feeling that the killing was done in desperation nor that it was the act of a psychopath. In fact, we do not see Michel's mind at work or grasp the degree to which he is aware of the moral ramifications of his act. He simply does it and goes on to other business. His girlfriend Patricia undoubtedly loves him (fig. 46), but at the end of the film she betrays Michel to the police, who gun him down in the street. We do not know why Patricia betrays Michel, though of course critics can speculate about it. Her decision opposes the normal response that we expect of similar narrative situations in other films and books. Her

**46** *Breathless*

thinking seems impulsive and, granted that in real life people will do impulsive and sometimes destructive things, we are still surprised to see this event on the screen. Nevertheless, we believe in it; it could happen, for life contains unexpected incidents of violence. It is convincing, too, in the sense that from what we have seen of the two main characters throughout, they might be psychologically prepared for an impulsive murder or an impulsive betrayal.

Very likely, Godard wants us to define the characters by what we have seen them do, not by what they might think they are. Michel would like to pattern his character after his American movie idol, Humphrey Bogart, which might tell us something about Michel. Yet what is important about him is that he really emerges as the total of what he does, not what he feels. It may not be a particularly brilliant reading of Albert Camus's existentialism, but *Breathless* succeeds in creating a detachment toward, and still an

interest in, the world of the two main characters. The documentary sense that occurs often in New Wave films is here not alienating but clinical: we watch and observe characters who may be themselves observing their own activities. In any case, we are not brought into direct contact with the characters' points of view. We see them interact, but we do not feel the presence of a director establishing a pattern of human conduct for our elucidation of the inner meaning of these characters. Godard does not leave us in the dark, but he does leave us on our own.

The clinical approach to cinema also typifies a movement that gained popularity about the same time that the New Wave got under way. This was the documentary style of Cinéma Vérité, which when employed by narrative filmmakers also causes us to respond to characters based on the way they appear from the outside. As the name implies, Cinéma Vérité is not designed as a fictional technique, but has evidently influenced the non-documentary film. It emphasizes casualness and spontaneity within a real setting, while de-emphasizing everything that seems elaborately planned. It has come to mean the attempt to portray reality without stressing the presence of an interpretive camera. This seems theoretically faulty, as it suggests an artlessness not conducive to great filmmaking, and in practice it has led only to a heightened sense of realism, of unposed and casual filming.

Although realism has long dominated film style, more and more films of merit break away from the pattern of complete fidelity to a physically real world. Fellini's 8½ and *Juliet of the Spirits* are largely attempts to portray inner states of mind, but like so many other psychological studies, these films are rather firmly rooted in a physical reality that serves as a touchstone for the nonrealistic sequences. Still, the frequent intrusion of overtly nonrealistic sequences in many contemporary films that are otherwise entirely constructed in plausibly realistic environments (including Kubrick's *2001: A Space Odyssey,* a substantially conventional film in regard to its narrative form based on the logical development of its premises) indicates more reliance today on the willingness and ability of an audience to adjust its traditional narrative expectations. The possibility of mixing styles is an aspect of modern cinematic art that is just beginning to be explored.

## Procedures of Modernism

This chapter has not attempted to deal with specific movements in the contemporary cinema in a categorical way, and no pretense is made here of surveying all the interesting procedures being tried out in our experimental age. A few of those developments which have so far proved most influential have been cited: the new intellectualism as represented by Bergman, which

significantly enlarged the "minority audience" so that the commercial possibilities of high art and intelligence were finally demonstrated (every age, however, will have to demonstrate this again); the externalized portrayal of modern man, as in the New Wave films, and the subsequent deliberate breakdown in the conventional structure of a film story; and the re-establishment of naturalism, as in Cinéma Vérité, where the character is firmly presented in his milieu, with no attempt to gloss over the unpleasing aspects of the character, situation, or environment.

Techniques, too, have developed, and the fashionable ones relate to the manner in which transitions can be made not only from sequence to sequence but within the sequence. Such techniques were pioneered by Griffith, but they strike us as new when they appear as "jump cutting" (the omitting of a portion of real time in a situation where one would expect more or less continuous visualized action). Godard in his early films, particularly *Breathless,* deliberately ignored some of the traditional links in the action. On the other hand, some modern films enjoy a leisurely pace, and in Resnais's *Last Year at Marienbad* it is difficult to evaluate whether any length of time has elapsed between scenes. In any case, many films demand that the public accept difficult transitions, whether they are dislocations of place and plot (chronologically progressive) or flashbacks, which are dislocations of time (chronologically regressive). Audiences are not confused by a few seconds' intercutting of an entirely unrelated image within a sequence. Even an Academy Award winner, the sure mark of popular favor, John Schlessinger's *Midnight Cowboy,* contained several quick flashbacks that were clearly related to the main character's recollections of some bizarre sexual episodes that occurred in his past, but were nevertheless insufficient data for an audience to attain a coherent understanding of what actually happened or what had been done to the hero's psyche or how this had affected his decision to become what he is. Yet this portion of the film, though incomprehensible visually, did not arouse adverse comment; it was typical of many confusions relevant to cutting in the modern film, and very few viewers are gauche enough to admit to interpretive difficulties in regard to such techniques.

Patterns can be discerned in the modern film, but few rules could be inferred from the different kinds of practices we find in such key filmmakers as Fellini, Buñuel, and Truffaut. What then is modernism in the cinema? A satisfactory definition would seem improbable were we to attempt to include all notions of experimentation. We could avoid the problem by noting that the modern spirit equals the sum total of all the interesting modern techniques. Or we could try to define modernism as a collection of attitudes about the contemporary film. In this latter sense, we would have to say that modernism entails a loosening of narrative patterns that have been employed since Griffith. For one thing, the exposition of character is cut down. Exposition, a stage term, is the verbal method of bringing before the audience

information about the previous conditions of character and plot that have led up to the present situation, and it usually occurs at the beginning of the work; its visual equivalent used to occupy a good portion of the film. Less of it is seen today in a film like Fellini's *8½* than in, say, Fellini's earlier works such as *La Strada* or *I Vitelloni* or *The White Sheik*. The action of a modern film begins virtually when the film begins.

Secondly, with exposition cut back, the kind of plot frequently tends to be less intricate. The filmmaker's attitude is that a minimal amount of plot action will serve to create a situation where much visual movement will be in evidence. Movement, or activity, in the modern film replaces some of the conventional plotting. This sometimes leads to the kind of film narrative where incident is the chief structuring device of the filmmaker. Incident, as distinguished from plot, is not a unifying structure by itself. Plot establishes a cause-and-effect relationship between its incidents; it predicates a logical concept. In comparison, a film without a unifying plot may contain a series of incidents that are similar or that are related by their featuring the adventures of a particular character. The attempt in modern films to throw the burden of a unifying structure onto a series of incidents creates a number of problems that will be considered in Chapter 18.

Thus, modernism as witnessed in the works of the most discussed filmmakers can be considered an attempt to approach form from new directions. The older, logical progression from one stage to another in the development of a story no longer signifies very much to most of the newer filmmakers. Instead, a character is depicted confronting a series of interesting situations, as in *Breathless,* or an ambiguous situation is presented in which the narrative progression in time is not particularly important, as in *Last Year at Marienbad*. In Antonioni's films, a segment of contemporary life is examined, with the development of character eventually becoming the equivalent of a plot. Modernism, essentially, endorses an attitude toward cinematic storytelling that is responsive to the modern vision of life: the lack of structure in life suggests unstructured films that trace the modern spirit as manifest in the lives of some interesting modern characters. Images of drifting and disorientation mirror the world we live in; therefore we can expect the temper of the times to influence the cinematic shape of stories that seek to reproduce contemporary reality on the screen.

## Voyeurism

By the end of the 1960's, it had become clear to the general public that the film had developed strongly voyeuristic tendencies, and to many this seemed a deplorable fact. A regrettable fact certainly, but still the development was a logical outcome of an original tendency of film: to show a mass audience

what they had not seen in a way that made the object or incident vivid enough to become part of the mass experience. Historical precedents are never excuses for undesirable present conditions, but they do teach us something about the current situation.

In America at the turn of the century, the large audience was composed mainly of urban workers, many of them immigrants who could not speak English well (no disadvantage in the silent film days). The early films appealed to many because they contained sights of things that were undoubtedly real, but just beyond the immediate experience of a great segment of the audience. In later days, particular attention would be paid to lavish interiors in numerous films about wealthy and glamorous characters. They manufactured romantic attitudes that were not completely detached from reality—just different enough from ordinary experience so that the audience could live vicariously in the darkened movie theaters, which were deliberately designed American baroque palaces of rich drapery and deep-piled carpets, huge mirrors, and grotesque statuary.

Developing a mass demand for a product obliges the manufacturer to fulfill the customers' expectations, and yet such expectations are difficult to satisfy because of the fluctuations of popular taste. What the movie audience always seemed to want was something new, but not so new as to hinder its being absorbed into the mainstream of contemporary culture. The fantastic costs of motion pictures and the repeated failures to prejudge public taste correctly tend to make the movie industry conservative. Thus, we readily understand why over the decades the industry has returned again and again to sexual themes, an eternal human interest, and financially a safe subject. The only controversy occurs in regard to explicitness, and nowadays, as in the past, the producers and distributors claim that they are only responding to the preferences of the majority of the public in dealing with sexual subjects in an explicit way. The problem in this country is complicated by current considerations of society as well as by strong competition from European films, which have a long tradition of graphic sex. Indeed, certain films seem to have box office success based simply (as far as anyone can see) on sexual activity; yet other films just as explicit are not successful. In any case, no one denies that commercial films today depict sexual episodes more explicitly than they ever did before. However, it cannot be said that the subject is depicted more frequently now than in the past, though before the 1960's, when censorship forbade much of the physical display common in the 1970's, there obviously was less time spent elaborating on the subject. When the lights went out in a 1940's film, they went on again only in the next sequence.

In a study of film as a contemporary art, we must deal with the subject of sex because it often contributes significantly to the delineation of the film idea, whether it is essential to the film's basic concept or imposed upon it. Sex as an inherent aspect of a film's design is not a new approach. From

the silent days to the present, most studios sought "sex symbols," actors and primarily actresses who conveyed a physical presence or, really, by suggestive photography were made to seem extraordinarily attractive. The epitome of the art, say, Joseph von Sternberg directing Marlene Dietrich, was seldom achieved but often attempted.

In the simplistic terms of publicity releases, there are two kinds of film that exhibit sexual activity, the exploitation film and the "serious commentary on life" film. The distinction hinges on the filmmaker's apparent concern either to titillate—to take advantage of the public's desire to see the erotic on film—or to communicate the truth of human experience. As of now, the American intelligentsia has pretty much accepted the distinction —certainly, the reviewers use it as a criterion for evaluation: exploitation films are bad, serious sex films are either good or at least honest. In practice, however, the distinction is truly blurred. Exploitation filmmakers like Russ Meyer are often as honest as possible in their avowed intentions to glorify standards of conduct that the general public would call at least questionable. That their typical level of ineptitude prevents any true glorification is irrelevant to their "honesty." The artistic incompetence of such films never posed a threat to the commercial industry, but their small success did awaken the industry to the possibility of a large commercial market for the erotic film. To the industry, good taste, like fine art, implies a luxury that is permitted only when the major requisite for filming is in evidence: commercial prospects. The industry's current assessment of erotic cinema resembles its assessment of the wide screen: neither overt sexual activity nor Cinerama can be projected on television, and the lack of each on television will presumably draw people to the movie theater.

The film experience revelant to exploitation films—frequently with overtly descriptive titles such as *The Seducers* and *Without a Stitch*—need not be analyzed, as these films really lie outside the narrative situation, though they have some sort of plot. Of undeniable concern is the so-called serious endeavor to depict modern life with explicit scenes of sexual encounters. Nudity justified by the context had not been the original issue, of course: the nude shots in *Intolerance* did not provoke calls for censorship. The later long-standing ban on nudity in Hollywood films that was removed in the 1960's undoubtedly had been at times an artistic hindrance. Censorship in Hollywood developed in the thirties as a reaction to the verbal suggestiveness of performers such as Mae West. The result of censorship was often a ludicrous imposition on a work of art of a rule that really was meant to restrain minor directors from offending the abstraction we call public taste. Indeed, sexual preoccupation flourished during the censorship period; for instance, everyone applauded the Busby Berkeley dance numbers of the 1930's, which involved prolonged and witty erotic fantasies and sexual symbols. In fact, the innocuous situation comedies of the 1950's frequently

relied on insidious sexual innuendos, but were promoted as family entertainments. Meanwhile, filmmakers developed an iconography of sex symbols that when overused seriously flawed their films: for example, a man
and woman embrace and the director cuts to an image of ocean waves
breaking. A cliché of this sort was in itself good reason to move away from
the censorship system to the rating system, which, though misused and unreliable, is theoretically an alternative to censorship because it might be a
guide to parents. The protection of children was the valid argument of
twentieth-century censors.

For the student of film, however, the problem of censorship is social,
not esthetic. What indeed qualifies as an esthetic problem for the modern
film is the conflict built into any narrative that employs explicit sexual scenes
that are not warranted by the film idea but are required because of commercial determinations. Certainly, some extremely complicated and highly
serious films can include explicit scenes in the film idea itself. Ingmar
Bergman's *The Silence* was one of the first serious films to do so. The
sexual incidents, the sense of death, the mobilizing of the military in the
background, the unintelligible language of the foreign country where the
women are temporarily stranded, all combine in *The Silence* into an image
of a desolate world of isolated individuals. Although the film was a landmark in that it was the first time a major artist had shown explicit sexual
sequences in some detail, the difficulties of the themes and the slowness of
the pace precluded its commercial success in this country despite a good
deal of publicity about its alleged eroticism. In any case, it was clear that
the film was conceived in terms that required explicitness or the sacrifice
of artistic integrity.

How many films since then, with equally high artistic ambitions, truly
relate their explicitness to the film concept? What we really see in the
modern film of serious intent is, almost always, a bedroom sequence
worked into a plot in order to assure that the film will be able to compete
commercially with films that include such sequences for purely sensational
reasons. Such a sequence, when it concerns main characters, cannot be detached from the narrative, regardless of the degree of its relevance. If, for
instance, a harassed filmmaker wanted to include such a sequence only for
the commercial value his producer thought it would have, he could not
dispose of it in the form of a disgression. In other words, he cannot decide
to spend five minutes or even three minutes with his major characters
running about undressed and hope that as a deliberate and obvious di-
gression it will not affect the rest of the film.

For the sake of comparison, consider the deliberate digressions that
were implanted in the Marx Brothers films. Today, those obligatory scenes
in which Harpo and Chico play their instruments are annoying flaws; the
films stop dead for a few minutes while comedy and the plot are suspended

for solo performances. We are bored, but the film does not irretrievably flounder, for the sequence, once past, is forgotten as the Brothers roll merrily through the rest of the film. If the sexual encounter could be handled the same way, it would create only a small artistic problem. However, the casual treatment of sex is improbable, since sex implies either the development of a passion or a calculated use of another person—and both alternatives incorporate meaningful human motivations. For every bedroom encounter, sequences leading up to and away from it must be made part of the film. In fact, a filmmaker cannot make a believable bedroom sequence irrelevant because it shapes our awareness of the characters; it sometimes tells us more about them than is intended for the artistic integrity of the work. As a clichéd attribute of modernism, the persistent use of sexuality in film after film results in an emphasis on characterization beyond every other aspect of the film—*and* an insistence that every film do the same thing (*i.e.,* stress personality). Constructing a story so that it will contain a bedroom sequence narrowly restricts the film idea.

Because of the graphic nature of the medium, its surface level will always dominate our attention. A narrative that stresses physical love is adversely limited with respect to other possible themes unrelated to its bedroom scenes. And in films most conducive to sexual encounters—films that are really about the love relationship between two people—even after we have been shown physical passion we have yet to be convinced that the story is about human love. A sexual encounter becomes perfectly clear literal imagery, but it says nothing in particular about the love between a man and a woman, and romantic idealism notwithstanding, a filmmaker had better not count on the audience's accepting so facile a premise as the equation of love and sex and applying it to his film. To create a sense of real love, the director has to establish the relationship in other terms too. Yet the time and effort expended in building toward a physical encounter and then unwinding from it directs our responses mainly to the surface relationship.

The movie industry's assessment of the contemporary interest in voyeurism results in a sense of obligation on the part of many producers to use sexual imagery for its pictorial interest regardless of its narrative relevance. That it may also have narrative relevance usually only partially justifies its use, for the considerable attention given to creating the surface glamour of sexual imagery often results in the subordination of the other, more important elements of the narrative and thus in the separation of the sex sequence from the overall film idea. In this respect the often sneered-at sex films aimed at New York's Forty-Second Street audience at least retain the integrity of the basic concept, though it may be a perverted concept. Artistic integrity and explicit sexual imagery have only very rarely gone

together, and that they do so in Bergman's *The Silence* or Fellini's *Juliet of the Spirits* or Pasolini's *Teorema* means nothing as an excuse for the ordinary filmmaker's turning to obligatory scenes to satisfy the voyeurism of the public or the producers' anticipation of the public demand for this kind of filming.

# Part Three
# Theory and Esthetics

In America, where cinematic theory has never flourished, any attempt to collect and structure observations toward a theory of the narrative film must be tentative and perhaps apologetic. In this country, every man is a film reviewer, and if he disseminates his reviews in print rather than just telling his friends about what he has seen, he is also a critic; and if the critic has seen *The Birth of a Nation* and *Potemkin,* his credentials as a scholar are established; further, if he dislikes those two films, he also qualifies as a theorist. Beyond this level of approach, relatively few have ventured. A main reason is that the study of film presents a difficulty in evaluating source material. Hardly anyone has seen all the important films, and even if he has, ninety percent of them cannot be talked about sensibly because they do not evoke particularized visual memories. We remember the subjects they dealt with, but we cannot trust our memories in speaking of how these films achieved their success. Unlike all classic books and reference texts, even great films cannot be obtained in stores or libraries; thus, they cannot be checked out easily.

Nevertheless, the film has unobtrusively become more than a vehicle of entertainment, more than an accepted art form—though such are no mean accomplishments; it has established itself as a body of knowledge, and even slipped past the fringes of the academic establishment. Yet without theoretical foundations, practical film criticism remains primarily a highly subjective and contentious exercise in doling out praise and blame.

In the chapters that follow, the narrative film will be considered from the standpoint of both form and content, separated for the convenience of analysis, as we do with drama, literature, and other narrative arts, and to a lesser extent with traditional types of painting and certain other visual arts (and one might add, too, program music). The aim here is to distinguish those characteristics of film which we can ascertain are peculiar to the medium. Always we will want to know how meaning is communicated cinematically.

**249**

# 13

# Specifications
# Through
# Camera Shots

## The Shot as an Informational Unit

The basis of a theory of narrative film form lies with the shot. By common consensus, the shot is accepted as the prime element of film, and yet seldom have the special modes of the shot been analyzed apart from its context. In other words, we need to explore the ways in which the individual shot functions as a basic unit of meaning. When we talk of a unit of meaning, we assume that the unit conveys something intelligible to us by itself; but this does not assume that ideas are conveyed completely by the unit. In studying the nature of a shot's functional possibilities, we recognize the limitation inherent in a *unit* of meaning; a shot usually functions only as a short part of a sequence, and that sequence itself as part of the whole film.

Essentially, the shot communicates a piece of information: it specifies facts or attitudes about something. By itself it does not amass its specifications in order to overwhelm us with a good deal of information about a person, place, or object. Of course, in the primitive film there were shots of considerable duration—at least in proportion to the total length of the film; frequently, the entire sequence was comprised of a single shot, and the early filmmakers indeed used the shot as a means of communicating many pieces of information. The artistic failure of the primitive film in

large part stems from an attempt to make the shot function for more than a limited number of specific pieces of information.

The ordinary shot must specify something, even if only a blank wall occupies the frame. Consecutive shots of blank walls would create a confusing abstraction, and in most films virtually every shot gives us particular visual information. (We are not talking now about the quality of the information, which may be trivial or repetitious.) Sometimes the material presented, either because it is unusual or because it is filmed from an unusual vantage point, is deliberately abstract, and thereby nonspecific. For instance, in *The Woman in the Dunes,* a rather remarkably photographed visual experience, the Japanese director Hiroshi Teshigaharu emphasized sand from various perspectives. At times it was unclear just what a particular shot was showing (sometimes even when it included a part of the human body). The context would clarify these individually abstract shots, yet evaluated by themselves certain shots communicated a visual ambiguity. This is extremely unusual. The much more common experience permits a viewer to understand the visual content of every shot as it appears before him. One reason is that the same places and people are shown over and over. On the other hand, the same shots taken out of their context might contain a greater degree of abstraction than we notice at the time we see them in context. Many close-ups are in fact little more than abstract geometric shapes; even an ordinary ashtray might be unclear in a close-up that isolated it from its environment. Nevertheless, most filmmakers and spectators assume a clear visual understanding of each shot as it occurs within the narrative film. In those cases where the content of a shot is not clear, the effect disturbs us and must be justified in light of the filmmaker's major intention within the sequence.

Thus, a film with three to eight hundred shots has bombarded our eyes with a quantity of images that could not easily be absorbed in a literary work, the verbal image creating an immediate demand on our conscious intellect. In comparison, we have no trouble absorbing the images of shots, for they are directly meaningful to us. Perhaps they would be less so if the narrative film were not so firmly entrenched in the realistic tradition, where the images reflect pretty much the world already familiar to us.

## Functional Specifications: Limitations and Discontinuity

The first consideration in evaluating the functional quality of the shot concerns the nature of the information it specifies. The second (which will be considered later in this chapter) concerns the built-in point of view of the shot in regard to that specification. For the moment we will consider each shot as if it were neutral in its presentation of the subject. The shot,

as we have seen, naturally particularizes its subject matter, which is another way of saying that within the frame objects and areas are depicted with surface realism. What we see are surfaces similar to those we would see if our eyes were in the position of a recording camera. From this it follows that the function of a shot in terms of its content is to specify an area or an object, with or without moving figures. The longer shots define an environment, but with the camera set closer to the subject, the environment tends to be less clearly defined; at the same time, the objects in closer shots occupy an increasingly prominent place. The close-up of a face, for instance, may exclude everything else within a room. As such a shot, which is limited to a rather small area of reality, becomes completely specific (*e.g.,* by showing only the face of an actress), it may also create a sense of abstraction in regard to the total environment (the room within which we have previously seen the actress). We believe that behind the head of the actress the wall still exists, the same wall that we saw in earlier shots of this sequence. Yet in fact, no wall is visible in the particular shot—only the disembodied face.

The kind of information specified by the individual shot is also limited to the given particulars, regardless of what may be implied by the total context. The visual specifications mainly relate to shape. The camera tells us that various parts of an area are rectangular or spherical. Distance and size may or may not be specified. In a close shot, we can tell hardly anything about real size, and virtually nothing about distance, for our sense of proportion is hindered by the exclusion of identifiable objects for comparison. However, even with a close-up we can receive plausible information if the shot includes some previously identified object of known size or a part of the human body. For instance, if we see a ball bouncing in a close-up, its shape is immediately conveyed to us, but how can we tell its size? If a hand appears, we have an immediate point of comparison. But suppose the following shot reveals that the hand belongs to a midget. Then the information relative to size has been misleading—perhaps intentionally for comic effect—and we have been tricked into evaluating an apparent fact on the basis of unreliable information. The point is not merely academic, for films as a matter of course rely on our disoriented senses in several useful ways. For example, the destruction of property, particularly of buildings, can be portrayed through the use of scale models that deceive us in close-up by appearing life-sized.

Visual specifications are further limited by the two-dimensional plane. The illusion of depth, however, works quite well. Even in the primitive film, the sense of three-dimensionality always dominated those shots in real environments, though not those in artificial settings. We cannot always estimate the distance of a character from the wall behind him, but careful cinematography can always avoid a disadvantageous camera setup in those few situations in which it is important for us to judge such distances. Never-

theless, it must be conceded that the camera specifies dimension less effectively than the human eye.

What the single shot does accomplish more effectively than the eye compensates for any of its limitations in specifying information. That is, the shot fragments the reality of nature to a greater extent than the eye can do. This creates an image of a segment of reality disconnected from the total reality that we assume appeared before the camera. We too look at the world selectively, focusing on different parts as our eyes scan our visual field. To say that the camera does the same thing is really to speak in terms of analogy, not of equivalents. For what the camera records will be broken down into shots, and the shots assembled in the final film are not merely selective—as are perceptions made by our eyes—but also discontinuous.

Our real-life perceptions are never discontinuous. The implications of this distinction are important. Because we see continuously (unless we deliberately distort our vision, or, say, close our eyes, turn our head, open our eyes, close them, turn our head, etc.), we rarely totally exclude the rest of the visual area when we concentrate on one object. The exceptions are notable, but they don't change the rule. By presenting an image disconnected from the entire visual field, the shot reveals itself to us as a highly selective unit. This selectivity usually manifests itself in an environment, for example the movie house, that has built-in factors that further concentrate our attention (*i.e.,* on the screen). Thus, we tend to see certain things on screens in movie theaters more intently than we do in real life, where neither the psychological condition for viewing, nor the physiological working of the eye, allows us to see as we do in film.

The discontinuous image is more emphatic than the same image seen within the continuous pattern of the eye's perception because each frame of the shot excludes all sorts of irrelevant details. Even a long shot of an interior is more limited than the view of a person actually sitting in the room. The most casually conceived shot naturally excludes something, and even in the hands of a careless amateur photographer, it almost always succeeds in including the focal point of interest somewhere within the frame; naturally, whatever is omitted is certain to be (visually, if not thematically) extraneous to the main point the cameraman has in mind. In fact, the usual artistic sense that characterizes great filmmakers like Renoir or Dreyer or Eisenstein requires excluding the irrelevant from the frame. The more indifference a director exhibits toward visual design, the less selective his image is likely to be.

The degree of selectivity is determined not only by the distance of the camera from the object (the size of the visual field) but also by the care the filmmaker takes to compose the elements so as to relate everything within the frame to the main visual point of the shot. With the proper attention to the elements within the frame, even the long shot may result

in a highly selective image. What more memorable detail do we have in the contemporary film than Bergman's long shot of the religious flagellants whipping themselves along the road in *The Seventh Seal?* The ordinary functions of long and close shots are certainly distinct, but it is important to note that both kinds of shot are by nature inherently selective because they present discontinuous images of the visual field, and are sometimes made deliberately more selective when all the details within the frame are controlled by a filmmaker for artistic effect.

## Camera Distance and Shot Specifications

Since long and close shots product distinct visual effects, the usual functions of these shots need to be noted. (We need not categorize exactly the function of the medium shot, for depending on the director's style, it can be among his closer shots or his longer ones.) The longer shot (*i.e.,* those shots commonly denoted by the terms "distance," "long," "establishing," "full," etc.) without human figures in the frame usually serves to specify an environment. Outdoors the use of such shots is commonplace: the grandeur of a canyon, the magnificence of a country estate, or the wildness of a jungle can be depicted as effectively as the impersonality of an industrial complex or the oppressiveness of a slum neighborhood. Indoors, longer shots often function to specify the economic status and esthetic taste of the occupant of a particular room.

With human figures in the frame, the primary purpose of the long shot is to specify the relationship of people to environment or of people to people. In the Western, the long shot of the landscape remains primarily scenic until the cowboy appears within the frame; then the intention changes to one in which the shot emphasizes, for example, the loneliness of the man riding along the canyon. The long shot establishes proportions relevant to man, as well as distances, sizes, and shapes. Longer shots are naturally particularly useful for the depiction of physical action; pursuit, fighting, racing, and the like are commonly photographed largely in terms of long shots with, of course, closer shots intercut to specify fragments of the scene.

The longer the distance between camera and subject, the more clinical the observation tends to be; that is, the farther away we are, the less emotionally involved we become. This is an interesting phenomenon, long recognized instinctively by directors who will rarely use only longer shots to convey the total experience of an event that involves a sympathetic character. For example, prizefights are always filmed from a variety of camera setups in fiction films (as distinct from newsreels or professional prizefights recorded as sports events), keeping us from really seeing the fighters slugging it out; this not only aids in the staging of what is, after all, merely a faked fight, but more importantly, it allows the director to use

close shots to remind us of the sympathetic fighter's predicament as he sees fists flying toward him or as he receives blows straight on. But we must also see the fighters in several long shots, or else the fight can hardly be made convincing—the actors must appear to be hitting each other.

Surely, the long shot, considered by itself, has an objectifying effect. It specifies action objectively, first because spatial relationships are self-evident. Even if tension is built up within the sequence, we are forced to observe the content of an individual long shot in terms of what the visual distance demands of our eyes: that we notice the specific relationship of objects and people. The long shot may be giving us specific information about the action it conveys, which in itself might be quite subjectively exciting; its visual appeal, however, comes to us in the form of objective information directed to our senses, and our eyes can be intrigued only by what is happening. Secondly, because the image reveals itself as discontinuous in regard to the entire sequence, each shot successfully filters out certain considerations of the previous shot, certain pieces of information: the boxing ring is seen first from one angle, then from another, and in the second shot, the background is different, even though the foreground (within the square ring) remains virtually the same. We analyze the action of the two men punching each other as we absorb the information from each shot. Thirdly, although we do not analyze every part with equal attention, we are still obliged to consider the relevant details as if each shot were itself a short tableau informing our eyes of some bit of specific information needed to comprehend the whole (the sequence). The long shot, because it contains more details to start with than the close shot, makes a greater demand on our senses, a factor in detaching us emotionally from the spectacle we are witnessing.

Although the long shot is not often selected with any particular artistic design, especially today when the whole tendency of shooting urges a closing in upon the actors (presumably a result of some dubious notions equating closeness with intimacy and involvement), still, the long shot can function subtly in the hands of a major director. In *Strangers on a Train,* Hitchcock uses a long shot with as much psychological effectiveness as the most carefully chosen close-up. The shot fastens on a crowd watching two tennis players practicing. All heads move in rhythm with the game, but amid the uniform turning of heads from one direction to the other, one man's head remains absolutely still, staring straight forward. We easily discern him at a considerable distance, although the camera moves in somewhat for greater emphasis. This shot rivets attention on the insane killer Bruno, thus doing at a distance what normally only a close shot can do. In addition, it is far more suggestive than a close-up could be because it does not exclude the environment. In fact, what Hitchcock aims for requires the presence of the numerous moving heads of the spectators. In the first place, the shot represents the point of view of one of the tennis

players, whom Bruno has been attempting to force into committing a murder, and serves to alarm him about Bruno's presence; just prior to this shot, the player looked at the crowd, and this shot clearly reveals what he has seen. Thus, the man's annoyance and fear are immediately impressed upon us. Secondly, the shot implies everything about Bruno's disturbance. His surface calm, seen in his failure to move his head as is natural while watching tennis, indicates not only rapt concentration on his singleminded goal but that he is psychologically unlike everyone else. The shot tells us both things at once, emphatically and with so much remarkable visual wit that it probably serves a third purpose: it provides a sort of comic relief at a moment of extreme tension.

The closer shot (including medium close, close, and close-up shots) generally involves us emotionally with characters to a greater extent than the longer shot. This is because the closer shot isolates an object or person from most of the environment; the information such a shot specifies differs in kind from that specified by a longer shot. The closer shot achieves a kind of underlining of a small portion of the environment, singled out not only to emphasize something about it but also deliberately to de-emphasize the surrounding context. The isolation of a part from the whole also requires our eyes to analyze the material specified, but the absence of obtrusive or irrelevant factors makes the visual inspection simple. Our objective interpretation of the literal image before us may be immediate and may therefore allow us more leeway for emotional response. And the usual lack of motion within the closer shots—not that they are without motion entirely, but simply that the motion has itself been fragmented from the larger motion —makes it still easier to absorb the specifications of the closer shot than the longer.

The isolation that occurs from the close shot's exclusion of most of the surrounding context must not be confused with alienation. A close shot of a man's face may stress his harmony with his environment. Whatever the purpose of a particular close shot, it functions to exclude spatial relationships for the purpose of detailing specifications about a particular thing or person. Medium shots, possibly, may specify both spatial relationships and details. However, it is difficult to emphasize both continually without so dividing the spectator's visual concentration that the overriding purpose of the sequence becomes less important than its parts.

## Point of View Within the Shot

The second function of the individual shot is to convey a point of view or attitude toward the subject within the frame. This attitude is most often neutral, which might be considered a "nonattitude," though actually the neutrality of a particular shot may be part of a much more meaningful

attitude suggested by the larger context. In any case, neutrality reveals a filmmaker's sense that the particular shot ought to convey its information without explicit directorial commentary. When we notice an attitude implicit within a shot, we are probably responding to a filmmaker's deliberate attempt to present a point of view other than the obviously objective view we ourselves would most likely take were we at the scene of the filming. Were we there we would undoubtedly take a variety of views corresponding to the distances of shots (*i.e.,* long, medium, and close). We would not, however, be likely to stand on our heads to view a particular event; but between such an extreme viewing position as taken by a cinematographer and complete neutrality, there is a range of camera setups and techniques that might suggest to an audience some implied commentary on the part of the filmmaker.

In other words, we can denote as neutral those shots in which the camera records the material that most people could be expected to view if they were witnesses to the matter being filmed. Surely all filmmakers instinctively respect this viewpoint and normally film everything from an unobtrusive camera angle. Except for special effects, the major directors are not interested in emphasizing camera method over style, content, theme, and characterization. However, almost all films contain shots that have built-in directorial attitudes toward material within the frame, and we are alerted to this by unusual angles and sometimes by unusual movements. In a scene between a boy and a man, particularly one involving tension, the filmmaker frequently resorts to high or low angles for the presentation of attitude. For example, a low-angle shot that includes both the man and the boy within the same frame informs the viewer that the man is intimidating the boy.

This differs somewhat from saying that the boy feels intimidated because the man towers above him. When both man and boy are shown together in a low-angle shot, regardless of other materials (such as dialogue), the filmmaker forces us to perceive the event from a nonneutral point of view. The filmmaker's subjective shooting overtly implies that intimidation. The intimidation could have been conveyed by having the actors mime the idea along with dialogue; for instance, the boy could be cowering and the man waving his arms. Such drastic overemphasis, however, is not necessary for film acting, especially if the gestures can easily be avoided either by dialogue or by implying an attitude by means of the camera arrangement. Ordinarily, the eye-level shot of a man and a boy in conversation is simply a neutral specification of the fact of their conversing. Even if the dialogue and the gestures specify conflict, the information can still be considered neutral in its presentation as long as the camera remains at eye level (fig. 47). Once the filmmaker insists, however, on removing the view from the ordinary perspective, he signals to us that he intends to emphasize an attitude toward the information within the shot.

**47** A neutral presentation of conflict (David Lean's *Great Expectations*)

The camera angle is not the only factor that can build a point of view into a shot. For instance, the placement of figures in unusual spatial relationships might determine an emphasis. A shot of the same boy and man conversing filmed in such a way as to show the boy dominating the frame by partially blocking the larger man might turn the attitude into one emphasizing the boy's defiance, even regardless of the dialogue. In this case, as in the previous example, the attitude is not necessarily based on the information specified by either the performers' appearance in the frame or

their dialogue. Here again attitude is primarily determined by the film-maker, for it results from his manipulation of the camera angle or the placement of his actors. As such, we might say that it is imposed upon the material of the shot, upon the information that could have been conveyed to us objectively.

Thus, the neutrality of the eye-level, normal-distance shot can easily be transformed into subjectivity. In a larger, theoretical sense, every shot is subjective to the extent that it is selective. Nevertheless, in practice film-makers obtain a high degree of apparently objective analysis of situations by expressing neutrality through the camera setup. In fact, the most personal films, those that we associate most frequently with the individual style of a significant filmmaker, are usually primarily neutral in the presentation of individual shots. This is not a paradox. The filmmaker deeply concerned with expressing his personal vision tries to do so mainly through the selection (and editing, of course) of the material that goes into his shots; he generally does not emphasize a peculiar presentation of these materials. The constant insistence of the director on interpreting each shot for us by forcing our attention to the attitude he wants to convey in each shot is the mark of a propagandist, who is more concerned with the clarity of his message than with the refinement of his art.

Another kind of subjectivity concerns the attitude of a particular character, not the filmmaker. To use the example referred to before, we assume that in the conversation between the boy and the man the camera may take alternating shots from high and low angles, depending on whether it photographs the man or the boy. If only the boy is in the frame, the camera could photograph from a high angle, the immediate suggestion being that we are viewing the boy from the man's point of view. Similarly, if only the man appears in the frame, a low-angle shot will clearly indicate the boy's point of view. This suggests a very easy formula, something that we seem to see in every film: for example, the person sitting looks up at the person standing. The technique requires no skill, no particular attitude on the filmmaker's part. Often enough it is perfectly correct filming, though perhaps not particularly imaginative, and we will find it in the work of the major artists when they are presenting a sequence in which conversation dominates any conceivable pictorial interest. The use of this particular example—the filming of conversation—is not meant to imply that suggesting the point of view of a character is always an uninspired technique. When the development of a character's point of view is basic to the film idea, as in *The Last Laugh* (see Chapter 9), such subjective filming is clearly desirable. But while it is certainly true that almost all films avoid the purely objective analysis of character—for that would force us to view life in a somewhat limited way—it is equally true that almost all films (*The Cabinet of Dr. Caligari* excepted) avoid concentrating our attention on the world as seen solely through a character's subjective view.

# The Shot in Relation to the Sequence

In dealing with the specifications and attitudes relevant to individual shots, we have, of course, been limited to the informational or surface level; we must also inspect the other dimension of the shot, its symbolic reference to a wider sphere of meaning. Nevertheless, the constant critical endeavor to treat this level without a proper recognition of the way in which the shot communicates has created its own problems in analysis. Primarily, the problem lies in a failure to discriminate between the expressive mode of the film and that of the older narrative art media, fiction and drama.

Considered in its functional sense, the shot serves to present a piece of information, not an idea. Ideas are sometimes contained within single shots, but only when the sequence has established the possibility of doing so. The impression received by a viewer is always affected by the context of the shot—the sequence, and the shot itself remains very much an informational unit of sight and sound. Since Griffith, attempts to make the shot function as the prime vehicle of ideas (in the style of Porter) have been extremely rare and even more rarely effective. Critical impressions to the contrary, not even Orson Welles has tried it very much. In a sound film, a single-shot sequence used to present an idea entirely through dialogue means, of course, the temporary abandonment of the cinematic mode. A couple of overtly ineffective attempts occurred in Mike Nichols' *Catch-22,* revealing in their talkiness the intransigence of the literary source. Saying that shots communicate information rather than ideas does not, however, denigrate the importance of the shot. The kind of information and the quality of its presentation within the shot remain essential, even when we agree that the total effect of the sequence ultimately justifies the validity of each shot.

The exception to the generalization about this functional limitation of the shot is notable: the great performers who were also filmmakers tended to rely more than other filmmakers on the shot as a block of meaning within the whole film. In other words, sometimes a Keaton or a Chaplin, for example, would conceive of important segments of his films in terms of a comic idea actually contained within a single shot. This use of the shot is really less common than a casual recollection of the two men's films might suggest. One remembers, for instance, a classic Chaplin piece of comedy in *The Pawnshop:* Charlie takes apart a clock in the process of examining it for its value and finally hands the separate parts back to the owner, for they are now worthless. The camera fastens on Charlie's various approaches to the dissection of the mechanism. In fact, this is not a one-shot sequence but a series of a few shots building up a comic idea, though the editing is hardly noticeable when we watch Chaplin's work. However, the very nature of comedy suggests a number of bits that can be portrayed within a shot, and some shots in the above sequence include rather fully conveyed ideas,

even without the shots of the reaction of the victimized clockowner. Although the communication of an idea within a shot is occasionally carried off superbly by the filmmaker-performer (for example, previously cited instances in Chaplin's *The Vagabond,* as well as Keaton's final resignation in *Cops*), generally speaking, even those filmmakers who use the shot from time to time for the portrayal of an idea do not *feel* the single shot as a sequence itself. In fact, Keaton and Chaplin are among those directors who most evidently construct their films with sequences in mind.

In summation, it can be said that a film idea, even a small one, needs some degree of development, usually more than can be cinematically portrayed within a single shot. The shot, then, is used to convey that information that will culminate in a conceptual presentation. The shot is the specification of the motivating idea, the detail of the picture, and the vehicle for the physical reality of the film.

## Shot Specifications in Buñuel's *Simon of the Desert*

All great filmmakers have this much in common: they do not film at random; obviously, they are careful in choosing what to include within each frame and what to exclude. Some filmmakers with a very high degree of pictorial sensitivity (*e.g.,* Kurosawa, Visconti, and Dreyer) actually compose their camera arrangements with the precision of a photographer or a painter, but more typical of even the greatest practitioners of cinematic art is an approach that stresses the human element in matters of composition more than configurations of things, of backgrounds and props. The shot is composed mainly according to the visual emphasis dictated by the characterization, theme, plot, or mood of the sequence. Since all filmmakers develop their ideas in sequences, the analysis of particular shots must always comprehend the relevant context of the sequence.

Luis Buñuel's *Simon of the Desert* (1965), a major film though it runs only slightly more than forty minutes, provides an excellent example of creating difficult but absorbingly interesting images within shots that are economical and yet allusive, moving effectively on the level of their specification and suggesting symbolic parallels by virtue of the filmmaker's attitudes conveyed through the camera. The pictorial style is essentially simple.* Most of the film takes place in a desert area where Simon stands on a platform atop a huge column for a period of years, a modern-day parallel of the fifth-century saint, Simeon Stylites. (Some critics seem to mistake Simon for Simeon Stylites and assume that the film shifts from the fifth century to the present day at the end. The screenplay also refers to

* All references are to the version of the film distributed by Audio Film Center. The screenplay published by Orion Press (New York, 1968) differs from the actual film in many minor ways that subtly change the entire meaning of the extant film.

**48** *Simon of the Desert*

him as Simeon Stylites. Assuming that the film was made after the screen-play was written, we can see why Buñuel significantly broadened the implications of his film by distinguishing between Simon and the fifth-century saint.) Since the conversations between Simon and his various visitors occur with Simon atop his pillar, the camera films frequently from a tilted position, many shots moving up or down. Also, since Buñuel needs to show Simon and his visitors in the same frame, a good number of shots are taken from a considerable distance. By the very nature of the spatial relationship of Simon to his visitors, the camera produces a sense of the hero's separation and superiority to those in his immediate environment. This desert environment enforces the visual emphasis on the human element, with only the column itself vying for attention in the landscape (fig. 48).

A film in which a man stands on top of a huge pillar in the desert might seem extraordinarily limited in its possibilities of movement, yet Buñuel's shots ideally locate the issues at hand, and the images of movement are charmingly carried off. Of course the basic movement is a spiritual one, a man's attempt to purify his soul from the various imperfections the flesh

is heir to (the devilish influences within are personified visually in the incarnate Devil, played by a beautiful actress, Sylvia Pinal). Atop his platform Simon appears severely limited in his movements—his single major physical action is the raising of one foot in a final, successful attempt to advance his spiritual state. However, in spite of his relative inactivity, he responds to movement on the part of others, much of which we see from his vantage point. The movement beneath his platform utterly fails to tempt him off the pillar. We see, for example, a happy novitiate from the monastery skipping up to the pillar to visit his idol, and the movements of a dwarf, grotesque and crude as the dwarf himself.

The most interesting movements are those of the beautiful woman who appears to tempt him. He recognizes her as Satan in spite of various disguises (the one disguise that temporarily fools him includes a beard and locks of hair that the woman puts on when she pretends to be Jesus). These visions of the Devil are theologically valid, though they may simply be dramatic projections of the psychological troubles that plague the mind of Simon. To other characters, Simon appears pure and saintly, but he claims unworthiness. To the modern audience this claim might seem insincere self-conceit, yet without question Simon means what he says. He practices asceticism for stated causes: he wants to develop charity and humility, and the truth is that Simon is deficient in both. We note his impatience at being interrupted while praying, his sternness toward the monk who looks at a woman, and his coldness toward his mother. Thus, the Devil, whether actual or merely intended as a visual manifestation of the inner trouble, represents Simon's struggle with his own spirit. The Devil's appearances and her movements around the column are fascinating modern re-creations of the temptations of Jesus. As a comparison, the New Testament setting in the wilderness (Matt. 4:1–11) itself symbolizes the struggle of man against the Adversary under the most basic conditions of barrenness and hardship. The Christian saints who went into the desert (including Simeon Stylites) must surely have had the New Testament narrative in mind: in the desert, the confrontation is direct and unavoidable. There, Jesus stands still and Satan comes to him. Sylvia Pinal is a highly suitable modern Satan, for the sexual temptation is the most blatant of modern inducements to set aside moral and psychological ideals (fig. 49).

The final sequence surprises and sometimes disturbs many viewers. An airplane flies over the desert, and Satan announces that the plane will take them away. A shot of the plane is followed by a shot of the empty platform. It almost seems as if Simon has been swallowed up by the force of evil. We feel that Simon, who is removed from his familiar environment to a New York discothèque, might not be able to withstand Satan, though the information we have received so far would indicate that he has won. Of course, the scene of the empty platform recalls a threatened temptation of Jesus by Satan. Typical of the film, the shot that surprises us by a fresh

**49** *Simon of the Desert*

visual image (a platform empty for the first time since the beginning) also alerts us to symbolic inferences.

The shots in *Simon of the Desert* are meant largely to specify a variety of predicaments stemming from the hero's attempt to purify his spirit, to exorcize his personal devil, which manifests itself as a lack of charity (*caritas,* that is, or selfless love) and a lack of humility. That he is only human in having such weaknesses, that in fact these flaws are not noticeably more apparent in him than in other men, is irrelevant. The point is that he sees himself as unworthy, for the superior spiritual man has a greater awareness of his shortcomings. As a result he sets himself up in the desert in an extraordinary situation, resulting from an almost unhuman attempt to purge himself. The shots demonstrate the nature of the predicament according to Buñuel's witty assessment of the inherent implausibility of any saint's motivations.

The point of view of the shots is basically neutral, though many spectators sharing a negative attitude toward the devotional life tend to see Simon from Satan's view. Simon is a hard man to budge, and we are almost made to feel it would be worth while for the Tempter (or Temptress) to shake him off the column. After all, she advocates motion, he stillness. At one point she appears on the platform trying to seduce him by lewdly placing her tongue on his face. His reaction to all her temptations is to turn away or say, "Get behind me, Satan." Since Satan in female form reacts with feminine outrage and frustration over the failure to attract Simon, we see shots of highly human feminine vexation contrasted with a male's indomitable virtue, and this by itself suffices to suggest an attitude to viewers, to make some think that we are supposed to sympathize with Satan. However, the content of each particular shot is recorded without any obtrusive commentary from the filmmaker. Buñuel indeed delineates the difficulty of man's fulfilling the obligations he feels are imposed upon him by his calling, which seem to require superhuman effort, unnatural dedication. The saint is paradoxically admirable for his strength and perseverance, yet held in suspicion for not being exactly like us and revealing all the flaws of the ordinary man. Ultimately, the unsuccessful allurements of the Devil are not pitiable but exposed as superficially enticing and inwardly ugly. (The Devil is not, after all, a pretty girl but an old witch, and her interest in Simon is not personal; she is challenged by the mere existence of every good man and must rise to defend the potentiality of sinful human nature, or else lose her kingdom in Hell.)

Resisting the Devil, however, constitutes only part of the process toward sainthood. What Simon went to the desert for was to improve on his spiritual condition in the most isolated environment, one that would be most conducive to meditation on the problem of greatest concern to him. Buñuel profits from the choice of setting. There is so little within the frame to distract us visually from the emphasis to which Buñuel directs us that small activities are felt to be significant even during the course of the film. The one possible exception occurs when Simon, annoyed at his continually reappearing weaknesses, resolves to stand on one foot until God signals him that he has overcome his shortcomings in charity and humility. Very little is made of this, though we do have a shot of the raised foot. Buñuel gives less visual emphasis to the gesture than it deserves, considering the fact that when Simon puts his foot down, acknowledging a change in his internal condition, we hardly notice it.

Yet in all other important points, the excluding of irrelevant gestures within the frame clears the way for sustaining focus on both visual and oral elements that bear on the theme. After the change in Simon seems to occur, he radiates an internal glow, a feeling of good will, or charity. He starts blessing things such as an insect. In fact, he notes that blessing is both a saintly exercise and an amusing and harmless pastime, a self-satiric

remark which in itself is a sign of growth in the overly solemn anchorite. When the dwarf appears asking for a blessing on his goat, Simon, who might hitherto have exhibited some sternness and impatience with the crude goatherd, proceeds to bless both the goat and the dwarf. When the dwarf objects to being named in the same blessing with an animal, Simon does not argue the point but simply smiles. The verbal contents of the individual shots are indeed simple specifications, but they are clear indications of a spiritual movement. The film's style establishes the importance of such pieces of information in regard to the general thematic material.

Film is, of course, an external medium, and the difficulty of conveying the real sense of an inner life (so often confined exclusively to dialogue) can be overcome effectively by depicting small gestures, though rarely in film can small gestures be relied on as a pattern of human activity duplicating an inner life. The reason for this usual limitation is that film presents so graphic a record of the total environment within each frame that a filmmaker has difficulty in separating the key gesture from unimportant gestures or background materials unless he resorts to close-ups. Buñuel succeeds without too many close-ups in *Simon of the Desert* because he has arranged for his shots to be patterned on small movements in an open environment with a minimum of distractions. The close-up is always an emphatic shot; it sometimes suggests an excessive emphasis on a gesture that is not borne out by the total meaning of the sequence. By avoiding a reliance on close-ups and still emphasizing small activities, Buñuel creates a film style that is particularly capable of expressing nuances to indicate changes in the atmosphere or spiritual condition of Simon or in Satan's psychological state of mind.

Therefore, the abrupt switch to the New York discothèque with its crowdedness within the frame and its blaring music might seem at first an unfortunate redirecting of the film's overall style. The increase in the surface excitement does not alter Buñuel's procedure of employing shots with visually simple specifications though highly subtle implications. The dance floor is filled with gyrating dancers, but the camera does not create a focal point; instead, it moves about, suggesting a similarity among all the couples, eventually specifying only a general impression of the kind of activity at this symbolic Black Mass. At a table, Simon in modern clothes is singled out, his face indicating his surprising ease in this environment— without, however, being an integral part of it. Having conquered temptations, he is not newly tempted; yet he has also worked out his inner spiritual problems, which parallel his external denial of Satan. Without overt signs of pride, he has now returned to the world of men, but here of course there is no particular place for the saint. The "radioactive" dance hints at a world on its way to extinction. (The screenplay, in fact, ends with a return to the column, which mysteriously explodes.) The outsider saint is not important to others, who are wrapped up in their world of unreflecting

activity. The intellectual Simon (and perhaps Buñuel) remains an observer of the unobservant. For himself, however, he has become worthy, and he needs the world as little as it needs him.

The neutrality of the camera enforces no attitude on us, but this does not mean that the filmmaker avoids presenting his commentary or particular attitudes. Buñuel's shots of a man devoted to his spiritual improvement serve both to attract and detach us in regard to Simon. We watch a man on a pillar in the desert, the basic image of the film. His appearance within the environment is towering and yet somewhat ridiculous. This is, certainly, any saint's predicament: to be like other men is not to be a saint; similarly, we are glad to have saintly men among us, but we do not exactly strive to imitate those men.

It is extremely difficult to convey cinematically the idea that a man's existence can be noble and comic at the same time because the explicit surface level of the medium tends to exploit each aspect as it appears, thus jarring our sensibilities by moving from contrasting shots. Buñuel largely overcomes this inherent difficulty by constantly returning to the central image of man on a platform and the paradox that it implies, for the platform is a universal stage. Simon's audience, just like the movie audience, comes to be amused as well as edified. The content of the shots justifies both of our attitudes. Simon telling a beautiful woman to get behind him is not merely exercising his Christian obligation to refuse temptations to evil because he knows the woman is Satan. The shot happens to show us a beautiful woman *literally,* and Simon's response to the threat creates a paradox within the visual frame; on film, a half-dressed woman, Devil or not, is still a half-dressed woman, and not entirely the threat to us that she poses to Simon. The shot is totally comic, though totally serious too.

In *Simon of the Desert,* the specifications of the shots are intellectually complex though actually simpler on the surface than shots in ordinary films. Certainly, Buñuel has the gift of presenting highly connotative materials regardless of their surface reality; perhaps his success results from his clearly detailed literalness, which is nevertheless mixed (without stylistic inconsistency) with unreal or supernatural activity. In his early films, the image level was itself unreal (*Un Chien Andalou* and *L'Age d'Or*), and the ambiguity was stylistic. The increasing complexity of his ideas in his later works required a realistic surface as a base for conceptual paradoxes and ambiguities (as in *Viridiana, Belle de Jour, The Milky Way,* and *Tristana*). The visual wit of his early films remains, but a work like *Simon of the Desert* becomes profound beyond its surface as we move from the reality of the specifications of the shots to the conception underlying Buñuel's total vision of the world within his films.

# (14)

# Filming
# Movement
# and
# Nonmovement

## Problems in Analysis

Since the major assumption behind the art of the film is the depiction of the concept of movement, the single great problem of filming is how best to depict that movement. Yet a narrative film of any length must be made up of images of people and things at rest as well as in motion. For the dramatic impact of the process of motion—as well as for the sake of realism—a filmmaker wants to portray nonmotion with as much expressiveness and perhaps as much emphasis as he employs to portray motion. He knows that the actual physical motion projected on a screen accounts for only a portion of the total concept of movement in a narrative film. In other words, a film contains not just externalized action, not simply people jumping about. A film also contains narrative in which movement, actual or implicit, must be integrated with the shaping idea that determined the film in the first place.

The problems related to the filming of movement and nonmovement seem generally and equally misunderstood. The possibility of using a great many shots of essentially nonmoving images has been established by Carl Dreyer in such films as *The Passion of Joan of Arc* and *Gertrud,* but Dreyer's influence has been minimal. In any case, images of movement and

nonmovement are usually combined intuitively or arbitrarily, hardly ever as a result of an intelligent application or exploration of theory.

Another factor complicating the analysis of filming movement is the current practice of using a flexible, moving camera for most shots. The influence of Murnau's camera fluidity in *The Last Laugh* led to a general attempt to film with cameras on easily moveable objects—platforms, elevators, tracks, cars, cranes. Unquestionably, a cameraman perched on a moving vehicle will always be moving his camera, panning, tilting, dollying about with the performers, for reasons that are physiological as well as psychological: the mind automatically tends to frame objects in the center of vision. Thus, if a performer standing in the center of the frame walks three steps to the side, the camera will move with him to keep him in center frame. The director himself very likely thinks in terms of center-framing images, and thus, no check is exerted on this tendency in the thousand ordinary films turned out each year in the major industries. The result is that the moving camera setup now seems more natural than the stationary arrangement, though the desire for perpetual center-framing is more a habit of mind than an esthetic principle.

## Camera Alternatives

The traditional reason for using a moving camera is to avoid having to cut from one camera setup to another. Obviously, people and vehicles must often cover a greater area than can be successfully captured in one stationary shot. The other method of photographing movement over a distance—the assembling of two or more shots—is, in comparison, more difficult to accomplish, except when some extraordinary tracking vehicle needs to be constructed; even then a single traveling camera shot may compensate for five or six stationary setups, all of which require lighting considerations as well, perhaps, as considerations of setting.

Theorists on film have had surprisingly little to say about the two different approaches to filming motion. Generally, all those who comment on the matter—and they do so rather casually—seem to assume that camera movement means fluidity, and that fluidity is a good thing. No popular antonym exists in the critical vocabulary for *fluidity,* and the adjective *static* is frequently pejorative, suggesting something old-fashioned. It is as if once the moving camera became available, it should have made the other approach obsolete.

Perhaps this critical oversimplification ties in with the modern tendency to disparage Eisenstein's approach to filming, for Eisenstein is supposed to have eschewed the moving camera in favor of editing. Two fallacies here should be dismissed before an analysis of the noncomparable values of the moving and stationary camera can be considered. First, Eisenstein actually

used the moving camera more often than has been noted, even in *Potemkin*. The second fallacy implicit in the criticism of Eisenstein is that those who employ a great many stationary setups conceive of film as the art of editing rather than the art of filming. In the following two chapters, it will be seen that, for example, Chaplin (who edits much as the current favorites of the school of moving-camera filming) relies mainly on stationary shots. On the other hand, even those filmmakers who use the fluid camera at its best— such as Kurosawa (who will be considered later in this chapter)—sometimes rely a great deal on the type of editing associated with Eisenstein.

Distinctions based on the practices of favored and unfavored directors become entirely too personal. What is truly important to consider is the different values implicit in each kind of filming. Four broad categories, not equally important, establish the general possibilities in regard to filming motion and nonmotion. As might be expected, actual practice usually consists of a mixture of these methods, but some attention must be directed toward the theoretical premises underlying specific practices.

The four categories, then, are (1) stationary cameras to film primarily stationary subjects; (2) stationary cameras to film subjects in motion; (3) moving cameras to film primarily stationary subjects; and (4) moving cameras to film subjects in motion. The relative merits of these categories are impossible to evaluate, since a good director, given a variety of subjects to film, has a choice of approaches, and the method he chooses will distinguish the presentation of the content in such a way that it will be essentially different and not readily comparable to the alternative ways. In examining the possibilities and their implications, we often discover that the effectiveness of the film idea is determined as much by the way the camera presents the subject matter as by the editing itself.

## Stationary Cameras and Stationary Subjects

Few people will dispute the value of a static camera arrangement when the subject is not in motion. The stationary camera functions well for such arrangements as conversations in interior sets and close-ups of faces. Moreover, for technical reasons most (but not all) close-ups are shot without camera movement, for details are more likely to be missed if the camera moves than if it holds still, and the detail is usually the main point of a close-up. However, the traditional stationary establishing shot is becoming rare. Generally, directors feel that to disclose a landscape with three or four stationary shots is wasteful when it can be done with one sweeping camera movement.

As present styles of filming go, the stationary camera for capturing stationary subjects is limited because it cannot be continually used without drawing attention to essentially noncinematic elements. After the coming

of sound, a large number of good but rather talky plays were filmed, but they were unsuccessful because they lacked movement. Standard procedure today attempts to hide the static quality of this kind of subject matter by either moving the camera or moving the speakers. To disguise essentially static images through sheer technique only avoids the problem of conceiving narrative ideas in a cinematic way in the first place. Nevertheless, the 1930's-style reliance on the stationary camera for uncinematic sequences, while perhaps more honest, was seldom more artistic. And some of the very early attempts of the silent film at drawing-room comedy were even more dreadful examples of filmed tedium, for the lack of cutting made the lack of motion within the frame readily discernible.

## Stationary Cameras and Moving Subjects:
## A Sequence from *The Mark of Zorro*

To generalize, then, we can say that the moving camera has to a large extent replaced the stationary camera in some of its traditional functions, such as the establishment of the scenic view. The esthetic justification for the replacement of several stationary camera shots with a single moving shot rests on the premise, surely debatable, that fluidity is one of the highest cinematic values. Another common premise, that the moving camera saves time by giving more information in one shot than would be possible in two or three equivalent stationary shots, requires us to define cinematic information in only one way. A moving camera following a man walking down the street may reveal information about the nature of the walk, but this information might well be given by a nonmoving camera. In fact, the three or four camera arrangements needed to record the walk might, by varying the angle, tell us more than a camera on a flexible crane. The moving camera tends to emphasize the motion in terms of its progress from point to point; the stationary camera does something quite different: it emphasizes the particular environment at any particular point during the walk and places the character against the background. In contrast, when the camera moves, the background becomes much less important.

An example of the way in which motion can be captured with striking effect by the stationary camera can be found in *The Mark of Zorro*.* The long chase sequence that occurs toward the end of this film is done almost entirely without camera movement. The sequence has several purposes. Least important for plot but of great interest to all viewers is the exhibition of Fairbanks' athletic prowess. The sequence is also part of the film's climax inasmuch as Zorro will finally achieve his aim of demoralizing the soldiers

* A general analysis of this Douglas Fairbanks film directed by Fred Niblo appears in Chapter 8.

by proving that they cannot catch him. And most important, Niblo manages to turn the hero's leaping and graceful running into a revelation of character.

The sequence begins with horses ridden across the frame, literally off the screen, since the camera does not move to follow them. Later we sometimes see Zorro running across the frame in one shot, followed by another setup showing the soldiers in pursuit. By separating the pursued from the pursuers through cutting, the camera makes time elliptical. That is, the few seconds that must elapse between the appearance of Zorro and the appearance of the soldiers is eliminated. The inherent capacity to manipulate time is probably the chief advantage of using the stationary camera over the moving camera. When the moving camera continuously follows a subject, it captures real time, inevitably slowing the action compared to the elliptical time of the multiple stationary camera arrangements. However, as long as the stationary camera films continuously, it produces the same effect as the moving camera in regard to duplicating real time.

When Zorro enters the town where the major part of the chase will take place, we see him riding swiftly from left to right, followed in the same shot by the soldiers; since this is a continuous single shot, we know exactly how far behind him the soldiers are, though he has ridden past the limits of the frame. Then in another shot we see him grab hold of a rope (his world, like Tarzan's, has a number of inexplicably convenient ropes for swinging) and in one motion reverse his movement. As the pursuing soldiers ride by from left to right, he swings above their heads from right to left (fig. 29) and arrives at a second-story landing. The effect could not be reproduced with a moving camera, for the beauty of the feat consists in the capturing in the same frame of two opposing motions. The shot is taken from a distance, too, in order to emphasize the extent of the swing. We need to see the full figures of Zorro and his pursuers, for part of his swing brings him to the same level as the soldiers, who—were they ever prepared for his goading of them—could have reached out and grabbed him as they rode by. Zorro's aim is to surprise and humiliate them. Niblo's goal is to provide a visual area that is absolutely still as the environment of a great deal of truly cinematic movement.

Similar patterns of surprise are recorded from stationary positions. Zorro eludes his pursuers by tricking them, not by outracing them, for he wishes to demonstrate superiority, not fear. Typically, he leaps over a wall and hides in some adjacent shrubbery; when the soldiers finally manage to struggle over, they stupidly assume that he has taken advantage of their slowness by running away, and they rush off oblivious of his actually being behind them. This pattern of movement, repeated several times, reflects the frantic state of the pursuers and the complete calm of the hero. Furthermore, it sheds considerable light on his sense of comedy. He has to think up variations to amuse himself and at the same time impress his pursuers with their stupidity.

One of the simplest variations is the running leap over a barrier. One sequence creates a cumulative visual effect that could not be achieved with a different style of filming by showing three such leaps in rapid succession, though in clearly distinguished physical areas. Niblo edits the shots of the leaps, each of which takes only a few seconds, without showing us Zorro's moving from one location to the next. First Zorro runs toward an entrance blocked by a donkey; he jumps over the donkey and disappears from the frame; there follows a close-up of the animal, then a return to the view of the donkey blocking the way. Onto the frame come the soldiers, who are afraid to try running around the donkey and, of course, are incapable of leaping over it. In the fourth shot of this series, the racing Zorro bounds over a wall in his usual fashion. Once he is off the frame, the soldiers run up to this barrier and struggle over. Are these the same soldiers from shot three, and if so how did they get past that donkey? The question is entirely irrelevant to the film as we watch it. Has a half minute elapsed, or perhaps five minutes? Again, no one watching the sequence could raise such a question. Niblo has clearly juxtaposed a shot of Zorro leaping over a wall with a shot of soldiers stymied by a donkey. In contrast, the moving camera would follow Zorro as he approached the wall and would inform us, perhaps, as to the geographic relationship of the town's buildings, streets, alleyways, and walls, but this sort of filming misses the point. Shot four serves as an abstraction: the graceful man successfully outleaps the clumsy soldiers; style humbles awkwardness. The stationary shots link together with a deliberate disregard for time; in fact the filmmaker annihilates real time in order to abstract the particular feat and to establish it as Zorro's characteristic pattern of movement.

Another variation at leaping over the barrier occurs when Zorro clears an empty animal pen with a magnificent somersault. The pursuers must laboriously climb over one side of the pen, walk to the other end, and climb out, which they do with their usual lack of inspiration. The last soldier gets stuck, unheeded by his companions. Zorro walks up behind the struggling soldier and frees him to rush on without having noticed who did him the favor (he assumes it was another soldier). Thus, Zorro plays a private joke on all concerned, actually aiding his pursuers, who clearly are no match for him.

The characterization has been established in purely visual terms. Zorro's grace, good humor, and even generosity appear and reverse the basic premise of a chase. If Zorro can continually end up behind his pursuers, he is really not being chased by them, but taunting them instead. Had Niblo tried to depict this with a moving camera, he would certainly have emphasized the *act of chasing,* and therefore lost some of the effects he gains from discontinuity. By cutting from stationary shot to stationary shot, he removes this episode from the realm of time and makes it stand as the symbolic activity of Zorro's life, the outwitting of his humiliated

pursuers, the forces of tyranny. By allowing his hero to move in and out of the frame, he further increases our sense of Zorro's facility within his environment. The action, obviously, is much quicker when portrayed by edited static shots rather than moving shots, which capture a longer segment of real time. Niblo wants to create the pell-mell sense because it allows him to string together related patterns of action with very little time between. Normally, a director would want that delay in time in order to emphasize the particular beauty of each variation. Niblo and Fairbanks do not. They have so great a variety of clever moves yet to make (the part discussed is not even half the entire sequence) that they do not wish to emphasize any single incident. Their procedure leaves the audience remembering a general style, not an event. For Zorro, style is the man. Thus, the movement as recorded from stationary camera arrangements achieves certain effects not attainable with a moving camera.

## Moving Cameras and Stationary Subjects

The basic purpose of a moving camera in a situation without movement or with only minimal movement, the depiction of a vast area, is commonplace and requires no elaboration. A second important function of the moving camera is to replace editing when the joining of shots and subsequent distortion of time would be less effective than the use of real time. There are other reasons to forego the usual process of cutting: for instance, the moving camera might be used to emphasize a subjective point of view in a three-sided dialogue; the camera, taking the consistent perspective of one character, might move back and forth between the other two.

The moving camera is frequently applied to a shot in which some visual revelation is meant to take place. The camera might dolly along a deserted alley and come to rest on a body that was not visible at the commencement of the camera's movement. The shot might be relevant to an observer—a character in the film—whose emotional condition at the time requires him to look slowly in the direction of the body. Sometimes, no particular character's point of view is intended, and such a shot simply increases suspense, but it is a trick of prolongation more than an esthetic determination.

Most sensitive moviegoers would agree that the continued use of a moving camera to film static images simply calls attention to the whole contrivance of the filmmaking process for no particular advantage. In the sound film, a continual problem for more than forty years has been the visual pointlessness of very many conversational sequences. They are simply dull to look at because the literary impulse to convey meaning primarily through words is still basic in a large part of the commercial industry. As a problem in filming it manifests itself in the desperation of directors to get actors to move around while they talk. Obviously, a great deal of

movement fully photographed might very well distract from the primary importance of dialogue; to compensate for this, the camera itself is frequently called upon to perform the movement. When a stage play is made into a film today, the filmmaker often transforms the one or two original stage sets into a dozen indoor and outdoor environments. In other words, the dialogue is broken down into exchanges, each to be set into a separate environment. What was done on stage in a single conversation can be spread out on the screen to fill a half dozen shots in as many speedily juxtaposed scenes. Sometimes the dialogue proceeds consecutively, but the people are shown in the separate locations with their voices doing the talking while they are seen, say, getting to know each other in different environments. However, such "montage" effects are still less common than the simple arrangement of proceeding with a conversation outdoors, strolling in the street.

The fallacy behind either approach lies in the belief that making dialogue accompany moving images is the equivalent of a film idea. Unless the narrative idea embodies moving images, no amount of camera movement will suffice to create material that is basically cinematic. In animation or in the short experimental film, the camera itself may indeed supply the visual interest, for in such a case the camera becomes the key to the film idea. But, as noted before, in the full-length narrative, the camera generally remains an inobtrusive recorder of events interpreted by a filmmaker, serving as his instrument, not his subject.

## Moving Cameras and Moving Subjects

For many years the moving camera has normally been used to handle significant movements. Still, the practices of earlier filmmakers like Griffith, Chaplin, and Eisenstein deserve study because their frequent reliance on stationary cameras for moving subjects will always be artistically relevant and offer viable alternatives to those practices of every ordinary director of our times. In fact, a moving camera is no more natural to the medium than a stationary one. The justification of either kind of shot must lie in the particular effects achieved.

Viewers sometimes assume that by nature the moving camera comes closer to our own way of watching subjects in motion than a stationary camera. After all, we always turn our heads or at least our eyes to watch a car drive off. In film, a car moving across the frame appears from nowhere and then disappears off the frame. If the camera does not move, our view of the car's motion is unnaturally restricted. On the other hand, viewers seldom notice that a moving camera will usually photograph moving subjects in a distorted relationship with the environment, and the distortion, though not necessarily crucial, is significant. The filmmaker employs the moving camera

to enlarge the scope of the spectator's field of view. Now the scope of any individual frame of a moving shot equals the scope of any comparable stationary shot; the only difference is that with the moving shot the environment changes with every frame, whereas the environment remains identical in every frame of the stationary shot. What is important to note is that what changes in the moving shot is the environment, not the subject.

For instance, if a camera follows a car as it drives down city streets, the car (*i.e., the subject*) remains in relatively the same position within the frame, and if the camera moves at the same speed as the car, the car's position might be exactly the same in every frame of the moving shot. The result on film is an image in which the background, the environment itself, does the moving while the subject stays relatively still. This is true even when the image is of a man running. A panning camera captures a man whose legs move but who himself remains in center frame. Yet the information our eyes receive when a man on screen is running from left to right and the camera panning or traveling with him is actually one of a background moving from right to left and a man standing still. Of course, we subconsciously transform the image of a moving background into the image of the moving subject. But while the distortion does not disturb our sense of reality during the film because it is not consciously perceived, it does prevent us from a complete comprehension of the environment through which the character moves. What *is* comprehended is the nature of that movement, observed pretty much without the distractions of the details of environment. Theoretically, at least, the moving camera to some degree always isolates the subject in motion (though the subject is actually the most stable element within the frame) from the background (which is actually constantly changing and disappearing off the frame).

On the other hand, a stationary camera, while limited in its ability to capture the full field of action, does not create distortions of subject and environment. Thus, when the main point of the shot has to do with the environment in relationship to the subject, a stationary camera alone allows us to focus on a stable environment through which a figure or an object moves. The spatial relationships are thereby clearer than with a moving camera, though the latter can usually make the sense of time clearer to us. In many situations the environment does share importance with the subject in motion, since the motivation for the movement usually has at least something to do with the surroundings. Yet if the environment is vaguely depicted, the aspect of place may lose some significance relative to the motion itself.

Everything depends on the effects desired of the shot. Sometimes the effect of an abstract notion of movement, running for instance, can be much more important than the background. At the end of *The 400 Blows*, Truffaut wishes to convey the absolute isolation of his young hero and shows him running along the deserted beach and finally frozen in a position that de-

liberately leaves the background somewhat vague. On the other hand, the modern tendency in the wide screen is to emphasize the background as one of the most valuable cinematic elements. The evident use of cities and picturesque scenes in order to fill the frame with colorful shapes and volumes is essential to the current practice of most directors. When the wide screen made the stationary shot of the human figure more difficult because the standing figure no longer filled a significant portion of the frame, the moving camera began to dominate the ordinary pattern of filming, serving to dissociate the human image from the natural environment: a man running in a specific area (*e.g.,* a specific street) followed by a moving camera tends to be recorded on film as a man running in a generalized area (any street). The two modern practices, the moving shot and the emphasis on background, became rather contradictory in many films.

An awareness of the implications of the four categories of shots for the filming of movement and nonmovement leads to the conclusion that the very selection of the approach most fitting for a particular image requires a clear conception of the alternative effects, not an arbitrary decision to move with the action or to stand still and permit it to pass out of camera range. In fact, the image itself ought to be conceived in terms of camera movement or stationary setups. There are, of course, other factors involved in such a choice. A director may feel that he has a certain style particularly suitable for a camera in constant motion; yet if his style is not to be merely a revelation of his own nervous energy, he has to justify it by a film idea suited to that style.

## Meaning Through Camera Movement: Kurosawa's *Rashomon*

One of the films most influential in the development of a pattern of consistently fluid camera movement was Akira Kurosawa's *Rashomon* (1950), a film that made a sensational impact upon Western viewers. With this film, audiences here learned that the Japanese industry was capable of both greatness and innovation. Kurosawa's marvelous tracking shots through the woods were perhaps the most striking technical achievement of *Rashomon*. Never before had a moving camera conveyed tremendous tension so gracefully; never had a camera moved so swiftly and yet so subtly. Although the movement inheres in the film idea and the filming was not designed to call attention to itself, the camerawork remains an outstanding example of technical skill controlled by a film mind of the highest caliber, capable of expressing perfectly the artistic end of each sequence.

The film contains four subjective segments in which individual characters relate their eye-witness accounts of a single event. These four personal accounts are themselves included in a narrative that contains a plot of its own, not necessarily connected to the central event described in each

of the four segments. The complexity of the structure requires a shifting in mode for almost each sequence, which Kurosawa manages to handle without splitting his style into bits and pieces. Throughout, the camera style reflects the filmmaker's unifying sensibility.

Although there had been films in which a situation or a location provided the framework for numerous unrelated stories concerning the characters who happen to be in the specific environment (*e.g., Ship of Fools, The High and the Mighty,* and *Grand Hotel*), Kurosawa's film did something that had never been done before: it shifted the emphasis slightly so that the framing story and the inner narratives become meaningful inasmuch as they shed light on each other. The narrative reminds us of Joseph Conrad's fiction because the story that is listened to has an effect on the listeners, who perform a small but decisive action at the end based on how they have been affected by the events discussed.

The inner story concerns three characters, Takehiro, a samurai, his wife Masago, and Tajomaru, a bandit (played with astonishing verve and variety by Toshiro Mifune, still the only Japanese actor widely known in the West). Before the film begins each of the three characters has told his own version of the events to a magistrate conducting an investigation into the samurai's death. (Since he is dead, the samurai's version is told through an intermediary, a medium.) These three accounts are related to the movie audience by a priest and a woodcutter, who speak to a man referred to in the screenplay as the commoner while they are all taking shelter from the rain in the ruins of the Rashomon, a gate or gatehouse outside the city of Kyoto, the ravaged capital of twelfth-century Japan. The woodcutter and the priest have heard the three versions of the participants during the official examination before the magistrate; throughout the film the woodcutter appears overwhelmed by the dishonesty of the testimony, and finally admitting that he was an eye-witness, he relates his own version of the events. He has become completely discouraged by his realization of human depravity, not so much because the incidents were horrible but because Takehiro, Masago, and Tajomaru felt compelled to make up lies that in each case put the narrator in the best possible light. In the woodcutter's view, all human honor is lost by each character's attempt to transform objective reality so as to support the needs of his ego. The priest also begins to feel discouraged about the readiness of men to do anything for their own ends, so that near the conclusion of the film he becomes highly suspicious of a gesture by the woodcutter. In other words, the woodcutter's version affects the one sensitive listener, the priest, while the other listener, the crude commoner, is either unaffected or inspired to commit a miserable theft at the end of the film.

Before we can analyze the technical and artistic achievement of the moving camera in this film, we must look in considerable detail at the complicated narrative content of the four variations on the basic episode. It

will be seen later that Kurosawa uses the camera to unify the plot and distinguish the four versions of the central story. The difficulty of this feat is compounded by the complexity of the narrative's raw materials. The first three versions, told by the participants, differ in many minor details, and even some essential facts are contradicted; only a few general premises seem agreed upon such as the fact that the bandit succeeded in overcoming the samurai and tying him to a tree and then made love to his wife in his presence. However, these three versions are exactly alike in their evident intention to make the speaker seem exalted by his part in the episode.

In the first version, Tajomaru the bandit explains to the magistrate how he cunningly tricked the samurai and his wife into following him into a remote part of the forest. After overcoming the samurai in a fight and binding him, Tajomaru attempts to take the woman by force. She determinedly and fiercely fights him off, gaining his admiration for her spirit; but suddenly finding the bandit desirable, she succumbs to him. Thus, Tajomaru's story up to this point has made the bandit (1) exceedingly clever at his trade, (2) sophisticated enough to appreciate an extraordinary woman even though she tries to kill him while defending herself, and (3) so masculinely attractive that he is capable of winning over this woman, not having to take her by force. Yet even at this, Tajomaru has not completed his description of his heroic escapades. The wife, he relates, insists that either the husband or the lover must die to salvage her honor. Tajomaru, understanding the validity of the suggestion, nobly cuts the rope from the samurai and engages him in a fantastic duel (fig. 50). Although earlier in this version he was

**50** *Rashomon*

depicted as being excessively cautious, perhaps even cowardly, Tajomaru performs like Zorro, and after a magnificent fight he slays the samurai. As he says to the magistrate, "We crossed swords over twenty-three times. Think of that! No one had ever crossed over twenty with me before." * He concludes by saying that the woman had run off during the fight, and he didn't bother to look for her. Thus, Tajomaru admits to the killing, for as a notorious bandit he would undoubtedly be executed even if he were innocent of this particular crime. He has managed to gain our sympathy because his nature is inherently heroic and dignified.

The dominant tone of the second version, that of the wife, Masago, is pathos—which is, to her, an equivalent for masculine heroics, for she becomes the epitome of feminine sensitivity and human dignity, the helpless victim of an outrage. As she tells it, the bandit did rape her, then laughed and ran off into the woods; there was no sword fight nor any suggestion on her part that one of the two men must die. In fact, she runs weeping to her husband, still tied to the tree trunk, and throws herself first on the ground and then on him, pathetically imploring some kind remark from him. He remains silent, staring at her contemptuously. In his eyes she has been dishonored, even though she could do nothing to prevent the rape. When she cuts the ropes she offers him her dagger to kill her. He still remains absolutely unmovable, still implacably scornful of her. The filmscript at this point describes the woman as growing more desperate, and then in close-up, "she moves steadily forward now; her world forever destroyed, she holds the dagger high, without seeming to be aware of it. The camera tracks with her in the direction of her husband until she suddenly lunges off screen." † She claims to have fainted, probably not consciously aware of having killed him. She says that later she tried unsuccessfully to commit suicide and concludes her version by asking, "What should a poor helpless woman like me do?"

The version of the dead samurai is told through a medium who conjures up his voice. (For the premise of the film, this conjuring must be accepted as a supernatural event; the story turns out as untrue as the other two versions, but not because of any interference with the materials on the part of the medium.) Takehiro, the samurai, claims that Tajomaru, after the rape, successfully consoled Masago, asking her to run off with him, as he really loved her. Takehiro describes his wife's reaction—"Never, in all of our life together, had I seen her more beautiful," ‡—as she obviously returned the bandit's love (the superb camerawork achieves the effect of making Masago look indeed more beautiful than she had elsewhere in the film). Masago agrees to go off with the bandit, but just before leaving she insists that Tajomaru kill her husband. From this point Takehiro shapes his

* *Rashomon,* translated and transcribed from the film by Donald Richie (New York, Grove Press, 1969), p. 86.

† *Ibid.,* pp. 97–98.    ‡ *Ibid.,* p. 109.

story, as Tajomaru did his, to show his adversary as noble. In other words, Takehiro has already described himself as the suffering husband shocked to discover his wife's perfidy; now, he must elevate himself and his reaction to this perfidy by elevating the bandit. Tajomaru is made to share Takehiro's shock at the revelation of Masago's character; thus, Takehiro's narrative makes the wife the villain and the bandit an upholder of the sort of code that Takehiro himself epitomizes. When Tajomaru throws the woman down and asks the husband whether he should kill her, the husband says that he almost forgave the bandit because of his assertion of the code of masculine honor. She runs away, and the bandit tries to catch her, returning hours later without having found her. Then Tajomaru, offering no explanation, cuts the samurai loose and walks off into the forest. Now Takehiro tells us that he heard someone crying, and in a close-up we see it is the isolated husband himself. Shortly thereafter, the husband commits suicide by plunging Masago's dagger in his breast. After that, he remembers someone pulling the dagger from his breast as he died. Thus, the husband's version, like the previous two versions, ends with the speaker's claiming credit for the death of Takehiro—that death being the only ascertainable fact up to this point. And like the other two versions, the purpose of Takehiro's account has been to show himself as a truly noble character, superior to the others.

The fourth version is told by the woodcutter, who hidden from view observed the episode without participating in it, although at the end it is apparent that he stole the dagger that was sticking in the ground (the other three versions agree that the dagger at one time was sticking in the ground, dropped by Masago during her encounter with Tajomaru; though the husband of course claimed it was eventually stolen from his breast). For having taken this valuable implement, a piece of evidence, the woodcutter feels incriminated to the degree that he did not tell his story to the police; instead he tells it at last only to the commoner and the priest. Kurosawa intends that this version stand for the truth, though many critics feel it is also a relative account.

*Rashomon* is not film about the relativity of truth, however; it is about the kinds of lies people will tell to protect their self-image, the most important possession a man believes he has. Normally, the final version of any controverted narrative represents the truth. For critics to doubt the fourth version, they must feel that the key to everything lies in the final remarks of the samurai that someone pulled out the dagger just as he died. First of all, if his remarks are true, then his story must be basically the truth, an impossibility here, for no narrative structure (literary or cinematic) could rest on a third version that contradicts two prior versions and is in turn completely contradicted by a following version. Some critics argue that the samurai's final remarks are either a pointless lie or the truth. It is clear that his concluding lie is not pointless: he lies to cover the loophole in his suicide story, which no one could believe without his accounting for the weapon.

He knows that objectively judged, he will appear to have been killed in a battle, the victor then removing the sword, which is what happened. The dagger later was stolen from the ground by the woodcutter, for it was a piece of valuable property that the poor man could not resist.

The fourth version is not only placed advantageously to set the record straight, but its tone as well communicates a sense of the reality of the characters as we are ourselves destined to think of them once we understand that they are liars. If they are lying yet eager to admit to the killing, then the truth of their conduct must be much worse than the capacity to commit the violent act they confessed to. The woodcutter reveals their nature to us without involving his own character one way or the other, and so, in the absence of any apparent motive for his lying or evidence of his having any relationship with these characters, we must conclude that he is telling the truth. Even if we are not certain about the question of whether he took the dagger from the ground or the body, we could hardly expect him to invent a complex variant simply to cover his petty crime from the eyes of the commoner and the priest.

The woodcutter's story is spoken without musical accompaniment, whereas music has brilliantly been used to help establish the mood of the three previous stories. The lack of music coupled with the lack of the narrator's participation in the version significantly distinguishes this narrative from the others. He relates the story after the rape: Tajomaru pleads with his victim to marry him: he is willing to reform, to give up thieving. In reply, the woman cuts her husband's bonds, indicating that the two men must fight over her. Immediately the samurai, a perfect parody of that brave warrior class Kurosawa has often depicted elsewhere, backs off, proclaiming his refusal to fight and put his life in jeopardy; then he calls his wife a whore and suggests that she kill herself. Next, as the two men stare at each other, the samurai offers to give the bandit his wife, but Tajomaru after some indecision decides instead to accept Takehiro's evaluation of the woman. At this point, Masago begins to taunt the two men with their cowardice and lack of manhood to such an extent that swords are drawn, and after much hesitancy and trepidation on the part of both men, the battle begins. In its depiction of incompetence, clumsiness, cowardice, and desperation tactics the battle stands as a burlesque of all the serious battles that Kurosawa went on to construct in such films as *The Seven Samurai, Yojimbo,* and *Red Beard,* in which the same actor, Mifune, was to partake with tremendous glory. Here the combatants' arms shake as they cross swords; when one swings, the other runs; every advance culminates in a stumble. Tajomaru hurls his sword at the cringing samurai, who screams, "I don't want to die! I don't want to die!" After the battle Tajomaru is stupefied and exhausted. He even swings the samurai's sword at Masago, who flees into the forest. Finally, he removes both his sword and Takehiro's from the grove, limping off into the forest.

Thus, the fourth version has the effect of revealing the abject nature of all three participants. We understand now why they prefer to claim credit for the violence, as long as they can shape the incidents to bolster their egos. We last see the three anti-heroes in positions of fear, the samurai dying ignobly, the wife rushing off frantically from the scene of the debacle, and the victor, "half-crazed," staggering away into the forest. The woodcutter has witnessed the mutual disillusionment and debasement of three people, and as a result has become skeptical of mankind in general.

In addition to the usual problems involved in adapting a literary source to the screen, Kurosawa was faced with a difficulty in transforming the theme of his literary source into the entirely different theme he wished to express. Ryunosuke Akutagawa's short story "In a Grove" was conceived in terms of the technique of multiple points of view: its theme and its technical presentation are the same, and for Kurosawa to use the story at all meant a commitment on his part to preserve what interested him (the multiple points of view) but to redirect the implications of the plot with respect to moral relativism, which is not part of Kurosawa's view of the world. Little or nothing resides beneath the surface of the Akutagawa story, and none of Kurosawa's other films are as simplistic as this source. Kurosawa turned the surface complexity into a mirror of the internal development of the director's ideas (not the story writer's). The first thing Kurosawa must have done was to evolve a frame for the personal narratives spoken by the characters, and he took it from another interesting Akutagawa story, "Rashomon." The humanistic idea of the "Rashomon" story has to do with the deterioration of human values under the pressures of deplorable external conditions (impoverishment). Thus, the main body of the film is taken from "In a Grove," incorporated into a framework based on "Rashomon," and structured so that the framing story and the personal versions of the rape and the death take their meaning from their juxtaposition in a newly created context.

This is an interesting technical achievement, but it is doubtful whether the mere power of even Kurosawa's intellectually evocative context could have held everything together in what is, after all, a short film (only 88 minutes). The real problem, once the intellectual concept suggests itself, concerns the way of approaching the materials. Highly literary and intellectual as these sources are, they have been turned into a totally cinematic event. Even while in the process of straightening out the intellectual procedure for this work, Kurosawa had to create a film style to embody the stories and all of the theme—in fact, to relate the theme and stories in spite of what might have been their tendency to seem disparate, hopelessly unsolvable, and so inwardly directed that they appear in Akutagawa's texts as essentially noncinematic.

It is in this respect that the fascinating use of the moving camera becomes not the tour de force critics at first admired it as, but more than that:

it holds the film together and clarifies that impressionism so deeply involved in any interested party's narration of highly emotionally charged incidents. We see a rapidly moving camera creating in certain sections a frenetic pace; moreover, the conditions under which each character receives his impressions—or at least the way in which he later tells the world he has received them—relates to the unstable internal conditions of the narrators.

To preserve the surface realism of each first-person version, Kurosawa does not distort the literalness of the image. The story exists in an environment that is real, and therefore the audience will believe what is shown; the given "facts" become the truth unless clear reasons exist for the viewer to doubt these facts. Kurosawa had to find a way of avoiding two extremes: first, that each participant's version might become so firmly rooted in objective reality that audiences would accept all versions as true and turn the whole film into a paradox of alternative structures of reality, and second, that the presented evidence might be so blatantly false that the audience would dismiss each version out of hand.

The film's style is designed around the use of a moving camera that continually clarifies to the viewer that the angle of perception in a particular version belongs only to the speaker. As any judge knows, the eye-witness account can be deceptive, unintentionally or deliberately, regardless of the degree of personal involvement of the witness. In *Rashomon,* we are very quickly alerted to the narrators' highly personal involvement by the style of the film, and so we tend to accept the testimony of each of the participants only tentatively once we discover (during the second narration) that the versions are contradictory.

The moving camera emphasizes narrative subjectivity by establishing different rhythms for each narration. For instance, even before the versions are given, the woodcutter describes his discovery of the body. It is this tracking-through-the-woods sequence that so astounded critics at the 1951 Venice Film Festival and immediately established Kurosawa's reputation. Yet, assuredly, to Kurosawa the style of filming was integral to the characterization. The woodcutter is a simple man. His swift movement through the forest prior to discovering the body presents him in a happy, unassuming mood, though the music suggests an undercurrent of tension. Following this, the first narrative is quite different, though it contains even swifter movement through the forest. The bandit Tajomaru tells his story from a highly eccentric point of view, which ought to put us at some distance from him right away. His erratic personality is duplicated by the quickly shifting camera movements, quite different from the speedy tracking of the woodcutter's sequence.

The more slowly paced second and third versions contain much less camera movement because the narrators, the wife and the samurai, do not see the events in terms of the motions of all three characters interacting; rather they both see themselves performing very meaningful dramatic

gestures. Each is the tragic figure in his own version. As the wife recounts her tale, she stresses her predicament and her sensitive response to it: thus, we see her occupying most of the frame. Exactly the same is true of her husband telling about himself in the third version. The relative proportion of static camera arrangements is higher in these two versions than elsewhere in the film because each character portrays himself as a solo performer (a key clue to the unreliability of the accounts, by the way). In the fourth version, which presents the basic truth of the interior plot, the woodcutter sees everything from a detached point of view, for he is not a participant until after the central action is completed. To suggest his objectified viewpoint, the moving camera becomes once again prominent, creating a distancing effect and a satiric commentary on the lies of the other three versions.

In its exploration of the individual point of view, the camera does not, in the first three versions, show us the situation as it would have objectively appeared to the narrator during his participation in the events. Instead—and this is of course the chief clue—the camera focuses on the narrator as he expands upon his role in the drama. What we see then is not the narrator's perception of the event but his dramatization of his part as he pretends it would appear to some objective observer. That no such observer existed was the obvious understanding of the three lying participants. However, the fourth version is just that objective observation: an intruder, the woodcutter, happening upon the scene witnessed the events, though because of his shameful stealing of the dagger, he has not told his version to the authorities.

In the first version, the camerawork emphasizes the exaggerated, romantically childlike world of the bandit, Tajomaru. In the second, it reveals the vain posturing of the wife, Masago, as she re-enacts her fantasy in which her purity and innocence are victimized by the masculine brutality and evil of the world. In the third, the husband pictures himself as a man of such overwhelming nobility and sensitivity that he must commit suicide because the world cannot achieve his standard of humanism. The first three versions, by emphasizing the movement of the speaker, de-emphasize the other two characters. Therefore, the camerawork implicitly enlists in a conspiracy of concealment under the controlled description of each narrator. The camerawork in the fourth version is premised on revelation. Here, the woodcutter reveals to us what we might have guessed from our common-sense understanding of human motives for lying: that the husband, the wife, and the bandit are all culpable and embarrassed at having demonstrated to each other their own contemptibility. They are not so much hiding facts from the rest of the world as protecting themselves. And what they need to protect is not their physical beings, not even their reputations, but their true selves, which exemplify horrifying life-styles; they may vaguely know what they are, but they surely don't want to face the truth of it (fig. 51).

**51** *Rashomon*

In the fourth version, the camera movement suggestively comments on all of the previous camerawork, whether moving or stationary, by turning the mood of the three "serious" versions into comedy for the purpose of revealing truth. Tajomaru is no longer heroic, dashing, and fair-minded; instead, he becomes a clumsy fool, inept with the sword and uninspiring as a lover. The wife is no longer the beautiful victim of female frailty but the instigator of trouble, an excessively proud woman with no concern for the lives of either man. The samurai falls from the noble pedestal he erected for himself and is seen as a craven coward, the anti-samurai, who when placed in a position to defend his wife's honor pronounces what must be one of the greatest comic lines in the Japanese cinema: "I refuse to risk my life for such a woman." Much of the revelation that we get from the fourth sequence is communicated purely by the objective camera's reversing of the carefully fabricated moods established by the subjective camera in the other three versions. We learn, finally, that what was recorded by the camera was not reality but the distortions of each character.

The fourth version, then, is crucial to our perspective on the preceding versions. We have already looked at some of the evidence for establishing the validity of the woodcutter's story, to which we can add that the whole satiric revelation of the bandit-samurai encounter would be gratuitous if the final version were not the truth. In addition, the framing story would have meant nothing, for the obvious agony of the woodcutter throughout, his claims that human beings are shockingly depraved, and his desire to find meaning in the chaos of lies would have been sheer pre-

tense on his part, and a waste of his own effort in misleading the commoner and the priest for no conceivable reason. It is our conviction of the truth of the final version that makes the concluding action of the framing story relevant to the whole film. To make sure that this version would not be weighed merely as one more relative interpretation of the incidents, Kurosawa switched the camera's point of view to omit the narrator's presence, directly dramatizing the objective reality of the situation.

Kurosawa does not use the moving camera as a substitute for continual cutting. In fact, the published filmscript contains 407 shots (averaging about thirteen seconds in length), as high a number as is found in most films of this length that feature stationary shots. Kurosawa's unusual effectiveness with the moving camera depends on cutting from one moving shot to another, a technical difficulty in most films even when the movement is slower than in *Rashomon*. Cutting on movement usually has a disorienting effect unless the area is perfectly clear from the context, which is the case here.

As the area is a general one—the particularity of this grove as distinct from some other grove is unimportant—the audience has no difficulty in comprehending spatial relationships. This might be contrasted to Kurosawa's method of establishing the area of the Rashomon for the framing story: the film opens with several shots, primarily stationary, at varying distances from the characters (the woodcutter and the priest), for it is extremely important for the audience to perceive exactly the peculiar area that serves as the environment of the framing story. In contrast, the moving camera in the interior stories limits the absolute clarity of our impressions of the grove, for if we were totally familiar with it, it might begin to seem boring; that it never does, even in the fourth version, is an indication that Kurosawa has taken great care to photograph it in a variety of ways, but in such a manner that we have not truly bothered to distinguish one tree from another.

In its separate functions within specific shots, the moving camera serves primarily to emphasize various discoveries made by the characters or to reveal dramatically to the audience certain aspects of the situation depicted. In the tracking scene in which the woodcutter finds the body, we have a series of moving shots cut together from a variety of angles and distances producing at first simply a sense of swiftness, and finally an effect of tension. The audience gradually becomes aware that the woodcutter's journey is heading toward a momentous discovery. The cutting includes some shots of the sun seen through the trees, an ominous suggestion of external observation, ours or nature's, of an event of some significance, a Conradian journey into darkness.

Where movement has been made normative, the stationary camera can be used with shocking abruptness, as it is in this sequence. After about fifteen shots, in most of which the man is moving as well as the camera, the

woodcutter in close-up comes to a complete halt and the music stops. This is followed by a stationary medium shot of the man looking at a woman's hat and a veil. He continues his movement, and the camera moves with him, until he suddenly makes another discovery, a man's hat. He bends down to pick it up; then another discovery, an amulet case. He begins to move forward but almost immediately he stumbles as the camera pans. He jumps back and we see a close shot of stiffly raised hands, obviously of a corpse, completing the initial discovery. By moving along with the wood-cutter in setting up this discovery, the camera puts us in immediate contact with the man's psychological state, which is absolutely simple: sheer frightened surprise. The simplicity of his reaction strikes us as normal enough, but it is actually a fabrication, a simulation of the elemental response he deems satisfactory to the police investigations. In order to make his story convincing to the police, he had to contrive the entire sequence of moving through the woods as a man with no concern in the world—just a man at one with nature in an environment perfectly natural to him—until he discovers the body of a person killed in some act of violence.

The movement of the camera to portray discovery can represent either a subjective or an objective view. When in the first version Tajomaru is seen sleeping under a tree, the audience shares his initial perception of the samurai and his wife. As the camera moves close to Tajomaru's face, we see his eye open, and then in a most gracefully executed movement, the camera quickly turns about at a right angle to reveal the samurai and his wife in the distance and Tajomaru's head close to the camera. We are made to see not only what Tajomaru saw (or said he saw), but the guise that he wishes us to see him in: the relaxed bandit so much at ease that he can pretend to be asleep at the approach of strangers, and a man much attracted to the pretty woman he sees through the corner of his eye but completely in control of his mannerisms at her approach. Tajomaru's discovery of the approaching figures is described so as to add to his self-characterization as a sophisticated, cunning bandit.

In the fourth version, the moving camera is used to reveal the anti-heroic movements of the three participants. In a series of comic shots that begins with Masago's accusing her husband of cowardice for not fighting for her, the camera pans with her as she moves away from him, eliminating him from the frame. Next, she advances upon Tajomaru, accusing him of the same kind of cowardice, even spitting in his face, and followed by the camera, she moves away, symbolically dismissing the two men who were about to abandon her. With the woman between them but back far enough so as not to be in the line of their movement toward each other, the men, properly embarrassed, draw their swords. Four mid-shots are intercut showing the men advancing timidly toward each other. Next comes a remarkably effective shot that starts as a close-up of Masago as she nervously watches the men. As the camera dollies back to reveal more of the area,

we see that in front of Masago the two men are about to cross swords. We do not see the men, only the tips of their swords, shaking extravagantly from their mutual fear of battle. As the swords touch, we discover the full extent of their fear in the long shot that follows: the two men stumble backwards, the samurai flees, Tajomaru follows and trips; the men swing wildly at each other and then run in opposite directions, as confused as they are frightened.

Another way in which Kurosawa's visual style affects our perception of the characters in this film is through the frequent dissociations of the characters from their environment, an effect brought about by quick camera movements. When characters' actions in the foreground necessitate frequent camera movements, the background is visually de-emphasized as our attention is focused on the physical activity. A stationary camera tends to relate characters to each other and their mutual background, and in this film such a procedure might work against the inherent subjectivity of the various narrations. For example, Tajomaru describes how, as the three characters first came together, he offered to lead the samurai to some valuable swords he pretended to have found. As Tajomaru crosses back and forth in front of the samurai and his wife, trying to size them up and perhaps intimidate them, the camera movement emphasizes the self-confidence conveyed by his gesture. A stationary shot would more likely have emphasized the drama inherent in the scene, giving more weight to the samurai's response than Tajomaru as narrator would have desired.

Although less noticeable there than in the four versions of the central event, the moving camera helps convey the meaning of the framing story as well. The frame filters the diffuse pieces of information we observe in the interior stories, simplifying the ideas into basically distinguishable attitudes toward the meaning of the narrative as a whole. The art of *Rashomon* requires both a commentary on and a reaction to the contradictory versions of the narrative, and Kurosawa determines to shape that commentary-reaction itself into a narrative, immediately enlarging the scope of the implications of all that we have seen.

The movement of the framing story concerning the activities of the woodcutter, the priest, and the commoner from an atmosphere of despair to one of hope is depicted in the most basic of all images, the weather: it rains throughout the film and finally stops. The symbol suggests that the human actions have taken part in a general movement toward a restoration of the normal order of things. As an external comment on the development of the film's mood, the symbol can be effective because it powerfully represents what we observe from the action itself.

The predicament is presented in these terms: living in the worst of all possible times, confronted with extraordinary examples of human treachery, failure, selfishness, and hypocrisy, should man live in continual suspicion of his fellow men, always expecting the worst of them, or should he—in

**52** *Rashomon* (The priest, the commoner, and the woodcutter)

spite of the reality of man's infinite capacity for evil actions—still retain his faith in men? To sustain this very broad issue, Kurosawa arranges for the camera to establish general positions swiftly and concretely in regard to the two key elements. First, he depicts the immediate environment as symbolic of the worst of all times; second, he uses his three characters to stand for the three possible reactions to the conditions of the age. At the beginning the woodcutter stands for the divided man who does not know what position to take about human nature, having just witnessed some incredible examples of dishonesty and distortion; he represents the man seeking the truth. The commoner is the cynic, who if he is influenced at all changes for the worse by the end. The priest starts as the affirming character who insists on believing in the better nature of man, though as a victim of his age he has seen enough to shake his faith even before the film begins (fig. 52).

As for the environment, clearly Kurosawa does not really insist on a specific time and place. He has no particular interest in twelfth-century Kyoto (the town is not shown). But Kyoto may have some symbolic value for the Japanese audience: as the title preceding the first shot says, it is a time "when famines and civil wars had devastated the ancient capital." We see none of this. What Kurosawa takes care to make us see in a number

of shots against which the film's opening titles are flashed is the Rashomon gate during a tremendous downpour. It could be any ruined edifice anywhere, and of course any time. But this is the gate of an ancient capital, the symbol of a civilization in decline. The world seems to have declined as far as possible; the disasters, as the priest mentions later, are not limited to man's sins: "Wars, earthquakes, great winds, fires, famines, plagues—each new year is full of disaster." Nothing is offered to counter the gloom so definitely conjured up by the characters. The camera at the very beginning establishes the area in a traditional way, using mostly stationary shots, first showing us the gate, then focusing on the priest and woodcutter. The sense of confinement is heightened by closer shots, capturing the men against some small but noticeably unattractive portion of the background.

After each version of the central incident, we return to the framing story and the re-establishment of the somber atmosphere in part depicted by the moving camera. For instance, after Tajomaru's version, we have a close shot of the rain pouring on top of the Rashomon, and the camera tilts down to reveal the three men below in an oppressive shot accompanied only by the sound of the rain. After Masago's version, the camera returns to the steps of the Rashomon, focusing on the effect of the rain beating down in a shot that reveals the men in the background, gradually tilting up to them. After the samurai's version, the camera switches to the interior of the Rashomon, this time panning rather than tilting to reveal the agitated motion of the woodcutter. On the return to the Rashomon after the fourth version, we see another long shot of the interior, half of it blocked by a large beam; but now the camera does not move as in the other re-establishing shots.

The tone for the final sequence of the film is at first despondent. The commoner, a total cynic, is not surprised at the depravity of the participants, which he accepts as natural conduct. In fact, he assumes that the woodcutter is lying, and eventually forces an implicit confession from him about the theft of the dagger. The commoner raises the underlying issue of the film. If men will normally lie when their own interests are involved, then, as the priest says, "earth becomes a kind of hell." And the commoner's immediate cynical reply to this possibility is: "You are right. The world we live in is a hell." The priest claims he does not want to believe this, but he knows that his spiritual surety is in deep trouble. Facing the realism of the commoner and the muddled shock of the woodcutter, he can offer no reasonable or instinctive argument against the prevailing gloomy evidence. He has only his will to believe.

At the moment when the three positions are fully presented and the argument seems to have reached an impasse, waiting upon an event that will transform the stated attitudes into cinematic action, we suddenly hear the crying of an infant. Although the introduction of a baby is unprepared for and does not grow out of the plot, the baby's being abandoned there is not

implausible. The baby, in any case, is intended as a test of the attitudes previously articulated: cynicism, doubt, and indecision. Certainly, it is an imposition upon the plot, but everything in the film is imposed artificially into a world meant to suggest a generalized allegorical setting rather than a historically distinct place and time.

Hearing the cry, the commoner rushes off to find the baby: he acts promptly, on the motive that there might be some gain for him if he can locate the infant first; the other two are less decisive. The camera moves with them as they go to investigate the sound and discover the commoner stealing the baby's clothes. Thus the situation has come down to the basic problem of how to respond to any new incident outside the normal course of events. Since this world hovers on the edge of chaos, something unusual ought to be expected: new disasters happen all the time, babies are abandoned, men killed, women attacked. The interior story, though melodramatic, poses the problem of how to react in the face of an unprepared-for event. The cynical commoner insists that in this age everyone lies and steals, and the only crime is getting caught; only the fool does not take advantage of his opportunities. Thus, the stealing of a baby's clothes, an atrocious moral action, becomes permissible, even advisable, conduct. The other two are shocked. When the woodcutter insists on moral condemnation of the commoner, the commoner accuses the woodcutter of stealing the dagger. The woodcutter is abashed by his guilt feelings, and the commoner, convinced he has won the argument, leaves the ancient gate laughing.

Left alone, the priest holding the baby and the woodcutter standing next to him, the two men watch the rain for an apparently long time, as indicated by three dissolves, the first a long shot, the second closer, and the third closer yet. Between the men and the camera, dominating the visuals and the sounds, falls the rain. The men stand silently, until the rain begins to stop. During the time they spend watching the rain they have been considering the adequacy of their positions. The question of whether to trust in man had been answered with an overwhelming negative by the commoner before he left. We see in the final sequence of the last four minutes of *Rashomon* that the priest has lost his faith, his simplistic belief in man's potentiality for unselfish action.

Therefore, the only possibility of redemption lies with the woodcutter, but he has experienced a moral crisis. He has been pushed into a paralytic position by the commoner, who made him grasp the similarity of all kinds of theft. Seeing his moral culpability and relationship to the commoner, the woodcutter is overwhelmed by sobering reflection. The theme Kurosawa is subtly affirming is that after all the commoner was wrong: men still retain the capacity for acting unselfishly. The woodcutter was right when he noted that all evil is committed by men ready to find excuses for their conduct, which means that regardless of their actions men retain a moral consciousness, and thus a potentiality for redemption.

As the priest starts to move away after the rain stops, the woodcutter approaches him and indicates that he will take the baby. At this gesture, the priest recoils vehemently and shouts, "What are you trying to do? Take away what little it has left?" Thus, in this remark, the priest's conversion to the commoner's view is confirmed. He is absolutely suspicious of the woodcutter, who has all along appeared a gentle man. The woodcutter immediately explains himself in so humble a way that he cannot be doubted. He says: "I have six children of my own. One more wouldn't make it any more difficult." This indirect answer quite eloquently summarizes the situation. The priest is suddenly made aware of his own lack of charity, his misconception of human nature. In a flash, his previous humanistic view is shown to have its justification in the woodcutter's unselfish offer to take the child.

It is a simple action, but the significance of this proof destroys the contention of the commoner that all men must act always in their own interest. That was the commoner's justification for his conduct, and also indirectly his explanation of the conduct of the bandit, the samurai, and the wife. Yet the film finally makes it clear that even in the chaotic disorder of that world, man can rise above his baser inclinations. Nothing is beyond the capacity of the depraved man, no evil unimaginable. Yet on the other hand, the film shows that it is not the circumstances that make men depraved but the weak character of man that makes him susceptible to committing evil under the guise of necessity (*i.e.,* self-interest).

Evil is not eliminated by any number of good actions, but the premise that evil is essential for human conduct is destroyed by a single good act. The last words are the priest's, and he underscores Kurosawa's theme by telling the woodcutter that because of him, "I think I will be able to keep my faith in men." In the next-to-last shot, the camera tracks with the woodcutter as he leaves the Rashomon carrying the infant. As he recedes, the powerful visual image of the sunny sky is seen behind him and the gate. When he moves outside the frame, the camera stops, leaving us with a long shot of the priest seen in the distance, watching after the woodcutter. The final picture is of the signboard over the gate. These last few shots of *Rashomon* reverse the impression of chaos and disaster established in the beginning. The sun replacing the rain reminds us that the sense of disaster and disorder implanted earlier had much more to do with the atmosphere created by the characters than with the weather. The state of mind induced in the characters may very well be reflected by the weather, but it is not determined by it. There can be no doubt that Kurosawa intended the final images of the film to suggest a restoration of moral order. The priest is left in a state of renewed hope, and the reason for it is clearly seen in the woodcutter's going off with the infant. The sunlight symbolizes the moral affirmation underlying the framing story, and it is revealed to us by a moving camera shot that is consistent with those moving shots that have determined the stylistic integrity of *Rashomon.*

# Editing
# Through
# Fragmentation

## Categories of Editing

The ultimate realization of the film idea occurs in the process of editing. Allowing for the real possibility that some directors rather fully edit their films mentally before shooting, we can still claim that the arrangement of shots is the key to the construction of the artistic work. The popular concept of editing as mainly "cutting"—reducing the length of film footage produced by a nonselective director—has never had much basis in reality. The process of editing entails more than just cutting away the excess. Since a film is shot entirely in fragments, editing becomes a way of conceiving the totality of those fragments. In the process of editing, the fragments are often themselves broken up (as when a shot is divided for the intercutting of a close-up). Finally, after extensive evaluation, the fragments are assembled in such a way that no reordering would express exactly the same meaning.

Many contemporary critics seem to denigrate editing by the dubious division of filmmakers into two schools: those who rely on editing to accomplish what they did not do in filming—that is, convey ideas in terms of the shots—and those who have basically expressed themselves without relying on the juxtapositions of the editing process in order to convey ideas. In the first group are Eisenstein, Griffith, and those silent film directors

who are out of favor with these critics. In the second group we find Renoir and many of their current favorites. The division creates a complete falsification and an essentially meaningless dichotomy, for all great filmmakers conceive of their materials in terms of edited sequences. If one counts the number of shots in a film by a supposed exponent of one method, he likely will find no great difference from the number of shots in any film by a supposed representative of the other school. Since shots are never simply strung together, even in the worst commercial products, all filmmakers must conceive of their films as becoming ultimately completely edited works.

Nevertheless, the persistence of so overwhelming a misconception among critics of some stature (it might in fact have started with the esteemed French critic André Bazin) indicates that indeed some difference exists in the way that filmmakers look at the business of constructing their sequences. Renoir, after all, differs from Eisenstein—though he is more like Eisenstein and every other important filmmaker than unlike them. The critics who try to establish a hierarchy of talent based solely on the difference between Renoir and Eisenstein are misdirected. In fact, they cannot retain a consistent esthetic standard in their categories because two of the currently admired filmmakers, Hitchcock and Lang, are much closer to Eisenstein in editing than to Renoir, and no system of strictly formalist categorizing can bring those two directors closer in line to Renoir than to Eisenstein.

Categories of some sort remain essential, however, for certain distinctions help us to understand how filmmakers differ in style. We are not speaking about content, though the choice of content is in part determined by the prior attitudes of a filmmaker; he will not willingly accept assignments (if he has the choice) that do not lend themselves to his view of the world. Yet categories established only by subject matter are misleading for the cinema, since the very nature of the industry system compels filmmakers to handle a remarkably wide variety of subjects if they wish to work frequently.

The categories on which this and the following chapter are based are two rather broad stylistic approaches that cut across any conceivable subject categories. These two basic approaches to editing characterize a distinctly different feeling for the film idea: one is analytic, the other synthetic. Nevertheless, among the major filmmakers, the analytic and synthetic processes frequently appear within the same film, which proves that the two approaches must be regarded primarily as conceptual tendencies rather than opposed styles. In other words, Renoir will usually put together his images in order to synthesize the various aspects of his ideas, but there are sequences in his works (such as the rabbit hunt in *Rules of the Game*) that show that from time to time he conceived of particular ideas from the analytic point of view. Similarly, Hitchcock, whose approach is largely analytic, creates a number of sequences based on the other method, as in the expository opening sequences in *Psycho*. In contrast, directors with no

noticeable stylistic consistency seem to edit films without any particular tendency to use one or the other procedure—both procedures may be used, but it is often hard to figure out which method dominates when a filmmaker's style seems indeterminate.

The majority of films from the sound era on are undoubtedly put together with a roughly formulated process of synthesis because the film idea commonly evolves from the dialogue. In most ordinary films, the editing of the visuals is determined by the ideas expressed in the dialogue in any particular sequence, which often means merely the simple splicing together of pictures to reinforce the sound. This and the following chapter assume some deliberate thinking on the part of a filmmaker rather than strict subservience to another man's literary scenario or a studio-appointed film editor.

## The Development of the Analytic Approach

The basic procedure for editing worked out by Edwin Porter relied on a synthesis of segments of film action. It remained a primitive method because it was not flexible enough to allow for any suggestiveness on the part of a shot. Instead, the shot in a Porter film had to be explicit to the degree that it communicated a meaningful part of the action, intelligible in itself even removed from the context. Porter's conception of editing was limited to the function of linking segments of a narrative together. The process of analyzing the segment itself was developed by Griffith, with the result that in a few years Porter's method fell into permanent disuse. The Porter film could never be totally cinematic because the unanalyzed segment (that is, the single-shot sequence) included so much pictorial information, so many surface details, that it could deal with life only in the most objective manner: it became a wide-ranging recorder of reality, but this was not to be the ultimate achievement of the motion picture narrative.

Porter's synthetic approach to editing was not the forerunner of the accumulative kind of synthesis discussed in the next chapter, for Porter's concept of a film did not include building up a film idea; rather, each self-contained segment was an equal aspect of the film idea. The boarding of the train and the robbing of the train certainly share equal cinematic interest in *The Great Train Robbery,* and both are aspects of a film idea that simply consists in showing how a robbery is carried out. Porter was concerned primarily with a continuously moving narrative, not with a film idea that revealed itself in progressive stages or with increasing complexity.

The film sense that Porter lacked and Griffith excelled in drove Griffith to experiment with the nature of the film idea as looked at from a point of view completely opposite from Porter's. Instead of seeing the filmmaker's job as simply the joining together of appropriate steps for completing the

narrative design, Griffith started with an idea and contemplated a method for breaking it down into constituent parts. At first the parts served to develop the plot in much the same way as in Porter, but eventually, as they became shorter, they began to contain the film idea in a fragmented form. By 1912, a film no longer consisted of distinct segments that could be put together to re-establish the narrative whole. Replacing the segments were clusters of shots—sequences—that stood for a part of the narrative idea, but were attached one to the other in so complicated a way that the idea was disrupted or made ambiguous by the omission of a shot or two in any cluster. In fact, some of Griffith's short films are today difficult to follow, either because some shots are missing or because Griffith's early technique was faulty, leading him to omit some materials he thought were obvious but turn out not to be.

If in Porter the film had been composed of segments of narrative action, in Griffith the film became fragments of human responses and gestures, brief selections of human activities that were made to reflect that larger sphere of life that art can never capture whole in any medium of expression. Whereas Porter had isolated an activity—a train robbery or a fire-fighting adventure—and depicted it in terms of its separate actions at each stage in the narrative, Griffith looked to the total environment to select images of parts of human activity representative of the larger context, we might say, of the stream of life.

Yet in Griffith's films, the sense of narrative structure is so prominent that audiences were able to follow his stories even though his technique was new. He never used his superb gifts to create "experimental" cinema or nonnarrative or purely poetic experience. He had no particular interest in moving away from the vision of life his films suggested into the realm of nonrepresentational art or unpatterned human activity. Therefore, some casual observers of Griffith's art regard it as an early attempt to derive a narrative form, in a mode that is today outdated. Actually, what fell out of fashion, though perhaps only temporarily, is the kind of Dickensian plot structure Griffith imposed upon the materials of his films. However, in regard to technique, Griffith did not merely introduce the analytical approach to editing, he also developed it virtually as far as it was ever to go. Nevertheless, because of the fact that Griffith originated this approach and the Russians of the 1920's continued the practice and analyzed Griffith's procedures, film historians have generally credited the Russians with the contribution of this kind of editing.

Therefore, the man most often associated with the analytic approach is Sergei Eisenstein, a great filmmaker and theoretician whose *writings* in fact go beyond the *practice* of Griffith's films. On the other hand, it seems questionable whether the actual effects of an Eisenstein film deviate at all from the effects of the similar techniques in Griffith's work. The real difference between the filmmakers probably lies in the distinct kind of nar-

rative structure each designed for his materials. Eisenstein, in spite of his considerable knowledge of English and American literature (surely he was a more perceptive and analytical reader than Griffith), did not work with the fictional story film. His completed film ideas reflected first mass social movements and later (when the official Soviet line changed) certain heroes, Alexander Nevsky and Ivan the Terrible, who summed up national qualities within a historical period. For the Western audience, however, Eisenstein's films do not provoke the kind of immediate emotional involvement associated with the style of the typical Dickens-Griffith American film. What American audiences see in a film like *Alexander Nevsky* is a marvelous display of film technique in an interesting story; but lacking a fictional framework or a national allegiance, Western audiences do not identify with any particular character. There is plenty of emotional material in Eisenstein, but without the strong sense of character identification, audiences were more conscious of the technique, the handling of the individual events, than they had been with Griffith.

## Some Characteristics of Fragmented Sequences: Hitchcock's *The Thirty-Nine Steps*

That faculty of mind most adaptable to the analytic approach habitually conceives of an idea that can be grasped all at once by some striking arrangement of details within a sequence. Before a viewer understands the total import of the sequence or segment of the sequence, however, he grasps merely the relationship of detail to detail. Thus, a viewer's perception of the total is restricted by the filmmaker's refusal to show everything at once. We undoubtedly see the elements of an idea more clearly when we study them in pieces than when they are presented all together. This theory is supported by the traditional development of the art of filming from the early exclusive reliance on the long shot to the increasing use of closer shots that isolated details of reality for emphasis and clarity.

The approach to filmmaking that leads to the dissection of the sequence, the analytic approach, tends at first to appear highly intellectual and scientific. It begins with the conception of an event in terms of its minutest meaningful particles, and when successfully executed it results in the construction (or reconstruction) of an episode in which the whole sequence depends on the exactness of each part. The sequence in the mind of an analytic filmmaker can be likened to a completed jigsaw puzzle. When scrambled, the separate pieces become almost meaningless, each piece in fact containing only a minimum of meaning in itself. But when assembled, the whole is evident and complete, and the process of putting the pieces together does not obtrude on the finished pattern. Removing one piece, however, attracts attention to the process and makes it seem markedly in-

complete or ineffective. The sequence, like the jigsaw puzzle with the missing piece, is then unsuccessful.

In theory, the filmmaker who proceeds to dissect an idea into its parts works backwards—that is, from the whole idea of a sequence he deductively seeks out the particulars; but since the practice is a matter of personal creative imagination, it need not concern us. In a movie theater, the film made by an analytic process reveals itself in much the same way as the one produced through synthesis in the sense that it must proceed shot by shot to build up each sequence. Obviously, then, for one method of film editing to be distinguished from another, we must concentrate on the effects, not the artist's derivation of his idea.

We have already seen that the single shot by itself functions as a unit of information rather than the vehicle for a fully articulated idea. If within a sequence each additional shot tends to develop a logical progression with the preceding shots, then the filmmaker is synthesizing his materials, accumulating his images in a way that is quite evident during the process. On the other hand, if the particular shot tends to present information that does not immediately seem an outgrowth of the points being developed by the previous shots, or if it simply presents one more piece of information we are to hold in abeyance until other shots complete the idea, we are perceiving an idea from an analytic point of view.

We are not confused by a sequence developed according to a process that has fragmented the idea for us because we do not look for the same things as we do with the other kind of editing. Instead, we become interested in the array of materials, visual and verbal, being structured for us by the filmmaker. The manner in which shots link up to form psychological connections may be particularly engrossing, as it seldom is in the process of synthesizing a sequence. However, most viewers will be less conscious of the direction in a film that presents them with a series of heterogeneous images that do not immediately join together in a self-evident progression. On the other hand, the bombardment of disjointed images in the analytic process frequently creates suspense and tension to a greater degree than the alternative process.

Even more characteristic of the two approaches is the nature of the specifications within the shots. The synthetic process tends to establish an environment and keep us constantly in touch with the spatial reality of it. In contrast, the analytic filmmaker tends to dissect the environment, to feature the part rather than the whole, and thus to some extent to remove the totality of the environment from our constant perception. Relying on synthesis, one director will choose to locate his characters firmly in a place in order to set up an action within the frame, whereas, relying on analysis, another director will prefer to cut from one part of the environment to another, the action really occurring along with the movement from shot to shot.

Hitchcock, one of the most consistently analytic directors, prefers to create an environment in terms of extremely meaningful details rather than through the usual techniques of establishing shots. This is because his highly developed sense of economy or precision allows him to select just those details from an environment that the characters themselves will either notice or use in the course of the film sequence. In *The Thirty-Nine Steps* (1935), the first twenty-minute segment, which serves to establish the plot movement of a spy-chase narrative, is an impressive example of how Hitchcock creates meaning through his style of editing. Almost all the shots revealing the environment in which the hero moves suggest confusion; indeed, no real distinction is made between the world as the audience sees it and as the character himself experiences it. The story concerns a Canadian visiting London. A sophisticated man alone in a large city, with no apparent acquaintances, he seems, in this crowded and impersonal environment, a passive observer of the multitude of barely connected images that impress themselves upon him, beginning with the opening shot of the flashing letters on a music hall.

The correlation between the visual images, sounds, and dialogue on the one hand and the mental state of the Canadian on the other derives from Hitchcock's selection of specifications that contain highly interesting cinematic details. Before seeing any faces, we see hands buying a ticket and feet walking into a theater. The hero sits in the hall watching a vaudeville show that features a fascinating memory expert. A riot ensues, which seems almost natural, given the confined area, the spirits of the crowd, and the general carnival atmosphere; the firing of a gun produces a panic, emptying the hall. Outside, the Canadian is accosted by a strange woman, who urges him to take her to his apartment. The man, who is both genial and experienced in the ways of the world, acquiesces but is quite surprised, for his head has not fully absorbed the previous impressions of the riot (fig. 53). At his apartment the woman insists that she is a free-lance spy, and though he does not believe her he allows her to stay the night in a separate room. Up to this point, like the hero, the audience has found all the events extremely interesting but thoroughly confusing.

Hitchcock has contrived, by means of the editing, to establish in the first sections of *The Thirty-Nine Steps* a sense of the fragmentation of city life, at least as it must appear to an outsider, an observer, an intelligent man who is intent on taking it all in but cannot because it all moves too rapidly and seems chaotic. The art behind this depiction of chaos is perfectly ordered, as we begin to understand once Hitchcock completes the exposition of the hero's predicament. The completion is the woman's murder during the early morning; she manages to get to the room where the man is sleeping and mumble something about the "Thirty-Nine Steps" before she collapses with a knife in her back. Instantly, the chaos of the preceding night's images begins to take some shape, and the hero is forced into an

**53** *The Thirty-Nine Steps*

involvement in an espionage plot. Before the murder, the images were mainly amusing. The man was entertained by the variety of the evening's experiences, but until the woman's murder he could not regard anything he had witnessed as significant.

Thus, the point of the Hitchcock film is brought home to the hero—and to the audience—with a sudden desperate immediacy. Hitchcock analyzes the same pattern in many films: an innocent man, with no particular problems, is suddenly thrown into a situation of imminent peril. The peril is accentuated in this film because the editing—which has the purpose of showing us the fragmented impressions of the hero's world—has also produced a sense of passivity in us and in him. Coming out of the vaudeville hall and meeting the woman, he never addressed the world with the question, What will I do now? but rather seemed to ask, What will I see next? *The Thirty-Nine Steps* concerns a man who suddenly awakens to find himself alone in the midst of an emergency (he will almost immediately be hunted by the police as a murderer and by the gang of spies as a threat). The dramatic question arises, then, as to how such a man will react to the dangers, or how he can meet the challenge of his existence. The effectiveness of the editing lies in its ability to involve us very deeply and dramatically in the hero's predicament so that we experience with him the sudden awareness of the implications of his situation.

# Eisenstein's Analytic Theory

The classic example of analytic editing through fragmentation of the idea of the sequence is found in Sergei Eisenstein's work, particularly *Potemkin*. Eisenstein himself, as a renowned theoretician, has written about sections of the film and commented on its structure, but neither Eisenstein nor anyone else ever really attempted to create another film in precisely the same fashion as *Potemkin*. Nevertheless, its style became the model for a certain type of approach to filmmaking. The word applied to Eisenstein's method is "montage"—a symbolic rather than apt description, since this French word meant more or less "editing," with perhaps a slight suggestion of assembling shots in distinction to the American word "cutting" with its slight suggestion of the elimination of the excessive.

As his basic principle, Eisenstein holds that *"the shot is a montage cell (or molecule)."* * The vehemence of his repeated assertions that the shot is a montage cell reflects his running disagreement with another director and theoretician, Vsevolod Pudovkin, Eisenstein's great contemporary. Pudovkin and others supported the concept of montage as a means of presenting an idea by a series of visual images, the rhythm being determined by the length of the shots. Therefore, to Pudovkin each shot stands as a fixed element of the montage. Eisenstein, scornfully dismissing this theory (which of course has obviously been accepted as the editing principle by many filmmakers) as "metric montage," which he calls a "completely false concept!" insists that the shot is not an element, but a montage cell, which both shapes the total context and derives its meaning from that context. The distinction lies in the degree of specification one comprehends in the shot. Pudovkin would seem to support the more popular view: the shot's information is absorbed consecutively by the spectator as each new image appears. In contrast, Eisenstein argues that since viewers perceive shots one atop another (see p. 13), the specifications do not produce an additive effect but virtually a simultaneous one.

He points out that shot $A$ followed by shot $B$ occurs only on the film celluloid itself. In the mind of the spectator, shot $A$ is not merely followed by shot $B$, nor do $A$ and $B$ together produce $A + B$ or $AB$. What is produced is $X$, an entirely new perception, the explanation of which lies in physiology (the brain's retention of visual images) and psychology (including the spectator's emotional response to the appearance of shot $A$ and shot $B$). The *collision* of shots $A$ and $B$ to produce the new element $X$ underlies Eisenstein's conception of cinematic art: images in visual conflict. But since the single shot is a cell, conflict also occurs within the single shot itself. Eisenstein lists nine such internal possibilities for the silent film:

* Eisenstein, *op. cit.*, p. 53.

(1) conflict of linear directions

(2) conflict of planes

(3) conflict of volumes

(4) spatial conflict

(5) light conflict

(6) tempo conflict

(7) conflict between matter and viewpoint (*i.e.,* through unusual camera angle)

(8) conflict between matter and its spatial nature (*i.e.,* through lens distortion)

(9) conflict between an event and its temporal nature (*e.g.,* slow motion) *

The shots, the montage cells, are not truly meaningful individually, even though each contains elements of conflict. Only when the cells are assembled in an organic relationship does meaning become possible. Each shot, however, achieves some emotional association in the mind of the viewer.

From his basic ideas about dynamic editing, Eisenstein went on in *Potemkin* and later films to evolve methods of editing the hundreds of individual shots that go into any film along the lines of his new principles, such as the principle of "shock attractions": for example, a shot of a baby carriage rolling down the Odessa Steps is followed by a shot of the horrified look of a man turning his head to watch the carriage. During the process of shooting the sequence, of course, the two shots were not filmed at the same time; later, at the time of editing, Eisenstein juxtaposed a shot of a child's carriage with a shot of a man turning his head. The associations of the carriage rolling and the man's head moving and of the catastrophe of the event and the horror expressed in the man's face are predetermined by the director according to his knowledge of audience psychology. In addition, Eisenstein employs other, more complicated methods of cutting, such as rhythmic montage, tonal montage, overtonal montage, and intellectual montage; these methods, though extremely technical, tend to enlarge our views of the possibilities for creating significant meaning in the film form.

## Eisenstein's *Potemkin*

What affected American viewers on first seeing *Potemkin* (1925) was mainly the remarkable technical facility demonstrated by the young Russian director. Certainly the subject of the film, an incident during the

* *Ibid.,* p. 54.

abortive revolution of 1905, could not possibly have engrossed Western audiences. On the other hand, Eisenstein's own commitment to Marxist doctrine and to the film as a mass medium designed to appeal to and educate millions of illiterate Russian peasants must have influenced his conception of the narrative. As intellectualized as the film may appear to Western viewers, especially if they know anything of Eisenstein's rather difficult theorizing based on the film, *Potemkin* has to be judged not merely as technique but as a film idea that addresses itself immediately to audiences of every level.

After all, in spite of his theorizing about the intellectual processes of filmmaking, Eisenstein communicates primarily by means of emotion or intuition. His strength lies in the skillful way he attaches an idea to a series of shots so that it becomes immediately understandable on an emotional level—long before the usual rational procedures of the mind can analyze the idea. The process of analysis is the filmmaker's; the result of this analysis, the finished film itself, does not require analytic perception while we watch it.

The early part of the film concerns the growing discontent of the sailors aboard the battleship *Potemkin*. The tyranny of the officers is portrayed visually in a number of ways that probably are not consciously noticed by most spectators until Eisenstein directs our attention to some overt tyrannical action; then, because we have been subconsciously prepared, we feel very strongly the emotional aspects of the men's predicament. For example, the visual design of the early sequences prior to the mutiny contains, among several other details, the following:

(1) The serious facial expressions of the oppressed crew, which indicate the men's continuous concern about conditions. In contrast, the officers' faces express scorn or contempt. Furthermore, the officers all relate to each other pictorially by the neat uniforms they wear, which become a mark of the class distinctions aboard the ship (the officers come undoubtedly from the upper classes, whereas all the sailors come from the lower classes).

(2) The appearance of the officers almost always on higher levels of the ship than the sailors. The sailors are frequently photographed so that their heads are lower than the level of the officers' feet.

(3) Several shots of a young sailor showing him facing an officer from such an angle that the sunlight catches him through some grillwork. The contrast between the officer in the light and the sailor with the shadows of the grille across his face and body suggests both mental and physical confinement.

Thus, when the first significant crisis arises, we grasp it in terms of a pre-established pattern of mistreatment of the sailors. The men who refuse

to eat soup made from maggoty meat are summoned to the quarter-deck by the commander in order to be punished. Because of the numerous corroborating details that we have perceived such as the memorable close-up of maggots on the meat, we assume that this particular injustice represents merely another outrage entirely characteristic of the ship's command. Yet all the details by themselves were not essentially meaningful except as Eisenstein structured them. Even the maggoty meat, as revolting as it looks, presents no clear idea regarding a pattern of mistreatment because it is a highly particularized incident. Yet by a clever juxtaposition of the maggoty meat sequence and the following sequence, which shows the men cleaning and polishing parts of the ship (which we assume is a regular occurrence), Eisenstein re-creates in our minds the former sequence as a symbol of the continual life aboard the ship. Shots of cleaning the cannons and polishing the engine parts by themselves relay entirely neutral specifications; however, the total sequence illustrates the conscientious effort of the crew to keep the ship clean—as a comment on the unconscionable effort of the officers to get the men to eat unclean meat, as seen in the previous sequence.

The sequence on the quarter-deck culminates in a readily understandable mutiny, set off by a sailor who intercedes just in time to prevent an official slaughter—the commander has ordered the malcontents shot (fig. 54). The sailor cries out to the guardsmen, "Brothers!" and they put down their rifles, refusing to carry out orders and recognizing their kinship with

the men about to be slaughtered. In the ensuing battle, the sailor is killed by an enraged officer, but the mutiny succeeds completely.

From the very beginning we have been gradually induced to yield our total sympathy to the suffering humanity aboard the ship. A great number of rather brief images merge to present us with various fragments of the men's day-to-day reality as they themselves might see it. The information proceeds at a pace too rapid to allow us to objectify the situation and consider the possibility of an alternative point of view. Actually, even if the pace of the cutting were much slower, we would still be unable to derive a perspective on the situation any different from the one intended by Eisenstein because the specifications we receive are not truly meaningful until the sequence is completed, or at least until the series of shots analyzing the particular incident is finished. The fragmented nature of the presentation indeed makes us somewhat passive recipients of the information until the filmmaker channels it in a certain direction. While we are still unsure of the direction of a particular theme within a sequence, we are storing up all the relevant information Eisenstein deems appropriate, and thus the sudden awareness of what the event signifies (not just a mutiny but a coming together of the oppressed seamen in their realization of their common bonds) creates the powerful emotional response on the part of the audience.

The film idea governing the organization unites all the parts in a formal manner so that each bears on the central theme of brotherhood and rebellion; no interesting irrelevancies are allowed. The structure of the whole film develops from the movement of the theme, and even the structure within each segment is likewise determined by the movement of the theme within the part.

In his own analysis of the formal arrangement of *Potemkin,* Eisenstein divided the film into five parts so that its form would be comparable to that of a stage tragedy; * although the content of the film suggests an epic or chronicle form, he intended to stress the tragic quality of the events by selecting and arranging the facts in order that "they answer the demands set by classical tragedy: a third act quite distinct from the second, a fifth from the first, and so on." † Each of the five parts is then divided into two almost equal segments. These segments are of *conflicting* quality in both mood and rhythm. "Not merely contrasting, but *opposite,* for each time it *images exactly that theme from the opposite point of view,* along with the theme that *inevitably grows from it.*" ‡

---

* The five parts correspond to the five reels. In 1925, a great many of the makeshift movie theaters throughout Russia could provide only one projector, and so Eisenstein's theatrical divisions are in fact justifications for the necessary intermissions while the reels were being changed by the projectionist.

† *Ibid.,* p. 162.     ‡ *Ibid.,* p. 165.

The "Odessa Steps" sequence from the fourth of the five sections of *Potemkin* is the most frequently cited example of Eisenstein's montage. The massacre of the citizens by the Czarist troops takes about six minutes of screen time, yet requires more than a hundred and fifty shots. (The average length of the shots—less than three seconds—is not important, since there is considerable variation, several shots lasting less than a second.) The great number of shots indicates the nature of Eisenstein's concept of a sequence. The kind of understandable information specified in a shot of brief duration must, to be effective, relate directly to the total idea and do so in a precisely limited way.

Eisenstein manages to go beyond the simpler types of connections in order to relate his shots to the whole, taking advantage of a pictorial sense that visualized conflicts between people in terms of conflicts, for example, between linear patterns and between physical movements. In other words, not only does the information specified by each shot relate to the content (the slaughter of innocents), but the pictorial form of the people and the steps relates image to image. The basic visual design in terms of movement contrasts the orderliness of the troops on the steps and the chaos of the fleeing citizens. The soldiers kneel together to shoot their rifles in a regular pattern suggesting mechanized slaughter. At the same time, the visual design, in terms of its linear patterns, opposes the horizontal lines of the rifles with the oblique or vertical lines of the fleeing citizens. With movement against movement and line against line, the form of the images itself symbolizes the physical conflict.

In a preceding sequence, the Odessa Steps had been introduced as a scene of celebration, as the citizens cheer the battleship in the harbor. An insert title announces an immediate change in tone and pace—"Suddenly"; the brevity of the message also signals an abrupt shift in the speed of cutting. We first see people scurrying down the steps. By withholding the cause of the movement, Eisenstein forces us to detect only one thing, the visual expression of panic. In fact, the very next shot following the insert title is a close-up of a woman's face showing terror. The fourth shot reveals the soldiers moving as a rank, and it is only their formation that appears threatening, for they are not yet shooting. Even before we see them shooting, we witness a man falling, obviously killed by a bullet, and now we know the people have reason to panic.

Thus, the filmmaker establishes an environment of terror before he has truly made known to us the nature of that terror. As it becomes clear that the situation is a massacre, the abstract sense of horror dominates our sensibilities. Whenever we are faced with killings on a massive scale, we tend to take refuge in statistics, which blunt the kind of emotional response Eisenstein thinks necessary for his film. The great problem in the depiction of a mass tragedy is that we objectify the horror into an intellectual concept so that it can be absorbed in its entirety. Unfortunately, one death more or less seems to lack significance in a general disaster.

**55** *Potemkin*

Wisely, then, Eisenstein isolates certain individual atrocities on the steps while at the same time making clear to us that a massacre is proceeding simultaneously. The sense of simultaneity becomes important as we begin to understand that the actual event we are witnessing has been prolonged beyond any plausible real time. Since it would take only a few seconds to race down all the Odessa Steps, the fact that several minutes of film time elapse indicates that Eisenstein had no intention of depicting the event as if it were a historical incident. In fact, the event never happened; it was invented by Eisenstein to show not a single massacre but the nature of a civilian massacre in general. This sequence remains one of the most ambitious attempts on film to dramatize an abstraction by means of extremely precise details and to leave the viewer with an absolutely clear emotional understanding of all that he has seen. The concept of slaughter would have been difficult to absorb were it filmed entirely in terms of the isolated atrocities on the steps. Similarly, the slaughter filmed from a distance in an attempt to objectify the whole scene would fail to make a significant emotional impression: the observation of a great many details from a distance requires a feat of perception that tends to objectify the event beyond its emotional impact. The solution—the simultaneous revelation of the total disaster and the individual tragedies—required an expansion of real time.

On first viewing, we feel the shots of this sequence as, somehow, chronological, not simultaneous. The events are perceived as they are projected: one after the other, with no apparent reservations about the impossibly long time it takes for people to get down those steps. This is an example of the realism of the content impressing us so powerfully that we instinctively filter out information that would reveal the impossibility of the chronology of events: for instance, at one point all the citizens have fled down the steps, clearing the way (aside from the bodies of the numerous dead) before the approaching soldiers, but one woman carries her child up toward them to make a personal plea for mercy. Shortly after this, the steps are once again filled with dozens of citizens rushing down; obviously, for the additional citizens to get onto the steps they would have had to come from behind the soldiers, leap over their backs, and run down the steps before them. Indeed Eisenstein devised the sequence so that viewers would not recognize an intellectual check on their emotional involvement in the de-piction of the massacre. After all, the main points Eisenstein wants to com-municate refer to the machinelike inhumanity of the soldiers and the panic of the citizens, the senseless murdering of civilians and the oppression of the Czarist regime (fig. 55). No one has any difficulty with these concepts, for the shots have been so structured that while watching the sequence we cannot avoid its meaning. Eisenstein's technique allows him to control the audience response.

In fact, only upon studying the sequence apart from the total film do we notice the *ways* in which the simultaneity is achieved. One way is by the expansion of time. Another is through the method of establishing witnesses to the event. Set against a background of people dashing frantically down the steps are the individuals Eisenstein sets apart for a closer look at their responses. In the preceding sequence, several of these people were seen in close shots or close-ups as they celebrated the rebellion aboard the *Potemkin* by waving toward the ship and cheering the crew. Once the movement of chaos begins, these same citizens become points of reference in the "Odessa Steps" sequence. By continually returning to the few individuals we rec-ognize from the preceding sequence, Eisenstein enables us to distinguish them from the mass. They are the human equivalents of "recurring mo-tifs." For instance, when we pass from shots of the fleeing citizens to a shot of an elderly woman wearing a pince-nez, we assume that she witnesses all that is going on; we can identify with her more readily than with the crowd, not only because we have seen her before, while the rest are vir-tually faceless victims of the terror, but also because she is watching rather than running—she shares our position as spectator, and her observations are simultaneous with the events on the steps. In the very last image of the sequence, a Cossack raises a sword and puts out one of her eyes; the image sums up the other irrational cruelties, merging the idea of the observer and that of the victim.

During the sequence two incidents receive special emphasis and form two movements that indicate the nature of the individual tragedies within the large-scale disaster. The first is the incident of the mother whose child is killed during the rush down the steps. As the woman proceeds to carry her child up the steps asking the soldiers for mercy, for her son, her ascent pictorially reverses the downward movement of the dominant oblique lines that characterize the plight of the citizens. Eisenstein changes the tempo here by employing shots somewhat longer in duration. When the mother has noticed her small son fallen on the steps, she turns to move against the crowd to pick up her boy; the crowd without noticing the child tramples over him in their panic. The camera, very close to the mother's face, reveals the crazed look in her eyes. Four quick shots of the crowd running over her boy are followed by another close shot of her horrified face; then Eisenstein cuts back and forth between the mother on her way up the steps, finally picking up her child, and the crowd rushing down. The mother proceeds up the steps, obviously out of her mind with grief over her dead son; at this moment the elderly woman in the pince-nez exhorts the women near her to make a plea to the soldiers. Now the images alternate between the elderly woman, smiling as though she anticipates the soldiers will cease shooting because of the mother's approaching them, and the movement of the mother carrying her dead son. An anticipation of some reaction to this pitiable plea builds up purely on the basis of the hopes of the victims,

for the soldiers have been depicted with the utmost consistency as machines of destruction. The mother, isolated on the steps, shouts to them, "My boy is badly hurt" (fig. 56). She poses no threat, of course, but the soldiers, reacting exactly as they have done to the crowd, fire in strict formation, precisely like a squad of executioners, as the officer in charge lowers his sabre, signaling them to kill the mother as well as the child. Immediately, we again see dozens of people fleeing at the bottom of the steps; the rapid pace has resumed, the slaughter proceeds as before.

The other episode developed within the sequence concerns a young mother caught on the steps with her baby, who is in a carriage. Eisenstein in effect duplicates the idea behind the first episode inasmuch as both depict the destruction of a mother attempting to save her child, though the two illustrations are presented in entirely different image patterns. This reinforcement of visual concepts is typical of Eisenstein's style in this film, and is particularly noticeable in the many literal duplications of shots in this sequence and elsewhere. Eisenstein uses the repeated shots—for example, of the soldiers' regimental strides down the steps—as images of relentless movement toward the inevitable end. The images serve also to create the sense of simultaneity; the recurring shots indicate that in spite of our sense of time passing, what we have seen before we must assume to be still occurring. As for the repetition of the idea of the two major incidents within the sequence, Eisenstein probably felt that the intellectual pattern required additional information so that the single death of the first mother and the killing of her child would not seem merely an outrage of fate, a disaster that resulted from the mere chance of the mother and child being on the steps. The second incident makes clear the deliberate notion behind the government slaughter. All the people are to be annihilated, no one spared, no life saved just because it happens to be that of an innocent bystander. In a massacre of this sort, no one is exempted because all of the living are collectively the enemy of the state.

The incident begins right after a group of old men are shot down. We see a young mother shielding a baby carriage with her body, her face expressing the terror she feels at her inability to protect her child. The soldiers fire, and in close-up the mother throws back her head in pain. This is followed by a shot of the carriage wheels resting precariously on the steps. In tandem the two shots contain a good deal of information that the separate images could not communicate, which of course supports Eisenstein's theory about the nature of juxtaposed images. The factual information from the first shot is that the mother has been wounded, perhaps fatally; the second shot merely shows the carriage on the steps. In a different context, the carriage resting on the steps might be an image of safety, but because it follows the information of the mother's being wounded we realize what must happen: the now unprotected carriage will be set into motion by the falling mother or one of the fleeing citizens and sent rushing down the steps.

**57** *Potemkin*

We make this assumption though in fact both shots were close-ups that excluded such considerations from the pictorial area. Indeed, Eisenstein displays several intervening images before completing the incident of the carriage rolling to its destruction. We see the mother clutching her stomach where she was wounded, the Cossacks attacking, the crowd running, and the soldiers firing. Tremendous tension is felt over the inevitable moment when the carriage will begin to roll down the steps. The actual event happens more than twenty shots after we first see the woman's head thrown back as a sign of her being wounded. In that time Eisenstein unfolds the scene before the eyes of those who are themselves in the process of being slaughtered.

When we finally see the mother fallen, her head pushes the carriage off the step it had been resting on, starting its precipitate movement. At this point, just before the carriage actually starts rolling down the steps, we look at the elderly woman in the pince-nez; her face instantly suggests that she has noticed the carriage and has realized that the child will be destroyed, and yet she is apparently too far away to prevent the fall. (In fact, we do not know whether the woman ever sees the carriage—the montage creates the relationship.) As the carriage descends, no one in the immediate vicinity notices it, for they are all fleeing the soldiers. Huddling on the side of a building, however, is a witness to the incident, a student, whose face exhibits a mixture of horror and helplessness.

Eisenstein uses the momentum of the carriage as a measure for pacing

the sequence. As the carriage bounces from step to step (fig. 57), it gains speed, naturally, but this increased speed could not easily be conveyed through the shots themselves, since the simultaneity of incidents requires Eisenstein to keep cutting from place to place. In other words, if he had chosen to photograph the carriage careening downwards, he could have recorded its exact increase in speed through a few stationary camera setups; however, since he cannot follow the movement of the carriage for any consecutive length of time without abandoning his predominant style of portraying simultaneous occurrences, Eisenstein suggests the carriage's speed primarily through the increased tempo of the editing. This has the effect of increasing the tempo of all events at the end of the sequence, whether or not they are in the immediate area of the carriage.

The unusually rapid pace of the last dozen or so shots of the sequence is successful not only because of the quick cutting but because the scene has become clearly fixed in our minds and we can recognize details and characters. Naturally, the repetitions and the great variety of camera angles have prepared us for the images at the end, which might otherwise flash by too quickly to convey their emotional content. Eisenstein has by this time in the sequence narrowed the range of our responses. The audience has been exposed very carefully to a few basic abstractions about the nature of the machinelike oppression, the helplessness of the innocents, and the terrifying presence of instant death dealt out with no regret or exception to all who were caught on the steps or, having descended them, were pursued by the Cossacks. The speed of the conclusion does not permit us to objectify the event but forces us to participate fully in the emotional impact of the massacre on the survivors and witnesses. The sequence concludes with the carriage overturning and the elderly woman's eye being put out by a Cossack. There are no alternative ways to respond but with a feeling of revulsion.

The next sequence is virtually an immediate answer to the horrors of the Odessa Steps massacre. The guns of the *Potemkin* fire upon the headquarters of the military. This short sequence contains the renowned three-shot series of the stone lions, one lying down, one rising, and one on its paws, snarling. The impact of the series accrues entirely from the context; the stones themselves have arisen to testify against the massacre. The final shot of the sequence, which shows clearing smoke, reveals the destruction of the headquarters.

The fifth and last part of *Potemkin*, which Eisenstein entitled "Meeting the Squadron," is a less spectacular but equally proficient example of his editing. Eisenstein must have enjoyed the technical problem involved in gathering material that would not be a significant letdown after the "Odessa Steps" sequence. His solution was to change the tempo entirely and build up a different kind of suspense. In the first half of the fifth part, the sailors on board the *Potemkin* are alerted to the fact that the

Russian navy, or a large part of it, is sailing to intercept and overcome them.* Determined not to surrender, the sailors can only await the attack. Eisenstein conceives of the pervasive tone of this sequence as one of anxiety. With great originality, the filmmaker takes a number of images that individually suggest repose or relaxation and edits them in such a way that they really suggest a concentrated effort to hide anxiety.

The scene is nighttime, the waters splashing gently against the ship. The shots feature sailors gazing into the darkness or sleeping. A recurring image is of the inactive needles on the pressure gauges. In spite of the searchlight on the waters, the prevailing pictorial information specifies calmness. However, we realize that the surface calm is projected upon an emotionally tense state of mind shared by all.

As soon as the watch cries "Squadron on the horizon," the pace changes abruptly. The "collision of shots" that Eisenstein speaks about finds a parallel in the collision of tones from sequence to sequence. In this sequence, the sailors awake quickly and hurry up the holdfasts. They run about the decks, and several hasten to the engine room. The numerous shots of the engines and the pressure gauges, which had been motionless in the previous sequence, are now repeated but with the needles showing a good deal of motion. In fact, Eisenstein manages to turn the ship's apparatus —including guns and engines and gauges—into the equivalent of a living organism. The ship comes alive, as do the men, to the danger of the confrontation and develops into a symbol of the communal society functioning on board. If the ship becomes virtually a breathing, excitable creation, it does so as a result of the teamwork of the sailors, their unified thoughts about the encroaching peril, their ability to function under an improvised command, and their confinement to an area, a little state, which makes them aware of their common humanity or brotherhood in the sense that the good of the individual is essentially tied to the good of the community.

The preparations of the cannons for battle, the ship's increasing to full speed, and the approach of the squadron build to an impressive conclusion through a great many shots edited to create the concepts of peril and courage. The procedure is similar to that demonstrated in earlier sequences. Numerous shots of the elements of danger are cut into the scenes of determined preparations. On the one hand we are shown the naval squadron in comparison to the *Potemkin,* and the editing imparts to us the idea that the *Potemkin* cannot possibly escape destruction in terms of the sheer power and force of the opposition. On the other hand, the men proceed as if there were some chance, or if not, they are all willing to face their destruction bravely without pleading for mercy. Their complete mutual understanding of the facts seems clear, and therefore we cannot avoid admiring their attitude. Believing in the rightness of their mutiny, these men will not yield

* Apparently, the government gave Eisenstein the whole Russian fleet, as small as it was, for use in filming this sequence.

an honorable position to save their lives—although the issue of what alternative they had never arises, since all of them instinctively seem to agree on taking this stand.

The film ends with the portrayal of the historic fact that the squadron refused to fire on the sailors of the *Potemkin* and allowed the ship to sail through to safety, a rare instance of a fraternal spirit unifying mutineers and loyal navy men in a common cause. It is therefore the happiest of endings to a work that had depicted some of the most brutal events ever filmed. The film idea emerges as an illustration of the potential accomplishment that men working together can achieve in the name of honor and justice. Such a mass determination to rectify injustices within society (as symbolized by the repressive hierarchy commanding the battleship at the beginning) leads to a situation where the best inherent qualities of men come to the surface under duress.

For students of film, *Potemkin* stands as a textbook on the art of editing through the fragmentation of the idea of a sequence. Starting with a concept in each sequence that would relate to the overall film idea, Eisenstein dissects his material in such a way that the abstract concept can be evolved only through the proper organization of the pieces, the shots. By restricting the length of each piece of information and, more importantly, constructing the pictorial design of each shot, he directs our attention to exactly that fragment of an idea which will lead us toward the predetermined total concept of the sequence. The shots cannot be conveniently rearranged to produce the same effect because (1) the specifications within the shots are themselves deliberately limited—that is, fragmented—and therefore only vaguely comprehensible without the context (many shots are in fact totally incomprehensible outside the context); and (2) the specifications are not presented merely in terms of content but in terms of pictorial form, which means that for a full grasp of the formal design (the total comprehension of the specifications) we have to see what the pictorial form of the subsequent shot will imply about the shot we are watching at any one moment.

The mind indeed boggles at the thought of a filmmaker designing hundreds of shots in terms of pictorial relationships so that, for instance, the horizontal lines of one shot precede the vertical lines of the next, creating a conflict that our subconscious mind assimilates while we consciously perceive the conflict in terms of the content. Much of the editing must have been done on a less rational basis—surely Eisenstein relied mainly on his instinctive pictorial sense while putting together the fragments of his film. Afterwards, in his lecturing, he used the film to illustrate techniques he probably was surprised to find so neatly arranged for him when he came to analyze as a professor what he had accomplished as an artist. Whatever the conditions of creation, we are thankful for the product. *Potemkin* remains one of the most impressively edited films in all cinema.

# 16

# Editing
# Through
# Accumulation

## The Synthetic Approach

Perhaps the most common way of conceiving a sequence involves the process of synthesis. Editing by means of synthesizing requires starting with pieces that in themselves are incomplete but still contain significant meaning and placing them together so as to reinforce the meaning within the individual pieces. In this way, the filmmaker tends to accumulate the pieces in order to establish the meaning of the total sequence. Much of that meaning can be located within some of the pieces accumulated, whereas in an analytic sequence, say, of Eisenstein, hardly anything can be discovered from the piece. Yet the unsynthesized shot does not, of course, begin to equal the meaning of the synthesized sequence.

In Pudovkin's *The End of St. Petersburg* (1927), a series of shots depicts the senseless horror of war. Russian soldiers sent off to fight for a false cause are shown suffering the hardships of war after an insert title, "In the name of the Czar." The subsequent shots clearly underline the bitter irony of the false cause. Another insert title is shown—"In the name of the Kaiser"—followed by a shot of German soldiers trudging along. The point of the sequence is that everyone engaged in war suffers because of the evils of the rulers who send young men to die for invalid reasons, though this

general theme cannot be grasped until Pudovkin shows us the German soldiers in the same predicament as the Russians. However, even before the sequence is completed, the gist of this idea—that war is horrible—is perfectly established. In this kind of accumulative editing, each shot adds something to what we know from previous shots, so that we know more and more after each shot, whereas in fragmented sequences we are not totally conscious of what we know while the sequence is unfolding.

All filmmakers presumably start with a film idea that takes shape in terms of images. In the process of making those images relate to one another, the filmmaker reveals his stylistic preferences for developing a sequence. If he believes that the sense of his sequence requires a leap beyond the specifications of the shots toward some abstraction, he will likely proceed in the manner of Eisenstein to fragment the sequence idea so that the individual specifications require psychological connections that are not primarily linked to logical progression; the viewer has to grasp the implications suggested by the facts of the shot. In the case of the director who connects his materials logically and progressively with the preceding and following material, the viewer is called upon to make connections, but they are the evident ones dictated by plot and dialogue. This is not to suggest that the synthetic process is essentially obvious as compared with the opposite, analytic process. After all, the content of the shot in a synthesized sequence may be highly sophisticated, regardless of the style of creating the sequence. In contrast, the close-ups of the maggoty meat in *Potemkin* are among the the least subtle shots in the history of the cinema. Everyone in the audience knows immediately that this is meat unfit for anything; its specifications are obvious, though it is part of a sequence that is conceived in highly analytic terms.

Subtlety is not the issue here. What determines the difference between styles is the way in which the film idea is either broken down into its constituent parts (analysis) or built up from them (synthesis). As we have said, these differences can be most clearly understood from the different effects they produce. We have seen how the dissection of an idea can emphasize details that might have been passed over were they observed either in reality or in a film that did not so clearly delineate the parts. On the other hand, in the synthesizing process, the specifications within each shot direct our attention toward a larger idea; we grasp the formation of the idea quickly, and what we look for is its development. Successful filmmakers accumulate information, without repetition, through the addition of new material based on previous material, and each shot adds to what we know. In contrast, the fragmented sequence relies on juxtaposition, the effects continually creating various kinds of tension so as to expand our awareness of the piecemeal evidence we have been receiving.

Unless a filmmaker habitually thinks in extremely analytic terms, which is unusual, he will probably tend to use an accumulative editing

procedure for many sequences that are intended to convey basic or simple ideas. The reason is that accumulative editing is the most direct way to place a single concept emphatically before the viewers. At the beginning of *Jules and Jim* (1962), Truffaut wishes to establish for us the relationship of his two main characters, and at the same time he wants the tone to be only half serious. The two men are good friends because they are essentially warm people, Jim quite ready to give of himself, Jules quite ready to ask for help. The film opens with a series of shots of their developing friendship. An off-screen voice describes the beginning of the relationship while the visuals dramatize their friendship in a consistent pattern: we see them playing dominoes, and the voice tells us that Jules asked Jim to get him an invitation to a masquerade ball; we see another shot of the two seated, with Jim cutting the pages of a book for Jules; then we watch them walking together, deep in conversation, as the voice tells us what interests they shared. Next they sit in a boat with two girls, and the voice informs us that "there were no women in Jules's life in Paris, and he wanted one. In Jim's life there were several. . . . Jim introduced him to a young woman. . . ." * Truffaut's point is made with some satiric reference to national traits of Germans and French (Jules is German, Jim French), but the basic method of the opening sequence directly establishes the foundation of the relationship. Following the editing principle of accumulating shots that have no particular relationship in space (and the time too is approximate), Truffaut makes the point swiftly and clearly.

## Comedy and the Accumulation of Materials

Most of the great comic artists seem to have created their sequences in terms of accumulation. And for an obvious reason: the comedy of performance is largely based on the accumulation of gag situations. The performing comedian, on stage as well as in film, establishes a personality or a situation on which he will build his routines. There are of course other kinds of comedians; those who relate jokes do not need to build on previous materials if each subsequent joke is good enough. However, this type lies outside the main tradition of the comic screen artist. The Hitchcock kind of horror or suspense comedy may very well be done in analytic terms, but the comedy of a Keaton or a Langdon depended greatly upon the development of comic patterns, which in turn were built on the accumulation of details.

Laurel and Hardy specialized in establishing a few situations and developing numerous variations of those basic ideas. In almost all their two-reelers, a standard environment is worked into material for the entire

---

* *Jules and Jim,* trans. by Nicholas Frey (New York, Simon and Schuster, 1968), p. 12.

**58** *Leave 'Em Laughing*

film, but even when the location changed, the original idea sustained the
film. For instance, in one film, *Leave 'Em Laughing* (1928), three locations
relate to the ordeal of going to the dentist. We see them first in their apartment trying to relieve Laurel of his aching tooth; a series of gags is built
around the attempt, such as tying a cord to the tooth and attaching it to a
doorknob so that the opening of the door will pull out the tooth (instead,
it pulls off the knob). Then the two go to the dentist, and the long sequence
culminates in an orgy of laughing gas, which overcomes everyone. The third
location is the city streets; the two hysterical men drive to an intersection
and help create a traffic jam. A series of minor traffic mishaps occurs,
involving them with an infuriated policeman who naturally can't understand
their incessant laughter; each bump of their car causes a repetition (with
small variations) of the reactions of their laughter and the policeman's
anger (fig. 58). Yet the comedy is by no means simply repetitive, for its
whole point is related to their helpless condition getting them ever deeper
into trouble. It is hardly the quality of the isolated gags that accounts for
the humor in the film, but our increasing familiarity with the ways in which
the aching tooth creates perpetual difficulty from sequence to sequence.

The effects of comic accumulation can be highly successful even when
we are so familiar with the pattern that we can begin to anticipate the gags.

Another Laurel and Hardy film, *Double Whoopee* (1929), contains a number of set-up scenes that could not be as funny as they are if the audience were surprised at the discovery of the comedy. For instance, a foreign prince dressed in a glittering white uniform, haughtily conveying his sense not only of superiority but of cleanliness, stands smoking in front of a hotel, dropping his ashes into the hand of his lackey; suddenly Laurel and Hardy walk in front of him, heedless of his impressive appearance, and enter the hotel. Immediately we know that in some way Laurel and Hardy will not only cause him humiliation for his haughtiness but—more important visually—they are going to dirty his uniform. The event occurs when the prince, standing in front of the hotel elevator to make a speech to a few guests, does not notice that the elevator has ascended; he turns and falls into the filth at the bottom of the shaft. The elevator having come back down, Hardy emerges, oblivious. When he is helped to his feet, the prince, outraged, once more turns his back on the elevator, this time to make some angry threats to the hotel management. A second time the elevator ascends while his back is turned, and once more he falls into the shaft. This time, when the elevator descends, the door opens and Laurel walks out, equally oblivious of the discomfort he has given his highness the prince. This sequence occurs early in the film. Every viewer senses that the prince is destined to fall a third time, though we are not sure when (of course it occurs toward the end of the film). The first two times, the slapstick fall is funny and serves the moral purpose of deflating pomposity. But the third fall—the event we all expect to occur—is much more significant, for if the audience knows what is coming, why doesn't the prince? Clearly, the man's pomposity and foolishness destine him to extended retribution. His character is his fate, and so to a certain extent is his accumulated punishment.

With Laurel and Hardy, the effect of accumulative editing tends to be the feeling of inevitability, which is one of the unifying stylistic elements of their films. Yet numerous other effects are possible from accumulation, depending upon the handling of the accumulated elements. Buster Keaton uses the same basic method to achieve surprise, which is practically the opposite effect. In *Balloonatics,* Keaton and his girl are rowing in a river that, unknown to them, contains a huge waterfall. The sequence creates tremendous suspense effects through continual cutting from the peaceful couple in the boat to the perilous falls toward which they are heading. The inevitable sense is that Keaton and the girl are going to be killed, an event not altogether out of the realm of possibility in a Keaton film. But just at the moment when the tragic plunge is about to take place, the boat keeps moving straight off into the air, having caught onto a balloon Keaton had ridden in earlier. The surprise could not be achieved through dissection, with each shot of the sequence conveying a separate piece of information. All the given information must indicate the inevitability of a particular conclusion (that the boat will plunge over the falls). Analytical editing

might lead us to believe that alternatives existed, and the danger would be mitigated. Similarly, if we were not absolutely sure early in the sequence of what everything was building to, we would not be prepared for the significance of the surprise, for our attention would have been misdirected to the process of the developing situation, not to the anticipated result.

## Accumulation to Establish Tone:
## Resnais's *Last Year at Marienbad*

One of the chief values inherent in editing through the accumulation of details emerges from the establishment of a prevailing mood or tone. A well-known modern example of this effect occurs in Resnais's *Last Year at Marienbad* (1961). In this peculiar film, Resnais reduces the plot to little more than a situation raised early in the film: a man insists that he knows a woman, that they met the year before and agreed to meet again this year and go off together, but she denies even knowing him. The plot interest concerns the possibility of his story being true, or if not, his being able to convince her to leave her husband (or the man she lives with) and go off with him anyway. All this develops rather quickly in the film.

Clearly, whatever it is that sustains our interest, it is not the many turns on the basic situation, since few objective clues are given, for obviously Resnais avoids developing a mystery story. Nor are the characters portrayed so as to suggest levels of psychological complexity. What does count is the structure of the interior of the grand baroque hotel in which the characters live (fig. 59). The film in some ways resembles a museum tour through an environment the man himself describes repetitiously at the beginning: "these halls, these galleries, in this structure of another century, this enormous, luxurious, baroque, lugubrious hotel—where endless corridors succeed silent, deserted corridors—overloaded with a dark and cold ornamentation of woodwork, stucco, moldings—marble, black mirrors, dark paintings, columns, heavy hangings. . . ." * The camera moves slowly over the scene and throughout the film introduces us again and again to the same type of environment containing the same type of conversation: the man urging the woman to admit they had met in the past and to leave with him. The accumulation of images of the hotel's aridity and the formal social patterns displayed there carry almost the whole of the film's impact so that the basic film idea emerges precisely in terms of the hotel setting: will she take the opportunity to flee the kind of existence we see here? The mood is tedious, and many moviegoers felt the film captured this mood by copying it rather than symbolizing it. In any case, the nature of the tedium and of the

* *Last Year at Marienbad*, text by Alain Robbe-Grillet for the film by Alain Resnais, trans. by Richard Howard (New York, Grove Press, 1962), p. 20.

**59**  *Last Year at Marienbad*

world of the hotel is brilliantly exhibited by the accumulation of patterns of images of the hotel interior.

The repetitiveness of hotel corridors and salons in *Last Year at Marienbad* is carefully contrived by Resnais to enlarge our sense of the particular place into a sense of the hotel guests' entire lives. The filmmaker goes beyond the accumulated details to a generalized observation about a way of life. The generalization results from handling details artistically so that they begin to seem symbolic of the life-style of the characters, rather than simply monotonous depictions of the ordinary. Of course, it is the quality of the film's shots, their internal arrangements, and the order of the editing that cause the specifications to accumulate into something more than a conglomeration of details.

## Accumulation to Establish a Film Idea: Antonioni's *Zabriskie Point*

The process of accumulative editing compares with inductive reasoning in that the filmmaker moves from particular images to a general or larger image that encompasses the specific materials of the separate shots. Often

this movement within the sequence corresponds to our increasing awareness of the total meaning of the sequence while it is still developing, which means our conscious participation in the formation of the film concept. By its nature, this kind of editing seems less manipulative of audience response than the analytic approach inasmuch as our expanding awareness is intellectual (*i.e.,* we could probably put it into words), not just instinctive. Accumulative editing might also place a viewer in a position to approximate a character's perception of the developing idea. This is particularly true if the developing idea has some sociological reference—that is, some reference that ties in with a character's commentary on or opinion of the world he lives in, the world of the film.

An example of an accumulated sequence that allows us to partake in the developing point of view of a character occurs at the end of Antonioni's *Zabriskie Point* (1970). A young woman has heard on the radio that her lover has been unnecessarily shot to death while trying to return a plane he had stolen earlier that day. She stands before her wealthy employer's luxurious home, which represents the commercial world (a major business deal is being transacted inside that would lead to a building development in the desert area that has earlier appeared as a refuge for the two lovers, who do not really fit into the commercial world), and envisions the destruction of the home. We see the house exploding as if it were dynamited, and the girl's expression tells us that she would indeed be satisfied to see the house explode in this way. Then the house is again shown in the process of destruction by explosive charges. (The blasting imagery of the girl's fantasy is a projection of the means that the commercial world would employ to civilize the desert.)

Several shots of explosions occur (fig. 60), and the film ends without returning to the girl, who is conceiving these images. The images themselves have to carry, as they easily do, the full weight of the girl's conclusion about the world that has destroyed her young lover. In addition to the exploding house, we see certain other images that expand the meaning of the first fantasy image. Had Antonioni ended with the house, the image would remain rather personal: a young girl's grief causes her to turn against a symbol of the world she rejects. But with each explosion, our awareness of the symbolic nature of the imagery enlarges. We observe a television set, a refrigerator, and a woman's wardrobe explode—in separate images. The camera lingers on the various articles, examining them in detail as they rise into the sky. Filming in extraordinarily slow motion virtually abstracts the scenes of debris scattering into the air. The final images of food, clothes, and (presumably) the insides of a television set form a beautiful, if grotesque, mosaic against the sky, for the camera seems to have practically frozen the objects in their descent, so slowly do they fall. We have moved from the girl's view of a house blown to pieces to an image of American society's opulence and extravagance and culture wildly destroyed, but strangely enough attractive when reduced to their simple elements.

**60** *Zabriskie Point*

The whole of *Zabriskie Point* had been rather obviously structured around the contrast of the primitive (the desert) and the civilized (the city, Los Angeles), to the detriment of the civilized. The final imagery merges our previous perceptions of a dehumanized civilization made up of commercial interests motivated by a desire to sell goods, and always on the verge of violence or committing violence. Escape to the desert is only a limited possibility, since the world of nature is continually impinged upon by the forces of civilization. In fact, the two lovers could get to the desert only by means of a car and an airplane, basic symbols of the industrialized world. Since escape is not ultimately successful, the other possibility is destruction. The final images are not only the girl's fantasies, but those of the revolutionaries, the campus radicals who at the beginning of *Zabriskie Point* plan the next day's demonstrations, which will lead to violence. In that sequence the shots accumulate primarily verbal information about the youths: their language itself is violent, their ideals nihilistic. The ending of the film takes us to a point in the development of a general spiritual condition that in an important sense precedes the film's first sequence. For at the end we understand the frustrations and hatreds that produce the demonstrated but previously inexplicable psychological condition prevalent in the college radicals at the beginning. The girl is finally like them inasmuch

as she sees no way of coming to terms with the commercial society except to destroy it. At the film's conclusion, the shots of magnificent debris accumulate to create an image of the widest reference, expanding from a view of the girl's personal bitterness to the general view of a materialistic order with its materials in wreckage.

As a style, accumulative editing within the sequence relies much more on similarities than on contrasts. Contrasts are established, of course, but the major ones occur from one sequence to another, rather than within the sequence. In *Zabriskie Point,* for instance, the primitive world and the civilized world are linked by an airplane flight from the city to the desert, but the development of the contrasting ideas of the impersonal city and the emotionally vital desert are portrayed in separate sequences. The contrasts in the film are easy to absorb visually, since the sequences are themselves built up of images that reinforce one another.

In certain weaker films, accumulative editing presents viewers with a series of images that repeat themselves for no apparent reason but to make sure the audience understands the point. In fact, unless a filmmaker is extremely conscious of his technique, this potential for repetition becomes a likelihood. The aim of this style of editing, of course, is to shape an idea from the relationship of its parts, which is the same as the purpose of analytic editing. It is in the nature of the *relationship* of shots that one style differs from the other.

## Accumulation as a Unifying Style: Chaplin's *The Gold Rush*

From the work of the first two great filmmakers to achieve international reputations, Griffith and Chaplin, we can trace the two basic styles of editing: Griffith is notable for his dissection of the idea of the sequence and Chaplin for his accumulative procedure. This is not to say that either man invented a basic editing style, for evidence of contemporary use may be found in others; but they popularized certain approaches to making an intellectual concept cinematic. It is interesting to realize that the two primary modes of film construction, fragmentation and accumulation, had been demonstrated masterfully as early as 1920, by Griffith in an impressive number of long films, and by Chaplin in his two- and three-reelers and his one feature, *The Kid* (1920). Griffith's editing style was strikingly complex in its day and generated much more study than Chaplin's, for the outward simplicity of the editing in Chaplin does not direct attention to method, only to performance. From our historical perspective, however, we see now that Chaplin was developing an approach to visual imagery which, though confined largely to the image of Charlie the performer, was to become one of the most sophisticated of film techniques.

The typical Griffith sequence consisted of an event that required

characters to respond to it, the sense of emergency or tension creating the forward thrust even in relatively leisurely-paced films such as *Way Down East* and *Broken Blossoms*. With Chaplin, the sequence would typically consist of a situation developed in terms of increasing complications; plot was less important as a source for the film's movement than the individual and relatively small incidents. As Griffith's plots tend to be more important to his film idea, his sequences take on a particularized direction leading inevitably to the next event. Chaplin's sequences often move toward an abstraction or generalization. Even when Griffith attempts some general implication about man or society, as in *Intolerance*, he always works through very specific story lines with highly individualized characters. Griffith thought in such grandiose terms that he required very specific materials to hang his ideas on—and when he got to working with the specific materials, he always turned them into the heart of his films (the original notions seem to have been reduced to insert titles). Chaplin appears to have worked the other way: he began with very basic incidents, putting them together in such a way that they always seemed to go beyond the mere details and incidents in the life of Charlie the film character.

The Gold Rush (1925), because it was longer than even *The Kid* or *A Woman of Paris* (which he directed but appeared in only briefly) and more complicated in what it attempted to say, marks a maturing of Chaplin's art—if one can use the phrase for Chaplin, who was a great artist within months of his debut. This film demonstrates his feeling for the sequence rather than the shot as the primary structural unit in the film. The great shots that characterize the short films are still there, but they are used to build toward a greater meaning within the sequence and the film as a whole.

In *The Gold Rush*, Charlie is still at the center of the situations, but now they are expanded in their scope, with a number of reference points to a larger world. The film opens with long shots of tremendous numbers of prospectors seeking gold in Alaska; they are climbing a mountain of snow, and not every prospector can make it. The situation is grim, not at all comic. Charlie appears on a mountain ridge, not near any of the other prospectors, and his familar traits and walk dispel the grimness of the first shots. Nevertheless, the nature of the prospector's condition, its peril and its futility, glimpsed in the opening, is soon reinforced by other shots: for instance, Charlie comes across the grave of a prospector who died when he got lost in the snow. The weather is terrible and extremely dangerous. Charlie struggles to make his way over this snow-covered wasteland to a cabin he comes upon. Very little can be described as funny in this sequence. In one shot a bear follows Charlie, but he never notices it behind him, and the visual combination of peril and unawareness has a comic, though threatening effect. In the context of this sequence, that shot becomes another example of the various dangers that confront the prospector.

Chaplin aims at the accumulation of a series of shots that will suggest

to us the perils of the enterprise without, however, turning the film into a melodrama. In other sequences Charlie will face more significant threats than a prowling bear. The beginning of the film establishes an individual within an alien environment. The next sequence, inside a cabin, introduces two other characters—a criminal, Black Larson, and a prospector, Big Jim. The images here illustrate another aspect of the environment and the difficulty of survival. The weather makes it almost impossible to move out of the cabin, and the men are starving. Since the situations that will develop later primarily relate to the environment, about a quarter of the film is devoted to creating our sense of this environment and Charlie's place in it. The emphasis in the earlier films such as *The Kid* had been on Charlie's isolation (moral as well as physical) within an environment. In *The Gold Rush,* he shares with Black Larson and Big Jim a perilous situation in which they could all die of starvation.

Inside the cabin, images are accumulated to foster the impression of the three men's increasing desperation. When the doors are opened, the wind is so tremendous that Charlie is blown through the house. We watch him moving between two men of much larger size in a place where physical strength is considerably important, and yet the other two have no special advantage in the cabin. For a while, Charlie gains no more of our sympathy than his companions, one of whom is a criminal and the other a somewhat brutish man, because in the cabin sequences, a single elemental idea dominates each of them equally: hunger.

The editing expands on the concept of hunger through the accumulation of images suggesting imminent starvation. After Black Larson leaves in search of help, the two most famous sequences are developed: the feast of the shoe and the vision of the chicken. The first occurs when Charlie makes a dinner of his shoe in a survival attempt based on his own psychological insight: if one pretends to be dining on a lavish meal, then it is possible to trick oneself into eating anything (fig. 61). As Charlie goes through the motions of a chef in preparing a soup by boiling the shoe in water, then serving the main course of shoe to Big Jim, we note that Jim too can be induced to partake of the pantomime. A little disagreement ensues between the two men over the larger portion of the shoe. When Charlie has to settle for the sole, which is lined with nails, he handles the nails as if they were chicken or pheasant bones, pretending to eat every last piece.

The chicken sequence develops mainly from the point of view of Jim during his increasingly apparent breakdown. Jim's vision is a rare bit of whimsy for a Chaplin film: Charlie turns into a chicken of gigantic proportions. After Jim tells of his vision and they have a good laugh at it, Charlie shrewdly takes the knife away from the table, reminding us that the comedy of the film can never completely hide the serious nature of the sequence. After all, Jim is starving, and his desperation will lead him to do irrational things. At one point, with Charlie again transformed into a

**61** *The Gold Rush*

chicken, Jim attempts to shoot him, but Charlie is saved at the last minute by Jim's regaining his sanity and realizing what is going on. But from this point on, Jim's illusions and the reality of his desperation merge. No longer does he care whether it is Charlie or a giant chicken sharing the cabin with him, and Charlie is alerted to Jim's cannibalistic intention. The sequence has moved from the chicken-chase with its element of the farcical to a struggle for survival, with Charlie kept alive only because he has the rifle. The images are all associated with the idea of hunger, even if the earlier ones contain aspects of the ridiculous. To Chaplin, man reduced to his most elemental state is always partially comic, even as his desperation mounts.

The achievement of the editing, then, is to allow for a good deal of comedy—a number of amusing, sometimes hilarious, incidents synthesized so as to provide for variations on a serious theme. At some point early in his career, Chaplin realized that his kind of comedy was an appropriate vehicle for conveying that certain type of essentially noncomic film idea that interested him. The secret does not really lie in his pantomime—his ability, often noted by critics, to make audiences cry as well as laugh—a performing style that he shared with Harry Langdon, a much smaller talent, and others who aimed only at "sentimental comedy." In contrast, Chaplin works out a basic humanistic analysis of a serious problem that derives

from the nature of the sequence. The comedy, however, does not work against the inevitable seriousness of each idea underlying every full-length Chaplin film because he takes care to shape every series of comic shots so as to relate it immediately to the basic theme of the sequence. The chicken episode may be hilarious comedy, but we do not forget for a second that a good deal of time has previously been spent developing the truth about Jim's starvation. Unlike his practice in his one- and two-reel comedies, no gratuitous comedy exists in the film. Chaplin does not rely much on surprise in his editing, preferring to keep the audience continuously aware of the development of the idea, which helps to sustain a serious moral tone throughout his depiction of comic events.

Of course, not all the events, even on the surface, are comic ones. Figures of various shades of villainy usually inhabit Chaplin's film world, sometimes seeming to dominate it. Black Larson goes off supposedly to get food or help, but actually shoots two policemen and is later killed when a mountain crumbles beneath him. Jim, struck on the head by Larson, loses his memory. Charlie enters a town inhabited by tough prospectors and the girls who provide them with entertainment. All together, Chaplin views the world of *The Gold Rush* as a rather dismal place, with Charlie himself being one of the few redeeming characters in it. The theme of gold, of man's mercenary ambitions, emphasized in the title, of course explains much of the villainy. Nobody would be there were he not desperate to find riches. In this sense, everyone, including Charlie, has an awareness of the dehumanizing conditions likely to be encountered by the gold-seeker. Charlie, however, maintains an innocence not clearly understandable in light of his sharing in the mutual goal of all the prospectors in this film.

Nevertheless, Charlie's pursuit of riches harms no one. If he is motivated by wealth (which is not apparent), he at least is not likely to do anything antisocial to attain it. In fact, he is highly idealistic. The central plot reveals his idealism and innocence, at the same time separating him from the conditions of evil that surround the community of people who have come to seek gold. Charlie meets a dancehall girl, Georgia, and falls in love with her primarily because he is so absolutely lonely and isolated; he creates a totally imaginary one-sided relationship without any indication from her that she has noticed his existence. Indeed, we see Georgia more clearly than Charlie does. To us, she appears as a hardened slut who could conceivably be reclaimed but is not worthy of the efforts of someone like Charlie, whom she can only scorn.

When Charlie sees her at the dancehall from the isolated position where he watches the dancers, an outsider with no friends and no money, his first impression is highly favorable. He is still walking around with rags bundled over one foot because of his having dined on his shoe. The editing makes the most out of the pathos inherent in the situation. He looks at the attractive Georgia, and she glances in his direction. Suddenly she smiles and

beckons toward him. Overwhelmed by her kind notice of him, Charlie starts toward her to dance, but it turns out that she has not even seen him; she had simply signaled to someone standing behind him. Later on she does ask him to dance with her, but only because she is quarreling with Jack (the "ladies' man"), and wants to insult her friend by choosing the lowest character around, Charlie, as a partner in preference to Jack.

So many of the sequences reinforce the idea of Charlie's isolation that Chaplin frequently verges on drowning himself in a sea of pathos. But reaching the limit of artistic sentiment, Chaplin converts that sentiment into moral force. That is, he refuses to let Charlie remain the passive victim of uneven odds; the victim insists on fighting back, and finally Charlie manages to defeat both the potentially destructive elements of the environment (*e.g.,* he shoots the bear that menaces him in the cabin) and the cruel human elements that cause him to suffer. In this sense, Charlie rises to become a figure of heroic capacity, neither bewildered by successive misfortunes nor destroyed by the deliberate antagonism he continually encounters.

One of the most effective sequences developing this characteristic of Charlie concerns the New Year's party that he arranges for Georgia and her girlfriends. In an earlier sequence, the girls visited Charlie in his cabin and found his gentleness and innocence a source of condescending mirth. To the girls, including Georgia, Charlie serves as a simpleton who will entertain them by acting as their foil, unaware that they are laughing at him behind his back. Chaplin's objective filming allows us to perceive Charlie's erroneous interpretation of the situation as a gesture of friendship on the part of the girls, as he is already in love with Georgia. They elicit from him the confession that he is lonely, an important point because it shows that their treatment of him is a violation of general standards of human decency; their bad nature (or their insensitivity) deliberately leads them to take advantage of his good nature. Thus, the sequence works to accumulate evidence of the girls', particularly Georgia's, moral unworthiness in comparison to Charlie's gentleness. The point is enforced with an emphatic visual image. After the girls agree to come for a New Year's dinner, Charlie in ecstasy starts jumping around his cabin, throwing the pillows around. As the cabin fills with feathers, Georgia returns (she has forgotten her gloves) and sees the man's evident joy at the anticipation of the dinner party. When she leaves to report the scene to her friends as if it were an example of Charlie's ridiculousness rather than of his love, we know that Charlie is infinitely her moral superior.

Thus, the "New Year's Eve" sequence that comes later, showing the girls ignoring or more likely completely forgetting their appointment at Charlie's cabin, develops into a classic cinematic symbol, first of inhumanity and then of spiritual challenge and moral awakening. Charlie sets the table for a splendid meal that he is preparing for the girls (he has earned money

**62** *The Gold Rush*

to buy the materials by shoveling snow), who are to arrive by eight o'clock
(fig. 62). As the time approaches for them to arrive he projects a vision
of the pleasant evening to come in which he and they equally enjoy themselves. This dreamlike episode contains one of his most famous mime scenes,
the dance of the bread rolls, in which Charlie ingeniously makes the rolls
serve as a dancer's feet to amuse his imagined guests. The vision ends with
Charlie asleep. Intercut into the sequence, a number of shots depict Georgia
and her friends wildly carrying on at a New Year's party in the dancehall.
Eating and talking to Jack, now obviously on good terms with him, she
clearly hasn't the slightest thought of Charlie or his dinner. When she does
think of Charlie (after midnight), she proposes to Jack and her friends
that they go and play some practical jokes on him.

The amazing achievement of the sequence is the effect Chaplin derives
from the mood generated by the pathos of the hero's condition. The climax
of the sequence occurs with Charlie absent—he has left to investigate the
dancehall party to learn why his company did not show up. His empty
cabin becomes the object of Georgia's midnight excursion for the purpose

of ridiculing him. She and her friends arrive with a vague plan to entertain themselves by some ruse, not knowing that Charlie has left. Georgia enters the cabin and sees the settings and gifts on the table. She senses that everything present in the cabin is a symbolic extension of Charlie. Suddenly made aware of Charlie's humanity and her own crassness in responding to it, she begins to suffer remorse. She looks at the little present for her that Charlie left on the table. Her capitulation to the sentiment previously achieved by numerous shots of the abandoned Charlie is practically equivalent to a tragic awakening inasmuch as she begins to understand not only the world around her but the flaw in her own character. When Jack tries to prompt her into continuing the joke, she tells him that she's had enough and that the joke is over.

The sequence is supposed to show the evolution of Georgia's character, an exceedingly difficult task since she has been portrayed as a superficial person, insensitive to the point of brutality, and indeed obviously brutalized by her profession (a dancehall girl is clearly a genteel equivalent for a prostitute). She is not going to change, we might argue, from any single event. Chaplin's editing succeeds here because the sequence in which the event happens has so carefully established the fact that this single incident is immensely important and totally indicative of the relationship between Charlie and the woman. She has had a few other opportunities to respond with some sympathy that would humanize her, particularly when she discovered Charlie in the cabin filled with feathers, but she has missed them all. Were she to ignore or miss the significance of the empty cabin with the glorious preparations laid out for her, she would be beyond redemption. Yet it would require someone thoroughly dehumanized not to respond with compassion to such an arrangement. Chaplin has so synthesized the sequence that all the shots build toward an emotional crisis: displayed are the tokens of the hero's kindness and, more important, his singular devotion to her. The audience knows that she is elevated by simply being the object of Charlie's love, regardless of her not deserving his feelings. If she reacted to the scene before her with her previous scorn or indifference, it would be, perhaps, in keeping with the realism of her character, so consistently developed in the film. But Chaplin readily sacrifices a literal realism for a reevaluation of her inner nature. We are hoping to see her recognize the mistakes she has made in her prior treatment of Charlie, and when she does, we are willing to forgive her in part for her prior unkindness.

There should be no mistake about the way that Chaplin as director has manipulated our emotional response to this sequence. It is not simply our obvious sympathy for Charlie to start with that determines our feelings toward the girl's conversion. Chaplin compounds the implications of the sequence by accumulating images of Charlie's disappointment and dawning awareness that his dream of entertaining Georgia for dinner is impossible.

From the dancehall, where everyone is having a good time, Chaplin crosscuts to the lonely cabin, creating a tremendous emotional tension by contrasting boisterous celebration with the growing misery of Charlie's isolation. Therefore, when Georgia later enters the empty cabin, we expect her to respond to the emotional condition (the misery) that the environment just previously represented; in reality, of course, the emotional condition belonged to Charlie, not to the unused place settings on his table, but the symbolic transference of the emotion to the objects is evidently accomplished. Georgia looks as if she understands the despair that Charlie has just experienced. Furthermore, she knows she is totally implicated in the victimization of the man. Jarred by her recognition, for once in her life she feels truly sorry about her bad conduct.

Being sorry in itself signals a deeply felt change of heart. However, Chaplin does not explore this in the film, for after all the main character is someone else, and we must return to the resolution of his struggles in this society. Georgia's change of heart comes about, certainly, because finally Charlie has reached her, has made contact with her as a human being. Clearly, Charlie's indomitable spirit, his refusal to be denied because of poverty or feminine indifference, has ultimately won the day.

The character of Charlie the tramp bears tribute to the human spirit, a portrayal of the possibilities of all men. In *The Gold Rush,* the hero achieves the unlikely success of winning over a girl like Georgia and becoming a "multimillionaire" by sharing in Big Jim's gold mine. Both achievements are just literal unwindings of the narrative structure; their real intent is symbolic of the possibilities of human achievement in general. Throughout the film the editing has been designed to accumulate a variety of images that accentuate the underlying film idea. Each sequence reveals a different aspect of the same thing, expanding our awareness of the implications with each variation of Charlie's relationship with an alien world. Charlie stands for everyman, not because he is average (for he is extraordinarily gifted in emotional sensitivity) or typical, but because he is the most human of all characters in modern narrative art.

## Editing for Poetic Effects: Pudovkin's *Mother*

Another theoretically possible kind of accumulative editing—a method so visually striking that it is sometimes considered a distinct approach to montage in itself—stresses the juxtaposition of images physically unrelated to each other but thematically so close that the audience very likely grasps the connection immediately. The similarity of this method to the use of simile in poetry was noted very early by the Russians and has since been associated with the "poetic" style of Alexander Dovzhenko and Vsevolod Pudovkin. However, this procedure on film stock creates much more

emphasis than even the astounding poetic similes of a John Donne on paper, and therefore, regardless of its artistic possibilities, such a film technique cannot be used exclusively in any one full-length film. Still, the technique is important because of its wide use, even by ordinary directors, though it rarely appears more than once in a single film and does not appear at all in most films. But it must be considered an aspect of the accumulative style rather than a style in itself, for not even Dovzhenko relied on it as a principle for unifying all his shots.

One of the most famous examples of the film simile in the American cinema is Chaplin's shot of sheep being herded, which occurs at the beginning of *Modern Times* to suggest society's herding of workers who in the next shot are seen rushing off to work in a typical urban scene. The implication is immediately clear in terms of both its humor and its satire. Yet the shot of the sheep arouses certain expectations of future shots that are not, of course, normal for the ordinary realistic environment of a Chaplin film. The impact of a simile is such that the audience wonders when they will see another. *Modern Times* has so many brilliant images of the industrial world that after a short while no spectator's mind is still mulling over the effects of the simile. In some ordinary films, however, such a technique might well be disruptive.

Eisenstein, like Pudovkin and Dovzhenko, would occasionally use a film simile, but because such a shot has to be synthesized into a sequence, it could not frequently be made to blend with his analytical approach to editing. After all, a simile is not a real part of the scene being dissected. Yet in *Strike,* Eisenstein shows the Czarist soldiers attacking the strikers and cuts into the sequence images of a bull being slaughtered in an abbatoir. The cuts are effective—almost too effective for the larger context, for what happens drives home a point with resounding force (a spectator may remember the image long after he has forgotten the film)—yet the visual content of the preceding and following images make the same point just as clearly, though with somewhat less emotional force. It does Eisenstein little good to reinforce his idea that the government treats workers like beasts with the overwhelming example of animal slaughter. So little is gained intellectually and so much is lost by drawing out the audience's pity and rage that we might claim that Eisenstein has overstated the obvious for the sake of melodramatic effect.

The fact that two great filmmakers who do not specialize in the use of film similes managed to create a similar image in two entirely different kinds of films presents us with a significant comparison between their techniques. The handling of animals readily indicates society's dehumanizing tendencies in the treatment of masses of people. In Chaplin the shot occurs in a comic context; in Eisenstein, a tragic one. Clearly the simile itself does not determine the mood but emphasizes or exaggerates whatever has been elsewhere indicated as an appropriate response to the sequence.

Since the simile is a fabrication of the filmmaker and does not exist naturally in the environment under consideration by him, its purpose must be to illuminate what is happening rather than to change its meaning or to introduce a new idea.

The degree of illumination causes the difficulty. To strike a correct intellectual and emotional balance between the idea being presented and the simple simile illuminating the idea raises a difficulty even in poetry, where the practice is more than two thousand years old and has always had a more vital and common use than in the history of cinema. In film the simile must be even more carefully chosen than in poetry because a physically visible image will tend to be both more unexpected and more dramatic in the nature of its presentation than an imagined visual image in a poem. But regardless of the lack of subtlety, many similes are worth including because they are so attractive in themselves. The clarification of the idea may be obvious, and yet may be impressive anyway.

Editing for poetic effects can be accomplished in various ways regardless of film similes and without abandoning the basic realistic surface of the medium. Pudovkin's *Mother* (1926) exhibits a filmmaker's essentially poetic approach to images as realistic, even as brutal, as we find anywhere in cinema. His procedure stresses the poetic values inherent in the image but not obvious until they are emphasized by a variety of techniques.

Pudovkin's work resembles Eisenstein's in the desire at times to suggest simultaneity of action. Pudovkin shares some of Eisenstein's editing techniques, but as a film poet he also has some devices of his own. In *Mother,* to depict the way the strike-breakers recruit a worker, he shows us the group pouring drinks for the worker in a tavern. Intercut are close-ups of musicians obviously playing at the same time that the worker is drinking. Finally, separate shots of musicians and the worker are shown together as dissolves. The effect is a combination of a sense of joyous and innocent tavern activities with the ominous sense of the man's being deceptively initiated into a devious organization. The liquor and the music intoxicate him.

In *Mother,* dissolves with very quick successive superimpositions can suggest a general condition (almost a poetic metaphor). Shots of factories and the working class's tenement housing within a dissolve imply a sense of cause and effect though perceived simultaneously. This series of shots precedes another related series of shots—but this time the shots are not dissolved but connected by cuts. They establish conflict but no sense of cause and effect: scenes of factory whistles blasting away, awakening poor workers in crowded sleeping quarters, join to images of a beautiful and serene countryside.

One of the best examples of rapid dissolves occurs when the mother watches her son reach for the floorboard under which, she knows, he keeps a small arms cache for his revolutionary friends. The dissolves include close-

ups of the mother's horrified expression, the guns, her son's chest, his hands clutching his chest (*i.e.,* after being shot), her son lying dead, and again the mother's face. All these dissolves last just seconds but clearly convey to us what is passing in the mother's imagination. They are accumulative inasmuch as they proceed chronologically, but so swift are the images that they project almost simultaneously and are thus in effect very much like Eisenstein's.

A few effective similes appear in the film, the most dramatic occurring when, at a crucial moment, a young man who is involved in a factory strike is cornered by the strike-breakers, who threaten to kill him. Frightened, he points a gun at them, and when they attack him the gun goes off, killing one of the strike-breakers. As the crowd pounces on him and begins to beat him, Pudovkin cuts away to the scenic countryside as he did earlier, but this time images of weather evoke a sense of violence: clouds gather, the wind provokes ripples in the river, trees shake. Then comes the most powerful image of all: an iris shot of an arm with a rivet through the hand, a suggestion of the Crucifixion and a parallel with the martyred young worker.

A poetic image created within a single shot is harder to achieve, but Pudovkin manages a few such images in this film. One of the most effective occurs after the son's sentencing to prison. We observe a table's surface: hands are placed on top of it, and another's hands placed comfortingly on top of the first pair. Then the mother's bowed head appears from the upper part of the frame and rests upon the hands in a metaphor of maternal grief.

Imagery between sequences can also be used to suggest a broader base for the ideology of the film. The mother's visit to the son in prison is followed by the title "Outdoors" and shots of water rushing in a stream or river. The next title, "Spring," introduces shots of the mother walking home and young children playing. The shots may suggest the same environment for the mother and the children, but Pudovkin's aim is to contrast the outdoors and the prison, which we are again shown. The son in his darkened cell is barely illuminated by the sunlight through the bars of the window. A series of close-ups is intercut showing water in a river, a small child laughing, and the prisoner's eyes filled with rage, immediately followed by a shot of him venting his anger by flinging a cup against the wall and banging on his door.

In the exciting "prison riot and escape" sequence, the son flees to a river filled with ice in the final process of breaking up. We have already had several cuts to scenes of ice in pieces floating or rushing down the river. Thus, the actual flight by the son onto the ice unifies much of the visual imagery of rivers that had earlier appeared merely symbols of the son's desire to be somewhere other than in prison. The son escapes on the ice, only to be killed in the arms of his mother amidst a crowd of civilians fired upon by soldiers. This concluding sequence, virtually a remake of

Eisenstein's "Odessa Steps" sequence, includes the mother bravely raising the workers' flag and marching toward the charging cavalry, who trample her to death. Once the literal action of the film concludes, Pudovkin returns to the breaking ice imagery and to shots of industrial edifices presumably reflecting the economic class distinction in the Czarist-capitalist society.

The film idea of *Mother* derives from the concept of the heroic nature displayed by ordinary people of the lower classes when confronted with the oppressions of the established order. To convey this idea, Pudovkin accumulates images within the sequence toward the development of abstract notions of both human potential and the oppression of the system. Although the film is a study of typical conditions leading to the unsuccessful 1905 revolution, Pudovkin's images constantly shift us from the realm of the immediate environment to the general condition he wishes to emphasize. The individuals remain clearly delineated, convincingly real. But their reactions or thoughts are at the same time particularized by their environment and abstracted by Pudovkin's poetic techniques.

# Verbal
# and Visual
# Interactions

## The Problem of Mixed Modes

The problems of the dialogue film cannot properly be separated from the problems of editing sequences or even of filming shots. Some of the practical difficulties have been discussed in Chapter 10, yet these difficulties are only effects of the theoretical problems that result from the adaptation of a basically visual medium to the communication patterns of the verbal narrative. Thus, the process of filming images and editing them into narrative shape has developed into the process of creating a visual context for speech. But film narrative was not originally created to subserve the purposes of dramatic literature. Since there have been at least an equal number of great and almost great dialogue films as silent films, certainly the best of the sound films may be considered as examples of how to cope successfully with dialogue problems; however, they cannot often stand as general models, for these good dialogue films are frequently examples of special situations not widely applicable. And indeed, some of the best sound films really do not have a great deal of dialogue, or when they do, the dialogue is not always among the most important cinematic elements.

The practice of combining two distinct modes of communication almost always leads to a situation in which either the dialogue or the image (more often the former) is thoroughly dominant. Since the storytelling

procedure of the silent film narrative was carried over in large measure at the time that synchronized sound was being developed, it remains possible to this day to create art of a very high caliber in films that present a dominant visual pattern of communication. The alternative extreme— the great film in which dialogue entirely dominates the visual imagery— can only rarely occur, if at all. Of course, in most films of above-average quality, filmmakers have taken some care to balance visual and verbal modes. Nevertheless, the theoretical problem is not solved by the common technique of resorting to alternating modes of communication for different parts of the film: that is, after developing one or two ideas in the dialogue, the filmmaker switches to a sequence emphasizing physical action (the crooks discuss the crime and then go out and perform it).

The difficulty inherent in transferring emphasis from one mode to the other, even when patterned consistently throughout a film, lies in the disparity of the functional role relegated to each mode. Since man has been conceiving narratives in verbal terms for at least the last four or five thousand years, and in visual terms only since the start of this century, we understand why the ordinary filmmaker quite likely discovers the origins of a film project in a written text or a verbal concept. During the early stages of developing the film idea, the creator may instinctively assign to the dialogue the task of conveying the intellectual and emotional content of the film. The mixing of the visual and verbal modes usually works out so that the latter contributes the gist of the film's meaning; the visuals merely establish the decor or the trimmings, the facial expressions that accompany the words.

Films conceived in such a way may very well contain shots, even entire sequences, that are stimulating cinema. But if the filmmaker's essential approach to his material fails to unify the functions of the modes, he likely limits the total effect of his work. After all, some implicit unity of sound and picture on the thematic level is necessary to convey a significant film idea. To relegate trivial functions to the image precludes the best opportunities to enhance the quality of the verbal idea. In fact, if the verbal idea is allowed to float over insignificantly related images, the idea itself is undermined; it has no support or confirmation in the world we see established on screen. The idea is simply hanging in space, and if it is crucial to the life of the film, the film is destined to fail artistically.

Thus, we return to the basic problem of trying to find a way to combine the separate modes of communication. What to say and what to show and how to achieve integration of the two modes are questions that are resolved in each individual case primarily in the process of conceiving the film idea. But for the moment we are less concerned with individual cases than with the general condition. Undoubtedly, almost all filmmakers deal with the subject intuitively, and their success depends on the quality of their intuition. It also depends—and this is something we can discuss

in regard to theory—on the basic approach to the subject matter. Essentially only two attitudes need be distinguished at this point. First, the filmmaker may use the visual mode to establish a context for the dialogue. Second, and much rarer (but standard in the silent film), the filmmaker may insure that the visual image determines the nature of the conversation. At first glance both attitudes may seem virtually the same. The difference lies in the emphasis: in the first, the dialogue dominates inasmuch as the filmmaker sets up his environment after he determines in a general way what the characters have to say, what the plot requires to be said; in the second, the visual element dominates because what has to be said is limited by the visual circumstances conceived beforehand or simultaneously with the dialogue.

## Verbal Emphasis and Visual Relevance: Shakespeare and the Dialogue Film

The filmmaker who conceives of his film idea first in terms of dialogue often has a literary feeling for what constitutes good dialogue. Very indirectly, of course, he might consider his standard to be the dialogue of Shakespeare, which is usually conceded to be the best in the Western tradition of dramatic narrative. In this connection, we might consider briefly the nature of the impulse that brings Shakespeare so often to the screen. We are led to believe that the cinematic transformation of a play by Shakespeare, even if it is not an essentially great film, cannot be faulted in one respect: the dialogue will be superb. Actually, if one examines the results of half a dozen of the best film versions of Shakespeare, the mediocrity is striking. And the truth is that the dialogue, far from being the one redeeming virtue of such works, usually stands out as the worst part of the film.

Shakespeare's failure as a scenarist lies much more in his writing than in his dramatic ideas—many of which are remarkably close to good film ideas, especially in his development of the chronicle structure. But his dialogue remains beyond redemption, as any schoolboy could tell who has been ordered to see such a film, his blithe English teacher indicating that this is the only kind of film experience worth sharing with his classmates. In fact, the literary greatness of Shakespeare's dialogue, and to an equivalent degree that of the dialogue of all the masters of dramatic literature from the Elizabethans to Shaw, is the obstacle to its success as film dialogue.

The special achievement of Shakespeare's stage dialogue lies very deeply in the sense of environment that it creates. Because of the precise establishment of the area in which the world of the play is contained, Shakespeare's dialogue can be abstracted from any setting and performed

with great success in an entirely oral situation, as on radio or records. The world of *Hamlet, Lear, Richard II,* of indeed even the lesser plays, is emphatically realized in terms of the dialogue, which comprises the carefully articulated ideas, characterizations, and plot developments, thus firmly establishing the conditions of the play. The dialogue, in other words, creates the context. For example, Act Five of *Henry IV, Part I* opens with this dialogue:

> KING: How bloodily the sun begins to peer
> Above yon busky hill! The day looks pale
> At his distemp'rature.
>
> PRINCE:          The southern wind
> Doth play the trumpet to his purposes,
> And by his hollow whistling in the leaves
> Foretells a tempest and a blust'ring day.

This dialogue informs the audience that the King and his party are near the scene of the impending battle rather than at court and that the weather is ominous. This sort of highly suggestive dialogue is always uncalled for on the screen. What can a visual image do but repeat what Shakespeare has described—or make the verbal image pointless by depicting the setting more precisely than the dialogue (more than Shakespeare, in fact, felt was advisable)? It is not merely the setting but the entire world of the drama that flows from Shakespeare's lines, and therefore to incorporate that world in the somewhat mundane reality of actual images of forests, battles, and storms seems an unnecessary belaboring of the imaginative reality so brilliantly established by the poet without the help of Cinemascope.

Akira Kurosawa, it might be noted, has made an excellent film out of Shakespeare's *Macbeth,* entitled *The Throne of Blood.* In that case, what the filmmaker did was merely to borrow the dramatic ideas of Shakespeare, as the poet himself did from his own sources. Kurosawa then took the Macbeth "myth" and applied it to a new context where its eternal relevance and power were exhibited cinematically. He let Shakespeare's text serve as the basis for a dramatic structure, which he blended into a medieval Japanese setting. The result is more Kurosawa than Shakespeare, but it is a fine film.

The language of poetry practically by definition suggests images even beyond the literal image; however, it is the literal image that will cause trouble in the film. Since the surfaces of the film are themselves images of the real world, they convey a literalness that hinders or obtrudes upon the suggestiveness of poetic dialogue. Certainly film tries to suggest ideas beyond its surface, but its suggestiveness lies primarily in the way in which shots are combined for predetermined effects. Forcing verbal images to fol-

low the literal image of a picture confines or distorts or undermines the words. This in turn means the undermining of the sequence, regardless of the quality of the visual images, for those have been made either vague or misleading by the dialogue.

The failure of spoken images to be assimilated into the visual pattern may indicate the impossibility of joining good dialogue to good pictures. Yet in theory, at least, the possibility does exist. What has yet to be discovered is a quality style for cinematic dialogue, a language that goes beyond the vivid and pragmatically effective dialogue of the 1930's gangster film, a genre that succeeded as well as any in integrating words and pictures harmoniously.

When we consider those good films in which the dialogue predetermined the nature of the visual context, we find certain revealing similarities. A diverse short list of such American films might include *She Done Him Wrong* (with Mae West), *The Big Sleep* (with Bogart), *Duck Soup* (with the Marx Brothers), *Body and Soul* (with John Garfield), and *Sunset Boulevard* (with William Holden and Gloria Swanson). First of all, the films are memorable primarily for the powerful presence of the stars, even when, as in each of the above cases, the directors are extremely talented; these are talking films, and the characters who do the talking (or create the noise, let us say, so as to include Harpo Marx) are the ones who determine the quality of the film, not the writers nor the editors, nor even the director who supervised the acting. Furthermore, and perhaps because of this, the films tend to take their shape from the presentation of personalities, not from plot or theme, nor from anything not tied directly to characterization as it either exists or develops. The world of the film lies, ultimately, not so much in what the characters say as in the style in which things get said. These are indeed good talking films because they are highly stylized in their talk. Certainly some of Mae West's lines are truly funny, but not all of them, or at least they are not all equally amusing; yet audiences laugh uproariously when she says "Peel me a grape" or "Come up and see me some time." Wit hardly matters once she has established her characterization, for at a certain point in the film everything has become the projection of her cynical sexiness.

Still, the general problem of full cinematic effectiveness arises whenever the film is so conceived that the dialogue controls the context, as with most literary adaptations. Of course, when a director starts with the words, his first business must then be to make the surfaces relevant. This can be done well, of course, but it requires material that is especially suitable for visual and verbal relationships. For instance, in *The Maltese Falcon,* the dialogue does indeed create the context—one of moral confinement: characters assemble in rooms to plan devious activities, and the rooms become visual representations of the evil environment; the conversation establishes the atmosphere of evil, which is sustained by the actions we witness. Yet the fact remains that such films are not plentiful, and when we have examples

of the successful film in which the dialogue establishes the context or dictates the nature of the visual imagery, we seem to be pointing to special situations.

## Visual Emphasis and Verbal Relevance:
## A Sequence from Bergman's *Wild Strawberries*

There is no turning back to the silent film, to that nostalgic—and largely imaginary—golden age when every film idea shone through with purely visual brilliance. Less often remembered is the fact that the "golden age" produced a preponderance of heavily titled films in which imperfectly conceived film ideas struggled in search of—not a purer visual expressiveness, but a more explicit insert title. The many sound films that prove ineffective cinema because they have no visual significance are probably paralleled by an equal percentage of silent films that failed because they sought a dialogue equivalent.

The creation of an artistically successful sound film requires a clear conception of place and situation: the characters have to be located somewhere for some specific reasons. Next, the filmmaker must conceive of words that belong to such a context. A good part of human life is talk, and the lack of it in a sound film seems unnatural and implies a theme (inability to relate and noncommunication) that might not at all be intended. By itself, conversation does not imply either cinematic or uncinematic material, though in practice it often leads to the latter. To be cinematic it must be responsive to the surface image or the cinematic idea under development, or both. (By surface image, we mean only the specific place or the people within the environment; by cinematic idea, we refer to the concept behind the sequence in which the conversation takes place.)

When we examine common types of sequences from ordinary films, we discover that indeed most conversations carry the total meaning of the sequence with no particular regard to other cinematic aspects of the film. Almost all conversations presented in cars fall into this category. Two people talking in a car are presumably going someplace, and that seems sufficient justification for the characters to be doing their talking while en route. Car conversations seem cinematic because the photography simulates a condition of motion, especially when the rear-screen projection device gives the impression of movement through the back or side windows of what is, after all, not a real car and not in motion. The esthetic questions are usually conveniently ignored. For instance, is the journey itself important enough to justify our having to sit through it? (Most journeys are not important—the action, we know in advance, is scheduled to take place after arrival.) Is the journey just a change of scene—that is, why couldn't the conversation be held someplace else? Does the situation of driving have

any bearing on the nature of the conversation? Or, do people say the same things in cars that they say in living rooms? While driving, people don't normally look at each other, and therefore the subjects of their conversations in cars may very well differ from what they discuss elsewhere.

Ideally, a shot, much less an entire sequence, should not be used merely for the convenience of the dialogue. Unless an image is deliberately abstracted—that is, either universalized, as in some John Ford Western, or made unreal, as in *The Cabinet of Dr. Caligari*—place always figures prominently in a film. It can't be escaped or ignored. Conversations must occur somewhere, obviously, but the fact of their being interesting or relevant to the *plot* cannot entirely justify their being irrelevant to the location and the immediate visual conditions.

The major filmmakers usually locate conversations specifically so as to associate the reasons for the characters' presence or movement with the environment; presumably they could tell us why the conversation takes place here and not there. As an example, we can consider the sequence from the early part of Bergman's *Wild Strawberries* (1957) in which the old Professor, Isak Borg, begins his long drive to the city where he is to receive an honorary degree. His daughter-in-law Marianne accompanies him to return to her husband, Borg's son, from whom she has been separated for a month because of marital difficulties (she has stayed that month in Borg's house). Bergman has made it clear that the journey is a long one and that this is a crucial day in Borg's life. At this point he introduces the first of many conversations that occur in the car. As always in Bergman, the se-

quence is well filmed, but no particularly artful camerawork distracts us from what is simply a conversation between two people (fig. 63).

Yet in the conversation we have material that is truly cinematic and truly meaningful in terms of the plot, characterization, and theme. A few lines from the beginning of the sequence will serve to establish the technique, though these lines are actually preliminary to the significant ideas that will develop later on:

> ISAK: Please don't smoke.

> MARIANNE: Of course.

> ISAK: I can't stand cigarette smoke.

> MARIANNE: I forgot.

> ISAK: Besides, cigarette smoking is both expensive and unhealthy. There should be a law against women smoking.

> MARIANNE: The weather is nice.

> ISAK: Yes, but oppressive. I have a feeling that we'll have a storm.

> MARIANNE: So do I.

> ISAK: Now take the cigar. Cigars are an expression of the fundamental idea of smoking. A stimulant and a relaxation. A manly vice.*

The dialogue appears casual, perhaps even trivial, and not related to the car or the driving (Borg would dislike cigarette smoking in his living room). And yet, as low-keyed as the dialogue seems, it perfectly and very obviously suits the visual material, which consists largely of two faces in a car. The small gesture of lighting a cigarette becomes a subject for Isak Borg to vent his irritation on. By expanding his personal displeasure at Marianne's lighting a cigarette into an attack on smoking only for the sake of the generalization against women (illogically conceived on the basis of the premise that smoking is unhealthy and expensive), he suggests an animosity toward his daughter-in-law that is uncalled for and not really derived from the immediate cause. His previous argument at home with his housekeeper, who objected to his making this long trip by car, has made him irritable, and the cigarette serves as a pretext for his self-expression.

Marianne's character is also revealed under the pressure of the circumstances. In these close quarters she can neither argue with the old man or keep silent all day, so she changes the topic to the innocuous subject of weather (which Borg can twist into an outer sign of his inner an-

---

*Four Screenplays of Ingmar Bergman*, trans. by Lars Malmstrom and David Kushner (New York, Simon and Schuster, 1960), pp. 177–78.

noyance: the weather is "oppressive"). Although *Wild Strawberries* is structured as a first-person narration by Borg, who we understand is in the process of reevaluating his life, we sympathize with the tactful woman in her predicament of being stuck for a long time in a confined area with Borg. We sense that the trip is likely to be miserable for her, since her attempts to pacify Borg are unsuccessful. First she agrees not to smoke; then she agrees with Borg's observation about the weather, though it contradicts her previous remark that it looked "nice." Yet even this does not placate Borg, who returns to the topic of smoking, though he had exhausted it before with his sweeping condemnation of her smoking.

There is no point in elaborating on the texture of the dialogue, since we are not here concerned with the complexity of the quoted passage (and it is certainly more complex judged within its context than as related here). What remains of interest is the way in which Bergman makes his conversation relevant to the fact of place. It sounds like the sort of thing one would say in a car, and yet it works as well in disclosing characterization as the more significant dialogue that two such intellectual people as Borg and Marianne might say in Borg's library, where this sort of conversation would be unlikely. Also, Bergman establishes a well-motivated tone for the ride, for it is a special kind of ride, one that has an unusual goal (the reconciliation of husband and wife and the receiving of an honorary degree to climax a distinguished medical career). Thus, the mood of petty irritation and the seriousness of the purpose of the long drive create their own tension. Eventually, Bergman will develop the film idea more clearly: this is a ride into Borg's past, a recapitulation of his spiritual decline, the dawning of a tragic revelation, and the movement toward a reordering of his present existence. Yet even if the car did not develop into a metaphysical symbol, the use of it and the journey are clearly significant in regard to characterization and theme.

## Specification of Environment in the Sound Film

In a sequence in which the filmmaker intends to stress the visual concept, the problem of verbal relevance is also the problem of the degree of tension allowable between sound and picture. Since it is extremely difficult for picture and sound to make the same point without obviously duplicating each other, and since both visual image and sound have special ways of communicating, the filmmaker needs to create an environment and a reason for being in that environment that will yield themselves to a certain kind of dialogue. Even if in real life people are apt to say anything anywhere, art is not a transcript of life. If the nature of the place where the conversation is occurring becomes totally irrelevant or indeed disappears from conscious awareness, then a tension will develop between sound and picture when-

ever (as always happens) the background environment obtrudes for a moment on the dialogue. This often occurs with films adapted from plays, for studio designers take great care to make the interiors of the apartments in which most of the action occurs seem visually quite opulent. We spend the first few minutes of the film getting acquainted with the place, and then it becomes irrelevant for three-quarters of the film. Every once in a while we recall the apartment, and of course this directs us away from the conversation. Apparently, dialogue can create its own environment, and when it does so the specifications of the visual environment are frequently a blatant annoyance.

This is less true when the environment has not been carefully specified. If the environment includes an element of the general or the abstract, it is easier for the verbal material to establish its relevance. For this reason, many ordinary films in certain genres like the Western present unified artistic wholes, though otherwise the artistry seems unintentional. From the campsite to the canyon, the Westerner traverses a familiar, unparticularized terrain, though one of eternal appeal. Only half articulate, the Western hero (a Jimmy Stewart or a John Wayne) moves about consciously aware of the environment and chooses his words so as to say directly and concisely what needs to be said. His horse and his guns speak visually for him, for they are extensions of the environment. Although one Western bar looks like every Western bar, it is always adequate for the film concept, and the dialogue that fills the room, without pretense to literary quality, usually fits right in. In contrast, the lavish interiors of many costume films simply create a particularized place in which nothing relevant is spoken, as the verbal remarks neither grow out of the environment nor correspond to it. (Such a film as Visconti's *The Damned,* where everything verbalized exactly suits the characters in the highly particularized places, is of course an exception. Visconti proves that visual emphasis and highly relevant dialogue are possible within a sharply defined interior environment.)

Similarly, the science-fiction film and the horror film abstract their environments because we have grown familiar with the mad scientist's laboratory; furthermore, one weird monster resembles the next. The verbal responses in the second-rate science-fiction films are always the same, and the dialogue is trite, but quite a number of them generate interest in part because the dialogue actually approximates the natural human reaction to the specified visual contexts. The woman screaming from a tree in terror of King Kong expresses exactly what the situation warrants (fig. 64). Of course a quality difference exists between *King Kong,* say, and some *Godzilla*-like film, and frequently the difference has to do with conflict between picture and dialogue for domination. In the truly cinematic *King Kong,* the monster ape becomes the star, and the dialogue remains functional; it consists of the sort of things members of the civilized world might say while intruding on the primitive. The presence of King Kong or the threat of his

**64** *King Kong*

presence (that is, the visual material) is always kept in mind. In the execrable science-fiction films based on the idea of the monster who intrudes on civilization, the environment revolves around human beings talking in offices or worrying in laboratories; when the monster arrives, the film is momentarily interesting, but most of the time the characters just sit in rooms and theorize about the matter. Here, the dialogue creates the content, but the monster, on his rare appearances, is much more interesting than the people. As a result the characters grow duller and duller while the audience eagerly awaits the next appearance of the monster.

## Integrating Dialogue and Visuals: Renoir's *Rules of the Game*

The sound track cannot usually be edited with the same economy one can employ with the visuals, largely because the specifications a filmmaker wishes to make through dialogue require logical development that normally takes longer than a visual image takes to impart its meaning. Therefore, the creation of a sequence in terms of sound alone is not common. The dialogue itself can seldom be edited so as to create the units of a sequence, as do the visual shots. Within a sequence the dialogue is frequently continuous, whereas the images are most likely discontinuous; that is, while two people partake in an ongoing conversation, many separate shots are employed to convey whatever visual information there may be.

The editing of the sound track to create a meaning parallel but not identical to the visuals has not been commonly practiced. Fritz Lang did a good deal of this in *M* (see Chapter 10), but his use of sound primarily

dramatized the significance of the visuals, even when the sound was itself dramatically effective, as when the mother calls for her child, whom we know has been led away by the murderer: what we remember is the child's name as it resounds against the image of an empty stairwell. Although Lang's use of the sound track is thoroughly effective, it did not include all the possibilities for editing sound.

In *Rules of the Game* (1939), Renoir constructed his sound track so as to develop ideas implicit in the visuals without duplicating them. Much of the film is edited to suggest dramatic scenes, short conversations between characters; yet the apparent dramatic base does not conflict with the truly cinematic nature of *Rules of the Game,* for much of what we see creates the meaning of what we hear (and vice versa). Renoir employs sound with considerable economy, at times even more economically than any equivalent visual shots could do to produce the same ideas. In introducing characters, for instance, Renoir's expository opening sequences concisely link all the major characters through visual and verbal reactions to a radio broadcast. The opening shots supply the source of the broadcast and suggest its implications. The film opens with a shot of a noisy crowd at the airport greeting André Jurieu as he arrives after setting a transatlantic flight record. The camera follows a female announcer broadcasting the event over radio. Jurieu, interviewed amid the crowd, stands with his friend Octave (played by Renoir), who is trying to explain to him why Jurieu's lover could not meet him at the airport. Then over the air the impassioned, romantic Jurieu makes the comically scandalous remark: "I am very unhappy; I have never been so disappointed in my life. I undertook this exploit because of a woman. She isn't even here waiting for me. She didn't even bother to come. If she is listening to me, I tell her in public that she's let me down." * While the announcer is left to supply some excuse for Jurieu's startling conduct and Octave to distract his friend and prevent him from enlarging on his personal problems, the camera cuts to a woman's bedroom. The voice of the broadcast is heard from a radio in Christine's room, and we assume she is the lover Jurieu referred to because of her evident concern about the broadcast.

The fact that Christine and her maid Lisette enter into a conversation seemingly irrelevant to the broadcast (she questions the maid about her lovers) only heightens the sense we have that the broadcast actually means a great deal to Christine, for the verbal details have been made exceedingly prominent and require some comment. Silence on the matter can only indicate that the radio interview had some extremely personal meaning for Christine. After her conversation with Lisette, she enters her husband's room. The first shot of him, the Marquis Robert de la Chesnaye, shows him absorbed in listening to the broadcast. The conversation between the hus-

* *Rules of the Game,* trans. by John McGrath and Maureen Teitelbaum (New York, Simon and Schuster, 1970), p. 29.

band and wife here relates directly to the broadcast: Robert reveals that he knows his wife has been having an affair with Jurieu, can understand sympathetically how it might have come about, and forgives her. Thus, we have his apparent interpretation of Jurieu's remarks: the fact that his wife has disappointed Jurieu, Robert feels, indicates that she can give up her lover.

Alone after this conversation, Robert calls up his lover, Geneviève, who is not listening to the radio, but who, as soon as she hangs up, walks into another room where four men playing cards are listening to that broadcast (this is still part of the same shot in which Geneviève was introduced on the telephone). Thus, each of the major characters is introduced in his own milieu against the background of the radio interview. The interview with its revealing comment on Christine's failure to show up inspires Robert to seek closer marital ties with his wife, first by excusing her and second by breaking with Geneviève. Geneviève hears the broadcast and presumably realizes its potential impact on Robert, for she says so in the subsequent sequence when Robert tells her that he wants to return to his wife.

Jurieu's unhappiness, Christine's hesitancy in regard to her relationship with him, and the affair of Robert and Geneviève are thus linked in a highly suggestive way, in the first twenty-five shots of the film. The complexity of the relationships is clarified by the unifying radio broadcast, but not truly explained by it. In addition to the broadcast, much dialogue is used to characterize each person involved, even the guests in Geneviève's house, who serve to reveal to us that everyone knows that Christine has been Jurieu's lover. (Indeed, the film is about the rules of the game of love among the middle and upper classes, as they are observed or broken by the participants and as the rules are made to appear in the eyes of the public.) The dialogue does not do it all; for in addition to focusing our aural attention on the relationships between speakers, Renoir wants us to see this world with considerable clarity.

For instance, Renoir requires us to grasp in a precise way the abstract notion that wealth leads to idleness and the social malaise of this society. He presents Robert's preoccupation with mechanical dolls and birds as a visual symbol of the man and his class. This suggests his partial detachment from the truly human and an excessive interest in the regulated, formalized style of life. Robert stands as the opposite of the erratic Jurieu and survives him. The visual symbol of the mechanical toys complements the kind of information we receive from his dialogue: Robert's calm, controlled speech implies that the rules of conduct exist to promote an orderly social surface. Marital infidelity, his own and his wife's, is unfortunate but acceptable as long as it remains within the concept of the rules and provided the patterns of good conduct are not violated. This too suggests the leisure-class preoccupation with a life-style that exalts external appearances of honor over passions and integrity. Indeed, the whole film seems to revolve

**65** *Rules of the Game*

around the apparent need to stifle real feelings and substitute a good deal of cynicism. The final entangled relationships lead to a situation where Jurieu, about to leave with Christine, is mistakenly shot and killed by Robert's jealous gamekeeper, who thinks he is protecting his own marriage. Ironically, Robert, who knew of Jurieu's destination, must cover up the sordidness by addressing the guests at his estate in these terms: "Gentlemen, there has just been a deplorable accident, that's all. . . . My keeper Schumacher thought he saw a poacher, and he fired, since that is his duty. . . . Chance had it that André Jurieu should be the victim of this error. . . . Gentlemen, tomorrow we shall leave the chateau weeping for this wonderful friend, this excellent companion who knew so well how to make us forget that he was a famous man . . ." * (fig. 65). Actually, Robert functions best as a self-appointed symbol of his class and the values of honor and order. This improvised eulogy, so contradictory to the implicit emotional response called for by the situation, typifies the attitude and surface calm of Robert that Renoir carefully established visually through the character's demeanor, his manners, and his hobby of mechanical devices.

Renoir's ability to create a meaningful dialogue film rests on a sensitive awareness of how people live within an environment and an age. *Rules of the Game* has a well-written, highly readable script, more so than most scripts of quality films, but it still remains essentially a visual experience

* *Ibid.,* p. 168.

because the visuals incorporate the language: sentences have meaning not only because they are spoken by clearly defined characters but because they say particular things in particular places—in airports and bedrooms, during a hunting party or a masquerade—and what they say is influenced by the place and the time, which helps establish a certain kind of plausibility for the drama.

Renoir's use of the sound track cannot of course be the last word on the subject. For other film styles, other uses of sound can be discovered. To edit a sound track so as to create meaning that does not negate or duplicate the visuals remains the key problem, but all the highly successful sound films have to some extent come to terms with it.

## Opposing Dialogue and Visuals: Buñuel's *The Milky Way*

A filmmaker may choose to counterpoint the sound track and the picture so that cinematic meaning results from the combination of the two in conflict rather than from integration or from the alternation in the mode of communication of the ideas between sound and picture. Such a technical feat is not often attempted for any prolonged segment of a film, even by great directors, for lack of subject matter suitable to this essentially disorienting process. But Luis Buñuel has achieved remarkable success in *The Milky Way* (1968) by combining intriguing, amusing visual images with some erudite dialogue. The immediate result naturally inclines toward the comic: a kindly priest has been elaborating on Christian doctrine to a police officer in a restaurant; when the officer points out that the priest a few minutes before had contradicted his present view, the good priest suddenly flings the contents of his cup in the officer's face. The contrast between the violent gesture and the dignified and pious remarks of the priest (who, it turns out, is a madman) is typical of comic incongruity. The humorous disparities disclose a serious theme. Buñuel's film idea as it emerges from such a sequence is the disparity between dogma and how one actually lives in this world. Neither the dialogue nor the image alone conveys the concept, but the clash of words and pictures does.

In *The Milky Way,* Buñuel succeeds several times in communicating ideas through conflicting sights and sounds. An extraordinary duel with swords occurs between two characters dressed in eighteenth-century costumes. Buñuel draws on our familiarity with dozens of such scenes from the costume-drama films of the past, but *The Milky Way* is intended as neither parody nor burlesque. The visual part is entirely straightforward. One man insults the other; they follow the ritual of arranging for an immediate duel, preceded by the customary slapping of the face with a glove. The duel is expertly staged; neither man is wounded. However, the extremely elevated level of the dialogue makes the sequence high comedy:

throughout, the men hold a running argument on theological issues, specifically the question of free will. Both argue like doctors of the Church, referring to authorities for examples. The argument, like the duel, ends inconclusively, and the men walk off as dear friends. Clearly, theological controversy is irrelevant to daily life, though Buñuel's point is not that simple. After all, these men are aroused by the theological issues to stake their honor and their lives. Buñuel manages to satirize the conduct (the visual image) by enclosing the duel in a high-minded debate; at the same time, the philosophy is itself undermined by the nonintellectual activity of the swordsmen.

Buñuel's technical achievement in *The Milky Way* is of a type not likely to become common practice, though the method of comic counterpoint is found frequently in individual sequences from sound films. Between Buñuel's studied irrelevance and Renoir's parallel development of picture and word, we notice in most films various kinds and innumerable degrees of relationships of sound and picture. The editing of a sound track does not require an *a priori* commitment to the superiority of either mode of communication, but primarily a realization that although film is basically a visual experience, the world of narrative art is frequently verbal. The unification of the two modes in the modern sound film probably requires a filmmaker to control the scenario to a greater extent than may have been necessary in the silent era or may even be feasible today. Yet such control is essential because the film idea must include the dialogue and visuals from the start—though not necessarily in detail, for many filmmakers like to improvise both dialogue and shots during the actual filming. What cannot be added, however, is either the visual sense or the verbal suggestiveness of a film idea if it was not part of the original conception. The extremes of modern filming are premised on either (1) the visual experience, which is conceived in terms of an interesting narrative, but one in which the dialogue seems a distraction, or (2) the literary work, usually a stage play, to which the filmmaker simply attempts to add an interesting visual area—to graft a picture onto the words. Renoir and Buñuel and other successful filmmakers of the sound era work out a pattern of language spoken in a clearly perceived environment, all within a narrative framework where characterization is revealed by actions and responses. The resulting interaction of the verbal and the visual is essential to the expression of the film's meaning, not additional to it.

# Structure
# in the Modern
# Film

## The Trend Away from Traditional Plotting

In a well-known study of fictional art, E. M. Forster draws an interesting distinction between story and plot that is essentially true for all narrative art, including the film. The story, he says,

> runs like a backbone—or may I say a tapeworm, for its beginning and end are arbitrary. It is immensely old . . . Neanderthal man listened to stories . . . gaping around the campfire, fatigued with contending against the mammoth or the wooly rhinoceros, and only kept awake by suspense. What would happen next? The novelist droned on, and as soon as the audience guessed what happened next, they either fell asleep or killed him.*

In regard to the modern film, the story may be said to consist of all the incidents regardless of their connections or importance, as long as they arouse the audience's curiosity about what will happen next.

Plot is something else. The term suggests a deliberate structuring of

* E. M. Forster, *Aspects of the Novel* (New York, Harcourt Brace Jovanovich, 1927), p. 26.

incidents in which the connections are essential. Forster defines plot this way:

> We have defined a story as a narrative of events arranged in their time-sequence. A plot is also a narrative of events, the emphasis falling on causality. "The king died and then the queen died" is a story. "The king died, and then the queen died of grief" is a plot. The time-sequence is preserved, but the sense of causality overshadows it. . . . Consider the death of the queen. If it is in a story we say "and then?" If it is in a plot we ask "why?" That is the fundamental difference between these two aspects of the novel.*

It is also the fundamental difference for the narrative film. Thus, all films will have something that can be defined as the story, but some films may not have a plot. Most films, of course, have both: the story equals the total of the incidents, while the plot is comprised of only those incidents that link together in a pattern of cause and effect.

One of the significant trends in the contemporary film is a movement away from the predesigned structure of a plot. Comparable modern movements might be noted in the novel and on the stage, though in both literary forms the major trend remains within the conventional definition of plot. But film may very well be turning toward the kind of plotlessness that many already see as typical of Bergman's later work, most of Antonioni's, and several of the more talked-about contemporary films. The avoidance of a plot as the controlling structure of a film seems to many viewers to threaten the basis of the art form; however, there are two considerations that might require us to revaluate the supposed basis for narrative film content in the first place: the literary antecedents of plot narrative require a structure not always suitable to films, and the disappearance of the plot narrative does not necessarily mean an end to the narrative film. But if plot goes, what kind of structure can a film have? Surely, it will not be the developed scenario that enforced a literary idea on so many conventional films of the past. At the other extreme, the random joining together of numerous incidents cannot substitute for a plot. Structure is not a limitation on an artist but an opportunity to unite form and content. What new form will film content take if the trend away from a story line continues?

Let us remember that stories are always about things that happen to people (and even animals are allegorical people). In the oral tradition, relatively little detail was given to setting. When the oral tradition became a written tradition, more attention was paid to detail, but never as much as in the most casually conceived film, where details (random ones perhaps) surround characters. The real question to ask about film form is whether a filmmaker can use the details of setting to replace a large part of the narrative structure. (The one filmmaker to have consistently succeeded

* *Ibid.*, p. 86.

in this manner, Fellini, will be discussed later, but his approach to narrative is distinct from that of his contemporaries.)

Certainly directors nowadays seem to think they can do without a plot if the setting creates sufficient interest. Intuitively perhaps, they seem to be showing us a background, then bringing a character or two into the foreground, and saying, "This character lives a certain way because he responds and has responded to backgrounds such as are revealed here." The possibility of revealing motivation by analyzing a character's reaction to his environment (which includes people and events as well as objects) is more difficult the more vividly depicted the background. For example, a brilliant attempt to depict a growing intellectual awareness on the part of a character who repeatedly comes into contact with the violence of our society in Haskell Wexler's *Medium Cool* (1969) remains essentially unsuccessful because the background overwhelms the audience's sensibility. The description of significant and terrible events of the recent past (the assassination of Senator Kennedy, the 1968 Chicago Convention riots, etc.) develops a relationship between the audience and the event, bypassing the character. Whether *Medium Cool* will become more effective as the background events fade into history is problematical (the film's sociological impact may also fade). In any case, it demonstrates the difficulty of structuring a film in terms of a character's relation to his environment when that environment is charged with more emotional life than the character himself.

Equally difficult would be the attempt to play up character by restricting the background or simply depicting it with a few vivid allusions that make it a convincing abstraction. Godard does so with some success, his films implying that a character exists as a product of his environment; however, not enough of the world is actually shown to prove anything, even in so comprehensible a film as *Breathless,* and especially in the more experimental works like *Le Gai Savoir*. The relation of character to environment, to the world he inhabits, may be essentially cinematic, but it does not suffice often as an artistic structure. Indeed, it often necessitates a choice between an emphasis on character to the exclusion of the necessary detailed look at his environment, and an excessive amount of documentation of the environment to the detriment of characterization. In the latter instance, it should be remembered that a man totally defined or determined by his environment must be of limited capacity.

The problem of formlessness is most evident in the film that emphasizes characterization in terms of incidents that seem only casually related, a structure premised on the view that life presents us with a series of unrelated events. Historically, the concept of narrative art as an ordering of experiences has always been accepted in theory and challenged in practice. Works of art that seem disordered in one age might seem perfectly comprehensible in the next. Therefore, quite possibly current films that do not on the surface develop a narrative idea toward a decisive denouement at

the end may yet be perceived as having a highly structured plot ten years from now (as is already true of such an originally confusing film as Hitchcock's *The Birds*). On the other hand, a stringing together of visual images (as in *Dynamite Chicken*), even when it is held together by a unity of place (as in *Putney Swope*), and even when it traces the developing relationship of characters (as in *Lions Love*) may very well be just a collection of film materials, not a real film. That is, such films may fall outside the narrative tradition, and if so they must justify themselves as other things— perhaps entertainments or sociological records.

The procedure of working out a narrative structure by the stringing together of incidents occurs more frequently than critics generally note, as we all become more and more used to such films. To provide a sense of "plot movement," this structure requires a hero who is unusual or in peculiar circumstances so that we continually wonder what he will experience next. Sam Peckinpah's *The Ballad of Cable Hogue* (1970) revolves around the adventures of an illiterate middle-aged Westerner without ties to the land or to other people, except for a vague desire to kill a couple of former acquaintances who left him to die in the desert. He is, however, what people call an "original American character," which means he is honest and irrepressible in his speech. After Cable discovers a water source and digs a well, the whole film centers on his business operations (a sort of roadside restaurant) in the desert. Assuredly, no one in the audience has any interest in the business, but what sustains the narrative is the unlimited possibilities of the situation, unlimited because the film is not restricted by any perceivable arrangement of events.

Anything could happen to the hero (or, conversely, nothing need happen to him). The shack he inhabits is situated along the main road; all types of people ride by in the stagecoach, and any kind of action or relationship could develop there, as long as the characters themselves are amusing once they are introduced into the film. (A prostitute and an itinerant preacher-con artist are the two who become most friendly with Cable Hogue). But the relationships are arbitrary determinations of the filmmaker, and can either be terminated simply by a character's moving on or begun by a new arrival. At the end, the two friends who double-crossed Cable at the beginning, nearly four years before, are brought onto the scene. Without any logical reason for their reappearing at this time (or at any time), and since the hero had never made an attempt to find them, the revenge motif really becomes irrelevant as a structuring device. The film finally ends with Cable run over by an automobile attempting to save the life of one of the men he had wanted to kill. One of the problems with the plotless narrative is that it never really ends, it only stops—and the most convenient way of simulating a real conclusion is the arbitrary removal of the hero. His time is up because the filmmaker decides to have done with his film.

# Structuring the Realistic Film:
## Olmi's *The Fiancés* and the Italian Neorealists

Since the structuring of a film is difficult to comprehend as an abstraction, we ought to consider the simplest type of contemporary content in terms of a specific model that has met with general approval. In Ermanno Olmi's *The Fiancés* (1962), the plot *seems* virtually unpremeditated, identical with the reality of ordinary lives. The secret of its success lies in the fact that environment and character seem to create the incidents naturally, without authorial manipulation. A welder and his fiancée are forced to separate for a couple of years because of a job opportunity that will send him from Milan to Sicily. They have misgivings about the separation, but he can't turn down the chance to earn a higher salary. He relocates in Sicily; they correspond; some letters create a misunderstanding; and finally he telephones her and they reaffirm their love in a strikingly inarticulate conversation. The film ends with the feeling that the fiancés will eventually be reunited. An audience leaving the theater has hardly noticed any plot at all.

Yet the plot is the essence of the film's conception. Visually, the film presents a study of alienation and the effects of loneliness on a man's spirit, but the theme ties in directly with the narrative. A simple story of lovers separating and reconciling, the narrative develops in a fundamentally straightforward manner, but it is never formless, as it might seem if it were the basis of a stage play. One of the features that distinguish a film plot from a stage plot is the ability of the former to shift ground consistently without becoming melodramatic; the latter, on the other hand, is primarily suited to a structured rising and falling action. Perhaps the flexibility of the film has something to do with its essentially inconsistent narrative point of view—the change from subjective to objective presentation is just a matter of course. Another distinction evolves from the fact that the realistic film emphasizes spatial relationships between man and environment, and man's responses to his environment are limited to three, in varying combinations: approval, disapproval, and indifference. These basic responses are shared by all of us, probably within the course of a day. The film frequently studies just these attitudes, whereas dramatic compositions depend on a verbalization of man's relation to events (the dramatic events themselves are frequently relevant to the background, but the emphasis is less direct than in film).

The plot of *The Fiancés* omits that single dramatic incident which in a stage play would be necessary to bridge the gap between the lovers' initial separation and their ultimate reconciliation: the climax. A play does not make much sense without the dramatization of that incident. A film, however, can substitute a series of responses of man to environment for the climactic incident—the method that Griffith made standard for the film. But the modern tendency (beginning in the 1960's) to break away from

the Griffith-Dickens sense of a highly structured narrative has valid theoretical premises as well, if what substitutes for the traditional plot also results in a structured plot—though it does not employ the same sort of overt major action we find in the more conventionally designed film. However, relatively few fine works like *The Fiancés* have so far appeared in such a form.

The problem for any stage play is to convince an audience that character change really occurs for good cause; people don't suddenly change unless they have a reason, and the theater, because of its verbal method, conveys its reasoning logically. The film must also depict character change through means natural to the medium—that is, by showing us the character moving from one intellectual or emotional position to another. Olmi shows this process in terms of a character's attempts to relate to his immediate environment. The movement toward reconciliation is depicted by small incidents that add up to the film idea of homesickness, portrayed simply but deftly by showing visually the small, daily defeats of a man not adjusting very well to the foreign industrial environment.

The Sicilian situation is, to the man, immediately alienating. The ride from the airport places him apart from the other employees in the car—two professional men whose conversation excludes him—on the way to the company hotel, where he boards until he finds permanent lodgings. The first night in the hotel contains several sequences that convey his isolation. Arriving late, he eats alone after the others have finished; a waiter tells him about family troubles, to which he can respond with nothing more than a sympathetic ear, though he himself badly needs sympathy. In his small room he finds nothing to do; he is bored and embarrassed. There is no one to talk to, and it is too early for him to go to sleep. From his room he hears music down in the restaurant across the way, and he hurries there to partake of the night life. His eagerness to see some life turns into desperation when he enters the restaurant and discovers it is closing up. The sounds were from a blasting jukebox, but no customers remain. All he wants to do after his long trip is talk, but everyone is asleep; besides, he is not a forward type and does not know how to make overtures of friendship without revealing his awkwardness.

He is not particularly verbal, but never in the cinema have we felt more interest in the working of a nonintellectual mind. With very little dialogue, Olmi has shown us exteriors and objects that supply all that is necessary to understand the man and to follow his development with concern. The clean but barren and functional hotel room symbolizes the man's mental state as he confronts an environment that is absolutely tedious, though it contains none of the discomforts so easy to complain about. Were he to be asked how he liked it, he would be unable to express his reservations without baring his soul (he misses his fiancée), and he is not the sort to talk about such things.

**66** *The Fiancés*

Throughout the film, Olmi shows the man constantly interacting with his environment, making a few friends, having some entertaining moments (one sequence in the hotel is a fascinating study of how the tedium drives the company employees to play infantile pranks as if they were all in a boarding-school dormitory). Every seemingly minor matter becomes an event because the background so clearly signifies the man's state of mind. His reading his fiancée's letters in his small, unattractive lodgings (fig. 66), his roaming the flat, unattractive countryside, and his walking through the town and wandering into church (as does a stray dog) are the iconography of his inner awareness.

The blending of the narrative into the environment has to some extent always been part of the cinematic tradition, but the emphasis on this as a deliberate style became notable with the Italian Neorealistic school of the 1940's and 1950's, probably the most artistically important European film movement of the sound era. Led by De Sica, Visconti, and Roberto Rossellini, the Neorealists de-emphasized contrived literary plotting in favor

of stories that grew out of the pressures imposed on individuals by the brutal conditions of war and its aftermath. Olmi and several other fine Italian filmmakers of the 1960's come from that tradition (Fellini's early films do, too), with the interesting difference that as post-war economic conditions improved, the most relevant human problems were not immediate threats of destruction or starvation but relationships with the new industrial environment. Antonioni is thereby directly linked to the evolution of the Neorealist movement. Since in Italy the cinema of realism was always humanistic, the Neorealists' concern was to focus on individuals within the social milieu, exactly as Antonioni does today, though his milieu entails not physical deprivation as much as spiritual emptiness.

The similarities between the Neorealists' concept of story line and the seemingly formless plot line that has become popular since Antonioni's *L'Avventura* (1960) are worth noting. In *The Bicycle Thief,* after the bicycle is stolen, De Sica's poor laborer, aided by his son, goes off in pursuit of his former possession, so necessary to maintaining his job. No real plot of the usual sort emerges once the situation is delineated. The film simply details the incidents of a hopeless search set against the background of the vast city, the size of which tends to depersonalize individual disasters and thereby its individual citizens (fig. 67). In one sequence, the laborer and his friends decide to check the outdoor bicycle market, where the thief might dispose of the merchandise. At the market, however, De Sica shows us thousands of bicycles, suggesting to us that many of them could have been stolen, that indeed the small tragic event of his hero's life is duplicated

**67**  *The Bicycle Thief*

daily throughout the Roman environment. Later, in fact, it turns out that the thief himself is more pathetic than anyone else, in this environment where man is victimized by the machinery of society, which makes everyone ineffective (including the government, which would like to offer more employment, and the police force, which would like to catch bicycle thieves).

Watching De Sica's film, audiences always feel the simple narrative suffices entirely for the subject. This is because the process of the character development always seems structured, though no resolution to the motivating incident actually occurs. Our original interest in the laborer's plight is sustained by the vivid sense of reality within an environment that seems to propose the futility of searching for the stolen bicycle. The laborer grows in stature as he responds to the challenge of the environment (the abstraction of society or "the system" versus the individual), and about three-fourths of the film merely unravels the initial conflict, without attempting to reach the kind of resolution of narrative typical of the closed-ended story that characterizes most of the films discussed in this book.

Antonioni's films logically extend this typical Neorealist practice. Even more than De Sica, Antonioni is fond of beginning with a significant event to start some activity that will substitute for the traditional plot movement toward a resolution. In *Blow-Up* a photographer accidentally snaps a picture of something that looks like an act of murder. This event starts him on a search—not for a bicycle, but for a dead body, which eventually disappears. In *L'Avventura,* the somewhat astounding disappearance of a girl from a tiny island, practically from under the noses of her friends, creates the narrative interest. Has she drowned, as most of them assume, or is the resulting search for her on shore justified, though she is never found? The difference between Antonioni's structure, which has been widely criticized, and the structure of De Sica's *The Bicycle Thief,* which is never criticized, may be minimal; the overt difference lies in the relatively obvious transformation of character in De Sica's film and the unobtrusive development of Antonioni's characters. And while character development is not the same as plot, audiences have gradually come to accept the one for the other in many fine films. With the popular success of *Blow-Up,* we have evidence that even the difficult structure of an Antonioni film can entertain the masses.

## The Nature of Plot Structure: Dickens Versus Antonioni

When the motion picture was in its infancy, no concept of narrative film art seemed feasible. First of all, the art of storytelling had been traditionally verbal, and without words it was not obvious that acting (mime) could convey a narrative idea clearly. Secondly, the films were necessarily short

so that when the first narratives appeared they gave the impression of being fragments of a larger narrative idea. *The Great Train Robbery,* for instance, told the story of a robbery, but that action itself did not relate to the lives of the robbers, as it would in the hundreds of Westerns to follow; it displayed merely a fragment of a story idea, or rather a fully developed episode.

In France, Méliès and a few followers had realized the possibilities of the nonrealistic narrative, but oddly enough, in the following seventy years the nonrealistic narrative developed only a very small tradition within the full-length narrative cinema. Jean Cocteau's *Beauty and the Beast, Orpheus,* and *The Testament of Orpheus,* while interesting in themselves, stand outside the main currents of the cinema. Surrealism, a major art movement and an important dramatic genre in this century, has not been a significant cinematic alternative to the realistic style, though it has produced a few films of greatness such as Buñuel's *Belle de Jour* (but even this film proceeds pretty much in terms of a realistic surface).

Thus, whether by chance or by nature, the film developed, under the dominant influence of Griffith, a narrative form very much in the tradition that Griffith acquired from Dickens and the nineteenth-century novel. (Dickens of course is just one major literary proponent of the plotted narrative—that is, the literary work with a narrative design determining its structure.)

In the Dickensian narrative mode, the author imposes a conceptual form upon his materials, though the materials seem naturally to sprawl about as life itself. In particular, contemporaries of Dickens, reading his novel as the chapters appeared serialized in a monthly magazine, may have felt that Dickens himself didn't know what he would eventually do with his characters. Innumerable characters seem engaged in diverse, barely related activities, which the author somehow manages to tie together. Even today, when one rereads a Dickens novel, he might feel that there is still a chance that it will somehow end differently from the way it did the last time. This feeling derives from the nature of the Dickens world, which, teeming with life as it does, implies formlessness; formlessness suggests reality; the world as we know it with its consistently unexpected developments. Yet the apparent formlessness is itself controlled by a master craftsman. Thus, the great achievement of Dickens' fictional world: the sense of reality and the actual imposition of artistic form. This narrative mode carried over by Griffith into the film manifests itself in a work like *Intolerance,* in which a superstructure absorbs innumerable details that seem chaotic or unrelated at one point but become meaningful later. Griffith, the seminal mind of the cinema, inherited the Dickensian tradition, and through Griffith the propagation of the major film tradition can be traced back to the nineteenth-century novel.

The value of a plot structure seems to have been understood from the

beginning of our narrative heritage. Homer did not conceive his poems with a vague sense of plot but deliberately structured his narrative into the total concept, as we can assume from the sophistication of the narrative design. In the *Iliad* and the *Odyssey* plot was not just a superstructure holding together the numerous disparate events, which would otherwise be related merely by place or character; furthermore, it did not serve just to supply a focal point for the activities of the characters or a means of relating characters to environment. It did these things, but in addition it functioned to present the epic idea centered around the "wrath of Achilles" or the "wanderings of the resourceful Odysseus."

In other words, the Homeric sense of narrative form required that plot be the most important element. It was from studying Homer that Aristotle undoubtedly learned this principle, for in the *Poetics* Aristotle makes plot more important for the narrative drama than character, theme, or language. This ancient theory has puzzled many modern critics, who prefer an emphasis on characterization and in fact read Homer and Sophocles, as they do Shakespeare and Dickens, as if the truth were that characterization preceded plot both in the derivation of the literary work and in importance for critical analysis. The misunderstanding stems from the basic premise of narrative art as an imitation of life. Regardless of what Aristotle may have meant by this premise, we can see in the practice of the masters of narrative such as Homer and Shakespeare and Dickens a similar emphasis on plot in this sense: since art deals with human beings, the chief function of plot as an imitation of life is to establish a situation that requires significant choice (*i.e.,* reaction) on the part of characters. Narrative art, in film as in epic verse, establishes predicaments in which we observe human possibilities; men become truly human in the process of becoming aware of their condition insomuch as the predicament demands of them some kind of action.

Art also becomes instructive and eternally relevant by the quality of the imitation of the action—or put in practical terms, the degree to which the created predicament applies to human life in all places and all times. However, the difficulty of great art, or the paradox of it, lies in the evident fact that the creation of a meaningful situation requires a high degree of specification. That specification—particularly in film, where it is visual—demands that an artist clearly demonstrate his sense of the reality of the predicament not in an abstract arena for the clash of the good man and the hungry lion, but in a fully conceivable, localized situation pertinent to a particular man or group at a particular moment. For this reason, narrative art has a beginning, a middle, and an end: a beginning to establish the credibility of the character's reaction, a middle to demonstrate that action, and an end to complete it—which does not necessarily mean to explicate it, but to signal to the audience or reader that the demonstration has not been abandoned in mid-course.

Thus, the four distinct narrative art forms of Homer, Shakespeare, Dickens, and Griffith, to the extent that they emphasize a plot, relate to each other in the sense that the narrative concept has been traditionally (1) a crucial part of the artistic design of the total work, and (2) a plot that contains a beginning, a middle, and an end. Given these similarities, we note of course that all the narrative arts differ in the formal presentation of their narrative materials, in their modes of expression, and in the particular emphasis placed on each aspect of the narrative. Naturally, this book has been concerned with the peculiar problems of narrative expression in the cinema. Nevertheless, any narrative serves in its abstract sense as a way of organizing human experience, a way of arranging patterns of human activity so as to make human life intelligible in a brief compass of time—in, let us say, the time it takes to sit through a two-hour movie.

In real life we have at least two broad organizing patterns, both of which take too long to portray in their totality: one is the seasonal cycle and the other is every man's movement from life to death. Narrative art aids us in understanding existence without having to study a man's life in such historical and biographical detail that it takes our total existence to grasp another's existence thoroughly. In fact, the arrangement of narrative has probably taught us to understand history and psychology inasmuch as the establishment of a narrative pattern means the extracting of the essence of an event—the distillation of its meaning—and the shaping of it into a form that allows us to follow it from beginning to end without worrying about the (literally) millions of omitted details of no major relevance. Therefore, the narrative artist at the least has two tasks in designing any story: (1) choosing a plot that reveals the ideas of the work, or allows the characters to move within a situation in which the ideas can be raised naturally; (2) selecting those details that are most meaningful to the life of the characters.

The problem is how much one can omit from the standard development of a situation and yet retain a sense of a beginning. Similarly, what degree of desirable ambiguity in plotting will still permit an artist to leave us with a sense of ending? Dickens' answer for the nineteenth-century writer was to include an overwhelming number of background details to fill in the biography of all important characters. He also ruled out most plot ambiguity, preferring to control the total development of his characters' lives, even to the extent of telling readers what happened to the characters after the plot was concluded. In contrast, many modern filmmakers seem to rely primarily on a sense of environment in establishing a situation or concluding it. The vividness of a film's surface makes it possible for an environment to be sketched quickly and to replace some explicit action. Still, the question remains as to whether substituting environment for plot will turn out to limit the communication of ideas. Traditional plot structure has for centuries developed the relationships

between a wide variety of ideas and actions. In comparison, the modern film structure that tries to develop relationships between setting or decor and characterization seems rather narrowly confined. After all, the camera can only show us a character either at ease or not at ease in an environment; and while this tells us something, it hardly seems capable of telling us as much as the traditional Dickensian plot once did.

Antonioni best represents the kind of director who studies character in relation to the modern world and sometimes (not always, of course) makes the setting a replacement for a developed action. In *Eclipse* (1962), Antonioni restricts the action to what might be considered virtual tableaus of the heroine; that is, the incidents that happen to her are not structurally determined by the preceding incidents. A relationship of event to event does exist, and granted that different events or different locations might be less interesting and less suggestive than the ones Antonioni used, they might still be equally valid from the standpoint of plot logic or cause and effect.

John Russell Taylor makes a valid summation of what we see in *Eclipse:*

> The décors play a vital part in the film and our understanding of it, since plot is reduced to an absolute minimum and is replaced by a study of mental states performed almost entirely by the use of objective correlatives, and for these to work properly it is necessary for us to be clear about what emotional colouring they should have for us. The plot can, in fact, be disposed of in one sentence: Vittoria, a beautiful young Roman who makes her living by translation, breaks off an affair with Riccardo and shortly afterwards drifts, at first unwillingly, into another affair with Piero, her mother's energetic young stockbroker.... [*Eclipse*] makes *L'Avventura* seem packed with action....*

The story follows the activities of Vittoria, none of which are particularly dramatic, and the plot becomes a series of small experiences that presumably lead to a new awareness, if not for the heroine, then for the spectators.

The trouble is that in following anyone's life a filmmaker conveys mainly a sense of disorder and drift, for in reality the day-to-day existence of almost anyone will seem like this. Very likely, a sample day taken from the life of the most orderly man will convey disorder and drift, simply because it is removed from the context of his life. Limited by its nature, narrative art cannot trace very many days in anyone's life, and the artist chooses certain days to represent all the other days. Realistically, a single

---

* John Russell Taylor, *Cinema Eye, Cinema Ear* (New York, Hill and Wang, 1964), p. 78.

day can hardly ever be a significant organizational unit, if for no other reason than that a man lives and thinks differently on holidays and working days. Antonioni does try to depict selected events in Vittoria's situation that will seem typical, yet significant and worthy, so as to make her life germane to a general examination of modern man's condition. Yet without a developed story, contrived by a filmmaker, how can we know whether we are observing random responses to random events? And if the events are random, even if typical, are we not left with a number of observations relevant to a single character but not to a single organizing film idea? Is it not possible that even the most skillful filmmaker who structures a film with regard to lifelike situations leaves us ultimately with a handful of particulars and details?

If such dubious results can be attributed to a work by a major artist such as Antonioni, it would seem likely that lesser artists would have even more difficulty in conveying anything other than a sense of the modern malaise in a plotless film. Of course, *Eclipse* is not so entirely plotless as several other films made since then. The heroine undergoes a process of self-evaluation, and this in itself supplies a sort of narrative development. Nevertheless, the literal shape of a film is its story, and in *Eclipse* the story does not by itself control character development or indicate the film idea.

The connection of the first two sequences, for example, is arbitrary because of a lack of causal relationships. Vittoria and her lover Riccardo part in the early morning in such a way that it seems likely that their affair is finished. As is frequently true in Antonioni, the first sequence seems to stress the portrayal of a minor character, Riccardo, as much as that of the major character, Vittoria. We have no reason not to expect the film to be Riccardo's story as much as Vittoria's, for indeed the subtlety of his character revelation is as good as anything in the film. (For instance, consider the delineation inherent in a small gesture: Riccardo knocks over a piece of pottery in his apartment, which suggests his current mood of abstraction in regard to his lover and his general indifference to the art around him.) Yet after this sequence Riccardo disappears from the film. The next sequence brings Vittoria to the stock exchange of Rome, where the camera emphasizes her mother's broker, Piero, as he goes about his business in the typical frantic atmosphere of such an environment (fig. 68). Perhaps the ultimately meaningless activity in the exchange is meant to be associated with the emotional emptiness Vittoria has indicated she experienced in her love relationship. Certainly, connections on a thematic and psychological level can be made, if only because, as we have discussed elsewhere in this book, shots in sequence tend to suggest connections; and of course sequential events too may suggest all sorts of connections, as nothing in life is ever totally dissociated from a given context. Nevertheless, we can still ask why Vittoria couldn't have gone to a racetrack or an amusement park? We would certainly have

**68** *Eclipse*

been able to make a series of perhaps as interesting thematic and psychological connections with the second sequence there as we can with it at the exchange.

The striking ambiguity of the ending, presented in a seven-minute sequence (usually partially cut by distributors because it annoys audiences or bores them), seems to bear no relationship to the story of Vittoria's and Piero's love affair, the outcome of which remains indecisive. The group of images without dialogue that conclude the film has led critics to a variety of interpretations, many of them contradictory. As there is no plot to substantiate one's interpretation of the ending, Antonioni seemingly invites completely personal responses to his film. Peter Cowie has described the ending as follows:

> It is a montage sequence of frightening power and complexity, united by the unnerving, echoing music of Giovanni Fusco. A pile of hollow bricks outside Vittoria's apartment that earlier in the film had been glimpsed in neat array is now crumpled in confusion (like a city wrecked by nuclear attack?); one sees a piece of wood that Vittoria had thrown casually into a barrel of water; streams of

water run down into drains; a nurse wheels a child in a pram along an empty street; a man descends from a bus and on his newspaper one notices headlines that hint at atomic war; blocks of flats loom menacingly against the twilight sky; trees seethe as if impelled by some hidden force; lights flicker on across the city, but the zebra crossing at which Piero and Vittoria had arranged to meet remains deserted; a final close-up shows the incandescent, elliptical form of a street lamp[,] an equivocal closing image that could refer to the title of the film or suggest the conflagration that will shortly engulf the arid, mineral world Antonioni has scrutinized. The predominant feeling engendered by these shots is, however, one of finality: everything comes to a halt or dies away, for the night or forever. The cold melancholy of this disputed sequence is strongly reminiscent of Ecclesiastes, with its dismal prophecies: "all is vanity . . . What profit hath a man of all his labour which he taketh under the sun? One generation passeth away, and another generation cometh; but the earth abideth for ever." *

Will images specifying aspects of "finality" suffice for a satisfactory ending to a film that did not lead toward any sort of climactic action? Without an action that originates in a starting point and moves toward another point by a series of cause-and-effect steps, perhaps no conclusion will draw together the strands of various activities that filled the film's sequences. Although we do have a narrative structured chronologically in terms of a woman's progress through life, the open-endedness of the presentation has made many viewers uneasy. However ingenious the interpretations, many remain skeptical about the ultimate sense of orderliness that some critics see in the film. *Eclipse* strikes us all as an interesting examination of contemporary life, well done within the particular sequences and containing some valuable insights into human relationships— but not quite an integrated artistic experience. Shaped too much like life itself, it becomes more a description than a distillation of life's meaning. *Eclipse* demonstrates the difficulties of communicating a film idea without a readily perceivable film structure.

## Structuring an Expanding Visual Idea: *Fellini Satyricon*

A *typical* modern non-Aristotelian structure for the narrative film cannot be discerned while we are still in the midst of several developing contemporary movements. However, at least three new patterns emerge from several films made today. We have already alluded to the structure that seems formless and consists mainly of joining incidents together; this

---

* Peter Cowie, *Antonioni, Bergman, Resnais* (New York, A. S. Barnes, 1963), p. 45.

tendency is found frequently in the experimental film, where the narrative may be totally unrealistic or, conversely, totally realistic (in which case it describes the random events of a person's day). Another pattern features the episodic chronicle in which related events occur but the plot development is restricted in terms of the adventures of the hero. We follow the hero from place to place, and the events stem from his personality, as in *Breathless*. These two types of structure are less popular than the traditional plot structure around which most films are still conceived. An interesting third possible alternative lies in the film constructed around an expanding visual idea conceived in terms of setting and mood and imbued with a moral tone, as in Visconti's *The Damned*, Penn's *Little Big Man*, and Bernardo Bertolucci's *The Conformist*. This moral idea seems necessary if the spectacle is going to substitute for the traditional plot, for pure spectacle detaches itself from human involvement. In a Cecil DeMille film, the spectacle, though the most important aspect, is only background, a setting to satisfy the eye; for this reason, all DeMille films have traditionally established plots acted out before the lavish backgrounds. What we are considering now, however, is the kind of spectacle that is fully involved with the meaning of the film.

The only major director to work consistently with this structure in several films is Fellini: *La Dolce Vita* (1960), *8½* (1963), *Juliet of the Spirits* (1965), and *Fellini Satyricon* (1969), are conceived in terms of a group of images that create the central situation. Only with the appearance of the fourth of these films has it become apparent that Fellini is developing a new cinematic form that takes its shape from the spectacle of human beings living in a certain way. The setting, indeed, becomes the life-style of the characters, not just revealing their background but defining the entire scope of their personalities.

The source of *Fellini Satyricon* is a first-century novel that exists only in fragments and is attributed to a courtier of Nero's empire, Petronius. Fellini's inserting his own name into the title of the film (presumably to distinguish his version from another film made around the same time) serves to emphasize the difference between his work and Petronius' *Satyricon*, though in many ways the film is a successful adaptation of its source and to a large extent seems faithful to the moral sensibility of the original. One aspect of the novel deliberately carried over into the film is the feeling of narrative incompleteness, at least as regards the plot. Characters reappear from time to time, but if they did not, little would be lost; even when they die, their demise is not a logical necessity growing out of the given events. The arbitrariness of the characters' movements further emphasizes both Petronius' and Fellini's lack of concern for developing any sense of plot or character awareness. Things simply occur in visually interesting places. The novel is narrated in the first person by Encolpius. Strangely, and at times awkwardly, the film employs a narrative

device simply by having Encolpius say, in effect, I next did this, or What a night that was! However, in the film (as compared to the novel), this device is not often or consistently applied, for the film in no sense attempts to portray Encolpius' subjective point of view; in some scenes this character does not appear. His perceptions rarely seem to be emphasized, nor do all of the important dramatic events concern him.

Fellini has remarked that the narrative suggests a dreamlike form, but the surfaces of the imagery seem more realistic than surrealistic. In fact, only the nature of the extravagances removes the activities from the realm of realism. Yet the film creates a reality of its own premised on a morally abandoned world in which only wealth and pleasure command attention. Given such a civilization—and it seems a plausible equivalent of either first-century Rome under Nero or Pompeii at the time of its destruction in 79 A.D.—the images of sexual perversions in the weird atmosphere of the Roman brothel, the fabulous gluttony at the feast of Trimalchio, the ritual of a mock funeral, the ceremony of the wedding of two men, and a dozen other excesses are all realistic possibilities within the depicted environments.

Furthermore, the inhabitants of such a world would not be expected to resemble inhabitants of classical cultures that adhered to moral norms. Thus, understandably, the world of the film is populated largely by people who seem to be grotesques. Still, they remain recognizably human in their insatiable appetites and restlessness (Trimalchio, the wealthiest, seems the most restless). Lack of restraint, in fact, probably drives them to seek new pleasures through excesses that demoralize rather than satiate. "What I want now," says Trimalchio, "is to add Sicily to my property so that if I decide to go to Africa I can sail on my own estate. You think I'm content as I am?" * Against the background of such lives lived in such places, the two main characters, Encolpius and his friend Ascyltos, move familiarly through all levels of society, partaking in the situations as they find them, usually without reservations, regardless of whether they are victimizing others or themselves being victimized. At one point Ascyltos addresses the audience directly and tells us that he had stolen Encolpius' slave Giton (a boy about sixteen with feminine traits, who is used by both friends for homosexual activities), forced the boy under threat of his sword to sleep with him, and later sold Giton to an actor (plate IV). "Then," Ascyltos continues in the same speech, "While I was wandering about the city, a good family man approached me and led me to this place and in one of those niches he began to insist on violating me. He already had his hands on me, but I pushed him into the pool." † Such conduct, common to their

---

* *Fellini's Satyricon* (New York, Ballantine Books, 1970), p. 136.

† *Ibid.*, p. 97.

world, provokes no surprise or sense of outrage, never a moral reflection on what has occurred.

Fellini has characterized the two young men as the equivalents of hippie students of our own times in a preface to the screenplay:

> Their revolt, though having nothing in common with traditional revolts—neither the faith nor the desperation, nor the drive to change or destroy—is nevertheless a revolt and is expressed in terms of utter ignorance of and estrangement from the society surrounding them. They live from day to day, taking problems as they come, their life interests alarmingly confined to the elementaries: they eat, make love, stick together, bed down anywhere. They make a living by the most haphazard expedients, often downright illegal ones. . . . They are drop-outs from every system, and recognize no obligations, duties or restrictions. . . . they don't even practice the cult of friendship, . . . and so are willing to betray or disown each other any time.*

The artistic premises of the film, however, preclude any voice of moral commentary within the environment; a society so depraved as the one depicted here can accept all sorts of characters on its fringes or even assimilate them without qualms. The two are not tempted to join that culture for any length of time because it offers nothing to them but what they choose to take or steal on occasion.

The action of the film is structured in terms of episodes that do not necessarily follow in any special order determined by the exigencies of plot, and conceivably the order could be rearranged. There are no dramatic progressions other than the ones that are developed within a few chronological sequences; once one episode is completed, another begins at some distinct and sometimes distant place (though all are within the Roman world). We do not always know how or why Encolpius has moved from one location to another, but we can assume that he travels because he has no particular reason for staying in one place rather than in another. In any case, the action itself grows out of the changing locations.

Since the action of each episode is more or less anecdotal—hinging on such dramatic questions as: Will Encolpius retrieve Giton from Ascyltos? or Will Encolpius be able to regain his sexual potency with women, which he has mysteriously lost?—the audience retains an entirely objective attitude. Fellini intends for us not to sympathize particularly with the characters, most of whom are thoroughly unpleasant, and even Encolpius is an essentially unattractive human being. Thus, the action and the characterization are continually less interesting than the spectacle of the film or the environment of the action. Indeed, the scenery stands

---

* *Ibid.,* p. 44.

among the most interesting ever captured on film, though it is not real (most of it was built indoors). Fellini has caught the landscape of a degenerate civilization, reflecting the immense corruption of wealth as well as the decay of classical culture. At the beginning of the film we are introduced to a theater in which the performers act out a series of vulgar comic bits that fail to amuse anyone in the Roman audience. Finally, some wretch is dragged on stage; then the leading actor takes an axe and cuts off the man's hand. This sadistic action brings forth a spontaneous show of approval and laughter from the entire theater crowd. Thus, Fellini immediately communicates his theme through our understanding of the environment and the kind of people who attend the theater; no structured dramatic action based on the conflict of individuals is needed here to convey the idea. We see at once that the great heritage of the classical theater has culminated in brutal, degrading entertainment approved by a dehumanized public.

From this point Fellini proceeds to lead us through the pleasure world of the Roman Empire, each sequence revealing some new aspect of the destroyed sensibilities of that era. We witness next the sexual preoccupations of the Roman population. The people we encounter seem to represent every segment of that population, from the prostitutes to the magistrates, the impoverished as well as the wealthy. The homosexual world in this film merges with the heterosexual in the personalities of Giton, Encolpius, and Ascyltos. At different times in the film, all three young men also have heterosexual relationships. Encolpius tours a brothel where we see all forms of sexual activities, some of them perverse and masochistic. The ambiguity of the homosexual-heterosexual instincts of Encolpius and Giton (who has the sexual allurements of a girl) is manifest in the relationship between master and slave. Encolpius loves Giton, but Giton acts the role of the coquettish girl, the unfaithful mistress, who on a whim chooses Ascyltos over Encolpius, a decision which practically destroys the latter. Left by himself in his ghettolike apartment house, Encolpius is almost killed in the building's destruction, which the screenplay claims is a visual reminder to viewers of "those who died in the ruins of Pompeii."

The most famous scene of Petronius' *Satyricon* occurs at the villa of the nouveau riche Trimalchio, where a feast has been prepared to entertain a large number of people, primarily for the purpose (from the host's point of view) of eliciting praise and admiration (plate V). Those who wish to dine well will offer the expected praise, but others, including some servants, laugh at him, recognize his garish vulgarity, and exploit him for their own entertainment. Fellini actually employs considerable restraint in depicting the bad taste and gluttony of the scene described in Petronius because he wishes to avoid the visual clichés long associated with the depiction of the Roman banquet orgy a la DeMille and others.

He has said, "We're so used to seeing the usual bloated bellies streaming sweat and stuffing themselves on legs of lamb and bunches of grapes, the usual greasy mouths kissing each other lasciviously. . . ." * Nevertheless, the sequence enhances Petronius' satiric thrust at the misuse of wealth and the depravity of luxury. But it goes beyond Petronius by using the inherent properties of the cinema: the great variety of guests, nameless minor characters, appear as visually real as Trimalchio, and therefore their appreciation of the innumerable courses of the meal, their marveling at the extravagant way the dishes are prepared (with food unexpectedly stuffed in other food or shaped like birds or fish), and their general bad manners enlarge the theme into an indictment of the entire society, not just of Trimalchio. In fact, the host sits before them as the envied ideal of that society and so symbolizes the values the others strive to attain.

Throughout the banquet, Encolpius eats and watches and listens to the cynical and ironic comments of an old poet. The young man seems to accept the adverse commentary and yet also to accept the entertainment as worthwhile. He indulges himself as much as anyone else and ends up exhausted and drunk on a beach, where he is bound and taken aboard a ship by an emissary of Caesar to begin another adventure. Such fortuitous connections link all the episodes. The abruptness and arbitrariness of the connections between sequences are not disruptive, for Fellini really wants to structure the film by means of diverse or independent visual experiences, each intended to shed a different light on the expanding image of a society in the process of spiritual collapse. Encolpius as an observer without moral interests (or perhaps without insight) could never function as a critical intelligence, as an interpreter of the spectacle of Rome life.

Indeed, the images are overwhelmingly clear in their thematic import and need no internal evaluation from any of the participating characters. Scenes of cruelty and sadism may be unrelated directly to scenes of gluttony, but all are related by the nature of the spectacle of Roman life; they simply supply different perspectives on the same theme of cultural decline. Fellini has stated that the film is not a historical re-creation of another age or a filming of a famous literary work, but a parallel with our contemporary Western culture. But the brilliant though horrifying parallel with modern life is only suggested, not depicted by the powerful imagery, which instead establishes the film idea in terms of its own particularized reality—the relevance of which is not dependent on historical authenticity.

The structural accomplishment of *Fellini Satyricon* is extremely rare in narrative art. Fellini has succeeded in communicating the film idea by presenting images unified thematically by their illumination of a central moral condition. He did not need to develop the images or intensify the evils as the film progressed. The early sequence that shows a man's hand

* *Ibid.,* p. 14.

being chopped off is surpassed as a symbol of deterioration by a sequence at the end in which a group of heirs are confronted with a dead man's will that reads in part:

> All those who are mentioned in my testament . . . can enter into immediate possession of what I have left to them on the condition that they cut my body into pieces and eat it in full sight of everybody.*

The heirs weigh the possibilities and decide that an hour's nausea is worth the inheritance, and thus one of the final images is of cannibalism. However, this can hardly be considered a development of the corruption demonstrated in the early sequences; rather it is a more revolting dramatization of the total debasement of human values exhibited everywhere in the imagery.

*Fellini Satyricon* is the most striking example in the recent cinema of a film taking its structure from a series of images gradually unfolding around a central theme. The audience does not arrive at any realization of the theme of the decline of a civilization as a result of the progressive unraveling of the story. Rather the implications expand from sequence to sequence as new images of a dehumanized world appear before us. Fellini had accomplished this in other films, but he always included a developing story as part of the film idea. Whether the structure of *Fellini Satyricon* becomes a feasible one for a variety of film subjects remains to be seen. Regardless of its ultimate influence, it will stand as a remarkable execution of the film idea in a new kind of structural context.

---

* *Ibid.*, p. 271.

# APPENDIX

# Glossary

Terms are nouns unless otherwise indicated. Verb forms derived from nouns and nouns derived from verbs have corresponding meanings: *e.g., to crane* means *to use a crane* or *to move a camera on a crane;* a crosscut results when the camera crosscuts.

**angle**  The position of the camera in relation to the subject being photographed. A shot taken from above the subject, looking down at it, is called a **high-angle shot.** One taken from below, looking up at the subject, is called a **low-angle shot.** In the majority of shots, the camera photographs the subject at approximately eye level, and no angle is noticeable.

**asynchronism**  The use of dialogue or sounds that do not seem to originate in the natural environment being shown on screen. It is a method of counterpointing sound and picture.

**cinematography**  The process of filming a motion picture, as distinguished from *photography,* the process of making a still picture. The distinction is not frequently made, and in American usage the movie cameraman is commonly called a photographer.

**close shot**  A shot in which the camera is slightly farther from the subject than in a close-up, yet nearer than in a medium shot. (See **close-up, medium shot.**)

**close-up**  A shot in which a person's head or a small object just about fills the screen vertically. Although loosely defined in terms of distance, a close-up generally excludes almost all background above and below the subject.

**crane**  A device used to move a camera up or down. A **crane shot** is one in which

the camera films while mounted on a device that is moving vertically; the camera itself does not pivot. (*Cf.* **tilt shot.**)

**crosscut** *verb* To cut, within a sequence, between two distinct locations.

**cut** *noun* The joining of any two shots without optical devices or intervening frames, by far the most common method of connecting shots. **quick cut** An inaccurate way of referring to either an abrupt switch to an unexpected shot or a shot of unusually short duration. Actually, all cuts take exactly the same length of time (about one-fiftieth of a second. *verb* 1. To connect shots, to edit. 2. The word used by directors during filming to halt the procedure.

**dissolve** A method of joining shots in which, during the transition from one to the other, the two visibly overlap for a second or so.

**dolly** A device for wheeling a camera around the floor. A **dolly shot** is one taken with the camera on a moving dolly.

**dub** *verb* To add sound—including dialogue, sound effects, and music—to a film after it is photographed.

**editing** The process of assembling shots into sequences and organizing the sequences into the completed film. It includes the process of matching the sound track and the visuals. The procedure is carried out by the editor, who is at least nominally under the supervision of the director, though often in fact accountable directly to the producer.

**establishing shot** Any shot at the beginning of a sequence that clarifies the location; it is usually a long or full shot.

**fade in** A technique in which a shot begins in complete darkness and gradually lightens to normal.

**fade out** A technique in which the picture gradually fades to complete darkness, ending the shot. It is a synonym for the less common term **fade.**

**fast motion** A technique whereby the image on screen is made to move more quickly than it did at the time the shot was taken. Often called **accelerated motion,** it is generally used for comic effects.

**flashback** A shot, series of shots, sequence, or series of sequences inserted into another sequence in order to depict events of the past.

**focus** The degree of definition or sharpness of a shot. **Soft focus** is an effect obtained by covering the lens with a filter or some material such as vaseline so as to give the picture a misty glow or a decorative lack of definition. The term is also used sometimes as a synonym for *out of focus.*

**frame** *noun* 1. Literally, the borders of the screen (*i.e.,* the frame of the picture), but more commonly the entire picture itself. 2. An individual picture on the film celluloid. Twenty-four frames appear on the screen every second in the modern sound film. The duration of a shot is measured technically in frames; thus, a shot of 480 frames has a duration of 20 seconds. *verb* 1. To move the camera for the purpose of keeping a moving subject within the picture area. Framing refers to slight, sometimes almost imperceptible, camera movements, not to dolly shots, though it is often a kind of dollying. 2. To adjust the movie projector so that parts of two frames do not appear on the screen at any one moment.

**freeze** An optical process whereby a frame is duplicated over and over, thus creating the effect of a still picture and "freezing" the action.

**full shot**   A shot in which a standing adult would occupy almost the entire vertical dimension of the frame. Commonly used in interiors, it is a type of long shot, but closer to the subject than that term might suggest.

**golden section**   A term borrowed from painting and applied to the dimensions of the screen that were standard before the wide screen was popularized in the 1960's. The proportions of the golden section were about 4 to 3 in the cinema, the width being longer than the height.

**insert title**   Words inserted into a sequence interrupting the visual images. Insert titles were most often used in the silent film, especially for dialogue and to mark transitions in time. The term is replaced by **subtitle** in most film books.

**intercut**   *verb*   To insert a series of shots depicting something occurring at one location at intervals in a sequence in which the action occurs at a separate location.

**iris shot**   A shot in which one area of the otherwise dark screen, usually in the form of a circle, is illuminated. Beginning or ending a shot by opening up or closing down the illuminated circular area is called **irising in** or **irising out,** respectively. The technique was used primarily in the silent film to create visual emphasis on a particular point within the illuminated area in the shot.

**jump cut**   A cut, usually unexpected, to a shot somewhat removed in time from the previous shot; sometimes, a cut in which time elapses but the place and the camera position in the two adjoining shots remain the same.

**long shot**   A shot in which the camera records a vertical area at least equal to a standing adult in height, and usually much greater, so that it encompasses an area of considerable size.

**masking**   An effect whereby part of the screen image is covered, usually in darkness, as in an **iris shot.**

**medium shot**   As used in this book, a shot that covers an area of which the vertical dimension is approximately equal to the height of a seated adult or an adult from the waist up. The term is relative and in general usage seems to define any area captured by a normal camera lens at a distance of five to fifteen feet. It can also be described as a shot that covers the area between that covered by full and close shots.

**mid-shot**   As used in his book, a synonym for **medium shot.**

**montage**   1. In Europe, the process of editing.   2. In the American industry, a sequence displaying a great number of shots of short duration, used frequently to show the passing of time, and in the 1930's and 1940's, usually to provide a transition of time or place. (This sense of the word derives from a misconception of Eisenstein's practices in *Potemkin.*)

**moviola**   1. (*capitalized*) A trade name for a popular viewing machine used in studio work for editing or in schools for film study, on which a small image of the film can be seen, stopped, reversed, and run at various speeds.   2. (*lower case*) Commonly, any viewing machine of a similar type.

**offscreen**   *adjective*   Of sound or dialogue, having the source of the sound not pictured on the screen during the shot in which it is heard.

**on location**   *adverb*   Elsewhere than in a studio, but not necessarily in the place supposedly depicted in the film: *e.g.,* a film that takes place in Spain may be shot on location in Arizona.

**overexposure**   A glaring effect or a complete negation of the color or contrast of

the film due to the recording of an excessive amount of light during the filming. Formerly accidental, it is now frequently used for special effects.

**pan shot**  A moving camera shot in which the camera pivots horizontally while mounted on a nonmoving base.

**parallel action**  A structure for a film or a sequence in which the filmmaker depicts two separate actions that are related by theme or plot and occur simultaneously. It is usually accompanied by crosscutting.

**reel**  The spool on which the finished film is wound. It was used as a standard for measuring the length of silent films. In America, a reel ran about 15 minutes, and so an eight-reel film would run about two hours. However, reels might contain anywhere from 10 to 20 minutes of film; therefore, the measurement was only an approximation of running time.

**scenario**  An early version of the narrative of a film, sometimes just an outline of a story that precedes the writing of the shooting script, but more often a version of the story with the sequences indicated.

**scene**  1. A term used sometimes (but not in this book) for a group of shots that constitutes a division of a sequence.  2. A technical term for **shot.**  3. Loosely, a synonym for *setting* or *location*.  4. Loosely, a **sequence.**

**sequence**  A group of shots related by time, place, and situation. It is a basic organizing unit of the film. The sequence is the equivalent of a scene in a play, but the latter word should not be used in this sense in regard to film. (See **scene.**)

**shooting script**  The final script for a film, in which all the shots are distinguished individually, usually with specific regard to camera placement and movement.

**shot**  Any length of film recorded by the camera without interruption. The fundamental unit of the film, its duration is theoretically unlimited, from a minimum length of one frame. The average full-length film contains well over three hundred shots. Most shots are either moving or stationary, but some alternate movement and nonmovement of the camera.

**short**  A film of less than forty minutes.

**single-frame photography**  The use of a motion picture camera to shoot only one picture (frame) at a time. The results of such filming may be fast motion or simply peculiar effects. For instance, a timing device may be used to snap a picture every fifteen seconds at a busy intersection. After ten hours, 2400 pictures will have been taken; they may be projected on a movie screen in little more than a minute and a half, producing the effect of extreme fast motion. The technique is also called **stop-motion** or **stop-action photography.**

**slow motion**  A technique whereby film is projected at a rate slower than that at which it was shot, producing the effect of slowing down the action.

**special effects**  Effects obtained by laboratory technicians employing optical equipment or scale models for the purpose of creating interesting visual images or simulating images not readily obtainable in the normal course of filming (as, for example, the destruction of a city).

**split-screen filming**  The technique of dividing the frame into two or more distinct images to create the effect of simultaneous shots. The dimensions of the images are often different.

**stereoscopy**  The technique of making three-dimensional images, which are usually perceived by wearing special glasses or using a viewer.

**stop-motion photography, stop-action photography**  Synonyms for **single-frame photography.**

**subtitle**  1. The translated dialogue appearing at the bottom of the screen in a foreign-language film.  2. An insert title.

**superimposition**  The technique of causing two or more shots to appear within the same frame, one atop the other. It is used to produce supernatural effects such as a character's walking through a wall, and formerly also to create the illusion of twins when one performer was to play both roles (an effect now accomplished by masking).

**synchronism**  The use of dialogue or sounds that originate from sources visible within the environment depicted in the frame or obviously close to it.

**take**  A single recording of a shot during filming. Usually several takes are needed for each shot, the editor selecting the best one for inclusion in the finished film. When the modifiers *long* and *short* are used with *take*, the reference is to duration, not distance.

**tilt shot**  A moving camera shot in which the camera pivots vertically while mounted on a nonmoving base.

**tracking shot**  A shot in which the camera films while mounted on an object moving horizontally; the camera does not move on its axis. Also called a **trucking shot**, it is distinct from a dolly shot in that it is usually employed when a significant distance is to be covered, as when the camera is mounted on a car. (*Cf.* **pan shot, traveling shot.**)

**traveling shot**  1. Usually, a synonym for **tracking shot.**  2. A shot sometimes (though rarely) distinguished from a tracking shot by the fact that the camera moves at a speed independent of the object being filmed, whereas in a tracking shot the camera moves at the same speed as the object being filmed. (See **tracking shot.**)

**underexposure**  An effect in which the images are dim because less than the normal amount of light has reached the film during shooting. It is usually the sign of poor lighting technique, but is sometimes deliberate.

**wipe**  A technique in which a new image appears on the screen and removes or covers (*i.e.,* "wipes away") the existing image.

**zoom shot**  A shot in which the image seems to be moving continuously nearer to or farther from the camera, though the effect is in fact the result of a lens adjustment.

# Filmography
# of Selected Directors
# of Feature
# Films

Dates of films are release dates; however, there is no authoritative list of release dates, and thus different sources will vary within a year or two. Foreign films are listed under their English titles if they are better known thereby in this country. Short films and documentaries are omitted except as noted.

**Michelangelo Antonioni** (b. 1912)

1950   Cronaca di un Amore
1952   I Vinti
1953   La Signora Senza Camelie; "Tentato Suicidio" (*episode in* Love in the City)
1955   Le Amiche
1957   Il Grido
1960   L'Avventura; La Notte
1962   Eclipse
1964   The Red Desert
1965   "Prefazione" (*episode in* I Tre Volti)
1966   Blow-Up
1970   Zabriskie Point

**Ingmar Bergman** (b. 1918)

1946   Crisis; It Rains on Our Love
1947   A Ship to the Indies
1948   Night Is My Future; Port of Call; The Devil's Wanton
1949   Three Strange Loves
1950   To Joy; It Can't Happen Here
1951   Illicit Interlude

| 1952 | Secrets of Women |
|------|------------------|
| 1953 | Monika; The Naked Night (Sawdust and Tinsel) |
| 1954 | A Lesson in Love |
| 1955 | Dreams; Smiles of a Summer Night |
| 1957 | The Seventh Seal (*completed in 1956*); Wild Strawberries |
| 1958 | Brink of Life; The Magician (The Face) |
| 1960 | The Virgin Spring; The Devil's Eye |
| 1961 | Through a Glass Darkly |
| 1963 | Winter Light; The Silence |
| 1964 | Not To Speak About All These Women |
| 1966 | Persona |
| 1968 | Hour of the Wolf; Shame |
| 1969 | The Ritual (*made for television*) |
| 1970 | The Passion of Anna |
| 1971 | The Touch |

## Luis Buñuel (b. 1900)

| 1928 | Un Chien Andalou (*short*) |
|------|---------------------------|
| 1930 | L'Age d'Or |
| 1932 | Land Without Bread |
| 1947 | Gran Casino |
| 1949 | El Gran Calavera |
| 1950 | Los Olvidados (The Young and the Damned) |
| 1951 | Susana; Daughter of Deceit; A Woman Without Love; Ascent to Heaven |
| 1952 | El Bruto; Robinson Crusoe; El |
| 1953 | Wuthering Heights; Illusion Travels by Streetcar |
| 1954 | The River and Death |
| 1955 | The Criminal Life of Archibaldo de la Cruz; Cela S'Appelle L'Aurore |
| 1956 | La Mort en Ce Jardin |
| 1958 | Nazarin |
| 1959 | La Fièvre Monte à El Pao |
| 1960 | The Young One |
| 1961 | Viridiana |
| 1962 | The Exterminating Angel |
| 1964 | Diary of a Chambermaid |
| 1965 | Simon of the Desert |
| 1967 | Belle de Jour |
| 1968 | The Milky Way |
| 1970 | Tristana |

## Charles Chaplin (b. 1889) *

| 1914 | Making a Living; Kid Auto Races at Venice; Mabel's Strange Predicament; Between Showers; A Film Johnnie; Tango Tangles; His Favorite Pastime; |
|------|---------------------------|

* The complete filmography of Chaplin given here includes the films he appeared in but did not direct prior to *Caught in the Rain,* his first directed film. Thereafter, he directed or codirected all the films listed except *A Busy Day* (which may have been made earlier) and *Tillie's Punctured Romance,* both directed by Mack Sennett. All the films before *A Woman of Paris* are shorter than feature length except *Tillie's Punctured Romance* and *The Kid.*

Cruel, Cruel Love; The Star Boarder; Mabel at the Wheel; Twenty Minutes of Love; Caught in a Cabaret; Caught in the Rain; A Busy Day; The Fatal Mallet; Her Friend the Bandit; The Knockout; Mabel's Busy Day; Mabel's Married Life; Laughing Gas; The Property Man; The Face on the Barroom Floor; Recreation; The Masquerader; His New Profession; The Rounders; The New Janitor; Those Love Pangs; Dough and Dynamite; Gentleman of Nerve; His Musical Career; His Trysting Place; Getting Acquainted; His Prehistoric Past; Tillie's Punctured Romance

1915　His New Job; A Night Out; The Champion; In the Park; The Jitney Elopement; The Tramp; By the Sea; Work; A Woman; The Bank; Shanghaied; A Night in the Show

1916　Carmen; Police; The Floorwalker; The Fireman; The Vagabond; One A.M.; The Count; The Pawnshop; Behind the Screen; The Rink

1917　Easy Street; The Cure; The Immigrant; The Adventurer

1918　Triple Trouble; A Dog's Life; The Bond; Shoulder Arms

1919　Sunnyside; A Day's Pleasure

1920　The Kid; The Idle Class

1922　Pay Day

1923　The Pilgrim; A Woman of Paris

1925　The Gold Rush

1928　The Circus

1931　City Lights

1936　Modern Times

1940　The Great Dictator

1947　Monsieur Verdoux

1953　Limelight

1957　A King in New York

1967　The Countess from Hong Kong


## Carl Theodore Dreyer (1899–1968)

1919　The President

1920　Leaves from Satan's Book

1921　The Parson's Widow; The Marked Ones

1922　Once upon a Time

1924　Mikaël

1925　Master of the House; The Bride of Glomdale

1928　The Passion of Joan of Arc

1931　Vampyr

1943　Day of Wrath

1945　Two People

1955　Ordet

1964　Gertrud


## Sergei Eisenstein (1898–1948)

1924　Strike

1925　Potemkin

1927　October

1929　The General Line (Old and New)

1931　Que Viva Mexico (*fragments of an incomplete project*)

| 1936 | Bezhin Meadow (*unfinished*) |
|------|------------------------------|
| 1938 | Alexander Nevsky |
| 1945 | Ivan the Terrible, Part I |
| 1958 | Ivan the Terrible, Part II (*completed in 1946*) |

## Federico Fellini (b. 1920)

| 1950 | Variety Lights (*codirected with Alberto Lattuada*) |
|------|------------------------------------------------------|
| 1952 | The White Sheik |
| 1953 | I Vitelloni; "Matrimonial Agency" (*episode in* Love in the City) |
| 1954 | La Strada |
| 1955 | Il Bidone |
| 1957 | Nights of Cabiria |
| 1960 | La Dolce Vita |
| 1962 | "Temptation of Dr. Antonio" (*episode in* Boccaccio '70) |
| 1963 | 8½ |
| 1965 | Juliet of the Spirits |
| 1967 | "Tony Dammit" (*episode in* Histoires Extraordinaires) |
| 1969 | Fellini Satyricon |
| 1971 | The Clowns |

## Jean-Luc Godard (b. 1930)

| 1959 | Breathless |
|------|-----------|
| 1960 | Le Petit Soldat |
| 1961 | A Woman Is a Woman; "Sloth" (*episode in* The Seven Capital Sins) |
| 1962 | My Life to Live; "Le Nouveau Monde" (*episode in* RoGoPaG) |
| 1963 | Les Carabiniers; "Le Grand Escroc" (*episode in* Les Plus Belles Escroqueries du Monde); Contempt |
| 1964 | Band of Outsiders; The Married Woman |
| 1965 | Alphaville; "Montparnasse-Levallois" (*episode in* Paris Seen by Six); Pierrot le Fou |
| 1966 | Masculin-Féminin; Made in U.S.A.; Deux ou Trois Choses Que Je Sais d'Elle |
| 1967 | "The Year 2000" (*episode in* Love Through the Ages); La Chinoise; Weekend |
| 1968 | Le Gai Savoir |
| 1969 | One Plus One (Sympathy for the Devil); Wind from the East |

## D. W. Griffith (1875–1948)

| 1914 | Judith of Bethulia; The Battle of the Sexes; The Escape; Home Sweet Home; The Avenging Conscience |
|------|---------------------------------------------------------------------------------------------------|
| 1915 | The Birth of a Nation |
| 1916 | Intolerance * |
| 1918 | Hearts of the World; The Great Love; The Greatest Thing in Life |
| 1919 | A Romance of Happy Valley; The Girl Who Stayed at Home; Broken Blossoms; True Heart Susie; Scarlet Days; The Greatest Question |
| 1920 | The Idol Dancer; The Love Flower; Way Down East |

* In later years, *The Mother and the Law* and *The Fall of Babylon* were borrowed from *Intolerance* and released as separate features.

| 1921 | Orphans of the Storm; Dream Street |
| 1922 | One Exciting Night |
| 1923 | The White Rose |
| 1924 | America; Isn't Life Wonderful? |
| 1925 | Sally of the Sawdust |
| 1926 | That Royle Girl; Sorrows of Satan |
| 1928 | Drums of Love; The Battle of the Sexes |
| 1929 | Lady of the Pavements |
| 1930 | Abraham Lincoln |
| 1931 | The Struggle |

## Alfred Hitchcock (b. 1899)

| 1925 | The Pleasure Garden |
| 1926 | The Mountain Eagle; The Lodger (A Story of the London Fog) |
| 1927 | Downhill; Easy Virtue; The Ring |
| 1928 | The Farmer's Wife; Champagne |
| 1929 | The Manxman; Blackmail |
| 1930 | Juno and the Paycock; Murder |
| 1931 | The Skin Game |
| 1932 | Rich and Strange (East of Shanghai); Number Seventeen |
| 1933 | Waltzes from Vienna (Strauss's Great Waltz) |
| 1934 | The Man Who Knew Too Much |
| 1935 | The Thirty-Nine Steps |
| 1936 | Secret Agent; Sabotage |
| 1937 | Young and Innocent (The Girl Was Young) |
| 1938 | The Lady Vanishes |
| 1939 | Jamaica Inn |
| 1940 | Rebecca; Foreign Correspondent |
| 1941 | Mr. and Mrs. Smith; Suspicion |
| 1942 | Saboteur |
| 1943 | Shadow of a Doubt |
| 1944 | Lifeboat |
| 1945 | Spellbound |
| 1946 | Notorious |
| 1947 | The Paradine Case |
| 1948 | Rope |
| 1949 | Under Capricorn |
| 1950 | Stage Fright |
| 1951 | Strangers on a Train |
| 1953 | I Confess |
| 1954 | Dial M for Murder; Rear Window |
| 1955 | To Catch a Thief |
| 1956 | The Trouble with Harry; The Man Who Knew Too Much |
| 1957 | The Wrong Man |
| 1958 | Vertigo |
| 1959 | North by Northwest |
| 1960 | Psycho |
| 1963 | The Birds |
| 1964 | Marnie |
| 1966 | Torn Curtain |
| 1969 | Topaz |
| 1972 | Frenzy |

## Akira Kurosawa (b. 1910)

| | |
|---|---|
| 1943 | Sanshiro Sugata |
| 1944 | The Most Beautiful |
| 1945 | Sanshiro Sugata, Part II; They Who Step on the Tiger's Tail |
| 1946 | Those Who Make Tomorrow; No Regrets for Our Youth |
| 1947 | One Wonderful Sunday |
| 1948 | Drunken Angel |
| 1949 | The Quiet Duel; Stray Dog |
| 1950 | Scandal; Rashomon |
| 1951 | The Idiot |
| 1952 | Ikiru (Living, To Live) |
| 1954 | Seven Samurai (The Magnificent Seven) |
| 1955 | I Live in Fear |
| 1957 | The Throne of Blood; The Lower Depths |
| 1958 | Hidden Fortress |
| 1960 | The Bad Sleep Well |
| 1961 | Yojimbo |
| 1962 | Sanjuro |
| 1963 | High and Low |
| 1965 | Red Beard |
| 1971 | Dodeska Den |

## Fritz Lang (b. 1890)

| | |
|---|---|
| 1919 | Halbblut; Der Herr der Liebe; Der Goldene See (*Part One of* Die Spinnen); Harakiri (Madame Butterfly); Das Brillanten Schiff (*Part Two of* Die Spinnen) |
| 1920 | Das Wandernde Bild |
| 1921 | Vier um die Frau; Der Müde Tod |
| 1922 | Dr. Mabuse, der Spieler (*Part One of* Dr. Mabuse, der Spieler); Inferno (*Part Two of* Dr. Mabuse, der Spieler) |
| 1924 | Siegfried's Death (*Part One of* Die Niebelungen); Kriemhild's Revenge (*Part Two of* Die Niebelungen) |
| 1926 | Metropolis |
| 1928 | Spione; Frau im Mond |
| 1931 | M |
| 1932 | The Testament of Dr. Mabuse |
| 1933 | Liliom |
| 1936 | Fury |
| 1937 | You Only Live Once |
| 1938 | You and Me |
| 1940 | The Return of Frank James |
| 1941 | Western Union; Manhunt |
| 1942 | Hangmen Also Die |
| 1943 | Ministry of Fear |
| 1944 | The Woman in the Window |
| 1945 | Scarlet Street |
| 1946 | Cloak and Dagger |
| 1948 | Secret Beyond the Door |
| 1950 | House by the River; An American Guerrilla in the Philippines (I Shall Return) |
| 1951 | Rancho Notorious; Clash by Night |

1952    The Blue Gardenia
1953    The Big Heat
1954    Human Desire
1955    Moonfleet
1956    While the City Sleeps; Beyond a Reasonable Doubt
1958    Der Tiger von Eschnapur; Das Indische Grabmal *
1960    The Thousand Eyes of Dr. Mabuse


## Friedrich W. Murnau (1889–1931)

1919    Der Knabe in Blau; Satanas
1920    Der Bucklige und die Tänzerin; Der Januskopf; Abend . . . Nacht . . . Morgen; Der Gang in die Nacht; Sehnsucht
1921    Marizza; Gennant die Schmuggler-Madonna; Schloss Vogelöd
1922    Nosferatu; Der Brennende Acker; Phantom
1923    Die Austreibung; Die Finanzen des Grossherzogs
1924    The Last Laugh
1925    Tartuffe
1926    Faust
1927    Sunrise
1928    Four Devils
1929    Our Daily Bread (City Girl); Tabu (*codirected with Robert Flaherty*)


## Jean Renoir (b. 1894)

1924    La Fille de l'Eau
1926    Nana
1927    Charleston; Marquitta
1928    La Petite Marchande d'Allumettes (*codirected with Jean Tedesco*); Tire au Flanc
1929    Le Tournoi; Le Bled
1931    On Purge Bébé; La Chienne
1932    La Nuit du Carrefour; Boudu Sauvé des Eaux
1933    Chotard et Compagnie
1934    Toni; Madame Bovary
1935    Le Crime de Monsieur Lange
1936    La Vie Est à Nous; Une Partie de Campagne; The Lower Depths
1937    La Marseillaise; Grand Illusion
1938    The Human Beast
1939    Rules of the Game
1940    La Tosca (*codirected with Carl Koch and Luchino Visconti*)
1941    Swamp Water
1943    This Land Is Mine
1944    Salute to France (*allegorical documentary*)
1945    The Southerner
1946    The Diary of a Chambermaid
1947    The Woman on the Beach
1950    The River
1952    The Golden Coach


* The two films of this year were combined and cut into *Journey to the Lost City* (*The Tigress of Bengal*).

1954    French Can-Can
1956    Paris Does Strange Things
1959    Picnic on the Grass
1960    The Testament of Dr. Cordelier
1961    The Elusive Corporal


**Alain Resnais** (b. 1922)

1959    Hiroshima, Mon Amour
1961    Last Year at Marienbad
1963    Muriel, ou le Temps d'un Retour
1965    La Guerre Est Finie
1968    Je T'Aime, Je T'Aime


**François Truffaut** (b. 1932)

1959    The Four Hundred Blows
1960    Shoot the Piano Player
1961    Jules and Jim
1962    "Antoine et Colette" (*episode in* Love at Twenty)
1964    The Soft Skin
1966    Fahrenheit 451
1968    The Bride Wore Black
1969    Stolen Kisses; The Siren of Mississippi
1970    The Wild Child


**Luchino Visconti** (b. 1906)

1940    La Tosca (*codirected with Jean Renoir and Carl Koch*)
1942    Ossessione
1948    La Terra Trema
1951    Bellissima
1953    *Fifth episode in* Siamo Donne
1954    Senso
1957    White Nights
1960    Rocco and His Brothers
1962    "The Job" (*episode in* Boccaccio '70)
1963    The Leopard
1965    Vaghe Stelle dell'Orsa
1966    "La Strega Viva" (*episode in* Le Streghe)
1967    The Stranger; La Vita de Giacomo Puccini
1969    The Damned
1970    Death in Venice


**Orson Welles** (b. 1915)

1941    Citizen Kane
1942    The Magnificent Ambersons

1943    Journey into Fear (*credited to Norman Foster*)
1946    The Stranger
1947    The Lady from Shanghai
1948    Macbeth
1952    Othello
1955    Mr. Arkadin (Confidential Report)
1958    Touch of Evil
1963    The Trial
1966    Chimes at Midnight
1968    The Immortal Story

# Selected Bibliography of Books in English

## General

Agee, James. *Agee on Film: Reviews and Comments.* Boston: Beacon Press, 1964.

*The American Film Institute Catalog: Feature Films 1921–1930.* New York: R. R. Bowker, 1971.

Bluestone, George. *Novels into Film.* Berkeley and Los Angeles: University of California Press, 1961.

Clarens, Carlos. *An Illustrated History of the Horror Film.* New York: Capricorn Books, 1967.

Durgnat, Raymond. *The Crazy Mirror: Hollywood Comedy and the American Image.* London: Faber, 1969.

Everson, William K., and George M. Fenin. *The Western.* New York: Bonanza Books, 1962.

Fulton, A. R. *Motion Pictures.* Norman: University of Oklahoma Press, 1960.

Gish, Lillian. *The Movies, Mr. Griffith and Me.* Englewood Cliffs, N.J.: Prentice-Hall, 1969.

Graham, Peter. *A Dictionary of the Cinema.* New York: A. S. Barnes, 1964.

Halliwell, Leslie. *The Filmgoer's Companion.* New York: Hill and Wang, 1967.

Jacobs, Lewis, ed. *Introduction to the Art of the Movies.* New York: Noonday Press, 1960.

————. *The Emergence of Film Art.* New York: Hopkinson & Blake, 1969.

Lennig, Arthur, ed. *Classics of the Film.* Madison: Wisconsin Film Society Press, 1965.

Lindgren, Ernest. *The Art of the Film.* New York: Macmillan, 1963.

MacCann, Richard D. *Film and Society.* New York: Charles Scribner's Sons, 1964.

Manvell, Roger, ed. *Experiments in the Film.* London: Grey Walls, 1949.
————. *New Cinema in Europe.* New York: E. P. Dutton, 1965.
————. *The Film and the Public.* Baltimore: Penguin Books, 1955.
McGowan, Kenneth. *Behind the Screen: The History and Techniques of the Motion Picture.* New York: Delacorte Press, 1965.
Montagu, Ivor. *Film World: A Guide to Cinema.* Baltimore: Penguin Books, 1964.
Nicoll, Allardyce. *Film and Theater.* New York: T. Crowell, 1936.
Sarris, Andrew. *The American Cinema.* New York: E. P. Dutton, 1968.
Stevenson, Ralph, and J. R. Debrix. *The Cinema as Art.* Baltimore: Penguin Books, 1965.
Talbot, Daniel, ed. *Film: An Anthology.* Berkeley and Los Angeles: University of California Press, 1966.

## History

Anderson, Joseph L., and Donald Richie. *The Japanese Film: Art and Industry.* New York: Grove Press, 1960.
Armes, Roy. *French Cinema Since 1946,* 2 Vols. New York: A. S. Barnes, 1966.
Bardeche, Maurice, and Robert Brasillach. *The History of the Motion Pictures.* New York: W. W. Norton and the Museum of Modern Art, 1938.
Baxter, John. *Hollywood in the Thirties.* New York: A. S. Barnes, 1968.
Ceram, C. W. *Archeology of the Cinema.* New York: Harcourt Brace Jovanovich, 1965.
Cowie, Peter. *Swedish Cinema.* New York: A. S. Barnes, 1966.
Durgnat, Raymond. *Nouvelle Vague: The First Decade.* London: Motion Publications, 1966.
Eisner, Lotte H. *The Haunted Screen.* Berkeley and Los Angeles: University of California Press, 1969.
Hampton, Benjamin. *A History of the Movies.* New York: Dover Press, 1970.
Higham, Charles, and Joel Greenberg. *Hollywood in the Forties.* New York: A. S. Barnes, 1968.
Houston, Penelope. *The Contemporary Cinema.* Baltimore: Penguin Books, 1963.
Jacobs, Lewis. *The Rise of the American Film.* New York: Harcourt Brace Jovanovich, 1939. Reprinted, New York: Teachers College Press, 1968.
Knight, Arthur. *The Liveliest Art.* New York: Macmillan, 1957. Paperback edition: New York, Mentor, New American Library, 1957.
Kracauer, Siegfried. *From Caligari to Hitler: A Psychological History of the German Film.* Princeton, N.J.: Princeton University Press, 1947.
Lahue, Kalton C. *World of Laughter: The Motion Picture Comedy Short, 1910–1930.* Norman: University of Oklahoma Press, 1966.
———— and Terry Brewer, eds. *Kops and Custards: The Legend of Keystone Films.* Norman: University of Oklahoma Press, 1968.
Leyda, Jay. *Kino: A History of the Russian and Soviet Film.* London: Allen and Unwin, 1960.
Low, Rachel. *The History of the British Film,* 3 Vols. (1896–1906, 1906–1914, 1914–1918). London: Allen and Unwin, 1948–50.
Mast, Gerald. *A Short History of the Movies.* New York: Bobbs-Merrill, 1971.
Quigley, Martin, Jr. *Magic Shadows.* London: Quigley, 1948.
Ramsaye, Terry. *A Million and One Nights.* New York: Simon and Schuster, 1964 (reissue; originally published 1926).

Robinson, David. *Hollywood in the Twenties.* New York: A. S. Barnes, 1968.

Rondi, Gian L. *Italian Cinema Today.* New York: Hill and Wang, 1966.

Rotha, Paul, and Richard Griffith. *The Film Till Now.* New York: Funk & Wagnalls, 1949.

Sadoul, George. *French Film.* London: Falcon Press, 1953.

Slide, Anthony. *Early American Cinema.* New York: A. S. Barnes, 1970.

Wagenknecht, Edward. *The Movies in the Age of Innocence.* Norman: University of Oklahoma Press, 1962.

## Theory and Esthetics

Arnheim, Rudolph. *Film as Art.* Berkeley and Los Angeles: University of California Press, 1957.

Balázs, Béla. *Theory of the Film: Character and Growth of a New Art.* New York: Dover, 1970.

Bazin, André. *What Is Cinema?* Berkeley and Los Angeles: University of California Press, 1967.

Durgnat, Raymond. *Films and Feelings.* Cambridge, Mass.: M.I.T. Press, 1967.

Eisenstein, Sergei. *Film Form,* ed. and trans. by Jay Leyda. New York: Harcourt Brace Jovanovich, 1949.

————. *Notes of a Film Director.* Moscow: Foreign Language Publishing House, 1958.

————. *The Film Sense,* ed. and trans. by Jay Leyda. New York: Harcourt Brace Jovanovich, 1942.

Hardy, Forsyth. *Grierson on Documentary.* London: W. H. Allen, 1945.

Jacobs, Lewis, ed. *The Movies as Medium.* New York: Farrar, Straus & Giroux, 1970.

Kracauer, Siegfried. *Theory of Film.* New York: Oxford University Press, 1960.

Lawson, John Howard. *Film: The Creative Process.* New York: Hill and Wang, 1967.

Manvell, Roger. *Film.* London: Penguin Books, 1950.

McLuhan, Marshall. *Understanding Media: The Extensions of Man.* New York: Mc-Graw-Hill, 1964.

Nizhny, Vladimir. *Lessons with Eisenstein.* New York: Hill and Wang, 1962.

Pudovkin, V. I. *Film Technique and Film Acting,* trans. by Ivor Montagu. New York: Crown, 1949.

Reisz, Karel. *The Technique of Film Editing.* London: Focal Press, 1958.

Spottiswoode, Raymond. *A Grammar of Film: An Analysis of Film Technique.* Berkeley and Los Angeles: University of California Press, 1950.

Tyler, Parker. *The Three Faces of the Film: The Art, the Dream and the Cult.* New York: Yoseloff, 1960.

Wollen, Peter. *Signs and Meanings in the Cinema.* Bloomington: University of Indiana Press, 1969.

## Important Filmmakers

Armes, Roy. *The Cinema of Alain Resnais.* New York: A. S. Barnes, 1968.

Barr, Charles. *Laurel and Hardy.* Berkeley and Los Angeles: University of California Press, 1968.

Barry, Iris. *D. W. Griffith: American Film Master.* New York: Museum of Modern Art, 1965.

Bogdanovich, Peter. *Fritz Lang in America*. New York: Frederick A. Praeger, 1969.
_____. *John Ford*. Berkeley and Los Angeles: University of California Press, 1968.
_____. *The Cinema of Alfred Hitchcock*. New York: Museum of Modern Art, 1963.
_____. *The Cinema of Howard Hawks*. New York: Museum of Modern Art, 1962.
_____. *The Cinema of Orson Welles*. New York: Museum of Modern Art, 1961.
Calder-Marshall, Arthur. *The Innocent Eye: The Life of Robert J. Flaherty*. London: W. H. Allen, 1963. Paperback edition: Baltimore, Penguin Books, 1970.
Cameron, Ian, ed. *The Films of Robert Bresson*. New York: Frederick A. Praeger, 1970.
_____ and Robin Wood. *Antonioni*. New York: Frederick A. Praeger, 1969.
Cowie, Peter. *Antonioni, Bergman, Resnais*. New York: A. S. Barnes, 1963.
_____. *The Cinema of Orson Welles*. New York: A. S. Barnes, 1965.
Donner, Jorn. *The Personal Vision of Ingmar Bergman*. Bloomington: Indiana University Press, 1964.
Durgnat, Raymond. *Luis Buñuel*. Berkeley and Los Angeles: University of California Press, 1968.
Finler, Joel W. *Stroheim*. Berkeley and Los Angeles: University of California Press, 1968.
Geduld, Harry M., ed. *Film Makers on Film Making*. Bloomington: Indiana University Press, 1968.
Gelmis, Joseph, ed. *The Film Director as Superstar*. New York: Doubleday, 1970.
Gibson, Arthur. *The Silence of God: A Creative Response to the Films of Ingmar Bergman*. New York: Harper & Row, 1969.
Gottesman, Ronald, ed. *Focus on "Citizen Kane."* Englewood Cliffs, N.J.: Prentice-Hall, 1971.
Graham, Peter. *The Cinema of François Truffaut*. New York: A. S. Barnes, 1970.
Henderson, Robert M. *D. W. Griffith: The Years at Biograph*. New York: Farrar, Straus & Giroux, 1970.
Higham, Charles. *The Films of Orson Welles*. Berkeley and Los Angeles: University of California Press, 1970.
Huff, Theodore. *Charles Chaplin*. New York: Schuman, 1951.
Jensen, Paul M. *The Cinema of Fritz Lang*. New York: A. S. Barnes, 1969.
McCaffrey, Donald W. *Focus on Chaplin*. Englewood Cliffs, N.J.: Prentice-Hall, 1971.
Milne, Tom. *The Cinema of Carl Dreyer*. New York: A. S. Barnes, 1971.
Moussinac, Leon. *Sergei Eisenstein*. New York: Crown, 1970.
Mussman, Toby, ed. *Jean-Luc Godard: A Critical Anthology*. New York: E. P. Dutton, 1968.
Nowell-Smith, Geoffrey. *Luchino Visconti*. New York: Doubleday, 1968.
O'Dell, Paul. *Griffith and the Rise of Hollywood*. New York: A. S. Barnes, 1970.
Payne, Robert. *The Great God Pan*. New York: Hermitage House, 1952.
Richie, Donald. *The Films of Akira Kurosawa*. Berkeley and Los Angeles: University of California Press, 1965.
Robinson, David. *Buster Keaton*. Bloomington: Indiana University Press, 1969.
Roud, Richard. *Godard*. New York: Doubleday, 1968.
Sarris, Andrew, ed. *Interviews with Film Directors*. New York: Bobbs-Merrill, 1967.
_____. *The Cinema of Josef von Sternberg*. New York: Museum of Modern Art, 1966.
Schickel, Richard. *The Disney Version*. New York: Simon and Schuster, 1968.
Sterne, Brigitta. *Ingmar Bergman*. New York: Twayne, 1968.
Strick, Philip. *Antonioni*. London: Motion Publications, 1965.

Taylor, John Russell. *Cinema Eye, Cinema Ear: Some Key Film-Makers of the Sixties.* New York: Hill and Wang, 1964.

Truffaut, François. *Hitchcock.* New York: Simon and Schuster, 1967.

Ward, John. *Alain Resnais, or the Theme of Time.* London: Secker & Warburg, 1968.

Weinberg, Herman G. *Joseph von Sternberg: A Critical Study.* New York: E. P. Dutton, 1967.

_____. *The Lubitsch Touch: A Critical Study.* New York: E. P. Dutton, 1968.

Wood, Robin. *Hitchcock's Films.* New York: A. S. Barnes, 1965.

_____. *Ingmar Bergman.* New York: Frederick A. Praeger, 1969.

# Index

Close-up shot, 88, 109, 121, 253, 255–57, 271; on a wide screen, 54–55
Color, in film, 58–64, 233
Comedy: and the advent of sound, 189–93; editing of, 319–22; feature-length, 144–53; of incident, 135–53; short, 139–44; in silent films, 135–66; of situation, 154–64
Commercial pressures, in filmmaking, 35–36
Conflict, within one shot, 303–04
Connection of shots, 32–34
Contemporary film, 222–46
Content, as the overriding interest, 28
*Cops*, 140–44, 262
Corman, Roger, 226, 228
Cost: of color films, 59; of major-industry films, 35–36
*Covered Wagon, The*, 52
Cowie, Peter, quoted, 369–70
Crane shot, 24, 54
Criticism, "auteur," 225–28
Cutting, 32, 288, 304

*Damned, The*, 61–64, 348, 371
*Death in Venice*, 61, 232
De Mille, Cecil, 134, 228, 371
Dept, in films, 55–58, 253–54. *See also* Three-dimensional films
De Sica, Vittorio, 77, 229, 361–63
Detective films, 210–21
Dialogue: asynchronous, 203; and characterization, 346–47; emphasis on, 341–42; film and stage, compared, 188; in gangster films, 208; integration of, with visual impact, 349–53; in *Maltese Falcon*, 211; opposition of, to visual impact, 353–54. *See also* Sound; Verbal and visual interactions
Dickens, Charles, 110, 298, 299, 364-70
Dickson, William, 89 and *n.*, 90
Director(s), film, 65–68, 74; attitudes of, expressed in camera shots, 258–60; ranking of, 225–28
Discontinuity, of camera shots, 254
Dissolves, 94, 336–37
Distance, of shots, 25, 255–57
Distortion, camera, 276–77, 304
Documentary film, 9, 91, 107
Donen, Stanley, 75, 77, 80
Double exposure, 30, 94
*Double Whoopee*, 321
Dovzhenko, Alexander, 334–35

*Dracula*, 205; pictured, 206
Drama: and the advent of sound, 193–203; in the silent film, 165–84
Dreyer, Carl, 205, 224, 225, 229, 262, 269; quoted, 59
*Duck Soup*, 191–93, 343
Dumont, Margaret, 191–93

Eastman, George, 90
*Eclipse*, 367–70
Edison, Thomas, 89–91
Edison Company, 15–16
Editing, film, 10, 20, 77, 172, 173, 260, 270, 271; through accumulation, 296–97, 300, 317–38; and Chaplin, 42–49; of comedy, 319–22; and the communication of ideas, 34–36; and connection of shots, 32–34; and Eisenstein, 303–16; through fragmentation, 295–316; and Griffith, 109, 113, 114, 135, 137; and Hitchcock, 299–302; machines, 52; and Niblo, 40–42; and Porter, 100–07; and Sennett, 135–38; of the sequence, 36–37; and the star system, 74–75; underlying premise of, 38–40
8½, 240, 241, 371
Eisenstein, Sergei, 13*n.*, 15, 27, 31, 35–37, 63, 77, 109, 110, 115, 173, 228, 270–71, 276, 295, 318, 335–336; and editing, 298–99, 303–16; and *Potemkin*, 304–16; quoted, 13, 303, 307
*End of St. Petersburg, The*, 317–18
Environment, 371; rather than plot, 356–57; specification of, 347–49
Erotic films, 242–46
European movie industry, and American, compared, 71
*Execution of Mary Queen of Scots, The*, 92–93
Exploitation films, 243–44
Expressionism, 171–72, 205, 207
Eye, human, and film, compared, 20–21

Fades, 32–33, 94
Fairbanks, Douglas, 72, 155–64, 272–75
Fantasy films, 94–95, 107
Fast motion, 29–30, 94
*Fatty's Chance Acquaintance*, 138; pictured, 139
Fellini, Federico, 61, 66, 71, 87, 229, 236, 240, 241, 357, 362; quoted,

373, 375, 376; and *Satyricon,* 371–76

*Fiancés, The,* 359–62

Fields, W. C., 78, 189–90

Film, narrative: comedy, 135–64; contemporary, 222–46; craftsmen of, 65–82; development of, 85–246; drama, 165–84; early inventions, 89–91; editing of, 32–49, 295–338; as an external medium, 20–31; and the eye, 20–21; genres of, 204–21; Griffith's contribution, 108–34; material nature of, 7–10; as motion and fixity, 7–19; movement and nonmovement in, 269–95; nature of, 5–82; physical properties of, 50–64; primitive, 87–107; realistic, 359–63; and sound, 185–203; specifications, 251–68; structure in, 355–76; technique and content of, 91–93; theory and esthetics of, 249–376; verbal and visual interactions in, 339–54

Film d'Art, 166

Filmmaker, 65–66, 68–82, 225–226

Fish–eye lenses, 21

Fixity and motion, film as, 7–19

Flashbacks, 30, 33, 241

Focus, soft, 54

*Force of Evil,* 71

Ford, John, 66, 78, 193, 207, 228, 345

Forster, E. M., quoted, 355, 356

*400 Blows, The,* 277–78

Fragmentation editing. *See* Analytic approach to editing

Frames, 8, 22 and *n.*

Frankenheimer, John, 30, 66, 232

*Frankenstein* movies, 171, 207

French New Wave, 237–40

*Freshman, The,* 144, 148–53

Freund, Karl, 174–75, 178–79

Gangster films, 208–10

Garfield, John, 69–71

*Gay Divorcee, The,* 82

Genres, film, 204–21

Gesticulation, in silent films, 11

Gish, Lillian, 73–74, 118, 126

Godard, Jean–Luc, 227, 237, 238, 241, 357

*Gold Rush, The,* 327–34

Golden Section screen shape, 53

*Grand Prix,* 30

Grant, Cary, 75–77

*Great Expectations,* pictured, 259

*Great Train Robbery, The,* 19, 35, 56, 100–07, 121, 297, 364

Greek theater, 52, 140, 156, 207

Griffith, D. W., 3, 15, 21, 31, 58, 66, 71–74, 85, 87, 89, 93, 94, 102, 104, 105, 138, 166–67, 228, 236, 241, 261, 276, 359–60, 364, 366; as an actor, 100, 111; and *The Battle,* 114–15; and development of the narrative film, 108–34; and editing, 109, 113, 114, 135, 137, 295, 297–99, 326–27; and *Intolerance,* 11, 122–34; and *The Lonely Villa,* 111–14; and *Man's Genesis,* 116–18; and *The Musketeers of Pig Alley,* 118–22, 208; quoted, 125

Hawks, Howard, 226, 227

Heiss, William, 92–93

*Henry IV,* 342

Hepworth, Cecil, 93

Hitchcock, Alfred, 13*n.*, 15, 22, 26, 36 and *n.*, 54, 60, 75, 193, 205, 226, 228, 256–57, 296, 319, 358; quoted, 76–77, 187; and *The Thirty–Nine Steps,* 299–302

Horror films, 205–07, 348

*Horse Feathers,* 148, 191

Horse racing, motion pictures of, 12

Huston, John, 210–21, 226

Idea, cinematic, defined, 344

Ideas, communication of, 34–36, 109, 116–18, 141, 261–62; structure, 122–34, 371–76

Incident, as distinguished from plot, 242

Influences on contemporary films: "auteur" criticism, 225–28; the new intellectualism, 228–36; public recognition of film as art, 223–24; stylistic movements, 236–40; techniques, 241–42; voyeurism, 242–46

Information, communicated by the shot, 251–52, 261

Intellectualism, new, 228–37

*Intolerance,* 11, 122–34, 167, 180, 244, 327, 364

Iris shot, 31, 32, 44, 54, 140, 172

Italian film industry, 78; neorealistic school, 361–63

A 2
B 3
C 4
D 5
E 6
F 7
G 8
H 9
I 0
J 1

**Cressman Library**
Cedar Crest College
Allentown, PA. 18104

## ④ THE PROJECTED FILM: PHYSICAL PROPERTIES    50

## ⑤ FILM AS PRODUCTION: THE CRAFTSMEN AND THE ARTIST    65

# PART TWO    The Development of Film Form    85

## ⑥ THE PRIMITIVE FILM UP TO PORTER    87

## ⑦ D. W. GRIFFITH AND THE DEVELOPMENT OF THE NARRATIVE FILM IDEA    108

# CONTENTS

meaning, since that meaning must be derived from the specific images and events of the narrative. The question raised in the extended analyses of various films is not "What does a film mean?" but rather "How is the meaning expressed?" The procedure throughout has been to interpret the particular ways in which meaning is revealed. Often, of course, the idea cannot be sensibly distinguished from the process that communicates the idea; in such cases the explication of the theme advances our perception of the filmmaker's method of structuring his materials in executing a film idea. The individual films analyzed are selected because they contain significant examples of the general film characteristics studied in the related chapters; in most instances, each analysis stresses only one or two aspects of a film as they relate to the film idea, though others might be equally important. Presumably, the neglect of certain aspects of each film will be understandable in light of a consistent purpose: to treat films as specific illustrations of general principles in order to work toward a theory of the nature of film.

I wish to express my gratitude to Erica Kaplan for her detailed and valuable editing of the entire manuscript as well as to Barbara Solomon for her helpful criticism. I am indebted to Dean Charles B. Quinn, C.F.C., and former President Joseph G. McKenna, C.F.C., of Iona College, for providing me with the opportunity to complete this book, and to the Museum of Modern Art for allowing me to examine films from its collection.

Stanley J. Solomon

# PREFACE

The purpose of this book is to examine the nature of the narrative film in regard to those characteristics that distinguish this art form from the other narrative arts. Hardly anyone these days will dispute the premise of *The Film Idea:* that the essential qualities of the cinematic mode differ significantly from those of any other mode. Furthermore, everyone agrees that the chief elements of film form are the different kinds of shot and their arrangement through editing. Beyond this point film analysts proceed in diverse ways, but sooner or later most of their written analyses turn into exercises in literary or dramatic criticism, thus confounding the distinction inherent in the identification of different expressive modes. Critics tend to strive after "film meaning" as if it were some disembodied conception breathed into a film by a creator, to be inhaled by a knowledgeable spectator, mulled over in the mind until it finds palpable form in language, and finally explicated for the public, who would otherwise miss the point.

This book predicates a different approach. Part One attempts to sort out the elements of the film medium and to examine their possibilities for cinematic expressiveness. In Part Two, the major procedures for shaping and organizing a cinematic narrative are discussed, mainly in terms of the historical development of the art form. Part Three deals with the theoretical and esthetic implications of the various elements and procedures that comprise a distinctive film idea.

The kind of analysis attempted here requires a good deal of description of specific occurrences in particular films because of the difficulty of translating a largely visual event into a verbal one. The difficulty cannot be ignored by simply talking about a film's

# For Barbara and Nancy Jane

## Picture Credits

On the Cover (left to right)

Picture credits continued on page 396.

© 1972 by Harcourt Brace Jovanovich, Inc.

All rights reserved. No part of this publication may be reproduced or transmitted in any form or by any means, electronic or mechanical, including photocopy, recording, or any information storage and retrieval system, without permission in writing from the publisher.

ISBN: 0–15–527375–2

Library of Congress Catalog Card Number: 77–190447

Printed in the United States of America

# THE FILM IDEA

STANLEY J. SOLOMON

IONA COLLEGE

HARCOURT BRACE JOVANOVICH, INC.

NEW YORK CHICAGO SAN FRANCISCO ATLANTA

# THE FILM IDEA

maybe two months' grace in the wallet. In the head, a doctor's news jockeyed for space with his plan.

At passing speed, squinting into the next few months, he hit the city limits, playing on his howling bungee an improvised, humble, speculative tune.

He woke. It was a Monday morning. He knew where he was, even the motel's name.

He did his stretches in front of the window, hanging on to the air conditioner. Okay. So what was all this worry about school? He'd done it before and always got himself over the hump. Ten, fifteen years had passed, so what. He had the way with words. Half Irish, half Italian — if that didn't make a poet, what did? If it took a while to get the pen looping and the tongue flapping, he could fall back on profs' mercy. Sir, I haven't thought seriously about literature in, let's see. Haven't really read a serious book in, let me think now.

Sir, it'll take a while to get the brain in game shape.

Start on push-ups today. He dropped to the brown shag, deciding to begin with two reps of thirty, add five more each day. Good it was a Monday. Monday was when you began something. And fall. A fall Monday was when you started school, or training camp, and where — one of his favourite things — you put on the new uniform and looked down your chest at the unfamiliar colours of your new second skin. You read the upside-down emblem, which in the old days was embossed with heavy, luminous thread: Express, Americans, Indians.

The secretary looked decent. Thirty, lanky, henna in the hair, baggy sweater, string of clunky wooden beads. She threw him a little smile while she dealt with two younger types ahead of him.

He smiled back, meeting her eye over these kids keeping two adults from doing business. If he was a "mature" student, then by extension these two in front would be immature. Maybe she'd laugh at that.

A prof buzzed through, head down in sheets of fresh xerox, rolling his eyes at some nuisance or other. It was going to be strange here, no question. The prof looked younger than him. He hoped he wouldn't have to call them "sir." Jesus, could he physically, actually do that? "Doctor" would be even worse. Doctor Paragraph, heal me. There goes Doctor Comma, off to lunch with Doctor Diphthong.

Better if he got women. For some reason the power struggle had different rules with women. Too often during his part-time undergrad stints the manprofs had seemed less than comfortable with the basic look of him, the scarface and Bonaduce bulk, maybe the perceived readiness of his muscles, who knows. In any case, they had been driven by some urge to give him grades lower than deserved, to meet him not in the alley but with a chickenshit mark in the mail. His essays were decent enough. That one course, the Modern British, a seminar affair with about ten of them around a table — he'd been at the weights all summer and wore a T-shirt the first day and the reedy prof had had furtive eyes for his chest and whatnots and at the end of it all he'd received the shittiest mark of his life.

"Bobby Bonaduce?" The secretary looked up from the file folder that no doubt held record of that very mark.

"Robert."

He had decided to be "Robert" here. He must have signed his forms out of autograph habit. In grad-school world the "Bobby" would not help his already shaky credibility. He wasn't exactly a goon at a tea party, but he wasn't not that either. Forty-year-old named "Bobby." Neck thicker than any other two around here.

"I'm definitely 'Robert.'"

"Well"—she handed him a course list—"I'm definitely 'Lorna.' Since you're so late—we're a week and a half into classes and—"

"Guess I'll have to buy a couple essays off somebody." He gave her a deadpan she didn't see.

"—since you're so late you have to get the professors' permission, so you'd better choose fast and go and—"

"Can you tell me which of these are women?"

"Sorry?"

"There's just initials here." He rattled the course list at her. Only when he saw the look on her face did he realize how the question must have sounded. Maybe she thought that he thought he was sexy or something and wanted women profs for that reason. Or that she had in front of her some old throwback who wouldn't be taught by a woman. Jesus, Lorna was looking at him hard. Maybe it was only that his morning five o'clock shadow was upon them both, and the scars were coming out bright white, and she had no clue about him whatsoever.

He woke up surprised at any number of things.

At the window's view he did his stretches, which sometimes did and sometimes didn't affect the stupidity in his right foot, and considered the town below. The cathedral had recently gotten a new copper roof. The newest part was still shiny, while the older part was already turning black, on its weird way to that green.

Yesterday's drive through town had sparked so much memory, things he hadn't thought about for years. The butcher shop where Leah had insisted they buy their meat. The church where the wedding was, all those quiet Moncton relatives of hers he didn't know and met only the once. That tavern, now a pizza chain, where the owner had set up a used electroshock machine on the bar, some customers laughing, others wary of it.

Up the hill, a glimpse of the hospital where Jason was born had put Bonaduce right back in that yellow room. Light from that window falling on that tiny squinty face. *My god it's a little old wrinkleman.* He'd watched it all, a fairly daring thing for the dad to do in those days, though apparently it was strange not to do it now. Impromptu, the doctor asked if he wanted to cut the cord. Scissors were handed over and he'd stood hesitating long enough for the doctor to ask if he was shy of blood. He shook his head, unable to voice questions to do with the cord there, its pulsing, its unearthly colour — and, and whose cord was it? Leah's or Jason's? Who would it hurt, the cutting? When the doctor reached for the scissors Bonaduce went ahead and did it, it was tough like steak sinew. The blood came rich and thick, and neither mother nor son seemed bothered.

Down the hill from the hospital was the corner gas station where on Christmas Eve they'd bought a tree, Bonaduce home from a road trip for the only Christmas the three of them would spend together. Gripping the crook of the lowest branch he'd dragged it home over the sidewalk snow, a perfect winter night, the heavy quiet. Leah carried Jason, who peered out from his ball of soft blankets, wide awake, watching it all. Two new parents agreeing that from the staring look in his eyes you could tell he was listening even harder, he was hearing more than seeing.

Twenty years later, driving in traffic, Bonaduce could see the eyes of his baby boy listening.

He hadn't meant to drive by her old place, but there it was, the tiny upstairs apartment, her window you could see from the street. All those early times there, her awful little bed, not much sleeping to do anyway, they couldn't get enough of each other. And that time — Bonaduce smiled, speeding up — her apartment door was unlocked and he'd walked in and surprised her at the kitchen table eating that unbelievable stuff right out of the can. Which had explained the mints she sometimes munched at the start of a date. A few months later that sober evening at the same table, her pregnancy news, his monotone proposal. Hustling out then after hugs and laughter and her tears, late for the team bus, shaking his head at life and breathing hard, fleeing this building, now painted a flaccid green, used to be white.

The station wagon was chugging a little, ominous. It wanted the highway, it didn't like this city stop-and-start. For a last taste of nostalgia he kept going, up to the arena, and the boxy old thing made him feel his first job again. He'd been twenty, Jason's age.

The pride. Paid to play. Paid to *play*. People buying tickets to watch. He'd gone straight out and bought the Datsun 240Z, grinning into debt. He was making a living that would only get better, the NHL only a year away, for sure. For now, the Fredericton Express. He'd had trouble keeping down the grin as he checked out the dressing room, shook hands with the guys, found his stall with his jersey hanging in it. For days he sang about it in his head, singing his jersey number to the tune of the Bee Gees' "Stayin' Alive." *Ha. Ha. Ha. Ha.* Number *five,* number *five.*


Stretching at the window, he scanned Fredericton's rooftops. She lived on Grey Street now. Where was Grey Street? Jason's addresses had been different from hers the last couple of years, good; he'd left the nest, no mamma's boy. Did he live in a party house, wading through pizza boxes, cracking rude jokes with the boys, or did he have solo, studious digs? There was so much to find out about Jason, so much of it so basic. The ever-kindling guilt of the wayward Bonaduce.

He packed the car, checked out, found a cheaper hotel, unpacked again. Cheaper was better so long as the bed was hard. After a lunch of cheese, crackers and two apples, he drove down

Waterloo Row to park by the river. Nice fall day. He recalled fall here to be a good one, breezy clear blue days, just the kind that helped the fresh start.

He got out of the car, looked at the river, took a breath. He'd done it. Fredericton. Here he was.

He had his jogging stuff on; he dipped down into groin and ham stretches before the run. It was stupid to be afraid of bumping into either of them, it wasn't that small a town. Though it hadn't grown much. A few more red-brick buildings downtown, a few fewer elms. Of course the river hadn't changed at all. Twenty years ago he'd parked here in the same spot, doing what he was doing now — getting ready to jog but also watching, smelling, this moving mass. Feeling the weight of it, the dark authority of a big river, the hugeness of its intrusion and, as it swept by, the impersonal departure. No hello or goodbye. Rivers were essentially foreign. Almost eerie. Bonaduce had always thought of rivers as the place people drowned.

Watching the water leaving town, he found the names coming unbidden: Rochester, Kalamazoo, Tulsa, Las Vegas, Utica. Fredericton again. Some by trade, some by choice, in two decades the places he had called home.

Staying down in a toe-touch, he tightened his shoes. Blood filled his head, he wasn't in shape. But some months ago in Utica his right hand had bungled this job of tying a shoe. Today the hand was a magician again, fingers so fast you could hardly follow them.

He erased the phony poetry — thought about a river taking him away and now bringing him back.


Jog. *Jog.* Onomatopoeia, a litword he remembered. Buzz, whack, yodel, they sound how they mean. *Jog.* Jog the legs, the spine, the body into a pleasant stupor, hardbreathing. Jog the brain into a scene he should have experienced but hadn't, Jason with him here, jogging this forest path, puffing along behind, unbearable sound of your child's pleading breath. *Hey, Jase, you, lookin', forward, to, puttin' on, the skates?* No answer but the boy's noncommittal grunt, the boy in pain, hung over from a night out with his buddies, and a non-jogger to boot, in youth scornful of these maintenance measures. But jogging anyway, knowing the truth of the father's example. *Son the, mortal coil needs care, the bone-rig needs, tending for the, long haul.* Parking lot in sight, the dad does the corny thing, letting his puffing boy catch up and pass him at the finish.

⤳

Pen and blank sheet of paper on the tiny formica table. Large McDonald's coffee. Printed at the top of the sheet:

TO DO:

He felt cold and crusty under his clothes from the run. And ridiculously winded — two days of solid driving, the body falls way out of tune. But full feeling in the feet. Running, he'd felt almost bloody graceful. Doctors are best at arrogance.

Sad to end up in a food court. He'd cruised the town hungry, passing little pasta parlours and coffee bars, for some reason not stopping. Why not just accept it as a comfort that you feel at home in a food court? In this mall, with this coffee, you were anywhere on the continent. To get a bit cosmic with it — or "postmodern"? He had to get to the bottom of "postmodern" — he was everywhere on the continent at once. McDonald's had done this, and Ted Turner had done this too, hiring his unidentifiably clean Yankee voices. These Fredericton mall kids wearing Nike hats — shoe company conquers the planet's feet and now does the head. It was like something out of *Batman*—Sameness Drops diabolically added to the water supply.

### 1. skates sharpened

Aside from these Freddie kids looking less dangerous than American kids, scowls a little less earned maybe, and almost no kids of colour, the people of Fredericton looked just as stunned as they did in Springfield or Kalamazoo.

Impossible not to look stunned in a mall. Automatically tired, skin pale under fluorescent sky. Suggestion of mouth agape even if closed. A dumb hunt. You could imagine a scene a million years ago wherein some Cro-Magnon entrepreneur stocked a forest clearing with tethered hare, mudpools of carp, mounds of fruit, a few big-ticket U-Kill antelope, and let the Neanderthals in to "hunt," provided they had the shiny rocks to exchange. This the birth of the Mall Age. Of the Vicarious Era, marked by rapidly devolving human muscle. Which led to sports fans, to people paying others to play their hard-body games for them, thus giving Bonaduce a job, and so what was he complaining about.

### 2. place to live

A question of balance here. If he went for the one-bedroom over the bachelor, he'd need a part-time job. If he got the meanest shared flop he could find, he could maybe make it on the assistantship they'd promised him today. He could get a thousand for the car if anyone believed him that it came from south of the Rust Belt. But carless he'd have to rent closer to campus, higher rent, vicious cycle. And how could you go carless? How, when midnight came and your foot started tapping, could you not have your car out there waiting with its roof rack and head-lights and map of the big picture...

Maybe he should sell the car as a gesture to roots here.

There was still the chance, a small chance, of the cheque. The Utica courts might come through. How could Wharton get away with it? How could a guy declare bankruptcy, fold a team and renege on the payroll, even as his car dealership stayed open and looked healthy as hell, rows of shiny Japanese cars and dayglo pennants flapping in the breeze? So what if during the period in question Bonaduce hadn't been quite up to playing. A contract was a contract. Eight thousand dollars — almost twelve Canadian — would be just fine. Fournier was still with his girl-friend in Utica and he'd promised to keep Bonaduce posted.

Rent, books, food, money money money. He'd never had a secure thing but here he was at forty thinking week-to-week. Hand-to-mouth Bonaduce. But a thought: while Canadian schools couldn't give athletic scholarships, there were rumoured "subsidies" for the best players. So maybe he'd get some under-the-table. He'd go see the coach, stick out his hand and announce his intentions. Bob Bonaduce, I'm back in school, I'm thinking of playing for you. Or, "trying out." Best be humble, polite. There was no question of not making it. The floppiness had almost left, the motor was fine thank you. At his age he had a good year or two left at this level, no sweat.

3. Get coach's name, call coach

Though once he announced himself to the coach, the cat was out of the bag. A less-than-cool way for Jason to find out about any of this.

4. Call Jason

Writing that, he caught himself feeling almost comically nervous. Jesus. So what else?

5. Buy books

He'd scanned the reading lists. Regardless of what courses he took, the number of books he was to have read over the summer was enormous in itself, and the number he was to read between now and Christmas was similarly impossible.

He studied number 5. What about not buying any books at all, see how that went. He crossed out number 5.

Jason's letter was what did it. The letter had come during one of those days, the kind which tell you from the start you're having a turn under luck's big magnifying glass: traffic lights would either all turn green for you, or all turn red; you could win the lottery, or be singled out in a mall and executed by a maniac. Anything *would* happen today.

First — he was just going out the door, to the doctor for test results — a call came from Fournier about Wharton folding the team and skipping out. Season over, no pay, no job. Then — he was back from the doctor, just in the door, feeling hollow and cold and shaking his head in recognition of what a lifespan is — Jason's letter clattered through the mail slot, hitting his knee, making him jump. Jason, whose letters came maybe every two years, one letter for every three of his own. Bonaduce would've written even more but didn't want to force the relationship more than his unanswered letters did already.

He picked up Jason's letter, looked at it, waggled it for weight, announced to its return address, "Hey, Jason. Dad's got multiple sclerosis."

He was being dramatic of course, in the throes of fresh news, not belief. He read his son's letter, barely skimming the surface of its content, seeing more the texture of his boy's typing, feeling its effort and intent, amazed that his boy could think, choose, punctuate. A recent big decision, said the letter, was to quit his last year of junior in favour of university, playing there. More and more guys, Jason explained, had been jumping into pro from college.

And Bonaduce, seconds later, phoning the University of New Brunswick for registration forms. It was one of those things you couldn't put much thought to. He knew it was utterly corny every whichway. Tiny Tim territory. In no direction could you escape the corn of it. While Bobby Bonaduce could still skate, he was going north to enrol in school and play on the same team as his long-abandoned son.

God bless him, every one.


He unhooked the roof-rack bungees and lugged his stuff inside. The guy named Rod had disappeared upstairs but the big girl, Margaret, helped. Things were finally taking a good turn — after six ugly days he'd found himself a place. Town full of students, what did he expect. But here he was, and you couldn't argue a hundred-forty a month. Over on the north side, or wrong side, of the river, and a few miles out of town, the old house was paint-thirsty and gap-shingled, and right on the highway. He'd be sharing its one bathroom with three girls and two guys. His room was so small that, in his head, he was thinking quotation marks around "room." He suspected his housemates were making a secret buck off the landlord by renting out what was perhaps an old sewing room — but you couldn't argue one-forty a month. Heat included. No closet, but furnished. Or, "furnished." He could find a board to put under the mattress. You could *panhandle* one-forty a month.

"We each keep our own food like, separate," Margaret was saying as he slid a suitcase under his bed. "But I mean, sometimes we make meals together. Not that much. Weekends. You could keep your food, I don't know, in like a box or something."

Margaret probably thought a bit about food. She was fairly tall but up around the one-seventy, one-eighty mark it looked like. But nice, smirking and gum-chewing like a guy. She was leaning on his door frame and he could smell her minty breath. When certain people are nice you feel bad noticing their body.

"Marg? I like your earrings." She had what must be ten of them, mostly small hoops, in her right ear.

"Of course you do." Smiling, chewing her gum, her sarcasm including her as much as him, and nothing but pleasant.

"Whatcha got, about ten in there?"

"About. I could make us some tea?"

"Great. GREAT." A roaring *whoosh* from the highway made him repeat himself. It wasn't rush hour yet.

"Herbal? Black? Gunpowder?"

"Herbal, great." He was tempted to go Gunpowder to see what he got, maybe some in-crowd concoction. Booze or drugs even, you never knew. Not hard to tell from Margaret or the decor what sorts his roomies were. Probably casual smokers. A little tokahontas never hurt anyone, he might even join them. Each room had a couple of arty candles. The rooms themselves were painted in the clash-colours of past tenants. Not overly clean. Without looking for them you could see cobwebs in ceiling corners, and the smell of incense arm wrestling mildew. Rod and Margaret had been asking one-fifty but dropped it ten when they saw his car and he said sure to her question, "Some of us are like, students too, and could we maybe get a ride in when you go?"

Margaret shouted from the living room that the tea was ready. Absurdly, first he checked his hirsute self in the mirror strung up on a hook on his wall. It would be too utterly bizarre to dig out his razor and shave. But he patted his hair down.

They sat blowing politely into their teacups. Margaret had closed a window, but they still needed to talk loud to overcrow the *whooshing*s, especially the semis, whose shadows also pounded into the room, preceding the *whoosh* by a split second. In the silences Margaret seemed a little nervous, and Bonaduce's stomach hollowed as he recalled the formula: three girls, two guys... Now three guys, even-steven. Newly alert, he looked up at Margaret just as she looked up at him too. He looked blinking back into his tea. Well, Jesus, don't be an asshole. Forty, broke, roughish face. No catch himself. Anyone studenting at his age had obviously foundered on one of life's more basic reefs.

"Actually at night I love it. My room's like, right above yours. Puts me to sleep."

"Sorry? It?"

She jerked her head toward the window. "Truck-noise."

"Ah." Bonaduce exhaled. "Well I keep a little fish bonker beside my bed for the same purpose." Bonaduce made as if to whack himself two hard ones on the bean and Margaret laughed.

"No, they're spaced apart at night. You can hear one coming, a low like, sort of something way in the distance. I pretend I'm sleeping on the beach in Maui and it's like, this wave coming, and it comes roaring in just like a breaker, *whoooOOOSSSHH-hhhhh*...So where'd you like get the scars? Rod said you were either an axe murderer or a hockey player."

The room had a pastel, thickened feel from the layers and layers of paint, the latest one pale lemon. Floating dust added a dreaminess. Margaret chewed her gum with confidence, eyeing him with an off-kilter but intelligent glint.

He rasped like Brando, "Rod was right. See, I never did get the hang of skating." He waggled demonic brows at her. She smiled, no more afraid of any of this than he was. She'd be fun, she'd be okay. He could play guitar and sing in front of her, no problem.

"So Marg. What sort of student are you?"

"Not good, if that's what you mean."

"What are you taking?"

"Archaeology, only they don't really have a program here."

"Ah."

"I'm thinking of packing it in."

"No way."

"Well, yes."

"Marg? There's this saying. And as your elder, you have to listen and obey."

"I have always obeyed you."

"Marg? 'You sign your name, you play the game.'"

"Okay, sure," she said, not considering the Bonaduce maxim for more than a second. "And so like, what if the game's the shits?"

"Doesn't matter. Quitting feels shittier. It's true."

Unconvinced, or maybe she'd stopped listening, she pointed out the window to the stand of trees across the highway, near the river.

"Look. A pileated woodpecker. *Wow* they're big. I think it is one."

He tried to picture Marg in the academic world and couldn't quite. It wasn't just the way she talked. It was her humanness. He imagined her walking the halls head down, ashamed, insulted. Perhaps there were some human profs there too, but this morning he hadn't met them.

·⌒

He'd sought out his preferred profs and got in to see two. First, Doctor Gail Smith and her "Canadian Writers of the British Diaspora." He liked CanLit.

Bonaduce had long ago become wary of that brand of person who strategically doesn't say much, leaving you to stammer in the articulate pressure of their gaze. Some reporters tried that. But reporters you just played dumb with.

Her door was wide open. He knocked anyway and she watched him do this. She was maybe five years his junior. He stated his business. After a silent stare of ten seconds or so, sizing him up, she turned to her computer screen to ask, "Why do you want to take my seminar?" She hadn't exactly emphasized the "you" in her question, nor was its tone quite "What is two plus two?" but nonetheless it threw Bonaduce for a loop. First he answered her silence with some of his own. No way a joke or knowing smile (she still wasn't looking at him) or chummy reference to their shared age would deflect the question. There were correct answers, and there were honest answers, and as usual the honest ones were ridiculous: Because I need to take something. Because you're a woman. Because, though the doctors are wrong, I might not have much ice-time left and I want to play hockey with my son.

"Because I wanted to find out, you know, more about it."

"It...?" Staring harder into her computer and starting to type.

"Canadian writing. And—"

The typing stopped. The room froze with intelligence.

"—and, you know, the, the British diaspora."

"*Dee*aspora?"

"Well, toma*y*to, tom*ah*to. But, sure, *die*aspora." He knew that she knew that asking him the word's meaning would be cruel, and of course fruitless.

Typing and reading her screen, speaking in a monotone that suggested jowls-to-come, Professor Smith used whatever portion of her brain it took to say, "Lowry this week. *Volcano*. Brian Moore next." She pronounced Brian *Bree*an. "Lorna has the reading list."

He held up his xerox sheet and smiled. "I already have…"
She was so busy not noticing him now that he didn't finish.

Maybe if he had shaved.


Professor Daniel Kirk, his course called "New Traditions in the Carnivalesque," was perhaps fifty. He leapt to his feet, he stuck out his hand, he was all bootlick and smile, saying, "Dan Kirk! Read your application! Used to go to the Express games!" but Bonaduce knew he'd be calling him "Professor." He was the kind of eager, buttclenched male animal who would smile and meet your eye while checking out everything about you, alert to danger. His office felt like a lair of radical pettiness.

Bonaduce felt himself mirror Kirk's beaming smile. Shaking the man's hand, he knew a shitty mark when he saw one.


A Coke in his fist, cubes rattling, he went table to table in the Student Union Building cafeteria asking questions. The team name had just been changed from the "Red Devils" to the "Varsity Reds," this reportedly having something to do with Frederic-ton being a fundamental notch in the Bible Belt. The season started in two weeks, a road trip to Nova Scotia against Dalhousie, then Acadia. The coach was Michael Whetter, and he could probably be reached through the Athletics Department. He was believed to be quite young, maybe even late twenties. No one knew if he had played any pro.

Bonaduce had hoped to find at the helm an old crony, or at least someone who'd heard of Bobby Bonaduce. At worst, and this might be the case here, it was some youngster who'd kept all his teeth, played college and then gone to coaching school to learn the European stuff: the jogging with medicine balls, the five-man rotating unit, the playing flimsy and falling down howling if somebody nudged you.

It's not like you wanted to be handed a spot on the team. It's just that when you're not in the greatest shape it would be easier for all concerned if you were dealing with someone who knew what you could do. Because in training camp you don't go out and bash. These guys were going to be your buddies; you had their knees, shoulders to worry about; you saved the bashing for the enemy. This was a concern because, from the look of things, he might be forced to go out and impress someone, show what he could do. And what he could do was bash.

The meal had an edgy, formal quality to it, and Margaret seemed almost nervous. Nervousness didn't suit someone like her. Bonaduce suspected she'd gone backstage and campaigned to have everyone eat together tonight and welcome the new guy. Not present was the other woman, Joyce, who apparently almost never left her boyfriend's. So much for Bonaduce's mating-math.

It was him, Marg, Rod, and he was introduced to the two others. One was a poor guy named Toby who had a withered arm held like a fleshy hook against his chest. Toby was a smiler, but behind the smile was that brand of whatever hell it was to grow up with an arm like that. The other person, Beth, turned out to be Marg's sister, and Beth was even bigger, and six feet at least.

Margaret brought their plates out two at a time. Unlike the others, Bonaduce waited for her to sit before he began, though he didn't think she noticed.

Marg looked beautiful next to her sister, Beth. Beth wasn't quite walleyed, wasn't exactly hulking, but those were words you'd use. She hunched over her plate, protective of her food.

Her thin, tightly curled hair made Bonaduce imagine her bald when old. He looked at Marg and saw her being bald too.

"So where's 'Ralph'?" Toby asked Beth, taking some bored pleasure in overpronouncing this name. Bonaduce had heard Toby refer to the boyfriend as "Ralph the Forestry Ape." He'd surmised too that Beth doted on him, and that Marg was a bit worried that her sister's love seemed desperate.

"At a funeral," Beth answered, shovelling a forkload. "One of his profs." She spoke with her mouth full, and Bonaduce had to look away.

They were eating something Marg had cooked and called "student gourmet"— mac and cheese with extras thrown in. Bonaduce embarrassed himself commenting on what tough but tasty tomatoes they had here in New Brunswick, meaning this as a sort of compliment, and Marg having to explain about sun-dried.

"So. Robert." Marg cleared her throat for the rehearsed question. "So like, what brought you up here? To do English lit."

"Well, that's"— he chuckled for her, shaking his head —"that's a complicated one."

"Oh, the chain," Toby said slowly, mocking no one in particular, "of pain."

"Well, yeah, it's always complicated," Bonaduce offered. "But I guess here I could say it was either push rust in Utica, or English lit here."

"'Push rust'...?"

"Sell cars."

"Sounds like a bad name for a band," said Toby, making a show of buttering with his good hand while holding the bread to the table with his bad elbow. "'Push Rust.'"

"No," continued Marg, "but like, why here? You've been all over. And apparently unencumbered. I mean, *New Brunswick*?"

"What you do is this." He smiled to tell them he was both joking and not. "You turn forty. You find an atlas, have a few beers, close your eyes and go"—he closed his eyes, twirled his finger, then stabbed—"Hey, New Brunswick!"

He dipped his head and ate. Dinner would soon be over. Things would settle in a week and be just normally friendly. He had no doubt now that this was Marg's work. She had asked Rod, who'd been reading a book in his lap, to put on one of his classical discs. It played quietly now in the background, making you want to sit up straight. Toby, proud to know, announced Vivaldi. Bonaduce had heard it before, it was a common one, almost elevator. Toby announced further that they were listening to "Spring." When Rod told him it was "Winter," Toby said it should be "Spring," because those plipping sounds were so totally like icicles melting.

This guy Toby, amazing. Suggesting Vivaldi had gotten his seasons wrong.


It was Krieger who changed Bonaduce's outlook on hockey as a job.

Krieger was finishing his career in Kalamazoo just as Bonaduce got there. A basher and a crasher and the team captain, he was one of the characters you meet. He'd had his nose broken a bunch of times and was fond of saying that on windy days he didn't know what side of his face his nose would end up on. If asked about his scars, Krieger might say someone had put out his face fire with a shovel. If you sat next to him at the restaurant and displayed an appetite, you might hear your dining style likened to a starving man sucking a dog through a keyhole. Krieger's hyperbole.

Bonaduce's second year there, Krieger retired but stayed in town as a car salesman, which is what lots of guys did, cashing in on what local popularity might have accrued. Also they were essentially homeless otherwise. Certainly jobless. Bonaduce easily pictured Krieger selling cars, leading a customer around, nodding at the car's back seat and making some outlandish sex joke, and the customer feeling included in the panache of professional sports.

The team missed the bruising Krieger. Certain tough guys come to be mother hens more than anything else. When play stops they check for scuffles, concern on their faces, protective. They are respected and don't have to fight much any more. In any case, with Krieger freshly gone, Bonaduce said what the hell and stepped up his grit to fill the void. He had to try something. He hadn't climbed leagues and he was twenty-five.

Slash, spear, elbows always up. I'm meaner than you. Drop the gloves first, get in the first punch. In front of the net be a constant menace, a fucking monster. Your goalie's your helpless naked mother and nobody gets near. It wasn't so hard: you'd been living on the edge of malice to begin with.

Though the face got messier, the style paid dividends. That first year he came close to the IHL penalty record, he got the loudest cheers at home and the loudest boos away, the local paper said it was like he'd miraculously come out of nowhere, and once suggested that if Bobby Bonaduce ran for mayor, well, hey. Until he was traded again two years later, a few of the guys called him "Mayor," or even "Your Worship," which is what the mayor of Kalamazoo was referred to, politics being as full of hyperbole as Krieger. But even though violence didn't get Bonaduce the phone call from above, he was now a known commodity, a leader, a mature influence some team would need. He'd been made captain.

Though what had really fuelled his new violence, if the truth were told, was the sight of Krieger selling cars. Bonaduce drove past on his way to the rink and he'd see Krieger in the floor-to-ceiling window, sitting there at a communal desk, waiting for customers, Krieger's boredom clear even at this speed and from this distance. It was the "Used" lot — they generally stuck the ex-players there, the idea being that hockey fans were more the Used than the New market. Krieger would probably sell a few cars, but still.

What Bonaduce had seen through the window was that, when you quit the minors, selling cars was about as good as it got. He'd seen a few retirees jump into assistant coaching, but they were the keeners, the hockey-Eddies. He'd seen others go into what turned out to be shady business deals. Some went into security, donning fake cop gear to walk empty malls at night. And he'd seen guys keep at the beer like they'd always done while playing, only now they ballooned, adding forty, fifty pounds in a few years. Some drank more than ever, more than beer, and some — you heard stories — got into dealing dope. Rumours of downtown violence, detox, bad guys from Colombia. Some of the names you heard had faces. You could remember crashing corners with some of them. You could remember the grace of so-and-so's stride, and you could understand the bitterness that maybe helped take him down, because he and everyone else knew he should have been in the NHL from the start but management was too stupid to see it.

You'd heard of other teams offering career counselling for older players. While it may have been coincidence, two weeks after an old 'Mazoo alumnus, a guy named Al White, was found dead in a Boston alley, such counselling was offered to a few of them, including Bob Bonaduce, who was now twenty-six, an *older player*. This was about as mood-enhancing as writing your law-school finals and on your way out being handed an application for employment at McDonald's. To attend a session was to finally admit you were not going to the bigs. No one signed up.

What Bonaduce did do by way of career enhancement was enrol in an English course.

His third prof he met the next morning in class. He stumbled in late and she rose from her chair in greeting.

"Jan Dionne" was all she said, giving him her hand in a clumsy, human way. Finally, a professor who didn't have to act like one.

"Jan? Bob Bonaduce."

This was "Creative Writing: Longer Narrative Forms." Bonaduce was registered in the creative-writing option, meaning this was his speciality, this was what he would do next year's thesis in. He had already decided to write a novel. According to her thumbnail bio, Jan Dionne was primarily a poet. This fact made Bonaduce sweat a bit, thinking of his application. But what were the chances?

He sat and took stock. A seminar, there were only three other students, and Jan Dionne, around a table. Hard to hide in this one.

The other male in the room looked maybe Jason's age, and he wore traditional artist's gear — tight black refuse and a glower. Name of Philip. Serious business, this guy. One young woman was uncomfortably pretty, blonde, with unforthcoming but potentially wild eyes, hard to read. Her name also happened to be Jan. (Bonaduce dubbed them "Big Jan" and "Little Jan," an age thing, because they were the same size.) And there was Kirsten. Glasses and, though she may yet turn out to be nice, she cast upon the room a constant lip-length sneer, one that wrinkled her nose and bared her upper teeth. They were never not bared. It was like she'd once been struck snarky by one of youth's big sticks and her face had set this way. Kirsten didn't look at him long enough for him to nod to.

"You look lost." Big Jan was smiling at him.

"Well, you know. I'll catch up."

"We can get a coffee after this and I'll fill you in?"

"Great."

Big Jan explained that they were doing "plot-building exercises" begun last week. She invited him to jump in if he cared to. She had given them a scenario whereby a person turns a corner and hears a scream. The idea was to come up with what happens next, the goal being something called "artful incongruity"—which Little Jan, perhaps seeing in Bonaduce's face something other than comprehension, explained was "some plot device that's unexpected but not so out there that it's just bizarre."

They went round the table with their incongruous plots and Bonaduce heard nothing too good in any of it. Kirsten's was actually sort of stupid, in that a woman screamed because the guy was naked, which was fine, but then she had the guy wake up, it was all a dream. Big Jan pointed out that using a dream to end a plot was clichéd and a cop-out, to which Kirsten, lip lifting and nose wrinkling, asked whether fiction wasn't a cop-out by definition. To which Big Jan said, while that may be true, such discussion lay in literary theory, whereas this course was about craft, about what worked dramatically. When Kirsten fell into an unconvinced, talentless stare, Bonaduce found relief in the knowledge that her presence in the class would take some of the pressure off him.

This relaxed him enough to contribute. They were about to move to the next exercise when he half-raised his hand.

"Bob?"

"This is off the cuff."

"That's fine. So: fellow comes around the corner, there's a scream and — First, your character's name? And occupation?"

"He's, you know, unemployed. Newly unemployed. Name of — Robert."

"What happens next?"

"Okay. First, it's his own scream. It's him screaming."

"Okay. Good. So what's he screaming at?"

"Well, everything. The details."

"What sort of details?"

"Well, it's sort of random. Just all the shitty stuff. All the details that sort of work at you —"

He put his hands up and worked his fingers like chaotic worms, half-noticing that those on the right hand weren't going as fast as those on the left... *and depending on the pattern of plaque it'll be one hand or the other, one foot or the other, thankfully not both...*

"— the details that suddenly get you. Make you scream."

"Okay, so what happens next?"

"He dies. Boom. Totally unexpected."

Jan's eagerness fell. "Well, cop-out. It's like Kirsten's dream, a convenient —"

"It's not the end. It's the beginning of a story about his afterlife."

Big Jan looked willing to be eager again.

"It's been done in movies and stuff, I know," Bonaduce continued modestly, "but if you write it really straight, the reader won't expect it, won't even know he's there, because there's no trumpets and stuff. That's your incongruity. That it's just ordinary."

"An afterlife..." Jan Dionne shrugged at the size of this.

"Another incongruity is that the same shitty details are there, but now he knows what they mean. He feels foolish for blowing it all his life. His main feeling in the afterlife is embarrassment, and" — what was that word — "atonement."

Bonaduce took in the details of Philip shutting down, Little Jan's ass shifting, Kirsten's teeth watching him.

Jan laughed again. "You've done some thinking about this."

"Jan? You hit a certain age."


Jan Dionne would be workable. She was an eye-to-eye prof, one who began by respecting you and then you could blow it or not. Over a coffee in the English Department lounge, surrounded by some definitely non-human types, she filled him in. The course was a workshop. You brought in your stuff, everyone discussed it, you took it home and fixed it. At year's end she had to — Jan whispered this bit — assign your stuff a grade, but only because academe — she shot the others in the lounge a dismissive look — demanded it. It's a struggle for us here, she added, meeting his eye, the "us" including him, and meant "writers." Her gaze lingered into uncomfortable silence, and it was in this moment that Bonaduce became aware of her hairless chin, her facebones, her breasts, and the rest of her difference and unknowability — her as a woman. He felt this as both a bridge and a distance.

"I forgot to mention that I enjoyed your poetry," Jan said as they stood. So sincere she wasn't smiling. "Very much. I didn't read the whole portfolio, but enough to know it was extremely good. 'Eclectic' is right."

"Hey." A slight shrug. What were the chances. Don't meet her eye. Let her misread fear as humility.

"'Till Death Do Us.' The sex/cannibalism ironies were so layered. 'My flesh, the salt of your kiss, the teeth of time. . .'"

"Hey." Jesus, quoting the stuff. He hardly remembered typing that one. "Do you remember one called 'Blades'?"

"No. Sorry." She paused apologetically. "But I remember lots. Have you thought about a collection? What I saw was certainly publishable. Here and there I was intimidated, to tell you the truth. That one, 'Aeolia,' my goodness, and so different from —"

"Stuff I worked at over the years. Long bus trips, not much else to —"

"That's right! I know! You're a hockey player! People are talking about that."

A shrug, a dull look away to deflect this direction. Afraid as he was, it was disappointing watching her turn into a hockey fan.

"Any newer work you'd like me to see? Poetry is my area."

"Actually I think I've packed it in. Fiction is all I do now. My new area. Writing a novel for my thesis."

"You've started it?"

"Thought I'd get the jump on it."

"You going to bring it to the workshop?"

"Why not."


To get into the creative-writing option, which let you do two fewer academic courses, he'd had to submit "a portfolio of recent creative work." He had no such work, recent or otherwise, save for two old poems, and no time to write more. He could write, he knew he could write. In the meantime, there in the college library in Utica were all these literary journals — *Mississippi Review, Ploughshares, Alchemy* — a slew of unread anthologies of unknown poets' unknown poems.

It took him an afternoon and evening to select and type twenty-eight pages of poetry. And his own two, "Blades" and "Black Hogs." Describing his work in the cover letter, he used the words "eclectic range," and "postmodern."


As arranged, he met Marg outside the library, where she'd been studying, and they walked out to the student parking lot together. An almost balmy night. He remembered that Maritime weather was nothing but change, consistent change. Also that the extremes could be entertaining but you got sick a lot.

He took off his sweater and carried it in his hand. His other hand squeezed two books. He had to get a briefcase. Time to hit the yard sales. Marg was bookless, her long arms dangling not quite in rhythm to her pace.

"Haven't quit school yet, eh?" he asked as she waited at the locked passenger door. He searched for the key.

"Not yet." She smiled as he opened her door for her. "You know, like, not a lot of people lock their cars here?"

"I've been in the States for twenty years."

"Especially, I mean," she continued, and he was already wincing with the punch line, "cars like this."

It was warm enough to ride with the windows down. Marg marvelled at the eight track, and played with the old air freshener. She brought her nose to it.

"I think this has lost its power."

"Well, it's acquired new ones."

"Oh — this is your rabbit's foot." She nodded and seemed happy, like this was her territory.

"That's it." He paused. "Keeps me a lucky mess."

She looked genuinely interested in the grey cut-out now, fingering it with respect.

Lucky mess. It was Fournier who had called him this. That accidental way non-native speakers make poetry. Fournier, his best friend ever? Who knows. And why decide such a thing. But Fournier, Fournier and his watch exactly three hours late. Ask the time and it took him that little calculation. It was one of those many-buttoned watches with beepers and such, and Fournier would go into pidgin English to explain how he didn't know how to set it. But it had been perfectly three hours late for years. Out of the blue, in a rare insecure moment, Fournier had confessed to him that he'd set it this way when he was still Vancouver property, playing for their farm club, Hamilton, three time zones away. He'd bought this watch and set it and kept it at Vancouver time. The silly hopeful bastard, it had probably cursed him.

It was eleven when they pulled off the highway into their gravel drive. A motion-sensing light over the kitchen door shone in their faces. Bonaduce envisioned a year of this: arriving home, this light, Marg beside him, the old-oil smell of the gravel. Arriving "home."

"You're limping."

"Stiff." He hadn't realized he'd been helping himself along, one hand on the car.

Inside she asked if he wanted tea and he said okay and took a seat on the couch. Rod nodded to him and went back to his reading. Rod was always reading. You could hear someone in the shower and, mixing with the musk of an old house, smell the distant steam and soapiness.

He may have nodded off. Marg delivered his tea. She put a disc on, some soft Celtic instrumental. He picked up the case, The Irish Descendants. Not your most imaginative name. What he felt like, he didn't know why, was some Shirelles. Even some Supremes.

"Do you play Yahtzee?" Marg asked.

"Well, I don't know."

"It's dice, but sort of like poker."

"I know poker."

Marg located score sheets and two pencils, and what looked like a handful of dice. This was okay, this student life. Late night, tea, music, good company, no real worries. Yahtzee. He'd missed all this.

Bonaduce asked Rod if he wanted to play Yahtzee. Rod declined, smiling. Rod said almost nothing but you could tell he was a good guy.

"Do we bet?" he asked Marg, who was rattling the bones, warming them up.

"We could bet."


The taskmaster morning sunlight of fall. It didn't sound like any of his housemates were up and there was no evidence of them yet in the kitchen. Moving quietly, still a stranger here, he plugged in the kettle. Or tried to, missing the socket, his eyes still fastened more to dream details than to those of the waking world.

It was the kind of dream that shapes your morning and fills it with feeling long after it's forgotten. Jason was a Jason the father hadn't known, a boy of a prime sixteen, and they were all in bed together: Bonaduce, Jason, Leah. Dad in the middle. He could feel their heat. They'd all been jogging, in bright white track suits, though his own was muddy-dirty. In bed they still had these track suits on, and they were covered with a heavy comforter. It was hot but Bonaduce kept the comforter gripped to his neck in case anyone wanted to throw it off. No one said anything. Jason seemed concerned with food, and Bonaduce and Leah shared a proud knowing look at their son's appetite.

Three adults lying in bed together. Bonaduce shook his head, smiling gently, blowing into his coffee cup. He took the coffee to his room and sat on the unmade bed. He put a hand down, the bed still warm from the heat of him sleeping, the heat of his dream. Out the window, the maples were hinting at red, the poplars at yellow. The start of their pretty death.


He had the name and number scrawled on a napkin scrap. This piece of paper felt so electric in his pocket after two days, he had to smile at himself, how nervous he felt, how like a teenager afraid to call the special someone.

He decided that when he did call he would contrive to leave a message, and not have to talk. Ashamed of this cowardice, he plotted nonetheless to call on a Saturday night, a time any healthy young guy would be out-and-about. Hey — the message would say, and its tone would be neither pathetic nor too clever — Hey, guess who? Well, you sitting down? I'm in town. And I think maybe here for a while. Anyway, got some weird and wacky news. Gimme a call. Let's have a coffee or whatever. Be great to see you! Hope things are good and all that. It's been a while, eh?

Something along those lines. There was no telling how he'd be, how they'd be, if the call happened live. Even worse, way worse, if it happened in the flesh, face-to-face. That could be a stammering, awkward disaster. Better get the boy on the phone, leave a message, let him prepare.

Noon public-skate. The Lady Beaverbrook Arena. He'd practised here with the Express a few times. Outside it reminded him of a swimming pool because of its low contours and walls of blue tile.

He hadn't public-skated since he was a child. Outdoors in Winnipeg, at night. Lights strung up, music piped through bad speakers — Juliette, Rosemary Clooney — and couples skating hand in hand. Once in a while the Beatles as a treat for the kids, and a sudden licence to go wild. The young Bonaduce flying around, near misses, showing off. He remembered being grabbed mid-wildness by the coat scruff, yelled at by some old hero whose wife had her hands hidden in a white fur muff, like in a Hollywood movie.

He laced his skates. The smells always got to him. The water-melt on wood or rubber, the Zamboni fumes, sometimes ammonia, the old socks or wet cigars, or just the after-stink of your buddies. You always knew you were in an arena. How long had it been, six months? This would hurt.

The wall sign said noon was an adult-skate, no kids. Through the glass doors he could hear piped music, "Maggie Mae." And it *was* late September and, hey, he was back in school. The nice coincidence, the teenage astrology, of music. A whiff of a song like that from the window of a passing car could make you feel her skin, smell her shampoo, see the bark of the tree she braced against.

You can smell ice. The broad white sheet in front of you. He stepped on, the tiny vertigo of first-time-in-a-while. Mostly middle-aged and old men, here for exercise, skating a slow circle. Two couples. No muffs, but both were doing the fancy hand-hold. Born of Holland. Maybe Hollywood.

It was cowardly coming here, public-skating before reporting to the Varsity Reds. But he had to get the worst kinks out. He'd never not been in shape but he had to admit he was forty. And doctors were sometimes right, whatever; something grim had indeed attacked him, who knows what. But the legs felt decent. Right calf wasn't all there but it seemed to be suffering no loss of thrust. Better slow it down in fact, some people were watching. Public-skate protocol. Awful that they might think he was showing off, like there was a need to. He pictured himself losing his mind, doing some bashing here at the geriatric noon skate, something out of Monty Python. "Berserk Skater Maims Twenty Before Turning Blades On Self." Did they still have the *Daily Gleaner* here?

Actually it was a challenge to skate this slow.

Nor was there any doubt now. She was fighting not to look at him. Marilyn Bauer. Had to be. The veiled way she was eyeing back. They'd partied together two decades ago. Leah's friend Marilyn Bauer. Husband Dale? Dave? Marilyn and Dave. Dave had been with Leah before Bonaduce arrived on the scene, then they'd continued as friends. This now-platonic connection had nonetheless given Marilyn coy reciprocal claims on Bonaduce and, that's right, they'd had that flirt once under the table with their feet.

Marilyn Bauer looked ready to break into a smile the next time he chugged near. Fredericton had suddenly shrunk. Bonaduce left the ice, an early exit he would not read about in the Sports pages.

Time to suck it up and make some phone calls. What could either of them say? He was respectable. He was a grad student. He was a published poet.

He'd actually often thought of writing. Writing something. And not just when bored — the road trips, the bus, Jesus, the endless bad TV in the what-town-we-in hotel. Sometimes he was simply inspired. He'd write a bus-poem, usually a funny rhymer, and maybe set it to guitar for later, or maybe he'd show it to the guy beside him, depending who the guy was. He wasn't hiding anything, it wasn't that, they already all saw him as a freak, it's just that only certain guys would appreciate the clever lines.

How many times had some guy, knowing he'd taken another English course over the summer, yelled at him across the dressing room: So when you gonna write a book about us? They'd laugh and mock him for the booky weirdo that he was, but in their eyes you saw that they did feel their lives were worth writing about, and that they hoped maybe he would.

Maybe he would.


Getting "home" that evening he saw tacked to his door frame, hanging from a leather thong, a many-coloured spiderweb thing in a metal hoop. A few feathers dangled from it. It looked Indian, and it was apparently a gift. A taped note said: For your window, Margaret.

He took it down and rehung it in his window. And in doing so realized that he'd be seeing sunsets from this room, here was an orange one now. It wasn't a bad view altogether, he hadn't noticed this. Early peerings out had depressed him a little because it had looked so barren — unkempt fields and stunted trees fronted by a neighbour's heavy-equipment trailer permanently parked there, the trailer barren too. Greys and browns and the fading greens of fall. The scene had made him think of Jan Dionne's term "emotional landscape," which was where the main character found himself, and into which the clever author would plant traps and rewards. Well, if this bland scene was his emotional landscape, there were no rewards in sight, and probably no traps either, and it looked like it'd never been planted by an author of any kind, clever or otherwise.

He scraped a crusty smidgen off the glass with a fingernail. If you wanted to, you could see this lack of drama out there as simplicity. This lack of colour as subtlety. More fuzzy than stark, like a watercolour. You could see it as an empty stage waiting for something to happen. Birds. Deer. They had to come. In two months, snow. There were worse things to watch than an empty stage. For now, this decent orange sunset. This Indian thing from Marg.


In the SUB cafeteria he thumbed through the *Daily Gleaner*, Fredericton's rag, searching for Sports, wanting to check up on the stats and lives of a few buddies. He couldn't help but notice the spelling mistakes, and the wildly bad headlines — "Seniors Pursue Recreational Pursuits"— and letters to the editor, half of which quoted the Bible while railing against a gay group's attempt to hold a Pride parade. Where was he, Montana?

Today's paper had a Health section, which he scanned, trying not to read "Kidney Symptoms and —" "Bowel Disease the Scourge of —" You get into reading this stuff and you turn hypochondriac, fearful every time you pee and things feel a little off. "Pancreatic Cancer Rare But —"

That's what Coach Murphy had had. Pancreatic. A fast one. The Tulsa players had taken turns in groups, it was easier that way, Murphy being a coach no one liked. Half-dozen guys shuffling around, trying to hide behind each other, no clue what to say. How ya doin' Coach. Can we get you anything Coach? We lost to Phoenix again last night, blew it in the third. Lame jokes about who blew it, shoulders punched, Coach Murphy manages a smile. In it you can see his corny gratitude and terror both. He cries, or maybe it was just pain, his face squeezing up like a baby's. He looked so weak, completely used up, no say about whether he cried or not, a leaf in some fatal wind. It didn't exactly cancel out their former sense of him, all that macho dressing-room bluster—it just made it seem pointless. The last time Bonaduce saw Coach Murphy, his head was turned to the window and he was unresponsive to them. He'd fallen to an even more basic state. Though *fallen* wasn't the word. His intelligence as such appeared gone, but you could see that his feeling for what he looked at—the light in the window—was deep. A yearning, but not even that complicated. A plant's basic connection to the sun.

One *Gleaner* article that caught Bonaduce's eye had him actually laughing out loud as he chewed his last french fry, kept him smiling as he sucked his large Coke through a straw. Doctors, oh they'd be duking it out over this one. It was about red wine, how someone had found something in it that looked damn close to a cure for cancer. Bonaduce could see the hypochondriacs arriving even now, sick line-ups at the liquor store, fists squeezing necks of plonk. Responses by other doctors would be a week away, articles about the dangers of guzzling, about how red wine *caused* cancer.

Doctors—he glanced at the young types slouched over their fries and bookbags, as yet unstricken with any of this—doctors were our gods. Doctors certain of themselves and lord how we're glad they are. It's just these damned second and third opinions.

*... Unfortunately for you it was a pyramidal attack...*

*... Good news: the attack was pyramidal...*

*... Now on the other hand, if you'd had a pyramidal episode...*

How, how could there be such basic contradictions?

*Mr. Bonaduce, multiple sclerosis is genetic, is hereditary. Bob, may I call you Bob, MS is a matter of diet. Hello there, sir, pleased* to meet you, multiple sclerosis is viral, something you caught as a child, and it flowers — I'm sorry, perhaps that's not a good word to use — twenty years later.

Well, doctors, I guess I don't really care how I got it as much as I want to know, how do I fix it?

Mr. Bonaduce, you don't. Your nerve roots are covered with a myelin sheath, which has been damaged, and blocked with this white crud, "plaque." It'll keep occurring, more and more. Bob? You fix it with diet, visualization and prayer. Sir, you can do any of the diets if you want, they probably won't hurt you, but mostly you rest, and take any number of drugs indicated by any number of symptoms.

Okay so I don't fix it. But if I have it — and I don't have it — give me the scenario. Tell me what would happen.

Bob, you will continue to experience deepening bouts of localized paralysis. Double vision or spot blindness. Fatigue. Fatigue is persistent. Pain. Later, aside from general immobility, of course incontinence must be provided for.

Incontinence? That's —

Yes. But, strangely, there's another, final thing.

What.

At this point euphoria is a common complaint. Well, since it's euphoria, "complaint" might not be the word to use in this —

That's funny.

But it suggests not only spinal and optic deterioration but also that somehow the actual brain tissue is —

He'd heard nothing more, frozen on the incontinence being provided for, on the image of diapers, unable to consider them and unable not to.

Sure, he probably shouldn't be drinking this Coke. Or having white bread, sugar, beer, Cheez Whiz, chips — right. Diet was one thing most of the gods agreed on, especially the alternative types. There was only one thing upon which all and everygod agreed: fatigue. *Don't, Mr. Bonaduce, Bob, sir, let yourself get overtired.*

Now how would a university student or hockey player ever get himself tired? Bonaduce rattled the cubes in his paper cup, sucking it dry, making the sound of a child finishing his milkshake. He savoured the dread possibility that Jason could come in here at any second. Bang, his son. His only blood family. Here's Dad hangin' in the SUB with a Coke, books scattered around. Hey Jace, how ya doin. Casual wave, like it hasn't been years, like Jason wasn't some unknown creature now, nothing remotely like the ten-year-old of their last handshake. Maybe nothing the same but the DNA.

Whoever Jason was now, he'd be thrown for the loop of his life. Off-balance and full of big questions. Frightened, in a word.

Well, better him than me.


Gail Smith's class was a secret hot room in hell Bonaduce hadn't known about. The intimate size of it, six, was extra-hell. Both black-mood Phil and glare-teeth Kirsten were in this one too.

Introductions were made for the latecomer. Bonaduce felt big and stupid already. In Winnipeg, because home room was French, if you were late you were *en retard*, and he hadn't dropped the association.

Gail Smith called everyone either Mister or Ms, and she herself was "Professor Smith." Bonaduce was about to witness her sitting up straight for three hours. He would not catch a smile, but to show she got a student's wry aside she did a thing where she turned down the corners of her mouth and jerked her head up and to the side, looking off into the sky with amusement and tolerance. It was like she saw herself as a seventy-year-old guy from Oxford. She could actually be kind of pretty except that she was so careful not to be.

Bonaduce would stay mum the whole time. The first hour was occupied by what looked like an argument, but probably wasn't, about what constituted "Britain." It seems that Professor Smith's inclusion of several South Asian writers on the list made Phil and Kirsten take offence on their behalf. Smith's point, that they were victims of British imperialism, and "forcibly adopted, as it were," seemed to rankle Kirsten in particular, in that she was certain the writers would be outraged at being thought victims. Smith countered that the only fact that mattered was that all these writers *had moved* — she almost shouted this. Which made Bonaduce wonder why she hadn't dropped the "British diaspora" thing and just called her course "Writers Who Have Moved." He also wondered if these writers — Vassanji, Ondaatje, Begamudré — would care what Smith or Kirsten thought. Luckily he didn't have to contribute this or any other musing, for these seminars were set up so that each week a different student did most of the talking, or "presented."

It wasn't as if Robert Bonaduce was afraid. Not overly. Humanly nervous in front of new humans. For all intents and purposes speaking a foreign language. People sat so alertly. Even Phil's dark slouch looked coiled and ready. Drawn blinds kept the sunlight outside where it belonged.

But all it was, really, was that these guys had worked up a decent act, all witty dash and brain-pizzazz. The ordinarys in the cheap seats could see this. But knowledge *was* power, and these types knew tons about that which the poor Bonaduce had no clue whereof nor whatsofuckingever. Phucking Phil, today's presenter, began his Malcolm Lowry spiel with shrugs and hand flaps as if to suggest he'd thrown some thoughts together out in the hall. Then launched into a sentence beginning, "Now of course the temptation is to foreground a reading of *Volcano* with a reading of Lowry's *life*, but those narrative contrivances in the text — linearity, closure, what have you — subsume in their very *artifice*, artifice by which the text, as 'novel,' derives, shall we say..." Phil was especially good at belittling certain notions by pronouncing quotation marks around certain words and getting people to smile, and Smith to jerk her head back.

The sentence continued for quite some time, and at first Bonaduce was spellbound. Then worried that this was the way you talked in this room. Was he supposed to "present" in this language? Then he smiled, enjoying the notion of *This is Phil presenting*. He remembered hearing the word used like this before, as a verb with no object, in TV nature shows. When a goat stuck its chest out, or a salmon turned itself bright red, or an antelope lifted its ass to another's face, they were *presenting*. Ten minutes in, Bonaduce was stifling his laughter — at Professor Smith's stupidity for allowing such a sentence to continue, at his own stupidity for not having a clue what was being said, and at Phil's stupidity for caring about any of this in the first place. He grinned picturing himself when his turn came three weeks from now, him with his upper dentures out, *presenting* with a sloppy lisp, dumb-on-purpose, saying "Well I theen the movie on thith inthteada the book but," and he was wearing his hockey gear, and three days' beard, his posture *presenting* so to threaten violence if anyone fell from wide-eyed attention at anything he said. He grinned harder and shook his head with an insight into the essential difference between his last career and this new one: if in the other game you disagreed with someone, you physically attacked him. What made him laugh aloud and got him reprimanded by Smith, who asked him, as if he were six years old, to "Please share it," was the image of him understanding something Phil said enough to disagree with it, then lunging across the table and grabbing Phil's arm and snapping it. Bonaduce decided against sharing this and mumbled an apology. Thinking himself understood, disagreed with and laughed at, Phil glared at him, and Bonaduce felt instantly overtired.

The ordeal was finally over. They gathered books and notes. Bonaduce had drawn a few decent pictures of his station wagon. He decided he could maybe do this course if he got serious and learned the rules, and the meaning of "postmodern," and next time read the book. Leaving the room, Bonaduce tried to be friendly to the other guy who'd just suffered through with him, a teammate if you will, a bespectacled Mr. Webster. Filing out, it was like the siren had gone, and they had lost but hadn't deserved to; they were bruised and weary and going for a shower together. Pointing to the slouched, exhausted Phil, Bonaduce threw an arm over Webster's little shoulders and whispered, "Guess we're gonna wanna buy our essays from *that* guy." Mr. Webster didn't look Bonaduce in the eye and his smile was nervous, but he did seem to know it was a joke.

In the department lounge, as usual, were the glances at the Bonaduce body as he scanned the bulletin board or stole coffee, dropping two loud nickels into the can instead of quarters. Young or old, prof or student, library nerd or nose-ring artist — up came whisperings of *professional hockey player*. Looking at him harder by not looking, Bonaduce the walking car accident. He'd expected this, body-people being exotic to head-people. Models, athletes, embodied some kind of ideal, so said the Greeks, though the notion had lately fallen from favour. And him doubly exotic — accepted into grad school, a jock who presumably wasn't stupid. These types were magnanimous enough to enjoy the little thrill of a preconception broken. But, hey, he'd show them: he could be stupid in ways they'd never dreamed of.

They wanted to know about the fights. Especially those who thought they didn't want to know. Those who so quickly shrugged off the ludicrous subject in fact looked a bit like deer alert to a trouble-noise. Or they were hungry for the information, if only to have theories refuelled. It had not been a surprise to Bonaduce that half the fans at a New York boxing match were intellectuals, many of whom were women.

Stupid rough hayseed hockey players. Bonaduce wanted to explain things. He pictured the guys in the dressing room, on the bus, in the bar. The levels of wit he'd heard. But mostly it wasn't words, it was the way a guy being interviewed taped a stick while spouting bad clichés on purpose, or waggled his ass below the gaze of the camera. It was shared looks at the swelling colour of a teammate's knee. It was hotel and nightclub and taxi savvy. It was sound public management of pride and envy, something academics were apparently inept at.

Language, simply, was a route not many of them took. Should he tell these loungers that in 1968 Eric Nesterenko scored thirty-two goals for Chicago and published his first book of poems? But that would be falling into their trap, accepting their definition of intelligence.

On the ice is where it really happened. The brilliance of some. All senses sparking, working at the widest periphery, aflame with danger and hope both, seeing the whole picture, the lightning-fast flux of friends and enemies, the blending of opportunity and threat. Words didn't stand a chance here. Words were candy wrappers, dead leaves.

Bonaduce took his two-nickel coffee over to the main table, ringed on three sides by couches, seven or eight people on them. Might as well get to know some of these guys. Especially since half of them were young women.

"Can I wedge on in here?"

All the bodies on all three couches flinched to make room. He sat in the largest gap, smiling and nodding at the stiff young woman on his left and the nervous young man on his right. He grabbed up a *New Yorker*, chuckling at its cover, its tight little in-joke, an urbane mocking of the urbane, in this case a bunch of businessmen hustling to work in a uniformly demented way.

True, sure, dressing rooms had their share of morons. Guys who would say *libary* if they ever had cause to say it. The stuff he'd heard come out of guys' mouths. *Twats, queers, hosebuckets,* and half the room laughing. But a dressing room was your basic cross-section, this seemed only reasonable. The fact remained that half the guys in any dressing room he'd ever sat in could have ended up here in this lounge, thumbing *New Yorker* cartoons and being wry. They had for various reasons taken a different route, the body-route. The logic and joy of having it work like that.

Out of the blue and apropos of nothing except their being inches apart, he stuck his hand out at the guy beside him, whose head was down in a book which smelled freshly purchased. *Lady Windermere's Fan.*

"Hiya. Bob Bonaduce."


French fries in the SUB and then a long evening bent up in a library carrel, reading Brian Moore, in his head pronouncing it *"Bree*an," which coloured everything. Home by midnight, and on the kitchen table, weighted down with a buttery knife, a scrawled note from Marg: "Friend of yours called long-distance. Fornay? Fornier? French accent. All excited. Said you MUST begin something called a yeast diet. Said to tell you it's a cure? He's sending you a book on it. I assume you know what he's talking about."


You wake up with vision so fuzzy it's like sleep's dreamscape has continued, and then you find the legs don't work too well. Couldn't even bloody walk, he was a big nightmare puppet with packed rag legs. It wasn't some awful new injury, because he'd been feeling so weak and weird lately he hadn't even been playing. Rolling and flopping himself across the floor, it was almost funny. There wasn't a lot of pain aside from some deep nervy stuff he recognized as having been there for a while. The hands didn't work either. Despite dumb eyes and sleeping fingers, he eventually got Fournier on the phone. *Fournier, Jesus, you're not going believe this.* Damn if he wasn't slurring his words as well. He made a joke about the mother of all hangovers. Fournier promised he wouldn't, but an ambulance came and the boys in dull green, all intent on his survival, in no mood to crack a smile at the Bonaduce jokes, packed him up and away he went. Halfway to the hospital he was halfway better; a few hours later he could walk, he could see okay and he was feeling foolish.

But tests, tests, tests. Sitting in the blood-sample room full of sick people, holding a number, waiting for his name to be called, exhausting the *Sports Illustrated*s, endless baseball and basketball, in your stomach a drone of worry doing a dance with your trust in a body that had never let you down.

Passed from doctor to doctor. (After many high-tech gizmos and scans, the test of choice turned out to be the cartoonish popping him on the knee with the rubber hammer.) Have you ever experienced double vision? Bonaduce ping-ponging his eyes from the doctor to the curtain and back, asking, Which one of you asked that? The doctor deciding to smile, but continuing, How about blurred vision? To which Bonaduce answered, actually serious, Do you mean like concussion-blurred vision, or the kind that's just sort of usually there?

Waiting for tests, feeling better, he half-enjoyed the image of him in the corniest of scenarios. He was lying in a hospital bed, adult-diapered, limbs mobile as breakfast sausage, a professionally flirtatious nurse spooning vanilla dessert into his yop, and he asked the doctor (who'd be checking things off on his clipboard, brow furrowed, when everyone knows there's nothing *on* the clipboard): Well, Doc, does this mean that's it for the NHL?

The doctor is a wise-ass hockey fan. He says, Hell no, Bobby — there's always the Leafs.

Answering the questions, he was made to recall his body-history, which in his work was more or less typical. Finger, rib, two noses, cracked a footbone, a hairline in the right collarbone (the most painful), lots of sprains and cuts. About a hundred stitches in the face, all healing well and looking just fine except the rubbery scar-mess over the left eye, and those white lines criss-crossing his five o'clock shadow. Like Krieger, he'd had a job as a fencing mask in Heidelberg.

The only bad one had been the leg. In Rochester, which is a broken-bone kind of town, an innocent shove had conspired with a rut in the ice. Deep in the skull you hear and feel the snap. A beloved leg suddenly foreign, angling off into new territory. The senses falling in another direction, into a deep inner black, into fainting. Embarrassing, but no choice in the matter.

Then the strangest thing: coming to, what he felt was, what he even said to himself was, *I'm out of it.*

The war was over. Tonight's game, but also maybe the season, maybe hockey altogether, the career. Balled up there on the ice, Terry-the-Trainer's whisky breath asking if it was a knee, he felt the descent of a peace, he could even smile a bit in the wincing. He must have looked macho being helped off — smiling while the leg dangled so ugly. The tough Bonaduce. No one would see in the smile a little kid Winnipeg home from school sick, in pyjamas, TV all day, a warm bed, Mom's bustle in the next room.

The year-of-the-leg he was back for the playoffs and he played ten more seasons. All part of the job. Everyone played with pain. Injuries were unsurprising. In fact they felt nothing but appropriate. If you played the game right, you were in their arena, so to speak. You were sort of asking for them.

Waiting at home for the test results, he began to see disease the same way. As life-injuries. We're alive, so we're in their arena, we're really just waiting. He thought about death and saw that being alive in the first place was sort of like asking for it. Waiting for test results you think all sorts of things.

But you can point your attitude one way or the other. He wrote everything off to a deep flu, to a stubborn virusy thing. The clumsiness was frightening, but viruses were getting weird, weren't they? He could still skate okay. Funny, he could skate better than he could walk.

It was like an injury that was taking time to happen. You could actually forget about it, forget it was still happening, until the dropped spoon, or the delay of the comb. Then you understood how big it was. You could feel how life itself had become a hovering that was nothing other than sick. The air around you an impending deadness. They said it was going to come back; relapse and remission were the poles of your new planet. The whole thing would, simply, get worse.

In hockey it was generally all nice and quick.


"Leah there by any chance?"

There. Done. Some things you have to just do.

"She is. I'll just go and locate her."

That would be Oscar. He sounded okay, kind of funny, mocking his use of "locate" as he said it. Oscar Devries. She was still Leah Miller, like she'd always been, eschewing the tuneful Bonaduce moniker on their wedding day, contemporary gal that she was. Phone to his ear, he could hear Oscar walk away, wooden floors it sounded like. Oscar was a lawyer with NB Hydro or something. Probably an elegant old house, reno'd from the rats to the rafters.

"Hello?"

"It's your best nightmare."

"Bobby?"

"So that was Oscar, eh? You still with Oscar?"

"That *was* you! You're in town!"

In her voice excitement and fear.

"I am."

"Marilyn called, said she saw someone she thought was you. Remember Marilyn Bauer? 'It *had* to be him, and he was *skating*, it *had* to be him.' So I guess it was! Is!"

"Here I am."

"You here playing?"

"No, hell no. Packed it in. Old age, eh? But don't tell Jason. That I'm here. Surprise."

"Sure. So — you here for a while?"

A definite note of concern behind the cheer.

"Could be. It's kind of a long story —"

"We really have to get together, but, look, I'm out the door. I'm really late. We're having a party Friday night. Oscar will tell you about it. 'Bye."

And Leah was gone. Leah who would never for as long as she lived ever have to apologize to him, because he was the one who'd left. Leah who felt that the distance between them was now great enough for her to be excited over the phone in front of Oscar, with no fear of anyone misinterpreting. For her to invite him to her party, easy as could be.

But he'd heard what he knew he'd hear. Not in her voice, but in her silences, and the way she breathed. He knew she'd been holding the phone with both hands.

"Hello?" Oscar again. "Now you'll be wanting directions, is that it?"

You could hear him smiling, an ironic, friendly guy.

It was a decent little bed, even though something was conspiring to keep him in it. His first single bed since he was a boy.

Maybe if you just stayed put, lying down, and eased your mind in the right direction, a pure and gentle going-in that almost erased you, this tender secret muscle the size of your body that turned you to air if you flexed it right — if you stayed here like this, you could be one of those people, and he knew they existed, one of those people who know only what matters, who can play life like the game it is, who know its movements — its tides and wind and forest smells — and understand all the efforts of the heart. You would know to keep in mind that everyone's lost and no one's to blame. You would be able to lie here in bed like this but be content with it, content to look out this window to see those birds leaving that branch, moving off one by one in a sprung rhythm that suggests music.

This morning he found his roomies at the kitchen table, puzzling over heating and phone bills and such. Rod was wondering what had maybe been paid and what could be "left again till next time."

It was raining outside, cars were *whooshing* loudly by, a tableful of roommates were talking house matters. Things had a homey, practical feel. Toby already had a beer going. Bonaduce rummaged through his assigned half-cupboard, looking for the can of smoked oysters he was sure he'd bought. He was politely invited to take part, so he shuffled over, and he listened to Toby's suggestion that he take his turn and pay the phone bill. He decided to hold off airing the logic that this particular bill, some of which was long distance, covered a time previous to him setting foot in this country, let alone this house. He wasn't sure how things here ran yet, so he wrote out a cheque. Doing so, he briefly eyed Toby, who openly eyed him back.

Then went to his "room" and searched his "closet" (six hangers hanging on a string strung between two nails) to "get ready" for tonight's party at "his wife's house." What did you wear to such a thing? Were they rich, casual, stiff-necked, hip, what? And did he want to fit in, or did he want to shine?

He went to the bathroom. Sitting, he looked toiletside and noticed dark, flame-shaped stains of wet rising from the floor up the wall. The drywall was permanently damp and thickened with it, whatever it was, a rank ecosystem of climbing swamp. Instead of paying a phone bill, he'd love to come in here with a sheet of drywall and can of paint. Point this house in a new direction. He would discuss it with them. In the meantime he had Leah to get ready for. He picked up a paperback *Hamlet* someone, probably Rod, had left lying upside down on the floor, beside the swamp.


He lay naked on his bed, looking out the window at the stars. The party wasn't until nine and he didn't want to be early. He was already tired. Hard to kill time this time of night.

Red, white and blue rubber balls in both hands, you squeeze until it hurts, get the ligaments popping out in the wrists, and on the forearms blue veins almost the width of a cigarette. You do lose a step or two, but keep the wrist strength up and you always had your shot. He'd seen oldtimer games, and some of the old boys could still rip it pretty good. Forty feet out, a flick of the wrists and, bingo, the biscuit's in the basket.

These stars in this clean New Brunswick sky were a treat. The whole eastern seaboard of America had basically erased its stars. City lights and a bit of carbon burning was all it took. Fournier, who'd gone up hunting in Labrador, had a story of a Japanese girl visiting Goose Bay and pointing in amazement at the night sky. The smiling host, about to explain the wonder of the aurora borealis, looked up and saw none. And then realized she was pointing at stars — she lived in Tokyo and had never seen stars.

Squeeze the balls. Look at the stars. Tyger Tyger. Looking at stars is a feeling that's probably identical to what a dog gets looking at the controls of a stereo. Twinkling stars. Feel them pull at your little mind in that gently eager way they have, let them remind you for the first time in years that what you are looking at you are incapable of truly seeing and that the only honest response to this is to drop to your dull and sorry knees.

Loud stars. Hungry stars. *Synaesthesia*, grad-student word for the day. This jazzy darkness. Your citrus heart. Sweet and sour Leah.


Montreal traded him to Toronto in the middle of the season, just after Christmas, so he'd had no time to get his affairs — such as moving, such as abandoning his wife and son — in proper order before reporting to the Rochester Americans.

His plan was agreed to by Leah. At least, that was his memory. That he would go check out the town of Rochester and ascertain his status there. Because everyone involved was fully confident he'd be getting called up to Toronto sooner rather than later. One little injury to one Leaf defenceman was all it would take. Why move Leah and Jason to Rochester when they'd only have to move again? Leah was still in school, third year, so she should stay put, stay in Fredericton.

There were lots of reasons why this plan was agreed to. No one dared raise the main question.

Sex was great, it was always great. But between sex and the next sex was that edgy lack of purpose, a waiting which seemed most of all to be a kind of vacancy. They did share some vital loves: the same food, the same luscious colours in a picture or a sunset, a French horn for the way it came lording in. Smells. And of course sex, its textures and pace. They shared the senses, the runes of body. He'd even understood her eating the dog food, understood her after she'd been caught so embarrassed with the can of it and she told him it was like eating meat from the centre of the earth. They were joined perfectly in bodies' routes of need and terminals of pleasure. But with most else — friends, politics, questions of whether happiness came more from a Cadillac or a hike — on little could they easily agree, and it was so loud a problem it never had to be discussed.

Jokes though, they could share jokes. They could always make each other laugh. At a party, eye contact to confirm something scandalous they'd laugh at later. Sometimes they even joked about real things, about which they had no business laughing. What's your name again? Smiling sadly at the truth after they asked, Do we even know each other? Have we been properly introduced? No, though I believe I've just been Bonaduced.

Their joking was probably something close to love. As she tucked into a steak he could gently bark and whine, even in company, though she'd quit the dog food by now, and she'd laugh. She understood; they both felt the loving comment on her carnality, and her deeper needs, which seemed funny in the midst of a boring chatty party and their bed waiting upstairs.

He made attempts. He did. He tried and tried to expand his love, and to harden it against the hard times to come. Now and then even falling to the corny — flowers, a necklace for no reason, once a poem set and sung to moody music. But finding himself stooped and corny, he could never follow through. Couldn't stay pure, had to screw it up — he'd mock his flowers while handing them over, and the poem he wrecked by tacking on a spontaneous raunchy verse. Or when he fertilized her lawn for her. He'd seen on a lawn across town how green a chemical fertilizer could make grass — careless spreading had left a dark green spaghetti-drawing on a field of yellow. He got a spreader and commenced to write a message in fertilizer on her rented lawn. But the bag was empty after the second word, and the I LOVE that appeared several days later was messy and lopsided, and read more like a saint's axiom than a corny guy's love note, and Leah laughed but wasn't roused in the larger way he'd intended.

Ten o'clock, Grey Street full of parked cars, a party. The cars mostly newer though nothing too luxurious. Their house was a pleasing old place not in overly tip-top shape. Something about it shaggy at the edges, though it was brick. Oscar, smiling and ironic at the door, said, "Big Bob Bonaduce!" Leah must have described him. What words would she have used, she who hadn't seen you in ten years, or loved you in twenty.

"You must be Oscar."

He seemed okay. He wore the constant smile-of-a-host, but his was gently wry, and he had a shagginess to him as well, a slight sloppiness that Bonaduce liked in friends, though he was never that way himself. Both of them were wearing jeans and a sweater, but Oscar's jeans were faded to weakness. He wore wire glasses, was getting bald, with the round face baldness gives. A deep, croaking voice for that small body.

And not an ounce of nerves. Apparently no fear of losing her back to the hockey guy.

"Your old wife's somewhere in that." Oscar hooked a thumb back toward the main crush of people. "Beer's in the fridge, every-thing else's on the counter. I fetch you your first one." He raised his eyebrows in question.

"I guess a beer. Thanks." Bonaduce was already looking in over Oscar's turning shoulder, and there she was.

Leah. Even the name. There she was. Even the word *she*, the way it divided the world in two. Then ripened and rose in the blood.

54 ·

She was lifting a dipped mushroom to her mouth, tense in the shoulders, pretending not to have seen him yet. Her body as aware of his. Frightening how clearly his body remembered. Seeing her confirmed how exactly remembered. Her skin, its planes and hollows, both hidden and seen. The feathery hair on her neck. The way she held herself, even when relaxed every motion verging on the next, more than ready.

Panic in her shoulders told him she remembered as well. The only question was, would she hate him all over again for this?

Maybe this wasn't the only question.

She was wearing jeans too, and a fuzzy black sweater, mohair, the kind you'd get at a Used store, mildly campy and showy. A thin, almost invisible gold necklace draped her collarbone and then fell on into the sweater. A bit of makeup it looked like. Funny how they'd spent years and miles apart, but something of them had stayed front to front, talking loud and clear. The mushroom was in her mouth and she made as if to consider something as she began to chew. The choice of a mushroom wouldn't have been deliberate. She was staring off, composing herself, or revving up, one of those, because he could see that once she stopped chewing she was going to swing his way, lift her face and see him.

A teammate in Tulsa had a weird wife, weird in that she had written a book. Bonaduce learned it was self-published, but that didn't matter to anyone: Buddy Simon's wife had up and wrote a book. As Buddy described it, looking vaguely afraid, as if listening for something behind him, the book was about "ideas and philosophy and that." All the guys' wives or girlfriends received one at the Christmas skating party.

Maybe the weirdest thing about the book was that it was actually pretty good, pretty entertaining. Bonaduce relieved his jealously scoffing Julie of her copy and thumbed through it, a collection of homespun theories about this and that, most attributed to local farmers and off-kilter thinkers and old almanacs. Why cows lie down before a storm, a talking albino crow, Native prophecies about drought and pollution, home remedies — one of which, the inside of a banana peel rubbed vigorously on a bee sting, the author herself had seen save an allergic teenage boy's life.

One idea, a few pages long, its source "a naturopathic healer in our general vicinity," made Bonaduce see himself, the distant Leah and twelve-year-old Jason in a new light.

The idea was that ideal mates were brought together by a combination of looks and gestures, and to a large degree smell. The result was that, when two compatible people got together, it felt like good sex. (Bonaduce provided some adjectives of his own: *dirty* sex, *breakfast-lunch-and-dinner* sex.) What the two bodies communicated via their smells and such was genetic compatibility, which would lead to superior offspring, kids strong of limb and agile of brain. (Buddy Simon's weird wife noted that "one might see a mix of both Darwin and Hitler in this view.") But the gist was that if Nature's purpose was the best baby, its slick lure was the best sex. Two naïvely compatible parents led blindly grunting along the path to procreation.

Lying on his latest couch in his latest apartment, reading this sex theory in Buddy's wife's book, two hours before a game, Bonaduce thought of Leah. It was no effort to remember her. Her body, with its imperfections that were perfect to him. The little gut, showing that her body knew how to enjoy itself. The fingers on the stubby side, but strong and curious. Thick ankles and calves, to better hold that body up for more curiosity, more pleasure. And her soft skin — her skin was the best, it was the place where giving pleasure and taking pleasure were one and the same thing.

Her eyes, her bright eyes. You looked in and saw she was smarter than you but also that this wasn't a bad thing. You could also see how she felt her body to be not quite hers, or not quite her. She could hold her body at arm's length. You could see she respected her body, but also that she saw it to be a kind of playground.

Smell — said Buddy's weird wife's book — was the key. Nature's graceful shove. Here he was in Tulsa and he could still smell Leah. Her body's *root*. Even now it made him ache. I would climb the highest mountain, swim the widest sea. The smell was urgency itself. They'd been helpless with each other. The very first night they did it three times and, not that kind of girl, she hated him for it, as early as that. He knew even while inside her that in his life he'd feel nothing else like this. It took them a year to catch their breath and begin to suspect that their bodies had duped them.

Lying on the couch, considering the body of this woman he hadn't seen in years, Bonaduce might have masturbated had Julie not been there in the kitchen. Plus he had a game. He closed his eyes and pictured Jason. Perfect Jason. Healthy, tall Jason, possessed of that symmetry Nature indeed seemed to favour. With the hard Bonaduce jaw, and noble nose; with Leah's light hairlessness, wide smooth face, slightly feline eyes.


The times he did come through Fredericton and saw Jason, one problem was what the mother and the father did for a living. How it defined them. Nothing was ever said but there it was: Leah the social worker, helping refugees settle in the Maritimes. Aiding victims of war and torture, far from family and home, their lives ripped from them like skin. Leah's days were filled with their stories and, in retelling them, her heart was so over-full she would sometimes have to cry. On a few occasions she told the stories to Bonaduce, a man who had dedicated his life to working violently hard at preventing people with different-coloured uniforms from putting a puck in his net.

He'd be in town a single night, now playing for the visiting team, and before or after the game he'd drop by. Jason would be off having a snack or something while Leah cried about someone she'd met that day through her work, and Bonaduce would see as if in a mirror the trivial ugliness he represented. Hockey. It wasn't as if Leah was asking him to consider who was the right or wrong role model (there being no question), but rather which one of them Jason might want to follow in the way he lived his life.

When he visited, it wasn't always clear what she was crying about.

He visited when Jason turned six. He'd been looking forward to talking with his son, reasoning with his growing boy, his kid, and he came away surprised at how naïve he'd been. The whole bus trip up he'd dreamed of what they'd do together, visions of skating on the river, himself showing off a little. Maybe a movie, he'd ask the mother. But they would definitely talk and talk, two guys wild about seeing each other. *Jason, I love you. Jason, what's it like being alive and six? What does life look like stretched way out like that in front of you? Hey, what's it like being my son? I'm sorry that I cannot live with you. You see, life is a tragedy for some. But we are connected by our blood and so it doesn't matter where or when we...*

Jason looked at ease in the shades of olive and mauve Leah had dressed him in. Bonaduce smiled, no yellow and purple for this kid. Jason was also at ease seeing him, more excited in the gift of the toy ambulance than in his dad, then quickly pouty because the toy didn't take batteries or "do anything." Clearly, Leah, who had after an assessing pause in the doorway left them alone, hadn't done enough to prepare the lad as to the significance of this visit.

Bonaduce couldn't help staring at his boy's body, couldn't help the out-and-out butterflies at seeing how the little arms turned in their shoulder sockets, how the lungs puffed in and out, and how fast the kid scrambled under the bed and back, how he *knew* the tarantula gun was under there in that mess. And how quickly Jason's moods went screwy and sought only the silliest things. How what at first seemed a respect for adult stuff — yes, for *fatherly wisdom* — was nothing of the kind.

"Is lightning the biggest thing?"

They were in Jason's little sky-blue bedroom, Bonaduce sitting thrilled on the boy-sized bed.

"Nope. It's not."

"Gareth says it is."

"Well it's not."

"What's bigger?"

"Well…air."

"No way."

"Well, it is. Air is way bigger. It —"

"Lightning could *kill* air."

There was nothing to say to this, and Jason waved the eight-barrel gun in the father's helpless face.

"If this had real bullets it still couldn't kill you."

"Really?"

"No way way way."

"What's your favourite season? Do you like winter?"

"No…But bullets fit. Do you think if the bullets will fit it could kill you?"

"You don't like winter? No way! Don't you like Christmas? Playing hockey?"

"Know what I'm getting for my birthday? *Laser bullets.*"

"Hey, good stuff. You know lasers, they're a kind of 'ray,' like a space — But your birthday's not for eight or nine mon —"

"Or night-vision goggles. Get me night-vision goggles for my birthday."

A mischievous laugh, looking the dad-man in the eye, aware of his own greed, doing exactly something Mom told him not to do.

"I'll send you a surprise, but it won't be night-vision goggles, so don't be dis—"

"I'm way stronger than you."

"You're probably right, big buddy. You—well—wait now—you probably shouldn't hit. You really—I mean it now—"

No doubt real fathers learned the key. But when did a kid start making sense? Bonaduce had no memories of being stupid himself.

But there were also times to cherish. It was never hard to find the good.

Jason was eight during one visit, and it must have at some point occurred to him that his father was a pro athlete, because he dearly wanted to impress Bonaduce with what his body could do. His friend Luke had a tramp and Jason could do a flip, *C'mon and see me do it.*

It was late fall and it had snowed and Bonaduce couldn't imagine who would have left a trampoline out, but he borrowed Leah's car and turned corners where Jason pointed. Jason described his flip and variations of it, and then it became a double flip, and he was the fastest skater on his hockey team, and he could do lifters that sent the puck right over the net, almost taking the goalie's head off.

"But if you shoot it over the net, you can't score a goal," wise father explained, then instantly regretted it, seeing he'd tossed some damp into Jason's fire. It wasn't about scoring goals.

Nor was it about trampoline flips. After too many wrong turns, always followed by what Bonaduce came to see was a too-theatrical puzzlement on Jason's face—"Gee, I thought it was over *there*"—he realized they wouldn't be finding Luke's trampoline. And though he remained curious about whether Jason could in fact do a flip, he saw it wasn't the point and never had been. He was only mildly saddened that he had been following a route of Jason's untruths, that the boy had thought it necessary to go this direction to impress the father when it hadn't been necessary to go anywhere at all.

But it would be great, Bonaduce decided, it would be fucking great to have the time and place to get out and play hockey with his boy. Skate fast, take a goalie's head off, whatever. Everything, even standing up all wobbly, would be great. Holding hands through mitts, Jason looking up at him, them gliding fast enough to scare him a bit, Jason's bright-eyed look full of body's pride and thrill. And it would be the one thing they'd ever truly *share*, because what did kids really know — in fact what did people really know — other than the feelings in their bodies?

How many times, on a bus, with a guy, had the subject come up? How many countless quiet talks about getting married and having kids, wondering together about that kind of future? Most guys saw it as a given, and it turned out they were right. But how many times had Bonaduce sighed deeply and announced, "Well I've actually *got* a kid, up in Canada. He's seven now." Or eight now, or eleven now. The sigh before the announcement was a complex sigh, not just a sad one. There was even a bit of pride in it. Under its tone of melancholy at having fucked things up, there was also a hint of satisfaction that, because of this son's existence, life would never be empty. His son was no longer a little kid, he no longer had a kid's blind respect for feats of body so he no longer blindly respected Dad. He was being pummelled by adolescence, sussing out life's many green routes, alive to and aware of Bonaduce only in some unknown measure.

But how often had the *fact* of his son saved him from the depths. Thanks, Jason.

You understood it was the cheapest immortality any man had ever clung to. But there it was, a comfort.

．⤳

He'd survived Leah's party. It was time to see Jason.

He'd been antsy all day with the good butterflies, those of spirit rather than fear, those that helped a sharp performance. Only amateurs aren't nervous.

This morning, feeling the phone in his hand, the black plastic against his head, he'd called. Timing it right, nobody home. He left a simple message: "Hey, I'm in town. See you later today at the rink."

But funny how his nerves were as much about hitting the ice this afternoon and playing some hockey as they were about seeing Jason. It was just that these young guys were going to be in top shape and Bonaduce wasn't. He'd gone for ten runs now, and public-skated three times at the Lady Beaverbrook. One leg laboured a bit, but you wouldn't call it a limp. He was almost over whatever it was. Doctors were the first to admit theirs was an inexact science. Hey, he was going to play with his boy, he was going to play for the Varsity Reds, he'd be charging out from behind the net, he'd spot Jace circling to split the defence, he'd send him in alone with a perfect bullet on the tape and Jace would score a fucking beauty and then with the rest of the guys gather smiling in a huddle on the bright white ice and Jason would whack Bonaduce on the ass like a buddy.

All these years he'd made little of the fact that there'd never been a divorce. That on paper he was still married to her and her to him. He'd mentioned it once in an early letter, offering her any route she wanted to go. But she never mentioned it back, and in the meantime you couldn't help but wonder why not. Women were generally so keen on clarifying anything to do with relationship status. Perhaps not Leah.

But why were they still married? She was Catholic but, except for the wedding, she'd not gone to church in the time he was with her and he couldn't fathom her being bound by those laws. Was it instead that she cared so little for the piece of paper that she couldn't be bothered? Had she married him in the first place to satisfy her parents, and him? A shrugging traipse through a dead institution? Leah was contemporary and left-leaning and this might indeed be the case. Did she care, had she cared, so little for the marriage in the first place that divorce didn't even occur to her?

Strange to think that the marriage meant either too much or too little for her to end it, and that he didn't know which.


Skates in hand, he stood twenty-five rows up in the stands and watched. He told himself this wasn't hiding. There was Jason down there flying around. Good strides, low centre of gravity, fast. Professional speed. Not great with the puck. Shitty shot, actually. But good sense of position, a decent head for the game.

All this took Bonaduce about a minute to see in his son. What was sad, this was his son's chosen career he was seeing and any scout would see just as quickly that this youngster didn't have the goods for the big league, or even the next-to-big league, the one the father had made. Father watched son swoop past a check but then lose the puck for no reason other than wooden-handedness.

He continued watching, mesmerized. The way Jason leaned on the boards, catching his breath. The way he turned to hear a buddy say something, nodded curtly, said nothing back. Bonaduce found himself thinking the words "Scorpio. Bedroom eyes. Soar like an eagle or crawl like a lizard." Then saw himself and Leah standing over their magic little son, Leah reading aloud about Scorpios from a book some friend had given her. Neither of them believed, though Leah seemed for the moment open to it, her new-mother's hunger for information of any kind. Still it was fun thinking of a one-month-old having bedroom eyes, or that he would grow up either noble or flirting with the ditch.

Hard to read someone from the way he played hockey, but the young man out there on the ice seemed maybe kind of bland.

He and Fournier used to mock this goalie, René Leblanc. Over two seasons they'd noticed Leblanc going over the other teams' programmes before games. Tightening his skates, he'd shout to his defencemen — "Hey, watch Peca, eh? Watch Peca, Peca an' Smythe, they gonna have good game. Stay on 'em." And after the game, if Peca or Smythe had scored, he'd give the guys shit. It turned out he had the whole astrology thing memorized, and by looking at players' birthdays he knew how they were supposed to do that night. After being found out, Leblanc eased off because Bonaduce and Fournier had taken to warning everyone that Number 6 had Pluto in Aquarius and he'd be throwing elbows tonight. Leblanc, a believer, did not crack a smile.

Bonaduce pivoted away from the pillar. Time to strap on the blades. Say hi to his young eagle down there. Time to do his Gordie Howe thing. He found the stairwell. It wasn't exactly a limp he was suddenly into, but he had to use the handrail and he had to laugh at the timing of how our bodies hate us. Pimples the night of the date.

In the lower corridor he searched for the Reds' dressing room. He had a notion. If the planets and whatnots actually did stamp a code on us, it wouldn't be at birth but at conception. The baby that came out pissed off and howling had obviously been long stamped, it'd been in there hiccuping and with its own style of punching Mom in the gut from behind. If you got stamped at all it was when you were a quivering single cell, a tender jelly wild with newness. Leah's parents used to embarrass her with their story of a train berth somewhere between Ottawa and Montreal, this her start. Two cells meeting in the middle of a rocky night. Nature's biggest deal, the merger of chromosomes, the trading fire for fire. Bonaduce couldn't remember the precise time of Jason's coming, but it would've been in Leah's old room there on Charlotte Street. He could picture the sky-blue room, the morning light through its small window. It could have been any night of many when something stamped the ooze that came to be Jason.

He rapped once and pushed in the dressing-room door. Liniment and sweat, it smelled like most. A young guy packing rolls of medical tape into a metal cabinet stopped to look at him.

"I'm Bob Bonaduce. I talked to Coach ah... I guess the assistant coach. Said he had some gear for me?"

"You talked to me. And I forgot."

The trainer went to a locker and started pulling gear out. He tossed it on the floor in front of an empty stall and pointed to it. Then he startled with a thought.

"You cleared all this with the coach, right?"

Looking down, Bonaduce gave him the thumbs up.

Just like at every training camp, the nameplates above the stalls had been removed. Make the team, your name went up. They'd need initials this time. J. Bonaduce. B. Bonaduce. Where in this room would they seat themselves? Bonaduce would enjoy it side by side, but it might be too embarrassing for the boy. J. Bonaduce.

Hey, obviously Leah stayed married so Jace could keep the good name. "Jason Bonaduce" was a good hockey name. Though it wasn't a great hockey name. "Bobby Bonaduce" was a great hockey name.

Was it an accident so many great players had the great names? Short muscly ones, gold on the tongue: Bobby Orr. Bobby Hull. Syl Apps. Others, despite their names, hadn't made it to greatness: Bronco Horvath. Morris Titanic. Merlin Malinowski. Others, like himself, who despite the great name hadn't made it out of the minors: Hal Cabana. Vic Pitt.

In this working-man's poetics there was the perception that a "Jason" was either spoiled or rich. A kid named "Jason" had grown up with brand-new hockey gear, had gone to summer hockey schools. "Jason" was almost grounds for other teams to run at you, or for your own coach to bench you at any hint of you being lazy, or selfish with the puck.

The gear was stiff with someone's old sweat. Blood swelled in his face when he bent to his skates. He couldn't quite work his right ankle, nor did the toes on that side have their power. Hey Jace, how ya doin there, thought I'd come out for a dangle.

He himself was a Leo. Leos can purr or they can roar, but they're best at shining quietly, knowing they are admired.


Leah, delicious Leah, there at the food table, nibbling. He joined her and it was the two of them chewing away, food to nourish their bodies, they'd always loved eating together. Damned if this wasn't also like seeing your best old friend. You hit a certain age and you find certain judgements have worn away or gone under-ground. Nibbling, happily pressed close together by the crowd, they talked about nothing serious. You're looking well. Nice house you have here, is that oak? Beside him her body. The small paunch. Her skin. He pictured her twenty years ago wearing his leather Express jacket, way overlarge, like wearing her big fella's own tough protective skin, in the manner of Fifties sports guys and their gals. Much more aware than him that it was the

Seventies, she'd humoured him. He did like her in it. Maybe she'd liked it a little too, though he remembered her erect posture in it, her look of patience and independence.

For Oscar's sake he tried not to stare at her. Good pâté, he said, nodding as he chewed, though he'd never been wild about organ meat. She laughed and told him, Guess what? She was vegetarian now. And they both laughed perfectly, knowing without saying that it had gone from dog food to this. He'd never forget it, he'd known her all of two weeks, catching her spooning it right out of the can into that cute little face. Leah horrified at being caught, but Bonaduce had felt strangely touched, not because he'd found a weakness but because something in this ultra carnality was akin to her hunger in bed, a horniness which felt so good to be a party to. Plus, Leah being refined, and petite — well, dog food was a contradiction that deepened her immensely. During that evening twenty years ago she came to know him enough that she could laugh about it. A few months later she said that telling him — he was the only one she'd ever told — had helped her drop it, her weird craving. After a year she reported in all seriousness that she was down to the occasional Gainsburger, which she ate more or less out of nostalgia.

Vegetarian now. He shrugged and she shrugged back, as if saying to each other, *Of course* apples become oranges.

"A minor shift from the Alpo diet." He pointed at the carrot she turned in the dip.

"My history is *not* for public consumption." The hissed mock-panic, a nudge of the shoulder into his chest.

But it thrilled him that maybe Oscar didn't know.

"You know Jason is too?"

"What, vegetarian?"

"It was actually him who got me into it." She went ironic, sounding just like Oscar. "I mean, the kids these days."

"Jesus, why?" He wanted to say "how." How do you play vegetarian hockey? His body felt sure that no meat meant a lack of something powerful.

"I think there's something moral going on. But I don't know what came first. He just stopped eating it, around fifteen, said he couldn't stand the taste. Except for chicken in Chinese food, then that went too. So how long are you in town for?"

"You still drink? Can I get you a beer or something?"

Leah stayed put while he sidestepped and squeezed his way to the kitchen. Oscar was there, laughing and chatting, and it was weird taking one of his beers out of his fridge for his girlfriend.

A woman was talking to Leah in low tones when Bonaduce arrived back. Eyes down, half-smile, she zipped away pretty quickly. He wondered what, exactly, the talking was about. Ex-hubby hockey guy. Leah's Jason's daddy back in town. There was a rich and tangy high-school taste to all of this.

"I've moved here."

"You—" Her face quickly shut off, became unreadable. "Did you get traded again? Traded here?"

"No, hell. I've retired. Actually..." He'd decided beforehand to be perfectly straight with her because she would find out in any case. And there was the chance she'd be an ally. "I'm going back to school, a master's degree. You know, English."

No response. Beautiful Leah, paused with celery stick. Unable to decide what dip, or wishing her celery was metal, sharpened.

He'd said "English" with a respectful weight he wanted her to hear. Sure, he wanted her to think of him in other than hockey terms, why not. But also he had changed his mind about English. Something good had happened in his bathroom that evening, him sitting there with *Hamlet*, the wet flames of swampwater crawling the wall beside his leg.

Arriving in Fredericton he'd been prepared to defend preconceptions of his violence and stupidity by mocking English literature itself. Hey, it's nothing special you're doing. In fact it's perverse. Your face in the blinders of a book, indulgently gorging on words despite this dying world, the starving masses. Someone you know is gasping in the terminal wing and you sit reading *Lady Windermere's* fucking *Fan*.

In the bathroom he'd thumbed the paperback *Hamlet*, remembering maybe liking it back in high school. Sitting on the toilet, free of any pressure, free of having to do something *with* the stuff—maybe that was why it clicked. How could you not be cowed? Here you were perfectly described, here you were crawling between heaven and earth, a dirt-bound angel. Caught up in the demands of heaven, yet helplessly mired in earth's crude gravities. Animal stink wafting up between your legs. Noble yet snuffling along for the next sandwich. Dull angel or special dog, take your pick.

This deepened the way he said "English." He wanted to free Leah of her celery and meet her eye and explain to her his new feelings about it. How our struggle can seem only tedious until someone like Shakespeare renders it worthwhile, and for their good words we must thank writers everywhere. English. You read *because* people are in the terminal wing and your turn is coming. Maybe you even read *Lady Windermere's Fan*.

"Why here, Bobby?"

"Well, the whole thing's wacky, but I'm going to play hockey here too, with UNB. With Jason."

This got her. Tucking back, giving herself a double chin, she began shaking her head. "Well that's...that's...I don't know..."

"What don't you know?"

"What to think. For one." She managed a little smile.

"Jason doesn't know what to think yet either—I haven't told him." Tiniest of jokes. "So, could you maybe not, you know, if you see him..."

"Hey."

Leah put both hands up as if warding off the food table. She wouldn't look at him. In the side of her eye he saw a flash hinting at what might be her reservoir of anger.

"He's an adult. You can both do whatever you want."

Funny, the last bit. Father and son as co-conspirators. Her uncontrollable boys. Bonaduce wasn't at all unhappy that she summed up the situation in this way.


Standing at centre ice with the coach, Bonaduce registered the instant Jason spotted him. It now became intensely difficult trying to talk some sense into this young fellow Whetter when you knew that, over your shoulder, catching his breath after a drill, the long-lost son was staring at you in bewilderment and who knows what else. He tried to listen to Whetter while sneaking sidelooks at Jason, whose plumes now gradually quieted. The lad was a plugger even in practice. Bonaduce shot him a wink he maybe didn't see.

"Thing is, our first game's in a week and a half." Whetter had his elbow cocked, whistle ready in his hand. He kept shaking his head, kept toeing a pylon with the point of his skate. He had on four-, five-hundred-dollar skates. Why did coaches need the best skates? Up top he wore glasses, and looked like a broad-shouldered accountant.

"You're not in shape and —"

"*Game* shape, no."

"— and the guys have been at it since August, dedicated from the start, and cuts were made a month ago..."

Whetter let the last bit rest, content with bureaucratic cowardice.

"You gonna make the playoffs?"

You hated saying such an arrogant thing, but time was awasting. Almost smiling, Whetter gave him a *touché* look, point taken. Bonaduce shrugged. The shoulder pads were too small and the helmet rode up too high. He whapped at it with his glove, then threw his head to his left shoulder, popping the vertebra that had been getting stuck since he couldn't remember.

Jason wouldn't come over as long as he stood talking to the coach.

"Bob, the other thing, maybe the only thing, is the pro rule."

"The pro rule."

"The sitting out a year."

"The what?"

"A pro comes back to school — it does happen — they have to sit a year out, don't ask me why."

Bonaduce felt the cold sweat of foolishness break out. He didn't respond because he couldn't.

"So first we have to find out if Utica — East Coast League, right? — if Utica constitutes pro."

"Of course it fucking constitutes pro." Now feeling himself turn red.

"Well okay, and if that's the case, you sit. A year before eligibility."

Say something. Focus. Ineligible? It was a creeping, bureaucratic word, nothing to do with this game. The hockey he knew, the best guys played, the others sat.

"Actually I wasn't playing, I haven't played since last December. I was injured. So — hey — maybe I'll be eligible in December."

"If you were still under contract I doubt it but —"

"Well actually the contract got all screwed up too. So maybe I'm free to play. The owner, this unbelievable sleaze, he just —"

"But anyway, hey, we'll get everything checked."

Whetter turned, bringing the whistle to his lips and saying, without looking at Bonaduce, "If you're ineligible you can't practise with us either, we'd get dinged. Get the gear off."

Whetter blew the whistle hard three times, skating away from him.

Hard not to move his body, dance around, as he waited in the concrete tunnel outside the dressing room. Hard not to plot hellos, hugs. It was all so —

Jason. Here he was, coming out through the door with a smile already set, breathless, flushed in the face. He stopped five feet away. Steam rising off his soggy longjohns in the slight cold.

"So what the hell," he said, almost yelling, much of Leah in his smile, "what the hell was *that*? A cameo? What you doing in town?"

It sounded rehearsed, but now they shook hands easily. Jason had become more slick in performing the rite than however many years ago it was Bonaduce had last had this pleasure, this hand in his.

The father smiled back. He should speak, but found himself taking in the son's lanky body, the shoulders not so wide, Leah's shoulders, they could take some added muscle and he'd still be mobile — he hadn't peaked, he could do more. Weight training, he'd make a decent power forward, bash the corners, crash the net, you don't need the good hands.

"Well, actually I thought I'd stay the year."

"Wow, no kidding!"

Bonaduce — as casually as he could, shrugging and smiling with self-deprecation, leaving out all medical news — explained his plans.

At first Jason said, "Really?" Then in the clutch of nervous laughing his eyes pulled away and something bubbled up in his tight gut — you could see it — and buckled his spine. Jason's stuttering inbreath filled the hall with his confusion. The boy just standing there, yet moving so fast. Looking at his father he brought a clawed hand up as if cradling and juggling a ball, a very Italianate gesture. Bonaduce could see Jason's grandmother in this.

Trying to laugh the same laugh again, Jason couldn't look at him now. Nor could he speak. His face went a new red.

Speechless and in trouble himself, Bonaduce watched his son spin away for the dressing room, double-palming the door with more violence than he'd shown on the ice.

That night, for the first time in his new home, he broke out the guitar. Slow picking, with interludes of languid strumming, at his feet a case of beer. At some point into the room came Margaret, Rod, Toby, and some other guy whose name he did not catch. They heard some Bonaduce versions of blues standards, some Howlin' Wolf stuff. They were patient with and then mocking of his dip into country, which was fine with him because humour went well with the genre, and Toby knew a few and warbled mockingly along. They were briefly intrigued when, beer done and time to think about bed, he dug deeper into his time-bag for Muddy Waters, then way back to Woody Guthrie, the room falling quiet for the simple good politics. Or maybe everyone had left. When he looked up and saw that all but him and the roaring Maui surf trucks had found their way to bed, he started his secret string of tunes from that alltime hardcore rag-top heartbreaker, Roy Orbison. And damned if Bonaduce didn't lose a tear or two, there at the end, head down, the candle casting a light less sad than perfect in the way it put a glow on the front of the guitar.

# II

Societies differ mostly in how each culls its herd.

F. A. D'AMBOISE

*Why* kill yourself to win? Sure as fuck not for me. And not for the fuckin' money in *this* league. *It's the guys.* Look at each other. Look around. *That's* why we put the fuckin' biscuit in the basket. *Now get out there.*

COACH MURRAY MURPHY, TULSA OILERS

*Margaret.*

At the sink she repotted plants. Like so many other jobs in this house, this was hers by default. She wondered, trying not to be too judgemental about her roommates, whether it was more a case of simply "not noticing" than "letting things die." One plant (mother-in-law's tongue?) was all roots, pale clean roots woven tight, shaped exactly like a pot. Amazing how it survived, just on water, with maybe the decay of its own skin as nourishment, whatever. She should stick it, potless, back on the windowsill, see if anyone noticed. Or let it die again.

Her back was to him and, because of last night, as he brushed past she half-expected a pat on the rear or some sexual tease. He looked the sort but apparently wasn't. He was a kind she really hadn't known before, a boomer who hadn't done the hippy thing or the business thing but instead had played sports. He seemed the least Sixties of anyone in this house, which was ironic, him being the only one alive at that time. All the same there was a sort of restless *On the Road* feel to him — she'd read Kerouac in Hawaii — but you weren't talking Sixties now, you were talking Fifties. Beats, the boys' club of the day, bunch of dads gone wild. There was also something about Robert more basically Fifties: you could see him with slicked hair behind the wheel of a smooth rod with stuffed dice dangling from the mirror and deep purple hoor-lures framing the back window. It was effortless to see him so. His smile, a smoke or toothpick in the James Dean mouth.

The dreamcatcher, he'd thanked her but joked about it, how this fancy new air freshener didn't smell hardly at all. When he saw she took it a bit seriously, and after she explained the psychology of it — how knowing it's in the room can trigger lucid dreaming — he seemed to reconsider. He wanted to know if it could affect luck. In fact now he seemed a bit in awe of it. The man's been out of the picture for a while.

It wasn't like someone's father living here, but it was close. The creased pants and polite manners and constant corny announcement of his limit of two-drinks-a-night, though after dusk he sometimes slurred. His lame "Time to hit the books, eh?" and then you could hear him snoring through his closed door. The others were still a little mad at her for renting the room to him, unable to kick all the way back with a guy like that around. Until his helpful ways and that goofy guitar night showed his harmlessness. That and the fact that he spent so much time in his room. He seemed generally tired.

But he didn't belong. Where did a Robert Bonaduce belong? In this he was a mirror for her because she was hanging on in this house by a thread herself. This house out on the highway, the traffic roaring east or west without doubt, and her life lacking any direction. The bare halls and rooms felt like a stage upon which she was acting out her limbo-life: between men, between jobs, between journeys. It was unhealthy to be banking on memories of Hawaii, to be nostalgic at twenty-four. She was at the wrong university to service her fading passion for archaeology. Which was probably good because she'd been understanding that bones and such were maybe best left buried, and that to search backwards in time was exactly what she should not be doing. In that school of thought, the whole world was a crypt.

When he'd driven up looking to rent, Rod had huddled with her and laughed, No way, looks like some sort of mafia guy. She'd shrugged and said, So what? Her whim was to give the house some range. Bonaduce might be a spark, a bit of colour. And a practical joke, why not. Rod's I-can't-believe-you're-going-to-jump-his-bones look put exactly that idea in her head and made Robert doubly interesting. Maybe a bizarre romance, Christ, who knows. He was old but in a dented way cute, and a grad student in literature, so smarter than he looked. He would have stories to tell.

As it turned out he would keep his stories to himself. Behind the corny cheer he carried a weight. He'd sit staring in the living room, then grin hiyas and howdys when he saw you. He worked his face a lot when people were near. Good in public, bad alone. Her opposite.

Toby didn't like him, but at least there was some strange respect. *Grudging* would be the word. In a way they were similar, stuff going on underneath they tried to hide. Indirect. Toby was funny with his new description for Robert every morning. "He's Moose, Reggie, Archie and Jughead all in one." Or, "He's what I would have been were it not for drugs." Hilarious him straight-faced saying that, his tiny body a hundred pounds less, his withered arm. Robert could tuck him behind an ear like a pencil.

Robert must have had some fine injuries — he'd grab his feet or legs as if to check that they were there. She caught him punching himself in the foot and he made a madman joke of it, punching calf, knee, thigh, tongue hanging out. He could be funny. Some days he limped and bumped hallway walls. He didn't like to talk about hockey unless to run an anecdote by you for the novel he's planning.

Then last night he came to her. It was way after midnight. He asked softly at the door if she was awake. He sat on the end of the bed. It felt fine that he'd come. He was shy. They both dropped their joking and she welcomed this. She tucked up her legs to make room, but then slid a foot back to tickle his thigh through the covers, she didn't know why, didn't know if she wanted this from him yet, or ever. The physical part alone might be okay, because he didn't seem selfish, and he had a worldliness and humour. But it seemed very likely that he'd go gushy on her. Thinking she needed that. And thinking he meant it.

He seemed not to feel her toe's welcome. Then, destroying all romance within a million miles, he asked, How close do you feel to your parents? At first she assumed it was a joke, a Groucho Marx sexual thing and a way to acknowledge their ages, but he didn't smile or waggle his eyebrows. Jughead Archie Reggie and Moose had asked her a serious question.

She thought a moment, then told him she couldn't put it into words. She apologized for being so lousy with words, thinking how he must always get that apology, being in English. He said she was great with words, and asked other questions: Did she think it was automatic for a child to love a parent even if the child didn't see the parent much. Did she love one parent more than the other. Animals were connected by smell and such — did she think humans had anything like that as well.

She spoke her thoughts to him for what they were worth. She didn't ask why he was asking. It was pretty obvious he had a kid somewhere. One thing she said made him stiffen and fall silent. What she said was, "There're plenty of assholes out there, and lots of them are parents," but she'd only been talking about her own situation. She worked her toe harder to get him out of his worry.

"You have a kid?"

"I do. Yes."

"You're not an asshole, Robert."

"Not to you."

"I doubt it's even possible."

"Oh it is," he said, and in the dark she could hear him shift his shoulders, could hear his tired smile. "I contain multitudes."

An old hockey guy, quoting what was probably literature.

———

In the department lounge someone whose name he didn't know had invited him to Rye's Pub, see you there. So now Bonaduce — get out of that sleepy little room for a change — found himself downtown in a bar, celebrating some guy named Murray's oral defence of his PhD being over and done with. Kirsten and Phil and others whose names he didn't know had claimed tables. Some surprise at seeing him. Sure, he didn't know Murray, or his "thesis area," or exactly what an "oral defence" was — if the subject came up he would resist his joke about spitting. Something in the air had told him that grad-student socializing was encouraged, which was not a bad thing at all, hang together. Maybe as the bar was closing they'd get in a brawl with those History bastards over there.

His mood was definitely better. He'd decided Jason didn't hate him, nor was it a snub. Jason was shocked. What else could you expect? He'd basically abandoned the boy. A beaming, *Hey! Great, Dad!* from a dumb-knob son would've been unnatural and disappointing. This setback showed Jason's dark depths. What parent wanted a child who was uncomplicated?

He was good at patience. Maybe there was nothing he was better at. Though let's not bring up the pathetic side of this, his twenty years in the minors waiting patiently by the phone.

Eventually Murray arrived, accompanied by Professor Daniel Kirk, who was Murray's thesis supervisor and who Bonaduce hoped wouldn't remember him, for he hadn't yet made it to class. People shouted and raised glasses to Murray. Murray was a homely tall-and-lanky, like a weed that towered over the garden. He looked myopic behind his glasses, perhaps partially blind, lenses thick as porcelain. He smirked cynically by way of general greeting. Bonaduce had the sense of Kirk trying not to look his way, which was good, let's both do that. And they both did, though when Kirk sat they had only Murray between them.

It proved a strange little time. A poor team party. Half of them left after a single beer. After the one bland toast there was a jerkiness to any conversation, a lack of tone or build. The table-talk broke into shadowy murmuring pockets, Murray not even in one. Bonaduce felt bad for him, though as the minutes crawled by and from Murray's few blurts he came to suspect that Murray was an unliked loner and the cause of this rhythm-lessness to begin with.

It took Murray ages to get his first beer halfway down, at which point Bonaduce ordered him a second. When it came, instead of a thank you, Murray glanced at it with what looked like annoyance. He dutifully poured some into his glass, glug-ging the beer from straight over-top so the foam rose fast and some spilled.

"In Germany the mugs are tapered at the top. Which"— Murray demonstrated with his hands as God might squeeze a volcano top to contain the eruption —"quells the climbing head."

"Ah." Bonaduce smiled. "So you did the beerfest?"

His damaged recall of his own Munich visit didn't include tapered mugs. Maybe he hadn't made it to the classier tents. Murray turned his head to him but didn't look up from the table.

"I haven't been to Germany, but I collect."

"Ah."

"My father travels. He gifts me with steins."

This was pretty good, *gift* as a verb, one of the better ones in the new language he'd been learning here. Other verbs he didn't like so much. *Dialogue*. Let's dialogue. Hell, why not get Sally and trialogue. Eight of us at Murray's lousy party, octaloguing away.

He went to the bathroom, to urine. Coming out, wondering if he shouldn't just go home, a waitress gave him a stern look and asked if he'd washed his hands. She was good, her coy smile delayed just right. She was attractive enough to make the joke racy and it all a bit exciting. Late-twenties, countryish, maybe a little wild. "Coral," said her name tag. How to answer. Coral, no, I didn't, I thought you liked them dirty. Coral, could you come and show me how.

He looked witlessly down at his hands for her. "You mean these?"

She made to snap him on his ass with her tea towel. She'd made it all a little dance, already moving off and smiling at the next guy.

Another one or two had left. Murray was talking loudly, to Kirk.

"—no. It's not racial, it's cultural. The reason there are no philosophers from the equator is because they allow *desire*."

"Nonsense."

"They have sex at puberty! What more could you want? What's left! What's left to puzzle at after that! You net fish for the kids to eat! Think about it for God's sake."

Murray was actually fairly funny. Ballsy too. Here he was lecturing Kirk, professor. Now he turned to Bonaduce to lecture him as well, though Bonaduce could see from the eyes swimming in their lenses and staring past his ears that he could have been anybody.

"*We* sit up in the northern climes, *squeezed* with unfulfilled craving. Of all kinds. So what we do is sit and *think*."

"But education has its—" Kirk began.

"No. As long as we continue to privilege restraint, restraint over pleasure, we will remain, as it were, 'philosophical.' And they will remain childlike and happy, happily non-abstract. They do what they *want*, for God's sake."

What are you thinking, trying to fit in with these types. *Privilege* as a verb now.

Coral came by to empty ashtrays and wipe their table with her snapping-towel. Her manner was a bit theatrical, knowing she was being watched by the likes of Bonaduce and whoever else. Wiping in his direction, she leaned over so far that — hey, she was probably only doing her job but it was the kind of thing you can construe as an invitation.

Nothing was clear tonight. The heav'ns felt rotten, or something. When Murray left — big stein-expert man making it through almost two beers in one sitting — those who remained started jabbering about him like he was some sort of genius. Murray was squeezed all right, just like Kirsten and Phil and all these guys, thinking so hard and long they'd thought themselves into some fancy corners. From the sounds of it they were in awe of Murray (well then why weren't they nice to him?) because he'd "tossed off" his thesis while working harder on his real interest, which was a journal.

"I heard him refer to it as his" — Kirsten dropped her voice to a whisper — "his 'commentaries.'"

"He's been prolific as hell," said Phil, with the most respect Bonaduce had seen from him. "Three volumes." He shook his head in amazement. "Three volumes."

"How long has he been journaling?" Kirsten asked, her airy teeth for once looking more beaverish than judgemental.

"Since coming to Fredericton. Five years."

*Journaling.* This was getting good. *To journal. To beer.* Let's really beer tonight. Hey: *to verb.* Let's verb another noun.

The only question here was why did these supposedly smart folks admire a guy who wasn't thirty who'd never been to Germany or anywhere else, yet who was insane enough to have written three volumes of what was for all intents a fucking auto-biography? "Prolific" just means you don't get out enough. Three books about himself. Sitting in a fevery hunch in the library, in love with his own brain and chewing at it like a worm. Egoing like crazy.

Coral swept by again, giving Bonaduce a look, knowing that at this dead table she had a good audience in one at least. She made as if to dab at her forehead with her little towel — Whoo ain't I hot an' workin' hard? — and giving it some sexiness to boot. Then gone, smiling at the next table, good at it and knowing how to have an okay time at a shitty job. Coral was a trueheart and a relief. He could handle a Coral.

He could Coral all night long.

⌒

## Post Game
### by R. Bonaduce

After violently winning that night, they went to the strip club. Canary Singh, a wiry little centerman not born in this country, but part of the Asian hockey diaspora, sat a row back of the action, while the other guys had their usual handhold on the beaver rail. Their hoots and hollers occasionally brought Singh's head up out of his newspaper and cup of tea.

"Hey buddy! Hey Canary!" a few guys eventually called out to him. "What ya think of *those*?" They hooted and pointed in glee at the bounteousness of Darling Doctor Gail, two parts of whom were looming over them.

"Well, I think that those would feed a great many people in my country," said Canary Singh, gently rolling his head like they do.

Those of the guys that heard this stopped smiling and instead looked slightly sickened.

"'Tis not a mysterious thing, these entertainments of yours," Canary continued, sitting up now and pointing at Gail. "The bull is but of course made stiff at the sight of the sacred, what, the sacred *ood*ers? ooders of the cow. And just as it is with the cobra, in its rising to —"

A fist knocks Canary Singh's face out of the picture, and another fist flashes through but you can only hear the smack. The guys turn back to Doctor Gail.

Rolling his head more slowly, fingering the stitches under his eye, which had been sewn in just that night but now were popped, Singh picks himself off the floor, spits some gore and a coupla teeth onto the butt-burned carpet, flips open his paper again, hoping his buddies haven't gotten any of his blood on the sports pages. His name is in the summaries tonight. Two assists. He always sends the summaries home to a cousin in Calcutta.

• ⟶

Marg had offered him the loan of her laptop, leaving it here in the living room. With a hundred books to read and family relations to repair, he'd opened the thing, shaking his head at the foolhardiness of deciding to begin his novel, a project he wasn't supposed to even think about for a year. And as if he'd still be here.

The beers from the PhD party had him a bit goofy, and any serious intention was gone by the time he got the machine figured out and the title tapped down. Years ago he'd played a few months with a guy named Singh, an arrogant bastard. Singh had been both a fighter and a lech, a cruel loudmouth in strip bars. It was fun to turn him into Canary. The rest of what he wrote made him smile, dumb as it was, the fault of another beer and the echoes of Gail Smith's class that morning.

The second class hadn't gone any better than the first and he verged on dropping the course. Or having it dropped for him, the more likely scenario. He had to find out if taking only two courses kept his student status full enough to let him play for the Reds. He also had to maintain a certain grade. He should find out what that grade might be.

His little quip this morning hadn't helped. They were hashing out the "diaspora" definition again, arguing whether certain names on the reading list deserved to be there. While it was gratifying that no one else appeared to like Gail Smith either (in the lounge he had heard Phil whisper acidly that "Smith's reading list is nothing but whimsical"), the day's discussion was another round of grand language and hooded spite.

Bonaduce made two contributions. Neither his first, "Well, a good book's a good book," nor his second, "Hey: we're all just mutts from away," seemed to secure his position as worthy participant.

It was really too bad about Smith's class because he did like Canadian lit. During the long and scattered path to his BA he'd managed to find CanLit courses in, of all places, Kalamazoo, which from the sound of it you'd expect courses in Popeye, or Aztec Cooking, not books by Canadians. During the classes he'd decided not to pull rank by revealing his nationality. But he felt he had insights into the material that the others lacked. Reading her novel, he'd felt a shovel-the-snow kinship to Atwood, though her tough-shit sharpness made him nervous; and to Davies, though he was a stuffed shirt. But you could just tell they'd both shovelled driveways.

And Leonard Cohen, his CanLit favourite. You couldn't quite picture Lenny shovelling out a driveway, or even having a driveway, but here was someone who knew the body and its deepblood longing, and he wasn't afraid to sing it into sweet words, hard for a guy. He could have been Irish-Italian. He even looked Irish-Italian.

The first time he came "home" and walked in on their game he thought he'd lost it, thought he'd left his brain in class. Going about their domestic business — which for Toby meant lounging, for Rod reading, and for Marg and her sister cooking while washing enough dishes to eat off of — his housemates conducting a conversation that went like this:

"Lobster trap," Toby said, for some reason.

After a moment's hesitation, Marg said, "Handicapped parking."

"The concept," said Rod, focused on his book, "I'm struggling with."

"Hell," offered Marg's sister.

To which Toby shouted, "Nope!"

Marg's sister, slouching in thought, stirred spaghetti sauce, looking a bit nervous. "Heaven!" she said next.

"Better," said Toby, "but, nope. Heaven's still a concept. C'mon."

Marg's sister looked angry now. "Fuck!" she tossed at him. "Cunt!" she added in defiance, while Toby, supercilious, nodded at her.

Toby settled grandly back. "Some of the Flemish painters," he announced.

"Let's stop growling," said Marg.

Toby and Rod looked at Marg, then at each other, in some sort of agreement.

"His future varicose vein operation," said Rod, nodding toward Bonaduce.

"Hiya," said Bonaduce.

"Howdy," said Marg's sister.

"Nope, nope, nope," said Toby.

Not looking up, Rod asked Toby, "Nope, what? Nope 'Hiya'?"

"'Hiya' was fine. Nope 'Howdy'."

"I was saying hello," Marg's sister explained. "Don't insult me."

"*That's* better," deemed Toby.

"Brad Pitt's bum," said Marg's sister, to which Toby closed his eyes and subtly shook his head, for some reason not pleased but deciding to let it go. Toby had lately begun to make Bonaduce think of a hamster cage. The seedy hair and the way it fell, and the frayed collar, and the colour of his skin, gave you the combined feel of dank and dusty shavings.

Understanding now that this was a game which, at a minimum, involved coming up with something weird, Bonaduce decided he was up for some fun. He was decent at weird. He jumped in.

"Trained hamster you keep tied by a string around your neck that's trained to, whenever you start choking on a chunk of food, it goes down your throat and eats whatever's stuck."

The housemates looked at one another for a moment, then explained to Bonaduce the notion of "non sequitur," how you had to say something that absolutely didn't fit. There could be no connection at all. Even opposites didn't work, because they had the connection of being opposite.

"And make it short," added Toby.

"Toby? Was that your turn?" asked Marg's sister.

"Was that yours?" Toby answered back.

Bonaduce had another go, answering a pretty good "Kangaroo high-jump record" to Marg's "Is the Lord's Prayer punctuated?"

But then he sidled off to his room, to read. No wonder these guys were good at irony — they came home at night and *practised*. They worked out like pros. They had non sequitur relationships, lived non sequitur lives. They even had a non sequitur diet: doughnuts, tofu, fresh basil, moonshine. Bonaduce recognized now why he'd found them in some way smarter even than the grad-school types: not giving a shit about normal stuff, like conversation, gave you a sort of intimidating power.

In the days to come the game continued on and off, in spurts, and Bonaduce understood that he'd been witness to earlier versions of it but hadn't cottoned on. You never quite knew when it might start. The next morning, in fact, he was in the kitchen putting on his shoes to this scene:

"Any of that left?" Rod asked, gesturing to the frypan Toby held with his good hand while scooping out bacon with his bad. The room reeked of old oil and scrambled egg.

"Tuesday," Toby answered.

"Melanoma," said Rod.

"I wasn't doing it," said Toby.

"Clinton didn't resign eventually," offered Rod.

*"I wasn't doing it. Tuesday. We have nothing. We shop tomorrow. Tomorrow is Tuesday. Today we eat shit. He"*—Toby pointed at Bonaduce—*"ate the last egg."*


Quit your fooling around. Quit your moaning. Get off your ass.

One shoe on, pause, breathe, take a gander out the window— Mr. Neighbour should really paint that old trailer of his—pull on the other shoe, work at getting that frayed lace licked and in through that damned eyelet. Time's a'wastin'.

It all comes down to, what do you accomplish within the clumsy grab of the day. What do you do between the calloused hands of dawn and dusk. What do you need, and find, and use. The squeeze is on. What do you do.

You could say it's a duty, either to others or to yourself. But a duty all the same.

Oscar Devries answered the door, waved him in, and as he ran upstairs shouted something about Leah being called out on an emergency, just make yourself at home.

Bonaduce removed his shoes and wandered into the living room. A Beatles song was on, but he noted an odd roughness to John's voice, then a harmony that shouldn't be there, then laughter — it was an outtake, this must be one of those anthologies. Great, let's hear it. From the party here a few weeks back, he recalled the wafts of music, old British-invasion stuff: Animals, Who, some Kinks you didn't normally hear. Now some connoisseur Beatles. He liked Oscar even more. This was a friendly house, a sweater dropped in the very middle of the living-room floor, and three dirty cups and orange peels on the coffee table.

He sat deeply into the couch and took note of his old man's sigh. Man he was tired... *Of course you will find that fatigue is the biggest day-to-day impediment*... and this fight was not the good fight, because the enemies were big and shadowy and there were too many to see. He put his feet up on the coffee table, nudged a cup with a toe and wondered if he would fall asleep here in his wife's house.

He might have. Last he remembered he was really liking an *a capella* version of "Because," and now here was Oscar coming in with coffees, and the cups at his feet were gone.

Leah had been called away to a church in Sussex, where a Guatemalan family, facing deportation, had last week taken illegal refuge. The little daughter had developed a fever and earache, and they'd wanted Leah's help, only Leah's, in getting a prescription filled.

"It's after hours, it's Sussex." Oscar shook his head, blowing into his coffee. "We can assume our Leah's having a red-tape kind of day."

Our Leah.

"So I'll call her tonight, set up another time?"

"No, she called and said she'd be back soon. She wants you to wait. She apologized profusely." Oscar smiled. "Actually, she didn't apologize. Nothing comes between her and their suffering. Her priorities are clear."

"Guess you can't blame her."

"Oh, I manage to." Oscar keeping up the smile.

The coffee was the strongest Bonaduce had ever tasted. Why did it feel odd to find out that Leah had ended up with a nice guy? Kind, with pleasant wise-ass tendencies. Balding and shortish like an Oscar should be, but also not caring about this, an Oscar worth his salt. Bonaduce felt revved up in his presence, could easily fall into friendship with this guy. Jesus, what would Leah make of that?

"Actually, she was on the news last night. Did you see it?"

Bonaduce shook his head.

"They mostly interviewed the father, who was typically tearful and amazed at our Canadian hospitality, and then there was Leah, large as life. They let her have a few sentences. She came off quite well."

"Hey, did you tape it?"

"I should have."

Proud Oscar. Leah the celeb. Bonaduce recalled the times in Fredericton they'd watched him on local sports highlights and a couple of times interviewed after games, major five-o'clock shadow, sweaty hair plastered to his forehead. Him wincing to see and hear himself, Leah joking not to worry, last week Tony the goalie had sounded even stupider. And there was the time he'd propped up a football-sized baby to see the screen. *Look, Jace! Look, Jace! See Daddy's pass?*

The Beatles finished and Oscar went to the CD rack. Bonaduce had come to talk to Leah about Jason, to see if the boy had said anything. To solicit Leah's help. At least advice.

"Any preferences?" Oscar asked, flicking plastic against plastic.

"Well, I'm definitely into the old stuff too. I liked what I heard at your party. Hey — so anything." He paused. "So how well you know Jason there, Oscar?"

Oscar was into a drawer of cassettes and he held up a hand for Bonaduce to wait. He popped one in, made some equalizer adjustments, and on came "Here Comes the Night."

"Hey. Early Van."

"You know it?"

"Sure, it's great. 'Them.'"

They sat and listened for a moment, attuned as much to the other man's listening as to Van Morrison's young throat hitting its raspy limits on the chorus.

"The Brit guys were pretty innocent, eh?" Bonaduce offered. "They all did the big attitude." Acknowledging Van's Irishness would only complicate things here.

"Sorry, I'm not following."

"It was all an act. Like the Stones. Everybody was five foot two and in art school."

Oscar smiled, his shoulders leaping in a silent laugh. He looked happy for this guy talk. Should have him out for a beer.

"Oh, now, well, I think the British have their fair share of tough guys, and psychotics."

"They love a stage is all I'm saying."

"You think"— Oscar pointed at the stereo, pausing then shaking a finger just as Van Morrison went into one of his wails — "you think that's an act?"

"I know it is." You could picture the wee guy in a booth, headphones on, holding the mike the exact proper distance for an undistorted howl, this his third take, he's warmed up now. "You don't scream like that for real unless, I don't know, you're watching your own blood pour out of you."

· 93

"Okay, I suppose." Oscar, enjoying this, searched for something to counter with. "But on TV, videos, you see these bands that look evil and I tend to believe it."

"They've had to think more, you know, visually. Can't just stand there and sing any more."

"Well, I guess, sure. Learned to act." He paused. "Okay. Have you seen Iggy Pop?"

"Hang on, I mean Brits. The *Brits* are the actors. All they did was put American R & B on stage. Iggy Pop's real."

"Oh, I see."

"No, it's true. Go ask any Brit superstar, go ask the Beatles who turned them on and it's always Chuck Berry, Elvis, Jerry Lee Lewis. Even Carl Perkins, for Christ sake."

"I suppose."

"Oscar? Americans couldn't fool anybody. They don't even try."

He was up with Oscar now, hunched shoulder to shoulder and peering into the music titles. Oscar was indeed an Anglophile. Stones, every Beatles you could think of, even Petula Clark, housewife with a ditty. Elton John, well of course, and Supertramp, the whiners. Lots of Moody Blues, who were The Lettermen on drugs.

"So you have it down to a kind of British-versus-American thing."

"Oscar? How many American bands can you recall who wore the matching, you know, 'outfits'?"

You had to admire the Brits for their imagination, but, well. If Jerry Lee Lewis was mad at you he'd shoot you in a second. If David Bowie was mad at you he'd put on a costume and stare.

Oscar had been thinking. "You got me."

"The Byrds did, for a while."

Bonaduce tried picturing Oscar and Leah together. They weren't a likely mix. He didn't feel jealous, in the way he sometimes did over sexy women he didn't even know, couples he passed in the street. He saw Leah being cheerful with Oscar, efficiently going about her day, threatened by nothing in the man at all.

"So the Brits only *look* like they suck blood from animals," Oscar mused, mildly imitating Bonaduce. "But they're in actual fact just — clarinet wusses." He grinned, pleased with himself.

"There you go."

"In all probability Ozzy Osbourne didn't bite chickens' heads off at home, true."

"That was great coffee."

Bonaduce slumped back on the couch. Two regular guys sitting here talking music. Oscar was getting more comfortable. Good thing he hadn't thought of Paul Revere and the Raiders. Or Kiss, Alice Cooper. It would've been all over.

"This body piercing's pretty spectacular though." Oscar shook his head in a kind of admiration. "How far is *that* going to go?"

"It's a contest, isn't it."

"I saw a nose ring the other day, not the usual tiny little thing in the side, but a big, thick hoop"— he pinched thumb and forefinger into both nostrils —"like a bull. She couldn't have been fourteen. And man? I saw a bone once, in Toronto."

"Hey — guy in Wheeling has one. Or had one. I mean a hockey player. He —"

"Nose ring?"

"Nose ring. He attracted some attention. Guys trying to get at it with their sticks. Guy had balls, I guess. Hockey player with a nose ring..."

Oscar smiled appreciatively.

"Earrings have been around," Bonaduce offered. "Guy can have an earring and still be a stud."

"The code." Oscar nodded to himself.

"That's right." Bonaduce lifted his cup, forgetting it was empty. "So. So how well do you know Jason?"

"Not well." He shook his head with self-judgement.

"Ah."

"Considering we lived together for three years. I mean, I can tell you what he doesn't like for breakfast."

"Right."

"I came in at a touchy age I think. Fifteen. I just made myself available if he needed me for something, but he never did. Well, the car, a summer job, that." Oscar pulled a bullied face and made as if to go for his wallet. "But emotionally, no. He's such a private kid. But you know that."

"Right."

No, you don't know that. You don't know that at all.

Hard sitting still at the highway house between classes, between *jogs*. Between the last thing and the next thing. Breaths.

The Maui trucks made it harder. Something adhesive in them, you could get dragged out of your thoughts by a big truck, get towed on down the road. Maybe it was just that he envied the driver his destination. Here he was, stopped, while so much of the last twenty years had been a road trip. Buses from Rochester to Muskegon, to Springfield, to Portland. Portland Oregon *and* Maine. On those endless purgatorial all-nighters he'd often be sitting up awake, eyes on the black window, generally unaware of but held anyway by the bus's constant muffled roar. No one else on the road except the big trucks, working the interstate. Catching up to one, buddy-buddy alongside for a while, the truck's whining, roaring insistence would blend in with and double that of the bus. You can see the driver lit up ghost-green behind his wheel, staring straight ahead, both of you rushing in the same direction. What's the guy nodding to, what beat? You try to guess the tape he's listening to, you almost hear it through the noise, hey it's Beefheart, no it's Johnny Cash, no the decades have flown by, it's Vince Gill now. You know in all likelihood it's Abba, or funk. Though a guy likes funk you don't automatically hate him, despite his obvious deficiency. At least it's not disco, or *Belafonte's Best*. It's probably Anthony Robbins, or Sri-somebody, the driver's probably nodding yes, inspired to be all the trucker he can be. Actually you can tell from his intent face that, like you, he's alone with nothing but his own rambling thoughts. Beside you on the road, in a sixty-mile-an-hour easy chair. The guy like a teammate you'd never meet.

Reaching across the table with his good arm, Toby poured the wine. He usually poured because the wine was usually his, homemade red bought from a friend for two bucks a bottle. The friend made a fifty-cent profit per bottle, so Toby didn't feel guilty.

Bonaduce lifted his jamjar for Toby to stop pouring.

"Studying tonight." He smiled but didn't know if he was joking or not. At night he'd been accepting the glass of wine Toby always offered. In training, he always stopped at two.

It was a decent domestic scene. Rod, never much of a talker, sat in a corner sipping and reading. Despite the slightly froggish set of his lips and eyes when he read, Bonaduce liked the look of Rod, the relaxed alertness as he sat, the graceful way his spine arced out of his collar. Tonight Rod was reading something by the Dalai Lama, and occasionally he would mutter a quote, some kind of gently wise truth you'd expect. Bonaduce and Marg had taken to keeping the Yahtzee game at permanent readiness on the coffee table and played it nightly, as they did now, a dime a game. Toby talked.

"It's not the best," Toby said, as usual, after topping up everyone's jar, "but it works. And it's cheap. Bloody booze tax. It's all taxes. Fucking, government, monopoly."

Bonaduce had lived with Fournier for much of the last decade — five, six years? — but otherwise alone. He'd forgotten that roommates weren't always a bowl of cherries. These young types were okay in general and Marg here was a jewel, but Toby — Toby was getting on his nerves. From the first he'd noticed that Toby had a certain nasty air about him. Then it dawned one night, listening to Toby speak, that every single thing Toby said was negative. Life was taxes, government monopolies, sleet. Even when he smiled it was hooked by a sneer. His chicken arm hard against his chest, blocking open laughter.

"Well, taxes, yeah." Bonaduce gave a little shrug. "But then we don't pay medical here."

"Yeah, right." Toby rolled his eyes and looked away, possessing information Bonaduce did not.

"Well you ol' *luck* bucket," Bonaduce exclaimed to Marg and her large straight. Marg liked his cowboy talk. He scooped the dice and rattled them loudly up at his ear. "Baby needs a new pair a feet."

You don't want to avoid the people you live with, skulking off to your room in the evenings like some kind of loner. You want to participate. But evenings, while drinking Toby's wine, you couldn't help but get his constant dark slant on things, his voice being the dominant one in the room. Some complainers you understand and forgive, others you don't. If Toby were to lean in and look you in the eye and say how God had given him a shitty arm and a shitty life, you could sympathize. But when a guy complains constantly, constantly, about the bad things we all shared — weather, politics, good food too expensive or cheap food tasting bad — it got a little tiring. Thank you, Toby, for always reminding us, for always making clear the lowest shitty denominator.

"Free medical? The drug companies charging sixty bucks for a bottle of pills it costs two bucks to make?"

"Yeah"—Bonaduce made himself nod—"I guess it is pretty bad that way."

"AIDS medicine costing thousands a month?"

"Right. That's wrong."

"Wrong, man, it's criminal. We're afraid to die and people cash in on that. No one should make more money than anyone else. It's immoral. With health it's criminal."

Bonaduce nodded absently, thinking about the drugstore today, where he'd gone for vitamin C, devil of a cold or something coming. He'd found himself in the geriatric row—walkers, trusses, canes, all beige and ugly-practical, easy to hose off. He'd had to force himself to walk the aisle, pretending he wasn't noticing the twenty feet of adult diapers, a whole fucking section for them.

"And everyone *knows* it's criminal," Toby said.

They'd had an argument once, almost a fight (Bonaduce had actually been able to picture them fighting, Toby attacking him with both arms, an ugly image). Toby, who was on unemployment insurance, had been ranting that the government changing just the name, from "unemployment" to "employment" insurance, was typical in that their solution to any problem they couldn't fix was to euphemize it. Toby was right, but Bonaduce made the mistake of joking that the government would soon be calling death "Afterlife Canada," and to this Toby said, "It isn't funny, man," and glared at him until he was forced to get up and go to his room.

Toby was uncorking another bottle of wine, as usual making a display of it. Bonaduce didn't like thinking it, but he suspected these one-handed shows of non-disability were why Toby had gotten into his wine habit to begin with. Toby was opening wine and staring accusingly, and it felt like gritty déja vu. Bonaduce sighed and looked away.

"That's how it is, I guess."

He hardly heard himself. He'd been halfway into a sip of wine when his own ditty, "We don't pay for medical here," came back to him, echoing. He stopped his sip at the possibility that on some deeper level he hadn't chosen Canada so much as he'd fled the medical bills of the United States.

"Your roll, there, Robert," Marg drawled. "Howse about a quarter a game? My ol' *luck bucket*'s gettin' full of your dimes."

*Oscar Devries.*

When, out of the blue, Bob Bonaduce called on a Friday night near the end of November and said in his way, Hey Buddy, let's do a pub crawl, Oscar was surprised and impressed with himself, first that he agreed and second that he felt glad for it. And when Bonaduce pulled up in his wreck and honked, he was actually doing it, he was pulling on his coat, smiling and shrugging to Leah, waving, going, incredible. Doing the male thing. Poor Leah, she no doubt had some complicated feelings about all of this. His "Honey, I have a date with your ex" seemed to get to her somehow and hardly let her smile. This outing apparently wasn't quite what she had in mind on those occasions when she suggested he go out and find himself some friends.

The idea was to hear some music. Over the phone they'd agreed on a bar called Chevys, which Bob had heard played nothing but oldies.

Considering they were middle-aged men who didn't know each other, in the car it was surprisingly smooth. Just two fellows venturing forth with what looked to be adolescent drinking intentions. He'd been made aware, during sessions with the counsellor he and Leah had seen, that with men his own age he was at ease only when the roles were clear, when the sign "Client" or "Employer" or "Sales," or what have you, was shined up and pinned to a chest. Oscar had nodded politely at the woman's exaggeration, but he did take her essential point home with him.

Declaring just how fine a beer sounded, Bob Bonaduce grinned, nodding at the windshield, and Oscar understood that he was going to a dance club with someone who was "ruggedly handsome."

So, this was the man Leah had married. And this was the father of Leah's son. Most of all, though, in the air was the fact of Bonaduce having slept with her. Twenty years ago or not. Leah had described it as "adolescent passion," as if these words dismissed it. On the contrary it made him consider this thing called animal magnetism, it made him remember how at the party Bonaduce had looked at Leah, the simple but profound gravity in his eyes, and it made him consider his own lovemaking, which was infrequent these days and which — under the glare of true animal magnetism — might amount to little more than feeble.

He glanced down at their two pairs of blue-jeaned knees. To his knowledge he had never been alone with someone who had slept with the same woman. It was a vague and queasy thrill, the proximity and palpable sense of their two laps side by side here in the car.

"Decent night," said Bonaduce, head tilting back in meditative satisfaction. "Decent fall."

Oscar agreed.

He had feared a heart-to-heart, some confession or plea from this man who couldn't help but have unrealistically romantic notions about Jason. The cheap pathos of absence. According to Leah, Bonaduce was orphaned at some young age, the father leaving, the mother dying. In any case Leah said she feared unresolved father stuff surfacing here in Fredericton in some kind of overblown way. What words had she used? "Walt Disney way." Play catch with me Dad, golly jeepers, atta boy Son.

But once in the car Oscar saw that Bonaduce would neither blurt nor plead. No, the man had slicked-back hair and he opened his window in preparation for lighting a small, thin cigar with a comic flourish. Bonaduce kept smiling. He exhaled luxuriously and announced with corny pleasure, "Only on special occasions." Which made Oscar feel good, to be called a special occasion. The fellow had some social grace. No doubt in his career he met people all the time. The smile appeared genuine. He could have been a successful minor politician, that small-town charisma. The clothes, the relaxed athlete at the wheel, the casual vanity of the man. Looking over at you for no reason, smiling and meeting your eye as if something were transpiring.

Other than ask directions to Chevys, Bob Bonaduce was happy to go on about nothing remotely serious. As with his blather about British musicians and nose rings. Tonight it was questions about Fredericton, about nightspots, about when Oscar thought the first snow would hit. He asked about "your lawyer job," nodding politely to the litiginous intrigues while not listening. He really did need to talk but the need had nothing to do with content.

Chevys revealed a side of Fredericton Oscar hadn't seen up close. Everyone was between forty and sixty, which was a nice surprise, and which made sense given the music. In the first ten minutes they played Young Rascals, Elvis and Dusty Springfield. But he'd be damned if this wasn't a singles bar. Tables of ladies sitting wide-eyed and available. Men standing posed in shadow with arm crooked, their beer bottles held pointed in comically suggestive angles. Quick, serious swigs as if suddenly considering something. Swallow, as an afterthought. Ripple your jaw muscles.

He couldn't help but smile — he had never felt so stared at. Women in their forties, even fifties, made up to the hilt but in tight jeans like it was 1975, giving him a hungry unblinking come-on. Oscar Devries, piece of meat. Great stuff. Bonaduce didn't seem to be noticing, though he was getting double the eyes. Well, the man must be used to it, scenes like this. What else does a man do? In Kalamazoo.

The volume went up for an old Doobie Brothers, and if it was hard to talk before, now it was impossible. He and Bob had more or less guzzled their first beer (it seemed to Oscar that they'd each been trying to keep pace with the other) and now Bonaduce appeared with four bottles, two for each of them. Oh-oh and oh well. The DJ behind smoked glass spun a slow platter next, "Ruby," that Kenny Rogers cowpat about a good old boy home from 'Nam sexually disabled, him watchin' his Ruby goin' out to git herself laid, poor him waitin' up, drinkin' the wine. With this song the mood changed as if the DJ had pulled a switch, some kind of perverse romance suddenly in the air, everybody's face taking on the cartoon loneliness and tragedy. The guys swigged with inner torture now, and the gals were stricken in their chairs, eyes wider than ever. And Bob Bonaduce — oh goodness, look at this — there was Bob Bonaduce, eyes downcast, disabled, suffering the same.

Oscar tilted a beer and decided to climb off his arrogant perch. This blue-collar watering hole had lain hidden somewhere in his oddly polar world of executive suits, on the one hand, and Leah's impoverished refugees, on the other. Despite the manipulative music it was elitist and hypocritical to stand here in disdain of the tabloid loneliness of Middle America. For apparently Middle America crossed the border. And you couldn't help but visualize the wanton middle-age sex. By the looks of things this bar would lead to a lot of it, all these divorced old —

"*This is great, eh?*" Bonaduce shouting in his ear.

"*Yeah.*"

"*Good music.*"

"*Yeah.*"

Except for the ubiquitous "Satisfaction" and the Hollies' "He Ain't Heavy," there'd been precious few good tunes. All Top Forty, the expected Motown, Creedence, nothing remotely obscure. Bob seemed bored too, eventually. He didn't seem interested in the women, of which, from the looks of them looking at him, he could've plucked his choice and taken home with the effort of one waggled finger. He'd already refused two women asking him to dance, but now accepted a third, she a rotund sixty-year-old who made her request a self-deprecating joke.

Weird being here. Leah's early husband. Weird watching him down there dancing. The grace of an athlete, the stiffness of having muscles like that. Somewhat flinging his arms around in humour and confidence, and also implied threat, though that would not be deliberate. How much of any dancer's dance was deliberate, exactly? There were questions he wanted to ask Bob now, because Bob was quite possibly not as uncomplicated as he seemed. Living across the river in a house of twenty-five-year-olds. Middle-aged grad student in English but who spoke and looked like a fellow who — what, owned a gun shop? ran a gas station? Apparently he was serious about the hockey with Jason. Jason had reacted negatively to the idea. How was that developing? Leah had not returned from Sussex the day Bob had come over to discuss it. Maybe they'd spoken since on the phone. Who knows? He was staying out of it. He thought the father/son hockey a sweet idea, but so completely innocent. Let's play catch, son. A given that Jason would find it awkward. "Lame" is the word he'd use.

"*Wanna head out?*" Bonaduce, puffing, limped up. Lame.

"*Sure.*"

Bonaduce led him out of Chevys. In the car he said he knew another good bar, Rockin Rodeo, which he then disparaged as "kind of hick." Oscar, who had just experienced the hickest scene of his life, wondered what was in store.

"I've had four beer, probably have the same there, we cab it after that," Bob announced, clicking on his seat belt.

"Taxi's on me." Oscar smiled because both of them were still almost shouting.

"Sounds good." He flashed the Bonaduce smile. "I'm on a student's salary these days. This is my big night out."

What salary would this man attract when school ended? An English MA, in his forties, God help him. Oscar had done an English BA, but only as a route to Law, and perhaps one shouldn't mention this. Bob Bonaduce had basic problems he wasn't dealing with. This constant good mood of his clearly strode on rickety stilts. And if any serious conversation was going to ensue tonight, now was the time, and maybe it was his job to start it.

"I've wanted your side of this and now I can ask you: how come you and Leah never did get divorced?" It wasn't that he didn't believe Leah's version. And he hoped this didn't sound in any way jealous, because it wasn't. Leah wasn't speaking fondly of the man.

Another Bonaduce smile. "I guess we weren't on good enough speaking terms to get one."

Oscar chuckled appreciatively.

"Yes, well. It goes with the territory. We've had some problems ourselves. An early affair..." He shrugged, content to leave ambiguous an affair that had only been Leah's.

"Ooo, hey, it happens."

"But — I love her, Bob."

Now, hell, what was this about? He'd shrugged as if casual but hadn't it come out like a plea? Four bottles of beer and he'd turned to pathetic mush, telling about affairs — he'd never told *anyone* else — and now confessing his love.

"That's good to hear, Oscar."

He and Leah did have a good one, a good relationship. They'd healed and worked through. They had an unspoken understanding of where they were headed, of what was *utmost* in a relationship.

"That's really good to hear."

Oscar looked over to him and smiled, though Bonaduce was staring straight ahead, driving carefully. His poise at the wheel. Big carnivore in graceful repose. He could picture Bob Bonaduce with Leah. To picture this was also to understand that, when sex was mindless, when sex was inevitable as gravity, *utmost* had no chance.

He waited a half-mile before asking the next one.

"So is this hockey thing with Jason important to you?"

Bob either shrugged quickly or suffered a neck spasm of some sort, it was hard to tell in the dark of the car. The man who had been an orphaned adolescent didn't otherwise answer the question, though the car was going faster.

Oscar regretted his question for what he now saw might be its latent cruelty. But Bob's silence was so turned in on himself that Oscar wasn't made to feel awkward. In fact he felt freed of any involvement. Outside, it had begun to sleet. Mixed with road grease and bugs already there, the windshield turned the colour of mud. Bonaduce didn't appear to notice.

"Can you — can you see? Do you have any wiper fluid?"

———

Bonaduce remembered the washer fluid running dry about an hour out of Fredericton on the long haul here, seemed like ages ago now. You always try the wipers anyway, make that same greasy mistake. He found a wad of paper on the floor, pulled over, got out, spit, wiped a face-size hole in the mess. Old Oscar could ride blind. I love her, Bob.

Too bad they didn't have a couple of road beers.

"Bob, can you see?"

"No. Why?"

"Good. Excellent."

Windshields were one of those things you don't think about until they make themselves known like this. He'd completely forgotten, but recalled now when it was that this windshield had last entertained him, and the reason he'd run out of fluid: the firefly. An hour out of Fredericton, middle of the night, he'd seen off the highway what looked to be a cloud, a swarm, of fireflies. He'd never seen a cloud of them before. Hundreds at least. Marvelling at the auspicious luck of seeing a cloud of fire-flies just as he was embarking on a new life, a sudden *splot* woke him up, a double-take wake-up because the fresh-dead bug was a firefly, its guts phosphorescent green on the windshield, eye level, right there.

The bug was dead but its guts were alive. Bright, bright as a tiny flashlight. Green fire undiminished. Again, though not a nice event for the bug, he saw it as his luck. A neat little story to tell, and some science to boot, a firefly's light outlived its life. The fire came first, and it was bigger. So what was the human equivalent?

All kinds of thoughts swirled as he drove at speed. He'd quit the bungee music for now and had rolled up the window. You could stare at the little green sun and at the same time see beyond it to the road. He was awfully tired, road-delirious, and his thoughts about luck took a turn. Because when the bug's light finally did start to fade, he saw this loss as the true image of his luck. So swirly and dream-caught was he, that it being a green light cemented the bad-omen deal, green being not only Irish but also part of the Italian flag. He watched it fade, he watched it fade, using the wipers to get it away, his luck draining, running out, bad choice coming here, bad sign this setting-sun fly, just go away. And there was no human equivalent.

Oscar silent beside him, he drove peering through his faced-sized hole. He knew he was superstitious. Firefly, dead air freshener, dreamcatcher. The luck of the Irish. Italian. In voodoo, scientists say, it's your own superstition that kills you. If that was true, what a truth it was. Because, if you could kill yourself with belief, it meant you could also fix things — anything. Well. Of course it was foolish to ponder these big questions, even when what might be an evil disease was shouldering you in that direction. Life throwing its gloves off, staring you down. But was more foolish not to ponder them, even if you know there are no answers. You let twenty years slide by without considering the big questions, you obviously haven't been doing enough wrong, or right.

He drove, enjoying Oscar's nervousness. He'd thought he might get into some stuff with Oscar tonight, but now knew he wouldn't. A good guy, but Oscar was simply too cynical about too much. Marg had the better ear for it and, incredibly, the better words. Lapsed Christians had a good take on things. In fact, watching her, it had dawned on him that, since there are no big answers available to the big questions, maybe the key was to go smaller. Ask questions less huge, questions not aimed *directly* at the big stuff. Not what is the meaning of life, but where is meaning found. Not what is the answer, but how should I ask it. Where in *hell* is the question.

Love, of course, was a place to start. Which was sort of why he was here.

At the instant Bonaduce thought this, Oscar asked a question about Jason, which startled him. Coincidence packs a jolt. Coincidence felt like religion's messenger-boy. Startling as well was the next insight supplied by his beer-fuelled reverie: Superstition was the only religion he'd ever had.

Another beer would be nice. Expose Oscar to a bit of country twang. He seemed to have a decent sense of humour.

*Oscar.*

When they pulled up in front of Rockin Rodeo and studied its neon sign replete with lassos and boots, Bob broke into the most superb westernisms. "Thar she be, Randy-buck. Settin' thar all purty as a rivershell." It seemed that in his years south his ear had absorbed some of the essential American tongue.

Bob found a parking spot a block distant. It was a beautiful night now. Decent indeed. A hard white moon had come out. Overnight would be cold enough to start ice on the puddles. He had not in a million years thought he'd end up in this country-and-western joint he passed with no curiosity each day on his way to work. What was disturbing was that after only four beer Bob — big beer-drinking Bobby Bonaduce — staggered walking the block to the bar. He actually didn't seem drunk; but Oscar felt offput, and then a little custodial. As they neared the bar, once again his friend launched the lunatic drawl, a cowboy rant that mixed cheek and nonsense.

"Why, this'n here hombre's dirt-mad enough"— Bob was pointing into the face of a scowling woman leaving the bar —"to take and kick the ass-tanks off'n a bull in a toad storm. An she'all knows it, too."

The blonde hombre decided to smile as she climbed into her taxi. Bob kept up the showoff as he pushed in the double glass doors, then the fake saloon doors, talking louder and louder over the music. He stood surveying the place. He pointed at various women.

"*She* was so purty that, wellsir, ever' bigbone weevil from all hunnert counties took and went on a stomp for her benefit, and her benefit too, and hers'n — spree the likes a which six yaller dang bitch coyotes couldn't howl 'nuff to keep *tam*."

Everyone was in jeans, half wore cowboy boots. Even a scatter of cowboy hats. One fellow in a shiny aquamarine cowboy shirt, thumbs hooked in his belt loops, stomped the floor with his big heels, quite serious. Oscar told himself that this was not unlike walking into a meeting place of the Klan, then he understood he only wanted to see it this way for the thrill of it, because he was already bored. This was loyalist New Brunswick and it was dress-up. Though there might possibly be fights.

Bob Bonaduce was loud enough that a few heads were turning, and while Oscar smiled broadly to show everyone it was all a joke, he really wanted Bob to stop.

"Well thar, mister, watcha thank of this'n har line-dancin' dude-pit?"

"If you shut up I'll buy you-all a beer, Big Bob."

Rockin Rodeo was fine from the point of view of studying exotic culture and its music, but two beers later it was very much time to go. Then it was later still and he'd had too much to drink, having stupidly agreed to the cowboy-macho thing of two tequila shooters back to back. Coupla manly men. It was fun drinking in this bar with this man but not worth sitting hung over in tomorrow morning's light. If anything it made him realize his love of Saturday mornings. Him alone with his coffee and paper in the sunroom, Leah sleeping in. The click of his cup, the smell of the coffee, and newsprint.

Outside, impatient with the task of getting a cab for each of them, what with these womenfolk flirtin' their way in front, he was foolishly manly again and drove Bob's wreck to Bob's house way out on the northside highway. He was afraid Bob would've driven himself if he hadn't. Bob's legs weren't working right, and his tongue was thick and slow. *Helll. Owwe. Ahhh-fisss-errr.*

Stupid. Cops did love to catch a lawyer. Why was he doing this?

Bob snapped on the radio and sought music, music being the string through this night's beads.

At Bob's house a clutch of kids dressed in black stood in the gravel parking area, staring into the sky. They yelled at Oscar to turn the car lights off, they were looking for the Hale-Bopp. Bob launched into a string of puns about Halley's comet and bebop music and Bill Haley and the Comets, none of which the kids seemed to understand or want to.

Oscar somewhat self-consciously stepped through their midst and into the house to phone a cab. But Bob Bonaduce took the phone from him and mannishly replaced it with a beer, screw Saturday. Some of Bob's tapes were truly classic, the fellow did know music. He had a big cardboard box packed with tapes. In his funny little room. Bob was enacting some sort of student-hell parody, living with these vampire kids, but he seemed to be enjoying himself. The box had Musswell Hillbillies, early Who, Fairport Convention, these the only good Brit stuff, for Bonaduce was indeed married to the early American white boys. Jerry Lee, some uncommon Elvis, Gene Pitney, Del Shannon, and anything pre-Dylan. Pre-complexity? The Brits had always been into complexity perhaps because, well, to give Bob his due, they were already at a remove, copying the Americans.

The gang of glowering youth came in from their comet and sat in the living room drinking tea and talking softly, more than likely stoned, definitely not wanting two drunken old men in their face. There was a small laughing argument about what went on the stereo, Bob laughing that he'd sue, and then goddamn renovate this place tonight and everyone in it, he had his own lawyer along too. Oscar for one would have been more than happy just to stay in Bob's room and flick through the tape indexes, sit on the bed and talk about whatever, but Bob had a guitar by the neck and insisted Oscar stay in the living room and sing. Bob bragged that he knew how to play every song off the first album of some band called Los Lobos. It was unclear whether or not they were about to hear every one of these songs.

This wasn't to be the case, but it was still largely awful because Oscar was forced to sing. This only after the young people had drifted off, and only after much ridicule and another beer, and another beer. Some of it wasn't bad funny-singing, Bob "doing Oscar Devries doing Mick Jagger," and then a spontaneous ode to the Hale-Bopp comet, except that some house-mate asleep above started pounding on his floor, and Bonaduce, hissing how he didn't fucking like that one-armed gimp, pounded the ceiling with the head of his guitar. Oscar was drunk enough that it was more amusing than scary to see Bonaduce's anger fire his muscles like that, the speed of it and the teeth-clenched smile, a rage that may have served his profession but rage nonetheless. Bonaduce left dents in the ceiling, and the guitar was sprung out of tune.

———

His eyes blinked, stayed open. Sure, this morning had to come. He realized he'd been expecting it. A morning when the truth dawned clear and hard and woke him before the sun did: There was nothing to do with his life but the thing he was doing now, and no one wanted him here doing it.

All he could manage under the weight of this truth was to go up on an elbow and look out his window. Scan the stage. It was grey, windy, shitty out. Nothing else. The comet had left for now. Right, he'd seen it last night, his first comet, and it had surprised him. Paler than starlight. It was fuzzy and playful, like a child's crayoned happy-thing. He'd read in the paper the previous day how comets were regarded as harbingers of doom, and standing with Oscar beside the car he'd had doom in mind as he searched the sky for the comet. Toby had impatiently grunted, There, and Bonaduce got behind him to sight along his good arm. His eyes found this softly glowing fuzzy-bunny thing. Now instantly doubly sinister. You are shown the face of death and it is Shirley Temple's.

Up on his elbow, Bonaduce could feel the entirety of himself gaining, by the moment, a dark and precarious weight. He knew he was one step away from going down and staying down. He willed the eyes to stay open. He looked through the rainbow threads of the dreamcatcher. Marg had called it this, explained its reason for being.

He looked through, seeing what he could, eyes zooming through blurring threads to focus on the distant treeline, the empty stage. Dreamcatcher in reverse. Hey, out there. Catch this one.

Well, with any luck you can find something specific to blame a lousy mood on. And he was a bit hung over. Quite a bit hung over... *and of course fatigue*...Lucky him, he could blame a variety.

Last night had been all right though, his date with Oscar, ending up back here for some tunes and a nightcap. The guitar, right. Toby's stereo had been eating and ruining his tapes for a month and Toby refused to demagnetize. His young roomies had nothing but CDs themselves and unfortunately it wasn't the right kind of music. In this he and Oscar had been in agreement.

But now how in anyone's hell could a successful lawyer in his forties be shy about singing the good oldies in front of a bunch of kids? They wear black and nod their snarky little heads to Nine Inch Nails but so what? Even Marg he didn't like last night. Young types who give no credit to anyone but themselves for anything. You laugh at the purity of Del Shannon, it's your loss. Live your lives in a snarkier-than-thou postmodern house of mirrors, go ahead.

Despite what it was speeding toward, there was something okay about age, there really was. Last night, him and Oscar like buds here in this romper-room house. At the writing workshop he and Big Jan sometimes caught each other's eye and almost smiled after a blurted youngism. In the halls at school, nineteen-year-olds ambling smug with all the latest trendy torn cool junk on their bodies and on their minds — it was stuff you knew nothing about, but you couldn't help feel sorry for them, looking down from your perch of age. Because you knew, and they didn't, that what they so absolutely believed in right now, what stiffened their spine and curled their smirk, would in twenty years be gone. You knew, and they didn't, that in twenty years they wouldn't know anything at all, and feel just like you.

Imagine telling this to Jason. Imagine the look.


He opened the fridge. Toast, toast would be good. With jam. Or maybe meat, this looked like meat, liverwurst. It didn't smell off, too much.

"There's a giant hole in the bathroom wall."

Here was Marg, standing in her big white terrycloth robe. The whole idea of her was hard to look at.

"Was that all that noise last night?"

Shit. That's right, the bathroom wall.

"Well, Marg, it was all rotten there. I decided to fix it."

"Looks like you kicked the wall in."

It came back now. He'd fallen hard against it for no reason and dented it with an elbow. Then he'd lost it a bit and started kicking, starting with the swamp-wall beside the toilet.

"It was all rotten." It was. Some of it the fist had gone through easy.

"But I mean we're renting. That's like, the landlord's job."

"So where is he? It was all piss-soaked."

"Well, now we have this totally screwed-up wall."

Marg's face was slack, her voice was monotone. She wasn't into reasoning.

"I'll fix it. I just couldn't stand it. I hated it. Can't see how anyone could sit down beside that and take a —"

"*He* might hate it, you kicked in his wall. It wasn't rotten all the way to the bathtub like that." Marg turned her back on him and started doing something fast at the counter with her hands, grabbing up papers or something. "I just cleaned it all up, so I know."

"Marg? I'll fix it."

·⌒

THE HOCKEY NOVEL
by
R. BONADUCE

It is not only species of animals that die out, but whole species of feeling. And if you are wise you will never pity the past for what it did not know, but pity yourself for what it did.

— John Fowles, probably talking
about old-time hockey

Oscar Devries, immigrant baby, was given his first pair of skates at age four weeks. Outside their sod hovel the prairie winter wind howled like a she-devil as Father laced Baby Oscar's skates up tight. So tight that blood began beading up at the lace-holes. But little Oscar didn't cry. He cried only when they removed the skates and he kept crying until they laced them back on, tighter. They taped popsicle sticks on for shin pads and stuffed his little rig into a thimble. Helmet? No helmet, Oscar thrashed his head until they gave up trying to put one on him, he wouldn't be a fancylad. And fuck the mouthguard too: he already had no teeth. They noticed he had come into the world with several facial scars.

Oscar's first game he played naked, save for his bleeding skates. His foul temper kept him warm and red and his skin unfrozen. He went goalless but, using his adult-size stick, he sent six players to the Winnipeg Regional Hospital.

　　　　　　　　　　　　•⌐

Religiously and soberly, always sticking to just two, Bonaduce poured himself his second glass. Red wine, hey, I feel a tumour coming on, pass the red. He wondered if Toby would miss this bottle, if he kept count. Downstairs, Toby kept his bottles stacked dusty on their sides as if it was a fucking wine cellar, not a rat cellar.

He was having nothing but trouble coming up with anything for Big Jan's workshop. He'd whined to her and she'd simply said, Write what you know. So he'd joked, Hard to write about nothing for very long. And she'd said, Nonsense. And he'd said, Nonsense it will be!

So, sure, he could write about hockey. But what? A pack of anecdotes? The exotic stuff? He'd seen a goalie's artery slashed. He'd seen teammates shit their pants during a game, one guy — who was that, O'Dowd? — forcibly trading the dirtied pants with a frightened Russian rookie, O'Dowd the satanic joker. (Here ya go, Jan and Phil and Kirsten, good stuff, eh?) Or Donny Carter, his nervous breakdown between periods. That nervous little look, the glancing around like a timid baby, not talking, took a few days for anyone to catch on, then a year on the sixth floor for Carter. Or should he just write a stupid Rocky story about a guy who overcomes the odds? Everyone liked that crap, maybe even Jan. Bill Spunska, clumsy immigrant, barely makes the team but scores the winning *yadda* with *yadda* left on the clock in the *yadda yadda* finals. Do you do the social comment? team-as-microcosm thing? Modern gladiators, boxed vicarious bloodwar, testosteronic bugs in a bell jar. Do you write for an audience at all? Or do you just scribble for yourself and hope someone else gloms onto your heartbeat? But how to convey the subtleties of a thing, how do you hold the good mirror up to the rink's old wet-cigar smell, or the sound of tape tearing off the roll as distinct from ripping off an ankle, or the kaleidoscopic personality of a dressing room? Or the game itself, the fresh ballsy chugging, the deepgut serenity of a solid hit and the guy going down. Or the danger of it all — you have the puck and you're lugging a bag of gold to market surrounded by fast bandits.

How do you know if anyone will care?

Tonight at the laptop, once again he'd begun with a legitimate beginning, the Fowles quote, then fouled it up going right into the Oscar joke. Well, Jan's other advice had been, just start writing, no goal, freeform. Maybe he'd try again tomorrow. Maybe he'd shove this in Oscar's mailbox in the meantime, why not. Too bad it wasn't this fun writing essays. Humour — humour was the antidote for all that wasn't humorous.


His first piece of mail. In the student general mailbox a message from Professor Daniel Kirk regarding the "New Traditions in the Carnivalesque" seminar he'd registered in but so far had not attended. Hard to say how old the note was because he hadn't been checking the box. Come to think of it, he'd passed Kirk in the hall a few times and the guy's stick-up-the-ass response to a friendly hello Bonaduce had written off to personality rather than circumstance. Sorry, professor, my mistake.

A word in the last sentence was underlined:

<u>What</u> are your intentions?

Nice, a catchphrase for him to go to sleep to and wake up with, a jingle for life. Come on, *what* are they?

His second piece of mail was old news. His grant had been turned down. He was to subsist on the assistantship alone. Once a week he met thirty students, Engineering types mostly, to work on writing skills. It was strange. The course was called "Aspects of the Novel." A Professor MacAphee, whom he hadn't met, gave twice-weekly lectures on novels the class was supposed to have read, then on Fridays the lectured-to students broke into groups for a session with a grad student, to work on essays about these novels. Bonaduce had questions about this. If they wanted these guys to learn how to write essays, give them subjects that mattered to them: movies, computers, sex, whatever. They lacked the tools to say the right things about the novels even had they read them. They wrote MacAphee's lecture insights down as best they could, and it was Bonaduce's job to help them hammer these notes into essays. He encountered poor slobs trying to work in "Apocalypse now was of course but the bastard celluloid son of heart of darkness the masterpiece," not knowing if this meant something was good or bad.

Bonaduce figured he was a decent teacher, because in their tongue-chewing labours he saw himself mirrored in Gail Smith's. He got on their good side, even the back-row sneer-doctors in the ball caps, by clapping his hands and saying, "Gotta do it so let's do it, let's fuckin' go get 'er, ya wanna be as dumb as ya look?" It at least got their attention. The only reason they bothered to stoop to try to put fancy sentences together was to pass the course, get the degree, the job, make as much money as possible. Bonaduce had chased rubber for twenty years, but compared with these guys he was a philosopher and bohemian. If teaching this course was depressing, its social forecast was scary. What had happened to the liberal fucking education?

Regarding his first piece of mail, Bonaduce decided his intentions hadn't changed — that is, he had no clue *what* they were — and he left Kirk no note.

That night, there it was, in the centre of his window, the comet. The Hale-Bopp happy face, all plague-spewing innocence. It had an intensity you could almost hear. Having it in your window was funny and not-so-funny. It was hard not to feel singled out. Apparently for the next month this comet would be exactly right there.

What can you make of a ball of nasty dirty ice millions of miles away framed perfectly in your very own bedroom window? Monster pulling a gaudy dirt-tail longer than lifetimes. Hanging there in your window utterly still — yet moving at a speed your mind can't take.

Absolutely no sound out there, ever.

*What* were its intentions?

### THE (HO)KKY NOVEL
### by R. L. Bonaduce

The history of hockey is actually herstory. Not many persons know this.

In 1846, on the outskirts of Halifax, little Gail Smith picked her nose out of her book and cast her steady regard through the window at the mess of boys playing out on the pond. Slipping and sliding in their boots, they chased a frozen turd around, batting at it with their bent sticks in hope that it might career betwixt two wooden pails. "Score!" they would shout with glee, as if it mattered, whenever this occurred.

They had rebuffed her again. Not that she wanted to play. But they'd made a point, when going their smelly way out-of-doors, to make sure she knew she wasn't allowed. Their taunts, directed at her size, her gender, her appreciation of books, only privileged her steely resolve. To the sounds of their faint, wolfish shouts of "Score!" she went to the cellar for the knives.

It had taken her a week of evenings, working away with file, with hacksaw, with Whitmans auger. Her one pair of boots were ruined — but sacrifices were necessary.

When she appeared on the pond, bent stick in hand, there were the expected hoots of derision, but these were now laced with anger at her daring to challenge. Those that weren't engaged in red-faced yelling might have noticed that she was newly taller; those with the keenest eyes may have had to squint at the glint of sun off something excellent and unimagined beneath her feet. But all noticed, and were struck dumb, when little Gail Smith swooped in amongst them, confiscated and held onto their turd, performing defensive twirls and offensive thrusts, dancing the turd back into their mass and out again, just to taunt them. And in the end, all the boys and girls — many of them were girls after all — all lying in pain on the ice, dismembered, impotent, decon-structed, she casually nudged the turd 'tween the buckets with her shiny toe, and shouted not the crude word the others had used, but stated her own, fairly and without closure: Hello

*Margaret.*
It was morning when Robert's French friend from the States called again, waking her up. Referring to himself only as Fournier, asking for "Bobby," then all sorts of guy jokes. How's the big Bonaduce doin'?

She went downstairs to get Robert. The call had become mixed with the dream she'd been having just as the phone rang. She re-pictured it, a dream so obvious it was silly. She had seen a shirtless Robert coming toward her, crawling toward her. He was emerging from some sort of hay loft, he was above her and grinning as he crawled out of the hay, his muscles glistening and defined by shadow, bits of straw clinging to them like beauty marks. He needed a shave, which was fine, which was even better, and as he grinned at her, crawling closer, his black hairiness turned blond and then longer, now great curling locks cascaded in rivulets in the valleys of his wet muscles, which got even bigger, and his smile grew even more perfect, and suddenly it was one of those strange ones where the dream is obviously goofing around on you, almost mocking, and the dream knows this before the dreamer does.

Robert wasn't in his room, and his coat was gone. Fournier, when told this, kept joking around. "Hey, so where is the guy, you hidin' 'im? You his wife? How many wives he have now? All with a flirting edge, just in case. The kind of guy who knows no other way with a woman.

Fournier calmed down when she had no answers to any of this. His questions turned general and sober. So how was he really? His health. Was he walking okay?

"Well, he'll like, bump into the fridge if he doesn't see it coming."

"Jesus H."

She'd meant it as a joke, exaggerating Robert's clumsiness, his occasional shoulder hitting a door, which might send him into a little stagger. His friend's concern surprised her.

"I just want to know, did he get the book I sent up. The yeast book."

"I don't know."

"Maybe it got stopped at the border. The herbs and pills and stuff, eh? Jesus H, I told this to Kim. He didn't get it then?"

"I don't know. I mean, I didn't see it."

"He didn't get it then."

"He keeps to himself. He might have gotten it."

"You gotta tell him to do it when he gets it."

"Sorry? Do what."

"What the book says. When he gets it, you make him to follow it to a tee. He's a proud sucker but it's important, eh? For sure he can get better. Kim's instructions for the herbs and pills are in there too, eh?"

"I'll tell him." And make him do the herbs and yeast and pills. Okee-dokee.

"Bobby'll laugh — my girlfriend Kim, she's into the alternative stuff, right? — Bobby'll laugh, but she says you can snip it in the bud if you get on it early."

"Robert has like a disease or something?"

Silence on the other end, Fournier finally sussing.

"He has, he has MS, eh?"

"MS. That's…"

"Jesus H. Didn't tell you, eh? He's got multiple sclerosis. Can kill the stupid bugger."

"He didn't say a word to me. Wow, that's awful."

"Hey, it's the shits. He's pretty depressed about it."

"Well, yeah," Marg agreed. Picturing Robert in his room, aware of his presence in this house as if for the first time, she added, softly, "He is."

"He didn't tell anyone?"

"I don't know."

"Didn't he tell his wife?"

This was getting good. Marg couldn't help smiling.

"Which one?"

Fournier laughed.

———

HOCKEY NIGHT IN THE KREMLIN

What has the game become? Money. In a brief time we have seen the game change to its corporate, crumbling state. The way owners buy winning teams, the way the players change teams…

It will get as bad as baseball, the money hunt. What are young kids making of this, seeing that their heroes' sights are set on anything but loyalty?

To win, a team has to work as one body. Gone are the days you would kill and die for a teammate. Guys hardly know each other now. All the Europeans, even in the minors. Foreign guys sitting lost in the dressing room, no much eenglish, touching fingertips to their freshly stitched wound, wondering what they've gotten into.

Nor can we understand them. Look at the those Detroit Russians, who our game privileged with the Stanley Cup this past year. Them taking the cup to Russia and right into Lenin's Tomb. How can you understand people like that? If it's humor, it's different from ours. What it looks suspiciously like is loyalty and tradition, and of a sort we no longer have, if we ever had it at all. Father, Comrade Father, we have successfully deluded them, they think we are like them, we now have their money and their cars. Father, look at this trophy, we will touch it to your face. Wake up, Father, we've won.


He didn't try to conceal the Salvation Army store bag. He laid it on the kitchen counter, took out the can opener and put it in the utensil drawer, which was otherwise filled with broken spatulas, crumpled bills, gummy screws, widgets. A month had gone by and these guys were still opening cans with a hammer and rusty hunting knife, no doubt another ploy of Toby's to force everyone to watch how dextrous he was.

In his room, it was time to lie down. But first he took out and once more tried on the leather coat and checked himself in the mirror. A classic: wool-lined, ass-length, a little beaten up. Buffed at the elbows and lapel, where you could see past the dye into the old cow herself. Forty bucks, but winter was coming, and it was a coat that would last many more years. He hung it on the biggest nail.

His favourite book growing up had been *Robinson Crusoe*, and his hands-down favourite movie had been *Swiss Family Robinson*. As an adult, the main positive in getting traded (aside from sometimes getting a raise, or escaping a brainless coach) was the fresh start, with nothing. Survival of the freshly marooned. Later trades especially, he'd taken this idea completely to heart and jettisoned everything — furniture, car, dishes, even the bulk of his clothes.

More often than not, a trade involved a player coming your way from the other direction; a pissed-off or elated phone call from the guy often came the same day you got your news. But Bonaduce would politely decline the offer of the ready-made, furnished, dish-stocked apartment. Instead he hoteled it for a while, then on a free day found himself something small, clean. The first week he might buy a couple of pots, maybe a solid chair. Goodwill and Used stores were fine if the stuff was well built. Adding to your nest bit by bit, this was the Crusoe feeling. Locating the best little grocery was Crusoe finding the breadfruit tree beyond the hill. The dented pewter mug was the half coconut shell, the yard-sale carving knife was the fish hook fashioned out of a bent ship's nail. Comforts growing. Bonaduce would sometimes even think *coconut*, and *survival*, as he drank his milk out of the mug in the morning.

He would picture women in his new place. And eventually one would come, and him with curtains, with dishes for four, with a rack of spices Bonaduce would have no clue when to use. Women seemed to like shopping for him in this way, maybe it was his dumb-dog trust. More than once he had a woman help him with his Crusoe-shopping before they'd even slept together and, generally speaking, this little burst of shared domesticity would lead her into the sack. Not that that had been his plan from the start, not exactly.

The Crusoe routine shifted when he was bought by Tulsa, and he met and roomed with the goalie Fournier. The arrangement was expedient and stop-gap. Here he was in Okie, the middle of nowhere, truly. Road trips were so long you were never home. In Tulsa it was common for four or five guys to room together, foamies and cots in the living room, save some bucks waiting for the next road trip or trade or call-up. Bonaduce saw how the guys here banded together more than usual. Oklahoma was a deeply strange place for a Canadian to be. Dust, heat, Okie-talk, pickup trucks downtown. Strange to be the home team here, trying to beat the shit out of a busload of fellow Canadians while all the cowboys in the audience hollered. They didn't shout here, they hollered, and sometimes they yipped. On the scoreboard the word HOME could tear your heart out. Within days of arriving in Tulsa, Bonaduce had all the lore about guns pulled out in bars, about places not to go. Safe in the dressing room, they enjoyed constant mock cowboy talk. *Wellsir, I reckon it's 'bout tam we should take and work up a lather out thar on the frozen ceement pond...*

It was common knowledge that all goalies were weird, no matter where they may be trying to fit in. But with his accent and Montreal suave, Fournier fit this place not one bit. His English wasn't great, but the glint in his eye leapt easily over language. He had a way of smiling at your subtle question, looking at you with understanding but saying nothing. He was the kind of guy you gave the benefit of the doubt to, both because you wanted to and because he may have in fact understood. He read so much. He and Bonaduce had more books scattered about their place than the rest of the team put together. Maybe, they joked, the league put together. Fournier was a little hippyish, and had "two professional-hippy brothers" in Vancouver who sent him flattened hashish in letters, which he used in moderation. Fournier frowned on cocaine or drunkenness.

A three-year veteran of Tulsa when Bonaduce met him, Fournier was desperate to get out, had been from day one. Immediately he'd bought furniture, car, and all the rest of it, riding the common superstition that as soon as you plant roots you get traded. When this didn't work he went the other extreme, making almost a religion out of his bare fridge, cupboards, apartment. Once he'd gotten to know Bonaduce enough, he stated shyly that his lifestyle was in keeping with the tradition of Zen. He shopped "only for the food of one meal." He had two sets of clothes, one clean, the other on. If he needed a car or a tennis racket, he borrowed. No TV. He was usually the best-looking guy on the team, and French to boot, but he avoided the bars and tended to meet his women in the grocery or library. These women tended to be Zen or health-food types themselves. They talked that talk in any case, though in those unlikely cowgirl accents.

But Fournier was a good guy and Bonaduce went along. It felt okay to go out in the morning to buy that day's food. (Not unlike a hunting-and-gathering Crusoe.) Made you feel focused, life so simplified. He kept his closet lean. (The ship would be coming soon, take him home.) No stereo, so he bought an old guitar, learned the basic chords, started making up his own ditties. Where the rest of the guys went into debt for a muscle car, he walked or took taxis. For all this he felt lighter, more ready for the game, or call-up to the bigs. He felt this leanness gave him speed. It was Tulsa where he began playing naked under his gear — longjohns in the heat made no sense, they soaked up your sweat and you carried these extra sopping pounds by game's end. Naked, skating blew you dry.

Here in his highwayside house in freshstart Fredericton —
which in the minors was called Freddie Beach! — he had two
shirts, two T-shirts, jeans, cords, sneakers, dress shoes. Underwear,
socks. Guitar, box of tapes. Skates. He'd bought a towel, now a
leather coat and can opener. He'd been given a dream-catcher.

## A Mirror

We're a rack with meat hanging off it. Sometimes you get
banged up or sick and the meat separates from the rack
a bit. Things puff up or flap and dangle. Sharp hurt or
bruise hurt or weird hanging-nerve hurt. Sometimes in
the crammed dressing room after a road game you look
at the other guys over thirty, those few that are left, and
they look like you feel. You sit there actually laughing at
what you have become, how at this very moment a shoulder and a lip, and a few ribs, and a foot, and maybe a
deep organ somewhere to the left, are smashed numb or
throbbing. Shaking your head in amazement, you sit
there dripping sweat. You can smell yourself, the naked
body there below your nose. You have a herpes flare-up
and a cold. You are being yelled at to hurry to climb onto
a bus, which you will ride all night sitting up.

Beside you a younger guy stands whistling, still eyeing
the NHL, and one foot from your face he's flicking talcum
powder onto his balls.

It's all more funny than not.

He woke in an instant. Brain abuzz. It was definitely the middle
of the night. The room was dark but somehow vibrant. Efferves-
cent, but beneath sight. He could hear that the highway was still.

He wondered if it was this pregnant silence that had woken him. No, he sensed something alive outside. He went up on an elbow to see it.

There. Fierce, bigger than the sun, the full moon rising over the treeline. Huge, loud as kettledrums you couldn't hear. Its light stolen, and more powerful for it. You could feel all this, important, in the blood.

When he arrived, Leah and Oscar were in the living room together. The curtains were closed. She was on the couch drinking coffee, feet tucked up under, the Saturday *Globe and Mail* spread around her. Hard to say, because he'd never seen them together before, but the room felt stern, jagged, as if they'd been fighting. Though maybe this sternness was their comfort zone, the kind of air they breathed. He had no inkling of how they got on. Or who Leah had become.

He'd called a few times, and Leah could never manage a time to do it, to get together to talk about Jason. Today, crossing the bridge into town, he'd decided to just drop by. The friendly Maritime way. It was Saturday and sunny so he stopped en route at the farmers market and spent the last of the month's money on a block of Emmenthal cheese.

Along with his leather coat, he handed the cheese gift to Oscar, whose thanks was a surprised raising of eyebrows. It actually even looked like a gift — a square wrapped in butcher's paper, tied neatly with string.

"Thanks," Oscar said. He hesitated, then smiled cautiously, not looking up. "And thanks for that little — I don't know what exactly you'd call it — that 'hockey story' about me. It was... strange."

"Fiddling around, thought you'd get a kick out of it. Hope it was okay I sent it to where you —"

"My secretary found it *extremely* strange. She opens my mail. She might want danger pay from here on in."

"Hey. Wait'll she reads about Oscar-the-Teenager."

"I had no idea I had such, ah, *robust* beginnings."

"You smaller guys are the meanest. There was this little guy, Amis? You wouldn't —"

But, laughing, Oscar had already turned and walked.

With Oscar fetching a coffee in the kitchen, Bonaduce turned to Leah and got to it. She'd been pretending to read the paper, but looked up as soon as his question was ready.

"I was wondering about Jason, if he's talked to you."

Leah actually seemed serious when she said, "Bobby, if you want to play hockey with him, why don't you just play outside? One of the rinks, they flood the tennis courts, always by Christmas. Take your sticks, you see lots of fathers and —"

"No. Jesus. That's not —"

"You'd really have as much fun just —"

"No, it has to be —" She really had no idea at all. "That's kids. That's just fun. It has to be way more, you know, I don't know, 'serious.'"

He shook his head, surprised at her. Danger. A team. It had to matter. Together, rushing the prize pig to market, bashing through deadly bandits, loving these guys who ran the gauntlet with you. Glory, laughter, sloshing tankards of ale at the inn.

Leah was quiet for too long. With no further word she uncurled off the couch and left the room. Oscar, who had returned, who had been wearing his ironic smile all along, shrugged and said, "It's a tricky one!" Then he fell to silence as well, staring at the floor, looking glad to be free of having to have an opinion.

The hall toilet flushed and, while Oscar didn't appear to hear, Bonaduce felt a little shy of it, of what it meant. He pictured Leah pulling up and zipping her jeans.

She returned and sat. In her stern silence the mother's love clearly reflected the son's troubles. Well, Bonaduce was here today to try to fix those. First he had to find out what they were.

"I came on too strong with him I guess. It was a little much."

"A little."

"Old Gordie," he said, smiling, "probably had a family powwow first, see how they all felt about the old guy coming to play." He looked up. Not even an indulgent smile from her. "Gordie Howe?"

"I know."

"I guess me coming here to live would have been heavy enough."

"Coming here to *visit* would have been heavy enough."

"Sure. I guess."

"And Gordie Howe was totally different."

"Well, yeah." Though what did she mean? "The principals raking in big money, the sentimental thing for the fans, sure, that really adds —"

"*No. Shit.*" Leah clapped her hands, once. He remembered seeing her do this to get Jason to listen. "He had the *right*. He was a goddamn *father*."

Oscar, rising and trying to flee gracefully, dropped the CD case he'd been handling and it clacked on the coffee table, another rude clap.

*A goddamn father.* What could you say to such a thing? Nothing that wasn't feeble. I want to try to be. I have to start somewhere. Maybe we could all just.

"Well, Leah, I'll think about that." Think about what, exactly. Maybe she wasn't wrong, but she certainly wasn't right.

"I mean, Bob, do you have any clue at all?"

About fatherhood? In Tulsa there was Cynthia, with Lisa, her seven-year-old, and the three of them did almost a year together. He knew Lisa's homework, what she ate for lunch. Lisa had let him hold her after she'd fought with her mother. He had never exactly lived with the two of them but —

"Do you have any clue what Jason wants, or what I want?"

Ah, that's what you meant. No, I guess I don't.

"No, Leah, I guess I don't." Do you have any clue what I want from Jason, or from you? Yes, you probably do. "I guess you got me there."

He shrugged softly from his chair. He waited, then aimed a little smile at her, like a wedge into her hardness, an invitation to the intimacy she was working like hell to avoid. But she wasn't looking his way.

He got up to go. Leah did nothing to stop him. In fact she pinched up a section of newspaper to get on with her morning. She was that mad. Jason was that mad.

The sun came out from behind a cloud and flooded the window behind her, backing her in bright light, turning her black. He could no longer see her clearly without squinting.

He left then in thudding awkwardness, not letting her see his eyes. He was aware of his legs in their long walk to the door, and then the sound of its opening and clicking closed.

He stepped out into the sun and the draining knowledge that, of the two people he had journeyed back so far to see, he was now on speaking terms with neither.


*Margaret.*

It was a week after talking at length to Robert's French friend. She still hadn't mentioned anything about it to Robert, finding neither the opportunity nor the nerve. Nor the feeling, not really, that it was hers to do.

Though maybe tonight. They were alone in the house together. In the spirit of devil-may-care they had declared all the food in the house fair game and were preparing something good. There was her own angel-hair pasta, plus some nice hot Italian sausage from what looked like Rod's spot in the freezer, and the rest of her over-dry sundried tomatoes. Robert found some half-good garlic at the bottom of the vegetable tray along with a romaine with enough crispy leaves in the middle.

Standing with him at the sink, washing and ripping, almost touching shoulders. Here she was, making dinner with a man who was deeply sad of late but who did a pretty smooth job covering it up with cheerfulness, a man Fournier had called *one of the world's greatest guys.*

It was ridiculous that Robert made her think of her father, they were so unalike. Maybe that was why! Her father had never stood at the sink with her like this, she couldn't remember once. Or if he had, he would have made a big deal out of it: Let's everybody smile, here I am at the sink with my daughter, what do you all think of that? His spotlight for a moment including her. Her father had taught her in the end that there were many styles of insanity, many of them acceptable. One style let you have a business, a family, respect, and then let you disappear — well, San Diego — with a cliché secretary. He had no conscience, none. She was unclear in herself if she ever wanted him to call, say, at Christmas.

And here was Robert, appearing, from the States. Let's not take the equation any further please.

Fournier had been amazed at a few of the things she'd been able to tell him about his friend — He goin' back to *school? No!* — which told her how private Robert had been with Fournier too.

He'd found a jar of beets, which he held out to her in question, and which she suggested might not be appropriate for the meal. Her adding that they were Toby's mother's seemed to decide it for him. He winced and bent his knees opening it.

"Can't beat Harvard beets," he said. She couldn't tell if the stupid pun was intentional. "We can crank the stereo, play some Yahtzee later," he said, hands in the sink, jerking his head in the direction of the living room.

*But he's a bit of a loner, eh?*

Yes and no. Last night, again just the two of them, he'd brought out his guitar. She was ready to be embarrassed for both of them, but he wasn't a bit shy as he sang. Occasionally he'd look up and smile at her. One song he said was from Lovin' Spoonful, "You Didn't Have to Be So Nice." This one he sang right to her, smiling coyly, holding her eye, meaning the words. It was all so ordinary and simple she thought her heart would break. She realized then that he was the best she'd ever seen at looking at you, and almost meaning it. He finished, saying how that song had made him buy an autoharp, which sounded like "an angel's guitar," and that it was too bad John Sebastian had turned out to be "creepy and a sheep."

She tested the sundried tomatoes and they still wouldn't bend. The water they soaked in had turned to thin brown blood. Robert hummed as he melted butter and found the sugar and scooped in a "guesstimate"— she was starting to like his corny words— with his cupped hand. She tried not to be obvious as she watched him move. He looked practised in the kitchen, no stumbling, almost graceful. Mincing the garlic, the way he set down a plate. She didn't add to her beet-criticism when he brought out the Louisiana hot sauce, which was all vinegar too and wouldn't fit Italian either.

*He really should not eat certain things, eh? And the main thing— don't let him get stressed, or tired.*

Okay, Fournier, I won't let him.

Marg had been staring straight into but now noticed the frost pattern on the window in front of her. It was truly spectacular, backlit as it was by the kitchen porch light. A thousand prisms, shifting if you did. Framed in the window, it was a display, a happenstance gallery. If you had the time, you could watch it grow. Intricate patterns, hundreds of geometric storylines. No artist could do that, Marg didn't think. An artist would miss the precision or else go overboard into foliage and elves, something human. But how could beauty be so obvious and so painfully subtle, both at the same time? Some saw beauty like this as proof of God. That was too simple, though calling it an accident was too simple too. Not that that window display was proof of an intelligence, but more that it was what created expectations. And what made us try. That window display was what made us think there was something better. In store.

"Robert. Look at the window." She pointed, shaking her head, the prisms shifting colours as she did so. "I mean, *look* at that."

"That's pretty cool."

"Remember when you had the time to like, look at stuff like this? Magic Jack Frost?"

He nodded but didn't look convinced. She could see him take her comment and go within. Memories, worries, what. He smiled and looked at her. He had his hands up in front of him, dripping and limp at the wrist, fingers turned toward his face.

"I do have the time. I call it 'time to kill.'"

No dishcloth in sight, he wiped his hands on his pants. Then went to the fridge and, drawing out two bottles of Heineken beer, fell into his cowboy talk.

"Some especial-occasion-type beer, little lady?"

"Great."

"Crack the heads off'n a couple foreign weasels?" He waggled the Heinekens at her.

"Go to it."

He looked suddenly speedy and impatient. *And, hey, you really don' wanna make him mad.*

She hadn't liked hearing that one. The build of the man. His blocky hands ripping salad like it was air. Though Fournier had said it in an admiring way, and added, *Oooweee.* When she asked what he meant exactly, he said, "Ask the people of Kalamazoo, they tell you, eh?" and laughed. To her silence he'd actually laughed and added, "Don't worry, you're safe."

The bathroom hadn't been safe.

How mad would he be getting? The day after Fournier's call — and it wasn't like she'd hurried to find out, she was in the library already — she looked up the disease. And read about it, horrible. What must be going through Robert's mind? The thing was, anything could happen to the man now. Including nothing.

As she began to serve up, Robert told her to wait, mumbling "Hang on, hang on." First he fussed two tea towels into napkins. Then he cleaned off the table with his hands, one hand brushing crumbs carefully over the edge into the other. Disappearing to the living room, he returned with a Christmas candle, a foot-high Santa with only a half-inch of his red toque melted down. She decided against telling him this was Toby's special candle. She watched him light it.

"*Mah* Oklahoma," said Robert, sitting down finally and jigging hot sauce on everything, including the salad, "includes fancy eatin'."

The accent was totally believable, and went with the way he tucked in.

———

### WHAT IT TAKES
### — By BoBo Bonaduce

There are three kinds of toughness.

The second kind is the famous kind American fans like, the toughness of the big guy who can fight. Each team has at least one guy like this. If he's won enough fights early on, he can skate through the rest of his career with his head high, face calm, sometimes even that cultivated look of boredom. Cocksure as a dog who gets paid to piss. Even the guys on his team fear him, sometimes hate him a little, because his job is to punch a guy's lights out with no provocation and if you get traded he'd do the same to you. Still, it is sad watching these tough guys topple, when the younger tough guys start beating them up on a consistent basis. The father bested by the child. It means the end of a career, at thirty, and these guys aren't going to any Hall of Fame.

The third kind of toughness depends on everyone's fear of the unknown. The game of hockey is license for some truly crazy men to inflict pain. These men can't be summed up or described. They're all different, because one aspect of crazy-toughness is that it's a kind of genius and it doesn't repeat itself.

He stopped typing. Picturing the guy's face, what it felt like to go into a game against him. Even thinking about him, the feather of fear tickled the gut. Shorty Amis. Bonaduce had seen no better practitioner of this toughness than Shorty Amis. He'd been on the receiving end of the rodent's abuse more than a few times himself.

The thing was, Amis and his kind were beyond tough. As in Amis's case, it often had to do with the shoulder-chip venom of being a little guy, but it was more a general condition of having an eagerly sick spirit. Amis had no teeth, and his assaults were two-voiced — a piercing shriek overtop a deeper, honking, ragged attempt at words. Guys fifty pounds heavier were unnerved by his voice. Before, during and after a tussle, Amis yelled at you and continued from the penalty box, shrieking until he lost his voice. Bonaduce had seen him shriek till he retched.

Amis had once been called up by Philly to play the Bruins in tough old Boston Garden, a kind of experiment probably, a let's-unleash-it-and-see-what-it-does. Amis knew why he was there, and his NHL career lasted less than a minute, during which time he speared one guy (sending him to the hospital for a spleen), started a fight with the guy who avenged the spear (Amis getting beaten up), finished two more fights (getting beaten up twice more), shoved the linesman (getting tossed for this), spit at a fan on his way off the ice, and spanked the hat off the head of a cop who got too close.

Amis would cut your face for no reason other than the colour of your jersey. He'd cut Bonaduce twice. The first time, Bonaduce fought him and, literally adding insult to injury, lost to the wiry prick. The second time, Amis's stick missed his eye by a hair, and Bonaduce was bleeding badly and too protective of his eye to fight. Other times they'd gone into corners together and ended up gloving each other's face and whatnot, and in the box the weasel-faced shit wouldn't stop shrieking. "Fuckin' stick your fuckin' eyes out, fuckin' chop your head off, fuckin' *shit* down your fuckin' *neck,* fuckin' *kill ya, I'll fuckin' kill ya, I'll fuckin' FUCK ya."* Retch.

Once, Bonaduce realized the shrieking had stopped. Feeling like an air-raid siren had ceased, he chanced a look over. And he caught in Amis's glaring back something like humour. Bonaduce met his eye. When he saw Amis's quick wink, the hair actually rose tingling on his neck. He sat back and caught his breath, and later looked over at Amis and studied his calm profile. He looked quite bright. If Amis hadn't been born in Timmins but, say, in New York City, he might've been a poet.


He cradled the green plastic pot in the drive-way wind, the spindly plant brushing his chest and tickling him under the chin. He hustled it to his room. There are plenty of substitutes for blood kin. Anyone who forms bonds with plants or inanimate objects knows this. The guy and his car. Even the *engine* of his car. Even a new engine *part* can be your special buddy.

Sure, it was a pathetic gesture to try to add anything to this little room, to try to make it more like a home. And a weakling plant like this one — a drooping pine-thing that lay somewhere between a bonsai and Charlie Brown's Christmas tree — a weak-sister plant like this could go the dangerous other direction and confirm a tawdry, lonely life, and cause fits of uncontrollable weeping, tears coursing the beard.

There was nowhere to place it but on the floor. He put it in the far corner, though nothing here was far, wedged it in tighter with his foot, and wished it well. It had been inevitable; at some point he always bought his house a plant.

His favourite, in Tulsa, he'd brought in under Fournier's wary gaze the day after teammate Lonny Miles went up on the rape charge. The rape charge had upset him, he wasn't sure why. The girl — Jennifer — was in fact a girl, or looked it and acted it at least, being only seventeen. He'd met her at a party the night before the alleged crime and liked her, perhaps because in certain ways she reminded him of Leah. It wasn't the clear skin and large-eyed cuteness they shared, it was more the brain-package, the depth and brightness and humour in the eyes, the basic read on the situation that made you wonder what she was doing with a bunch of hockey players, himself included, and Lonny Miles in particular. A crunchy little detail, one Bonaduce would be willing to offer up if he was called as a witness at the trial, was that, from the look of them sitting there on the couch, Jennifer didn't seem to like Lonny much. It looked like she wanted to be at the party but not stuck with Lonny, thin-lipped, brash, loud laugher Lonny.

Bonaduce sensed some connection between yesterday's rape news and today's walking down the sidewalk with a new plant. He'd liked Jennifer, however briefly, and he'd never liked Lonny Miles. What made him like Lonny Miles even less was the way he'd smiled when he'd said this morning at practice, "She got into it." He'd spent the night in jail, been bailed by the owners, came to practice almost gloatingly. When asked by the guys what the hell happened, he picked up his head and superciliously scanned the room, which fell quiet, uncharismatic Lonny Miles from Sydney Mines getting maybe his first spotlight ever. The little smile was an arrogant smile and, when mixed with the Clint Eastwood–like "She got into it," worked to suggest a whole slime-bucket full of things: he was irresistible, she couldn't help liking it, the bitch was deranged and the rape charge was absurd and wouldn't stick, he was so hot-damn he didn't care anyway because all that mattered was that she "got into it."

The piece of slime that stuck to Bonaduce was the literal meaning of those words. For the words did admit to rape, or something close. Because they said this: at the beginning, she wasn't into it. How not-into-it she was was anyone's guess — Bonaduce couldn't help remembering her looking at Miles with something between tolerance and disgust — as was the kind of seduction, more like coercion, probably physical force, used by Lonny Miles.

Bonaduce realized that this — even *wanting* sex with a woman who was very not into it and didn't fucking even *like* you — was foreign territory to him. Jesus, who'd enjoy that sex? Why not go stick your dick into some gravel?

Thoughts such as these walked with him down the sidewalk with his new plant. It was almost three feet tall and rustled beside his ear. Her age wasn't an issue apparently, perhaps this being the South. But in the newspaper were blatantly disparaging remarks about hockey players and Canadians, and the fact that hardly anyone went to see these games anyway, as if the converse would somehow have excused the rape, as if the star quarterback from Oklahoma State would be above such charges.

He brought in the plant and Fournier, man of material simplicity, looked up like a lean wolf, instantly alert to excess. Bonaduce had recently joined his religion and yet here he was carting in this extraordinary bauble. It may as well have been a neon sculpture or ornamental barber's chair. Fournier watched him place it on the floor under the living-room window.

"Who will water this when we're gone?"

"I'll get someone."

This is all they ever said about it, Fournier being as sensitive as Bonaduce had always suspected.

It was called an umbrella plant. It was bushy and looked nothing like an umbrella, and he had no idea where it got that name. He looked down on it, fiddling a leaf between thumb and forefinger and on the verge of meditation, Fournier holding his tongue.

Here, this little Charlie Brown fern — Bonaduce had decided it was a fern — would not likely grant him the depth of friendly relationship the umbrella plant had. He'd kept it alive over the remaining Tulsa years, and bundled it off to his next stop back east, violating his own rule about starting fresh. It had uneven patches and rust spots now, but it stayed his buddy until, in his new place, a girlfriend poisoned it with tequila. He knew it was her and he knew it was deliberate. She secretly wanted control of his decor and didn't like that plant, or maybe it was his pure and simple affection for it.

### WHAT YOU NEED, CONTINUED

The first kind of toughness — it's what you need just to play the game. More a state of mind than body, you learn it as a kid or not at all — though you can see its birth in some Europeans over the course of a few seasons. It lets you play with a broken foot bone and not complain; it gives you dignity as you walk your chin to the dressing room to get it stitched, no freezing, so you miss no more than one shift. It lets you see pain as just another pebble in your shoe.

That's the key: it lets you see pain rather than feel it.

It's not as macho as it seems. In fact it's a trick. In the clash and speed of a game, things hardly hurt anyway. (I once took a skate on the forearm and didn't even know it until a guy smiling on the bench pointed at my blood-soaked sleeve.) But it's more than that. Like in war, where it's said a soldier's biggest fear is fear of cowardice, so it is on the bench surrounded by the guys: it's harder to show pain than it is to just sit on it.

In this way your pain is absorbed by the team. It's not a bad little trick.

And this first kind of toughness: when you walk into a bar, say, even if you aren't particularly witty, or sexy, or tough even, it lets you believe you're all of those. This belief shows in your face and in the way you speak, and makes people think you are those things too. Not all people, but enough so you get the rewards. You see this in guys again and again. You see complete schmoes almost become what they believe they are. It's not a bad trick, actually. It's one more thing you can do.


A hard and hurtful sun cut through the narrow ice-house windows, its rays deflecting off the saliva of Kirsten's bucking teeth into Big Jan's poetic goddamn hair, which baffled and trapped it.

God he was angry. He couldn't blame his mood on his little two-wine hangover. Nor could he blame it on this writing class. At least he wasn't afraid in it. People spoke English, he could hold his own. Though the day was coming when he would have to bring in a smash of work for them to tear apart. So far all he had were snippets, nonsense attempts at a novel that wasn't looking like a novel at all.

He even liked where the class was held, this old renovated ice house. It had thick stone walls you could lean your chair back against. It had *rafters*—how often could you use that word any more? The best part was this ancient oak table, must be fifteen feet long, for all to gather around, the kind of table you could imagine royalty supping at and tossing bones to dogs from.

He'd even almost enjoyed what they'd done this morning, spontaneous drills to sharpen their "artful incongruity." The more twisty and stupid-on-purpose he got with his stuff, the more Jan seemed to approve of it. This morning he'd come up with lines that went nowhere and fit into nothing:

My nose points to what isn't me

It was a shit-climb to the mountaintop, upon which sat a shit-shaped rock, which could well have been shit's temple

Life is a Cyst in Death's Immortal Flesh

Who put the Hale in the Bopp-shoo-Bopp-shoo-Bopp?

But this morning, because he suddenly liked Jan less, he liked his lines less, and the class less too. He'd thought her an ally, all her talk in class about getting at real stuff, the heart, and fuck everything else. Quote unquote. You trusted her saying this. She would've made a decent coach.

Before class they'd congregated in the lounge for coffee. Despite the hostile potential of Phil and Kirsten, something like camaraderie had been tempting the spirit of this group lately, maybe due to their "creative" as opposed to "academic" status. They'd begun referring to their academic counterparts as "inmates," this evolving from Bonaduce's joke that you didn't see those types much because they'd had themselves committed to the library. He'd said "libary," and they seemed to get it, appreciating self-deprecation though never going near it themselves.

The little creative team had huddled at the lounge bulletin board, sipping, reading a fresh notice of a PhD thesis having its oral defence. Bonaduce crowded in — some of these things were amazing, the language in them. This one you could understand. It was on Shakespeare. But it wasn't about themes, or poetic language, or characters. It was *speculation* about *possible* uses of the *trapdoor* in *early versions* of *some* plays Shakespeare *might* have written. The thesis was more than three hundred pages long, and Bonaduce suggested while hunched there that they should find this inmate and rescue him before he wasted the rest of his life. Phil supported Bonaduce with a snort, but otherwise no one said a thing.

Sure, maybe he'd been arrogant in saying it, and maybe you shouldn't make jokes in a public place about wasted lives, since the inmate in question turned out to be Kirsten's boyfriend. He couldn't blame her; in fact he admired her balls when she turned to him, the scabbard of her lip lifting to reveal her sword of teeth. She said simply, "Shakespeare's a waste of time. Hockey isn't. Oh." Her eyes were already dull, having dismissed him in advance.

He was ready to do sheepish and admit he was a pot caught calling her kettle-boy black, but before he could, Jan jumped in to lead Kirsten away by the shoulder, leaning into her like a friend, with a stage whisper for everyone's benefit that "our Robert has given up chasing his silly pucks, though perhaps a little late."

Well, now stop. *He* could belittle his life and his game, and it was only fair that Kirsten had her little whack at him, but Jan was not allowed. So, in class, still pissed off, ignoring most of the creativity drills, he wrote and reworked this:

Not that they ever will, but if anyone ever asked me which was more important, playing hockey or reading

Shakespeare, I will declare free from doubt: When you read a book you are nothing but a fan. And fans of books have nothing — nothing — over fans of hockey. That a puck is an utterly meaningless thing to chase is exactly the point. They might never think of it this way, but hockey fans are drawn to the spectacle of men who are the best in the land at using their bodies to fulfil *pure desire*. Pure, because these are guys who will basically kill to get at a puck, this chunk of dumb rubber the perfect symbol of worthlessness. It is so abstract, so pure in its meaninglessness, it is almost Japanese.

It got him thinking about them — fans. Generally, players didn't like them and didn't think about them much. But they didn't like to think about that either, about not liking the people who paid your salary, admired you, in some cases adored you. It was pretty simple, really. How can you respect anyone who likes you and doesn't even know you? If people hate you for your skin or uniform colour, it's of course more painful than if they *love* you for the same reason, but the scenario is similarly stupid.

There were lots of decent fans of course. Appreciators of the game. Guys who used to play themselves. Mums and dads who took their kids. The row of folks in their wheelchairs, some with heads resting over on their shoulders, others done up with team jackets, waving pennants. There were memorable, funny fans as well. Here, in Freddie Beach, twenty years ago, he'd forgotten about her — she was maybe sixty, floppy homemade hat in team colours, cowbell, tartan blanket on the lap, and most of all the big whisky-voice. She would pick quiet spots, ring her bell twice, and the fans would fall quieter still to hear her yell her weird stuff. *Hey, Seven. Yer mother still stink?* Another one he remembered, *Hey, Ref, that a banana?* Years later in a bar in Dayton the subject of this fan had come up and Bonaduce was surprised that other guys had all assumed that she was a weird old *he*. Anyway, lots of fans used the game to get their ya-yas out. Ripping shirts off and jumping up against the glass, leading cheers, picking fights, grenading the visitors' bench with cups of beer, whatever. In the Des Moines penalty box, Bonaduce had taken an empty mickey bottle off the helmet. His team went into the stands after the guy while he rested for a bit with his head between his knees.

In the lounge Bonaduce had nodded to Jan after her traitorous quip and said, "Yeah, me grow up." Then refilled his coffee and started down to the ice house. It was as close to a fight as he was going to get. He would be only nice. To Jan, to Kirsten, to Phil. To Toby and Leah and everybody. You get too tired for anything else.

He drove home with a kink in his neck after an awkward snooze in the library reading room. The chairs there were designed for sitting up; a guy should complain. Downtown at an intersection he found himself staring at a pack of kids. It took him five seconds to register that they were dressed as a witch, a Darth Vader, a what might have been Robin Hood. Jesus, Hallowe'en.

He pulled into a convenience store and spent far too much money on their whole stock of Mars bars. Screw the bags of little Hallowe'en-size bars, it was one night you could be a hero for not a lot of money. A real bar falling heavy from your hand, surprised muffled shout through the monster mask: *Wow, thanks.*

Marg and her sister and Toby were home, Marg and her sister on their way to a costume party. It was also a Friday night. In her white robe and pants, black belt and headband, Marg was a karate person, while her sister was a Bad Santa — your basic Santa outfit but with stitches on the face, toting a machine gun, bottle of whisky sticking out the pocket. Toby, slumped in the

living room starting a bottle of wine, and who Bonaduce realized was a sort of natural Bad Santa, wasn't going anywhere.

"Wanna come, Robert?" Marg asked, martial artist forcing
down a quick beer at the kitchen counter.

"Don't think so, thanks. I don't have a costume."

At this Toby snorted, and Marg shot him a look, the exchange
making Bonaduce see his creased pants and tight haircut. Not
bad, Toby lad.

The invitation was tempting, especially as he'd be here alone
with Toby otherwise. But he wouldn't know anyone, and Marg's
voice in asking hadn't been enthusiastic. He found an old salad
bowl in a kitchen cupboard, dumped the bars in it and came
back to the living room with that and an empty glass. Because
Toby would offer him some wine, he would accept, and Toby
would say, Well, go get yourself a glass then. Bringing the glass
in advance risked looking presumptuous and might lose him
his offer of wine, which would be fine. He set the bowl of bars
on the floor by the front door and switched on the porch light.
He found the Yahtzee score sheet and the dice, one still lost. He
hated playing with four, you had to reroll one die and remember
too much. He did like solo Yahtzee, however. It gave you a feel
for averages, and the duration of luck, which felt less like stamina than grace.

"No kids'll come," said Toby matter-of-factly, in the act of
rising to fill Bonaduce's glass.

"Why not?"

A car crunched into the drive, Marg and her sister banged
beer bottles on the counter and rushed out the back door, calling
goodbyes.

Toby answered as though Bonaduce were a kid himself.

"It's the Trans-Canada Highway, there's no streetlights, there's
a house only every hundred yards. The people around here are
poor and they drive their kids to the rich suburbs."

Well shit. Bonaduce eyed the bowl of Mars bars. As he did so the doorbell rang. He opened the door onto a two-and-a-half foot devil, a three-foot grim reaper and their Satanic mom. Ooo, Toby would hate him for this. He dropped a chocolate bar in their bags, empty so far, and in a childlike voice their mother sang a thank-you on her children's behalf.

"Maybe if," Bonaduce said, closing the door, "you know, maybe if the porch light's on, they'll come."

"Well there's going to be a *few*."

In the ensuing hour he was ready to concede this round to Toby, because only one more kid had come, and he was alone, tall enough to be fourteen, and under the tossed-on costume you could see quick hot eyes that looked less intent on candy than on vandalism.

Bonaduce picked up the empty wine bottle to take to the kitchen to rinse while Toby went down for another. Some CD of Toby's by a band called Dead Can Dance was on in honour of the night, though the music sounded basically Middle Eastern, a quarter-tone-wailing female singer backed by spacey ambient organ. As he washed out the bottle, he noticed the homemade label said "Mountain Frog '99," and he got a chuckle from it.

In the bathroom he found a garish red lipstick Marg's sister had used for her face blood. He smiled as he applied it to his nose. He liked Hallowe'en. He almost never got to enjoy one, there always seemed to be a game scheduled, the arena full of clowns and witches and team-colour harlequins, an extra buzz in the air. The nose began with just a small dot on the tip and then, what the hell, the whole schnozz, bright red. What was he? Maybe a wino.

He used to like those houses back in Winnipeg where instead of just dumping some candy in your bag they'd make you come inside and do something: sing, or a joke. Often they were European, or foreign-sounding at least, and they'd be dressed up too. Ten-year-old Bonaduce stumbling to get a song or a joke out, his buddies nervous or pissed off beside him. At one of these houses in his neighbourhood lived a boy — maybe he was twelve, maybe much older — in a wheelchair, and he'd sit there smiling like crazy, his head sort of flopped over and his fat hands palm up and unmoving on his thighs. Hallowe'en was the only time in the year you'd see him. Rumour had it his name was Jordy. Then one year Jordy wasn't there. In any case — Bonaduce finished the nose, even going up into the nostrils a tad — these people who invited the ghosts and goblins inside and made them come alive for their candy seemed to know something more about Hallowe'en than the rest did. Because, otherwise, these big-eyed four-year-olds upon whose heads parents had slammed a hat and mask, these little first-timers must be thinking, Holy, alls I do is go up there with this bag and they throw candy in it, why haven't we been doing this every night?

Toby snorted a kind of approval at Bonaduce's nose when he looked up from his display of bottle uncorking. Bonaduce lumbered over to read the label and this one was an Earth Spit '53. He laughed aloud at this and commented to Toby that his friend was pretty funny, to which Toby shrugged, noncommittal. The music got cranked up so that conversation was made difficult, and Toby wasn't pleased when the doorbell rang again and Bonaduce invited a Zorro (a Zorro! They must have a big ol' attic) and a princess inside. With a pretty good Irish wino accent, he demanded a joke or song of them, their teenaged sister or babysitter looking on nervously. They sang a quavering Row, Row, Row Your Boat, got three full-sized Mars bars each, and that was it for trick-or-treaters that night. Though Bonaduce himself hung in there till one a.m., the radio turned to what twenty-year-olds might be listening to at this moment, eating bars and sipping intermittently from a bottle of "Tidal Flats '02." No, he wasn't sipping, he caught himself gulping.

He put his hand over his mug, as if it was someone else offering to pour, then laughed, took his hand off.

This morning he'd been reading a book by Ven Begamudré, a male Asian Canadian writer writing about being a female soldier/ gourmet in Scotland. It was decent writing, but for some reason he'd grown cold and he couldn't get warm. He had been cold a lot lately. He saw how the bit of wine at night had helped warm him and smooth things. Beer was good after games with the boys, get the grin on, but wine was good alone, in the night. Mornings he felt gritty and more tired for it, even after two glasses. Last night he'd had a bucket-full. How soothing was alcohol, how thick the bandage, but then the bandage gets ripped off in the morning, how clear and hurtful this part was. His body felt beaten and shocked. So, no more drinking. It was just boredom. He shouldn't be drinking at all, he was in training, and he was, he was possibly — it just wasn't good for him right now. But no worry about making it a habit, he was too poor. Nor could he afford to keep stealing Toby's.

Nor was he all that worried he'd tossed last night's last swallow of wine against his wall.

This room, this bed, had become his place. His nasty little niche. Jesus, look at it. My, how he'd come down in the world. You get used to anything. Tired all the time, of company in general and Toby in particular, he read here, strummed here, lap-topped here, sipped wine here.

Paced here. He stopped himself. A three-step pace is ridiculous anyway. And it was a sham, an act — you can pretend all you want that you're a martyr and a prisoner but you're not and you know it.

He lay on his bed. Eyes can pace too. He pictured himself as a wolf in his forest den, a wolf who has eaten and is lying on his stomach, head on his paws. His eyes are open and looking, and his ears twitch at this sound or another, but the wolf is otherwise quite calm. Apparently waiting for something. But, being a dumb animal, he doesn't have a clue what it is.

He remembered last night deciding that his room was green. Years faded, it was one of those industrial almost-colours. Depending on the light, it was grey, or yellow, or even blue. But it was green, barely green. Last night he'd added the splash of red wine, a sudden impulse to see if wine would sink in, or drip down. It did both, a blob sinking in and the rest running down, an octopus body with skinny legs dangling to the floor.

If the ways of your own damn heart are hard to know, what dumb grin of red-lipped stupidity leads you to think you can know the heartways of anybody else?

How much of their anger is just anger at the past?

He ached picturing Jason's face. In the concrete corridor, in wet underwear, the steaming body. He'd seen clear as life that something of the father had created the boy and swelled in the boy's flesh...

But arrogant to assume this, and infantile to need it.

He lay back on his bed and closed his eyes. With the light off, his room was so dim that closing his eyes gave him perfect darkness. Which, if you cared to see things a certain way, could be a desirable and perfect thing. No comet, dreamcatcher, wine octopus. No stage.

⁌

*Oscar.*

Leah rose and quickly stepped into her clothes. Mornings it was her wont to linger here, choosing blouses, hair clasps, trying things in the mirror. Turning away from him — modestly? unconsciously? coyly? — when she removed underwear. Either not caring that he watched — because she did know he liked to watch — or perhaps understanding that a committed relationship legitimized his brand of voyeurism, if that is what it was called. Then she would stand at her writing desk and consult her day planner, review the human disasters on her schedule this week. After which she liked to lean on the windowsill, take in their view of the river over to the north side, gazing out, perhaps contemplating human suffering and the potential for freedom from it. It occurred to him this morning that maybe it was because Bob Bonaduce was over there on the north side that lately she hadn't been doing this.

This was simply not good. She was so knotted about Bob's being here and she could not talk about it. It was not good keeping such things inside. With prodding, Leah usually opened up. It didn't appear that Bob Bonaduce was going to take a hint and leave town. Or even well enough alone. Jason was knotted as well. Though it was harder to tell with him, due to Jason's knottiness in general. That was a horrible pun. It was like something a Bobby Bonaduce would say.

Wafts of coffee drifted up the stairs, his wake-up call. The timed coffee-maker one of the century's underappreciated inventions. Leah descended to pour herself her half-cup, which she would top with hot water, the coward.

He leapt up and peeked at her day planner, saw she likely wouldn't be heading out for an hour. She sometimes came back up with her coffee, so he quickly put on his robe and sweat pants. He no longer liked to be caught undressed. He realized he had become content to just cover up the ten pounds he seemed incapable of losing. Maybe it was fifteen pounds now. Maybe this year he would dust off the NordicTrack ski machine, or the stair-stepper.

Leah arrived back in their room. He felt the slightest hurt that she hadn't brought him up a cup of coffee. Not that she wouldn't happily do so if he was to ask. Would she just as happily doff her clothes if he were to ask?

"Leah?"

She raised her eyebrows for him while continuing to jot notes in her planner.

"I really think you should make amends with him."

Leah put her pen down flat and lifted her gaze out the window, across the river.

"What exactly does that mean? 'Make amends.'"

"Well, air it out. Talk. Make peace." He came upon a smart idea. "You know, instead of popping his balloon, you could help him pop it himself."

"He makes me see what a teenager I was."

What?

"Well, maybe that's not a bad thing."

Leah didn't respond. Uneasy, he was tempted to make a joke about Bobby Bonaduce the fountain of youth, but humour didn't seem right, didn't seem to enter into her current relationship with her ex. Her mood also prevented him from telling her what he'd planned to tell her, which was what an odd duck he'd decided Bob was during his last visit. After putting the strange gift of Dutch cheese in the fridge, he'd returned as she and Bob were blurting at each other about Gordie Howe. What he'd seen was Bonaduce as an Eighties man, being out of touch with every-thing dire about the Nineties. But then he seemed more Seventies, because he was so impractically naïve. On third thought, make that Sixties — the fellow was absurdly idealistic. No, wrong again, he was Fifties, just look at him. Okay, let's keep this going: the post-war simplicity of the Forties supplied the best description yet. Simplicity, or simplistic? He envisioned the pictures of sailors docking, getting off their ship, the certain looks on their faces, soon to be genuinely happy with wife and job and new barbecue.

Watching Leah and Bob hard at their argument, he'd still considered Bonaduce a good man, and maybe in the right, but he'd also understood that, twenty years ago, Leah had been intellectually slumming.

"Leah, I think you should call him."

"Why."

"For Jason. Even though he's twenty"—Oscar found himself voicing what he'd formulated—"and even though he never did have the man around as his father, the psychology of broken homes is complex, and gluey, and so maybe for Jason's sake you might consider, I don't know, normalizing diplomatic relations."

Leah stood gazing at the north side of the river.

"I will act as your ambassador if you like."

Leah staring across.

"Call the man. I can't stand your, your *mood* any more."

———

Sitting cross-legged on the bed, he glanced out his window, at the leafless trees through to the river. Knees sticking stiffly way up, he cradled a notepad over his crotch. Time to write something serious. Beside the bed a first cup of coffee steamed on a table he'd banged together out of two-by-fours and a serving tray he'd plucked from roadside garbage two houses down.

After a couple of sips and some staring into space, he wrote:

> The leafless trees looking black against the
> morning's frost.

He reached for his coffee, took a sip. It was a decent observation. Where it would go, who could tell, but those trees looked extremely black this morning even though you knew they were brown. Leafless? He crossed out "leafless." Jan's rule number one said that every word had to count. If there was frost, readers would assume leafless, wouldn't they? Unless they were evergreens. Hey, that-there frost was so white, even the *evar*greens looked black.

He changed it to:

The treetrunks looked black against the snow.

Because the idea, the effect, was snow, rather than frost. Then he crossed out "looked." Why did you need it? They *were* black against the snow. Though without the "looked" you might think the trees were in fact black, whereas "looked" suggested the optical illusion. Well, but, so what was the sentence about — the blackness, or the illusion of blackness? What *should* the sentence be about? Well, what should *any* fucking sentence be about. Settle down. Maybe once the paragraph got going he'd know. Maybe you shouldn't dwell too long on any particular —

"*Hey Marg.*" He heard Marg stop walking up the staircase.

"Yes?"

"*Get in here.*"

She came in smiling at his yell, she was a buddy. He had no shirt on, but he sensed this was okay, though some women weren't enamoured of body hair. And his, from the belt to the tops of his cheeks, didn't give your eye much of a break.

"What colour are those trees out there?"

"*Wow* this room is small."

"Welcome to my coffin."

"You hardly fit."

"Tell me what colour those trees are."

"That's a nice place for it." Margaret was looking at the dreamcatcher hanging low in the window. "Though if you hung it higher it'd, you know, be more up in the sky. Framed by the sky."

"No, there I can look right through it from bed."

"Why do you look through it?"

"So what colour are the trees?"

"Those?"

"What colour."

"I dunno. Brown?"

"No, I mean right now. Sitting against that white frost like that."

"Grey? The frost is almost gone."

"Shit. No, c'mon."

"How should *I* know. Charcoal? Charcoal. No, don't cross out what you had. What are you writing?"

"My novel. Until you ruined it."

"I just —"

"Marg. I'm kidding you."

Some people, when they go serious, it's like all their skin suddenly falls off and everything hurts. And they aren't so great to be with. He would've liked to tell Marg this, but she was serious at the moment.

### BOBO DOES THE TREES

BoBo Bombsaway was right tuckered after cuttin seven cord a hardwood usin only a ax. Choppin all them trees into finnicky eighteen inch chunks. But the wife Marg liked hers eighteen inches, heh heh. Though she yelled at him, why'd ya fuckin cut all them trees down? Cause they was too fuckin BLACK! he yelled back. An buy me a new chainsaw, woman! BoBo kicked at the old one, lyin there on the bed. These saws, once their teeth are mostly broke off, all they're good for is fixin cars.

•⤳

*Margaret.*

Robert opened her door and poked his head in like he knew she was awake. It was past midnight, maybe close to one. She'd heard him downstairs playing Yahtzee by himself, which he did a lot lately, head down and immersed sometimes for a couple of hours. Like he said, killing time. But she hadn't heard him climb the stairs, maybe she'd fallen asleep after all. She'd been lying in bed trying to decide whether or not to move out. Lately she'd gotten very tired of the general slovenliness of the place. Her sister was not around much, and Joyce was not around ever, and these bastards were trying to leave the cleaning to her, screw them. Jesus H, there was still deepcorner grunge from the tenants before them. And the aura of depression here lately, or was it just aimlessness? It had changed from what she first took to be a cool, healthy open quality, a letting things fall as they may. A "don't worry be happy" house mood. No TV, and that uniquely open gesture of Toby's when he unpinned his bedroom door and stashed it in the basement. But gradually this good house *mañana* had fallen to a lazy and wheedling "So I wonder what's to eat and who might get around to cooking it?" The guys, Robert too, would too easily tip into dinosaur ways and let themselves get waited on hand and foot and not even notice it was happening. Robert you might expect this of, and you might forgive it. Robert was kind, he would make it up in little ways he had. He would get all concerned, for instance, about how you talked — gently joking about how you, like, talked — and he would sincerely try to help you. Corny bugger.

Food smells too. She suspected she was allergic to the food smells of this house, they actually seemed to plug her up. When one of them did cook, it was all onions and grease smell for hours after. It went into the curtains, it smelled like years of grease in those curtains. Lately Robert had gotten into a habit of midnight popcorn. She could smell it again tonight.

And tension. Toby and Robert at each other, who knows why. They were quite a pair. Boys, play nice.

Toby was the last straw. She had slept with him three times now, and he was beginning to make demands and have expectations, though they'd promised well before the clothes were off that this would not happen. Rejection was such a hideous monster to him. Which was to be expected. But it would be impossible ever to tell him the truth, that his arm bothered her less than his drinking, or his being two inches shorter than her. He would still blame it on his arm. You could see how he used it as a magnifying glass, all hurts coming through it and burning him. Life was probably simpler that way.

As life would be simpler if she moved.

But then Robert's knock on the door, Robert poking his head into her plans. Her first thought was that he was going to read some of his novel to her. The second was that he'd discovered she'd slept with Toby and felt a little lonely because of it. The third was that they were going to talk about his illness.

He sat not at the foot of the bed this time but in the middle, and when she sat up, his arms opened and he was hugging her. All heavy and serious, his heart and body both. He felt even bigger than he looked. She had never felt a man like this. Hard as wood. Solid as ground. But denser, the moving blood in him somehow making him seem denser still.

Her breasts moulded to his shape, and she could feel his awareness of them. She pulled back a little and kissed him on the neck, small and soft, not clear what she wanted. There was something so passive about him and, despite the heaviness, so ready to change. To be led away like a dog.

He answered with his own identical little kiss on her neck. He removed his hand from her shoulder. What was he going to do with it? So softly she could hardly feel it, the hand was on her hair. Then it was pressing, huge and sad and gentle, spanning the back of her head, cupping it ear to ear. She resisted falling against the hand, trusting it fully, the way it cupped her head, holding all the thoughts she might ever have.

Then he sighed, long and low. The release of something deep. At its sound she knew nothing more would come of this night, nothing physical. But neither did he speak. He squeezed her head again, and once more kissed her neck. She pecked his neck back, identically, almost as a joke, but one he didn't get, because he sighed again sadly. It was all quite dramatic, really, as he got up in a hurry then and stood watching her in the darkness, and then went to the door and watched her some more, then left. Alone once more, she felt herself glad it had happened, whatever it was.

Still she thought of moving. Where to go. Jesus H, after this house, where. Alone?

The image of Robert and her sharing a place scared her. Not because it was a naturally bad idea, but because of how the image grew, and flipped. First it was them at home, a living room, smiling together over a glass of wine that wasn't Toby's, the Yahtzee dice on an elegant table. Then it was her standing behind him, able to see only the back of his head, which wobbled with the movement. She was pushing his wheelchair.

———

Bespectacled Patrick presenting. After these couple of months, Bonaduce understood half of it. Bits and pieces he caught himself actually enjoying. Getting the hang of it was no small source of pride. You spend time with this stuff, you witness yourself falling into word-mode too. In class on occasion he even caught himself clucking and taking ironic offence, a regulation grad student.

Normally shy Patrick had worked himself into a fever of confidence. Speaking, he looked over people's heads lest errant eye contact dam his stream of words.

"Ideologically embodied in object." That mean "symbolic," Patrick? A Marxist hidden inside every shovel? A dope in every hockey stick?

"Sub-meta-fictional." Patrick, c'mon Patrick, that translates as "under above the story."

Presentation finished, fielding questions, Patrick fell to nervous defence. He stuttered into sentences that began "I didn't mean to imply," which was like tossing blood bags to sharks. Phil slouched diagonally in his chair, radiating boredom, eyes taking in the shape of the room, as in: This discussion occupies not a lot of my brain. The posture worked. The others, Patrick too, were as hungry for Phil's approval as they were for Gail Smith's. In hockey as well you saw the one or two guys who worked the attitude and got to be daddy, backing it up not with words, but with goals or violence.

It was still mostly bullshit. The circle of wristwatches ticked, and Bonaduce sat occasionally in awe, generally asleep, other times nodding as if he agreed, but hating these long dips into fakery. He was intimate with everyone's jewellery, hair-habits, moles. (Phil had a hefty wart on his temple, at which he pictured himself pointing and laughing if things ever got rough between them.) He let himself x-ray Kirsten's limp sweater, arriving at a likely sense of her pair, and shame when this image stirred the nether zone. Sometimes he winced with the wasted time — What was Jason doing right now? Where was, where was his fucking Utica *money*? — but stayed willing to encounter language at its best, hearing new groups of words and feeling little wafts of oxygen coming off his understandings. He'd begun jotting down phrases, and words to look up. You never knew what you might use writing a novel, even one about hockey. But mostly he suffered a drifting mind, one which was repeatedly elbowed in the snout by fear. Once he woke hearing someone quote, "as he waited for his cataracts to develop so he could have the operation," and he decided that this described the sensation of sitting in this room with these people.

"Disfunction of the male–female." This from Doctor Gail, summing up. Disfunction at Gender Junction. Almost an old blues line there, What's the function, of the junction? Hey, what's better, Gail, "Disfunction of the male–female" or "Smash-up at the hairy-ugly"? C'mon, Gail.

Look up:

> nascent
> concomitant (sp?)
> self-reflexive (sounds kinky)
> quotidian

Neat Phrases:

> delicate with parody
> gently hyperbolized diction
> rife with serious play

It was UNB's third or fourth home game. Dalhousie in town to do battle. Bonaduce lined up like a loner to buy a single ticket. Not looking right or left. Checking out his shoe tops.

He sat surrounded by empty seats in the thirtieth row, feeling foolish, collar turned up, flinching into himself whenever Jason skated back to the bench. Averting his own eyes as if this would hide him from his son's.

He still hadn't tried calling him, not since outside the dressing room. The longer he left it, the more foolish he felt and the harder it got — it was one of those.

Doubtful that in the heat of the game the boy would catch sight of him. And Jason's back was almost always turned — he wasn't getting off the bench much. Jesus, the fourth line. Number 19. BONADUCE in red letters.

This arena could seat four thousand, and tonight there were maybe three hundred, clustered at ice level behind the benches. A few scattered, like Bonaduce. He knew the players could feel it too: like a lone rider on a bus, like a BB in a boxcar. Sounds echoed, haunted. Most of the crowd were students who wanted to cheer and party, but what should have been a crowd's roar was thin and tinny and worse than nothing, a reminder of what it wasn't. It made everything you did on the ice feel a little apologetic.

Fourth line and killed penalties. Here was a guy with pro ambitions, a nobody in a league not bothered much by scouts to begin with. Though you never knew. He did have the size and speed. And guys did suddenly "get good," as if their bodies found some dormant source grace or oomph that clicks like it had been there all along. But for now Jason was likely on the fourth line for a reason.

There was Whetter, pacing behind the bench in his cheap suit and tie, as nervous and frustrated as any coach anywhere. Bonaduce hadn't called him either. Had Whetter bothered to pursue the matter of his eligibility, or had his disappearance been a relief? Maybe he would saunter down after the game, have a chat. Maybe he wouldn't. Some avenues of life here were embarrassing to walk.

By the third period he understood. Jason was a right-winger, and the three right-wingers ahead of him were maybe the three best guys on the team. Jesus, luck of the draw. All Jason needed was somebody to get injured. Then step in, pop a few goals, make the newly healed guy work to dislodge you. It could happen. The first-line right-winger, guy named Harrington, Bonaduce hated from the getgo. A bony, haughty guy, wouldn't go near a corner, and both times after both his goals he cruised to centre ice doing a white man's try at a touchdown dance before letting the other guys high-five with him. Harrington was the kind of guy who could break an arm and no one on the team would mind.

The Reds won six-four. For a close game it was boring. Dalhousie was a bunch of small skill-guys in yellow uniforms. The refs let the bigger Reds get away with lots of clutch-and-grab. Jason would have been effective in a game like this. If he focused on defence he could be a small Bob Gainey, a guy so unflashy yet so bothersome he was noticed only by the other team.

Bonaduce rose from his seat ready for a beer. But, wait, he hadn't earned it, he hadn't played. Smiling, he saw he was nothing but a dog, salivating at a buzzer at the end of a game.


*Oscar.*

Bonaduce called just as Peter Mansbridge announced the top stories on the ten o'clock News. Bob had a knack for putting a wedge in a man's routine, which, while theoretically not a bad thing, could be irritating. Phone to his ear, Oscar tried to watch the News as well.

"So how're things there, Oscar old man?"

"...Great..." Kosovo had proved a shameful mess. Another mass grave with all fingers pointing to—

"Sorry for that bit of kerfuffle with Leah the other day. Last week, whenever."

"Not a problem..." He should tell him it was Leah who had felt badly about it. Leah should be apologizing to you. The look on her face, the staring-at-nothing for ten minutes. It had given him a jealous pang.

"How was the cheese?"

"Absolutely fantastic. Thank you."

"Oscar, I was wondering. I really have to get in shape here before playing with UNB and I was wondering if you knew of any oldtimers' teams. I need a contact. You know, our age, guys who play, friends of yours—"

Oscar sighed and muted the TV.

"—someone I could call to see if I could get on a team. My eligibility's still up in the air, but if I don't get on the ice soon, well..."

There was loud laughing and banging in the background, and he noticed now that Bonaduce had been close to shouting all of this.

"Where are you?"

"At the arena. Aitken Centre. Jason just had a game."

"Oh! Right, right!" He probably should be going to these games but he was fairly certain Jason didn't want him to. And Leah wouldn't go near the place. He could go with Bonaduce, of course. Join the mess.

"Did he win?"

"You know it."

His attempt, last week, to talk with Jason about this mess had been a parody of concerned parent interrogating mute youth. "So your father's in town!" "Yeah." "Quite a surprise?" "I guess." "And I understand he's going to be playing on your team?" "I dunno." "Well, how do you feel about that?" Jason at the fridge gulping milk from the carton and, to complete the sitcom scene, shrugging. Impatient, Oscar had repeated himself. "No, how do you *feel* about it?" Equally impatient, Jason met his eye and said, "I don't *know*." And Oscar felt stupid. As if knowing how you felt was a simple thing, and Jason hadn't been accurate the first time.

"And Jace had a few good shifts. They're playing him on sort of a checking line. And penalty-killing. I guess he's your basic digger."

Oscar could tell from the man's voice that he and Jason still hadn't spoken. Bonaduce was slurring, it sounded like. Not good. You could imagine the fellow in the bleachers sipping rum from a flask. He had the compassionate urge to tell Bob he shouldn't take Jason's silences personally because his son was as a rule quiet and, on top of that, simply shy, emotion not being one of the lad's skills. But Oscar couldn't locate the delicate way to tell a father something so elementary about his own child.

"Well, that's right, he's certainly always been eager about the game." He felt awkward having nothing more technical to offer. He also would've liked to add that Jason was especially shy around other men. But this might imply the equation of Jason having grown up with the role model *in absentia*. There was so much you couldn't say.

Jason had smiled and shrugged again for him as he put back the milk, shut the fridge and left the kitchen. There'd been something of the father in this and other gestures — Oscar could see this now. Traces of Bonaduce in the latent power of Jason's legs and arms, and in his almost musical striding away. Jason "carried himself well." As in Bonaduce dancing. In such synchronization one could sense invisible, internal juggling, bowling pins kept effortlessly in the air. There are those who can walk and chew gum at the same time.

In any case, in the kitchen, watching Jason move, Oscar had suddenly felt a more solid presence of Bob Bonaduce in town.

"I do know a couple of oldtimers players. Not friends exactly. I don't know if their teams are filled up or whatever, or how that might work, but there's this fellow at the office, Andrew Frenette. Andy Frenette."

"Great."

"You want his number?"

"Please." A pause. "Actually, I don't have a pen or anything."

Oscar suggested that he'd get Andy to call him. Bob sounded doubtful, indeed he pulled away to ask passersby for pens, but in the end he let himself be assured that Frenette would call.

"From the sounds of it" — Oscar heard himself chuckle raucously into the phone — "they have quite a colourful crew. Andy tells me a good many of them are rural lads, as he calls them, and the little trips they take for tournaments and what have you tend to the, shall we say, wild-and-crazy."

"Sounds good."

"One fellow, in fact, according to Andy, one fellow, a tough character, was convicted, along with his uncle — this was some years back, but — convicted for raising fighting dogs. Outside of Moncton. Dogs for dogfights, gambling. Can you imagine?"

"Well you probably wouldn't want to tangle with a lad like that."

"I should say you wouldn't." Not that "tangle" was something Oscar imagined doing with any lad at all.

"Oscar? I should go. But hey, we should do it again some night soon. Whatever it was we did the last time. Rockin Rodeo."

"Some night soon, Bob." Actually, why not? Beer, music, discussions never remotely crucial. Though why was it that talking to this man made him feel lonelier, more friendless, than ever?

"Oscar? Sounds good."

———

Everyone was asleep when Bonaduce got home. In the arena parking lot, his car hadn't started and he'd fiddled under the hood with it and ended up wearing down the battery. He'd had to collar someone for a jump. He'd cut his finger on the cable. He was tired, gritty and cold.

He washed his hands at the kitchen sink, eyeing the bottle of wine on the counter. White wine, a rare thing, labelled "Beard Filtered '72." He left the wine and took the half-bowl of cold popcorn into the living room. Marg's laptop was there.

story about a guy, in the kitchen cuts his finger to the bone and washing it sees his bone is made of what turns out to be pure diamond. After some thought he amputates it, sells the diamond-bone, gets enough to buy a house, etc. Gets used to the house of course, cuts off and sells another finger. Lives high for a year, nice car, sea cruise. Sells off a little toe, another finger, etc., gets to the point where he weighs lifestyle against healthy body, ends up with one arm and legless in a motorized wheelchair, but has private jet, tropical island, servants, women. Maybe end it with him waggling his lower jaw in the mirror, wondering if he needs it. Rife with play, use gently hyperbolized diction.

He woke earlier than usual, senses already attuned to — what? Maybe it was the muffled highway traffic. Maybe it was the soft light coming through the window frost.

No, it was outside. He got up to an elbow and looked. It was snow. The first real snow. Wonderful, a wonderful sight. As always. Didn't matter where you were, what your life was like. Look at that. Winter wonderland, get the toboggan, the skates, the hot chocolate.

Pause first, settle the kid-in-you. Look at the world turned white. It felt like everyone's good fortune. You could almost smell it through the window.

This wasn't much more than an inch or two. It was only early November. You could still see the spikes of cut hay. But nice all the same. He wanted to wake somebody up, get Marg up and tell her. It was still snowing lightly, they might get a proper dump after all.

What was that red blotch? Who'd spilled paint in the middle of — There was blood out there in the field. Blood is what it had to be. He dressed quickly, plugged in the kettle on his way through the kitchen, pulled on his leather coat. He had no gloves or scarf or boots yet. He went round back, past the pile of beer cases, now with snow on it, the cardboard would shmush when it melted, a nightmare taking them back — he'd get on that today. He'd claim the money for gas for all the trips to town.

Through sneakers you could feel the snow's cold. He approached the red, a two-foot splotch that faded to pink at the edges. It was some animal's smeared meal. He stood over it. He wouldn't have seen it without the background of snow. Canvas for an intense little painting. Bits of fur, anonymous brown. One thin clean bone, curved, a rib. Just beyond the smear a furry foot. He found a twig and stooped to prod what might be the foot of a rabbit? gopher? cat? He decided rabbit. It must have happened recently, no more than an hour ago, judging from the way this lightly falling snow was covering it up. Bonaduce thought he could remember hearing, in his dawn dreaming, the faint ragged growls, the piping screams. It had happened under the fuzzy cartoon comet.

He stood and surveyed the surrounding fields. For what, he didn't know. Cold, he tucked himself deeper into his coat and walked back for his coffee. Maybe this happened all the time, you just needed snow to see the blood, it was a battlefield out here, a charnel ground. Almost funny: this was the first wildlife he'd seen from his window.

He considered going back with a baggie for the foot. Let it dry, hang it from his rearview all stained and beaten up, and kind of intense for that. Though what would such a thing have to do with luck?

Ideas:

she looked at him with eyes that were two tunnels to the sun. (tunnels to hell?) (tunnels to nothing?)

Man stroking a rabbit's foot with a vigour unknown to the sane

The Maritime region's lack of good restaurants is a sure indicator of cannibalism in some form. Possibly only psychological. Or even psychic.

The night of the big grad party he started out shaky but got calmer with time. The shakiness came from two phone calls. The second call, right before the party, was Oscar's buddy Andy Frenette calling about oldtimer hockey. According to Frenette, not only his team but all the oldtimer teams in town were to his knowledge full, too full in fact. Guys paid to play and were protective of their icetime. Bonaduce asking, You sure? and finally as a last resort sliding in how he'd played pro, so maybe some team would...But this guy Frenette says, No, no, I heard about ya, Oscar told me, thing is we got some pretty good fellas too, and winning ain't all that important in this league here, just a good time. Bonaduce is now gutfrozen with shame. Hanging up, he heard his Tiny Tim words to himself: Nobody, not even old hackers, wants me on their team.

He shrugged that call off and showered, and got Marg going, and the party turned out well enough. Nice just to relax in wealthy digs for an evening. The solid comfy chairs, the sinky cream carpet. Grad students' eyes going big at such finger food: shrimp, fancy cheese, the see-through ham with the Italian name, toothpicked to green melon. Everything tasteful. On the stereo a medium jazz no one could argue with.

Marg didn't say much, maybe she was intimidated. Maybe in their midst she could hear herself and how often she said "like" and "I mean." Marg working on that wouldn't be a bad thing. She'd earn more respect, people would see past the valley girl to someone most likely smarter than they were. In any case, despite her looking at him a bit too close for his comfort these days, she seemed okay being left pretty much on her own while he nibbled, and sipped his limit of two beers, and listened in on conversations more than added to them. He had nothing much to say. And he couldn't quite get over the morning's phone call, Leah.

She had called him, finally. Her voice warm, soft. It followed him now to the fridge as he hunted more shrimp. It followed him to the bathroom, her voice was in the mirror behind his face as he washed his hands. Leah apologizing. Admitting to her confusion about him being here in general. Suggesting they meet. Somewhere where they wouldn't be seen and interrupted and nudged off the matter at hand. She named a motel restaurant off the highway, twenty minutes out of town.

The party rolled along fine, any nastiness being confined to the professors, of which there were eight. The main participants of one duke-up were none other than his own Gail Smith and Big Jan Dionne. The spat — all smiles and edge — was about creative writing versus literary criticism, which Bonaduce considered apples and bananas but didn't say so, and good old Jan stated the obvious, that without the creative there'd be nothing to crit, but she said it in the properly deluxe way. Apropos of something else, Jan got off another one, something that made him reconsider the books he was up to his eyeballs not reading. She said, "If what you read doesn't change you for the better, why read it?" Bonaduce and a few gathered others gave this rhetorical grape some silence and a nod. But Gail Smith turned it into a raisin by asking how one could possibly know what might change one until one's read it? She looked Jan Dionne in the eye and shook her head. Eager nods now, a snicker. For the *coup de grâce* Smith turned to the nut dish and said, "Plato died, get over it," and walked away.

Bonaduce found other sparring matches worth attending. He almost liked this world. They had guts and a willingness to scuffle. The party was at Doctor Professor Daniel Kirk's house, and another prof — a Professor Tillmann, Classics — arrived wearing no less than a black cape. He entered, took in the furnishings and then host Kirk, and announced in a fey, ballsy way, "A retentive, at play!" You could see Kirk's tight humour had no room for this, or maybe they knew each other's secrets and the remark was a get-back. Kirk mumbled something about the phantom of the opera, but it was clear that Tillmann was the type who loved anyone saying anything about him.

Other than Smith, no professors talked to Big Jan, or maybe it was the other way around. In any case she was surrounded by students, and seemed part and parcel with them, though cerebrally taller perhaps, something of Socrates-in-the-grove about her, except that she laughed too much, too eager with the young jokes. Once, on her way to the bathroom, Bonaduce grabbed her and pulled her into the dining room to dance to a dumb old Dr. Hook song. She was game enough, though disturbed by the question of sex — them so close in age, of course it's going to be in the air. He had no way of reassuring her that his intentions were only fun, that she was nice but — but she could in no way compete with Leah, whose soft voice wasn't leaving him tonight, whose body he —

Where was his head, what was he thinking? It had only been a phone call. As if it meant anything. Someone treats you like a human and you respond like a dog. And what about Oscar?

But a decent party. He even had a word with Phuckphace Phil, Bonaduce first humbling himself by plunking down on the couch and asking him outright, "What the hell does *deconstruction* mean, Phil?" In this world such a gesture was the animal equivalent of approaching with underbelly exposed. Bonaduce sort of knew the answer, but Phil enjoyed the chance to say, "If we liken any given piece of text to a sphere, around which one visits its context, historical and current, as well as the reader's pre- and misconceptions," and so on. When Bonaduce, friendly hockey guy, asked near the end if this meant keeping an eye peeled to just who's doing the reading and the writing, Phil paused and thought and nodded in tentative agreement. When Bonaduce asked if Phil'd mind getting him a Moosehead, because his leg had for some reason gone all wobbly, Phil did so in good humour, and Bonaduce knew he had maybe an odd friend in the making, one who would in any case laugh when asked if he'd sell him an essay.

Otherwise he enjoyed his second beer and came downstairs with the guitar he found. It surprised everyone all to hell, like they'd never seen a guitar or heard Jerry Lee Lewis before. He had a way of doing a guitar like Jerry Lee did a piano, the machine-gun thing and, despite each of them having an old dusty book up their ass, since this was the Maritimes they eventually did get into it.


*Margaret.*
He was boyish asking her and had to joke about it. Pointing to where it said "Mr. Bonaduce and Friend" on the xerox sheet, he said if he went Friendless it would be a waste of free booze and food, and she was looking frail these days, which they both knew was so not true. He said she didn't have to see it as "a date" if she didn't want to, him using that word at all showing their ages again. She told him, "Robert, I am definitely seeing this as a *date*." He seemed embarrassed enough, asking at all. She wondered what it meant, though, the difference between date and non. A corsage? A smooch goodnight at her bedroom door? He was acting as though the other night in her bedroom had never happened.

Robert explained that this was a yearly event, the profs hosting the students. A prof supplied a house, the English Department supplied supplies. On the drive over, more than once he asked himself aloud why he was even going. He liked no one, he didn't fit in. He did want her to meet his creative writing prof, Jan, who he described as "a regular guy." He looked serious saying this. Knowing she still played with the idea of grad school, he added that this was a chance to see for herself how boring that world was, how amazingly neurotically boring. A real spectacle, the rest of the world wouldn't believe it, especially how they talked, it was like a Monty Python parody. Archaeology might be different — it was bones, not words — but he bet it was the same. This rant seemed to get Robert excited about going.

She'd planned to use the drive over to get into the illness question. And the wife question. And their long and serious hugging too. But watching him jolly at the wheel, joking himself out of his nervousness about this bad-party and their non-date, she decided to wait till the drive back. She hadn't told him about his friend Fournier's call, it had been weeks now and she'd left it too long. But she'd been watching him closely, how he moved and spoke. When she'd proposed to Fournier that maybe he was getting better, Fournier had paused and at least considered this. He told her his girlfriend, Kim, said MS could go into remission but it never went away. Mostly Fournier emphasized, actually raising his voice at her, that "if you're a friend, Bonaduce has to fucking look after himself, okay?"

These words had stayed with her as she watched Robert and his late nights, his obvious bouts with Toby's wine, and now through the party. Late in the evening she heard him drop a beer bottle in the kitchen — Was that him drunk or sick or an honest mistake? He laughed, he was confident, he'd either drunk away his nervousness with these people or he knew how to hide it. He and his professor, Jan, were the only ones who had the guts to dance, and he was stumbling as he twirled her. He had to be pretty drunk to go right into a bedroom upstairs and come down with a guitar. He started to sing, and everyone was embarrassed for him, and then a guy named Phil started to sing along mockingly and now she hated these people. She started to sing too, but seriously. She wasn't good at it, but hell she was on a *date* here and this was her fella, and ten minutes later everyone but the most shy were bellowing away and it got uncool *not* to sing. Good for him.

The last to leave, they drove home at three, trying to see Hale-Bopp through the dirty windshield. Robert was funny, declaring astronomers had the best jobs in the world, "teams of mountaintop nerds and throb-heads" up in their observatories, where they invented liqueurs and named things Dog Star and Hale-Bopp and Johnson's Worm Hole, which they claimed *sucks in everything, including light and time*; giggling, their eyes swimming behind lenses like plums in milk, they put out press releases saying that that comet out there, let's see, what should we tell them? yeah, it's made of *dirt and ice*, yeah, but that's only what we can *see* — inside, we suspect there's this giant magic *surprise*, something that should, if our predictions are right, make cults in California castrate then shoot themselves.

When they finally clattered into the kitchen she was an inch away from joking to him that he partied pretty hard for a *married man*. Or even venturing, Care to come up for another *hug*? But Robert's velocity through the door kept him going down the hall and lurching off to bed. He did look suddenly exhausted, as if all evening he'd kept his body propped up to perform, and at last he could relax. He slurred a goodnight, and when he slowed up to look back over his shoulder and smile at her, he was staggering.

Saturday night, UNB versus St. Mary's. Jason had one shift in the first period and none in the second, after which the game was tied at three. Close games you don't play your weaker players.

If UNB lost, he'd go down and talk to Whetter. If they won, he wouldn't.

The Reds lost six to three. Jason got on near the end, only to take a cheap shot in the face and leave the game with a towel pressed to his mouth. At the buzzer the guys clomped mad down the tunnel to the dressing room while Whetter lingered at the bench to argue a bad call with the ref, who listened patiently, eyeing his tunnel across the ice, looking like he wanted a beer. Whetter finished with a friendly enough "I dunno, Dave." He turned away and found Bonaduce there waiting with his hand out.

"Hiya. Too bad there's a third period sometimes."

"God, yes." Whetter shook his hand and stared angrily at the wet rubber floor. "But it'll come. It'll come."

"It will. I was wondering if you looked into that matter of my—"

"Only two games left."

Bonaduce nodded as if he knew what this meant.

"February fourteen, you're free. We phoned around. You left a sinking ship there in Utica, eh?"

"Sure did."

"Since you didn't play from mid-February, it seems by then you'll have sat out your year in effect. You were still under contract of sorts, but it's a technicality I think we'd survive."

"Hey. Good stuff." Only by feeling good news flood his body did he realize how rare good news had been.

"Not that it'll be an issue."

"No?"

"Because by then we only have two games left in the season."

"But, and the playoffs."

"We need more your kind of optimism." Whetter smiled and looked up at him for the first time.

"I'll be there."

"Well, hang on. Thing is, you still can't practise. Not officially. So no way you'll be in game shape. Two games won't give you that either."

"I'll get on with an oldtimers team, skate my butt off."

"Maybe. Sure." Whetter hesitated. "What I really wanted to ask is a favour. After we talked, it hit me. But no one had your phone number. Not even Jason." A brief but questioning look from the younger man. "He said you were here incognito."

"I've been hittin' the books, eh?" Bonaduce smiled so as to let Whetter know he'd also been having himself some fun. It was suddenly strange, the two of them talking here, tiny in the bottom of this immense building shaped like a funnel, surrounded on all sides by empty seats. Two men in blue uniforms with brooms were way up top, beginning with the highest row. When they knocked over an empty Coke cup, you could hear it.

Jason could have got his number from all sorts of places.

"Anyway, the obvious thing was to ask you to be an assistant coach. The defence coach. Ever thought of coaching?"

They turned and started through the mouth of the tunnel. Bonaduce lagging behind, wanting to hear this but not wanting to go all the way to the dressing-room door.

"Thought of it." Thought he'd hate it. Telling the guys what to do, shoved you right out of the loop. Guys, management. "Sounds good."

"And that way you could get some ice. Practise without really practising. Scrimmage even, who's gonna know."

"Sounds good."

"So maybe you get in shape and maybe we use you."

"Sounds great."

"Puts Jason in a position, the boys might poke a bit of fun, but he wouldn't mind that, I don't think."

"No problem there."

"He's a good lad."

"Hey."

"Took a good one on the mouth tonight."

"Happens."

"And he'll get his chance to play."

"Good stuff."

"Whoops, gotcha—" Whetter had him by the arm.

"Tripped on piece of mat there."

Bonaduce stamped his foot on the culprit. He'd tripped, sending Jason in alone with the perfect pass, Jace tucks it upstairs to win the game and send them into the playoffs, he circles back to whack Assistant Playing Coach Dad on the ass like a buddy.

Set a guy up, no matter how much he hates you he has to come and whack you on the ass.

·⤙

Ideas:

> Castrated men shed their containers to chase the
> holy comet. We see them as the silly-dead.

> Ball of ice, keeping its distance from the sun. Snow-
> ball in hell.

> these words become a line
> that turns into a poem I need
> for Big J to give me an A
> so I will be allowed to stay
> and play
> wiff the boy I wuv

"Whatever happened to subtlety?" Toby says, chewing, the blank face of the professional passive-aggressive.

Sometimes you know you've been insulted. Toby. Man. He could get to you.

You cash your little teaching cheque, you make a choice between the used snow tires you're going to need any day now and a Mexican take-out spree for the house. To celebrate your new, secret, unpaid job of assistant coach — and also Frenette calling you last night after all and you going out with his team, a weird experience despite scoring your first official oldtimer goal. To celebrate all this you arrive with a double box of beer and four bags of Mexican, spiced extra hot. The start of a good night for the house: Marg, Beth, Rod, even Joyce was home to sit down for this. A hissing of beer tops and clinking of bottles, and everyone's just fine, except Toby, who suddenly hates spicy. He informs his housemates that its only purpose is to hide the taste of bad meat in poor hot countries and bullshit like this, pure Tobyness to knock in one fell swoop not only you for buying his dinner, but also any country, from Thailand to Togo, for enjoying a bit of pepper in the mouth and sweat on the brow. Then, Whatever happened to subtlety? Looking right at you as you shovel the rellenos in. You can now not brag, as you'd been gearing up to, about how in Tulsa you would chop jalapeños right into your scrambled eggs and could even gobble one of the buggers straight. Sure, macho sneer at boredom perhaps is all it was, but why not give the mouth a little hip-hop.

You had to hand it to Toby. It's a rare spice-wimp with the pills to turn the tables on everyone else. Almost made you stop chewing and feel your numb tongue, almost made you feel like a tasteless beast because it was true, you could in fact no longer taste the refried beans. Which almost made you say something very unsubtle to the one-armed bastard. But there he was, opening up another of his bottles of wine for everyone. Then going to his cupboard and coming back with a big bag of ketchup potato chips to eat.

He watched Toby eat his junk, his two-buck bag of treasure wedged in his lap, not offering any. Greasy shitty red-coloured crispies. You could see the link between food and body. It wasn't hard to connect Toby's shit-food with his shit-spirit. It wasn't farfetched. You are what you stuff down the hatch.

In Rochester, briefly, there'd been Yoshi, that Japanese winger. Purportedly a huge star in Japan, the best there ever. He had NHL speed, for sure, but aside from speed he had nothing. Too scared to relax into the flow, too used to stardom to recognize his new status as average guy, and therefore unable to adapt and learn. But the main thing was his undeniable foreignness — which Bonaduce put down to food. You could see it. The way he skated wasn't meat, it was fish. You could see seaweed in the way he sat inscrutably in the dressing room. Noodles in the attitude, tofu in the shyness. You knew you couldn't really see anything so exact as that, but Yoshi was definitely marked by a general dietary weirdness. Same with the Russians. Wooden bread, tough bad meat. The spoke like they ate.

Toby sitting here with his rancid, pinched, cellophane thoughts.

•➔

## Fuel
### — by Robert Bonafide

Whether dogfood or spice, food is a window on the soul, so on roadtrips, in restaurant after restaurant, it's impossible not to get to know your teammates in this way. Tommy, your defense partner, with his taboo about any vegetable — amazing he stayed alive let alone so nimble and bashing. There was Ray, who loved pizza, but only without the tomato sauce, said he couldn't stomach it (no matter how many times he got yelled at for contradicting himself by *eating the tomatoes in his fucking salad*). A lot of pizza goes down in motels after games, but with Ray around you couldn't just say "large works" into the phone, you had to explain twice to some guy with a heavy accent. Or you'd be in a real city and want to hit a sushi place and two thirds of the guys won't even bother responding to the suggestion, won't even try the word out in their brain, even after you explain how they can get teriyaki there, which they'll love, it's barbecue. But the unstated thing looms about hanging together as a team, and once more you have to forgo sushi for the steak joint, all dark and done up like a gold chain in black chest hair.

Guys who never eat breakfast, guys who only eat breakfast. Some guys, enormous cheapskates, banking their per diem while in the restaurant they order nothing and eat the table's basket of buns and breadsticks and butter, and then half your fries. Some guys with what might be actual allergies, JD with a bad one for anything wheat, maybe it was even Crohn's, he did eventually have an operation after getting traded to Phoenix — no matter, he was hated for being a pain to find a restaurant with. Some guys eating ugly with their mouths open. Some prim with little knives and forks in big hammy hands. Some eating at private tables — coaches, management. Some dumping ketchup without caring what it landed on. Some don't talk while they eat, some can't shut up. A few have a butt going in the ashtray while they stab at six a.m. eggs — though you don't see this much any more. Nor do you see as much carefree guzzling after games.

It seems the younger guys have learned about food, what it does. You hear words like "amino acids." "Complex carbohydrates." Last year, last road trip in my playing career perhaps, enough guys expressed interest in hitting a health-food store on the way out of Wheeling that they actually got the bus driver to stop. I watched the old coach sitting waiting for them, brow knit and staring, like his guys were in there looking at porno or astrophysics or something equally out of his league.

He was exhausted, he should sleep. Leah tomorrow. Leah, road-side motel.

He closed the laptop, thinking: Recipes. He should put in some recipes, these days every novel had them. So put some in, put in some genuine hockey player recipes: Mac 'n' Cheese With Big Chunks of Meat. Spagetty With Tomato Sauce On It. Potatoes Cut in the Middle With Butter In There. Ham Samwidge With Two Slices of Ham.

Probably shouldn't have stolen the bottle. Why steal wine that costs two bucks? Because you spent all your money on the guy's dinner and he took you down, that's why. And because it was impossible to out-and-out ask him for it. Better to steal the guy's wine than say something truly hurtful, like challenging him to an arm wrestle. He'd sipped his two glasses of it, then had to pour the rest out, hide the evidence.

He could hear Toby upstairs now, bumping around the bathroom. It was maybe three. You could somehow tell it was Toby. And Toby was probably aware of him down here typing. Toby didn't seem to sleep much either.

Leah. It really was not the best time for this. He'd hardly slept. He didn't feel good about much. Tired, gritty in the eyes, unsteady top to bottom. Thoughts not coming clear. His inner ugliness showed. Whenever he'd pictured today, he looked his best.

But why? *What* are your intentions?

He showered and shaved. Somehow he was late. It was cold, the coldest day yet, the bleak time of year, with the leaves long down but no snow. He felt thankful for his leather coat.

One of the chest buttons popped when he got into his car, and this made him sit and stare out the window, shaking his head. He cupped the big black button in his hand, examining it. He checked where it had come off, the circle of darker, shinier leather, the four pinholes and ragged broken thread.

And he had been somehow prepared for his car not to start. He ran his battery down trying, then faced the choice of hitching or calling a taxi. He'd be late either way. Maybe he shouldn't go. He shouldn't go.

And felt cheap as hell taking his sixty cents change from the ten. Sixty cents is sixty cents. He said, Sorry, I need it, but the taxi driver said nothing and wouldn't look at him, a mopey martyr for sixty cents, something to gripe about with the boys at the stand.

Bonaduce stood in the parking lot. This was like out of a movie. It certainly wasn't real, in any case. Roadside motel, and fronting the row of rooms her red car, its little ass pointing up. There in the big window of the café, Leah sat alone in a black-leatherette booth. Thinking hard at something as she sipped through a straw. Seeing him approach, looking quickly down, then looking up again and smiling.

The booths even had those private chrome jukeboxes on the wall, and when he sat across from her he had to resist the urge to search the titles, maybe find something corny for them to hear, something she'd recognize and they'd laugh.

"You're limping."

"No I'm not."

"I thought you were."

"Well I've been working out a bit."

Her lips, you couldn't tell if she had something on them or not. Wasn't that exactly the point, the art — But what was he thinking here? And what about Oscar.

He'd promised himself he wouldn't read anything into her idea of meeting at, well, at a motel. But here they were, together at a motel. Her suggestion. Back in those days, their days, when beds *meant* sex, motels meant beds. Look at her. Shy? Sad? Her silence thick with what? Jeans and a fuzzy sweater again, like at her party, his favourite, he might have told her this once and she might have remembered.

*Was* Oscar a buddy?

"So. Hi, Bobby."

Apology in her smile. A sad summing-up.

"Hiya." Look at her. "So, how's work? How're those guys down in that church?" He felt twenty again with her, inarticulate. He didn't mind this.

"They're still 'down in that church.' They might be there a year. But they're safe. Donations have been good and they have a nice little apartment set up. We even had to turn down a new living-room suite from Wal-Mart."

"Hey, I'll take it."

Leah smiled. "It gets so complicated. Wal-Mart is American, and its investment portfolio includes, you know, 'the usual.'"

His look prompted her to say more.

"Well, Juan admits to his involvement in a group that pamphlets against the monoculture — bananas — that's destroying all other agriculture there, and the whole pesticide health issue, and it's all American-owned, all Chiquita and a couple of others, so his real fight was against the U.S. So, Wal-Mart? Sorry."

"Maybe Wal-Mart's trying to make it up to him?"

"Right." Leah smiled with him.

She'd used *pamphlets* as a verb. She was a professional, and he no longer was. He shook his head at twenty years.

"What?"

"I dunno. A year in a basement. Holy."

A waitress came for their order. Leah ordered a sandwich and tea. He asked for a glass of icewater. He was desperate for a coffee because the cupboard had been bare and he'd done without, but coffee was eighty cents plus tax. You couldn't borrow a quarter from her. If you want a relationship with her son, you could not be a destitute bum.

And maybe you want more than a relationship with the son.

"Half a year easily. Ottawa's sitting on it. If they get in, the rednecks argue everyone'll get in. As if we can't tell the heroin smugglers from the — Juan has *scars* on his back. The kids saw their *uncle* killed."

"Who put the scars on his back?" He resisted a Wal-Mart joke.

"It's complicated."

The last thing you want to do is blow this. She hates you enough already, even if for a while there back in history she was your home. The last thing you want to do is misread the situation, come on to her just when she's got herself ready to talk and treat you like a human. You could blow it by looking at her wrong, by raising one cool sexy eyebrow, don't forget how well she knows you. Blow it when you don't even know what you want yourself, you can't put your finger on your intentions long enough to see whether your need is to get the mother in your camp so she'll get the son to come too, or whether this mixed-up welling of sadness and tears and breathing at the sight of her has to do with her alone or with you not being with a woman in God knows how long and needing, Christ, maybe just needing to be touched like this on the arm by someone.

"What's wrong?" Leah leaning in with tilted head. "Bobby? You crying?"

"Ah, hey, you know. No." He felt her eyes still on him, though no one spoke.

"Well, Bob. Jason . . . he lost a tooth. The other night."

"Really?" He looked up. She didn't look like she was blaming him for it.

"Did you know? A front tooth?"

"I didn't know. He okay?"

"At least it wasn't from a fight."

Didn't *look* like she blamed him. Fighting. The subject had been heavy in her silences, her distant look when it was celebrated in the bar with the guys and their wives after the game. If he'd studied her more closely that first season, he would have learned sooner that the few times she was not in the mood coincided with the few times she'd seen him fight. And here he'd been feeling jealous whenever Jim Murphy got into one and from behind the bench his Cindy would yell *C'mon, Murph, C'mon, Murph*, the good warrior's-wife. He imagined a Cindy more eager that night in bed, her black-and-blue knight gallant on top of her. He'd joked once to Leah something about how you'd figure a gal who fanged into the Alpo wouldn't be opposed to a small display of brute force from her man. But Leah had no use for it, and it was not one of her secrets. She smiled politely when he dismissed fighting as two tempers in a teapot. Or when he shrugged and said simply, "Consenting adults." Sure there were loose screws out there, guys who might try for an eye. In general, fighting was a war-in-a-box where no one got hurt. Black eyes, the odd nose or helmet-broken finger. And how many times did you see guys who'd fought that night clink glasses later in the bar?

It wasn't until he'd left Fredericton that he realized she may have been afraid. Not for him. Of him.

Well, hell. He wanted so much to tell her how that just wasn't in his makeup. Also how he suspected that hockey players in general were less likely to get violent with their women. It only made sense. At home on the couch the guy had no reason to be anything but a pacifist: hockey his outlet for whatever violent streak he had. He was happy to be home and at rest, a gentle sigh at the wife's ministrations.

Bonaduce had since dropped this theory, and not just because of all the athletes in the news for domestic stuff. Things had changed. The pressure. The frustrations at not making it. These days, to play in the minors was seen as nothing but failure. Fighting was more calculated now, a career tool, a spectacle, no real honour left in it. And steroids. He could imagine women in the awful privacy of their homes getting whacked because of that shit. Jesus, but he'd seen some young guys on the 'roid rage, flailing away, 220-pound tantrum, anger unheld as a child's, all teeth and paranoia, guy's face with its spread of telltale pimples oozing bad hormones and grease.

"Shit, a front tooth. But he's okay?"

"If he wasn't okay, he wouldn't have told me."

"Well, are *you* okay?"

Leah looked down, nodded. When she looked up again he could tell the subject had changed. She had dismissed their son, she had not invited him here just to talk about Jason. Her eyes were deep and clear, and rich with what she had become in the last twenty years. She was checking his eyes for what he had become during that time too, and it was hard not to look away.

Now it seemed that she might cry.

"Bobby, let's — let's not be in a hurry."

The words gave him an instant erection, though her eyes showed nothing but openness and sincerity. Her sandwich came, and his water. When her coffee arrived he said it smelled so good, could he have a sip? and he drank some, and when she took it back and drank some too, he saw how her lips touched the same spot.


He stood in his driveway, her car getting smaller, his hand still up in a wave. When he'd gotten out, neither of them had smiled.

His dead car with its hood open. In his hurry to the cab he'd forgotten to put the damn thing down. What did Leah think, seeing this yard, this house, this car with its hood up. White trash. In class Kirsten had given Phil shit for using that term, saying it implied that expected trash was black.

The keys were still in the ignition. Another picture of Bonaduce in a hurry. He decided against trying to start it, and closed the hood. None of what happened would have, had this car not died. Should he thank it or pound on it with a hammer? He would go in and have a bath, let it all percolate.

They'd ended up in her little car, Leah about to give him a simple ride home. They had talked and talked, Bonaduce ordering his fill of coffee, having decided to play the dufuss who'd forgotten his wallet. He'd come expecting a business-like discussion about Jason and for that alone he would have been grateful. But she had met him this morning to make a connection. They talked like ordinary people, they talked more about her work and he talked about his school, and she laughed at the stories of his fumblings. They talked about Oscar and Jason, but not in the sense that there was anything to *do* about either of them, and Bonaduce had only the slightest pang at the news that Jason's sights were set on Law, Oscar encouraging this. It was them simply catching up, enjoying each other's company, though of course they both knew that underneath it all was the blood-beast that erupted in Leah's car. It was a tiny car and he was a clumsy hulk climbing in. He couldn't remember whose fault it was that their knees touched, and then he simply patted it, her knee, safe there in her jeans, and he thanked her.

"Leah? Thanks for this," he'd said, and meant it. Both for the ride, but also more. And it worked because she looked up at him and he down at her and their faces were so close that the kiss was both their faults. At first neither of them betrayed anything other than a friendly kiss, a smack with the eyes open. But the kiss continued, and deepened, and got gently wild and down to business. Leah pulled away and, alone with herself for a moment, swore and slapped the steering wheel. Then she laughed, they both laughed. They kissed small again, then got right into it this time, and they were almost out of control there in the parking lot.

He did feel the dumb dufuss while she paid for the room. When they walked in, he wondered if she'd envisioned — maybe even planned for — this moment, too, this thrill, the delicious doom of the door locking shut behind them, then the brief relapse into shyness, their eyes falling on anything but the bed.

It was the best possible time. Right now. With his fingers on her neck and cheeks, the skin so soft he could hardly feel it through his own roughness. With her breasts and her legs teasing him with its clothing. With her head falling back under the full weight of this moment, with her fingers finding his belt loops, gently taking hold and drawing him to her.

# III

At first light, the old men upright and drooling.
CORMAC MCCARTHY, *SUTTREE*

He was consumed by doubts as to his own identity,
as to the nature of his body and the cast of his
countenance. In what manner did he relieve these
doubts? By the sensory perception of his ten fingers.
FLANN O'BRIEN, *AT SWIM-TWO-BIRDS*

December 1, Bonaduce bought a Christmas tree. It was early, he knew he was pushing things, but there they were as he drove by. You could smell the shaggy stack from the street through his open window, reek of pine after-life. If he wasn't supposed to buy one, they wouldn't be there. That it was the same gas station where he'd bought his only other Fredericton tree twenty years ago clinched it.

He interrupted an old guy who was just finishing the job of unloading the trees from the flatbed. He was skinny, unshaven, and permanently asquint from the smoke of the cigarette dangling in his mouth, surprising he could move one tree, let alone a stack. Anywhere but a jobsite he'd be taken for a derelict.

"You're the first." He gave Bonaduce a congratulatory nod and pocketed the twenty. He may have chuckled as he watched Bonaduce wrestle the tree onto his station wagon.

"Got some rust, eh?" the man added, indicating with his chin and cigarette the bottom of the driver's door.

Bonaduce searched in the back-seat mess for the bungees. What do you say to such things? You're wearing clothes, eh? You have yellow eyebrows, eh?

"I guess."

"Well, get 'er in some water quick."

It took a moment to realize he now meant the tree, not the rust. He tried to picture what kind of tree stand might be scroungeable back at the house. A big bucket, full of stones, bricks. Maybe he'd have to buy a proper rig.

But the car wouldn't start. He tried and tried, then got out. He didn't open the hood, because it wasn't flooded. The old guy standing beside him, he stared at his station wagon sitting there mulishly stubborn, as if it didn't like its burden of the tree.

"There's a good one right in there." The old man jerked his head back toward the garage. A sign read: Mechanic On Duty.

What money he might have had for tree rigs was now gone. Only because he was at a gas station to begin with did he decide to spring for a proper job. The old guy helped him and the mechanic push his car into the bay. If it was something major, kiss the car goodbye, he'd have to walk away from it. And the tree.

Well, but. He'd been trying not to think about it, the American Express card in the back of his wallet. He'd maxed it out before coming north. What sort of trouble could you get in for just trying it? Oops, silly me, wrong card, jeez I thought I'd lost that. And what about these guys you read about who, in debt to six maxed-out cards, declare bankruptcy and in a month receive invites for new cards? What if his card worked, what if he had three thousand U.S. to spend? Hey and while you're at it, throw in all those doughnuts, and that case of pop. And that bin of ice scrapers, please, I go through them.

It was a strange sight, his wagon rising on the hoist, Christmas tree on top. Two worlds strapped together, one fresh and green, the other stinking of oil and rust. Both in their way half-alive. Or half-dead, depending on your mood.

He walked and ran all the way home, adjusting his pace to the waves of fatigue as they rose. You could get on them, surf them. It was not unpleasant to slow life down, letting the cars *whoosh* on past. The noises, the smells. This was fine. It all depended on your mood. Moods were upon you, no choice in the matter. Sometimes you could stick-handle your way out of a bad one, sometimes you couldn't.

That Christmas in Tulsa, with Fournier. Christmas, never a good time for Bonaduce, was that year awful for Fournier, whose mother was sick. How sick, Fournier didn't know, and this was the crux. He hadn't made it back the previous year, and once again their game schedule was rotten. A travel agent helped him calculate that, with Christmas congestion and changing planes, he'd have a total of minus five hours to spend in Chicoutimi with his mother. So Fournier was down in the dumps. Sitting in a chair in the middle of the kitchen, he told Bonaduce with great gravity that Christmas in Tulsa was hell on earth.

Misery secretly loving company, Bonaduce went out and bought four bottles of champagne. Well, bubbly white. He'd once seen Fournier get near silly on the stuff. He also bought a funny Christmas card. In the background was the lower part of the tree and spread of presents. In the foreground, a guy's feet dangled in the air. It took you a second to see he'd hanged himself.

The card worked and Fournier got near silly on the wine. They gathered at a teammate's with eight or ten others who were suffering Christmas in Tulsa. A couple of them snickered but, unlike Fournier, they thought the card was sick.

A mile to go, along the Trans-Canada. Freezing rain was falling now and Bonaduce had to stop and turn his face away when a semi roared by. Some guys just didn't get black humour, had no talent for fire-with-fire. They didn't understand that sometimes you could slap a mood in the face and win.

### The Birth of Hockey

Because it is dark and smoky inside. Because Granddad drinks and after he wakes from his sour moanings his mood is prickly and his eyes follow you, looking for reasons to shout. Because outside it is bright and clean, and the pond gives you magical speed, and the faster you go the bigger the thrill, till it scares you. Because inside, the smell of a cooked onion takes all day to leave the house. Because Grandma gets sour herself when Granddad doesn't talk all through supper. Because it's only December and already she's hanging on for spring. Outside, your friends escape their hot houses and drift by with plans. Because you are too young to hunt and there's no money for bullets in any case, but there is the pond. Because inside, you can't read the Bible any more for it reminds you of inside and winter, of where you were, yet there is no other book. The catalogue is five years old and ripped, and the dreams it gives are tired. Because outside the rules are clear, to the point that if McIlhargy busts your shins again with the club he calls a stick you will fight him. Because inside, you cannot play another game of cards beside the flickering candle, tobacco smoke smarting your eyes and stinking so bad your nose can no longer smell it. Because outside you make sure your little sister played, and that the teams are even because it's more fun that way. Because sometimes, as the sun goes down, you find yourself hugging each other and cheering: McIlhargy falls, but not before the puck slides between his legs and through the holy posts, to nudge up against the backing snow.

On the phone. Out of the blue.
"Hello?"
"Hi. I was just wondering—"
*Jason.*
"Jason, hi."

"— if you wanted to go see Bob Dylan."

"Bob Dylan?"

"He's on the fifteenth. I've got these —"

"Bob Dylan's coming to Fredericton?"

"It's in two weeks, so —"

"That's incredible. Bob Dylan. This is the real Bob Dylan?"

"Yeah, do you want to go?" A trace of impatience. Things to do, fast twenty-year-old life.

"Hey, well yeah! Sure I do. Thanks. And I'll grab the tickets — so where do I —"

"Well, I sort of already got them."

"Hey. Okay. Great. Wow. Bob Dylan." Jason, Jason taking him to Bob Dylan, in Fredericton.

"Okay, see ya."

His boy hung up. No small talk, no further arrangements. No apology for the time in the corridor. All of which was fine. What Jason had just done had been hard for him, what he had just done was a great thing. From his voice you know it had been hard. Good lad.

And Bob Dylan. He sort of liked him, certainly had never loved him. The folky extraordinaire. The kind of guy if you went to high school with would be too arty and distant to like. But you couldn't deny he'd changed the world. He'd been reduced to Fredericton? A superstar demoted to the minors. But it would be great. Bob Dylan. It would be like seeing the *Mona Lisa*. The mummified body of Lenin. He'd get Jason over for a beer before the show and tell him what Bob Dylan meant to the world.


A world full of messages today. He'd just put the phone down, his ear full of Jason's echoes, hungry to replay them, when Marg was handing him a box, its surface colourful with U.S. stamps and Customs stickers.

"There was like a note for you from the post office that something was, you know, there for you. But, I mean, I was in town anyway so I just picked it up."

Why the nervous concern?

"No, I'm glad! Thank you. Great. Thanks."

He plucked the rusty hunting knife from the junk drawer and took it and the box to his room.

On his bed, looking at the window, he tried to hear and feel Jason's voice, but felt nothing more than a jittery stomach. He'd see him on the ice tomorrow night in any case. It was great the boy had called, the timing perfect. Fearing another disaster, Coach Bonaduce had been thinking of not showing up.

He hacked carefully at the parcel, half its top covered in stars-and-stripes stampage. Like he was opening a box containing his past twenty years. Amarica. His fellow Amaricans. Three months here had shown him how he'd become used to them. Their way of talking, proclaiming. Even their hesitations had a showy certainty. They were brave, it was true. Bashers on the biggest rink. Cradling this box, he realized in a mostly physical way that the America he'd left behind contained a neat two decades, a career, a game.

Why dwell on it? What was there to figure out? Over. Finished. Buzzer's gone. What of those past twenty years was even useful to think about? That this box was small seemed appropriate. You could pop it into a closet. You could flick it, *flick* it, out the window.

He put the knife to it. Inside was a health book about yeast infections, a letter from Fournier and a stern note of instructions from the girlfriend. Six bottles, vitamins looking like foliage crushed and capsuled. The two-page typed instructions said first you did the kidney cleanse, then the liver cleanse, then you started the main — You drank this at eight, that at noon, then you took — After the two-week juice fast you started the brown rice, introducing one different steamed vegetable every —

Fournier's note made no mention of their possible last paycheque except to say, "Wharton he's fucking unbelievable." Referring no doubt to continuing dirty legal manoeuvres. Fournier had finished his real-estate course and was about to start his new profession. "I wonder if buyers will trust a handsome Frenchman." Bonaduce pictured Fournier in a suit trying to sell something. Fournier would look good in a suit. If he relaxed and didn't smile all the time. Fournier could do the little charismatic eye-glint if he slowed down and didn't want something out of a situation.

Bonaduce restuffed the box. He placed it on the floor and, without looking, heeled it under his bed. What sounded like a vitamin bottle fell out and rolled to a stop somewhere. He didn't have a yeast infection. In fact he was feeling pretty damn good. Yesterday from the garage he'd more or less trotted all the way back here. It had to be four miles. He'd walked maybe only a mile of it and today his legs felt okay. Appropriately stiff and achy. In his general soul it did feel something like a flu rising, but he hadn't had a cold in a while so he was due. He was fine. Tomorrow was the start of his playing-coach career. Things were picking up, the towering gears of the universe were clunking more harmoniously of late. Though you couldn't deny the logic of it all: You sleep with the mother and, bang, the son calls, asking, Hey Dad, wanna go to a show? Had Leah spoken to him, put in a good word? Well, why the hell wouldn't she. She sleeps with you it means she at least likes you. Something about you.

Hey Dad, wanna go to a show? Hear some music? Just like it should be. He smiled, shaking his head. Life was a running stumble in the dark forest, truly wild. Bear pits, trip roots, cannibals. Sometimes you got a berry patch, a surprise waterfall, a sunlit clearing.

Bonaduce had to laugh, taking in his tiny bed and tiny room. He reached out like Jesus on the cross, and his hands almost touched both walls at once. Fournier had ended his letter saying that he and his girlfriend were thinking of driving up, pay a visit, could he put them up at his place, was there room?

Did Fournier think that when he'd left Utica he'd been called up to the bigs or something?

God he was tired. Time for a long nap, stay in bed all day, happy enough, but hope for no more boxes or messages.

The time he played in the NHL. "The Show" the kids called it now, copying baseball. His third season he was called up from Rochester to join Toronto on the road, meeting them in Philadelphia to play the Flyers that night. He would always remember the limo from the airport. Him with skates and overnight bag. That it was a plane at all was a taste of the bigs. He would always remember walking into the Leaf dressing room, the scattered greetings from guys who remembered him from training camp. There were three trainers, instead of one, taping ankles, giving rubdowns. Everything a bit newer, the gear better, lighter, cleaner, no thought of budget. Towels thicker, everything laid out, a choice of shampoos. There was Sittler; there was Lanny, who, when he said hi through that moustache, you couldn't see his lips move; and there was Tiger Williams, not as dumb as he came across on TV. They were as pale and bruised and mortal as the guys you left in Rochester. Same habits, same morals or lack thereof. As funny, and as limited in their speech. But there was something different in their eyes — a loftiness, a genuine knowing. Which posed a question you needed to answer for your own professional future: Was this confidence their reward, or was it what got them here in the first place?

From the bench Bonaduce watched his teammates get beaten by Philly, six-one. Clarke was fierce, and television didn't show how fast Leach could fly. But Bonaduce saw he could play in this league, these guys weren't all great, there were grinders like him. He was put on for the hell of it with two minutes to go. His shift lasted forty, fifty seconds and he didn't touch the puck. After the game he was informed of more travel arrangements. He had to hustle in and out of the shower and leave the dressing room just as the guys, sitting in their steaming gear, started to shake off the loss and joke around a bit. He was put on a smoky overnight train to rejoin his real team. And in the years that followed, whenever anyone asked if he'd ever played in the NHL, if he'd ever been called up, he simply said not yet. Because it hadn't really happened, not in the way it was going to.

He wouldn't know whether to remember it as life's treat or life's tease, this feast he'd been allowed only to smell. It was, as they say, a learning experience. The curt impersonality taught him that no one cared. Getting traded that second time — rupturing whatever family feel the team had given him — taught him he was alone.


Last night a dream about going with Jason to Dylan. Though in the dream it became the Harlem Globetrotters, as Dylan's warm-up act. Jason was thirty and paunchy, unshaven and surly. He smoked. And, damn, Bonaduce realized it was the kind of event you brought far younger sons to. The girl took their tickets. Father and son navigated the crowd, checking their stubs against the numbers over the tunnels. They passed a group of midgets, and Jason laughed at them cruelly and openly. This father–son thing, who said it would be easy? Bonaduce asked, "Ever seen these guys?" and Jason's answer, "Can't remember," irritated him. To say the Globetrotters could make so little impression that maybe he'd seen them, maybe he hadn't, was rude. He'd said it with a slackness of face that was ruder still. But he was being honest, they were beyond fake politeness at least. And they had the great seats. Couldn't help but love the Globetrotters, look at them warm up, shooting casual hoops, God they were loose, all high-five and whoop-up. How could you not love a seven-foot guy leaving the floor at full speed, faking a shot and cruising mid-air beneath the basket to come out from under and spin in a no-looker? You didn't see big guys like this in Canada. Sitting beside them suddenly, a tiny black man, the team clown, birthed a full-sized wet basketball from his hinged, snake-like mouth and Bonaduce knew this was a dream. He turned to Jason to tell him, and Jason was a huge fat older guy, stuffing a hotdog in his frowning maw, his belly resting on his thighs, one big repulsive bad mood. It was all funny now, just a dream, none of it true.

•⤳

In the morning he arrived humming in the kitchen. It was incredible but his lack of a car and a ride to give seemed to be sparking resentment in his housemates. Toby's deadpan, Well, what the hell else ya good for? was dangerous but funny, and Bonaduce shot him an approving wink. They leafed through the junk-drawer paper for a bus schedule they doubted they'd ever had. They grumbled about pooling their dimes for a taxi. No one was at all enthused by his smiling invitation to join him in his jog-and-walk to campus. He knew they found him idiotic in his sweatpants as he bolted his coffee and did his stretches hanging on to the counter edge. Even Marg was disturbed with him. Her asking, So what was in the box from the States? arose with a clunk out of some strained need to make conversation, and his reply, "One big yeast infection," didn't put the kind of smirk on her face it normally would have. Maybe she took it as sexist sass, and not a decent non sequitur. Maybe he shouldn't have had that tender moment with her up in her room.

He sometimes shortcut through fields and leapt ditches, feet crashing in brittle leaves, their crisp and perfect December sound. His steady breathing was the sound of health itself. The smell of smoke and pleasant garden-rot wafted over from what looked like a cauliflower farm, lots of unpicked white–brown bodies. Pungent smell of gravel kicked up by his feet. Soon all would go into the deepfreeze, this could be the last day of the sun warm on the face. Crows yelled at him from nearby trees and chickadees made him smile with their mournful, *geeez*er. If you're going to go schiz and let the world start talking to you, let's hope at least some of the voices are funny.

Things were coming together. The son. The son's mother. Even the hockey. Maybe even the school, why not. Next week, the last week of classes before the Christmas break, his stuff was being done in Big Jan's workshop, and then he would present *The English Patient* at Gail Smith's. He'd whined successfully to get both delayed and now time was up. He'd done only peripheral work on either, but pressure was his middle name, in the playoffs just drop the puck and turn the Bonaduce loose.

He was jogging first to the garage to pick up his car. If it wasn't ready today he'd jog in again tomorrow. It could only be good to fight through this tiredness. Put some teenage back in the legs. Things were moving and things were okay, everything pretty much as he'd wished, pretty much as he'd foreseen.

Luck, often you don't know you've had it till it's gone, but sometimes, like today, you can feel the blossoming, and you can feel that it's way bigger than you. That time, a solid month in 'Mazoo, when the goals just started coming, first a bunch of flukes and deflections, and then he actually started trying to score, turned into a bit of a rushing defenceman, and they kept coming. Basher turned offensive threat. He anticipated a call from on high. Call they did, but only to suggest that he stick to his game, not try to do too much. At which point he started to doubt himself, just enough to knock him off his edge and put a stop to the goals. Doubt can kill luck all by itself.

Jogging, he discovered he was whistling. It was a phony whistle. Trying to distract himself.

He made a quick trespass over the highway, to the river-edge where a stand of cattails promised entertainment. Holding his hands up like a boxer, he took left-handed swipes at the brown cigars, *whap*, he'd read the Natives used to eat these things, *whap*, made a kind of flour, *whap*. There were frogs down there in the muddy roots, *whap*, didn't they freeze, *whap*, solid?

Shit, why is it, *whap*, in middle age, *whap*, even the good times, *whap-whap*, are only iffy?

Right, damn, so let's have a look. Why the doubt. I'm jogging along, happy as a fast clam, yet here's doubt and here it had been all along. Doubt making the breath sound only hopeful. Doubt rising up deep from muscle and bone. Here was the sun full on the face — why the dark and the chill?

Because of the look on Leah's face.

Because of the sound in Jason's voice.

Because doubt has brought up the one and only question: Why jog, why do anything, when you're only going to die.

It's like there comes a time when, if you haven't been honest with yourself about certain questions, they get fed up and stand and shout at you all by themselves.

At Leah's insistence, communicated only through her hands, which moved as though caught in a graceful trance, the clothes had come off slowly. They did each other's, tugging at foreign buttons and clasps. In the delicious pace and clumsiness of this, he could feel all the more the hunger of twenty years. Slower, her hands said. I want to remember this — her mouth explained slowly into his ear — because it's going to be the only time.

While her saying this didn't dent his ardour, if there was darkness about their coming together, her words darkened things further. It was her right. She had the partner. Bonaduce was only free.

They stood in their underwear lightly embracing, pulling back a little in the semi-dark to take each other in, coming together to kiss and squeeze and almost lose control again because it was too much. If time had drained and scuffed their bodies, it wasn't noticeable in this light, and time hadn't hurt their urge at all. Leah was shaking. As for him, he was almost there from just the hard hugging, which would be a shame, a waste of this. She was smiling down at his underwear and what it could hardly contain. The straining thing in its ridiculous push, Leah looking a bit proud of herself.

She took further control, which again was fine and for the same reason. Shakily she whispered that if they didn't "literally" make love she could maybe live with herself. She had them retreat to separate beds. She pulled off her underwear, he pulled off his. Looking at him from across the two-foot chasm she played with herself. He did the same, though carefully, intermittently, because it was still almost over. He forced his thoughts to wander. He'd noticed that above both beds hung what appeared to be identical pictures of lake-and-distant-snowy-mountains. He checked now and they were in fact identical. What was the thinking.

"What's that?"

"What?" He stopped his hand and looked at her. Leah was pointing at his inner thigh.

"That."

"Oh. Bruise." From the oldtimer game. It was purple as a birthmark, fresh as a stamp, the size of a saucer and growing. Maybe it was age but he'd never had one quite like it, its centre almost black. He wished she hadn't seen it. Hockey was so much of the reason they had stopped —

But Leah could no longer stand it. She pulled her hair, she screamed, she laughed, and then she was in his bed. She had him promise that they wouldn't actually, *actually* — He said "fuck" for her but felt tainted for it, though it was a word they'd once used in play. Oh but now the deep taste of her, her soft and helpless moans, he could feel both in the pit of himself. The rules of their touch were further circumscribed when he lifted back his head and warned her not to, not to do *that*, stop, he was too close. It's been a while since the last time, he said, which she took as a joke, meaning since them.

In sweet frustration they continued what they allowed each other and neither could stand it for long. After a look from her and a look from him, in a blur of greased decision and a groaning roll they were on the floor between beds, furiously coupled, rocking now in the heartblood root of each other, and even as they both came she was already hissing, *Oh shit, shit.*

She was quick dressing. She had to meet a lawyer and with him drive a Chilean woman to Nackawic. The woman had all her belongings, there was a question of whether they could do it in just one trip. Leah tried to be cheerful, but couldn't quite pull it off, couldn't look at him squarely. The guilt on her face was plain and, Chilean woman or not, her hurry had more to do with getting away from him and what they had just done.

·⸺

"...for this reason one can see the text as an interrogation of the *pretence* of romantic ritual rather than as a interrogation of the ritual *per se.*"

Kirsten's sneer dropped like a theatre curtain as she ended her introductory sentence. Bonaduce had read the novel and liked it but had seen no interrogation of romantic rituals, never mind their pretence. It was basically about some East Indian guy in Canada landing only grub work and walking around moony-eyed but too shy to get laid, too shy for the romantic rituals to ever happen. Kirsten's sneer opened on her second sentence and the words "If we consider that" and the next two hours loomed large. The sun was bright outside the window and Bonaduce felt close to panic that life was racing by with him stuck here, a bug pinned writhing, impaled by words so empty they felt evil. Leah was out there cruising highways, alone, passing churches and motels, her ass restless on a car seat.

What was real was his headache. He never got headaches, but now he had a doozy. It was maybe the result of his run to the garage, sometimes a good workout will hock up the toxins. Of which no doubt he had plenty. Toby's wine. He hadn't been eating well. He felt akin to a sink strainer after the week's dishes were done, a carrier of oily rinds and pallid blasted fat.

"...clearly the point is that the rites of matrimony in the old country had become, here in Canada, mere farce. But he believed in the farce and she didn't..."

Or the headache came from the American Express card. He'd been helpless. The car was ready. Sitting out there in the lot, Christmas tree on top, in fine running order. The mechanic smiling at a job well done, praising the vehicle and all the miles left on her. Bonaduce staring at his car, still seriously puffing from the run. Apparently by signing the work order he'd okayed any necessary work. So they'd planed his warped head, changed the gasket, flushed the rad and replaced all fluids. Sure, he nodded, reading the smudged work order, Sure, I guess it had to be done. When the mechanic said, "I'm surprised it was still running," Bonaduce had to peer at him to see if this was a joke, because, well, the reason the car was there was because it hadn't been. The mechanic assured him that five hundred was a deal and looked ready to get angry if Bonaduce had a question about this.

He slid the credit card from his wallet with what he hoped resembled bored efficiency, handed it over between two fingers like a habit, like a cigarette, jeez I've used this thing five times today. He signed his name with delicate pressure, hoping a too-faint carbon imprint might save him. His stomach went empty and his sweating felt colder, less healthy than it had jogging. The mechanic punched some buttons and inserted the card. The intolerable wait — Bonaduce pictured a severe woman in Washington, D.C., scowling at a beeping computer screen — ended with his card being handed back along with a receipt. Both were smudged with grease, it was that ordinary. The mechanic had already turned away when Bonaduce called him back, holding his card out again and saying, I forgot to ask you how much those snow tires are. And could you fill it up?

"...what could possibly be wrong with her expectation of equal and consensual sex? Well, as we see at this point in the text, *both* cultures find plenty wrong with it, and though her crime was, at most, *naïveté*, the world will extract from her the penalties ritual demands..."

Leaving the garage lot, car shod for winter, he waved to the old Christmas-tree guy, who stabbed a finger at his roof rack and yelled, parental concern in his raspy voice, Get 'er in some water! Late for his seminar, he risked a ticket by parking in the professors' lot, right up against the building. Who cared about a parking ticket when you were on the Most Wanted list? That's his car, sheriff, the rusty one tied to that Christmas tree.

He'd gotten good at checking his watch without moving either wrist or head. Ten minutes had passed. Next week was his turn, and he would begin it with this: "*The English Patient* is a masterful, poetic work about the tragedies of war and love, and it poses this difficult moral question: Does love excuse a traitor?" After that he had no idea. Other than to say, Well, of *course* love excuses a traitor. Somewhere along the line he would slide in a coy "All's fair in love and war, eh?" But could he talk about nothing real for two hours? He began to sweat again, for the third time today. He realized he could smell himself. This smell was real too. Moronic to dress in track gear and run five miles before sitting shoulder-to-shoulder in a cramped room with this bunch of lily-whites. Some of whom probably wore a nosegay while pooping. Maybe next week if he smelled this bad nobody would notice what he was saying. He'd eat garlic wings and drink heavily the night before, sleep in his clothes, then run five miles and sit right next to Doctor Gail. And oh shit, there she is now, glaring, thinking yet again that he was smirking at today's presenter, not at the presenter to come.


Do you call her? He lolled like a big old morose teenager on his bed, the new phone on the floor beside him by virtue of the thirty-foot extension cord, both of which he'd charged at Radio Shack. His face felt puffy from lying around so much. Might as well lie around in here as slump around out there.

He'd also bought a little cassette player, and *Simon and Garfunkel's Greatest* was on softly, good old-fashioned candy.

Do you call? The signs — not eating, not sleeping too well — probably meant a teenager was supposed to do something.

She'd whispered, *This is the only time.* Nothing more had been said about the possible shape of their future together.

He pictured her after their beautiful fury was done, piecing herself back together, the static crackling of clothes hurriedly pulled on, Leah all too soon a social worker again. Him reclined on the bed, far from sated, but shy now like Adam, the sheet pulled over. He could still smell her in the bed, which was both a balm and a stimulant, and she was getting away. At the door, drawing on her long coat, rifling her purse for keys, about to leave the room's darkness. Then — like she didn't want to but felt she should — she looked back at him and smiled. The smile was worried and therefore false, and you could see her eyes were already focused on problems to come. The door closed behind her. Then opened again.

"How you getting home?"

Looking after him like he was a boy. He'd tried waving her away but she sternly told him to hurry, don't be silly, and so she drove him home. Sitting quietly beside her as she worked her car out of the parking lot onto the highway, he could feel how his letting her drive him cancelled whatever power he may have gained, and that she knew this too. They drove in silence, except for a few small jokes, as when they passed the bright pink car, and when nearing his house he stuck out his hand and introduced himself as Ray and she introduced herself back as Suzy Wong. They'd always had the little jokes.

So do you call her? Bonaduce flopped onto his stomach, his chin deep into the pillow and its strong smell of his hair. He really should start washing things, really shouldn't live like this, the student life should not mean disintegration. Do you risk ruining her trust that you understand her need for distance right now? Or is that just your imagination, the paranoid sore of lying bug-eyed in bed for too long. Look out the window at the flaccidly falling snow. Could easily be she wants you to call. Even if she doesn't know she wants it. Oscar's "There was an early affair." Maybe it was all no big deal, maybe she screwed around all the time. Could even be she feels fucked and forgotten, she's waiting by the phone like the other half of this teenage cartoon, staring off, curling a finger in her greasy neglected hair, which she will wash, grinning, after you two speak, after you get off your ass and call her.

No, she doesn't want you to call. Some things you know.

He cocked his left leg, touching his knee to his ear, and bent his head forward to his groin as far as his grabby old spine would allow, not so far these years, to check out the Bruise. There it was, its rainbow of bruise-hues, but blacker, and yellower, and still growing. He'd started thinking of the Bruise as having a capital B, because he'd never had one quite like it. And he'd had bruises everywhere. He'd had bruises *on* bruises. He'd never had a week during the season without one. Simple impact crushing and killing a tiny chunk of your body. Dead blood gone black, days to flush. He'd had bruises you couldn't see — the kidney, an eyeball, esophagus. Testicle. Never his penis though. Maybe his unit was his only virgin bit left, all safe there behind the tinny. Dumb little contraption, the balls hanging a bit below it, dangling this huge pain potential. The time, it was first-, second-year junior, when he took a shot full on the rig and it caught an edge of unprotected balls. There was the second or two of delayed hell, during which time he fell off the ice onto the aisle beside the bench and spent the next minute trying not to vomit, the pain simply ridiculous, no reason for it at all, but the funny part was the erection. Instant, surprising. Why sprout a hard-on at such a time? What was the possible point? Was it linked to whatever sick biology it was that caused hanged guys to spring one as they drop through the trapdoor and ejaculate at the stop? What was *that*? Either an extremely positive preview they may have just had of the afterlife, or maybe more likely their body's pathetically feeble last attempt to replant itself. Jesus.

Enough to make you shudder in the warmth of your teenage bed. Body's attempts to replant itself and what it makes you do.

Absently fondling his Bruise, now Bonaduce pushed it, pushed two fingers hard into the deepness of dead blood until he gasped with the hurt and shot into a wakefulness. He pictured a blood clot dislodged and rushing to his brain. He waited.

C'mon Leah, you did feel it. Pretty little angel eyes. Angel eyes, what a perfect two-word description of love, love that went both ways.

There were only two people, two friends, he could ask advice of. The first, Marg, still carried this apparent torch and her advice would be bent wonky. The second friend was Oscar, which was even funnier.

That evening at practice he began his career as a coach. The on-ice part was fine, almost fun. The players showed him friendly respect, though whether it was due to a pro background or a position of power was hard to say. The defencemen in particular acted like a word from Bonaduce might get them on the power-play or benched, though he himself didn't know if this was the case. He and Whetter hadn't really talked. But it was fun taking shots on the goalies and laying down passes during drills, great to get some puck-work in a non-pressure situation, get the timing going, the small muscles tuned. Fun even to pick up the pylons and crack the odd joke and generally be useful.

He wore nylon warm-ups instead of full gear. Helmetless and unburdened, he felt the wind in his hair, and on a few glides he got the baggy pants to snapping behind the knees, could imagine little pennants trailing. He felt faster than he likely was, because he had no real oomph and one leg was playing a little dumb. Jason he treated like one of the guys, and Jason treated him like one of the coaches, a distance which in this situation was perfectly right.

His favourite time was giving the defencemen pointers about nullifying the enemy in front of the net. He said, "Okay, I've watched you in games and some of you don't know this stuff, or if you do know it you don't do it," to get them listening. He showed them the skate-nudge, then the back-of-the-pants thing, where a two-inch down-thrust with your stick buckles their knees without toppling them, resulting in them fighting to keep their feet but not in you getting a penalty. The guys seemed to appreciate it and laughed when, demonstrating, he went quickly guy-to-guy and sent each of them into helpless little flails.

In the dressing room it was harder. Protocol. Did a "playing coach" dress in the coach's room or out here with the players? He hadn't done the full workout, so did he shower or not? The more frightening protocol was the father–son kind, of course, though Jason was pretty adept at ignoring him. Which was fine, probably the way of any coach's son in any dressing room. When Bonaduce had first arrived he and Jason had acknowledged each other with a nod and Bonaduce offered a quick "So, the fifteenth, huh?" and Jason had looked richly blank. He supplied the missing information, mouthing "Dylan," and Jason tossed his head back and said, "Right, right." At which point Bonaduce thought it best to leave well enough alone.

Maybe, Bonaduce decided — unlacing his skates in the players' room but on the bench closest to the coach's room, in this way straddling worlds — maybe it was all any parent could expect from any child, this sort of minimal attention. Why should the young pay attention to the older? Much more exciting were lives yet unlived. The young instinctively knew this. As a parent there was much for him to learn. Another utterly basic idea he had to keep in mind was something Marg had told him just last night — that all children are different. Bonaduce had been amazed that such an obvious truth could catch him off guard. At some level, sure, he knew all kids were different, but he hadn't been operating like he did. No, he'd been asking himself what nineteen-year-old boys did at ten o'clock Tuesdays nights instead of asking what it is Jason might do. "I mean," Marg had added, adding obvious onto obvious and making him feel stupider still, "they're, like, just like you and me." She pointed back and forth at each of their chests, their basic differences, and Bonaduce sat smiling and shaking his head, at his own stupidity but also at the proximity of her two "likes," and wondering if she'd ever stick two right together. I really, like, like you.

He decided he would shower, show these punks a body twice their age, expose them to the hideous consequences of playing this game. His groin bruise had flowered in grand new directions, its basic colour settling down to mauve while taking on an encircling yellow aura that wrapped his entire thigh. Naked, he thought he could feel his son's furtive eyes on him, checking him out, it was only natural. He was trying not to do the same with Jason. Lined up waiting for a free nozzle, he chatted with Tommy, a centreman, and Mike, the spare goalie, about their chances of making the playoffs. Playing it straight, he asked Mike what was each player's share of playoff money if they went all the way.

He heard Jason's low chuckle. He turned and saw his son naked, in line, laughing not at the Bonaduce quip but at something unrelated, some jibe from around a corner.

Maybe it was Bonaduce feeling only average in this roomful of sizable men and muscles, bodies you might in another situation take time to admire; maybe it was the being naked, everyone simply naked. Because the catchphrase he'd for two hours been breathing to himself, "We're both pretending I'm no one special," now transmuted to the thought *He's not pretending.*

Mike the spare goalie chattering in his ear, sucking up a bit, Bonaduce stared past his son's shoulder into the room's centre, into the pile of sticks and pooled meltwater. Why, how, was he in any way special to Jason? How was he any different from any other rutting deer or porcupine or slug who'd done the deed then empty-headed wandered away? Maybe Jason harboured none of the delusions Dad did. "Dad." Yes. Let's put that one in quotes.

Or maybe Jason, who owned a fine scowl and whose expertise at ignoring "Dad" was starting to bug "Dad" a little, maybe since Jason's relationship with Father was still so young, maybe he was only now going through the Freudian phase, the wanting to kill the him and sleep with the her...It would be so great to be able to joke with the kid about this stuff, run back out to the shower line, grab that naked shoulder and look him in the eye and plead, deadpan, Do what you have to do to me but *please* don't sleep with your mother, son.

You couldn't help suspecting by now that this kind of joking might never happen.

Whetter there watching him, smiling at him staring off.

"You look a little tired."

"Took a beating out there, those pylons, I dunno."

"So you want to work the bench against Acadia Friday night?"

"Sounds good."


This morning he woke out of a truly wild bad dream, heart pounding, hot sweat, everything. He'd been in the campus bookstore, browsing. Suddenly the whole row of novels was by Kirsten, her face on the cover jackets, a different sneer for each. Now there were books by Gail Smith, and everyone he knew, Marg and Toby and Jason, and even a trainer from Dayton he hadn't thought of for ten years. Everyone had written books except him. He sidestepped to the next rack, it was health books. One title was MS *and You*. Another was *Multiple Sclerosis*. The whole rack was on nothing but. One, SCLEROSIS!, had letters embossed, backlit and flashing like a cheap marquee. He picked up one, YOUR SYMPTOMS!, and tried to open it but—ha ha, very funny—his hands no longer worked. They didn't work and didn't work and still didn't work, flop flop thud, two slabs of dead baloney, he couldn't scream and couldn't scream and couldn't scream.

Marg's fucking dreamcatcher was turning out to be some kind of comedy machine.

"Your dreamcatcher's turning out to be some kind of comedy machine."

He said this to her big behind as she stooped to sweep under the kitchen table. As soon as he said it, he realized he'd have to avoid some details. Though he had his suspicions now about what Fournier may have blabbed to her. He was just basically trying to engage her in conversation, for it felt like they hadn't been talking much lately. He'd been in his room a lot. He hated the feeling of fading friendship.

"How so." Marg was breathing hard, arms working away. Toby, at the table finishing his scrambled eggs, lifted his legs for her to sweep there. A rustle and scrape of wrappers and beer-bottle caps.

"I had a wild dream. You were in it."

"What was I doing."

"You were an author."

"That's comedy? Thanks."

"No — everyone I knew was a famous author, except me."

Marg was putting the broom away in the closet. She turned her head and smiled for him.

"'S not funny," Toby said, leaning back, mouth full of egg and toast, "'s pathetic."

It is funny *because* I am aware just how pathetic it *is*, you mean and gimpy twerp. Marg was wrapping a lunch sandwich in wax paper. Bonaduce, hungrily aware that his cupboard was bare, said in singsong: Make me a samwidge an' I'll drive you to school?

214 ·

In the car she stared out at the riverside underbrush. Looking for winter birds. Some time ago she'd told him how birds bored her except in winter, when she loved seeing those that stayed.

Whatever she saw out that window was keeping her quiet. She commented neither when he slapped his forehead for always forgetting to take the damned tree off the roof, nor when he complained about how noisy his new snow tires were.

"But I guess they'll plough through anything winter can throw at them."

She turned to him with a no-nonsense look.

"Are you bothered by me and Toby?"

"Sorry?"

"No, please just say if you are. Are you bothered by me and Toby."

"Well, I'm sure as hell bothered by Toby."

Not missing a beat, Marg said in identical tones, "Well he's sure as hell bothered by you stealing his wine."

Ooo. Yikes. Damn. An embarrassment best left alone. How did he know? He didn't seem the type to keep count. Bonaduce leaned down to snap the radio on and fiddle for a station.

"You know Toby has lupus, and he had a stroke when he was sixteen? Can you please maybe see why he's a little bit bitter?"

"Well hell. I didn't know that." He was prepared to feel like an asshole, and indeed sat prepared for the feeling to dawn. But he felt fine. He saw that, at the mere mention of lupus, he had instantly decided there were others with lupus who weren't mean.

"So it doesn't bug you that he and I sleep together."

Then snapped the radio off. Marg and Toby? Was he supposed to know this? *Did* he know this? He didn't think so.

"You're both adults. No, it doesn't bug me." Did it? He didn't think it did.

"That's good. I'm glad."

She didn't seem it.

"Well, sure, yes it does bug me—that it's Toby. I mean, it's only natural for me to want you to be with someone I liked. Someone who's good for you."

Marg met this, his decent declaration of friendship, with more of the same severity. Only when he bent forward to threaten turning on the radio again did she speak.

"I mean like, you've been awfully distant lately."

"I guess."

"Sitting there in that room."

"How do you know I've just been, you know, 'sitting'?" He winked, but no humour in the lady today.

"Marg, I'm in a phase. It's a strange time of life for me." Try her again. "I like to think of my room as, you know, a cocoon. And out of cocoons come, you know…" She wasn't budging.

"I want you to talk to me, okay?" It was as if she hadn't heard him. Her voice descended into warmth as she said this, and her hand slid across the fabric of the seat and took his right hand, which had been at rest on his thigh.

"Hey. What ya wanna know?" He smirked for her but his hand and senses were afire, the hair on the back of his neck bristling. Young people could scare the hell out of you with their directness. Your own words could get stunned in the surprise and glare.

"Your friend Fournier says you're really sick."

"*Oh* hell. Hey. Fournier's all over the map. Don't listen to Fournier. He's French. He's a goalie."

"He thinks you're not taking care of yourself. And, Robert, *I* think—"

"You can't play university varsity fucking hockey if you have a serious fucking disease."

"I didn't know you were playing."

"I'm about to start."

"Maybe if you just looked after yourself a tiny bit better, and waited to—"

"There's nothing wrong with me."

"There is and I worry about you. Fatigue? Fatigue and depression are two first big symptoms, and all the time you spend in your room?"

"I've been writing."

It felt like punishment the way she withdrew her hand.

"Even if I did have it, which I don't, there's nothing you can do. So I'm not going to get myself in a knot about it."

"Well, I mean, that's not true. There is stuff you can do."

"Think positively. Swing a rooster over your head."

"All your joking," she said softly, making him sit up a little straighter, "all your humour is gallows humour."

Oh, she wanted morbid, did she? Well, he could help her there. In his sweaty little cocoon with the octopus-stained walls, he'd become a grad student of morbid.

"Marg? Where we're all going? *All* humour is gallows humour."

It was his turn to shut her out, some of her own medicine. They were at a red light. A gust of wind hit the back of the car, and a scatter of Christmas tree needles rained on the windshield.

"You know, like, I'm moving out?"

Marg all softness again. Bonaduce nodded for her.

"Well, and sometimes I've wanted to ask you if you want to get a place together."

Bonaduce became very aware of his driving.

"And sometimes I don't. I mean we've become good friends but I guess if we lived together I'd want to be able to talk about stuff that matters."

"That only makes sense."

He didn't enjoy Marg like this. Like she had completely lost control of herself. Her seriousness bugging out all over the place, staring at him. Nor did he like what was expected of him in this conversation. They were nearing the campus. He would either drive her to her building first, or she would tell him to go park and she would walk in with him.

"Living together might, you know, be 'dangerous,'" he said, giving in. "Just the two of us?"

"I know. I don't care." Her voice husky and fatalistic and unsurprising.

"There's all sorts of stuff you don't know about me."

"I know. I don't care." Repeating this, she smiled, more a smirk, the Marg he liked. She started chewing some gum they both knew wasn't there. "Like what?"

He almost said, Like I'm in love with someone.

Stopped at a crosswalk while a string of students Marg's age filed in front, he played with the sound of this soap-opera sentence. He checked out the feel of its main word. He couldn't tell if it was true. He hadn't used the word in a while. What a word it had turned out to be, it, too, growing so complicated with age. All the guys and their wives who'd had counselling to help them find it or get it back, who learned the words for love's fool's gold: obsession, dependency, habit. These days, on bus trips you could actually hear such words murmured through the drone, guys with fat lips, black eyes, earrings.

Marg nervous beside him as he pretended to be frustrated by all these pedestrians. He would love to ask Marg where good old lust fit in. He would love to describe to her what he could still clearly picture, he and Leah lying in the motel bed not knowing what to do with their eyes. Each time they met eyes, they got a version of each other that was surprising and too too full, a potency forcing them to look away, except for a brief few times when they made themselves hold it. One time he told her it felt like looking in a mirror. However corny it sounded, he felt it was true, and her angel eyes staring deeply back he took to be her agreement.

"Wanna just park? I'll walk in with you."

They walked through the lots, past student housing, and damned if he wasn't limping again but worse, like the hip joint had lost its little brain. Marg seemed lighter in mood, but she still wanted to hear about how dangerous living together would be. Bonaduce didn't announce his soap-opera sentence less out of fear of hurting her than of having to talk about it. Best talk to himself about it first.

As for living with Marg, the notion felt undeniably cozy. He could see, as though it were already happening, the pots of spicy pasta, the games of Yahtzee, the endless talk. Bohemian friends dropping by. He liked the idea of looking for used furniture with her, joking about each other's bad taste. He could be buddies with her, with a woman. Why not? He could be a Nineties guy. Apparently all the kids were doing it. Boys and girls playing together. Who needs sex, we're friends. If you believed what you saw on TV, it was like the war was over.

He pictured Jason coming by, checking out his place and thinking Dad a pretty cool dude.

"But like, definitely we'd get a two-bedroom place."

"— Whoops! Ouch. Fuck *off*."

He shouted at the foot that was still on the other side of the snowbank, it having refused to take part in his little leap over. He'd caught his fall with his hands, scraping his palms on the sanded sidewalk ice; it looked like he was doing a spread-eagle push-up. When they got going again, good old Marg took his arm in a nursy way, as if supporting him. They both smirked at this, but she left her hand there, and he went on the alert again, feeling through her mitt and its soft squeeze the expectations that must be smoothed away before moving in together could be an option. It wouldn't be fair for anybody.

"Well, hey, let's definitely talk about it."

Nurse Marg squeezed his arm.

"But do me a favour and leave Toby where he is. We don't want to be living with Toby again."

Damn, it had been a joke, a simple "I don't like the guy." Not at all a "I want you to break up with him." But through her mitt you could feel all the way up to her head, thoughts shifting into high rev over it.

## ROMANCE
### — by Lady Bonaduce

You might not think it, but what a soap opera the minors are. Consider the mix: you have a pack of young men whose only goal is to be somewhere else and who, if in their third or fourth year in the minors, are staring a life's failure full in the face. You have women who, while not exactly groupies, are attracted to these men mostly for their bodies and the fact that you have to pay to watch them. You have road trips and bars and more not-exactly-groupies, and young, tireless men-in-motels glad for the team's code of secrecy. You wouldn't say that many minor-league romances begin on a firm foundation, unless you're talking about the quality of the bed.

Soap opera. You see some good scenes before road trips outside the arena as the bus idles impatient diesel fumes, its cargo doors open. Shouting matches, public demands, mascara-blasted eyes. A guy stowing his gear in silence, the girlfriend conspicuously not there, the whispered rumors. There are the usual couples who milk a crisis to get things up, but most of the displays are painfully real. But the bus has to leave, and as it reaches the outskirts of town, you can look back at the rows of guys in their seats, a whole smack of them just staring into space, maybe shaking their heads in awe of what soap operas their lives had become. Jesus H, they were just down here to play till they got called, hadn't planned on meeting *her*, hadn't wanted these questions of loyalty. But soon enough the cards come out, or if it looked like a guy·was ready for a laugh Bombsaway might haul out the guitar and do a hurtin' song. Soon begins the quiet talk about tonight's team, which asshole to watch for in the corners, and the new nightclub two blocks from the hotel where you can get two, three quick ones in before curfew, and hey isn't Toledo where they have that little place with the lasagna? Mother Tucker's? with that waitress? she still there? what, traded to a Pizza Hut in Des Moines? Bullshit a relief from the jagged sourness left behind. Later that night on the ice, sometimes you find a good heartache fuels your game, and sometimes you find it drains you.

Someone up cooking bacon. Out his window, a frigid morning like so many back on the prairies, sunny, windy and hard-assed. The term "freeze-dried" came to mind.

He considered his wardrobe hanging on its hooks, the choices available to him. He recalled Whetter behind the bench in the standard sports coat and tie. Okay, did an assistant coach wear a tie. Or did he go casual like a trainer. Would the guys respect him more, or less. Would they even notice. Would Jason. Did any of this in the slightest way matter.

Clothes. He used to like clothes, what they did.

Noon he paid a visit to the English Department office to drop off the stuff to be xeroxed for the writing workshop — a manila folder of his collected observations and aborted beginnings to novels, most of them silly. In the mailbox he found a memo from the registrar informing him of his revised status, from full-time to part-time student. It showed him listed only in Gail Smith's and Big Jan's, meaning Kirk had officially pulled the plug. The note asked him to confirm this status or inform them if an error had been made. If he was in fact part-time, said the note, "overpayment of tuition monies might be owed and subsequently reimbursed."

Wearing a dress shirt under his leather coat, and a tie rolled tight in his pocket, Bonaduce frowned at the piece of paper in his hand, seeing right through it to the clear horns of his dilemma. He would love to be owed and subsequently reimbursed. Otherwise, unless he tried his credit card again, he would not eat today or all weekend. This horn was already goring his stomach. The second horn was more fuzzy: if he confirmed his part-time status, he would officially not be allowed to play for the Varsity Reds.

He ripped, balled and tossed the memo. Deny he'd seen it. He'd knock around in academic limbo a while longer. Limbo could last a long time, being the one thing bureaucracy excelled at.


There's no thrill in coaching. You stand behind the defencemen. They're yours, you oversee their changes and pairings. You can feel what a masochist's game coaching is. If the team won, who takes credit? It's the guys out there with the blades who take the hit, feather the pass. If the team lost — well, why didn't the coach have a system that worked?

It was a tight game, they were up two-one early in the third period, hanging on. Acadia was small, fast, gutsy. Anything could happen. Coach Bonaduce did catch himself growing excited. But it was nothing like being out there working your guts out to be the hero, working even harder not to be the goat.

When the guys were filing through the corridor on their way to begin the game, Coach Bonaduce had shouted, "Lean and mean, guys, lean and mean!" and he hadn't felt out of place doing it. (He hadn't eaten and it was how he felt.) But he saw he wasn't one of them. At the edge of the tunnel he stopped and let them pass by, into the arena light and scant cheers. Red and white warriors, tall and anonymous in their helmets and face cages, clomping the rubber with their contrived steel feet. They yipped, hollered and punched each other's shoulders, a nervous herd urging itself to become something carnivorous.

The few shifts Jason got, Bonaduce found himself so intent on the boy he forgot his coaching duties, but so what. At ice level you got a better feel for the play, and Jason was fast, very fast, he could play in this league, maybe a bit beyond, who knows. What he needed was a break. The asshole right-winger Harrington stood in his way. You tried not to hope for an injury to anyone, but. Your heart lifts when the Reds score to make it three-one, then you understand it was Harrington who tipped it in and you wish it was still two-one. Jason just needed a chance. And — Bonaduce's gut sank for an instant — Whetter might be the kind of coach who feared showing favouritism to the point that he might play Jason *less* now that Dad was coaching. Jesus, maybe Jason saw this too.

During the game he spoke to Jason once — a simple "Go hard, Jace" as he jumped on for a shift. And touched him once. His general yell, "*C'mon guys!*," followed by his cupped palm — *whop, whop* — onto the shoulder pad of someone who just happened to be Jason, though Bonaduce had sort of known this out of the corner of his eye. Jason answered with the half-fierce nod of a player who hasn't been on for a while and might not get on again and whose disappointment is battling his team spirit. Had he known whose hand it was on his shoulder? Of course.

What struck Bonaduce a second later — he couldn't tell if it was pathetic or funny, where was Toby when you needed him — what struck him was how, while clopping his son on the shoulder, he'd had his nose wide open wanting a smell of the boy.

Hanging alone by the red line, Harrington picked up a loose puck and scored an empty-netter to clinch the deal.

He got home late, having gone for beers with three of the Reds, who apparently didn't hang together as a team. This was a known and significant liability and he'd have a cautionary word with Whetter about it. He'd heard Jason beg off in the shower, a cold coming on, gotta watch it, exams coming. (Coach Bonaduce raised his eyebrows at the boy's priorities: the worry about exams, not next week's games.)

On his arrival home, as soon as his tired body landed on the bed, too swirly in the head to account for two draft beer, a fight broke out upstairs, Marg and Toby going at it. Marg yelled a few times and you could hear Toby's monotone scorn. You couldn't quite make out the words, though he did think he heard his name. Beth's softer voice began moderating. Eventually Marg's door slammed, right overhead.

You couldn't hear her crying but you knew she was.

Coming suddenly out of all that noise, silence. The absence of noise had its own weird force, a rising steadiness. Bonaduce perked up. Out his window the night felt wide and deep. He looked and the stars were brighter because there was no moon at all. Having fun, aiming his gaze through the dreamcatcher, he studied the sky long enough to make sure the comet was gone. Taken its cold warm-and-fuzziness elsewhere.

There's a feeling you get for disintegration, how it sometimes feels right. Or at least inevitable, which was maybe the same thing. The house felt that way now. Though no one knew it at the time, they'd enjoyed a modest golden age, then a falling, now a falling apart.

Someday soon they'd all be in different bedrooms and circumstances, new loyalties, feeling all right. It all had a rhythm to it, as predictable as a song.

Leah, I want to do it again. I just want to do it again. There's nothing I want to do more. I can now admit this to myself.

And maybe I want more than just it. And maybe Oscar should be told. And maybe Jason should be told. Leah should definitely be told.

He found himself punching her phone number, hearing its coyly flat music. Don't think. Take the puck and go with it.

Oscar answered, a friendly singing hello.

"Oscar, buddy. It's Bonaduce. How's it goin'?"

"Great! How are things with you?"

"Great! Leah around by any chance?"

"Well I'll just go and locate her."

The teasing airiness again, but could you not hear something nervous in it, maybe an anger? Had she dropped the bomb on him?

"Bobby?"

Oh, there's the proof, when her voice alone can get you half-way there.

"Leah — why are we still married?"

She was long to answer. He couldn't hear if she was smiling or not.

"Well, Bobby, you tell me."

"Maybe I will, another time. I have my version. Maybe we, maybe we should talk about it." His chest swelling with romance.

"When I didn't get them back, I just figured, I don't know, I figured that —"

"What back?"

Silence, and then slow, incredulous laughter, not completely friendly.

"Didn't you get them?"

"Get what?"

Leah explained. Her business-like manner no doubt had to do with Oscar being in earshot. She explained how she'd mailed divorce papers long ago. She'd assumed, when her lawyer didn't get Bonaduce's signature back, that he didn't want to.

"Leah, I didn't get any papers. So I thought the same thing. That you didn't want to." He forced a little chuckle.

Leah laughed lightly. "Imagine. All these years."

"Imagine." How, how lightly entertaining.

"So, well, I'm getting dinner ready here, but what do you want to do?"

"I want to sleep with you as soon as possible."

Her silence was dense and unreadable, but as five seconds became six he could hear a direction in it.

"Don't hang up, Leah."

"It's — not really the best time to get into these sorts of details," she said, instantly relieving and arousing him. Oscar, within earshot, wasn't the one getting the truth here.

"When's a good time? To get into every detail we can."

More silence, through which Bonaduce didn't breathe.

"No, I really don't see it coming to that. I don't think, I don't think they would be that ridiculous."

He could hear Oscar's muffled enquiry. Leah pulled away from the phone and said, "Bob never did get the divorce papers, and now someone's, they seem to be after him about marital status or some such at the university, something about tuition." More muffled Oscar words, and then Leah's "Here, you talk to him."

Leah, you bastard. He had to stop himself from hanging up. This wasn't fun. The phone being passed to Oscar. I love her, Bob.

"Bob? Legal difficulties? Here, I'll just turn my meter on."

"Oscar, yeah. But not really. Just, well, there's this form, when I signed up here, registered, it said 'marital status,' and I left it, you know, left it blank"— several coils of phone cord had at some point gotten wrapped tightly around his elbow and he saw his forearm was swelling up —"not knowing *what* the hell status I was, right? And they sent it back, and there's, there's —"

"Why would they send it back?"

"Well, who knows."

"That kind of thing doesn't matter much these days. None of their business. Legally or otherwise. Unless it's for benefits, or taxes. Spousal deductions. Curious."

Oh, Oscar knows. The sly dog knows.

"Well I did apply for a loan. And stuff. Good old bureaucracy, eh? Go figure."

"I'll look into the divorce status if you want."

"Nah — like you say, it doesn't matter."

"It's no problem, really. I'm having a half-price sale."

"Right. No, it's okay."

"It probably is. Well, hey. I hear you're going with Jason to see Bob Dylan."

"Sure are."

"Well, let's get together some time soon. You and me."

"Sounds good."

"No. I mean it."


Dylan was upon them and he'd heard nothing from Jason about arrangements. Where, when to meet, at what bohemian café, I'll be the one wearing the beret. He had a tape for him too, a *Dylan's Greatest Hits* he'd bought new and in the meantime scuffed up the cover, as with new running shoes, no sense embarrassing the boy with expensive gifts.

He forced himself to call.

"Jason. Hi. It's —"

"Hi."

Interrupting quick, hearing the father's wondering how exactly to identify himself. He'd been toying with "It's your dad," but feared Jason's possible anger there. "It's me" assumed intimacy. "Hi, it's Bob" made him queasy.

"It's your assistant coach here."

"Yeah. Hi."

"Anyway, couple of, couple of things." He stumbled, he was a teenager asking someone to a dance. "I was wondering if you wanted to borrow some Dylan music. You know, before going to hear him. I've got this tape you can have."

"Nah, thanks. I don't have a player."

His son's voice was deep, deep as his. Children did not have voices so deep. So resonant through the plastic, vibrating the bone of your head.

"No stereo at all? I mean, I could lend you the same thing in a CD."

"Nope. I'm music-less. Doesn't matter. Thanks."

"Okay." He'd told himself to not be instructive, yet here he was, launching in. "Maybe it's better that way, you won't be disappointed if he isn't as good as on record."

Jason agreed with his logic. They arranged to meet at eight, outside the main doors.

"You gonna wear full gear, or just your helmet?"

Bonaduce had had his two glasses of Toby-wine, and this had just come out. Jason chuckled, politely or not. Maybe their senses of humour weren't that far off.

"Another thing, Jace. A hockey thing."

"Yeah?"

"Now, *as your coach*," he said in a good deep comic voice, though there was no answering chuckle this time. "No, but really, I've been wondering about how much ice time you're getting, and it's the shits, eh?"

"Well, sure. But that's the way —"

"No. Bullshit. You deserve more. And I'm not saying this just because I'm, you know, on your side."

228 ·

Nothing from Jason.

"Anyway, so I was thinking of saying something to Whetter about how if you're moved up to the third line, even the second, it would add your punch in the corners, you could dish it out to the fancy guys in front and in no way would it —"

"Jesus, no. Don't."

"No?"

"No way. C'mon. Thanks, but no."

"Yeah, you're probably right."

Why, why had he gone with a ploy he'd all along known was pathetic, the worst?

"Okay then. I guess I'll see you, you know, when I see you."

"Okay."

"See ya buddy."

"Yup."

See ya buddy. He felt barely tolerated, indulged. Some things you know you'll be cringing about in darker moments to come.


He rifled the medicine cabinet for aspirin. Nothing but a bottle of Midol, which he'd heard of guys using.

The hole in the wall beside the toilet was even more embarrassing on these frigid days when the exposed boards grew a white sheet of frost and you could feel the cold as you sat on the throne. He could imagine the girls cursing him, feeling like white trash as they suffered their icy morning pee.

He rattled under the sink, knocking Marg's and Beth's bottles this way and that. A clue to love here, him under this sink. Because how you felt about a female's cache of stuff was definitely linked to how you felt about her. The creams the scents the soaps the brushes — was it vain clutter or was it sexy mystery?

If you're in love, it doesn't even matter if she's clean.

He hadn't lived with anyone before Leah, and her discreet lotions and bath oils (pre-Bonaduce gifts, from who knows) and makeup; even her styling combs and hair dryer and, God, even her tampons, had been a surprising source of shy joy and horniness. That he was living with someone who used this stuff was proof of their difference, the difference that fuelled the fire. Under the sink this junky palette of Marg's and Beth's and maybe earlier tenants' was only irritating. There was nothing for him except the Midol, two tablets of which he pocketed in case the pounding got worse. Dylan tonight, but before that the workshop of his stuff, his "novel," no two pages of which fit together. Three hours of Bonaduce roasted. His brain's balls kicked and forked apart.

He closed the cabinet with a foot. What he really needed was some amphetamine. He was starving, and about to go into the kitchen to steal someone else's food. He'd lost weight and his lousy diet had been making him tired, he could feel it. *Jesus* it would be nice to bring home a few bags of groceries. He eyed the gaping wall, the frost, the roll of toilet paper sitting stuck in the ice on a two-by-four.

Had he ever gone grocery shopping with Leah? He couldn't remember ever doing that together. There was always practice, or road trips. It would have been nice. Choosing a lettuce, cuts of meat, aren't we out of dish soap? How would you know? she'd quip. He'd be coy in the pet-food aisle. Bring a huge load of food home and over the days put it all in their mouths. How basic and sexy can you get?

He realized that he would love nothing better, save having sex with her, than to go with Leah to a drugstore and watch her buy lipstick, watch her try it on, wipe it off, another colour, that one, choosing the colour of his lust.

"Marg. G'mornin'." He spoke to her baby-blue-bath-robed back, elbows going up as she lifted bacon out of the pan.

"Morning."

"Any spare crusts of bread for a fella to catch the drippings?"

Before the workshop Big Jan found him in the lounge, having a nervous coffee. A bunch of writers were about to discuss his writing. He knew it wasn't spectacular. It sure could have been better. But he did care about it so he should have sat down and put way more effort in.

He looked up, Jan standing right over him. He grimaced for her and made as if biting his nails. Jan didn't crack a smile back. Which wasn't like her. Maybe on the day you were being roasted you got treated with nothing but professional —

"Come out in the hall. We need a word." Unsmiling, in fact shaking her head, she turned and left the lounge. He took another sip of coffee and glanced at Phil, who shrugged.

Out in the hall, a glaring Jan Dionne met him. She shook her head again, this time baring her teeth. Before she spoke she stopped to glare again.

"I was going through Manuel Diaz's new collection yesterday, Robert." She stared him in the eye, waiting.

Nothing occurred to him, save the tiniest seed of panic at the guy's name, Diaz. Diaz.

"A poem called 'Eye of the Cross.'"

His memory churned, caught, then blasted apart in panic. He'd forgotten all those poems he'd borrowed to get in here.

"I mean listen, fuck you, Robert, you didn't even spell the title right."

"Well, I think I was trying to fix it. 'On the Cross' gave it two mean —"

"I don't need this. I could easily, *easily*, have you kicked out. Out of the whole program."

"Jan? What it was, was me having no time to get enough of my own stuff together."

"Last night I felt betrayed, Robert. But right now I don't feel anything."

How clear his own feeling was. He cared less about getting kicked out than he did about being hated by the one person in school he liked. And yet in the back of his mind a childish voice was telling him, Doesn't matter, I'm going to Dylan with Jason tonight.

"Jan, I know saying sorry won't do it, I know that. Do what you have to do."

"Don't worry. I will."

"I guess, I guess if I could ask a favour, it would be that you look at my real work, the work I've done for the class, and let it rest on that. I swear *that's* my work."

"Robert? I know *that's* your work because it's not very good. If I do you this favour your chances aren't much better."

He didn't say touché. He knew she liked his work better than that. She was a hard one, staring at him not out of teacherly anger but something worse, an emotionless, clear-eyed dismissal, the kind that rings so true you take it home with you on your skin. And avoid mirrors for a while.

This was the shits, because he still liked her. He could probably still talk to her.

"Hey, buy you a dinner some night?"

He'd meant it as a joke, he was pretty sure of this, though things were blurring. Jan wasn't up to humour right then and, after her disbelieving look, she turned and walked.


The arena, where a few nights previous he'd helped coach the Reds to a sloppy victory under bright lights amidst scattered fans, was now crammed full, dark, and rowdy with expecta-

·tions. Jason's tickets were great. They were sitting off to the side a few rows up, overlooking the ice surface, which had been tarped and floored. On it sat perhaps a thousand. Up and down the aisles people moved, a bemused ambling. Lots of little kids running and pushing through. It was a hidden side of Fredericton, all these old Jerry Garcia, Gandalf, Che Guevara guys, their kids or maybe even grandkids wearing similar gear. And womenfolk in ankle-length gingham, unbelievable. Lots of ten-year-old girls with hippy bandanas around their heads. Probably lots of these older guys had come from the woods, back-to-the-landers trucking here in amazement that the Man had chosen Fredericton.

But there were also lots of regular sorts, even hockey-jacket types like him and Jason. Holy moly, him and Jason at Dylan. Who would've —

"See anybody selling Cokes?"

Bonaduce craned around, searching the aisles.

"Doesn't look like the vendors are out tonight. Probably have to hit the concessions."

Jason got up without a word and squeezed past people's knees.

The pressure off for a moment, Bonaduce sighed and stretched and looked around. This was fun, Jason or not. The steady deep buzz, the happy rumble, you could actually hear the smile in it, it was the noise of several thousand people who thought themselves lucky. You could smell marijuana — it wasn't hard to spot people passing joints. He hadn't seen this since Pink Floyd in Boston about a hundred years ago. He tapped his inner pocket, feeling the outline of the lighter and Rod's two joints in there, and the nauseating tickle of illegality. The stuff did make music stand out more brightly. Those times after a toke with Fournier, Fournier would go off and read and he'd lie back with the headphones and welcome a new take on songs he'd heard plenty of times before. He remembered one time listening stoned to Los

Lobos and thinking he was able to distinguish, just through the way they played, not only their personalities, but also who were best friends and why. But dope could sure take the ambition out of a fellah. And playing your own guitar while high was too, somehow, complicated, a brain busy watching itself watch how fast those fingers —

"Coke?" Jason was handing him down a drink. Jason, decent, respectful son.

They sat sipping for a while, taking in the scene.

"Hey, aren't these great seats?" Off to the side like this they were actually too near the stage for good sound. But they'd be able to see faces, and who played what. They'd see Dylan squinting, they'd see his cheeks hollow to suck his harmonica.

Jason nodded and said, "Yeah, not bad," and seemed to look around for the first time. He even glanced up at the ceiling.

"And thanks again, eh? It must have cost a bit. You sure?" He started going for his wallet, the twenty in it he'd borrowed from Marg.

"No. Oscar bought them."

"Ah. Good man. Oscar."

This was fine. Of course it was. They were together, who cares how. Oscar, good man.

"So how's the school going?"

"Okay."

"You switched to Forestry, right?"

"Second-year Forestry."

"So, so is it mostly about the business? Or, you know, the biology. The way they teach Forestry. What they prepare you for."

Jason tilted his head and appeared to consider something he hadn't before.

"Well, it's lots of stuff. You have to have Chemistry, and Statistics, lots of different stuff."

"So it's not just bigger guys with bigger axes."

"I just hope there's jobs still out in B.C. when I'm out," Jason said, shaking his head wistfully, not hearing the little joke.

Jobs, foremost in Jason's mind. Well, you did have to think about jobs. Though what about that last letter, Jason communicating some kind of desire to play pro? Maybe his time on the bench this year had snuffed that. Which wasn't fair. That asshole right-winger Harrington. A selfish one-way game, scores a few goals. Fans don't see through that, and apparently some coaches don't either.

Because they'd started talking, this pause was painful. They shouldn't be sitting in this clumsy hell.

"B.C.?"

"I guess."

"Why B.C.? Seems to me they have quite a tree infestation right here."

Jason was studying a hash pipe as it moved right below them, cloying in the nose. He didn't seem at all shocked. The smell, for some reason, made Bonaduce think of Jethro Tull, Montreal, the prancing Brit with the codpiece and flute. A decent show, though.

He reached into his pocket not knowing if there was a good way to broach this. It definitely straddled parent and buddy territory. You didn't want to come off like you were just trying to be cool.

He nudged his son and pointed down to the guys passing the peace pipe.

"Ever smoke any of that stuff?"

Jason shrugged. "Nah. Parties maybe."

"Yeah, me neither. But, hell, I figured, Hey, it's Mr. Dylan. Spirit of the occasion. I brought some."

Jason frowned and nodded in a way that could have meant yes, so Bonaduce slid the joint out of his leather like a sliver out of a wound. In the little ritual of lighting it and inhaling semi-fiercely he realized he looked too practised. My dad, he didn't make the NHL probably because of his drug problem.

It tasted strong and went right to his head. He held it out to Jason.

"Tokahontas?"

Jason considered the smouldering thing for a second before shrugging and saying "Nah."

Well, hell, bad idea, and what to do with it now. He took another drag, then sat with it. The guy to his left was his age and had a ponytail, so he nudged him and offered it. The guy took it but didn't smoke any. Instead he passed it further along, and Bonaduce watched Rod's joint go hand-to-hand a few more times before anyone took a puff. And then it kept right on going.

"So I wonder when they're going to start this party."

"Dunno," mumbled Jason, staring straight ahead.

"So, you very familiar with, with, you know, his music?"

"A little. Not much."

"Well, what do you think, do you *like* it?"

"It's okay."

Laconic little bastard. If there was one word that perfectly didn't describe Bob Dylan's music, it was "okay." This boy of his had taken bad lessons in Clint Eastwood. The one question was, was Jason always like this? Was this Jason, or was this Jason being angry? Was this his normal cool, or was this him punishing a wayward father? More to the crux of the matter, was this shitty silence a call for the same distance from him, or a demand that amends be made?

Bonaduce was on the verge, but felt that a gushing apology, here and now, would be ridiculous. But maybe not. Maybe one good sentence. One perfect phrase. Jason, let's. Jason, why don't we. This silence was ripe, was torture. God this dope was strong.

"Jason —"

His son turned to him, they met eyes. But the lights fell, and the crowd roared. Bonaduce felt the relief whoosh forth in his huge exhaled breath. Those *eyes.* He'd never seen into them before, and why was it that he was so surprised to see himself? And Leah, but mostly himself. But the boredom in them, the aggressive neutrality, it felt — It ripped your —

The band walked on, a bunch of young guys in T-shirts. Then on stepped the Man. No warm-up act, no announcer even, just him. Casual, classy. You want Dylan, you get Dylan. His band could have been his children, age-wise. Two were black. Bonaduce had forgotten how he'd wanted to joke with Jason about what he'd read in the paper that morning, the description of Dylan's voice as sounding like a bee in a jam jar, which was pretty good. Then the gossip about how the band members were under instructions never to look Dylan in the eye. Yikes, what did that say about him? Either major paranoia or some kind of insane regal —

They started playing: bass riff, drum walking itself in, organ noodling over top, rhythm guitar comes chunking along in back, ooo this was nice. Bonaduce leaned over, whapped Jason's shoulder and yelled.

"*This is nice, eh?*"

Woops. The music stopped. It was only a tune-up.

"Only a tune-up I guess. But it sounded good, eh? I think this is going to be good."

"Sounded good."

"Isn't it funny how music, how music can, you know, 'resolve itself'? You know, how sounds can sort of ask a kind of question, and then come up with an answer? and we can *hear* that? I mean, in *noise*? The art of noise."

Jason nodding, staring at the stage, a little smile. Don't get paranoid yourself. But slow down.

What might have been the stub of Rod's joint was being passed hand-to-hand in the aisle below him.

Finally they did start, a song he didn't recognize. You couldn't hear the lyrics, the sound system was not great. Which was, c'mon, this was awful, the guy was basically a poet, his words his strength, and you couldn't make them out. Why hadn't they — Or maybe it was his voice itself, that nasal whining, it was hardly human, maybe no microphone could translate it, maybe with Dylan distortion was automatic. Man this dope was strong, but man this man was bad. Bee in a jam jar — guy who wrote that was the best poet in the English language.

Whoops, was that a little stagger? Dylan addled, to boot. Who knows what the guy's done to himself, booze and drugs fit for a king. Probably a travelling good doctor with him, keep him alive and tuned. Quick, yells the doc, get me my bag, the drummer just looked at Bobby, he needs a sedative, get the cane toad.

After two songs Dylan took a short break, it looked like to replace a guitar string and fiddle with the sound mix. It was a laid-back show, no sense of hurry or trying to keep the crowd happy. Well, with the Man no one was going anywhere. People looked as attentive to how he sipped from his cup as they were to his music.

Bonaduce made a loud gush noise sucking his own cup dry. It sounded better than Dylan. This was fun, he was definitely having fun. Not even Big Jan could steal his fun right now. Though why was he on her case, it wasn't her fault. But it wasn't his fault either, Jesus Christ. He wouldn't be here having fun if he hadn't lied his way in. The workshop had gone okay, considering. He hadn't been keen on continuing after what had come to pass with Jan, but you sign on the line, you pay the fine. As expected, Jan was not too praising, and the others picked up on this and followed like the righteous lemmings they were; though Phil, good old Phil, had laughed and liked his stuff, liked that it wasn't connected, called it a "revealing pastiche." Next term, if there was a next term, he would prove to them that he could write up a big fine piece of—

A woman, a wild-bodied Asian beauty, was bouncing up the steps, all eyes on her. He nudged Jason with an elbow, feeling instantly foolish for it. Well, will you look at her. She was in stylish rather than idealistic hippy gear and in full body-stocking flaunt. He turned to Jason and Jason smiled and nodded and facetiously waggled his eyebrows, and Bonaduce had to tell himself not to feel insulted and stupid. God this kid of his was a quiet bugger. The thought that he might be gay struck him. It felt suddenly possible. He'd never heard mention of a girlfriend, and come to think of it he hadn't been part of any dressing-room sex banter Bonaduce had heard. Well. He knew he was entering a stoned tangent now as he interpreted all of Jason's silences to be akin to shame. Don't get close to Father because then Father will find out. This was all nonsense, of course. Jason was too — what? — too boring to be gay, gays had a spark. Though what if he was? It would be fine with him. You wouldn't *choose* it for your son, but hell he wouldn't hesitate marching in a Pride parade with him, why not? hell, he'd wear his team sweater to bug the guys — maybe a goalie mask too, stay hidden, ha ha — but you wouldn't choose it, I mean why subject your kid to the roll of the dice when it comes to AIDS, and you don't want him to suffer the social thing, the life of paranoia about what people think. Then that switching over to snark and hate, you couldn't blame gay guys for hating everything that wasn't gay. Come to think of it, maybe life was easier that way, something to focus on, and anger for fuel. This dope is extremely strong. It's fun. And the *main* reason you don't want Jason to be gay is because — there she's heading back down the stairs and the horny little bugger is stealing glances at her — is because then Jason wouldn't grow up and have children and have *this same joy inside, this joy of having a son of his very own!*

"What's so funny?" Jason staring, smiling at the dad's endless laughter.

Bonaduce was about to try to explain, that is, lie, when the band began again. A huge relief, moving the load from inside the head to outside. And it sounded beautiful, it truly did, until the Man stopped sipping whatever was in that cup and got up off a chair and began to play along. Bonaduce noticed something else when Dylan began to play. The band had been having a great time, but as soon as Dylan wanged out a couple of bars they went sober and rigid and watched him — actually turned as a group to face him so they could see his guitar work, and not because it was good. It was bad and unpredictable and they were on the lookout for accidents. Bonaduce saw it actually happen, Dylan springing out of sequence and the guys having to stutter with their fingers to compensate. A few times Dylan was simply unfollowable and the song had streaks of chaos. Luckily the speakers were cranked up to fuzzy. You had music more polished than this at any bar in town.

Between songs Jason leaned over. "That one was one of his radio hits wasn't it?"

"Yeah."

He'd been unsure what song he'd been listening to. But — Jason, asking. It might be a first. Cherish this. It's beginning. He sat back in his seat and watched Jason from the side of his face. Watched him nodding to the beat; took in the bobbing nose, the blinking, the parted lips, the jaw working the gum. Jason knew he was being watched and seemed to accept it, naturally the long-lost dad's going to check him out. Maybe he liked being checked out. Maybe he had the Bonaduce ego. What's in a DNAme? This was great, this concert was great. Thanks, Oscar. What was the question? Radio hit.

"I think it was one of those he had right around his stupid Christian —"

The song erupted in what became an embarrassing barrage of what turned into the Man playing a five-minute lead. Acting out senile old dreams of Clapton grandeur. *This* was Spinal Tap. The guy had been playing guitar for decades and hadn't learned how. He'd love to get Jason back to the house and play for him, a few tricky ones, maybe even sing a bit — could he sing to Jason? Might be a bit queasy for both of them. A crooning dad, yuck. Dylan was blowing notes now and, c'mon, even his harmonica-playing — it was his trademark and his trademark was bad playing. The guy was maybe a great songwriter but that was all. People had mistaken eccentric delivery for great performance. This was also the guy who put deep meaning into rock and roll and in doing so took out the humour. After Dylan everyone had to be a philosopher, you couldn't rock around the clock any more. Guy takes some nice old Woody Guthrie stuff and lays the oblique snark to it and sings it like a hornet in a bean can and gets studied in English classes across the land. People forget this was a guy who had himself baptised in Pat Boone's white-shoe swimming pool. Not that you wanted consistency, and maybe Dylan did it as a huge tipsy wisecrack, but here he was playing lead guitar like an emperor wearing not one stitch of —

Jason was leaning into him, yelling.

*"Guy rocks, eh?"*


He dropped Jason off after Jason declined the offer of a beer back at his place, which was fine, it was late, the boy had a cold and had to study.

"See ya later. Thanks for the ride."

"See ya Jace. See ya on the ice."

Jason wanged the door shut, and a dump of needles hit the windshield, the strong bugger.

He watched Jason's lope on the snowy walk, pleased with the notion that after Christmas he'd be playing an actual game with the boy, let's not forget why he was here. Jason turned and waved in the glass door of the shabby three-storey building, not unlike the place Leah and himself had occupied when they first met, where Jason had been planted.

He had had enough family for one night, truth be told. However nice it had been, however nice a start.

Back home, no way he could sleep. He walked the house lightly, aimlessly, ears still droning full. He checked Marg's room and she was out. Lots to tell her, where was she?

Well, damn, the dad also had to study. Time to put some major thought into Friday morning's presentation. In two days he'd have his ass up in the air in Doctor Gail's class. Here he was all dope-addled and tomorrow he'd be mud. In the living room — no more little coffin bedroom for him — he set up his Ondaatje notes and opened the special-occasion Heineken, one of the six he'd picked up in case Jason had come back. A beer to counteract the high, hopefully downshift to the pace of words on a page. It would've been so much more fun Friday to be a Bob Dylan critic than an Ondaatje critic. If Jason were here he could have practised, lobbing grenades into the Dylan myth, converting Jason with precision, rigour, the new academic Bonaduce tongue. Sad the boy didn't have a feel for music, but then neither did Leah, there'd been a sense of her putting up with rather than enjoying his record collection.

Another Heineken in Jason's honour. Then a third — take the night off — in honour of not worrying about Ondaatje. He'd read the book twice, how prepared can you get. He had the notes, the major points to make. He would have to fill in blanks, wing the bulk of it, but that was the nature of discourse, it wasn't a speech. He even had a way to get in the word *postmodern*: this book is not postmodern, but good old-fashioned storytelling. So there.

In the spirit of winging it, he lit up the other joint, because it helped words fly in his head. He'd stick a butterfly net up there and bring some down, get some insights pinned to the page. Friday he'd have a fighting chance.

He put on some of their snark music, not too loud, and stole another of Toby's bottles too, but came to his senses and cut himself off after one glass, remembering that not only was he not in shape, but that Christmas layoff would put a further dent in what shape he had. Tomorrow night was the last practice until the New Year. Actually it was a game, something called the annual Red–White Fight, where they divvied the guys in two, and the losers bought the winners pizza and beer. A little tradition, sounded good.

After tomorrow night, and Friday's presentation, it was two weeks off, no hockey no school. Then he'd have plenty of time for. He could do whatever he damn well.

He slouched deeply into the couch. His foot accidentally nudged Ondaatje off the coffee table. A Fredericton band, Modabo, was on. Nice harmonies. You could tell they were good guys. A clue about Fredericton, what it engendered in its sons, what kind of spirit. Despite his many sins, he'd left Jason in a decent nest.

He was glad he'd come back.

He caught himself sitting motionless, smiling, staring slightly up at nothing. A gleaming swirl in the gut was flooding up the neck, taking leaps into his face. Sometimes you cannot deny your happiness, there's a big happy fish looping in your stomach, you're on the verge of an idiot guffaw.

He had to move his body, something. He dove to the floor for push-ups. He counted. He did either fifty-six or sixty-five.

Still high, still happy, he brought his box of tapes from his room. He settled back with a homemade compilation of oldies. "Little Latin Lupe Lu" made him laugh, did these guys know how funny they were? Demanding sex, *shouting* for it, wailing, then a wheedling plea, pure pure jungle need. All in five-bar simple. Then "Stay," another pleading classic, hard-penis falsetto, some black Italian guy from New York City. Next a Woody Guthrie, his ultimate get-back song, "Little Black Train," about death, all of us being in the same boat, the train's a-comin' fer ya. Here, rich folks, you kin fight mah politics but you cain't argue this'n. Next was something Fournier had insisted he throw on the tape, some hot new poet type, Beck. One of these guys, like Cher, had only the one name, really cheap parents. Beck proved pretty negative, a Toby with a song to sing. But decent lyrics, "toxins won't kill your day job." Maybe a double negative makes a positive, who knows. But at my funeral, play "Pretty Little Angel Eyes" please.

No sleep yet. In deference to Oscar he tried some *Best of Pink Floyd*. It was okay; sure, they were good at ominous. But their druggy calculations told him they weren't playing from their balls, they really weren't. This thing Oscar had for Brits was a fundamental wall between them, it was worth calling the guy on, it would be a good argument over a beer. British was head, American was heart. You can't get much more apart than that. Earth and sky. Though Lennon's "Well Well Well" could scrape your guts out and cure your indigestion.

Coming out of a dream of what would've been the world's greatest song, Slim Whitman singing a cameo on Pink Floyd's "Money," he realized he was head-lollingly tired. He tilted the wine bottle for more but it was empty. He remembered having lots of insights, some about Ondaatje, but he couldn't remember what they were. He hadn't liked Dylan and Jason had. Unless he was being polite, wanting the both of them to be having a good time, a thought which took Bonaduce back up to glad.

This — Jason wanting them both to have a good time — was the closest he'd come to what Jason's love might be like. A fearsome thought, and enough for tonight.

He whistled — he never whistled — on his way to the bathroom. He almost went down, grabbed at a wall without looking. He liked it here, he knew this house's bones and didn't really want to leave it. Marg was bailing early. Kick Toby out, it'd be a decent place to live.

Howling, now he was howling. He heard Rod or someone yell *Shut-up* but he couldn't stop laughing. Because he'd found himself standing at the toilet, pointing the wrong way. Busy thinking of Marg moving, of life without Marg, he'd unzipped and taken his dick out, then half-asleep wondered if maybe he didn't have to do the other, so he'd pivoted, but still with his pants up and dick out, but now pointed at the bathtub, then he awoke to the situation and howled.

He turned to successfully pee. He'd once had a girlfriend who he'd *twice* found sitting backwards on the toilet, peeing. Elbows on the porcelain reservoir, hands in her hair, calmly deranged. He suspected a serious drug or alcohol problem and gently ditched her.

Still whistling, but sincerely bound for his room, he found himself stopping at the phone. It couldn't be all that far past midnight, maybe it was one or two. The idea was to thank Oscar for the tickets, for the idea to begin with, maybe give him shit about Pink Floyd. Good man like Oscar wouldn't be asleep yet. He pressed the buttons which his hands knew by heart, and wouldn't you know it but at the other end after some fumbling with the receiver it was her who picked up the phone tonight.

"Hello?"

"Hi, it's me."

That's all he said and all he planned to say, but her voice, all cozy and warm in the way she said hi back, the lovely sleepiness and the sweet concern, made Bonaduce simply lose his mind.

"I have to be with you."

Silence, a shuffling, then, "Hello?" From Oscar.

Bonaduce hung up, heart racing. Had Oscar heard? Had she passed the phone? Had Oscar grabbed it? What had just happened? Did Oscar know?

Did he want Oscar to know?

Why, damn, why did he have to call? What kind of guy are you, anyway? You don't do that to people.

Why do you want it *all*?

Right now, as he was finding a kitchen chair with his hand and Oscar was going upstairs to her, to ask about the call, who would she be truthful to? Neither answer made him feel good. What had he done?

The happy fish looping in the gut was gone. So was sleep.

•‿

Lat e

What am I good for, what am I good at, what's the point of m.

Can't help but wondering. Been wondering twenty years. The thing with playing in the minors, youre always wreslting mediocrity. As a description of yoursel. Worse because when a kid you were the best on your team etc. You grow up assuming youll always be that. Suddenly you arent, and there's a whole other league up there that wont even look at you.

To make it, you have to be the best, the very best, at one thing. Just one. In the minors its guys like me, jack of all, master of nothign.

Famous people are all like that, they have the one big thing. Can Bob Dylan skate? Who cares — he had the best words to put the tunes to. Could Ghandhi do anything else? Could he cook? Tell a decent joke? No but he was the best at taking punches without ever punching back.

Could the Buddha drive a jeep.

For a couple of years in Kalamazooo I was the best at being an asshole in front of the net. Was called The Zookeeper. I was a master. It was an act. Almsot worked though. Almsot got me called up. I was almsot a famous asshole.

So whats Jackofalltrades Bonaduce the best at. It isnt hockey. It isnt literature or writing. It isnt women. It definitely isnt fatherhood. Friendship has come under serious doubt, too.

No — how could I have missed it? Its right in front of my face. It made me phone her. Im the best in the world at staying up all night feeling sorry for myself. So, quit it. And typing is getttting

·⤿

Panic.

It had taken him hours of steady breathing, of hard focus, to get this far. The meanest work he'd ever done, meaner than push-ups this getting out of bed, getting enough clothes on, getting to the bathroom after asking God to let you please just not piss on your floor. Fighting panic the whole while. Finally making it to the kitchen table. Easy to flip back into panic at any moment here. Pick up that fork.

Steady breaths. Normal life. Hold your fork. Keep dead hand on lap under the table. Marg is watching.

"Tomorrow night, Regent Mall, eight-thirty?" she asked from the door. Wearing a big absurd beaver hat, the RCMP kind he hadn't seen since Winnipeg. It was apparently freezing outside. She had the earflaps down and the ribbon tied under her chin.

"Regent Mall. Eight-thirty," he repeated, softly, because even his tongue was gone this morning and eight-thirty was *ay-thiry*.

He was trying to eat the eggs she had made him, hoping she wouldn't notice he was using his left hand.

It was almost noon. He had stayed in bed as long as possible, wishing it wasn't true. So deadbody tired that even lying down felt like a strain, so tired that staying alive took effort.

"I think it'll be four, five places at most. We can do it in an hour." She was talking louder with her earflaps down. "And I mean, thanks, eh?"

"Hey. For nothing." She'd lined up appointments to view apartments, and he was driving her around to them.

"Taxi's here. 'Bye."

It was her first day of a Christmas-rush job in the mall bookstore, the same bookstore he'd had his bad dream about. Here he was with a floppy right hand, what a humorous meshing of worlds.

"Two of them aren't two-bedrooms," she was saying, pausing in the open kitchen door, frosty air billowing in. Her eyes were impish, fun-filled, at her best. "Just in case you wanna, you know, tie the knot."

He worked up a smile. Said something approximating "We'll bring along the preacherman."


It was the kind of deeply frozen world he hadn't walked into in many years. It was a childhood morning, a prairie morning, arctic. Your face burned and, in a minute, ached. Well, today only half the face: ha ha, the hidden rewards. He saw the tree on his car roof and looked away because it seemed only dead. Too scant of needle to consider any more. Last night, Jason hadn't mentioned the tree on his roof.

The mucous in his nose had instantly frozen and his eyes were tearing and blinding him. He went back in, found someone's mauve scarf, came out again with it awkward and ugly around his face and head, a bad wrapping job, done with more awareness of a dangling right arm than of the left clumsily working, self-pity rising out of panic to erupt in a sob. He sobbed just the once and stopped it. Poor me. Feeling sorry for yourself — it felt like warm soup, you saw guys fall into it and never get out, you could see them wearing it on the face for all to see.

The idea was to walk it off.

Limping mummy, a slit in the thick bandage for his ancient sick eyes. Muted grunting at every right footfall. Why not drool through the scarf, scare some kids.

He worked his way along the highway, bypassing the snow for a while, heading for a distant field he'd seen all along from his window but had never visited. In this cold even the truck noise was thinner, muffled. Tires sounding hard as plastic on the cold concrete, you could feel the crisp sound right in your nerves. Jesus, what did the truckers think of him, hobbling maniac out on the road, heading east. He thought of his occasionally entertaining bus window, its flashing frame of car wrecks, grass fires, chicken yards, barefoot kids and gawking trashy idiots, roadside tragedies like himself.

There wasn't much traffic. The quiet was nearly peace if he could keep from thinking. He lurched up onto the snow. You could see the tree and its cluster.

As he approached, it sounded electric. It crackled, rice crispies freshly in milk. It soon grew louder than his crunching steps, louder even than his fear. When a pause and tremor appeared to rifle through them *en masse*, he stopped. He was a hundred feet away. The tree's branches were full and heavy with them, weighted down. He could see now what he'd suspected, that they were all one species of bird. All noisily eating, clusters of orange berries. The words *mountain ash* came to mind. You made hockey sticks from ash.

He took smaller steps, trying for a harmless-looking rhythm. His right mitt he tried to keep from smushing dumbly against his thigh. Hundreds of birds eating, frenzy in the extreme cold. Massed crackle of their plucking, beaking, biting. Closer, looking hard, he saw he didn't know what they were. Crested head like a cardinal, with what looked like yellow over the eye, and their bodies were a nice, a subtle, an almost unnatural kind of tan.

Like a child's view of things. In one black tree identical birds eat orange berries. On the snow a man with a scarf around his face watches, arms out because it's so cold.

He'd probably gotten as close as he could anyway, but at his faltering half-step they all leapt away, making him jump. A sudden flapping *whoosh*, the whole instantly apart in so many pieces, birds exploding away in all directions.

The full moon up there, frozen pearl bouncing at his shoulder.

He stabbed three times before hitting the doorbell, with his right hand. All day it had improved to the point where now a doorbell was possible.

From the street he'd seen their Christmas tree in the window, all lit up and heartbreaking. Wonderful, now he was invading their home. He could see in the door window many coats hung, boots on cardboard stretching well into the hallway. A gathering of some sort. Maybe an office party. Great, he was bashing and crashing a party on top of things. He just wanted to take her aside and — He didn't know what he wanted.

"Bob! Just in time."

"Oscar buddy." His tongue was back. He slowly unwrapped his scarf.

"Our little festival-of-nations party. Come right on in."

Oscar was good at not showing surprise, at showing nothing at all. Maybe he greeted criminal clients like this. Polite to murderers, thieves, adulterers.

"I just came by to —"

"Come on, come in, it's cold. Everyone's here. Jason's here. I hear it was a fantastic concert."

"Sure was. The Man. Thanks for that."

Oscar waved away the thanks and took his leather coat, didn't seem to notice that it was a while coming off. There was no friendliness, no eye-to-eye before he rushed away toward the kitchen, yelling behind his back to make yourself at home.

He stood in the entranceway. Everyone's here. He hadn't wanted Jason in on this. Whatever this was. But maybe it was okay. Maybe Jason was a buddy now. Maybe it was best, in fact. Had to happen sometime.

About twenty men, women and children sat around, the majority of them Latino. Many had gifts unwrapped and sitting in their laps. Cutlery sets looked like the popular item, that and ceramic teapots. Board games for the children. They kept their gifts cradled in the wrapping paper. They looked too tropical for either the gifts or the Christmas tree, which swelled in the corner with bright ornaments and smell, that essence sharp in the nose always reminding Bonaduce of snow.

You thought "Mexican," but of course, being refugees, they were probably anything but. The women tended to favour lots of makeup, like TV women from the Fifties. Soon enough you could see the range of nationality, or race. Long faces, round faces, darker, lighter, some looked Indian, some almost Chinese. A few of the young men looked solo, and sad for it. A fair number looked like they felt themselves above this quaint gathering, their eyes bored and condescending. It may have been his nerves but some seemed to be watching him with suspicion. Well, he was the biggest guy in the room. Big tough hairy face. He didn't have the energy to think about this.

He felt like a huge fool and wished he hadn't come. This had nothing to do with him. There would be no talking with Leah here, if that is what he had come for. But how could he just run? At least say hi, Merry Christmas.

He took a seat on a couch beside a plump woman who looked his age. Though when he smiled at her and she smiled back, she looked younger. He noticed a scar on her head, on her temple, that looked like it had once been a hole. You don't come to Canada after a bullet to the temple. It was probably a pox scar, a vaccination scar. Though they don't vaccinate you in the head.

"Bob," he said, nodding. He'd almost put out his right hand, offering the limpest handshake in history. Here in Canada, we are very gentle.

The woman smiled and nodded back.

"Where are you from?"

"I from Chile." *Chee-lay.* Big professional immigrant smile.

"Ah," he said, tilting back his head as if she had explained something.

She added nothing more. He saw how much he didn't know this person, let alone these people. And people are not alike. He'd gotten to know Finns, and they were nothing like Swedes, who were nothing like Russians.

"How long have you been in Canada?"

"I here two day." Her non-stop smile, unfelt.

"That must — You must be in shock. Have you found — Have they found you a place to —"

"I just visiting." She smiled for real now, something of the imp in her, knowing his presumptions.

"Ah."

He should really get going. That clatter in the kitchen might be Leah. He could go in, say his hello, make his apology, go. That's why he was here, to apologize.

"My brother." The woman pointed to a man helping himself at the punch bowl. Oscar was suddenly at the man's side, holding a bottle of vodka. Oscar laughed and made some kind of moaning noise, glugged some into the punch.

Jason appeared bearing a tray of glasses. Was he wearing an ascot? The boy didn't look up, though by now of course he knew his father was here. Instead he went back to the kitchen and reappeared with a plate of something, some pastry Bonaduce didn't recognize. Jason said something to a woman who stood surveying the food, and they both laughed.

Jason had grown up with this, with these people. His son went back to the kitchen.

"He come ten years. Now he wife. Now he kids." She pointed to a Caucasian woman delicately fingering tree ornaments, many of which looked handmade.

"Now he help others come. With the worker Leah."

"Ah." He pictured himself shouting to her, a dumb American tourist, *Leah my wife!*, stabbing his chest with a finger.

Now here was Jason, approaching him with a beer, striding the room self-consciously. He looked nervous. Jason, take your father a beer, will you? Bonaduce gave him a little left-hand wave of greeting. Voices, what sounded like Oscar and Leah, arguing in the kitchen.

"Jace."

"Hi."

"What's with the neck?" He saw it wasn't an ascot but a towel, and Jason's watery eyes.

"I got this lousy cold."

"Looks like some kind of giant weird poultice." The image of ascots as poultices was amusing for some reason, ascots giant poultices for intellectuals, absorb any unworthy, common notions trying to rise to the head.

"No. Just a shitty cold." He either didn't know the word *poultice* or didn't find it funny.

"Jeez. And the Red–White game tonight."

"I'll probably be there."

"Jace, you sign the name, you play the game, eh?"

Hey, Jason, want to see your father try to sign his name?

From the kitchen, Leah definitely said "Bob." Something loud about "Bob."

"But hey, you gotta watch your health, nobody's gonna watch it for you."

"I guess."

"Though I *am* looking forward to you buying me my pizza and beer."

"No way." Jason finally cracking a sleepy smile.

"Way." This was good, this was all right. "Just keep your head up."

"Yeah, right. As if."

This was really okay. Jason, eyes down, but smiling and joking back. Hard not feeling like a loud fool around him but maybe that would be their way, these the roles they would play. It felt good just to have a role.

"Helpin' Mum a bit. Gotta go do some stuff."

"Okay. Go for it. See ya later."

Go for it. Loud fool.

Jason went for it, went to help the mum you could no longer hear arguing. Not a trace of cynicism about helping mum in the kitchen. Jason was a good kid. And if he was a momma's boy, what the hell else could you expect after —

What came next was fast and furious. Jason had no sooner left when Leah was loud again and he was at the party table again with another platter of food. Oscar was at Jason's side with the vodka, pouring. Neither smiled or talked. Bonaduce was startled to see Leah in the hallway, pointing a finger right at him. She turned on her heel, looking nothing but angry. Apparently he was to follow. She looked so pretty, heavily made up like these women she was hosting.

He followed her into the laundry room, limping stupidly past her with his beer as she stood in the door with her hand on the doorknob. She closed the door, locked it. Absurdly, the faintest notion of sex stirred below his belt. Who knows what she and Oscar do, allow, pursue. Ridiculous, because her face was set. She bent down, scooped up two sneakers and a plastic cat-food dish, wrenched open the dryer door, threw them in, slammed the door and hit some buttons on the control panel. The dryer roared into thuds and clatters that shook the walls.

"*What the hell are you trying to do?*"

"I just, *I just wanted to —*"

"*What was last night all about?*"

"*I'm sorry I —*"

"*Are you a complete moron?*"

"Did you, did you tell him?"

"No, thanks, *you* told him."

Ah, man, hated by Oscar. Didn't want that.

"*And now here you are at my party!*"

If sarcasm could kill, he'd be dust. He'd forgotten how good she was at mean. Her eyes cut away the two decades easily, and he saw it again, in her glare the knife that had severed and kept them apart in the first place. He'd forgotten but now could feel it, the truth of her, the truth of him and her. The truth he'd known while leaving Fredericton for Rochester, that this knife had finished off their hearts.

"*I just wanted to thank Oscar for the tickets. For Dylan.*"

Leah's eyes wide and incredulous, her head tilted to deal with a moron.

"You mean for *paying Jason to go with you?*"

"Well —"

"*He had to pay Jason fifty dollars before he'd go with you.*"

Ah shit.

"*Oh, good, you're drunk.*"

Stooping in the foaming beer to pick up the shards of brown glass, he cut himself, then had to lean back against the washing machine.

"*Don't step in it. Jesus.*"

She moved past him to an open closet where the household brooms and mops were kept, good proper convenient household. He leaned against the washer and breathed. He thought he could smell burning plastic. Burning plastic cat-food dish.

"Okay. I'm sorry. *I'm sorry. I'm sorry for what we did, and I'm —*"

"*Don't worry. So am I.*"

"*— sorry for Oscar. I just want to get to know Jason. I won't bug you any —*"

"*Bobby?*" Smiling, shaking her head, not looking at the drunken moron as she swept up his broken bottle. "*Why do you even think Jason's yours?*"

Falling to all fours, he helped himself up to standing. He didn't look at her. One sock was wet with beer and he limped it past, to the door. He fumbled at the knob, swatting her hand when she shouted *Jesus* and made to help him. Burning plastic making them both cough.

Wet sock on the linoleum, a little counter-slap to the beat of his limping, you could almost smile walking past, in view of the living room. Concerned rising murmurs, they had heard the yelling and now they smelled strange smoke as you smacked by with your beer-sock. From a peg in the entranceway he plucked his coat, didn't want to, but while struggling with it one-handed he looked up and nodded to the swirl of Mexicans, Incas, Mayans. He went for his boots. What do you know. All this time, a cat he couldn't feel had been rubbing up against the leg.

The next morning, sitting in his car outside the building supply store, waiting for it to open, he thumped the wallet on his thigh and wondered what a chunk of drywall might cost these days. He also reviewed last night's Red–White game, how it had gone, how the Zookeeper had appeared out of nowhere. Though maybe he'd always known the Zookeeper would arrive, maybe that's why he'd come north to begin with. Can't build bridges, you might as well burn them.

It was storming pretty hard and traffic was slow on the way to campus. Despite the snow he walked quickly in from the parking lot. He could feel the flakes hooking onto the whiskers, he hadn't shaved in a while. The limp was glaring at this pace, no avoiding it, but you didn't want to be late. Didn't want to give them the chance to start talking without you. They'd all read the book, they'd probably read all Ondaatje's books. Someone like Phil would grab the reins and take over, and you don't want to walk in on that. You want to get in the first punches.

Moving through such benevolent big-flaked snow, you could almost feel that things were normal and good. Up all night, he'd slept no more than a fretful two or three hours. The fatigue and the worry that kept him awake was gone now, he was ready for the game. This kind of snow, like the sky is softly falling on your head. Its silence so deep it is a sound, *hush*. An awareness to it all. Snow like this made him think of the words *the baby Jesus*, and — he could see it clearly — a white embossed Christmas card he'd touched with his fingertips as a child. He could remember the card's smell.

Up all night with Ondaatje, he could riff off whole paragraphs if called upon. To back up his points. Take, for instance, when Kip says. Well, this kind of metaphor can also be found in the passage where Hana imagines that.

He can even quote a critic on the book. Last night in the shaky two hours between Leah's delightful Christmas party and his spectacular Red–White game he'd found himself in the library, at the keyboard, searching. *The English Patient* was new enough that there wasn't much on it. Apparently it takes years for academics to work stuff up. But he found a few articles. One by a guy named Bird suited him perfectly, having to do with Ondaatje's good old-fashioned storytelling techniques of withholding information. In the stacks he located the journal and tore Bird out of it, and now in his bookbag on his shoulder Bird felt like the Bible. With Bird as ammo you could start the presentation with something like "It's all very ordinary. Behind the poetry *The English Patient* is a spy story, and a love story, only the whole time James Bond is lying mortally wounded in bed."

He could feel the melting snow as cold ointment against his old dead skin.

It was two minutes before class time when he got to Carleton Hall. As usual they'd all be early. They'd be up there in their strategic chairs, sipping coffee, firing up their synapses, whacking their wit on the ass, flexing their little shoulders. But no one will have gotten started on a good sentence quite yet.


So here you were at the annual Red–White game. Here in a room with a bunch of guys, throwing jokes about winning the beer and pizza. You're taking a while with the gear, the trainer tightening your skates for you after your story about dislocating a knuckle shovelling snow, bizarre how these things happen. The guy kneeling at your feet, grunting. Hey, I like this, says the Bonaduce, what else can you do while you're down there? He tells you to fuck off, guys laugh. You look and notice Harrington isn't laughing, in fact he's rolled his eyes and maybe that's what cements it for you. He's wearing red and you ask for a white jersey. You have fuel to burn.

Jason wasn't here. No surprise, and so what.

You step on. Whetter's suited up too, and they've got some guy dressed as Santa to ref. Girlfriends and scattered others in the stands. Though it's fun bullshit it's the closest thing to a game you've played in a year and the butterflies are going a little, despite everything else. Which makes the game of hockey such a wonderful thing.

You warm up, take a few shots. You can move okay, maybe you can hold your own. In any case here you are starting at right defence. A local TV station has sent a camera guy and he soft-steps to centre ice to catch the ceremonial face-off. A Moosehead rep, whose company has funded the beer, stands ready to drop the puck. He actually looks a little nervous. In the penalty box is a three-foot dented mock-up Moosehead beer can, the trophy. One centreman is the team captain, a red-haired pepperpot named Sullivan but called Maniac, and the other is Harrington, who's an assistant captain and has no nickname. The puck gets dropped. Sullivan smiles and doesn't budge, while Harrington, whose teeth are gritted, actually slashes for the stupid thing.

No hitting to speak of, an unwritten code. So lots of goals. Bonaduce himself picked up an assist on his second shift, nice little pass over the Red guy's stick, laying down flat for your streaking White buddy to send him in alone. On the bench then, breathing hard, respite from a world where there's no time to think. A world you're so familiar with, though it's always swiftly brand new. Catch your breath, feel your age, heart pounding, sweating freely, watch the game go by, involuntary groan when your guy hits the post. This is great, take a deep catch-up breath. Look down at your white jersey, look at the shiny lights coming off the black helmet beside you, look at the row of guys identically slumped. Just look around.

Third shift, Harrington put it through his legs trying to go around him, trying to suck him out, make a fool of the stumbly old guy enjoying his first game in a year. Wonky as he was it wasn't hard to fall into a curl and get his ass out to submarine the guy, catch his knee just right, you could feel it bend in the wrong direction, hear the second or two of surprise before the scream.

They carried Harrington off. Bonaduce, Whetter kicked off. Little Christmas present for you there Jace. Whoever you are. Gets fifty bucks, buys me a fucking Coke. Which I accepted with the dumb smile and big eyes of a dog. A Coke.

They'd already put Harrington into a car. In the dressing room there was no one to make Tonya Harding jokes to, except for the silent trainer, who actually smirked a bit — this Harrington was simply not well liked — and who was kind enough to help Bonaduce off with his skates. His skates which, after the good hot shower, after dressing and climbing into the heavy leather coat for the storm out there, after a moment's empty-handed meditation in the hall, he went back for. He picked the blades up out of their pool of water on the dressing-room floor, tucked them under his arm and, out in the parking lot, threw them in the back of the wagon.

This morning, inside Carleton Hall, he could feel snow melting on one side of his face, though you had to assume it was melting on both. Between classes the hallway was crowded. Out of the blue he was bone-deep exhausted, and dizzy in the sudden thudding heat. He paused a moment. Now he was moving sideways, now a wall thankfully against his shoulder. He took a few deep breaths. Something vital was sinking inside. He blinked, closed his eyes, and when he opened them, one eye was almost blind. As if one lid hadn't come up. He touched, and felt eyeball. Blindness was that fast, it was almost as if blinking had done it. Maybe it had.

Grab a little rest here, against the wall. He looked around, pretending to search for some notice announcing some event, a poster on these walls, the ceiling, trying to will his dead eye back.

There was the sense of vision's potential, not unlike the sense of something familiar yet at the same time forgotten, like a dead memory and tip-of-the-tongue hunger for it. With the good eye he noted the bland colours, the grey, the beige, the ceiling the colour of nothing but shadow. He shouldn't be standing staring like this. Unshaven Bonaduce, studying walls. Security please, I'd like to report a staring mess loose in the halls of academe.

He'd caught his breath. The eye hadn't come back, but it would. There'd be no more hockey after Harrington, so why was he even doing this, going to talk for three hours about a book? It wasn't the first time he'd asked this question of himself. Well, you sign the name you dah the dah. As you stare into the grey shadows, on the constant verge of teetering because half of you can't see, whispered phrases sweep in and out, grey *English Patient* insights insistent as jingles. Of *course* Caravaggio had claws for hands, the guy *wanted* everything so much... One vial of morphine equals one chapter of memory... You can see why writing is appreciated in a grey place like this. Literature wouldn't have a chance anywhere else. You need boredom, you need quiet. Poetry wouldn't survive an arcade. You'd put Ondaatje down, you'd dump your quarters in the slot. The world had turned arcade. He was searching for a silent, beige classroom to talk about something that was rich and sinewy but could only be born in quiet.

The hall was crammed with hurrying bodies, and loud with everyone saying excuse me and brushing his shoulder, which for no reason had come away from the wall. He was late, and Gail Smith would be up there shaking her head, making a display of looking at her watch, and maybe she had already made her head go back, while here he was comically flailing mid-aisle. Before he went down he grabbed a water fountain, managing a graceful dip to take a drink. Keep moving kids, I just wanted a sip here.

There was just no way for those stairs. There might be an elevator somewhere in the building, but could he get to it? And he was already so late, so late, and damn but it felt like the good eye could be dead in another blink. Time to turn back and get gone.

But ah, damn, he had some good stuff to say.

# IV

There is something in this more than natural,
if philosophy could find it out.

*HAMLET*

Maybe we're going a bit too hard on him,
he warned. You can easily give a man a
bigger hiding than he can hold.
We're only starting, man, said Shanahan.

FLANN O'BRIEN, *AT SWIM-TWO-BIRDS*

*Oscar.*

This Margaret had been in the bathroom a long time. It was strange being on a trip with an unknown young woman. Here at the café of a roadside motel barely a half-hour outside of Fredericton. Would anyone see him with her? As if it mattered now, as if it were anything but a bitter joke that such news might get back to Leah.

Why was he doing this?

He only vaguely recalled her as one of the scruffy kids in Bob's driveway looking for the comet, that night he'd driven him home. The sing-along with Bob, the mock-along with Bob.

Maybe she was in the bathroom doing some kind of drug, something for the nerves. If anything, theirs was a nervous mission.

It was a relief to be free of her talking. When he picked her up she'd been shy, but after a few minutes she'd settled down to talk and talk, about Bob of course, Mr. Bonaduce their one thing in common. But how kids communicated these days — I mean, like, y'know, cool. For each word of substance, five fillers, hesitators. Apparently she was in university. Perhaps Jason talked like that with his friends, but one wouldn't imagine so. Though when he'd asked Jason how the Dylan concert went he'd said, "*It ruled,*" bobbing his head, genuinely happy about it. Seeing this rare effusiveness, Oscar had been surprised and felt happy for Bonaduce. At the time.

"Sorry."

Margaret slid into the leatherette booth, facing him. Still in the momentum of the slide, she clasped her coffee and brought it to her mouth, slopping some over the rim.

"Not to worry. In fact I ordered us each some apple pie. That okay?"

Margaret shrugged but appeared irritated by something in this. Maybe she was on a diet. Well then, it was good he hadn't ordered the clubhouse sandwiches. She had small eyes in a wide, unreadable face. One of her ears suffered a wild scatter of earrings that was uncomfortable to look at and resisted counting.

"I just thought, who knows when we'll be eating next?"

"Right, so I guess there's no, like, giant hurry."

"No." Woodstock was an hour and half from Fredericton and they were halfway. It wouldn't take a minute to find the hospital, and as hospitals go it would be extremely —

"I mean like, it's not like he's going anywhere without his toes."

She was sort of smiling, a first. And, like a teenager, chewing away on some gum.

"Doesn't sound like he is, no."

"No but I'm just, I mean, I feel like I'm in a hurry because I have this feeling he's afraid."

This hadn't occurred to him, Bob Bonaduce afraid. Well, there would be the general fear of mortality, certainly, and fear of what sounded like a diabolical disease. But not the kind of fear that was assuaged by two friends showing up. One friend showing up.

"Like, he wakes up in a ditch almost dead, and by now he's been alone for two days."

He realized that this Margaret was giving him subtle shit. His one sign of a dip from reverential concern for Mr. Bonaduce — in the form of a man simply wanting some pie — and her voice takes on the tone of, What kind of friend are you? (Would you like me to explain, Margaret?) Clearly she loved Bonaduce. What other entanglements had Mr. Bonaduce wrought here? Perchance tupping the white youth. Whom hadn't he tupped?

Hard to know how to feel about this. His guts were, in fact, churning.

It was like his own ambivalence was being held out to him on a platter. The sequence of events had, by turns, found him angry, cruel, impatient. Then selfish, then sad. How could you wish such a thing on anyone? He had at last, and at least, been forced to admit what he and Leah both knew — that it was nothing personal, that Bonaduce could have been anyone, and that his and Leah's problems were their own.

"How well do you know Bob?"

This got her. She stopped and thought, then smiled.

"I don't know."

"I think it's exactly the same with me." He nodded instructively for her.

"No, we were like, thinking of getting a place together." Looking him in the eye. Pie was placed in front of her. "Thank you. But I don't know if it was going to be a platonic place or a nonplatonic place."

"Ah, I see."

"That's why I phoned your wife. We were going house-hunting, he was supposed to pick me up, and he didn't."

"I see."

"I mean, when he didn't, I knew something was up." She held a forkful of pie under her mouth, which kept itself open between words, just in case pie was forthcoming. "So, I mean, I know Robert *that* well, anyway. That you can trust him."

"Okay. I see." *Robert*, right.

"Sorry." Margaret put her forkful down and pushed the pie away. "I really don't think I can eat. Can we just go?"

Certainly. Oscar wished he could just give her the car. (And what was this almost superior air about those who hadn't learned to drive?)

Why was he doing this at all? Whatever made him nervous about people in general was further exacerbated by sickness and hospitals.

When he'd first asked Leah, challenged her about the affair, she'd denied it. Only after Bonaduce called her in the middle of the night a week later had she confessed. His rage was simple and he'd threatened to leave. She'd parried with marriage counselling. Oscar, it's happened before, let's fix it so it won't happen again. Him incredulous. *Let's* fix it? As in *us* fix it, as in plural? What was his part in this fixing, go to Canadian Tire and fix her up a chastity belt? But, after some time he came to see that, though hurtful, it was not unwise of her to delegate some blame. These failures did take two.

But he was in no mood for the continuing story, including Jason's worried news of Bonaduce stumbling around drunk at some intersquad game and breaking a player's leg, apparently on purpose. Then Jason smiling and shaking his head in amazement, almost admiration. "Dad's a madman," he'd concluded, shrugging, as uncomplicated a gesture as one of Bonaduce's own.

How does one break a leg on purpose? He'd reached down and felt the dense weight of his own leg bone. Good lord. He imagined Bonaduce attacking that too.

Then the big news. At first he'd been only mad when Leah called to him to the kitchen, where she stood hunched over the phone, wide-eyed and mouth open, her hand covering the receiver. She told him that this was someone named Margaret, a friend of Bob's — Oscar was already enraged at the tears rising in Leah's eyes — and Bobby was in a hospital up in Woodstock, his car had gone off the road. Oscar felt his anger drain as her other words spilled out, multiple sclerosis, hypothermia, coma, amputated toes.

He'd been found near the U.S. border in his car, in a ditch, he was there overnight. He's, they think he might be paralyzed.

"I see."

"Margaret wants to know if one of us can go to Woodstock with her. She needs a ride. She'll take a taxi if she has to. But she wants to go now. And I—I shouldn't, Oscar. Not yet. I think he's angry that..."

She was crying and couldn't finish, and he saw that Leah was already deeply involved in a simple new equation that included him: their relationship was less important than Bonaduce's life.

To his surprise, he'd said, "I'll go."

Jittery with too much coffee, he paid the bill. It was his turn to go to the bathroom. Why he was doing this, he still didn't know. Did he want an apology? Maybe. Or maybe his animal side just didn't want Leah near the man again, though the man was very seriously on his back, and though Leah was going to see him in any case, tomorrow or the next day, depending on Oscar's report. Amazing, though, the jealous animal. Could there be something in him that wanted to see his rival lying there crushed and defeated? One could see now how one could be jealous even of the dead. For he'd been jealous anew even after hearing Bob's condition, when he'd asked Leah how it was that this Margaret knew to call her at all and Leah had told him about her calling Margaret first, the day before, to apologize to Bonaduce for things said at the Christmas party. Leah apologizing to Bonaduce? If there was anyone in morality's jurisdiction who should be apologizing it was Bonaduce and Bonaduce alone. From the sounds of it Bonaduce should be apologizing to everyone with whom he'd come within ten feet.

His question led to other questions.

"You mean Jason isn't even his?"

"Jason's his." Leah couldn't look at him. "I was angry."

"Ah. I see. I think you probably got him with that one."

He snorted derisively—he still had enough upper hand for that. It wasn't until he was alone later that he realized she blamed herself for putting him in that ditch, and that this entanglement wouldn't go away but was about to get deeper in ways no one could predict.

He and Margaret climbed back into Leah's little red Neon. His Jeep was in for a starter transplant. It was freezing today, it was unbelievable, this cold snap. He and Margaret huffed and puffed in the bucket seats while the thing warmed up, their breath frosting the windows, Margaret with a pie-shaped styrofoam doggie bag on her lap. She was actually too big for this car. She was a fair bit bigger than he was. Backing out, he twisted around to look and their shoulders pressed, his shoulder and a twenty-year-old young woman's, and he thought of Bonaduce touching her. Had Bonaduce touched her? Of course he had.

"Can we, like, stop at a store?"

"Sure. Of course." The gas station where they'd just eaten had had a store. He tried not to sound impatient. "Do you want to go back?"

"No I mean a sort of big one. One that might sell dice."

"Dice."

"He likes Yahtzee, and I could only find four at home."

"Sure. Okay. A dice store."

It's not like we're like in a giant hurry, Margaret. With his mitt he scraped frost off the inside of the windshield. Hard to imagine anyone surviving this kind of cold. Apparently Bob's old car had kept running till the gas ran out, sometime in the night. The tailpipe was in snow and enough carbon monoxide had floated in to do some damage, Margaret wasn't sure which kind or how much. You couldn't help but think brain damage.

"Were you on the phone with him yourself?"

"No. Like, he wasn't quite there yet."

"He wasn't... quite there?"

"He wasn't able to. Wasn't up to it."

"Right."

Oscar tried to picture how it was going to be, seeing him. What he'd look like, what he'd do. He reviewed the MS symptoms Margaret had listed for him. Curious, the last one, the euphoria, at end stage. Euphoria, perhaps mind shielding itself from its dying body. Clever, the alternative being horror and agony. Euphoria was curious also because at the beginning there was apparently much depression. Margaret claimed Bonaduce had been here in Fredericton depressed for months and no one had known it. Oscar certainly hadn't. The man had seemed happy enough.

"I wonder if he's talking now?"

Margaret shrugged, staring straight ahead. As though to suggest, why would talking matter?

Oscar's gloved hands shifted on the steering wheel. The way Bob smiled, looked at you. In his first anger he'd decided Bob Bonaduce had befriended him only as a way to get to Leah. But he knew now that wasn't the case. He'd always known it wasn't. One look at the man and you could see he wasn't like that.

He supposed he was driving to Woodstock because maybe something about him and Bob Bonaduce had survived, something that had nothing to do with Leah.

———

*Margaret.*

Woodstock was tiny, and the mall wasn't far from the hospital. On her way from the Shoppers over to the Zellers, she had to double back past the car, where Oscar sat reading the paper. She waved as she crossed in front, but he didn't see her. Maybe it was just his mood. Robert had called him a good guy, but the man was almost a parody of uptight. He'd actually gotten out and fed the parking meter so that he could sit there in the space. When she'd bought him the gift of the newspaper, he'd thanked her, but slowly, like he was worried she might want something in return.

How hard could it be to buy dice in Woodstock? That Robert would want to play was certain, though whether he could play was not, so maybe this was foolishness. She could roll for both of them, he'd like owning one of her arms as his dice slave, he'd like that joke.

Don't worry about Oscar, let the fellow wait. And yet she'd liked Leah, she'd liked the wife. "The wife." Leah had sounded concerned, decent. Apologetic. "If I had only known he was sick…" "Why did he feel he had to…?" "I wouldn't have been so…" Leah felt more like Robert's friend than Oscar did.

Oscar's nervousness at seeing Robert. He who Robert called the best buddy he had here. What kind of friend was that? She pictured Oscar reading his *Globe* in the car, severe little lawyer with the croaking deep voice. Did he stand up in court and accuse people? She had in her pocket Robert's little essay, which at first she wanted to read to Oscar but then decided he wouldn't care, so screw him, great friend. She found it in her laptop and printed it out to bring, on the chance Robert hadn't left it behind on purpose, his painful little thing about Mahatma Gandhi and Bob Dylan and whether they also knew how to skate. Buddha and the jeep, Robert as usual being funny and sad at impossibly the same time. But to suggest he wasn't good at anything. A professional hockey player! And who played an instrument like that, and sang like a tough angel. Though she knew what Robert meant. And that he was talking for her, too.

She groaned at the image of him not being able to roll dice. She walked, angry, wiping away a tear. Between Oscar and Toby, and the hockey team kicking him off, no wonder Robert was fleeing back to the States.

She'd almost cried seeing the bathroom. At first she was angry when he didn't arrive for the apartment-hunting, fuming while she paced, but that soon changed to worry. Robert wouldn't simply forget. She taxied home and saw his clothes gone, the dreamcatcher taken from the window. And new bathroom drywall put up, a clumsy but thorough job that brought tears to her eyes. No letter, not surprising. Robert wouldn't be one for goodbyes.

Here. Chess, Scrabble, cheap little plastic travel games. Eureka, dice. They were small, four of them in a package. They looked weighty though, well made. Good dice. It was absurd to think of some dice being more lucky than any others, but these did. She bounced them in her hand and found herself wondering if Robert was religious.

Only four to the pack. She plucked a second. If Robert was religious it was in a non-conceptual way, like her. Lately when she wondered whether she was still religious or not, the image of a spade pushing into soft fragrant earth came to mind, a memory from the dig in Hawaii. The good smell of God in that earth, wet, dark, as much rot as growth. Robert would agree. On his deathbed if you asked him if he wanted a priest or a really good sandwich, there's no doubt he'd go for the sandwich. Or a bowl of steaming soft ravioli with three kinds of cheese. Drizzle of spiced olive oil. Shit, she hadn't meant *deathbed*, not literally, not aside from the joke.

She realized she hadn't eaten in far too long. She didn't want Oscar's pie. She could go back to the sub place she'd passed. Was Robert feeling religious now? If he was, she wouldn't try to discourage it. She had some books he might like, ecumenical forays from hard dogma, which old friends had given to her, hoping to keep her with them in spirit, intelligent books that had almost worked their way on her but no. In any case her only plan for Robert, her only strategy, was to try to make him feel good. That was the bare religion she followed now: seeing your way to anything good, in spite of the facts.

If it looked and felt right, even if only to make him feel good she'd offer him the second bedroom in the place she'd just —

The man who grabbed her arm wasn't big, but his fingers dug in and you could feel his anger in them. She had just gone through the glass doors and had stood looking around for the car.

"Come with me, please." He was leading her back into the store.

She had walked out with the two packs of dice. They were so small and cost so little and she'd forgotten them with Robert waiting for her a few blocks away in a hospital bed. She didn't know what to say, how to begin. You couldn't explain things to people. She resisted the man's pull, turned around and waved and yelled *"Help!"* to Oscar's car. Oscar was looking at her, rolling down the window. She laughed while shouting *"Sorry."*

———

It doesn't take a lot of body to drive. The right leg was dead but one eye worked, and one arm was pretty good. He sat back and tried to relax. As long as he didn't have to brake for a moose, the left heel pressing dumbly down on the gas was all the foot he would be needing. Around Woodstock, with the border a half-hour away, he began to practise clearly saying "Utica, New York" and "visiting relatives." This he changed to "on business," which came out less floppy. After you passed the breathalyser, what would a cop do when he discovered a slurring man hadn't had a single beer?

He was freezing, and even in the depths of his leather coat he couldn't get warm. He pushed at the heater controls incessantly, maybe that was why he went into the spin. Or maybe it was the search for music. Each time he lost another station to static he wedged his knee up under the wheel to free his hand for the dial. Whatever caused the spin, when he woke in the ditch classical music was on, and he would spend the rest of the night with the CBC.

He'd lost consciousness but came to remembering the feel of the black ice, the sick angling-off, the vertigo, the windshield framing all the wrong things, the car pointing backwards, neither steering wheel nor brakes affecting the slide one bit. Big helpless hunk of fast metal loose in the night. Had he actually thought, "If only the tires were skates," or was he just thinking it now?

The car was on its side. The bump on his head showed him how the driver's side window had been broken. Not much blood. His good shoulder was wrenched from its socket. The seat belt held him in position still. He could not feel his legs.

The windshield was in place but fissured along a thousand lines, a Jack Frost pattern, opaque. The passenger window, his lone view out, pointed straight up. Through it he could see shadowy tree branches and, beyond them, stars.

It took a while to understand that the car was still running. Old slant-six just idling away. Then his hand was on the key, thinking *explosion*. Then thinking *freezing to death* if he turned it off. If it hadn't caught fire yet maybe it wouldn't. He could smell no gas. If he turned it off, would it turn back on when it got cold? He took his hand off the key. He had maybe a quarter-tank, at most. He'd been waiting to fill up more cheaply over the border.

He did turn off the radio. He quieted his breathing, and listened. He'd left the road on ice, so no skid marks pointing the way. He couldn't remember hitting any trees. Had he ploughed a visible path? Not a lot of people would be making the journey, at midnight, into northern Maine. Maybe some drunks from Woodstock going to Houlton for the strippers. He imagined an oldtimer hockey team, a string of three or four rowdy cars, we'd all be lucky if they noticed the road, let alone the ditch beside it.

It was maybe half an hour before he heard a car and it was faint. It sounded like he was well off the highway, and maybe down an embankment. If that was a truck he was hearing, he was even further away. In the branches overhead there was no hint of head-lights as it passed, its noise fading into the fucking quiet of the idling car. His eye moved to the steering wheel, the rubber panel you pushed to honk at a car in front of you, to honk at a passing car as you lay freezing in a ditch. He couldn't even remember what his horn sounded like, some wire rusting through ten years ago.

He began renewed attempts to get himself out of his belt. Even if he succeeded in this, with no decent arms or legs what were the chances of him climbing up, pushing open that door against gravity, hauling himself out?

He knuckled the radio back on, it was a classical piece he knew, a famous Christmas one, something from the *Nutcracker*? He was halfway into seeing sugarplum fairies, into making the best of this bad time, when the smell kicked him in the nose.

He had shit himself. There was no mistaking it. It hadn't happened during the skid, it hadn't happened during the crash, it hadn't happened when he'd been out cold. It had just hap-pened now. It was still happening, the acrid stench building. His body emptying itself, muscles he couldn't feel.

Only one thing in the car was moving. He could see it, lit by the newly risen moon. The defrost fan was blowing on it, tick-ling it — the old good-luck charm air freshener. The cardboard tree shape was doing a little dance.


When the car died, the sound of its absence was awful, God it really was awful, and partly for this reason he groaned and groaned to fill it.

He didn't know if he'd been asleep. Terror and panic, if it went on and on, was a sort of huge sleep, so wild and full it was like bad, bad, dreaming. You could control it or not control it like you could or couldn't a nightmare. If you can see your own panic, who is it panicking? But you can get exhausted with panic. Too tired to be afraid. Too tired to be or do anything. Except die, the one thing that takes no effort at all.

His brain could still babble to itself like an idiot. Monkey-mind, in and out of sleep, chattering, even making lists, too stupid to know it should be nothing but afraid. He found his brain wondering if it should buy a Christmas present for Fournier's girlfriend or not, and what was her name again? He watched his brain fall into a dark, wet crater with Kip, defusing a bomb, over and over. He woke once in the middle of seeing himself writing in Marg's computer, he was writing something that he may have in fact written or maybe was composing only now, about all the guys and their superstitions. The famous ones you saw on TV, Patrick Roy jumping over the blue line on his way off, step on a crack break your mother's. That pitcher who throws an inning then races to the dugout and brushes his teeth at the water cooler, not caring who sees, superstition bigger than shame. The good zone you seek is delicate and there's nothing of it to hold on to, which is why guys have their little thing, they have to be first out or last out of the dressing room, hoping some other guy won't push in, being on the same charm. Shamrock, Buddha, girlfriend's bandana, lucky rock. Trinket in the pocket to keep luck near your body. Eat a salad, spaghetti, a peach, exactly four hours before the whistle. Have sex don't have sex, drive a car take a taxi. In the d-room some interesting ones, most of them camouflaged in the hubbub getting ready. A guy whose job grants him daily laundered underwear dons a stinking undershirt that's nothing but stringy rags, more dirt than fibre, last washed in 1986. A guy always slaps his face hard, twice, or it's his skates laced up then taken off then laced up again, and he'll be late on the ice rather than interrupt this. Number 12 whacks the goalie's pads twelve times. In the road-restaurant at the pre-game meal no one's surprised to see a teammate freak out over his baked potato when he's told, Sorry, we're out of chives. Bonaduce reflecting a moment, then typing that it's like you're with a bunch of fishermen all dangling different lures to entice the big luck trout. You've been doing your thing for so long you no longer see it. Your left skate is always first. You can't not start with the left. Sometimes you catch yourself, and ask what would happen if I just went ahead and put on my stupid right skate? You don't even risk it. It feels like doom. You don't want to play around with this stuff. You're typing in her laptop that you understand nothing about luck, meaning you know nothing about anything.

Except that you're so tired you're on the other side of everything you've known. You're cold and living off something vital, draining it. You want advice, you want magic, you want your luck back, any luck you've ever had, especially now that terror has arisen, terror that isn't crazy and has delivered you through the crust of dreams into clear time, terror that claws this present moment as though it were the inside of a coffin.

◦〜

They were apparently real. Or as real as sight was real. They were lit up from within and impossible, because he knew that it was night and that real life was sideways in a car.

Maybe his screams had brought them, maybe he had screamed, and screamed himself backwards into dreams. They were lit up and sometimes alone, sometimes together, appearing out of nowhere and through no effort on his part that he knew of.

At first he thought they were here to help him get out of the car, thought they had real bodies and could help. He could hear them as they approached, one by one, he could hear them and he probably yelled, *Who's here! Who's here!* and then here they were, right in the car but not looking at him, not helping at all, knowing he was there and even his situation but doing nothing. Guys he hadn't thought of in years. His grandmother. An aunt whose name he couldn't for the life of him. Jan Dionne, Gail Smith, Whetter. Toby. Fournier. They all came, each in their time, or perhaps all at once, none of them looking at him. Here was Leah, and here was Jason with her, but they were just faces in the line of teachers, friends and teammates, and they ignored him in no way more special.

He woke out of his own gibberish into a melting roomscape, into fragments that began and ended in dream-swirl. Once, the content of wakefulness was nothing more than the prodding spike of a headache. Another time it was knowing that he was finally warm. When he opened his eyes, seeing with only the one, what he saw was good because it was less frantic than his dreams.

Waking meant a different kind of seeing. The sun hard through the orange curtains was best, the light making the fabric magically more orange than orange, you could taste it, it quenched the hunger for all other sights.

Sometimes vision leapfrogged a dark tangled hump and landed him in sudden clarity, where he understood not only the mechanics of seeing, but also the profound friendship between the seer and the seen. The radiator under the curtain was white, unless curtain went brighter orange and radiator turned grey. The change took place as much in his eye as it did outside of it. The one eye made this a simpler certainty, though these understandings, and clarity itself, may have been drug-induced. In any case the lucid times were but pinholes in the swirl, respites from endless slogging through mud.

Drugs were a dam, and pain a swelling reservoir behind it, deep and vast and ready to drown him if the dam gave way. Sometimes pain did push through a crack and overcame him with such ease it was terrifying. Body's terror. Quick nod to the nurse's offer of morphine. Christine wouldn't look at him, she would administer the IV injection with sober efficiency and an air of withholding. Joyce though, Joyce was with him eye to eye, and she would joke how some guys just wanted to keep partying.

Drugs could do anything. They could make you content with diapers and stupidity. Oh yes the unbearable lightness of peeing whenever and wherever. Drugs could roll you over and sponge your fouled nether zone and your dead unit, so dead it ignored all nursely attention. Drugs would not allow the tiniest bit of shame to stick.

He woke, one eye staring up at the little TV set, hanging from its mechanical arm. In one of his home towns he'd watched such a thing from a dentist chair. Waking up this way irritated him — without his consent they'd turned it on and plugged him in — plastic earphone was jammed in his right ear — them assuming he preferred the jokes of *Frasier* to the less-staged ones unfolding out the window, or in his body, which was maybe or maybe not coming back to him, a finger or a foot too long hidden from sense but now uncurling, unwrapping itself like a gift. Who knows, though — perhaps he had consented to the TV. Perhaps *Frasier*, these jokes, perhaps distraction was part of the cure. The most irritating thing about this TV was that the noise was so close, wedged into his headbone in fact, while the action it was supposedly connected to hovered up there near the ceiling. In the tinny earphone the acting sounded like barking. Punctuating each joke, the canned laughter was so loud it was only static. It sounded exactly like surf. Each time the distant Frasier pulled a face, in your head the surf roared.

He woke to Marg and Oscar at the foot of the bed, whispering about whether or not to leave.

He smiled, but didn't know if it showed on the face.

They were quiet and nervous at first, afraid of looking at him. He managed to meet Marg's eye and they held it for a second, and when she understood he was okay she loosened up and could laugh a little. Oscar, poor Oscar, had to begin with a speech about Leah wanting him to say how sorry she was and such, and that she would visit soon. Infected by Oscar's formal tone, Marg added that Fournier was also on his way, and that he had a cheque for him, from his old hockey-team owner, and that it was a lot of money.

It was good to see his friends. Though odd to see these two together. Two worlds. And Fournier coming, a third. Leah would make it four. It would be too much. All the smiling.

Silence fell as they sussed he wasn't too good at speaking. Marg elbowed Oscar and said that, well, the important news here was that she'd just been arrested for shoplifting.

"I was so out of it I totally forgot the thing about *paying* for things." She dropped two rattling Baggies onto his chest. "These'll be ready when you are."

"Bones," he said, in a voice of inventory. Though it sounded more like "bo's."

"Yeah, and here"— Marg dug into her book bag —"Toby brings you this. We should probably hide it." She placed a bottle of home-made wine on his side table.

"Less see." He tilted his head at it. Marg understood, and spun the bottle by the neck so he could read the label. It read, "Gift Horse '98."

"I brought something too," said Oscar, again taking his cue from Marg. He rifled through a Zellers' bag.

Bonaduce tried for "Merry Christmas" but said, "May Chriss," which they didn't hear over Oscar's rustling.

"He decides to like, 'do some shopping' while I'm being interrogated." Marg snapped her gum.

"I realized," Oscar said, bringing out a new walkman, encased in its package, "that here you were, stuck up here in nowhere with no music. Leah had these two in her car. She stole them from me, I stole them back." He took two cassettes from his coat pocket and put them on his side table, then began tugging at the walkman's vacuum-formed packaging.

Bonaduce made his head fall to the side. He read Oscar's printing. One tape was "Van Morrison," the other "Early Bowie."

"Suck here, wih, briss."

"Sorry? What?"

"Stuck, here, wih, *Brits*."

"Bob, when I come back up I'll bring —" Oscar visibly stilled his panic by taking a breath. He looked up at Bonaduce, meeting his eye for the first time. He smiled ironically. "Next time, I'll bring you your damn Everly Brothers or whatever it is you like."

"Than's, Ah'car."

Bonaduce managed what might be a smile too, and a little waving finger of demand. Bring me something pure. Roy Orbison. Gene Pitney. Something that doesn't make your thoughts for you.

"Well, so where'd they, like, put your stuff?" Marg suddenly getting all stern with an idea. "Your tapes. Your guitar."

He shook his head and raised his brow just enough for her to see.

Marg walked off on her mission. Right, indeed, where was the car, where was his stuff. He remembered getting hauled up, out of the passenger door, the pain of this, the pain forcing him beyond relief into bad clarity, it was almost like leaping right out of his damn body into the bitter night. But, yes, he'd seen the strewn back seat. Leaving town he'd pretty much just thrown it all in, but now it looked liked someone had hit the blender switch. When they lifted him out of his own mess he'd been embarrassed by his smell, but then also by the brown skeleton of a Christmas tree bungeed to the roof.

"Bob?"

Oscar hovered nearer and hunched in, his deep voice hushed to a conspiratorial croak. He was going to get serious now, which was fine.

"Bob?"

Bonaduce lifted his eyebrows for him. You don't want to talk too much.

"Leah, she wanted me to tell you —"

"No. Ah'car? *Oss*-car."

"Yes? What?"

"Sorry."

He tried to show with his eyes that people, friends, don't do to each other what I did to you. You just don't.

"It's — it's not your fault. You had — you two had unfinished business."

Right. So we did. But that brand of business is never finished.

"Leah said, she wanted me to say, about the fight you two had, that Jason, well hell man, Jason *is* yours. Is your son." Oscar shook his head, smiling at the lunacy he hadn't witnessed. "And that she's sorry. She was pretty angry, I guess."

Bonaduce had known, of course. How could he have ever not known? Just look at the boy's body.

"No he'sh not." He tried to smile wisely. Oscar didn't know what to make of this.

"And, and also that, Leah said to say also that Jason wasn't paid to go to see Bob Dylan with you."

Bonaduce smiled. His muscles felt it to be a grin.

"In fact, he loved it, he loved the concert, he raved about it, and he loved going with you, I'm not just —"

"Ah'sar? Does' mahher."

"Sorry? Does…?"

"Doesn't. Matter."

He tried to show with his eye all he'd learned trapped in his car. How phantoms had arisen before his face, and how, when they dissolved, he was free of them and had always been free of them, for they were just phantoms all along, and isn't it funny how you have to keep learning what you already know. He tried to show with his face, too, that what mattered here was not Jason but you, Oscar, *you*, because it is you leaning over the bed, blinking, tender. Just like you don't matter when it's Joyce sitting here on her stool, skipping the grey peas for the decent dessert, attuned to him, knowing when he's geared up ready for another spoonful, whereas doing the same duty Christine's mind would be elsewhere and so in fact she wasn't here at all. What matters is this light streaming glory through the orange curtain, lighting up half your face, Oscar, dramatic, noble blood-colour, the rest of your face in shadow, it's —

"Ah'sar, you…"

"What? Bob?"

"You look *grea*'."

Poor Oscar, on the verge now. Sometimes you really shouldn't say anything.

He may have dozed because the light was different and Marg was clomping back in, and Oscar seemed to have moved his chair further back. Marg put a sack of his cassette tapes on his bedside table, beside Oscar's two. She stood over him, shaking her head.

"You broke your guitar."

*Twank.* He remembered, yes. The sound. First the spinning. Tumbling. Then hitting a final something, the ground probably, with a pow and a *twank* of the thickest snapping string.

He nodded for her. He'd heard its death song.

Oscar was grateful to go through the tapes and organize them for him while Marg disappeared into the little bathroom.

He cocked his head to the sound of the water running, its rush interrupted by something moving under it, being washed. Marg was hugely entertaining. Now paper towels ripped from the dispenser. Sounds of Marg drying, dabbing, then periods of no noise, of some kind of care.

She used the stool to hang the wet dreamcatcher, fastening its cord to the curtain rod, tying it tightly and well, setting up house, betraying that she had talked to someone and had learned he would be in this room for a while.

She clambered down, saw he had been watching her and smiled, pointing back to the dreamcatcher. She sighed, looked around, sat happily on the foot of his bed. When she realized she was sitting an inch from his feet, from his fresh wounds, she gasped, leaped up.

"Sorry! Sorry! Did I—?"

"Did' feel a thing. S'okay." He paused. "Si' a'ywhere on me y' wan'."

No one laughed at what was a decent joke. They were more numb than he was. He laughed at this, laughed again, then coughed, and started coughing, he hated the coughing because at the base of the deepest ones you could taste exhaust, and the taste filled his head with a memory and fact of poison.

He tried to sleep. Fournier coming with lots of money. Pack his bags with money, buy a new car, drive Marg to Maui, she could show him Maui. This he would love, because so would she, wild about him. Lie on the hot sand, he was wearing a big huge wacky bathing suit, cover his delicate condition, his diapered nether bulk. He'd listen to the surf, and decorate the tree, finally. The canned laughter, the Maui trucks. Marg is soothing his burned face, her vials of morphine lined up in the sand. Frasier's funny little brother is everywhere. He's still thinking of Leah, because it feels so good. Marg content pointing out parrots flitting tree to tree, God aren't they big, perched shoulder-to-shoulder. In trees black against the sand.

"Robert? Did — What? 'Parrots'?"

He could hear himself laughing.

But poor Marg was crying, he'd made her cry, she was grabbing her face, trying to stop.

"Mar'? 'S okay. Cry."

"I'm not." She smiled, her face wet, her body lurching with sobs.

He could feel his laugh, deep and poisonous. He could also feel his tears, not on the side of his face but when they landed in his ear.

"Mar'? Me either."